HarperCollins **POCKET**

WORLD**ATLAS**

HarperCollins Pocket World Atlas

Copyright © 2004 HarperCollins*Publishers*.
All rights reserved.

HarperCollins books may be purchased for educational, business, or sales
promotional use. For information please write: Special Markets Department,
HarperCollins Publishers Inc., 10 East 53rd Street, New York, NY 10022.

First published as Collins World Atlas Mini Edition 2004 by HarperCollins*Publishers* Ltd

Maps © Collins Bartholomew Ltd 2004

Printed in Singapore by Imago

ISBN 0-06-059531-0

04 05 06 07 08 IM 10 9 8 7 6 5 4 3 2 1

HarperCollins **POCKET**
WORLD**ATLAS**

HarperResource

An Imprint of HarperCollins*Publishers*

world

states and territories	8-23
countries	24-25
physical features	26-27
climate	28-29
land cover	30-31
population and cities	32-33
timezones	34-35

europe

physical features	1:35 000 000	36-37
countries	1:35 000 000	38-39
western russian federation	1:20 000 000	40-41
baltic states and moscow region	1:8 000 000	42-43
ukraine and moldova	1:8 000 000	44-45
scandinavia and iceland	1:10 000 000	46-47
british isles	1:8 000 000	48-49
scotland	1:4 000 000	50
ireland	1:4 000 000	51
england and wales	1:4 000 000	52-53
northwest europe	1:4 000 000	54-55
central europe	1:8 000 000	56-57
france and switzerland	1:8 000 000	58-59
spain and portugal	1:8 000 000	60-61
italy and the balkans	1:8 000 000	62-63
southeast europe	1:8 000 000	64-65

asia

physical features	1:78 000 000	66-67
countries	1:78 000 000	68-69
southeast asia	1:30 000 000	70-71
malaysia and western indonesia	1:15 000 000	72-73
myanmar, thailand and indo-china	1:15 000 000	74-75
philippines	1:15 000 000	76
north korea and south korea	1:9 000 000	77
japan	1:10 000 000	78-79
china and mongolia	1:30 000 000	80-81
central china	1:15 000 000	82-83
southern asia	1:20 000 000	84-85
pakistan, northern india, nepal and bangladesh	1:15 000 000	86-87
central asia	1:20 000 000	88-89
arabian peninsula	1:15 000 000	90-91
eastern mediterranean	1:15 000 000	92-93
russian federation	1:42 000 000	94-95

africa

physical features	1:60 000 000	96-97
countries	1:60 000 000	98-99
northwest africa	1:26 000 000	100-101
northeast africa	1:26 000 000	102-103
central africa	1:20 000 000	104-105
southern africa	1:20 000 000	106-107
republic of south africa	1:10 000 000	108-109

oceania

physical features	1:65 000 000	110-111
countries	1:65 000 000	112-113
australia	1:25 000 000	114-115
southeast australia	1:10 000 000	116-117
new zealand	1:10 000 000	118
antarctica	1:60 000 000	119

north america

physical features	1:65 000 000	120-121
countries	1:65 000 000	122-123
canada	1:30 000 000	124-125
western canada	1:15 000 000	126-127
eastern canada	1:15 000 000	128-129
united states of america	1:25 000 000	130-131
western united states	1:11 000 000	132-133
north central united states	1:11 000 000	134-135
northeast united states	1:11 000 000	136-137
southeast united states	1:11 000 000	138-139
south central united states	1:11 000 000	140-141
mexico	1:15 000 000	142-143
the caribbean	1:20 000 000	144-145

south america

physical features	1:50 000 000	146-147
countries	1:50 000 000	148-149
northern south america	1:25 000 000	150-151
southern south america	1:25 000 000	152-153
southeast brazil	1:10 000 000	154-155

oceans

features		156-157
pacific ocean	1:100 000 000	158-159
atlantic ocean and indian ocean	1:100 000 000	160-161
arctic ocean	1:60 000 000	162

index

	163-256

INTRODUCTION

The atlas is introduced by details of the world's states and territories and by maps and information on major geographical themes. The reference maps which follow this world section have been compiled to provide the best coverage for each part of the world through careful selection of scales and map projections. Maps are arranged on a continental basis, with each continent being introduced by maps and statistics on the continent's physical features and countries. Maps of Antarctica and the world's oceans complete the worldwide coverage.

Map symbolization

Maps show information by using symbols which are designed to reflect the features on the earth that they represent. Map symbols can be in the form of points – such as those used to show towns and airports; lines – used to represent roads and rivers; or areas – such as lakes. Variation in size, shape and colour of these types of symbol allow a great range of information to be shown. The symbols used in this atlas are explained here. Not all details can be shown at the small map scales used in this atlas, so information is generalized to allow easy interpretation. This generalization takes the form of selection – the inclusion of some features and the omission of others of less importance; and simplification – where lines are smoothed, areas combined, or symbols displaced slightly to add clarity. This is done in such a way that the overall character of the area mapped is retained. The degree of generalization varies, and is determined largely by the scale at which the map is drawn.

Scale

Scale is the relationship between the size of an area shown on the map and the actual size of the area on the ground. It determines the amount of detail shown on a map – larger scales show more, smaller scales show less – and can be used to measure the distance between two points, although the projection of the map must also be taken into account when measuring distances.

Geographical names

The spelling of place names on maps is a complex problem for the cartographer. There is no single standard way of converting them from one alphabet, or symbol set, to another. Changes in official languages also have to be taken into account when creating maps and policies need to be established for the spelling of names on individual atlases and maps. Such policies must take account of the local official position, international conventions or traditions, as well as the purpose of the atlas or map. The policy in this atlas is to use local name forms which are officially recognized by the governments of the countries concerned, but with English conventional name forms being used for the most well-known places. In these cases, the local form is often included in brackets on the map and also appears as a cross-reference in the index. All country names and those for international features appear in their English forms.

Boundaries

The status of nations and their boundaries are shown in this atlas as they are in reality at the time of going to press, as far as can be ascertained. Where international boundaries are the subject of disputes the aim is to take a strictly neutral viewpoint, based on advice from expert consultants.

MAP SYMBOLS

Settlements

Population	National Capital		Administrative Capital		City or Town	
over 5 million	⊡	**BEIJING**	⊙	**Tianjin**	⊙	**New York**
1 million – 5 million	☐	**MADRID**	○	**Sydney**	○	**Madurai**
500 000 – 1 million	☐	**BANGUI**	○	**Douala**	○	**Barranquilla**
100 000 – 500 000	☐	WELLINGTON	○	Mansa	○	Yong'an
50 000 – 100 000	☐	PORT OF SPAIN	○	Lubango	○	Puruliya
under 50 000	▫	MALABO	○	Chinhoyi	○	El Tigre

Styles of lettering

Country name	**FRANCE**	Island	*Gran Canaria*
Overseas territory / Dependency	**Guadaloupe**	Lake	*Lake Erie*
Administrative name	SCOTLAND	Mountain	*Mt Blanc*
Area name	PATAGONIA	River	*Thames*

Physical features

☐	Freshwater lake
☐	Seasonal freshwater lake
☐	Salt lake
☐	Seasonal salt lake
☐	Dry salt lake
	Ice cap
—	River
⋊⋉ 2188	Mountain pass
△ 6960	Summit

Other features

∴	Site of special interest
⌇⌇⌇	Wall

Communications

═══════	Motorway
───────	Main road
- - - - -	Track
▬ ▬ ▬ ▬	Railway
✈	Main airport
┼┼┼┼┼┼┼	Canal

Boundaries

───────	International
- - - - -	International disputed
───────	Administrative (selected countries only)
··············	Ceasefire line

EUROPE COUNTRIES		area sq km	area sq miles	population	capital
ALBANIA		28 748	11 100	3 166 000	Tirana
ANDORRA		465	180	71 000	Andorra la Vella
AUSTRIA		83 855	32 377	8 116 000	Vienna
BELARUS		207 600	80 155	9 895 000	Minsk
BELGIUM		30 520	11 784	10 318 000	Brussels
BOSNIA-HERZEGOVINA		51 130	19 741	4 161 000	Sarajevo
BULGARIA		110 994	42 855	7 897 000	Sofia
CROATIA		56 538	21 829	4 428 000	Zagreb
CZECH REPUBLIC		78 864	30 450	10 236 000	Prague
DENMARK		43 075	16 631	5 364 000	Copenhagen
ESTONIA		45 200	17 452	1 323 000	Tallinn
FINLAND		338 145	130 559	5 207 000	Helsinki
FRANCE		543 965	210 026	60 144 000	Paris
GERMANY		357 022	137 849	82 476 000	Berlin
GREECE		131 957	50 949	10 976 000	Athens
HUNGARY		93 030	35 919	9 877 000	Budapest
ICELAND		102 820	39 699	290 000	Reykjavik
IRELAND, REPUBLIC OF		70 282	27 136	3 956 000	Dublin
ITALY		301 245	116 311	57 423 000	Rome
LATVIA		63 700	24 595	2 307 000	Rīga
LIECHTENSTEIN		160	62	34 000	Vaduz
LITHUANIA		65 200	25 174	3 444 000	Vilnius
LUXEMBOURG		2 586	998	453 000	Luxembourg
MACEDONIA (F.Y.R.O.M.)		25 713	9 928	2 056 000	Skopje
MALTA		316	122	394 000	Valletta
MOLDOVA		33 700	13 012	4 267 000	Chişinău
MONACO		2	1	34 000	Monaco-Ville
NETHERLANDS		41 526	16 033	16 149 000	Amsterdam/The Hague
NORWAY		323 878	125 050	4 533 000	Oslo
POLAND		312 683	120 728	38 587 000	Warsaw
PORTUGAL		88 940	34 340	10 062 000	Lisbon
ROMANIA		237 500	91 699	22 334 000	Bucharest
RUSSIAN FEDERATION		17 075 400	6 592 849	143 246 000	Moscow

languages	religions	currency
Albanian, Greek	Sunni Muslim, Albanian Orthodox, Roman Catholic	Lek
Spanish, Catalan, French	Roman Catholic	Euro
German, Croatian, Turkish	Roman Catholic, Protestant	Euro
Belorussian, Russian	Belorussian Orthodox, Roman Catholic	Belarus rouble
Dutch (Flemish), French (Walloon), German	Roman Catholic, Protestant	Euro
Bosnian, Serbian, Croatian	Sunni Muslim, Serbian Orthodox, Roman Catholic, Protestant	Marka
Bulgarian, Turkish, Romany, Macedonian	Bulgarian Orthodox, Sunni Muslim	Lev
Croatian, Serbian	Roman Catholic, Serbian Orthodox, Sunni Muslim	Kuna
Czech, Moravian, Slovak	Roman Catholic, Protestant	Czech koruna
Danish	Protestant	Danish krone
Estonian, Russian	Protestant, Estonian and Russian Orthodox	Kroon
Finnish, Swedish	Protestant, Greek Orthodox	Euro
French, Arabic	Roman Catholic, Protestant, Sunni Muslim	Euro
German, Turkish	Protestant, Roman Catholic	Euro
Greek	Greek Orthodox, Sunni Muslim	Euro
Hungarian	Roman Catholic, Protestant	Forint
Icelandic	Protestant	Icelandic króna
English, Irish	Roman Catholic, Protestant	Euro
Italian	Roman Catholic	Euro
Latvian, Russian	Protestant, Roman Catholic, Russian Orthodox	Lats
German	Roman Catholic, Protestant	Swiss franc
Lithuanian, Russian, Polish	Roman Catholic, Protestant, Russian Orthodox	Litas
Letzeburgish, German, French	Roman Catholic	Euro
Macedonian, Albanian, Turkish	Macedonian Orthodox, Sunni Muslim	Macedonian denar
Maltese, English	Roman Catholic	Maltese lira
Romanian, Ukrainian, Gagauz, Russian	Romanian Orthodox, Russian Orthodox	Moldovan leu
French, Monegasque, Italian	Roman Catholic	Euro
Dutch, Frisian	Roman Catholic, Protestant, Sunni Muslim	Euro
Norwegian	Protestant, Roman Catholic	Norwegian krone
Polish, German	Roman Catholic, Polish Orthodox	Zloty
Portuguese	Roman Catholic, Protestant	Euro
Romanian, Hungarian	Romanian Orthodox, Protestant, Roman Catholic	Romanian leu
Russian, Tatar, Ukrainian, local languages	Russian Orthodox, Sunni Muslim, Protestant	Russian rouble

EUROPE
COUNTRIES (continued)

		area sq km	area sq miles	population	capital
SAN MARINO		61	24	28 000	San Marino
SERBIA AND MONTENEGRO		102 173	39 449	10 527 000	Belgrade
SLOVAKIA		49 035	18 933	5 402 000	Bratislava
SLOVENIA		20 251	7 819	1 984 000	Ljubljana
SPAIN		504 782	194 897	41 060 000	Madrid
SWEDEN		449 964	173 732	8 876 000	Stockholm
SWITZERLAND		41 293	15 943	7 169 000	Bern
UKRAINE		603 700	233 090	48 523 000	Kiev
UNITED KINGDOM		243 609	94 058	58 789 194	London
VATICAN CITY		0.5	0.2	472	Vatican City

EUROPE
DEPENDENT TERRITORIES

			area sq km	area sq miles	population
Azores		Autonomous Region of Portugal	2 300	888	242 073
Faroe Islands		Self-governing Danish Territory	1 399	540	47 000
Gibraltar		United Kingdom Overseas Territory	7	3	27 000
Guernsey		United Kingdom Crown Dependency	78	30	62 701
Isle of Man		United Kingdom Crown Dependency	572	221	75 000
Jersey		United Kingdom Crown Dependency	116	45	87 186

ASIA
COUNTRIES

		area sq km	area sq miles	population	capital
AFGHANISTAN		652 225	251 825	23 897 000	Kābul
ARMENIA		29 800	11 506	3 061 000	Yerevan
AZERBAIJAN		86 600	33 436	8 370 000	Baku
BAHRAIN		691	267	724 000	Manama
BANGLADESH		143 998	55 598	146 736 000	Dhaka
BHUTAN		46 620	18 000	2 257 000	Thimphu
BRUNEI		5 765	2 226	358 000	Bandar Seri Begawan
CAMBODIA		181 000	69 884	14 144 000	Phnom Penh
CHINA		9 584 492	3 700 593	1 289 161 000	Beijing
CYPRUS		9 251	3 572	802 000	Nicosia
EAST TIMOR		14 874	5 743	778 000	Dili
GEORGIA		69 700	26 911	5 126 000	T'bilisi

languages	religions	currency
Italian	Roman Catholic	Euro
Serbian, Albanian, Hungarian	Serbian Orthodox, Montenegrin Orthodox, Sunni Muslim	Serbian dinar, Euro
Slovak, Hungarian, Czech	Roman Catholic, Protestant, Orthodox	Slovakian koruna
Slovene, Croatian, Serbian	Roman Catholic, Protestant	Tólar
Castilian, Catalan, Galician, Basque	Roman Catholic	Euro
Swedish	Protestant, Roman Catholic	Swedish krona
German, French, Italian, Romansch	Roman Catholic, Protestant	Swiss franc
Ukrainian, Russian	Ukrainian Orthodox, Ukrainian Catholic, Roman Catholic	Hryvnia
English, Welsh, Gaelic	Protestant, Roman Catholic, Muslim	Pound sterling
Italian	Roman Catholic	Euro

capital	languages	religions	currency
Ponta Delgada	Portuguese	Roman Catholic, Protestant	Euro
Tórshavn	Faroese, Danish	Protestant	Danish krone
Gibraltar	English, Spanish	Roman Catholic, Protestant, Sunni Muslim	Gibraltar pound
St Peter Port	English, French	Protestant, Roman Catholic	Pound sterling
Douglas	English	Protestant, Roman Catholic	Pound sterling
St Helier	English, French	Protestant, Roman Catholic	Pound sterling

languages	religions	currency
Dari, Pushtu, Uzbek, Turkmen	Sunni Muslim, Shi'a Muslim	Afghani
Armenian, Azeri	Armenian Orthodox	Dram
Azeri, Armenian, Russian, Lezgian	Shi'a Muslim, Sunni Muslim, Russian and Armenian Orthodox	Azerbaijani manat
Arabic, English	Shi'a Muslim, Sunni Muslim Christian	Bahrain dinar
Bengali, English	Sunni Muslim, Hindu	Taka
Dzongkha, Nepali, Assamese	Buddhist, Hindu	Ngultrum, Indian rupee
Malay, English, Chinese	Sunni Muslim, Buddhist, Christian	Brunei dollar
Khmer, Vietnamese	Buddhist, Roman Catholic, Sunni Muslim	Riel
Mandarin, Wu, Cantonese, Hsiang, regional languages	Confucian, Taoist, Buddhist, Christian, Sunni Muslim	Yuan, Hong Kong dollar, Macau pataca
Greek, Turkish, English	Greek Orthodox, Sunni Muslim	Cyprus pound
Portuguese, Tetun, English	Roman Catholic	US dollar
Georgian, Russian, Armenian, Azeri, Ossetian, Abkhaz	Georgian Orthodox, Russian Orthodox, Sunni Muslim	Lari

	area sq km	area sq miles	population	capital
INDIA	3 064 898	1 183 364	1 065 462 000	New Delhi
INDONESIA	1 919 445	741 102	219 883 000	Jakarta
IRAN	1 648 000	636 296	68 920 000	Tehrān
IRAQ	438 317	169 235	25 175 000	Baghdād
ISRAEL	20 770	8 019	6 433 000	Jerusalem *(De facto capital. Disputed)*
JAPAN	377 727	145 841	127 654 000	Tōkyō
JORDAN	89 206	34 443	5 473 000	'Ammān
KAZAKHSTAN	2 717 300	1 049 155	15 433 000	Astana
KUWAIT	17 818	6 880	2 521 000	Kuwait
KYRGYZSTAN	198 500	76 641	5 138 000	Bishkek
LAOS	236 800	91 429	5 657 000	Vientiane
LEBANON	10 452	4 036	3 653 000	Beirut
MALAYSIA	332 965	128 559	24 425 000	Kuala Lumpur/Putrajaya
MALDIVES	298	115	318 000	Male
MONGOLIA	1 565 000	604 250	2 594 000	Ulan Bator
MYANMAR	676 577	261 228	49 485 000	Rangoon
NEPAL	147 181	56 827	25 164 000	Kathmandu
NORTH KOREA	120 538	46 540	22 664 000	P'yŏngyang
OMAN	309 500	119 499	2 851 000	Muscat
PAKISTAN	803 940	310 403	153 578 000	Islamabad
PALAU	497	192	20 000	Koror
PHILIPPINES	300 000	115 831	79 999 000	Manila
QATAR	11 437	4 416	610 000	Doha
RUSSIAN FEDERATION	17 075 400	6 592 849	143 246 000	Moscow
SAUDI ARABIA	2 200 000	849 425	24 217 000	Riyadh
SINGAPORE	639	247	4 253 000	Singapore
SOUTH KOREA	99 274	38 330	47 700 000	Seoul
SRI LANKA	65 610	25 332	19 065 000	Sri Jayewardenepura Kotte
SYRIA	185 180	71 498	17 800 000	Damascus
TAIWAN	36 179	13 969	22 548 000	T'aipei
TAJIKISTAN	143 100	55 251	6 245 000	Dushanbe
THAILAND	513 115	198 115	62 833 000	Bangkok
TURKEY	779 452	300 948	71 325 000	Ankara

languages	religions	currency
Hindi, English, many regional languages	Hindu, Sunni Muslim, Shi'a Muslim, Sikh, Christian	Indian rupee
Indonesian, local languages	Sunni Muslim, Protestant, Roman Catholic, Hindu, Buddhist	Rupiah
Farsi, Azeri, Kurdish, regional languages	Shi'a Muslim, Sunni Muslim	Iranian rial
Arabic, Kurdish, Turkmen	Shi'a Muslim, Sunni Muslim, Christian	Iraqi dinar
Hebrew, Arabic	Jewish, Sunni Muslim, Christian, Druze	Shekel
Japanese	Shintoist, Buddhist, Christian	Yen
Arabic	Sunni Muslim, Christian	Jordanian dinar
Kazakh, Russian, Ukrainian, German, Uzbek, Tatar	Sunni Muslim, Russian Orthodox, Protestant	Tenge
Arabic	Sunni Muslim, Shi'a Muslim, Christian, Hindu	Kuwaiti dinar
Kyrgyz, Russian, Uzbek	Sunni Muslim, Russian Orthodox	Kyrgyz som
Lao, local languages	Buddhist, traditional beliefs	Kip
Arabic, Armenian, French	Shi'a Muslim, Sunni Muslim, Christian	Lebanese pound
Malay, English, Chinese, Tamil, local languages	Sunni Muslim, Buddhist, Hindu, Christian, traditional beliefs	Ringgit
Divehi (Maldivian)	Sunni Muslim	Rufiyaa
Khalka (Mongolian), Kazakh, local languages	Buddhist, Sunni Muslim	Tugrik (tögrög)
Burmese, Shan, Karen, local languages	Buddhist, Christian, Sunni Muslim	Kyat
Nepali, Maithili, Bhojpuri, English, local languages	Hindu, Buddhist, Sunni Muslim	Nepalese rupee
Korean	Traditional beliefs, Chondoist, Buddhist	North Korean won
Arabic, Baluchi, Indian languages	Ibadhi Muslim, Sunni Muslim	Omani riyal
Urdu, Punjabi, Sindhi, Pushtu, English	Sunni Muslim, Shi'a Muslim, Christian, Hindu	Pakistani rupee
Palauan, English	Roman Catholic, Protestant, traditional beliefs	US dollar
English, Pilipino, Cebuano, local languages	Roman Catholic, Protestant, Sunni Muslim, Aglipayan	Philippine peso
Arabic	Sunni Muslim	Qatari riyal
Russian, Tatar, Ukrainian, local languages	Russian Orthodox, Sunni Muslim, Protestant	Russian rouble
Arabic	Sunni Muslim, Shi'a Muslim	Saudi Arabian riyal
Chinese, English, Malay, Tamil	Buddhist, Taoist, Sunni Muslim, Christian, Hindu	Singapore dollar
Korean	Buddhist, Protestant, Roman Catholic	South Korean won
Sinhalese, Tamil, English	Buddhist, Hindu, Sunni Muslim, Roman Catholic	Sri Lankan rupee
Arabic, Kurdish, Armenian	Sunni Muslim, Shi'a Muslim, Christian	Syrian pound
Mandarin, Min, Hakka, local languages	Buddhist, Taoist, Confucian, Christian	Taiwan dollar
Tajik, Uzbek, Russian	Sunni Muslim	Somoni
Thai, Lao, Chinese, Malay, Mon-Khmer languages	Buddhist, Sunni Muslim	Baht
Turkish, Kurdish	Sunni Muslim, Shi'a Muslim	Turkish lira

COUNTRIES (continued)		area sq km	area sq miles	population	capital
TURKMENISTAN		488 100	188 456	4 867 000	Ashgabat
UNITED ARAB EMIRATES		77 700	30 000	2 995 000	Abu Dhabi
UZBEKISTAN		447 400	172 742	26 093 000	Tashkent
VIETNAM		329 565	127 246	81 377 000	Ha Nôi
YEMEN		527 968	203 850	20 010 000	Şan'ā'

ASIA
DEPENDENT AND DISPUTED TERRITORIES

DEPENDENT AND DISPUTED TERRITORIES			area sq km	area sq miles	population
Christmas Island		Australian External Territory	135	52	1 560
Cocos Islands		Australian External Territory	14	5	632
Gaza		Semi-autonomous region	363	140	1 203 591
Jammu and Kashmir		Disputed territory (India/Pakistan)	222 236	85 806	13 000 000
West Bank		Disputed territory	5 860	2 263	2 303 660

AFRICA
COUNTRIES

COUNTRIES		area sq km	area sq miles	population	capital
ALGERIA		2 381 741	919 595	31 800 000	Algiers
ANGOLA		1 246 700	481 354	13 625 000	Luanda
BENIN		112 620	43 483	6 736 000	Porto-Novo
BOTSWANA		581 370	224 468	1 785 000	Gaborone
BURKINA		274 200	105 869	13 002 000	Ouagadougou
BURUNDI		27 835	10 747	6 825 000	Bujumbura
CAMEROON		475 442	183 569	16 018 000	Yaoundé
CAPE VERDE		4 033	1 557	463 000	Praia
CENTRAL AFRICAN REPUBLIC		622 436	240 324	3 865 000	Bangui
CHAD		1 284 000	495 755	8 598 000	Ndjamena
COMOROS		1 862	719	768 000	Moroni
CONGO		342 000	132 047	3 724 000	Brazzaville
CONGO, DEMOCRATIC REP. OF		2 345 410	905 568	52 771 000	Kinshasa
CÔTE D'IVOIRE		322 463	124 504	16 631 000	Yamoussoukro
DJIBOUTI		23 200	8 958	703 000	Djibouti
EGYPT		1 000 250	386 199	71 931 000	Cairo
EQUATORIAL GUINEA		28 051	10 831	494 000	Malabo
ERITREA		117 400	45 328	4 141 000	Asmara

languages	religions	currency
urkmen, Uzbek, Russian	Sunni Muslim, Russian Orthodox	Turkmen manat
rabic, English	Sunni Muslim, Shi'a Muslim	United Arab Emirates dirham
zbek, Russian, Tajik, Kazakh	Sunni Muslim, Russian Orthodox	Uzbek som
etnamese, Thai, Khmer, Chinese, local languages	Buddhist, Taoist, Roman Catholic, Cao Dai, Hoa Hao	Dong
rabic	Sunni Muslim, Shi'a Muslim	Yemeni rial

apital	languages	religions	currency
ne Settlement	English	Buddhist, Sunni Muslim, Protestant, Roman Catholic	Australian dollar
West Island	English	Sunni Muslim, Christian	Australian dollar
aza	Arabic	Sunni Muslim, Shi'a Muslim	Israeli shekel
rinagar			
	Arabic, Hebrew	Sunni Muslim, Jewish, Shi'a Muslim, Christian	Jordanian dinar, Israeli shekel

languages	religions	currency
rabic, French, Berber	Sunni Muslim	Algerian dinar
ortuguese, Bantu, local languages	Roman Catholic, Protestant, traditional beliefs	Kwanza
rench, Fon, Yoruba, Adja, local languages	Traditional beliefs, Roman Catholic, Sunni Muslim	CFA franc*
nglish, Setswana, Shona, local languages	Traditional beliefs, Protestant, Roman Catholic	Pula
rench, Moore (Mossi), Fulani, local languages	Sunni Muslim, traditional beliefs, Roman Catholic	CFA franc*
irundi (Hutu, Tutsi), French	Roman Catholic, traditional beliefs, Protestant	Burundian franc
rench, English, Fang, Bamileke, local languages	Roman Catholic, traditional beliefs, Sunni Muslim, Protestant	CFA franc*
ortuguese, creole	Roman Catholic, Protestant	Cape Verde escudo
rench, Sango, Banda, Baya, local languages	Protestant, Roman Catholic, traditional beliefs, Sunni Muslim	CFA franc*
rabic, French, Sara, local languages	Sunni Muslim, Roman Catholic, Protestant, traditional beliefs	CFA franc*
omorian, French, Arabic	Sunni Muslim, Roman Catholic	Comoros franc
rench, Kongo, Monokutuba, local languages	Roman Catholic, Protestant, traditional beliefs, Sunni Muslim	CFA franc*
rench, Lingala, Swahili, Kongo, local languages	Christian, Sunni Muslim	Congolese franc
rench, creole, Akan, local languages	Sunni Muslim, Roman Catholic, traditional beliefs, Protestant	CFA franc*
omali, Afar, French, Arabic	Sunni Muslim, Christian	Djibouti franc
rabic	Sunni Muslim, Coptic Christian	Egyptian pound
panish, French, Fang	Roman Catholic, traditional beliefs	CFA franc*
igrinya, Tigre	Sunni Muslim, Coptic Christian	Nakfa

		area sq km	area sq miles	population	capital
ETHIOPIA		1 133 880	437 794	70 678 000	Addis Ababa
GABON		267 667	103 347	1 329 000	Libreville
THE GAMBIA		11 295	4 361	1 426 000	Banjul
GHANA		238 537	92 100	20 922 000	Accra
GUINEA		245 857	94 926	8 480 000	Conakry
GUINEA-BISSAU		36 125	13 948	1 493 000	Bissau
KENYA		582 646	224 961	31 987 000	Nairobi
LESOTHO		30 355	11 720	1 802 000	Maseru
LIBERIA		111 369	43 000	3 367 000	Monrovia
LIBYA		1 759 540	679 362	5 551 000	Tripoli
MADAGASCAR		587 041	226 658	17 404 000	Antananarivo
MALAWI		118 484	45 747	12 105 000	Lilongwe
MALI		1 240 140	478 821	13 007 000	Bamako
MAURITANIA		1 030 700	397 955	2 893 000	Nouakchott
MAURITIUS		2 040	788	1 221 000	Port Louis
MOROCCO		446 550	172 414	30 566 000	Rabat
MOZAMBIQUE		799 380	308 642	18 863 000	Maputo
NAMIBIA		824 292	318 261	1 987 000	Windhoek
NIGER		1 267 000	489 191	11 972 000	Niamey
NIGERIA		923 768	356 669	124 009 000	Abuja
RWANDA		26 338	10 169	8 387 000	Kigali
SÃO TOMÉ AND PRÍNCIPE		964	372	161 000	São Tomé
SENEGAL		196 720	75 954	10 095 000	Dakar
SEYCHELLES		455	176	81 000	Victoria
SIERRA LEONE		71 740	27 699	4 971 000	Freetown
SOMALIA		637 657	246 201	9 890 000	Mogadishu
SOUTH AFRICA, REPUBLIC OF		1 219 090	470 693	45 026 000	Pretoria/Cape Town
SUDAN		2 505 813	967 500	33 610 000	Khartoum
SWAZILAND		17 364	6 704	1 077 000	Mbabane
TANZANIA		945 087	364 900	36 977 000	Dodoma
TOGO		56 785	21 925	4 909 000	Lomé
TUNISIA		164 150	63 379	9 832 000	Tunis
UGANDA		241 038	93 065	25 827 000	Kampala

languages	religions	currency
romo, Amharic, Tigrinya, local languages	Ethiopian Orthodox, Sunni Muslim, traditional beliefs	Birr
rench, Fang, local languages	Roman Catholic, Protestant, traditional beliefs	CFA franc*
nglish, Malinke, Fulani, Wolof	Sunni Muslim, Protestant	Dalasi
nglish, Hausa, Akan, local languages	Christian, Sunni Muslim, traditional beliefs	Cedi
rench, Fulani, Malinke, local languages	Sunni Muslim, traditional beliefs, Christian	Guinea franc
ortuguese, crioulo, local languages	Traditional beliefs, Sunni Muslim, Christian	CFA franc*
wahili, English, local languages	Christian, traditional beliefs	Kenyan shilling
esotho, English, Zulu	Christian, traditional beliefs	Loti, S. African rand
nglish, creole, local languages	Traditional beliefs, Christian, Sunni Muslim	Liberian dollar
rabic, Berber	Sunni Muslim	Libyan dinar
alalagasy, French	Traditional beliefs, Christian, Sunni Muslim	Malagasy franc
hichewa, English, local languages	Christian, traditional beliefs, Sunni Muslim	Malawian kwacha
rench, Bambara, local languages	Sunni Muslim, traditional beliefs, Christian	CFA franc*
rabic, French, local languages	Sunni Muslim	Ouguiya
nglish, creole, Hindi, Bhojpurī, French	Hindu, Roman Catholic, Sunni Muslim	Mauritius rupee
rabic, Berber, French	Sunni Muslim	Moroccan dirham
ortuguese, Makua, Tsonga, local languages	Traditional beliefs, Roman Catholic, Sunni Muslim	Metical
nglish, Afrikaans, German, Ovambo, local languages	Protestant, Roman Catholic	Namibian dollar
rench, Hausa, Fulani, local languages	Sunni Muslim, traditional beliefs	CFA franc*
nglish, Hausa, Yoruba, Ibo, Fulani, local languages	Sunni Muslim, Christian, traditional beliefs	Naira
nyarwanda, French, English	Roman Catholic, traditional beliefs, Protestant	Rwandan franc
ortuguese, creole	Roman Catholic, Protestant	Dobra
rench, Wolof, Fulani, local languages	Sunni Muslim, Roman Catholic, traditional beliefs	CFA franc*
nglish, French, creole	Roman Catholic, Protestant	Seychelles rupee
nglish, creole, Mende, Temne, local languages	Sunni Muslim, traditional beliefs	Leone
omali, Arabic	Sunni Muslim	Somali shilling
frikaans, English, nine official local languages	Protestant, Roman Catholic, Sunni Muslim, Hindu	Rand
rabic, Dinka, Nubian, Beja, Nuer, local languages	Sunni Muslim, traditional beliefs, Christian	Sudanese dinar
wazi, English	Christian, traditional beliefs	Emalangeni, S. African rand
wahili, English, Nyamwezi, local languages	Shi'a Muslim, Sunni Muslim, traditional beliefs, Christian	Tanzanian shilling
rench, Ewe, Kabre, local languages	Traditional beliefs, Christian, Sunni Muslim	CFA franc*
rabic, French	Sunni Muslim	Tunisian dinar
nglish, Swahili, Luganda, local languages	Roman Catholic, Protestant, Sunni Muslim, traditional beliefs	Ugandan shilling

AFRICA
COUNTRIES (continued)

		area sq km	area sq miles	population	capital
ZAMBIA		752 614	290 586	10 812 000	Lusaka
ZIMBABWE		390 759	150 873	12 891 000	Harare

AFRICA
DEPENDENT AND DISPUTED TERRITORIES

			area sq km	area sq miles	population
Canary Islands		Autonomous Community of Spain	7 447	2 875	1 694 477
Madeira		Autonomous Region of Portugal	779	301	242 603
Mayotte		French Territorial Collectivity	373	144	171 000
Réunion		French Overseas Department	2 551	985	756 000
St Helena and Dependencies		United Kingdom Overseas Territory	121	47	5 644
Western Sahara		Disputed territory (Morocco)	266 000	102 703	308 000

OCEANIA
COUNTRIES

		area sq km	area sq miles	population	capital
AUSTRALIA		7 692 024	2 969 907	19 731 000	Canberra
FIJI		18 330	7 077	839 000	Suva
KIRIBATI		717	277	88 000	Bairiki
MARSHALL ISLANDS		181	70	53 000	Delap-Uliga-Djarrit
MICRONESIA, FED. STATES OF		701	271	109 000	Palikir
NAURU		21	8	13 000	Yaren
NEW ZEALAND		270 534	104 454	3 875 000	Wellington
PAPUA NEW GUINEA		462 840	178 704	5 711 000	Port Moresby
SAMOA		2 831	1 093	178 000	Apia
SOLOMON ISLANDS		28 370	10 954	477 000	Honiara
TONGA		748	289	104 000	Nuku'alofa
TUVALU		25	10	11 000	Vaiaku
VANUATU		12 190	4 707	212 000	Port Vila

OCEANIA
DEPENDENT TERRITORIES

			area sq km	area sq miles	population
American Samoa		United States Unincorporated Territory	197	76	67 000
Cook Islands		Self-governing New Zealand Territory	293	113	18 000
French Polynesia		French Overseas Territory	3 265	1 261	244 000
Guam		United States Unincorporated Territory	541	209	163 000
New Caledonia		French Overseas Territory	19 058	7 358	228 000

languages	religions	currency
English, Bemba, Nyanja, Tonga, local languages	Christian, traditional beliefs	Zambian kwacha
English, Shona, Ndebele	Christian, traditional beliefs	Zimbabwean dollar

pital	languages	religions	currency
nta Cruz de Tenerife, Las Palmas	Spanish	Roman Catholic	Euro
nchal	Portuguese	Roman Catholic, Protestant	Euro
aoudzi	French, Mahorian	Sunni Muslim, Christian	Euro
Denis	French, creole	Roman Catholic	Euro
mestown	English	Protestant, Roman Catholic	St Helena pound
âyoune	Arabic	Sunni Muslim	Moroccan dirham

*Communauté Financière Africaine franc

languages	religions	currency
English, Italian, Greek	Protestant, Roman Catholic, Orthodox	Australian dollar
English, Fijian, Hindi	Christian, Hindu, Sunni Muslim	Fiji dollar
bertese, English	Roman Catholic, Protestant	Australian dollar
English, Marshallese	Protestant, Roman Catholic	US dollar
English, Chuukese, Pohnpeian, local languages	Roman Catholic, Protestant	US dollar
auruan, English	Protestant, Roman Catholic	Australian dollar
English, Maori	Protestant, Roman Catholic	New Zealand dollar
English, Tok Pisin (creole), local languages	Protestant, Roman Catholic, traditional beliefs	Kina
amoan, English	Protestant, Roman Catholic	Tala
English, creole, local languages	Protestant, Roman Catholic	Solomon Islands dollar
ngan, English	Protestant, Roman Catholic	Pa'anga
valuan, English	Protestant	Australian dollar
English, Bislama (creole), French	Protestant, Roman Catholic, traditional beliefs	Vatu

pital	languages	religions	currency
gotogo	Samoan, English	Protestant, Roman Catholic	US dollar
arua	English, Maori	Protestant, Roman Catholic	New Zealand dollar
peete	French, Tahitian, Polynesian languages	Protestant, Roman Catholic	CFP franc*
agâtña	Chamorro, English, Tapalog	Roman Catholic	US dollar
uméa	French, local languages	Roman Catholic, Protestant, Sunni Muslim	CFP franc*

OCEANIA DEPENDENT TERRITORIES (continued)		area sq km	area sq miles	population
Niue		Self-governing New Zealand Territory	258	100	2 000
Norfolk Island		Australian External Territory	35	14	2 037
Northern Mariana Islands		United States Commonwealth	477	184	79 000
Pitcairn Islands		United Kingdom Overseas Territory	45	17	51
Tokelau		New Zealand Overseas Territory	10	4	2 000
Wallis and Futuna Islands		French Overseas Territory	274	106	15 000

NORTH AMERICA COUNTRIES		area sq km	area sq miles	population	capital
ANTIGUA AND BARBUDA		442	171	73 000	St John's
THE BAHAMAS		13 939	5 382	314 000	Nassau
BARBADOS		430	166	270 000	Bridgetown
BELIZE		22 965	8 867	256 000	Belmopan
CANADA		9 984 670	3 855 103	31 510 000	Ottawa
COSTA RICA		51 100	19 730	4 173 000	San José
CUBA		110 860	42 803	11 300 000	Havana
DOMINICA		750	290	79 000	Roseau
DOMINICAN REPUBLIC		48 442	18 704	8 745 000	Santo Domingo
EL SALVADOR		21 041	8 124	6 515 000	San Salvador
GRENADA		378	146	80 000	St George's
GUATEMALA		108 890	42 043	12 347 000	Guatemala City
HAITI		27 750	10 714	8 326 000	Port-au-Prince
HONDURAS		112 088	43 277	6 941 000	Tegucigalpa
JAMAICA		10 991	4 244	2 651 000	Kingston
MEXICO		1 972 545	761 604	103 457 000	Mexico City
NICARAGUA		130 000	50 193	5 466 000	Managua
PANAMA		77 082	29 762	3 120 000	Panama City
ST KITTS AND NEVIS		261	101	42 000	Basseterre
ST LUCIA		616	238	149 000	Castries
ST VINCENT AND THE GRENADINES		389	150	120 000	Kingstown
TRINIDAD AND TOBAGO		5 130	1 981	1 303 000	Port of Spain
UNITED STATES OF AMERICA		9 826 635	3 794 085	294 043 000	Washington DC

capital	languages	religions	currency
Alofi	English, Polynesian	Christian	New Zealand dollar
Kingston	English	Protestant, Roman Catholic	Australian dollar
Capitol Hill	English, Chamorro, local languages	Roman Catholic	US dollar
Adamstown	English	Protestant	New Zealand dollar
	English, Tokelauan	Christian	New Zealand dollar
Matā'utu	French, Wallisian, Futunian	Roman Catholic	CFP franc*

*Franc des Comptoirs Français du Pacifique

languages	religions	currency
English, creole	Protestant, Roman Catholic	East Caribbean dollar
English, creole	Protestant, Roman Catholic	Bahamian dollar
English, creole	Protestant, Roman Catholic	Barbados dollar
English, Spanish, Mayan, creole	Roman Catholic, Protestant	Belize dollar
English, French	Roman Catholic, Protestant, Eastern Orthodox, Jewish	Canadian dollar
Spanish	Roman Catholic, Protestant	Costa Rican colón
Spanish	Roman Catholic, Protestant	Cuban peso
English, creole	Roman Catholic, Protestant	East Caribbean dollar
Spanish, creole	Roman Catholic, Protestant	Dominican peso
Spanish	Roman Catholic, Protestant	El Salvador colón, US dollar
English, creole	Roman Catholic, Protestant	East Caribbean dollar
Spanish, Mayan languages	Roman Catholic, Protestant	Quetzal, US dollar
French, creole	Roman Catholic, Protestant, Voodoo	Gourde
Spanish, Amerindian languages	Roman Catholic, Protestant	Lempira
English, creole	Protestant, Roman Catholic	Jamaican dollar
Spanish, Amerindian languages	Roman Catholic, Protestant	Mexican peso
Spanish, Amerindian languages	Roman Catholic, Protestant	Córdoba
Spanish, English, Amerindian languages	Roman Catholic, Protestant, Sunni Muslim	Balboa
English, creole	Protestant, Roman Catholic	East Caribbean dollar
English, creole	Roman Catholic, Protestant	East Caribbean dollar
English, creole	Protestant, Roman Catholic	East Caribbean dollar
English, creole, Hindi	Roman Catholic, Hindu, Protestant, Sunni Muslim	Trinidad and Tobago dollar
English, Spanish	Protestant, Roman Catholic, Sunni Muslim, Jewish	US dollar

NORTH AMERICA DEPENDENT TERRITORIES			area sq km	area sq miles	populatio
Anguilla		United Kingdom Overseas Territory	155	60	12 00
Aruba		Self-governing Netherlands Territory	193	75	100 00
Bermuda		United Kingdom Overseas Territory	54	21	82 00
Cayman Islands		United Kingdom Overseas Territory	259	100	40 00
Greenland		Self-governing Danish Territory	2 175 600	840 004	57 00
Guadeloupe		French Overseas Department	1 780	687	440 00
Martinique		French Overseas Department	1 079	417	393 00
Montserrat		United Kingdom Overseas Territory	100	39	4 00
Netherlands Antilles		Self-governing Netherlands Territory	800	309	221 00
Puerto Rico		United States Commonwealth	9 104	3 515	3 879 00
St Pierre and Miquelon		French Territorial Collectivity	242	93	6 00
Turks and Caicos Islands		United Kingdom Overseas Territory	430	166	21 00
Virgin Islands (U.K.)		United Kingdom Overseas Territory	153	59	21 00
Virgin Islands (U.S.A.)		United States Unincorporated Territory	352	136	111 00

SOUTH AMERICA COUNTRIES		area sq km	area sq miles	population	capital
ARGENTINA		2 766 889	1 068 302	38 428 000	Buenos Aires
BOLIVIA		1 098 581	424 164	8 808 000	La Paz/Sucre
BRAZIL		8 514 879	3 287 613	178 470 000	Brasília
CHILE		756 945	292 258	15 805 000	Santiago
COLOMBIA		1 141 748	440 831	44 222 000	Bogotá
ECUADOR		272 045	105 037	13 003 000	Quito
GUYANA		214 969	83 000	765 000	Georgetown
PARAGUAY		406 752	157 048	5 878 000	Asunción
PERU		1 285 216	496 225	27 167 000	Lima
SURINAME		163 820	63 251	436 000	Paramaribo
URUGUAY		176 215	68 037	3 415 000	Montevideo
VENEZUELA		912 050	352 144	25 699 000	Caracas

SOUTH AMERICA DEPENDENT TERRITORIES			area sq km	area sq miles	populatio
Falkland Islands		United Kingdom Overseas Territory	12 170	4 699	3 00
French Guiana		French Overseas Department	90 000	34 749	178 000

capital	languages	religions	currency
The Valley	English	Protestant, Roman Catholic	East Caribbean dollar
Oranjestad	Papiamento, Dutch, English	Roman Catholic, Protestant	Arubian florin
Hamilton	English	Protestant, Roman Catholic	Bermuda dollar
George Town	English	Protestant, Roman Catholic	Cayman Islands dollar
Nuuk	Greenlandic, Danish	Protestant	Danish krone
Basse-Terre	French, creole	Roman Catholic	Euro
Fort-de-France	French, creole	Roman Catholic, traditional beliefs	Euro
Plymouth	English	Protestant, Roman Catholic	East Caribbean dollar
Willemstad	Dutch, Papiamento, English	Roman Catholic, Protestant	Netherlands guilder
San Juan	Spanish, English	Roman Catholic, Protestant	US dollar
St-Pierre	French	Roman Catholic	Euro
Grand Turk	English	Protestant	US dollar
Road Town	English	Protestant, Roman Catholic	US dollar
Charlotte Amalie	English, Spanish	Protestant, Roman Catholic	

languages	religions	currency
Spanish, Italian, Amerindian languages	Roman Catholic, Protestant	Argentinian peso
Spanish, Quechua, Aymara	Roman Catholic, Protestant, Baha'i	Boliviano
Portuguese	Roman Catholic, Protestant	Real
Spanish, Amerindian languages	Roman Catholic, Protestant	Chilean peso
Spanish, Amerindian languages	Roman Catholic, Protestant	Colombian peso
Spanish, Quechua, other Amerindian languages	Roman Catholic	US dollar
English, creole, Amerindian languages	Protestant, Hindu, Roman Catholic, Sunni Muslim	Guyana dollar
Spanish, Guaraní	Roman Catholic, Protestant	Guaraní
Spanish, Quechua, Aymara	Roman Catholic, Protestant	Sol
Dutch, Surinamese, English, Hindi	Hindu, Roman Catholic, Protestant, Sunni Muslim	Suriname guilder
Spanish	Roman Catholic, Protestant, Jewish	Uruguayan peso
Spanish, Amerindian languages	Roman Catholic, Protestant	Bolivar

capital	languages	religions	currency
Stanley	English	Protestant, Roman Catholic	Falkland Islands pound
Cayenne	French, creole	Roman Catholic	Euro

World extremes – capitals

Largest national capital (population)	**Tōkyō**, Japan	26 849 000
Smallest national capital (population)	**Vatican City**	472
Most northerly national capital	**Reykjavík**, Iceland	64° 08'N
Most southerly national capital	**Wellington**, New Zealand	41° 18'S
Highest capital	**La Paz**, Bolivia	3 630 m 11 909 ft

AL.	ALBANIA
A.	ANDORRA
ARM.	ARMENIA
AUS.	AUSTRIA
AZ.	AZERBAIJAN
B.	BURUNDI
BE.	BENIN
BEL.	BELGIUM
B.H.	BOSNIA-HERZEGOVINA
BN.	BAHRAIN
BUR.	BURKINA
CAM.	CAMEROON
C.A.R.	CENTRAL AFRICAN REPUBLIC
C.D'I.	CÔTE D'IVOIRE
CR.	CROATIA
CYP.	CYPRUS
CZ.R.	CZECH REPUBLIC
DEN.	DENMARK
EQ.G.	EQUATORIAL GUINEA
FR.G.	FRENCH GUIANA
GEOR.	GEORGIA
GER.	GERMANY
GH.	GHANA
GUY.	GUYANA
HUN.	HUNGARY
ISR.	ISRAEL

JOR.	JORDAN
K.	KUWAIT
KYR.	KYRGYZSTAN
LEB.	LEBANON
LITH.	LITHUANIA
LUX.	LUXEMBOURG
M.	MACEDONIA
MO.	MOLDOVA
NETH.	NETHERLANDS
NI.	NIGERIA
POL.	POLAND
Q.	QATAR
R.	RWANDA
SLA.	SLOVAKIA
SL.	SLOVENIA
S.M.	SERBIA AND MONTENEGRO
SUR.	SURINAME
SW.	SWITZERLAND
T.	TOGO
TAJIK.	TAJIKISTAN
TURKM.	TURKMENISTAN
U.A.E.	UNITED ARAB EMIRATES
UZBEK.	UZBEKISTAN

1:180 000 000

0   1000   2000   3000 miles
0   2000   4000 km

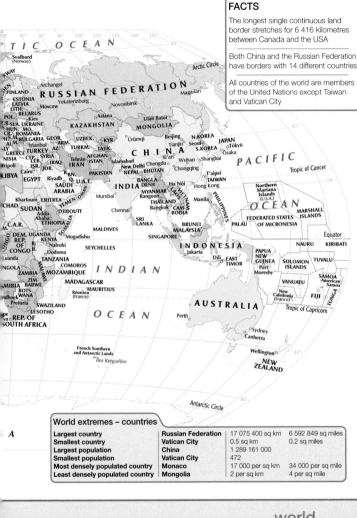

World extremes – countries

Largest country	Russian Federation	17 075 400 sq km	6 592 849 sq miles
Smallest country	Vatican City	0.5 sq km	0.2 sq miles
Largest population	China	1 289 161 000	
Smallest population	Vatican City	472	
Most densely populated country	Monaco	17 000 per sq km	34 000 per sq mile
Least densely populated country	Mongolia	2 per sq km	4 per sq mile

FACTS

The Pacific Ocean is larger than all the continents' land areas combined

52% of the earth's land surface is below 500 metres

Lake Baikal, in the Russian Federation, is the world's deepest lake with a maximum depth of 1 637 metres

Earth's dimensions

Total area	509 450 000 sq km	196 699 746 sq miles
Land area	148 721 936 sq km	57 421 861 sq miles
Water area	360 728 064 sq km	139 277 885 sq miles
Equatorial diameter	12 756 km	7 927 miles
Polar diameter	12 714 km	7 901 miles
Equatorial circumference	40 075 km	24 903 miles
Meridional circumference	40 008 km	24 861 miles

Map labels: Greenland, Iceland, British Isles, Baffin Island, Hudson Bay, Labrador, NORTH AMERICA, Mt McKinley △6194, Mt Logan △5959, Rocky Mountains, Missouri, Great Lakes, Newfoundland, Appalachian Mts, Rio Grande, Mississippi, Azores, Sa Madre Occidental, Hawaiian Islands, Gulf of Mexico, Cuba, Hispaniola, Canary Islands, Atlas Mount, Caribbean Sea, Cape Verde, ATLANTIC, S a h, Line Islands, PACIFIC, Galapagos Islands, Orinoco, OCEAN, A, Gulf of Guine, OCEAN, Amazon, SOUTH AMERICA, Ascension, Polynesia, Andes, Brazilian Highlands, St Helena, Tuamotu Islands, Tubuai Islands, Cerro Aconcagua △6959, Tristan da Cunh, Patagonia, Falkland Islands, South Georgia, South Sandwich Islands, Isla Grande de Tierra del Fuego, Cape Horn, Antarctic Peninsula, Amundsen Sea, Weddell Sea, Vinson Massif △4897, ANTAR

1:180 000 000

0	1000	2000	3000 miles
0	2000		4000 km

ARCTIC OCEAN

Arctic Circle

EUROPE

Scandinavia
North European Plain
Ural Mountains
Danube
Black Sea
Caspian Sea
Mediterranean Sea
El'brus △ 5642

West Siberian Plain
Yenisey
Ob'
Irtysh
Central Siberia
Siberian Plateau
Lena
Lake Baikal
Amur
Gobi
Tien Shan
Kunlun Shan
Himalaya
Mt Everest 8848
Aral Sea
Volga
Zagros Mts
Red Sea
The Gulf
Arabian Peninsula

A S I A

Sea of Okhotsk
Bering Sea
Sea of Japan
Honshū
Yellow
East China Sea
Yangtze
Ganges
Indus
Deccan
Arabian Sea
Bay of Bengal
Maldives
Sri Lanka
Mekong

PACIFIC OCEAN

Tropic of Cancer

Mariana Trench
Challenger Deep 10920 •
Micronesia

Equator

AFRICA

Nile
Ethiopian Highlands
Congo Basin
Great Rift Valley
Lake Victoria
Kilimanjaro 5892
Zambezi
Kalahari Desert
Cape of Good Hope
Madagascar

Seychelles

INDIAN OCEAN

Philippines
South China Sea
Borneo
Sumatra
Java
Celebes
Puncak Jaya △ 5030
New Guinea
Arafura Sea

Melanesia

Coral Sea

AUSTRALIA
Great Victoria Desert
Great Australian Bight
Great Dividing Ra.
Darling

Tropic of Capricorn

Tasman Sea
Tasmania
New Zealand

Îles Kerguélen

Davis Sea

Antarctic Circle

ANTARCTICA

World extremes			
Highest mountain	**Mt Everest**, China/Nepal	8 848 metres	29 028 feet
Longest river	**Nile**, Africa	6 695 km	4 160 miles
Largest lake	**Caspian Sea**, Asia/Europe	371 000 sq km	143 244 sq miles
Largest island	**Greenland**, North America	2 175 600 sq km	840 004 sq miles
Largest drainage basin	**Amazon**, South America	7 050 000 sq km	2 722 005 sq miles
Lowest point	**Dead Sea**, Asia	-398 miles	-1 306 feet
Deepest water	**Challenger Deep**, Pacific Ocean	10 920 metres	35 826 feet

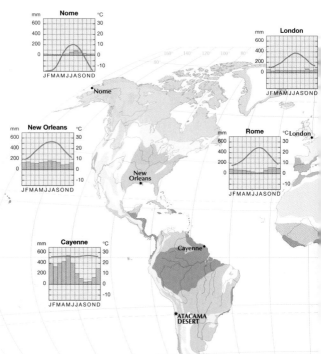

Nome

mm		°C
600		30
400		20
200		10
0		0
		-10

J F M A M J J A S O N D

London

mm		
600		
400		
200		
0		

J F M A M J J A S O N D

New Orleans

mm		°C
600		30
400		20
200		10
0		0
		-10

J F M A M J J A S O N D

Rome

mm		°C
600		30
400		20
200		10
0		0
		-10

J F M A M J J A S O N D

Cayenne

mm		°C
600		30
400		20
200		10
0		0
		-10

J F M A M J J A S O N D

Nome

New Orleans

London

Rome

Cayenne

ATACAMA DESERT

Climate graphs

Average monthly rainfall

Average monthly temperature

Weather extremes

Highest recorded temperature	**57.8°C/136°F** Al 'Aziziyah, Libya (September 1922)
Hottest place (annual mean)	34.4°C/93.9°F **Dalol**, Ethiopia
Driest place (annual mean)	0.1 mm/0.004 inches **Atacama Desert**, Chile
Lowest recorded temperature	**-89.2°C/-128.6°F** Vostok Station, Antarctica (July 1983)
Coldest place (annual mean)	-56.6°C/-69.9°F **Plateau Station**, Antarctica
Wettest place (annual mean)	11 873 mm/467.4 inches **Meghalaya**, India

So
Po

1:180 000 000

0   1000   2000   3000 miles
0   2000   4000 km

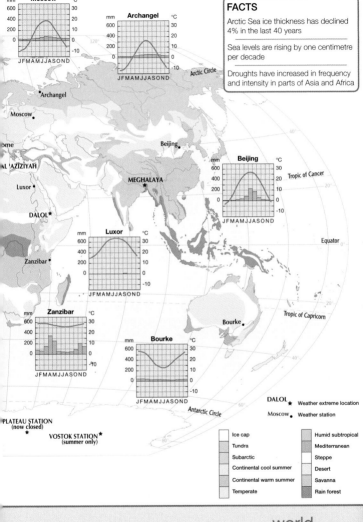

FACTS

Arctic Sea ice thickness has declined 4% in the last 40 years

Sea levels are rising by one centimetre per decade

Droughts have increased in frequency and intensity in parts of Asia and Africa

DALOL ★ Weather extreme location

Moscow • Weather station

Ice cap
Tundra
Subarctic
Continental cool summer
Continental warm summer
Temperate
Humid subtropical
Mediterranean
Steppe
Desert
Savanna
Rain forest

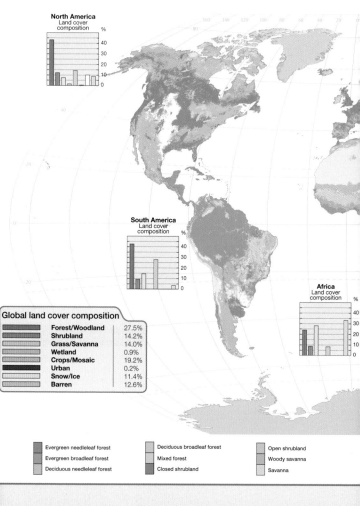

North America
Land cover composition

South America
Land cover composition

Africa
Land cover composition

Global land cover composition

	Forest/Woodland	27.5%
	Shrubland	14.2%
	Grass/Savanna	14.0%
	Wetland	0.9%
	Crops/Mosaic	19.2%
	Urban	0.2%
	Snow/Ice	11.4%
	Barren	12.6%

Evergreen needleleaf forest

Evergreen broadleaf forest

Deciduous needleleaf forest

Deciduous broadleaf forest

Mixed forest

Closed shrubland

Open shrubland

Woody savanna

Savanna

1:180 000 000

0 1000 2000 3000 miles

0 2000 4000 km

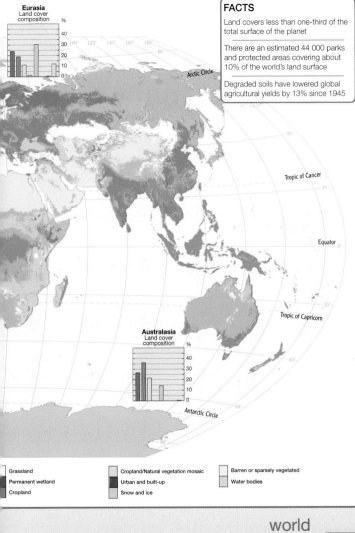

Eurasia
Land cover composition

Australasia
Land cover composition

FACTS

Land covers less than one-third of the total surface of the planet

There are an estimated 44 000 parks and protected areas covering about 10% of the world's land surface

Degraded soils have lowered global agricultural yields by 13% since 1945

Arctic Circle

Tropic of Cancer

Equator

Tropic of Capricorn

Antarctic Circle

Grassland

Permanent wetland

Cropland

Cropland/Natural vegetation mosaic

Urban and built-up

Snow and ice

Barren or sparsely vegetated

Water bodies

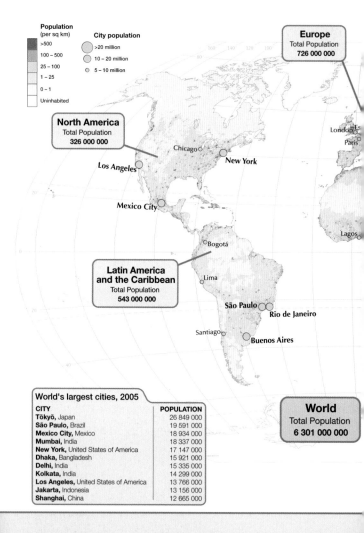

Population
(per sq km)

>500
100 – 500
25 – 100
1 – 25
0 – 1
Uninhabited

City population

⬤ >20 million
◯ 10 – 20 million
○ 5 – 10 million

Europe
Total Population
726 000 000

North America
Total Population
326 000 000

Chicago ○
New York ○
Los Angeles ○
Mexico City ○

London ○ Es
Paris ○

Lagos ○

Bogotá ○

**Latin America
and the Caribbean**
Total Population
543 000 000

Lima ○

São Paulo ○○
Rio de Janeiro

Santiago ○

Buenos Aires ○

World's largest cities, 2005	
CITY	POPULATION
Tōkyō, Japan	26 849 000
São Paulo, Brazil	19 591 000
Mexico City, Mexico	18 934 000
Mumbai, India	18 337 000
New York, United States of America	17 147 000
Dhaka, Bangladesh	15 921 000
Delhi, India	15 335 000
Kolkata, India	14 299 000
Los Angeles, United States of America	13 766 000
Jakarta, Indonesia	13 156 000
Shanghai, China	12 665 000

World
Total Population
6 301 000 000

1:180 000 000

0 1000 2000 3000 miles
0   2000   4000 km

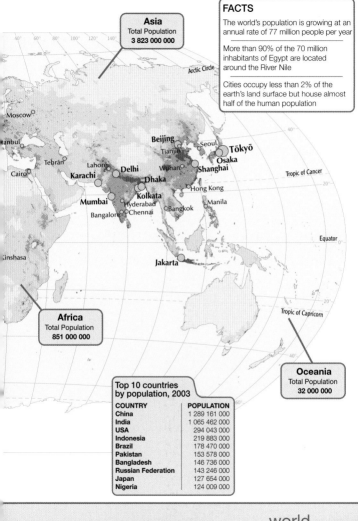

Asia
Total Population
3 823 000 000

FACTS

The world's population is growing at an annual rate of 77 million people per year

More than 90% of the 70 million inhabitants of Egypt are located around the River Nile

Cities occupy less than 2% of the earth's land surface but house almost half of the human population

Africa
Total Population
851 000 000

Oceania
Total Population
32 000 000

Top 10 countries by population, 2003

COUNTRY	POPULATION
China	1 289 161 000
India	1 065 462 000
USA	294 043 000
Indonesia	219 883 000
Brazil	178 470 000
Pakistan	153 578 000
Bangladesh	146 736 000
Russian Federation	143 246 000
Japan	127 654 000
Nigeria	124 009 000

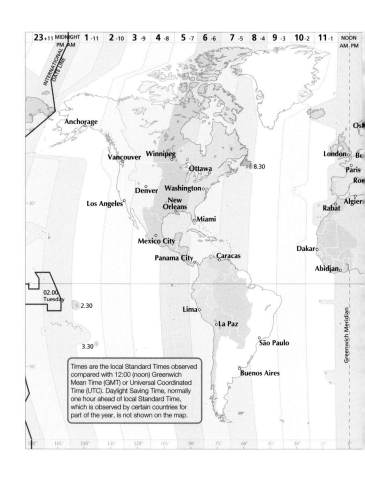

23 +11 MIDNIGHT 1 -11 2 -10 3 -9 4 -8 5 -7 6 -6 7 -5 8 -4 9 -3 10 -2 11 -1 NOON
PM AM   AM PM

INTERNATIONAL DATE LINE

Anchorage

Os▮

London○ B▮

Vancouver   Winnipeg

Paris
Ro▮

Ottawa   8.30

Denver   Washington

Algier▮

Los Angeles○   New Orleans

Rabat○

Miami○

Mexico City○

Panama City○   ○Caracas

Dakar○

Abidjan○

02.00
Tuesday   2.30

Lima○

Greenwich Meridian

La Paz○

3.30○   São Paulo○

Buenos Aires○

Times are the local Standard Times observed
compared with 12:00 (noon) Greenwich
Mean Time (GMT) or Universal Coordinated
Time (UTC). Daylight Saving Time, normally
one hour ahead of local Standard Time,
which is observed by certain countries for
part of the year, is not shown on the map.

180°   165°   150°   135°   120°   105°   90°   75°   60°   45°   30°   15°   0°

34   1:180 000 000   0   1000   2000   3000 miles
                     0   2000   4000 km

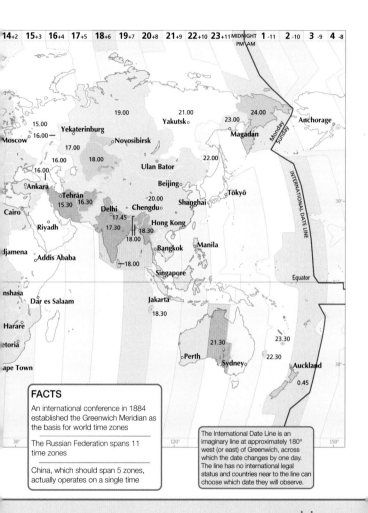

19.00
21.00
Yakutsk
23.00
24.00
Anchorage

15.00
Yekaterinburg
16.00
Moscow
Magadan
Monday
Sunday

17.00
Novosibirsk

16.00
18.00
Ulan Bator
22.00
INTERNATIONAL DATE LINE

Ankara
Beijing
Tōkyō

Tehrān
15.30 16.30
20.00
Shanghai

Cairo
Delhi
Chengdu
17.45

Riyadh
17.30
Hong Kong
18.30

18.00
djamena
Addis Ababa
Bangkok
Manila

18.00
Singapore

nshasa
Dar es Salaam
Jakarta

Harare
18.30

etoria
23.30

ape Town
21.30
22.30
Perth
Sydney
Auckland

0.45

FACTS

An international conference in 1884 established the Greenwich Meridian as the basis for world time zones

The Russian Federation spans 11 time zones

China, which should span 5 zones, actually operates on a single time

The International Date Line is an imaginary line at approximately 180° west (or east) of Greenwich, across which the date changes by one day. The line has no international legal status and countries near to the line can choose which date they will observe.

Horn

Vesterålen

Fontur

Lofoten

Faxaflói **Iceland**

▲Snæfell
1833

Vestfjorden

Vestmannaeyjar

Vatnajökull

*Norwegian
Sea*

Faroe
Islands

S c a n d i n

Galdhøpiggen
2470

ATLANTIC

Shetland

Cape
Wrath

Outer
Hebrides

Orkney

Vänern

OCEAN

**British
Isles**

Grampian
Mountains

*North
Sea*

Skagerrak

Kattegat

Vätter

Jutland

Pennines

Zealand

Ba

FACTS

Lakes cover almost 10% of the total
land area of Finland

The Strait of Gibraltar, separating Europe
from Africa, is only 13 kilometres wide
at its narrowest point

The highest mountain in the Alps is
Mont Blanc, 4 808 metres, on the
France/Italy border

Irish Sea

Ireland

**Great
Britain**

Weser

N o r

Elbe

Sud

Thames

Rhine

Danub

English Channel

Channel Islands

Ardennes

Böhmer Wald

Seine

Loire

Vosges

Jura

Lake
Geneva

A l p s

*Bay of
Biscay*

Rhône

Dolomites

Po

D

Cape Finisterre

Gulf of
Gascony

Massif
Central

Mont
Blanc
4808

A d r i a

Apennines

Pyrenees

Azores

Douro

Aneto
3404

Ligurian
Sea

Cordillera Cantábrica

Golfe
du Lion

Corsica

Vesuvius
1281

Tagus

Iberian

Ebro

Balearic
Islands

Sardinia

Peninsula

Golfo
de
Valencia

Minorca

*Tyrrhenian
Sea*

Cabo de
São Vicente

Sierra Morena

Mulhacén
3482

Ibiza

Majorca

Mou.
Etna
332

Sierra ▲Nevada

M e d i t e r

Sicily

Strait of Gibraltar

Sicilian Chan.

Madeira

r a n

Malta

AFRICA

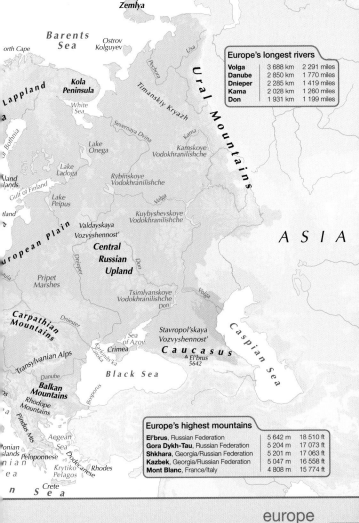

Novaya Zemlya

Barents Sea

Ostrov Kolguyev

orth Cape

Usa

a Lappland

Kola Peninsula

White Sea

Timanskiy Kryazh

Pechora

Ural Mountains

of Bothnia

Severnaya Dvina

Kama

Lake Onega

Kamskoye Vodokhranilishche

land lands

Gulf of Finland

Lake Ladoga

Rybinskoye Vodokhranilishche

Volga

tland

Lake Peipus

Kuybyshevskoye Vodokhranilishche

Valdayskaya Vozvyshennost'

ropean Plain

Central Russian Upland

Dnieper

Don

Pripet Marshes

ula

Tsimlyanskoye Vodokhranilishche

Don

Volga

Dniester

Carpathian Mountains

Dnieper

Stavropol'skaya Vozvyshennost'

Caspian Sea

Transylvanian Alps

Sea of Azov

Crimea

Caucasus

△ El'brus 5642

Kerkitis ka Zatoka

Danube

Bosporus

Black Sea

Balkan Mountains

s

Rhodope Mountains

a

Pindus Mts

Aegean Sea

Dodecanese

Rhodes

onian lands

Peloponnese

Krytiko Pelagos

Crete

an S e a

ASIA

Europe's longest rivers

Volga	3 688 km	2 291 miles
Danube	2 850 km	1 770 miles
Dnieper	2 285 km	1 419 miles
Kama	2 028 km	1 260 miles
Don	1 931 km	1 199 miles

Europe's highest mountains

El'brus, Russian Federation	5 642 m	18 510 ft
Gora Dykh-Tau, Russian Federation	5 204 m	17 073 ft
Shkhara, Georgia/Russian Federation	5 201 m	17 063 ft
Kazbek, Georgia/Russian Federation	5 047 m	16 558 ft
Mont Blanc, France/Italy	4 808 m	15 774 ft

europe
physical features

Europe's countries

Largest country	Russian Federation	17 075 400 sq km	6 592 812 sq miles
Smallest country	Vatican City	0.5 sq km	0.2 sq miles
Largest population	Russian Federation	143 246 000	
Smallest population	Vatican City	472	
Most densely populated country	Monaco	17 000 per sq km	34 000 per sq mile
Least densely populated country	Iceland	3 per sq km	7 per sq mile

Reykjavík **ICELAND**

Norwegian Sea

NORWAY

SWEDE

ATLANTIC

OCEAN

Tórshavn **Faroe Islands** (Denmark)

Bergen
Oslo
Stockholm

Glasgow Edinburgh *North Sea*
Belfast **UNITED** Aalborg
REPUBLIC KINGDOM **DENMARK** Malmö
OF Dublin Copenhagen Balt
IRELAND Manchester

AL. ALBANIA
B.H. BOSNIA-HERZEGOVINA
CR. CROATIA
CZ.R. CZECH REPUBLIC
HUN. HUNGARY
LIE. LIECHTENSTEIN
LUX. LUXEMBOURG
M. MACEDONIA
NETH. NETHERLANDS
S.M. SERBIA AND MONTENEGRO
SW. SWITZERLAND

Birmingham **NETH.** Hamburg
Cardiff The Hague Berlin
London Amsterdam Essen Poznań
English Channel Brussels **GERMANY**
Channel Islands **BELGIUM** Frankfurt Prague
(U.K.) **LUX.** am Main **CZ.R.**
Paris Luxembourg Danube Vienna
Nantes Orléans Strasbourg Munich **LIE.** Bratisla
Loire Zürich Vaduz **AUSTRIA**
Bern **SW.** **SLOVENI**
FRANCE Geneva Ljubljana
Bay of Lyon Milan **Po** Zagr
Biscay Turin **ITALY**
Bordeaux **SAN** Split
MARINO

° **Azores**
(Portugal)

Oporto Marseille **MONACO**
Andorra la Vella **Vatican City**
Tagus **ANDORRA** *Corsica* Rome
Lisbon **Madrid** Barcelona
SPAIN Palma Naples
de Mallorca *Sardinia* *Tyrrhenian*
Seville Valencia *Balearic Sea*
Islands
Cádiz Cartagena Palermo
Gibraltar (U.K.) *Sicily*
Madeira *Mediterr*
(Portugal) Valletta
AFRICA **MALTA**

FACTS

The European Union was founded by six countries: Belgium, France, Germany, Italy, Luxembourg and the Netherlands

Europe has the 2 smallest independent countries in the world – Vatican City and Monaco

Vatican City is an independent country entirely within the city of Rome, and is the centre of the Roman Catholic Church

Novaya Zemlya

Vorkuta

Barents Sea

Ostrov Kolguyev

Pechora

Lappland

Kola Peninsula

White Sea

Archangel

R U S S I A N

Severnaya Dvina

FINLAND *Lake Ladoga*

F E D E R A T I O N

Perm'

Helsinki

Gulf of Finland St Petersburg

Izhevsk

Tallinn

ESTONIA

Yaroslavl'

Volga

Nizhniy Novgorod

Kazan'

Ufa

LATVIA

Riga

Moscow

Ul'yanovsk

Samara

ASIA

LITHUANIA

Vilnius

Tula

Orenburg

S. FED. Kaliningrad

Saratov

BELARUS Minsk

Dnieper

Homyel'

Voronezh

Warsaw

Brest

Volgograd

dź

Rivne

Kiev

Kharkiv

Don

LAND

Katowice

U K R A I N E

Donets'k

Astrakhan

L'viv

Dniester

Dnipropetrovs'k

Rostov-na-Donu

Caspian Sea

OVAKIA

MOLDOVA

Budapest Chişinău

Odesa

Krasnodar

Groznyy

N.

ROMANIA

Danube

Constanța

C a u c a s u s

Belgrade Bucharest

Niš

B l a c k   S e a

Sarajevo

BULGARIA

gorica

Sofia

İstanbul

irana M.

Skopje

AL

Thessaloníki

T U R K E Y

Aegean Sea

GREECE

Athens

nian Sea

S e a

Crete

Europe's capitals

Largest capital (population)	**Paris**, France	9 753 000
Smallest capital (population)	**Vatican City**	472
Most northerly capital	**Reykjavík**, Iceland	64° 39'N
Most southerly capital	**Valletta**, Malta	35° 54'N
Highest capital	**Andorra la Vella**, Andorra	1 029 metres 3 376 feet

europe
western russian federation

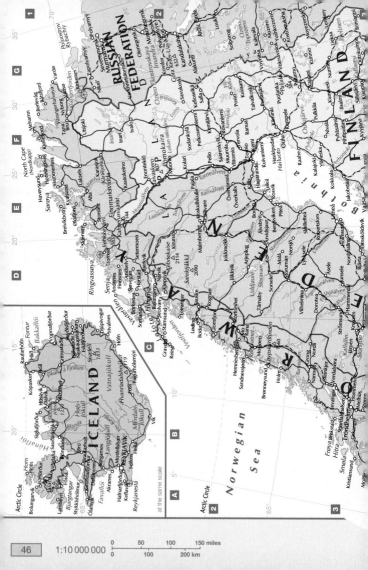

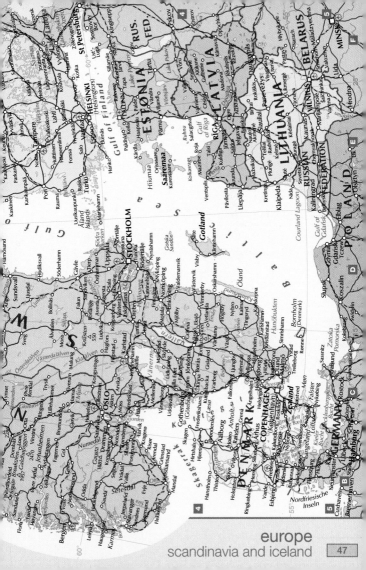

europe

scandinavia and iceland

47

48

1:8 000 000

| 0 | 50 | 100 | 150 miles |
| 0 | 100 | 200 km |

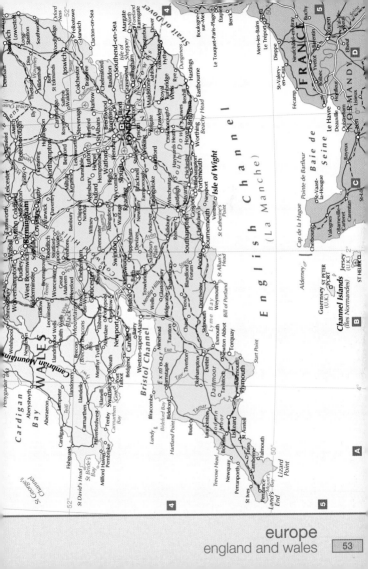

europe
central europe

57

europe
spain and portugal

SWITZERLAND
AUSTRIA
SLOVENIA

FRANCE

PROVENCE
MONACO

Turin (Torino)
Milan Monza
Genoa (Genova)

Lausanne
Morges
Vevey
Montreux
Frutigen
Chur
Davos
Pfunds
Vipiteno
Merano
Bressanone
Spittal an der Drau
St Veit an der Glan
Grosser
Speikkogel

Geneva
Aosta
Matterhorn
Zermatt
Brig
Blasca
Chiavenna
Bolzano
Bressanone
Villach
Klagenfurt
Maril

Annecy
Aix-les-Bains
Chambéry
Ivrea
Biella
Como
Lecco
Bergamo
Trento
Rovereto
Belluno
Udine
Trieste
Gorizia
LJUBLJANA

ALPS
Dolomites

Grenoble
Oulx
Susa
Asti
Pavia
Piacenza
Parma
Verona
Vicenza
Padua (Padova)
Venice (Venezia)
Rovinj

Briançon
Cuneo
Alba
Alessandria
Reggio nell'Emilia
Modena
Ferrara
Bologna
Ravenna
Forlì
Rimini
Pesaro
Fano

Ligurian Sea

La Spezia
Massa
Pistoia
Florence (Firenze)
Arezzo
Siena
Perugia
Ancona
Senigallia
Macerata

SAN MARINO

Cap Corse

Corsica (Corse) (France)

Calvi
Bastia
Vescovato

Isola d'Elba

Grosseto
Orvieto
Viterbo
Terni
Rieti

ITALY
APENNINES
Monte Como
Monte Corno

Pescara
Chieti
Vasto

Ajaccio
Sartène
Bonifacio

Strait of Bonifacio

Tarquinia
Civitavecchia
Guidonia
Montecelio
Tivoli
Avezzano

VATICAN CITY
ROME (Roma)

Pomezia
Aprilia
Anzio
Latina
Frosinone
Campobasso

Sardinia (Sardegna) (Italy)

Sassari
Oristano
Nuoro
Macomer

Golfo di Orosei
Orosei
Capo di Monte Santu

Gulf of Naples
Naples (Napoli)
Pozzuoli
Vesuvio
Salerno
Agropoli

Isole Ponziane
Isola d'Ischia
Isola di Capri

Cagliari
Golfo di Cagliari

Tyrrhenian Sea

Mediterranean Sea

Sicilian Channel

Sicily (Sicilia)
Isole Lipari

Palermo
Trapani
Marsala
Mazara del Vallo
Castelvetrano
Sciacca
Agrigento
Gela
Caltanissetta
Enna
Catania
Ragusa

A   **B**

1:8 000 000

0   50   100   150 miles
0   100   200 km

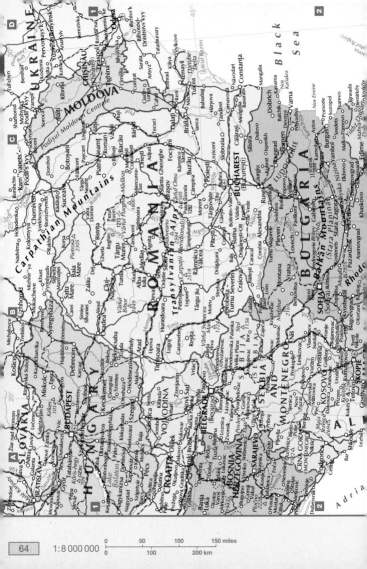

64 1:8 000 000

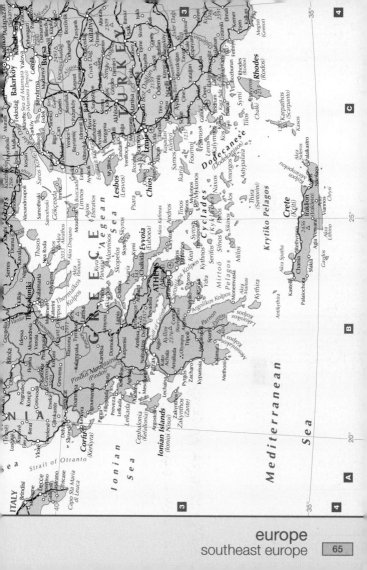

Asia's extremes

TOTAL LAND AREA		45 036 492 sq km	17 388 589 sq miles
Largest lake	Caspian Sea	371 000 sq km	143 243 sq miles
Largest island	Borneo	745 561 sq km	287 861 sq miles
Largest drainage basin	Ob'-Irtysh, Kazakhstan/Rus. Fed.	2 990 000 sq km	1 154 439 sq miles
Lowest point	Dead Sea	-398 metres	-1 306 feet

Asia's highest mountains

Mt Everest, China/Nepal	8 848 m	29 028 ft
K2, China/Jammu and Kashmir	8 611 m	28 251 ft
Kangchenjunga, India/Nepal	8 586 m	28 169 ft
Lhotse, China/Nepal	8 516 m	27 939 ft
Makalu, China/Nepal	8 463 m	27 765 ft

EUROPE

AFRICA

Mediterranean Sea

Black Sea

Anatolia

Cyprus

Caucasus

El'brus 5642

Mount Ararat 5165

Dead Sea

Syrian Desert

Euphrates

Tigris

Red Sea

Ad Dahnā'

The Gulf

Arabian Peninsula

Rub' al Khālī

Gulf of Aden

Socotra

Gulf of Oman

Arabian Sea

Volga

Caspian Lowland

Caspian Sea

Aral Sea

Turan Lowland

Syrdar'ya

Amudar'ya

Elburz Mountains

Zagros Mountains

Hindu Kush

Ural Mountains

Ob'

West Siberian Plain

Irtysh

Kazakhskiy Melkosopochnik

Lake Balkhash

Tien Shan

7439

Pobeda Peak

Karakoram Range

K2 8611

Kunlun S

Tarim Basi

Indus

Thar Desert

Plate of Ti

Himal

Mount Everest 8848

Ganges

Deccan

Western Ghats

Eastern Ghats

Bay of Ben

Laccadive Islands

Cape Comorin

Maldives

Sri Lanka

INDIAN OCEAN

Chagos Archipelago

Zeml Frantsa-

Novaya Zemlya

Kara

1:78 000 000

0 500 1000 1500 miles
0 1000 2000 km

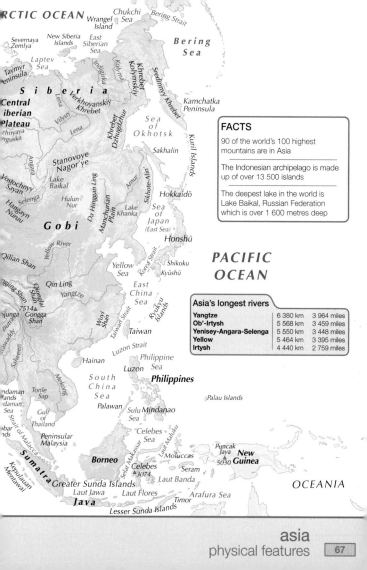

ARCTIC OCEAN
Wrangel Island
Chukchi Sea
Bering Strait

New Siberia Islands
East Siberian Sea

Severnaya Zemlya

Bering Sea

Taymyr Peninsula

Laptev Sea

Indigirka

Khrebet Kolymskiy

Kolyma

Sredinnyy Khrebet

Kamchatka Peninsula

S i b e r i a

Lena

Verkhoyanskiy Khrebet

Khrebet Dzhugdzhur

Central Siberian Plateau

zhnyaya nguska

Lena

Sea of Okhotsk

Sakhalin

Kuril Islands

Vilyuy

Angara

Stanovoye Nagor'ye

Vostochnyy Sayan

Lake Baikal

Selenga

Hangayn Nuruu

Hulun Nur

Da Hinggan Ling

Manchurian Plain

Amur

Sikhote-Alin'

Hokkaidō

Lake Khanka

Sea of Japan (East Sea)

G o b i

Honshū

Qilian Shan

Yellow River

Qin Ling

Qongtai Shan

Yangtze

Qionglai Shan

7514△ Gongga Shan

Yellow Sea

Korea Strait

Shikoku

Kyūshū

East China Sea

Wuyi Shan

Taiwan Strait

Ryukyu Islands

Taiwan

Luzon Strait

Hainan

Philippine Sea

Luzon

Philippines

njunga

utra

wadd

Salween

Mekong

South China Sea

Palawan

Sulu Sea

Mindanao

Palau Islands

ndaman ands daman Sea

Tonle Sap

Gulf of Thailand

Celebes Sea

bar ds

Strait of Malacca

Peninsular Malaysia

S u m a t r a

Kepulauan Mentawai

Greater Sunda Islands

Laut Jawa

J a v a

Borneo

Selat Makassar

Celebes ▲3074

Laut Maluku

Moluccas

Seram

Laut Banda

Laut Flores

Timor

Lesser Sunda Islands

Arafura Sea

Puncak Jaya 5030

New Guinea

OCEANIA

PACIFIC OCEAN

Asia's longest rivers

Yangtze	6 380 km	3 964 miles
Ob'-Irtysh	5 568 km	3 459 miles
Yenisey-Angara-Selenga	5 550 km	3 448 miles
Yellow	5 464 km	3 395 miles
Irtysh	4 440 km	2 759 miles

Asia's countries

Largest country	Russian Federation	17 075 400 sq km	6 592 812 sq miles
Smallest country	Maldives	298 sq km	115 sq miles
Largest population	China	1 289 161 000	
Smallest population	Palau	20 000	
Most densely populated country	Singapore	6 656 per sq km	17 219 per sq mile
Least densely populated country	Mongolia	2 per sq km	4 per sq mile

EUROPE

Mediterranean Sea

Moscow

Nizhniy
Novgorod

□ Volga

Samara

Yekaterinburg

RUSSIAN

Ob

Ural'sk

Ural Mountains

Omsk

Novosib

Black Sea

Ankara

TURKEY

Adana

Nicosia

CYPRUS □

LEBANON

Beirut □

Jerusalem □

ISRAEL

Damascus

Amman

JORDAN

SYRIA

T'bilisi

GEORGIA

ARMENIA

Yerevan

AZERBAIJAN

Baku

Tabriz

Aral
Sea

Astana

KAZAKHSTAN

Lake
Balkhash

Bishkek

Almaty

Tashkent

UZBEKISTAN

TURKMENISTAN

Caspian Sea

Tien Shan

Urür

KYRGYZSTAN

Baghdād

IRAQ

Tehrān

Ashgabat

Dushanbe

TAJIKISTAN

AFRICA

Red Sea

The Gulf

KUWAIT

Kuwait □

Shirāz

IRAN

Herāt

Kābul

AFGHANISTAN

Islamabad

Plate
of Til

Kandahar

Lahore

Himala

Jeddah

Mecca

BAHRAIN

Riyadh

QATAR

Doha

Manama

Dubai

Abu Dhabi

U.A.E.

Muscat □

Delhi

New Delhi

Agra □

Mount Everest
8848

NEPAL

Kathmandu

Allahabad

Patna

BAN

Dhal

SAUDI
ARABIA

Hyderabad

Karachi

PAKISTAN

Ahmadabad

Ganges

San'ā □

YEMEN

OMAN

INDIA

Kolkata

Aden

Arabian

Sea

Mumbai

Socotra

Hyderabad

Bay
of Ben

Bangalore

Chennai

Laccadive
Islands

Madurai

Sri Jayewardenep
Kotte

Colombo □

Male

SRI LANKA

MALDIVES

INDIAN

OCEAN

British Indian
Ocean Territory

Asia's capitals

Largest capital (population)	Tōkyō, Japan	26 849 000
Smallest capital (population)	Koror, Palau	14 000
Most northerly capital	Astana, Kazakhstan	51° 10'N
Most southerly capital	Dili, East Timor	8° 35'S
Highest capital	Thimphu, Bhutan	2 423 metres 7 949 feet

1:78 000 000

0	500	1000	1500 miles
0	1000	2000 km	

ARCTIC OCEAN

Bering Sea

Magadan

il'sk

Lena

EDERATION

Sea of Okhotsk

Petropavlovak-Kamchatskiy

Irkutsk

Lake Baikal

Sapporo

Hakodate

Ulan Bator

MONGOLIA

Harbin

Vladivostock

Sea of Japan (East Sea)

JAPAN

Shenyang

NORTH KOREA

Tōkyō

Yellow River

Beijing

Dalian

P'yŏngyang

Tianjin

Seoul

SOUTH KOREA

Osaka

Hiroshima

Fukuoka

PACIFIC OCEAN

Lanzhou

Yellow Sea

CHINA

Xi'an

Nanjing

Shanghai

East China Sea

Chengdu

Yangtze

Hangzhou

Chongqing

Wuhan

u

Kunming

Liuzhou

Guangzhou

T'aipei

Nanning

Hong Kong

TAIWAN

Kaoshiung

Hạ Nội

Luzon Strait

Hai Phong

NMAR

LAOS

VIETNAM

Quezon City

PHILIPPINES

ln

Vientiane

South China Sea

Manila

goon

THAILAND

Bangkok

CAMBODIA

PALAU

Koror

daman nds (ia)

Phnom Penh

Hồ Chí Minh

Davao

icobar ands dia)

Kota Kinabalu

Celebes Sea

Jayapura

Medan

Bandar Seri Begawan

MALAYSIA

BRUNEI

New Guinea

Sumatra

Kuala Lumpur

Putrajaya

Kuching

Borneo

SINGAPORE

Singapore

Pontianak

OCEANIA

INDONESIA

Palembang

Banjarmasin

Laut Banda

Jakarta

Laut Jawa

Makassar

Bandung

Surabaya

Semarang

EAST TIMOR

Dili

Java

FACTS

Over 60% of the world's population live in Asia

Asia has 12 of the world's 20 largest cities

East Timor is Asia's newest independent country – founded in May 2002

asia
countries

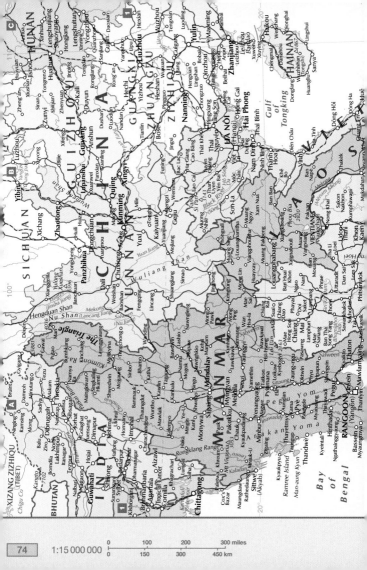

South China Sea

Natuna Besar (Indonesia)

Panarik

VIETNAM

Quang Ngai
Sa Huynh
Qui Nhon
Song Cau
Tuy Hoa
Vinh Hoa
Nha Trang
Cam Ranh
Phan Rang

Ngoc Linh 2598
Kon Tum
Pleiku
Phan Thiet
Buôn Mê Thuôt
Da Lat

Song Da Rang

Attapu
Saravan
Phou Bia 2819
Phouphieng Bolovens
Xékong
Pakxé
Kông
Kon Tum
Babu

Cheo Reo
Thuyên Quang
Duc Trong

CAMBODIA

Stung Treng
Kratie
Kâmpóng Cham
Ho Chi Minh City
(Saigon)
Vung Tau

Mouths of the Mekong
Côn Son

Champasak
Stoeng Trêng
Rôviëng
Kâmpóng Thum
Kâmpóng
Sâmbôr
Phnom Penh
Kâmpóng Cham
Svay Rieng
My Tho
Cao Lanh
Can Tho
Long Xuyên
Rach Gia
Bac Lieu
Soc Trang

Sisophon
Siemréab
Pursat
Battambang
Pouthisat
Kâmpóng Thom
Krong Kaoh Kong
Takêv
Kâmpôt
Kâmpóng Saôm
Sihanoukville
Doc
Ca Mau
Mui Ca Mau

Gulf of Thailand

MALAYSIA
Peninsular Malaysia

Kota Bharu
Pasir Putih
Kuala Terengganu
Cukai
Dungun
Kuala Lahan
Kuantan
Pekan

Narathiwat
Yala
Pattani
Sungai Petani
George Town
Butterworth
Ipoh
Teluk Intan
Kampar
Bagan Datok
Gunung Tahan 2189
Kuala Lipis
KUALA LUMPUR

Thailand

Nakhon Si Thammarat
Phatthalung
Songkhla
Hat Yai
Sadao
Kangar
Alor Setar

Khao Chum Thong
Thung Song
Trang
Satun

Surat Thani
Ban Na San
Ko Samui
Ko Pha-Ngan

Chumphon
Lang Suan
Ranong
Kapoe
Ban Takua Pa
Takua Pa
Phangnga
Thalang
Phuket
Krabi

Prachuap Khiri Khan
Bang Saphan Yai

Andaman Sea

Mergui Archipelago

Letsok-aw Kyun
Lanbi Kyun
Zadetkyi Kyun
Bokpyin

Tavoy
Myeik
Palaw
Tenasserim

Strait of Malacca

INDONESIA

Medan
Belawan
Tebingtinggi
Binjai
Pangkalansusu
Langsa
Kuala
Tanjungbalai
Tangsa
Pareula

Banda Aceh
Sigli
Calang
Takengon
Gunung Abongabong 2985
Blangkejeren
Gunung Leuser 3145
Meulaboh
Lhokseumawe
Bireun

Tapaktuan

INDIAN OCEAN

Preparis North Channel
Preparis Island
Preparis South Channel

Great Coco
Narcondam Island

North Andaman
Middle Andaman
Ritchie's Archipelago
South Andaman
Wrightmyo
Port Blair
Andaman Islands (India)

Little Andaman
Ten Degree Channel

Car Nicobar
Nachuge
Terresa Island
Camorta
Katchall
Nancowry
Little Nicobar
Dakoank
Great Nicobar
Nicobar Islands (India)

Tillanchong Island

asia
philippines

76

1:15 000 000

asia
north korea and south korea

9 000 000

0   50   100 miles
0   100 km

77

78

1:10 000 000

| 0 | 50 | 100 | 150 miles |

| 0 | 100 | 200 km |

E

Ostrov Kunashir

Yuzhno-Kuril'sk

Shiretoko-misaki

Nemuro

1

2

40°

145°

Yuzhno-Sakhalinsk

Kholmsk

Korsakov

Mys Aniva

Zaliv Aniva

Mys Krilon

Sakhalin

La Pérouse Strait

Moneron

Rebun-tō

Rishiri-tō

Sōya-misaki

Wakkanai

Hokkaidō

Monbetsu

Abashiri

Kitami

Shibetsu

Akkeshi-ko

Meaken-dake

Oshiri

Kushiro

1,503

Asahi-dake

Asahikawa

Nayoro

Teshio-gawa

2,290

Bibai

Yūbari

Hidaka-sammyaku

Erimo-misaki

Samani

Takikawa

Iwamizawa

Tomakomai

Otaru

Ishikari-wan

Sapporo

Chitose

Muroran

Hakodate

Iwanai

Suttsu

Yakumo

Mori

Shirija-zaki

Mutsu

D

140°

Shakotan-misaki

Okushiri-tō

Ō-shima

Oma-zaki

Matsumae

Goshogawara

Hirosaki

Aomori

Towada

Ninohe

Hachinohe

Miyako

Kamaishi

Morioka

Kesennuma

Ishinomaki

Kinka-san

Kitakami-gawa

Hamamaki

Kitakami

Ichinoseki

Akita

Honjō

Noshiro

Odate

Oga-hantō

Funakawa

Sakata

Tsuruoka

Tendō

C

Svetlaya

Amgu

RUSSIAN FEDERATION

Sikhote-Alin'

Bikin

Vostok

Bikin

Dal'nerechensk

Rudnaya Pristan'

Dal'negorsk

Kavalerovo

B

135°

CHINA

Jiamusi

Shuangyashan

HEILONGJIANG

Yilan

Wanda Shan

Baoqing

Qitaihe

Huilin

Mishan

Boli

Linkou

Jixi

Mudan Jiang

Mudanjiang

Muling

Hengdaohezi

Dongning

Pogranichnyy

Dal'nerechensk

Bezozavodsk

Spassk-Dal'niy

Arsen'yev

Chuguyevka

Yaroslavskiy

Lake Khanka

Kirovskiy

Lesozavodsk

Chernigovka

Ussuriysk

Artem

Bor'shoy Kamen'

Nakhodka

Vrangel'

Zaliv Petra Velikogo

JILIN

Pan Ling

Suifenhe

Tumen

Wangqing

Hunchun

Slavyanka

Zarubino

Vladivostok

NORTH KOREA

Unggi

Najin

Chŏngjin

Yalu

Tumen

Sea

of

Japan

(East Sea)

A

130°

1

45°

40°

PACIFIC

OCEAN

Liancourt Rocks
(South Korea)

Oki-shotō
Dōgo
Dōzen

Tsushima

Gōtsu
Hamada
Masuda
Hagi
Nagato
Shimonoseki
Kita-Kyūshū
Nagasaki
Sasebo
Hirado
Imari
Karatsu
Saga
Ōmuta
Makurazaki
Sendai
Kagoshima
Kanoya
Ōsumi-kaikyō
Ōsumi-shotō
Nishino-omote

Matsue
Izumo
Yonago
Tottori
Kurayoshi
Chūgoku-sanchi

Iwakuni
Tokuyama
Ube
Ōda
Matsuyama
Fukuoka
Kurume
Ōita
Beppu
Kumamoto
Yatsushiro
Isa
Miyakonojō
Miyazaki
Nobeoka
Saiki

Kyūshū

Hiroshima
Kure
Fukuyama
Okayama
Kurashiki

Hyōno-sen
1510

Sakaide
Takamatsu
Imabari
Tokushima
Kōchi
Anan
Nakamura
Sukumo
Uwajima
Ashizuri-misaki
Muroto
Muroto-zaki

Shikoku

Bungo-suidō

Kawatahama

Niihama

Kii-suidō

Tsuruga
Fukui
Takefu
Maizuru
Ōtsu
Kyōto
Ōsaka
Sakai
Wakayama
Kainan
Tanabe
Shingū
Shiono-misaki

Biwa-ko
Tsu
Ise
Owase
Matsusaka

Nagaoka
Niitsu
Nagano
Ueda
Matsumoto
Takada
Jōetsu
Kashiwazaki
Toyama
Takaoka
Kanazawa
Komatsu
Takayama

Noto-hantō
Nanao
Suzu
Noto-misaki
Wakasa-wan

Gifu
Nakatsugawa
Toyota
Nagoya
Okazaki
Kariya
Ichinomiya

Ōmachi
Kiso-sammyaku

Nagaoka
Niigata
Aizu-wakamatsu
Iwaki

Inawashiro-ko

Uonuma-sammyaku
Kōriyama

Kiryū
Maebashi
Takasaki
Utsunomiya
Oyama
Kawagoe
TOKYO
Chiba
Kawasaki
Yokohama
Sagamihara
Odawara
Hiratsuka
Atami
Numazu
Itō
Ō-shima

Hitachinaka
Hitachi
Mito
Tsuchiura
Chōshi
Narita
Kashima-nada

Fuji
3776
Fujinomiya
Shizuoka
Shimizu
Yaizu
Hamamatsu
Okazaki

Nojima-zaki

Irō-zaki
Nii-jima
Miyake-jima
Hachijō-jima

Sumisu-jima
Tori-shima
Sōfu-gan

NIPPON

HONSHŪ

140°

135°

30°

35°

asia
central china

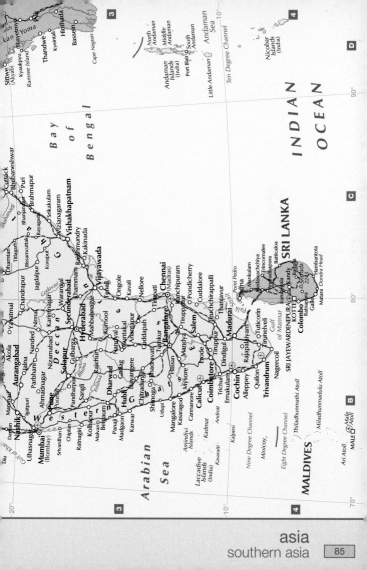

TURKMENISTAN

Torbat-e Jam
Herāt
Gushgy
Bālā Morghāb
Meymaneh
Shebberghān
Mazār-e Sharif
Kholm
Tāloqān
Feyzābad
Qullai Karl Marks 6726
Buzai Gumbad

Karakoram

Torbat-e Jam

Paropamisus

Hari Rūd

Chaghcharān
Bāmīān
Charīkār
Chitral
Drosh
Tirich Mīr
Gilgit
Barikot
Dir
Dangal
Mingora
Nanga Parbat 8126

K2 (Qogir Fer/Godwin Au 8611 2)
Astor
Skardu

JAMMU AN KASHMIR

AFGHANISTAN

Shindand
Farah
Delaram
Gereshk
HAZARAJAT
Kūh-e Bābā Shah Fulādī 5143
KABUL
Jalālābad
Khyber Pass
Peshāwar
Nowshera
Mardan
Haripur
Abbottābād
Srīnagar
Anantnag
Kishtwar

Chalap Dalan
Farāh Rūd
Ghaznī
Gardēz
Khowst
Kohāt
Talagang
Rāwalpindi
ISLAMABAD
Jhelum
Chamba
Kathua
Udhampur

Zābol
Zaranj
Dasht-e Mārgow
Helmand
Kandahār
Kalāt
Arghandāb
Tarnak
Bannu
Daud Khel
Mianwali
Khushāb
Gujrāt
Sialkot
Jammu
Sujanpur
Gujrānwāla
Hoshiārpur

IRAN

Shīndand

Dasht-e Arbu Lut

Gīand-i-Zureh

Mirjāveh
Amir Chah
Chagai
Dalbandin
Nushki
Mastung
Quetta
Mach
Sibi
Loralai
Dera Ismāil Khan
Tank
Bhakkar
Sargodha
Jhang
Faisalābad
Chiniot
Lahore
Amritsar
Ludhian
Ferozpur
Chandīgarh
Bathinda

Nok Kundi
Qila Ladgasht
Kalāt
Khuzdar
Kharan
Jacobābad
Shikārpur
Larkāna
Sukkur
Khairpur
Khānpur
Rahīmyar Khan
Bahāwalpur
Fort Abbas
Anupgarh
Hanumāngarh
Ganganagar
Sirsa
Hisar
Panipat
Kait
Del
NEW DEL

Nagha Kalat
Wad
Bela
Panjgur
Turbat
Gwadar
Pasni
Ormara
Sonmiāni
Karāchi
Thatta
Hyderābād
Mīrpur Khās
Tando Adam
Nawābshāh
Jaisalmer
Pokaran
Bīkāner
Nokha
Sujāngarh
Churu
Ratangarh
Sīkar
Jaipur
Tonk
Bundi
Kota

Makran Coast Range

Arabian
Sea

Tropic of Cancer

Rann of Kachchh

Gulf of Kachchh

Bhuj
Gāndhīdhām
Morbi
Surendranagar
Rājkot
Jāmnagar
Dwārka
Porbandar
Junāgadh
Keshod
Veraval
Mahuva
Bhāvnagar
Ahmadābad
Gāndhīnagar
Nadiād
Vadodāra
Bharuch
Surat
Nashik
Aurangābad
Jalna

Gulf of Khambhat

asia

pakistan, northern india, nepal and bangladesh

87

1:20 000 000

asia
central asia

89

Shahreẕā
Yazd
Bāfq
Nehbandān
Zābol
Zard
Dasht-e
Mārgow
Zaḡros Mountains
(Kūhhā-ye Zāgros)
Abarqū
Zarand
Gīrd
AFGHANISTAN

Masjed
Soleymān
Rāmhormoz
Ahvāz
Kūh-e Dīnār
4432
Zarand
Noṣratābād
Hormak
Gand-e Zūreh

Aṣra
Khorramshahr
Bandar-e Emām Khomeynī
Kūh-e Tābask
Arsenājān
Rafsanjān
Bardsīr
Kermān
Kūh-e
Ilazarān
Khūrāsa
Zāhedān
Amir Chāh
PAKISTAN

Ābādān
Ḡanāveh
Kāzerūn
Daryāchy-e Tashk
Bam
Nahrūd
Vakīlābād
Kigan
Kūh-e
Taftān
4042
Khāsh
Nok Kundi

Būshehr
Borāzjān
Farrāshband
Fasā
Neyrīz
Ābādeh
Jīroft
Bampūr
Vakīlābād
Kigan
SARHAD
Sarāvan
Hāmūn-i
Mashkēl

IRAN
Khvormūj
Dowlatābād
Qīr
Jahrom
Sa'ādatābād
Kahnūj
Kūh-e Bazmān
3489
Zābolī
Iranshahr
Bazmān

Kangān
Zīr Rūd
Jūyom
Hājjīābād
Rostāq
Kūh-e
Furgūn
Dowlatābād
Hāmūn-e
Jaz Mūriān
Qasr-e
Qand
Pishīn
Tump

Hāleh
Lāmerd
Evaz
Khonj
Fāryāb
Bastak
Lār
Bandar-e Abbās
Mehrān
Sūzā
Sīrīk
Remeshk
Nīkshahr
Bāhū Kalāt
Pozm Tiāb
Suntsar
Gwādar

Gāvbandī
Bandar-e
Maqām
Bandar-e Chārak
Qeshm
Angohrān
Marākī
Kālāt
Chāhbahār
Jīwani

Kūh-e
Kūhrān
Mināb
Eshpakh
Esbakh
Sarbāz
Dasht
MAKRAN

Ra's al Khaymah
Strait of Hormuz
2161
Jāsk
Kūh-e
Bandar-e Lengeh

OMAN
Dibā al Ḥiṣn
Fujairah
Adh Dhayd
Ash Shāriqah
Sharjah
Mina Jebel Ali
Adh Dhayd
Aṣh
Shinaş
Gulf of Oman

ABU DHABI
(Abū Ẓabī)
Dubai
(Dubayy)
Ash
Shināṣ
Şuḥār
Al Khābūrah

Trucial
Coast
Ṭarīf
Al Burayml
Sunaynah
As Suwayq
Barkā
MUSCAT
(Masqaṭ)

UNITED ARAB
EMIRATES
Ruweis
N U 'A Y M
Ar Rustaq
Rumaïl
Quraiyat

Al Mariyyah
Al Mudaibī
Nizwā
Ibrā'
Tīwī
Şūr
Ra's al Ḥadd

Al Khunn
Adam
Al Kāmil
Bilād Banī
Bū 'Alī

Al Jamālīyah
Al 'Ar'ānah
Salwah
Hājmā?
Jazīrat Maşīrah

Dammām
(Ad Dammām)
Dhahrān
Al Khawr
QATAR
DOHA
(Ad Dawḥah)
Fuwayriṭ
Dukhān
Al Ḥuwaylah

BAHRAIN
MANAMA
As Sayḥ
A R R I M Ā L
OMAN
Khalīj Maşīrah
20°

AL NUFÜD
A l   K h ā l ī
Jiddat al Ḥarāsīs
Al Qa'āmīyat
Dawqah

Ḥaraḍ
Thamarīt
Jūzur al Ḥalānīyāt
3

Al Ghaydah
Ṣalālah
Mirbāṭ

Tarīm
Shibām
Wādī al Maṣīlah
Ghubbat
al Qamar
A r a b i a n
60°
D

YEMEN
Al Qaṭn
Sayḥūt
S e a

Ash Shiḥr
Mukalla
(Al Mukallā)

Gulf of Aden
Socotra
(Suquṭrā)
(Yemen)
1503
Ra's Momi
C

Qalansīyah
Qāḍub
Ḥadīr
Ra's Shu'ab

1:15 000 000

asia
eastern mediterranean

93

asia
russian federation

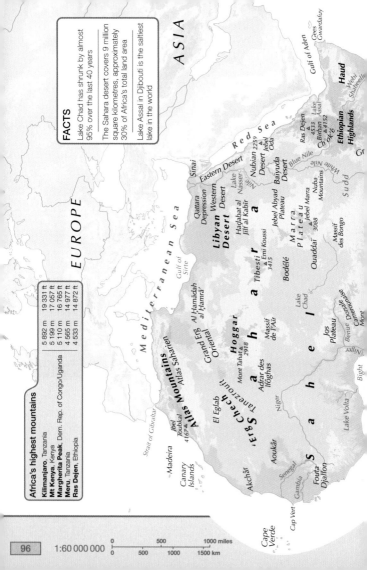

1:60 000 000

| 0 | 500 | 1000 miles |
| 0 | 500 | 1000 | 1500 km |

Africa's highest mountains

Kilimanjaro, Tanzania	5 892 m	19 331 ft
Mt Kenya, Kenya	5 199 m	17 057 ft
Margherita Peak, Dem. Rep. of Congo/Uganda	5 110 m	16 765 ft
Meru, Tanzania	4 565 m	14 977 ft
Ras Dejen, Ethiopia	4 533 m	14 872 ft

EUROPE

ASIA

FACTS

Lake Chad has shrunk by almost 95% over the last 40 years

The Sahara desert covers 9 million square kilometres, approximately 30% of Africa's total land area

Lake Assal in Djibouti is the saltiest lake in the world

Gulf of Aden

Gees Gwardafuy

Mediterranean Sea

Gulf of Sirte

Strait of Gibraltar

Madeira

Canary Islands

Atlas Mountains
Atlas Saharien

Jbel Toubkal ▲ 4167

Grand Erg Oriental

Al Hamādah al Ḥamrā'

Red Sea

Sinai

Eastern Desert

Qattara Depression

Lake Nasser

Nile

Nubian 239
Jebel Oda

Hadabat al Jilf al Kabīr

Jebel Abyad Plateau

Bayuda Desert

Blue Nile

Ras Dejen 4533 ▲

Birhan 4152 ▲
Chokē

Ethiopian Highlands

White Nile

Libyan Desert

S a h a r a

Tibesti ▲ Emi Koussi 3415

Bodélé

Marra Plateau

Jebel Marra 3088 ▲

Nuba Mountains

Sudd

Gr

El Eglab

Tanezrouft

Chèch Erg

Hoggar

Mont Tahat ▲ 2918

Adrar des Ifôghas

Massif de l'Aïr

Lake Chad

S a h e l

Ouaddaï

Massif des Bongo

Niger

Jos Plateau

Akchâr

Aoukâr

Senegal

Gambia

Fouta Djallon

Lake Volta

Benue

Cameroun Mont

Dorsale Camerounaise

Bight

Niger

S a h e l

Cape Verde

Cap Vert

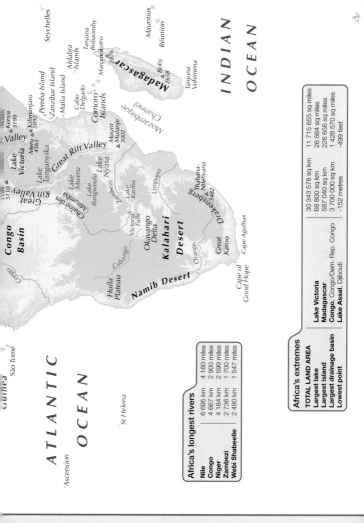

Africa's longest rivers

Nile	6 695 km	4 160 miles
Congo	4 667 km	2 900 miles
Niger	4 184 km	2 599 miles
Zambezi	2 736 km	1 700 miles
Webi Shabeelle	2 490 km	1 547 miles

Africa's extremes

TOTAL LAND AREA	30 343 578 sq km	11 715 655 sq miles
Largest lake	Lake Victoria	68 800 sq km	26 564 sq miles
Largest island	Madagascar	587 040 sq km	226 656 sq miles
Largest drainage basin	Congo, Congo/Dem. Rep. Congo	3 700 000 sq km	1 428 570 sq miles
Lowest point	Lake Assal, Djibouti	-152 metres	-499 feet

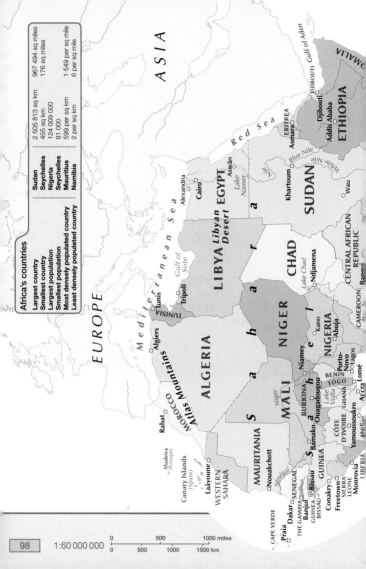

1:60 000 000

	0	500	1000 miles
0	500	1000	1500 km

Africa's countries

Largest country	Sudan	2 505 813 sq km	967 494 sq miles
Smallest country	Seychelles	455 sq km	176 sq miles
Largest population	Nigeria	124 009 000	
Smallest population	Seychelles	81 000	
Most densely populated country	Mauritius	599 per sq km	1 549 per sq mile
Least densely populated country	Namibia	2 per sq km	6 per sq mile

ASIA

EUROPE

M e d i t e r r a n e a n   S e a

Red Sea

Gulf of Aden

Gulf of Sirte

SOMALIA

DJIBOUTI
Djibouti

ETHIOPIA
Addis Ababa

ERITREA
Asmara

Blue Nile
White Nile

Nile

SUDAN
Khartoum

Wau

Lake
Nasser

Aswân

EGYPT
Cairo
Alexandria

Libyan
Desert

S a h a r a

LIBYA
Tripoli

TUNISIA
Tunis

Algiers

Atlas Mountains

MOROCCO
Rabat

ALGERIA

Madeira
(Portugal)

Canary Islands
(Spain)

WESTERN
SAHARA
Laâyoune

MAURITANIA
Nouakchott

Senegal

CAPE VERDE
Praia

Dakar
THE GAMBIA
Banjul
GUINEA-
BISSAU
Bissau
Conakry
GUINEA
Freetown
SIERRA
LEONE
Monrovia
LIBERIA
Abidjan

SENEGAL

MALI
Bamako

BURKINA
Ouagadougou

Niger

Niamey

NIGER

CHAD
Ndjamena

Lake Chad

S a h e l

NIGERIA
Abuja
Kano
Lagos

CENTRAL AFRICAN
REPUBLIC
Bangui

CAMEROON

BENIN
Porto-
Novo
TOGO
Lomé
GHANA
Accra
CÔTE
D'IVOIRE
Yamoussoukro

Lake
Volta

ATLANTIC

OCEAN

INDIAN

OCEAN

Ascension

St Helena

St Helena and
Dependencies
(U.K.)

Victoria SEYCHELLES

Aldabra
Islands

MAURITIUS
Port Louis
St-Denis Réunion
(France)

MADAGASCAR
Antananarivo

Mount Kenya
5199
Nairobi
Kilimanjaro
5892

Zanzibar Island

Dar es Salaam

COMOROS
Moroni
Mayotte **Dzaoudzi**
(France)

Lake
Victoria
Kampala

DEMOCRATIC
RWANDA **Kigali**
Bujumbura BURUNDI
REPUBLIC OF CONGO

Lake
Tanganyika

Dodoma
TANZANIA

Lake
Nyasa

Nampula

Mozambique
Channel

Lubumbashi

MALAWI
Lilongwe

MOZAMBIQUE

Brazzaville
Kinshasa

Zambezi

GABON

CONGO

Libreville

São Tomé

Guinea

Luanda

ANGOLA

Huambo

Cubango

ZAMBIA
Lusaka

Okavango
Delta

Harare
ZIMBABWE
Bulawayo

Limpopo

Maputo

Mbabane
SWAZILAND

Durban

BOTSWANA
Gaborone

Pretoria
Johannesburg

Maseru LESOTHO

Namib Desert

Windhoek

NAMIBIA

Orange

REPUBLIC OF
SOUTH AFRICA

Port Elizabeth

Cape Town
Cape of
Good Hope

Cape Agulhas

Africa's capitals		
Largest capital (population)	**Cairo**, Egypt	9 462 000
Smallest capital (population)	**Victoria**, Seychelles	30 000
Most northerly capital	**Tunis**, Tunisia	36° 46'N
Most southerly capital	**Cape Town**, Republic of South Africa	33° 57'S
Highest capital	**Addis Ababa**, Ethiopia	2 408 metres	7 900 feet

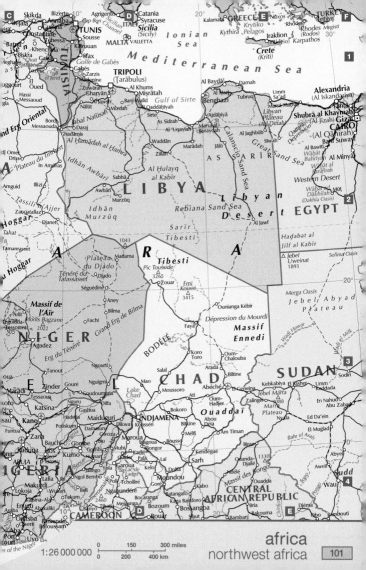

1:26 000 000

0	150	300	450 miles
0	200	400	600 km

1:20 000 000

ATLANTIC

OCEAN

WINDHOEK

NAMIBIA

Namib Desert

GREAT
NAMAQUALAND

NAMAQUALAND

Kalahari

Desert

BOTSWANA

REPUBLIC

GRIQUALAND
WEST

NORTHERN CAPE

SOUTH A

NORT

WESTERN
CAPE

CAPE
TOWN

0   50   100   150 mile
0   100   200 km

ASIA

Oceania's longest rivers

Murray-Darling	3 750 km	2 330 miles
Darling	2 739 km	1 702 miles
Murray	2 589 km	1 608 miles
Murrumbidgee	1 690 km	1 050 miles
Lachlan	1 480 km	919 miles

Wake Island

Northern Mariana Islands

Pagan

Saipan

Guam

Micronesia

Marshall Islands

Ralik Chain

Ratak Chain

Kwajalein

Majuro

Gaferut

Yap

Chuuk

Pohnpei

Caroline Islands

Kosrae

Gilbert Islands

Tarawa

Nauru

Onotoa

Kingsmill Group

Nanumea

Bismarck Archipelago

New Ireland

Bismarck Sea

Bougainville I.

Choiseul

Santa Isabel

Solomon Islands

Puncak Jaya 5030

Mount Wilhelm 4509

New Guinea

New Britain

Solomon Sea

Guadalcanal

Malaita

Santa Cruz Islands

Rotuma

San Cristobal

Banks Islands

Arafura Sea

Torres Strait

Cape York

Louisiade Archipelago

Rennell

Espíritu Santo

Fiji

Melville Island

Cape Arnhem

Cape York Peninsula

Gulf of Carpentaria

Great Barrier Reef

Coral Sea

Malakula

Éfaté

Viti Levu

Kadav

Timor Sea

Arnhem Land

Erromango

Tanna

Hun Islan

Cape Londonderry

Cape Lévèque

Lake Argyle

Kimberley Plateau

Barkly Tableland

Nouvelle Calédonie

Îles Loyauté

INDIAN OCEAN

Great Sandy Desert

Great Dividing Range

Gibson Desert

Macdonnell Ranges

Simpson Desert

Norfolk Island

North West Cape

Musgrave Ranges

Uluru 867

Lake Eyre

Lord Howe Island

North Cape

Australia

Great Victoria Desert

Lake Torrens

Darling

Nullarbor Plain

Great Australian Bight

Murray

Mount Kosciuszko 2230

Tasman Sea

New Zealand

Nor Islar

Cape Leeuwin

Kangaroo Island

Bass Strait

South Island

Aoraki 3754

Southern Alps

Tasmania

South East Cape

Stewart Island

Antipo Isla

Auckland Islands

Campbell Island

Macquarie Island

Oceania's highest mountains

Puncak Jaya, Indonesia	5 030 m	16 502 ft
Puncak Trikora, Indonesia	4 730 m	15 518 ft
Puncak Mandala, Indonesia	4 700 m	15 420 ft
Puncak Yamin, Indonesia	4 595 m	15 075 ft
Mt Wilhelm, Papua New Guinea	4 509 m	14 793 ft

1:65 000 000

0	500	1000	1500 miles
0	1000		2000 km

Hawaiian
Islands

PACIFIC OCEAN

Palmyra Atoll

Line Islands

Howland Island
Baker Island
Phoenix
Islands   Kanton
            Orona

Jarvis Island

Kiritimati

Malden
Island

Tokelau
Nukunono
Manihiki   Penrhyn   Caroline   Nuku Hiva   Marquesas
Pukapuka   Island   Islands
                                                   Hiva Oa

P o l y n e s i a

uti
ulaelae
Îles
Vallis   Savai'i   Suwarrow   Îles   Îles du
          Upolu   Samoan   Palliser Désappointement
Îles   Islands
de Hoorn
a Levu   Vava'u   Motu One   Fakarava   *Tuamotu Islands*
Tofua   Group   Niue   Palmerston   *Society Islands*   Tahiti
         Tonga   Cook   Hao
     Tongatapu   Islands Atiu
         Group   Rarotonga   *Tubuai Islands*
                                   Ruruta   Groupe
                                   Tubuai   Mururoa   Actéon

                                                      Îles Gambier

Raoul Island
                              Rapa   Pitcairn Island
ermadec   Marotiri
slands   Ducie Island

Chatham
Islands

Wake Island
(U.S.A.)

Pagan

Northern
Mariana Islands
(U.S.A.)

Saipan
□ Capitol Hill

MARSHALL
ISLANDS

Guam
(U.S.A.) ■ Hagåtña

Gaferut

Yap □

Chuuk

Pohnpei ■ Palikir

□ Delap-Uli
Djarrit

Majuro □

Caroline Islands

Kosrae

FEDERATED STATES
OF MICRONESIA

Gilbert
Islands □ Tarawa
■ Bairiki

ASIA

Kingsmill
Group

Yaren
■ NAURU

TUV

New Ireland

Rabaul

New Britain

Bougainville I.

Mount
Wilhelm
▲ 4509

New
Guinea

PAPUA

NEW
GUINEA

Solomon
Sea

SOLOMON ISLANDS

■ Honiara

Malaita

Santa Cruz
Islands

Fur

Arafura
Sea

Torres Strait

Port
Moresby

Banks
Islands

VANUATU

Rotum

FIJ

Espíritu Santo

Malakula

Timor Sea

Darwin

Gulf
of
Carpentaria

Cairns

Coral Sea
Islands Territory
(Australia)

Coral

Sea

Éfaté
■ Port Vila

Viti Le

S

Cape Léveque

INDIAN
OCEAN

Broome

Lake
Argyle

Townsville

New
Caledonia
(France)

Îles
Loyauté

■ Nouméa

North West
Cape

AUSTRALIA

Uluru
▲ 867

Alice Springs

Brisbane

Norfolk
Island
(Australia)

Lake Eyre

Lord Howe
Island
(Australia)

North Cape

Lake
Torrens

Darling

Auckland □

Canberra ■

Sydney

North
Island

Kalgoorlie

Great
Australian Bight

Adelaide

Murray

Mount
Kosciuszko
▲ 2229

Tasman

Wellington ■

Perth

Kangaroo
Island

Melbourne

Sea

Cape Leeuwin

Bass Strait

Tasmania

Hobart

Aoraki
▲ 3754

Christch

South Island

NEW
ZEALA

Stewart Island

Auckland Islands
(N.Z.)

Campbell Island
(N.Z.)

Macquarie Island
(Australia)

Oceania's capitals		
Largest capital (population)	**Canberra**, Australia	387 000
Smallest capital (population)	**Vaiaku**, Tuvalu	5 100
Most northerly capital	**Delap-Uliga-Djarrit**, Marshall Islands	7° 7'N
Most southerly capital	**Wellington**, New Zealand	41° 18'S
Highest capital	**Canberra**, Australia	581 metres 1 906 feet

1:65 000 000

0   500   1000   1500 miles
0   1000   2000 km

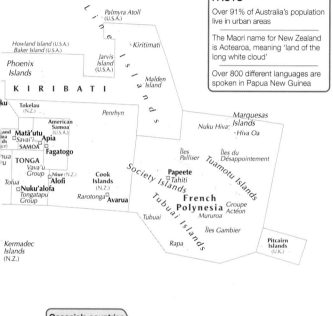

Hawaiian Islands (U.S.A.)

PACIFIC OCEAN

Line Islands

Palmyra Atoll (U.S.A.)

Kiritimati

Howland Island (U.S.A.)
Baker Island (U.S.A.)

Jarvis Island (U.S.A.)

Phoenix Islands

Malden Island

K I R I B A T I

Marquesas Islands

Nuku Hiva

Hiva Oa

Tokelau (N.Z.)

Penrhyn

American Samoa

Matā'utu
□*Savai'i* □
Apia

SAMOA

Fagatogo

Îles Palliser

Îles du Désappointement

Papeete
□*Tahiti*

TONGA

Vava'u Group

Niue (N.Z.)

Alofi

Society Islands

Tuamotu Islands

Tofua

Nuku'alofa

Tongatapu Group

Cook Islands (N.Z.)

Rarotonga □ **Avarua**

French Polynesia

Groupe Actéon

Tubuai

Tubuai Islands

Mururoa

Îles Gambier

Rapa

Pitcairn Islands (U.K.)

Kermadec Islands (N.Z.)

Chatham Islands (N.Z.)

Oceania's countries

Largest country	**Australia**	7 692 024 sq km	2 969 907 sq miles
Smallest country	**Nauru**	21 sq km	8 sq miles
Largest population	**Australia**	19 731 000	
Smallest population	**Tuvalu**	11 000	
Most densely populated country	**Nauru**	619 per sq km	1 625 per sq mile
Least densely populated country	**Australia**	3 per sq km	7 per sq mile

INDIAN

OCEAN

A 120° **B** Timor 130°
Sea
Melville
Bathurst Island Island
Beagle Gulf Darwin
Cape Londonderry Rum Jungle Batchelor Jabiru
Admiralty Joseph Adelaide Pine
Bonaparte Bonaparte River Creek
Archipelago Gulf Wyndham
Collier Kimberley Kununurra Victoria Timber
Bay Plateau River Creek
Cape Lévêque King Leopold Mount Ord Downs Mai
1 Ranges △936 Halls Creek
Broome Derby Liveringa Lake Lajamanu Lake
Roebuck Bay Fitzroy Sturt Creek Woods
Lagrange Crossing Tanami NOR
Eighty Mile Beach Desert TERR
Lake Gregory Tenr
Port Hedland Shay Gap Great Sandy Lake Cre
20° Barrow Island Karratha Marble Desert White
Roebourne Bar Lake Wills
Onslow Pannawonica Nullagine Lake Mackay Yuendumu Barro
North West Cape Chichester Range Cre
Exmouth Hamersley Range Mount Meharry Mount Mount
Tom Price △1250 Newman Lake Liebig Zeil Alic
2 Coral Bay Paraburdoo Lake Disappointment Macdonald Macdonnell R 1510
Minilya Mount Augustus Gibson Desert Lake △867 Erldunda
△1106 Ashburton Hopkins Lake Ulurů
Dorre Lake MacLeod Neales (Ayers Rock) Musgrave Ranges
Island WESTERN Lake Petermann Ranges Mount
Gascoyne Carnegie Warburton Woodroffe 1440
Dirk Denham Robinson Range Lake
Hartog Wells Great Victoria
Island Meekatharra Wiluna Desert
Murchison Lake S
Mount Maurice Coobe
Magnet Laverton AUS
Kalbarri Leonora Lake Carey
Northampton Geraldton AUSTRALIA Menzies
Mullewa Lake Leonora
Dongara Moore Barlee Maralinga Ta
Bonnie Rock Kalgoorlie Rawlinna Forrest Hughes
3 Wongan Coolgardie Nullarbor Plain Per
Yanchep Hills Merredin Kambalda Eucla Fowlers Bay Cedur
Perth Southern Lake Cowan Mundrabilla Streaky
Fremantle York Cross Anxie
Rockingham Noseman Great
Mandurah Hyden Balladonia Australian
Bunbury Katanning Bight
Geographe Bay Esperance
Busselton Hood Point
Margaret River Archipelago of
Cape Leeuwin Denmark the Recherche
Flinders Bay Albany
Point d'Entrecasteaux

110° **A** 120° **B** 130°

1:25 000 000 0 150 300 450 miles
0 200 400 600 km

oceania
australia

135° **B** **140°** **C** **QU**

Alberga   Macumba   Cooper Creek   Noccundra   Thargomindah

1
Oodnadatta
Edward's Creek
Lake Eyre (North)
Mungeranie
S t u r t
S t o n y
D e s e r t
Grey Range
Bulloo Downs
Hungerford

Coober Pedy   William Creek   Lake Eyre (South)   Etadunna   Lake Blanche

Ingmar   Marree   Tilcha   Lake Callabonna   Hawkers Gate   Tibooburra   Wanaaring

Millers Creek   S O U T H   Milparinka

30°
Tarcoola
Roxby Downs
Leigh Creek
Balcanoona
White Cliffs
Momba
Tilpa
D

A U S T R A L I A
Woomera
Parachilna
Lake Frome
Frome Downs
Barrier Range
Mootwingee
Wilcannia

Lake Harris
Roxby Downs
Lake Torrens
Flinders Ranges
Curnamona
Cockburn
Mingary
Broken Hill
Euriowie

Island Lagoon   Perdirka Lagoon   Woocalla   Hawker   Quorn   Olary   Menindee Lake   Menindee   Mount Manara

N E W
Lake Eyre
Lake Everard
Lake Macfarlane
Nonning
Port Augusta
Wilmington
Yunta
Coombah
Darnick
Ivai

2
Poochera
Streaky Bay
Gawler Ranges
Buckleboo
Iron Knob
Orroroo
Peterborough
Oakbank
Popiltah
Pooncarie
Gampung Lake
Mossgiel

Talia   Kyancutta   Kimba   Whyalla   Port Pirie   Jamestown   Boo

Anxious Bay   Lock   Cleve   Crystal Brook   Burra   Lake Victoria   Wentworth   Hatfield   Oxley

Eyre Peninsula   Arno Bay   Ungarra   Snowtown   Clare   Darling   Murrumbidgee R

Tumby Bay   Moonta   Wallaroo   Blyth   Balaklava   Murray   Berri   Renmark   Red Cliffs   Mildura   Tooleybuc   Moula

Port Lincoln   Maitland   Ardrossan   Kapunda   Waikerie   Merbein   Robinvale   Balranald   R

Gambier Islands   Yorke Peninsula   Gawler   Alawoona   Loxton   Deni

Cape Carnot   Spencer Gulf   **Adelaide**   Mount Barker   Murray Bridge   Ouyen   Lake Tyrrell   Swan Hill   Moula

Gulf St Vincent   Tailem Bend   Lameroo   Murrayville   Sea Lake   Ultima   Kerang   Echu

35°
Marion Bay
Yorketown
Willunga
Goolwa
Victor Harbor
Meningie
Keith
Hopetoun
Warracknabeal
Wycheproof
Charlton

Investigator Strait   Lake Alexandrina   Coonalpyn   Nhill   Dimboola   Donald   Bendigo   V I C

Cape Borda   Kingscote   Younghusband Peninsula   Bordertown   Padthaway   Horsham   St Arnaud   Stawell   Castlemaine   Ma

Cape de Couedic   Kangaroo Island   Naracoorte   Edenhope   Glenelg   Mt William 1167   Ararat   Beaufort   Kyneton   Sunb

3
Kingston South East
Cape Jaffa
Robe
Penola
Casterton
Coleraine
Skipton
Ballarat
Bacchus Marsh
Geelong

Millicent   Mount Gambier   Hamilton   Mortlake   Campervon   Colac   Corangamite   Lorne

Heywood   Discovery Bay   Portland   Port Fairy   Warrnambool   Port Campbell   Apollo Bay   Cape Otway

Cape Nelson

A **135°** **B** **140°** **C**

oceania
southeast australia

117

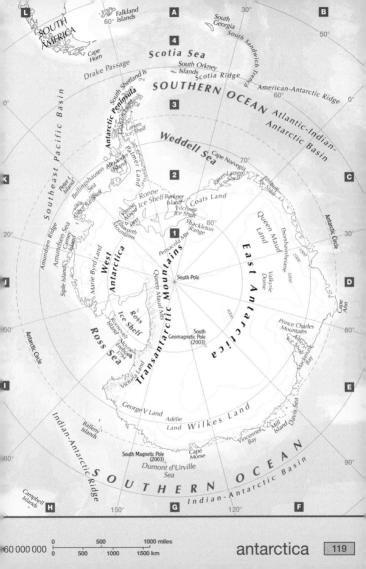

antarctica

ASIA

ARCTIC OCEAN

Axel He Is
Qu

Chukchi
Sea

Attu
Island

St Lawrence
Island

Bering Strait

Point Barrow

Beaufort
Sea

*Melvill
Island*

Norton Sound

Brooks Range

Banks
Island

Nunivak
Island

Yukon

Victoria
Island

Mount
McKinley
▲6194

Bristol
Bay

Aleutian Range

Mount
Logan
▲5959

Mackenzie
Mountains

Great Bear
Lake

Aleutian Islands

Alaska
Peninsula

Kodiak
Island

Gulf
of
Alaska

Great Slave
Lake

North America's longest rivers

Mississippi-Missouri	5 969 km	3 709 miles
Mackenzie-Peace-Finlay	4 241 km	2 635 miles
Missouri	4 086 km	2 539 miles
Mississippi	3 765 km	2 339 miles
Yukon	3 185 km	1 979 miles

Alexander
Archipelago

Peace

Lake
Athaba

Queen Charlotte
Islands

Coast Mountains

Rocky Mountains

Saskatche

▲3954
Mount
Robson

L
Winnipeg

Fraser

PACIFIC

Vancouver
Island

Misso

OCEAN

Mount Rainier
▲4392

Cascade Range

Bitterroot
Range

Cape Blanco

Coast Ranges

Great
Salt Lake

Kauai
Oahu
Hawaiian
Islands
Maui
Hawaii

Sierra Nevada

Great
Basin

Colorado

▲4398
Mount
Elbert

Death
Valley

Grand
Canyon

Lla
Estac

Guadalupe

Gulf of California

Baja California

Rio Grande

Sierra Madre Occidental

Sier
Orien

Cabo
Falso

Cabo
Corrientes

Vo
Popocat

North America's extremes

TOTAL LAND AREA		24 680 331 sq km	9 529 076 sq miles
Largest lake	Lake Superior, Canada/USA	82 100 sq km	31 699 sq miles
Largest island	Greenland	2 175 600 sq km	839 999 sq miles
Largest drainage basin	Mississippi-Missouri, USA	3 250 000 sq km	1 254 825 sq miles
Lowest point	Death Valley, USA	-86 metres	-282 feet

0   500   1000   1500 miles
0   1000   2000 km

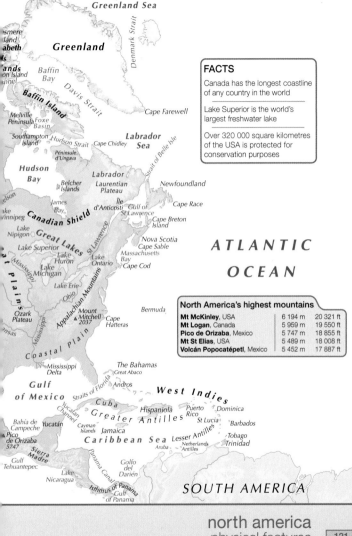

Greenland Sea

Greenland

Denmark Strait

smere
land
abeth
s
ands
on Island
annel

Baffin
Bay

Davis Strait

Baffin Island

Cape Farewell

Melville
Peninsula Foxe
Basin

Labrador
Sea

Southampton Hudson Strait Cape Chidley
Island

Péninsule
d'Ungava

Hudson
Bay

Labrador
Laurentian
Plateau

Newfoundland

Belcher
Islands

nelson

ake
winnipeg

James
Bay

Île
d'Anticosti Gulf of
St Lawrence

Cape Race

Canadian Shield

St Lawrence

Cape Breton
Island

Lake
Nipigon

Great Lakes

Lake Superior

Lake
Huron

Lake
Ontario

Nova Scotia
Cape Sable

Massachusetts
Bay

l Plains

Lake
Michigan

Mississippi

Lake Erie

Cape Cod

ATLANTIC

Ohio

Appalachian Mountains

OCEAN

Ozark
Plateau

ansas

Mount
Mitchell
2037

Cape
Hatteras

Bermuda

Mississippi

Coastal Plain

North America's highest mountains

Mt McKinley, USA	6 194 m	20 321 ft
Mt Logan, Canada	5 959 m	19 550 ft
Pico de Orizaba, Mexico	5 747 m	18 855 ft
Mt St Elias, USA	5 489 m	18 008 ft
Volcán Popocatépetl, Mexico	5 452 m	17 887 ft

Mississippi
Delta

The Bahamas
Great Abaco

Gulf
of Mexico

Straits of Florida
Andros

West Indies

Yucatán
Channel

Cuba

Hispaniola

Puerto
Rico

Dominica

Bahía de
Campeche

Pico
de Orizaba
5747

Yucatán

Cayman
Islands

Greater Antilles

Jamaica

St Lucia

Barbados

Sierra
Madre

Caribbean Sea

Lesser Antilles

Tobago

Netherlands
Antilles

Trinidad

Gulf
Tehuantepec

Lake
Nicaragua

Golfo
del Darién

Aruba

Panama Canal

Isthmus of Panama
Gulf
of Panama

SOUTH AMERICA

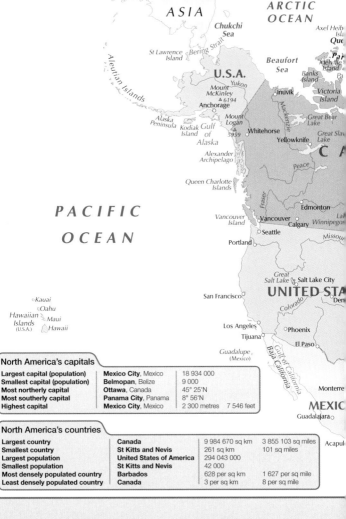

ASIA

ARCTIC OCEAN

Chukchi Sea

St Lawrence Island   *Bering Strait*

Axel Heib Isla   Que

Beaufort Sea

Melville Island   Pa

Banks Island

U.S.A.

Yukon

Inuvik

Victoria Island

Mount McKinley ▲ 6194

Anchorage

Mackenzie

Great Bear Lake

Alaska Peninsula   *Kodiak Island*   Mount Logan ▲ 5959

Whitehorse

Yellowknife

Great Slav Lake

Gulf of Alaska

Alexander Archipelago

Peace

C A

Queen Charlotte Islands

Fraser

Edmonton

PACIFIC

OCEAN

Vancouver Island   Vancouver   Calgary

Lak Winnipegos

Seattle

Missou

Portland

Great Salt Lake   Salt Lake City

San Francisco

UNITED STA

Colorado

Den

Kauai
Oahu
Hawaiian Islands   Maui
(U.S.A.)   Hawaii

Los Angeles

Phoenix

Tijuana

El Paso

Guadalupe (Mexico)

Gulf of California   *Baja California*

Monterre

MEXIC

Guadalajara

Acapul

North America's capitals

Largest capital (population)	**Mexico City**, Mexico	18 934 000
Smallest capital (population)	**Belmopan**, Belize	9 000
Most northerly capital	**Ottawa**, Canada	45° 25'N
Most southerly capital	**Panama City**, Panama	8° 56'N
Highest capital	**Mexico City**, Mexico	2 300 metres 7 546 feet

North America's countries

Largest country	**Canada**	9 984 670 sq km	3 855 103 sq miles
Smallest country	**St Kitts and Nevis**	261 sq km	101 sq miles
Largest population	**United States of America**	294 043 000	
Smallest population	**St Kitts and Nevis**	42 000	
Most densely populated country	**Barbados**	628 per sq km	1 627 per sq mile
Least densely populated country	**Canada**	3 per sq km	8 per sq mile

122   1:65 000 000

0   500   1000   1500 miles
0   1000   2000 km

Greenland Sea

Greenland

Denmark Strait

Baffin
Bay

Davis Strait

Nuuk

Cape Farewell

Baffin Island

esmere
and
beth

ands
on Island
nel

Foxe
Basin

Southampton
Island

Hudson Strait

Labrador
Sea

A   D   A

Hudson
Bay

Belcher
Islands

James
Bay

Newfoundland

St John's

Île
d'Anticosti

Gulf of
St Lawrence

St-Pierre

St Pierre and Miquelon
(France)

son

ke
nnipeg

Lake
Nipigon

Québec

innipeg

Thunder
Bay

Halifax

Ottawa

Montréal

Cape Sable

Minneapolis

Detroit

Great Lakes

Toronto

Portland

Boston

Chicago

Columbus

Cleveland

New York

Pittsburgh

Philadelphia

OF AMERICA

Ohio

Washington

St Louis

Memphis

rsas

Cape Hatteras

Bermuda
(U.K.)

Dallas

Atlanta

ATLANTIC

OCEAN

uston

Jacksonville

New Orleans

Orlando

Gulf
of Mexico

Miami

THE BAHAMAS

Nassau

Turks and
Caicos Islands
(U.K.)

Virgin Islands
(U.S.A.)

Virgin Islands
(U.K.)

ST KITTS AND NEVIS

ANTIGUA AND BARBUDA

San
Domingo

Santo
Domingo

San Juan

Puerto Rico
(U.S.A.)

Guadeloupe (France)

DOMINICA

Havana

CUBA

Mérida

Yucatán

Cayman
Islands
(U.K.)

Kingston

JAMAICA

HAITI

Port-
au-Prince

DOMINICAN
REPUBLIC

Martinique (France)

ST LUCIA

BARBADOS

ST VINCENT AND THE GRENADINES

co City

Veracruz

de Orizaba

BELIZE

Belmopan

Caribbean Sea

GRENADA

TRINIDAD
AND TOBAGO

atemala City

GUATEMALA

HONDURAS

Tegucigalpa

Aruba
(Neth.)

Netherlands
Antilles

San Salvador

EL SALVADOR

NICARAGUA

Managua

Pico

Guatemala City

Lake Nicaragua

San José

COSTA RICA

Panama
Canal

Panama City

PANAMA

SOUTH AMERICA

FACTS

Mexico City is the highest city in North
America and houses approximately
18% of Mexico's population

The Panama Canal, opened in 1914,
cut the journey between the Atlantic
and the Pacific by over 14 000 km

The territory of Nunavut is Canada's
newest administrative division,
created in 1999

north america
western canada

127

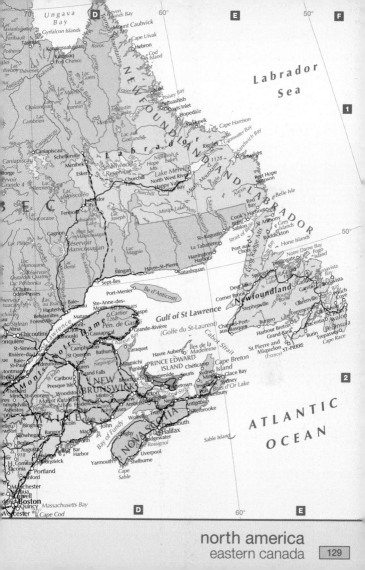

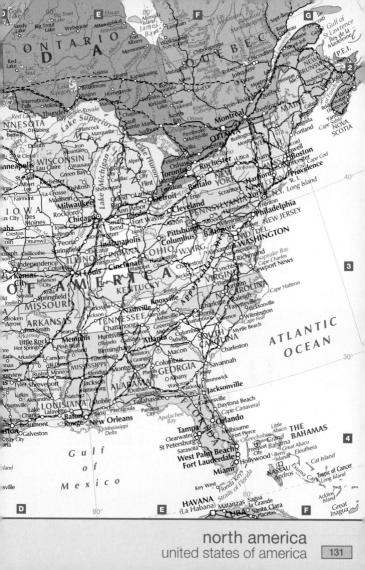

1:11 000 000

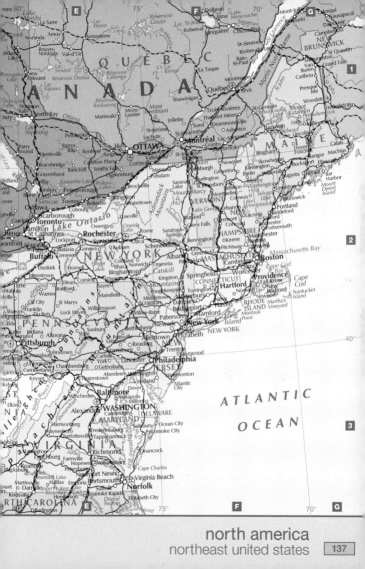

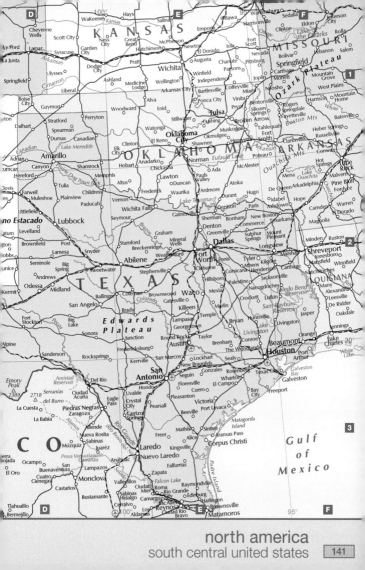

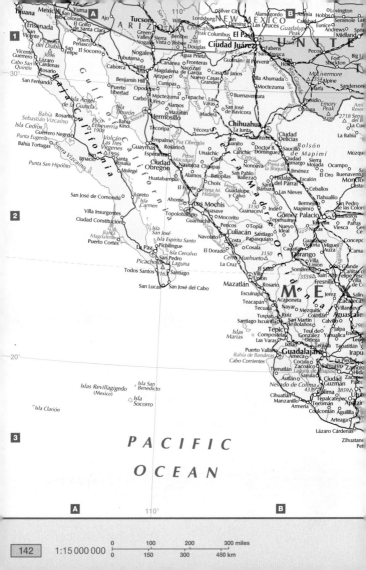

north america
the caribbean

145

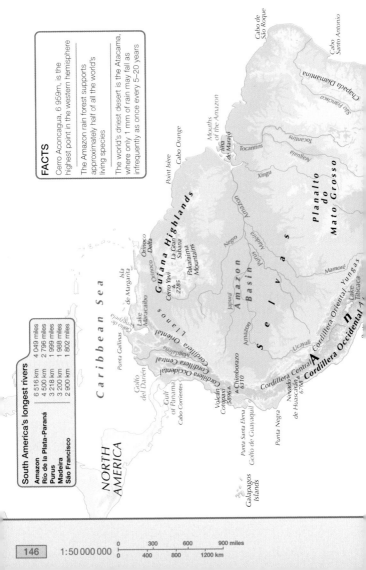

NORTH AMERICA

Caribbean Sea

FACTS

Cerro Aconcagua, 6 959m, is the highest point in the western hemisphere

The Amazon rain forest supports approximately half of all the world's living species

The world's driest desert is the Atacama, where only 1 mm of rain may fall as infrequently as once every 5–20 years

South America's longest rivers		
Amazon	6 516 km	4 049 miles
Rio de la Plata–Paraná	4 500 km	2 796 miles
Purus	3 218 km	1 999 miles
Madeira	3 200 km	1 988 miles
São Francisco	2 900 km	1 802 miles

1:50 000 000

| 0 | 300 | 600 | 900 miles |
| 0 | 400 | 800 | 1200 km |

Galapagos Islands

Punta Santa Elena
Golfo de Guayaquil
Punta Negra

Volcán Cotopaxi
Chimborazo 6310
Nevado de Huascarán 6 768

Cordillera Occidental
Cordillera Central
Cordillera Oriental

Punta Gallinas
Golfo del Darién
Gulf of Panama
Cabo Corrientes

Isla de Margarita
Península de Paraguaná
Lake Maracaibo
Magdalena

Orinoco Delta
Orinoco

Guiana Highlands
La Gran Sabana
Cerro Yavi 2285
Pakaraima Mountains

Point Isère
Cabo Orange

Mouths of the Amazon
Ilha de Marajó

Cabo de São Roque
Cabo Santo Antonio
Chapada Diamantina
São Francisco

Negro
Japurá
Putumayo
Amazon
Ucayali
Madeira
Mamoré
Iguaçu

Amazon Basin
S e l v a s

Cordillera Oriental
Yungas
Lake Titicaca

Tocantins
Xingu
Tapajós
Araguaia

Planalto do Mato Grosso

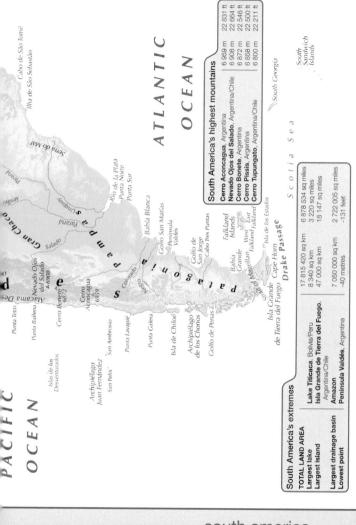

South America's highest mountains

Mountain	Elevation (m)	Elevation (ft)
Cerro Aconcagua, Argentina	6 959 m	22 831 ft
Nevado Ojos del Salado, Argentina/Chile	6 908 m	22 664 ft
Cerro Bonete, Argentina	6 872 m	22 546 ft
Cerro Pissis, Argentina	6 858 m	22 500 ft
Cerro Tupungato, Argentina/Chile	6 800 m	22 211 ft

South America's extremes

TOTAL LAND AREA		17 815 420 sq km	6 878 534 sq miles
Largest lake	Lake Titicaca, Bolivia/Peru	8 340 sq km	3 220 sq miles
Largest island	Isla Grande de Tierra del Fuego, Argentina/Chile	47 000 sq km	18 147 sq miles
Largest drainage basin	Amazon	7 050 000 sq km	2 722 005 sq miles
Lowest point	Península Valdés, Argentina	-40 metres	-131 feet

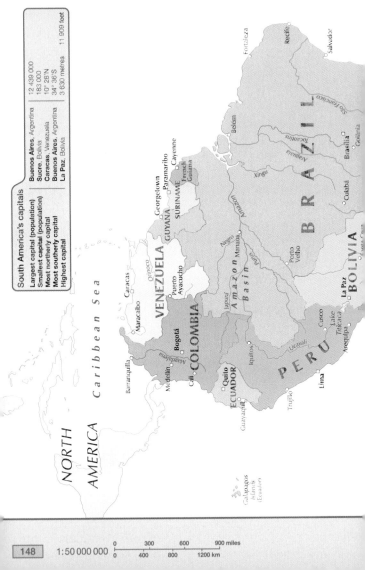

South America's capitals

Buenos Aires, *Argentina*	12 439 000	
Sucre, *Bolivia*	183 000	
Caracas, *Venezuela*	10° 28'N	
Buenos Aires, *Argentina*	34° 36'S	
La Paz, *Bolivia*	3 630 metres	11 909 feet

Largest capital (population)
Smallest capital (population)
Most northerly capital
Most southerly capital
Highest capital

NORTH

AMERICA

C a r i b b e a n   S e a

Barranquilla

Maracaibo

Caracas

Orinoco

VENEZUELA

Puerto
Ayacucho

Georgetown

GUYANA

Paramaribo

SURINAME

Cayenne

French
Guiana

Medellín

Bogotá

COLOMBIA

Cali

Magdalena

Quito

ECUADOR

Guayaquil

Galápagos
Islands
(Ecuador)

Japurá

Iquitos

Amazon

Negro

Manaus

Amazon
Basin

Purus

Belém

Xingu

Tocantins

BRAZIL

São Francisco

Fortaleza

Recife

Salvador

Porto
Velho

PERU

Ucayali

Cusco

Lake
Titicaca

La Paz

BOLIVIA

Cuiabá

Araguaia

Brasília

Goiânia

Trujillo

Lima

Arequipa

Santa Cruz

148

1:50 000 000

0   300   600   900 miles

0   400   800   1200 km

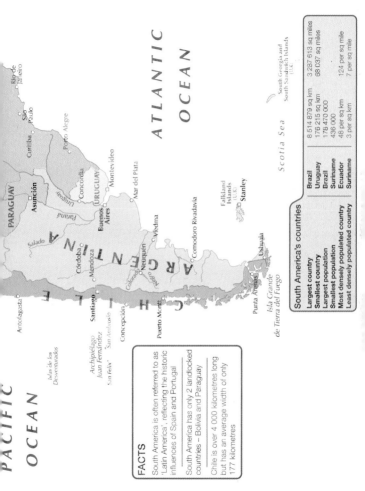

PACIFIC OCEAN

Islas de los Desventurados

Archipiélago Juan Fernández
San Félix *San Antonio*

Antofagasta

Santiago
San Antonio
Concepción
Puerto Montt

Isla Grande de Tierra del Fuego

Punta Arenas
Ushuaia

C H I L E

Salado
Córdoba
Mendoza
Neuquén
Colorado
Negro
Río

A R G E N T I N A

Buenos Aires
Mar del Plata
Viedma
Comodoro Rivadavia

PARAGUAY

Asunción
Paraná

URUGUAY
Uruguay
Concordia
Montevideo

Río de Janeiro
São Paulo
Curitiba
Porto Alegre

ATLANTIC OCEAN

Falkland Islands (U.K.)
Stanley

Scotia Sea

South Georgia and South Sandwich Islands (U.K.)

South America's countries

Largest country	Brazil	8 514 879 sq km
Smallest country	Uruguay	176 215 sq km
Largest population	Brazil	178 470 000
Smallest population	Suriname	436 000
Most densely populated country	Ecuador	48 per sq km
Least densely populated country	Suriname	.3 per sq km
3 287 613 sq miles
68 037 sq miles
124 per sq mile
7 per sq mile

FACTS

South America is often referred to as 'Latin America', reflecting the historic influences of Spain and Portugal

South America has only 2 landlocked countries – Bolivia and Paraguay

Chile is over 4 000 kilometres long but has an average width of only 177 kilometres

south america
northern south america
151

ATLANTIC

OCEAN

south america
southern south america

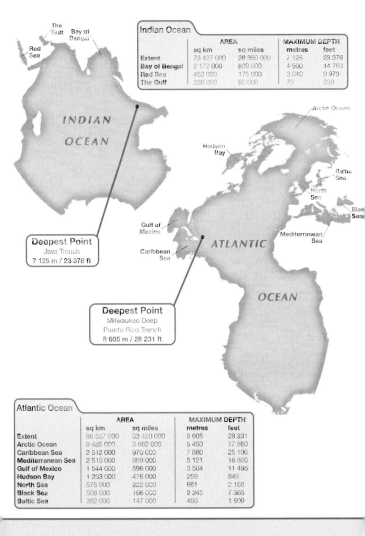

Indian Ocean

	AREA		MAXIMUM DEPTH	
	sq km	sq miles	metres	feet
Extent	73 427 000	28 350 000	7 125	23 376
Bay of Bengal	2 172 000	839 000	4 500	14 763
Red Sea	453 000	175 000	3 040	9 973
The Gulf	238 000	92 000	73	239

The Gulf Bay of Bengal

Red Sea

INDIAN OCEAN

Arctic Ocean

Hudson Bay

Baltic Sea

North Sea

Bla[c]k Sea

Gulf of Mexico

Mediterranean Sea

Caribbean Sea

ATLANTIC OCEAN

Deepest Point
Java Trench
7 125 m / 23 376 ft

Deepest Point
Milwaukee Deep
Puerto Rico Trench
8 605 m / 28 231 ft

Atlantic Ocean

	AREA		MAXIMUM DEPTH	
	sq km	sq miles	metres	feet
Extent	86 557 000	33 420 000	8 605	28 231
Arctic Ocean	9 485 000	3 662 000	5 450	17 880
Caribbean Sea	2 512 000	970 000	7 680	25 196
Mediterranean Sea	2 510 000	969 000	5 121	16 800
Gulf of Mexico	1 544 000	596 000	3 504	11 495
Hudson Bay	1 233 000	476 000	259	849
North Sea	575 000	222 000	661	2 168
Black Sea	508 000	196 000	2 245	7 365
Baltic Sea	382 000	147 000	460	1 509

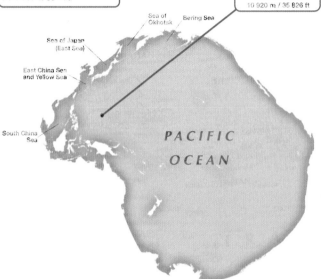

Deepest Point
Challenger Deep
Mariana Trench
10 920 m / 35 826 ft

Sea of Okhotsk

Bering Sea

Sea of Japan (East Sea)

East China Sea and Yellow Sea

South China Sea

PACIFIC OCEAN

Pacific Ocean	AREA		MAXIMUM DEPTH	
	sq km	sq miles	metres	feet
Extent	166 241 000	64 186 000	10 920	35 826
Bering Sea	2 261 000	873 000	4 150	13 615
Sea of Okhotsk	1 392 000	537 000	3 363	11 033
Sea of Japan (East Sea)	1 013 000	391 000	3 743	12 280
East China Sea and Yellow Sea	1 202 000	464 000	2 717	8 913
South China Sea	2 590 000	1 000 000	5 514	18 090

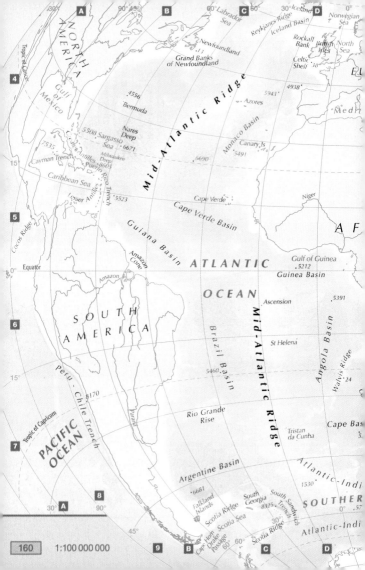

atlantic and indian oceans

arctic ocean   1 : 60 000 000

INTRODUCTION TO THE INDEX

The index includes all names shown on the reference maps in the atlas. Names are referenced by page number and by a grid reference. The grid reference correlates to the alphanumeric values along the edges of each map which reflect the lines of latitude and longitude. Names are generally referenced to the largest scale map on which they appear. Each entry also includes the country or geographical area in which the feature is located. Where relevant, the index clearly indicates [inset] if a feature appears on an inset map.

Name forms are as they appear on the maps, with additional alternative names or name forms included as cross-references which refer the user to the entry for the map form of the name. Names beginning with Mc or Mac are alphabetized exactly as they appear. The terms Saint, Sainte, etc, are abbreviated to St, Ste, etc, but alphabetized as if in the full form.

Names of physical features beginning with generic geographical terms are permuted – the descriptive term is placed after the main part of the name. For example, Lake Superior is indexed as Superior, Lake; Mount Everest as Everest, Mount. This policy is applied to all languages.

Entries, other than those for towns and cities, include a descriptor indicating the type of geographical feature. Descriptors are not included where the type of feature is implicit in the name itself.

Administrative divisions are included to differentiate entries of the same name and feature type within the one country. In such cases duplicate names are alphabetized in order of administrative division. Additional qualifiers are also included for names within selected geographical areas.

INDEX ABBREVIATIONS

admin. div.	administrative division	**Ger.**	Germany	**Port.**	Portugal
Afgh.	Afghanistan	**Guat.**	Guatemala	**prov.**	province
Alg.	Algeria	**h.**	hill	**pt.**	point
Arg.	Argentina	**hd**	headland	**r.**	river
Austr.	Australia	**Hond.**	Honduras	**reg.**	region
aut. reg.	autonomous region	**i.**	island	**Rep.**	Republic
aut. rep.	autonomous republic	**imp. l.**	impermanent lake	**resr**	reservoir
		Indon.	Indonesia	**rf**	reef
Azer.	Azerbaijan	**is**	islands	**Rus. Fed.**	Russian Federation
b.	bay	**isth.**	isthmus		
Bangl.	Bangladesh	**Kazakh.**	Kazakhstan	**S.**	South
B.I.O.T.	British Indian Ocean Territory	**Kyrg.**	Kyrgyzstan	**Serb. and Mont.**	Serbia and Montenegro
		l.	lake		
Bol.	Bolivia	**lag.**	lagoon	**str.**	strait
Bos.-Herz.	Bosnia Herzegovina	**Lith.**	Lithuania	**Switz.**	Switzerland
Bulg.	Bulgaria	**Lux.**	Luxembourg	**Tajik.**	Tajikistan
c.	cape	**Madag.**	Madagascar	**Tanz.**	Tanzania
Can.	Canada	**Maur.**	Mauritania	**terr.**	territory
C.A.R.	Central African Republic	**Mex.**	Mexico	**Thai.**	Thailand
		Moz.	Mozambique	**Trin. and Tob.**	Trinidad and Tobago
Col.	Colombia	**mt.**	mountain		
Czech Rep.	Czech Republic	**mts**	mountains	**Turkm.**	Turkmenistan
Dem. Rep. Congo	Democratic Republic of Congo	**mun.**	municipality	**U.A.E.**	United Arab Emirates
		N.	North		
depr.	depression	**Neth.**	Netherlands	**U.K.**	United Kingdom
des.	desert	**Nic.**	Nicaragua	**Ukr.**	Ukraine
Dom. Rep.	Dominican Republic	**N.Z.**	New Zealand	**Uru.**	Uruguay
		Pak.	Pakistan	**U.S.A.**	United States of America
esc.	escarpment	**Para.**	Paraguay		
est.	estuary	**pen.**	peninsula	**Uzbek.**	Uzbekistan
Eth.	Ethiopia	**Phil.**	Philippines	**val.**	valley
Fin.	Finland	**plat.**	plateau	**Venez.**	Venezuela
for.	forest	**P.N.G.**	Papua New Guinea	**vol.**	volcano
g.	gulf	**Pol.**	Poland		

1

100 Mile House Can. **126** C2

A

Aabenraa Denmark **47** B4
Aachen Ger. **54** C2
Aalborg Denmark **47** B4
Aalst Belgium **54** B2
Aarschot Belgium **54** B2
Aba China **80** C2
Aba Nigeria **101** C4
Ābādān Iran **93** C2
Ābādeh Iran **93** D2
Abadla Alg. **100** B1
Abakaliki Nigeria **101** C4
Abakan Rus. Fed. **95** I3
Abakanskiy Khrebet *mts* Rus. Fed.
    89 F1
Abancay Peru **150** B4
Abarqū Iran **93** D2
Abashiri Japan **78** D2
Abaya, Lake Eth. **103** B4
Ābay Wenz *r.* Eth./Sudan *see* Blue Nile
Abaza Rus. Fed. **89** G1
Abbasanta Italy **62** A2
Abbeville France **58** C1
Abbeville U.S.A. **138** B3
Abbot Ice Shelf Antarctica **119** J2
Abbottabad Pak. **86** B1
Abéché Chad **101** E3
Abengourou Côte d'Ivoire **100** B4
Abeokuta Nigeria **100** C4
Aberaeron U.K. **53** A3
Aberchirder U.K. **50** C2
Aberdare U.K. **53** B4
Aberdaron U.K. **52** A3
Aberdeen S. Africa **108** B3
Aberdeen U.K. **50** C2
Aberdeen *MD* U.S.A. **137** E3
Aberdeen *SD* U.S.A. **135** D1
Aberdeen *WA* U.S.A. **138** B1
Aberdeen Lake Can. **127** F1
Aberystwyth U.K. **53** A3
Abez' Rus. Fed. **40** F2
Abhā Saudi Arabia **90** B3
Abiad, Bahr el *r.* Sudan/Uganda *see*
    White Nile
Abidjan Côte d'Ivoire **100** B4
Abilene *KS* U.S.A. **135** D3
Abilene *TX* U.S.A. **141** E2
Abingdon U.K. **53** C4
Abinsk Rus. Fed. **45** E3
Abitibi, Lake Can. **128** E2
Abohar India **86** B1
Abomey Benin **100** C4
Abongabong, Gunung *mt.* Indon.
    72 A1
Abong Mbang Cameroon **104** B2
Aborlan Phil. **76** A3
Abou Déia Chad **101** D3
Abrantes Port. **60** B2
Abra Pampa Arg. **152** B3
Absaroka Range *mts* U.S.A. **134** A2
Abşeron Yarımadası *pen.* Azer. **93** C1
Abū 'Arīsh Saudi Arabia **90** B3
Abu Deleiq Sudan **90** A3
Abu Hamed Sudan **102** B3
Abuja Nigeria **101** C4
Abū Kamāl Syria **93** C2
Abunā *r.* Bol. **152** B1
Abunā Brazil **150** C3
Abu Road India **86** B2
Abū Sunbul Egypt **102** B2

Abu Zabad Sudan **103** A3
Abū Zabī U.A.E. *see* Abu Dhabi
Abyei Sudan **103** A4
Acambaro Mex. **143** B2
A Cañiza Spain **60** B1
Acaponeta Mex. **142** B2
Acapulco Mex. **143** C3
Acará Brazil **151** E3
Acarigua Venez. **150** C2
Acatlan Mex. **143** C3
Acayucán Mex. **143** C3
Accra Ghana **100** B4
Accrington U.K. **52** B3
Achalpur India **86** B2
Achicourt France **54** A2
Achill Island Rep. of Ireland **51** A2
Achim Ger. **55** D1
Achnasheen U.K. **50** B2
Achuyevo Rus. Fed. **45** E2
Acıpayam Turkey **65** C3
Acireale Italy **62** C3
Acklins Island Bahamas **145** C2
Aconcagua, Cerro *mt.* Arg. **152** A4
A Coruña Spain **60** B1
Acqui Terme Italy **62** A2
Ács Hungary **57** D3
Actéon, Groupe *is* Fr. Polynesia **111**
Actopán Mex. **143** C2
Ada U.S.A. **141** E2
Adam Oman **91** C2
'Adan Yemen *see* Aden
Adana Turkey **92** B2
Adapazarı Turkey **65** D2
Adda *r.* Italy **62** A1
Ad Dafinah Saudi Arabia **90** B2
Ad Dahnā' *des.* Saudi Arabia **91** B2
Ad Dakhla Western Sahara **100** A2
Ad Dammām Saudi Arabia *see*
    Dammam
Ad Dār al Ḥamrā' Saudi Arabia **90** A2
Ad Darb Saudi Arabia **90** B3
Ad Dawādimī Saudi Arabia **90** B2
Ad Dawḥah Qatar *see* Doha
Aḍ Ḍiffah *plat.* Egypt *see*
    Libyan Plateau
Ad Dilam Saudi Arabia **90** B3
Ad Dir'īyah Saudi Arabia **102** C2
Addis Ababa Eth. **103** B4
Ad Dīwānīyah Iraq **90** B2
Adelaide Austr. **116** B2
Adelaide River Austr. **114** C1
Adelebsen Ger. **55** D2
Adélie Land *reg.* Antarctica **119** G3
Aden Yemen **90** B3
Aden, Gulf of Somalia/Yemen **91** B3
Adenau Ger. **54** C2
Adh Dhayd U.A.E. **91** C2
Adi *r.* Indon. **71** C3
Ādīgrat Eth. **102** B3
Adilabad India **87** B3
Adirondack Mountains U.S.A. **137** F2
Ādīs Alem Eth. **103** B4
Adjud Romania **44** F1
Admiralty Gulf Austr. **114** B1
Admiralty Island U.S.A. **126** B2
Admiralty Islands P.N.G. **71** D3
Adour *r.* France **58** B3
Adra Spain **60** C2
Adrar Alg. **100** B2
Adrian *MI* U.S.A. **136** D2
Adrian *TX* U.S.A. **141** D1
Adriatic Sea Europe **62** B2
Ādwa Eth. **102** B3
Adycha *r.* Rus. Fed. **95** L2
Adygeysk Rus. Fed. **45** E3
Adzopé Côte d'Ivoire **100** B4
Aegean Sea Greece/Turkey **65** B3
Aerzen Ger. **55** D1
A Estrada Spain **60** B1

Afabet Eritrea **102** B3
Afghanistan *country* Asia **86** A1
'Afif Saudi Arabia **90** B2
Africa **66**
Afyon Turkey **92** B2
Agadez Niger **101** C3
Agadir Morocco **100** B1
Agadyr' Kazakh. **89** E2
Agar India **86** B2
Agartala India **87** D2
Ağdam Azer. **93** C2
Agde France **59** C3
Agen France **58** C3
Aggeneys S. Africa **108** A2
Agia Vervara Greece **65** C3
Agios Dimitrios Greece **65** B3
Agios Efstratios *i.* Greece **65** C3
Agios Konstantinos Greece **92** A2
Agios Nikolaos Greece **65** C3
Agirwat Hills Sudan **90** A3
Agnita Romania **44** B2
Agra India **87** B2
Ağrı Turkey **93** C2
Agrigento Italy **62** B3
Agrinio Greece **65** B3
Agropoli Italy **62** B2
Água Clara Brazil **154** B2
Aguadulce Panama **144** B4
Aguanaval *r.* Mex. **142** B2
Agua Prieta Mex. **142** B1
Aguascalientes Mex. **142** B2
Águas Formosas Brazil **155** D1
Águeda Port. **60** B1
Aguilar de Campóo Spain **60** C1
Aguilas Spain **61** C2
Aguililla Mex. **142** B3
Agulhas, Cape S. Africa **108** B3
Agulhas Negras *mt.* Brazil **155** D2
Ağva Turkey **65** D2
Ahar Iran **93** C2
Ahaus Ger. **54** C1
Ahlat Turkey **93** C2
Ahlen Ger. **54** C2
Ahmadabad India **86** B2
Ahmadnagar India **85** B3
Ahmadpur East Pak. **86** B2
Ahmadpur Sial Pak. **86** B1
Ahome Mex. **142** B2
Ahram Iran **93** D3
Ahrensburg Ger. **55** E1
Ahun France **58** C2
Ahvāz Iran **93** C2
Ai-Ais Namibia **108** A2
Aigialousa Cyprus **92** B2
Aigio Greece **65** B3
Aiken U.S.A. **139** D2
Aimorés Brazil **155** D1
Aimorés, Serra dos *hills* Brazil **155** D
Ain *r.* France **56** B3
Aïn Azel Alg. **61** E2
'Aïn Ben Tili Maur. **100** B2
Aïn Defla Alg. **61** D2
Aïn Oulmene Alg. **61** E2
Aïn Sefra Alg. **100** B1
Ainsworth U.S.A. **134** D2
Aïntab Turkey *see* Gaziantep
Aïn Taya Alg. **61** D2
Aïn Tédélès Alg. **61** D2
Aïn Temouchent Alg. **61** C2
Aïr, Massif de l' *mts* Niger **101** C3
Airbangis Indon. **72** A1
Airdrie Can. **126** D2
Aire-sur-l'Adour France **58** B3
Aisch *r.* Ger. **55** E3
Aishihik Lake Can. **126** B1
Aisne *r.* France **54** A3
Aitape P.N.G. **71** D3
Aiud Romania **44** B2
Aix-en-Provence France **59** D3
Aix-les-Bains France **59** D2

izawl India **74** A1
izkraukle Latvia **42** C2
izu-wakamatsu Japan **79** C3
jaccio France **59** D3
jdābīyā Libya **101** E1
jmer India **86** B2
jo U.S.A. **140** C2
kbulak Rus. Fed. **41** E3
kçakale Turkey **92** B2
kchār *reg.* Maur. **96**
kdağmadeni Turkey **92** B2
kersberga Sweden **42** A2
keti Dem. Rep. Congo **104** C2
khalk'alak'i Georgia **41** D4
khdar, Jabal *mts* Oman **91** C2
khisar Turkey **65** C3
khtubinsk Rus. Fed. **41** D4
kimiski Island Can. **125** G3
kita Japan **78** D3
kjoujt Maur. **100** A3
kkol' Kazakh. **89** E1
kmenrags *pt* Latvia **42** B2
kmola Sudan **103** B4
kobo Sudan **103** B4
kola India **86** B2
kordat Eritrea **90** A3
kpatok Island Can. **125** H2
kranes Iceland **46** [inset]
krathos, Akra *pt* Greece **65** B2
krehamn Norway **48** E2
kron U.S.A. **136** D2
ksai Chin *terr.* Asia **87** B1
ksaray Turkey **92** B2
ksay Kazakh. **88** C1
ksay Rus. Fed. **45** E2
kşehir Turkey **92** B2
ksu China **89** F2
ksum Eth. **90** A3
ktau Kazakh. **88** C2
ktobe Kazakh. **88** C1
ktogay Kazakh. **89** E2
ksayrski Belarus **42** C3
kure Nigeria **101** C4
kureyri Iceland **46** [inset]
kyab Myanmar *see* Sittwe
labama *r.* U.S.A. **139** C2
labama *state* U.S.A. **138** C2
laçatı Turkey **65** C3
lagir Rus. Fed. **93** C1
lagoinhas Brazil **151** F4
lagôn *r.* **93** C2
l Ahmadī Kuwait **91** B2
lakol', Ozero *salt l.* Kazakh. **89** F2
lakurtti Rus. Fed. **46** G2
l 'Alayyah Saudi Arabia **90** B3
l 'Amādīyah Iraq **93** D2
l 'Amīrīyah Egypt **92** A2
lamo U.S.A. **133** C3
lamogordo U.S.A. **140** C2
lamos *Sonora* Mex. **142** B3
lamos *Sonora* Mex. **142** B2
lamos *r.* Mex. **142** B2
lamosa U.S.A. **134** B3
land Islands Fin. **47** D3
lanya Turkey **65** C3
l 'Aqabah Jordan **92** B3
l 'Aqīq Saudi Arabia **90** A3
larcón, Embalse de *resr* Spain **61** C2
l 'Arīsh Egypt **92** B2
l Arṭāwīyah Saudi Arabia **90** B2
las Indon. **73** C2
laşehir Turkey **65** C3
laska *state* U.S.A. **124** C2
laska, Gulf of U.S.A. **124** C3
laska Peninsula U.S.A. **120**
laska Range *mts* U.S.A. **124** C3
lät Azer. **93** C2
latyr' Rus. Fed. **41** D3

Alausí Ecuador **150** B3
Alavus Fin. **47** E3
Alawoona Austr. **116** C2
Alba Italy **62** A2
Albacete Spain **61** C2
Alba Iulia Romania **44** B2
Albania *country* Europe **64** A2
Albany Austr. **114** A3
Albany *r.* Can. **128** B1
Albany *GA* U.S.A. **139** D2
Albany *NY* U.S.A. **137** F2
Albany *OR* U.S.A. **132** B2
Albatross Bay Austr. **115** D1
Al Bawīṭī Egypt **102** A2
Al Bayḍā' Libya **101** E1
Al Bayḍā' Yemen **90** B3
Albemarle U.S.A. **139** D1
Albemarle Sound *sea chan.* U.S.A. **139** E1
Albenga Italy **62** A2
Alberga *watercourse* Austr. **116** B1
Albert France **54** A3
Albert, Lake Dem. Rep. Congo/Uganda **105** D2
Alberta *prov.* Can. **126** D2
Albert Kanaal *canal* Belgium **54** B2
Albert Lea U.S.A. **135** E2
Albi France **58** C1
Al Bi'r Saudi Arabia **90** A2
Al Birk Saudi Arabia **90** B3
Al Biyāḍh *reg.* Saudi Arabia **90** B2
Alborz, Reshteh-ye *mts* Iran *see* Elburz Mountains
Albufeira Port. **60** B2
Albuquerque U.S.A. **140** C1
Al Buraymī Oman **91** C2
Albury Austr. **117** D3
Alcácer do Sal Port. **60** B2
Alcalá de Henares Spain **60** C1
Alcalá la Real Spain **60** C2
Alcamo Italy **62** B3
Alcañiz Spain **61** C1
Alcántara Spain **60** B2
Alcaraz Spain **60** C2
Alcaraz, Sierra de *mts* Spain **60** C2
Alcaudete Spain **60** C2
Alcázar de San Juan Spain **60** C2
Alchevs'k Ukr. **45** E2
Alcobaça Brazil **155** E1
Alcora Spain **61** C1
Alcoy-Alcoi Spain **61** C2
Alcúdia Spain **61** D2
Aldabra Islands Seychelles **103** C5
Aldama Mex. **143** C2
Aldan Rus. Fed. **95** K3
Aldan *r.* Rus. Fed. **95** K2
Alderney *i.* Channel Is **53** B5
Aleg Maur. **100** A3
Alegre Brazil **155** D2
Alegrete Brazil **152** C3
Alekhovshchina Rus. Fed. **43** D1
Aleksandrovsk-Sakhalinskiy Rus. Fed. **95** L3
Aleksandry, Zemlya *i.* Rus. Fed. **94** F1
Alekseyevka *Belgorodskaya Oblast'* Rus. Fed. **45** E1
Alekseyevka *Belgorodskaya Oblast'* Rus. Fed. **45** E1
Aleksin Rus. Fed. **43** E3
Aleksinac Serb. and Mont. **64** B2
Além Paraíba Brazil **155** D2
Ålen Norway **46** C3
Alençon France **58** C2
Aleppo Syria **92** B2
Alerta Peru **150** B4
Alert Bay Can. **126** C2
Alès France **59** C3
Aleșd Romania **44** B2
Alessandria Italy **62** A2

Ålesund Norway **46** B3
Aleutian Islands U.S.A. **158** E1
Aleutian Range *mts* U.S.A. **120**
Alevina, Mys *c.* Rus. Fed. **95** M3
Alexander Archipelago *is* U.S.A. **126** B2
Alexander Bay S. Africa **108** A2
Alexander City U.S.A. **139** C2
Alexander Island Antarctica **119** K2
Alexandra Austr. **117** D3
Alexandra N.Z. **118** A4
Alexandreia Greece **65** B2
Alexandria Egypt **102** A1
Alexandria Romania **44** C3
Alexandria S. Africa **109** C3
Alexandria *LA* U.S.A. **138** B2
Alexandria *MN* U.S.A. **135** D1
Alexandria *VA* U.S.A. **137** E3
Alexandrina, Lake Austr. **116** B3
Alexandroupoli Greece **65** C2
Alexis *r.* Can. **129** E1
Alexis Creek Can. **126** C2
Aleysk Rus. Fed. **89** F1
Alfaro Spain **61** C1
Al Fāw Iraq **93** C3
Al Fayyūm Egypt **102** B2
Alfeld (Leine) Ger. **55** D2
Alfenas Brazil **155** C2
Al Fujayrah U.A.E. *see* Fujairah
Algeciras Spain **60** B2
Algemesí Spain **61** C2
Algena Eritrea **90** A3
Algorta Spain **60** C1
Al Ḥadīthah Iraq **93** C2
Al Ḥajar al Gharbī *mts* Oman **91** C2
Alghero Italy **62** A2
Al Ghurdaqah Egypt **102** B2
Al Ghwaybiyah Saudi Arabia **91** B2
Algiers Alg. **100** C1
Algoa Bay S. Africa **109** C3
Algona U.S.A. **135** E2
Alger Alg. *see* Algiers
Algeria *country* Africa **100** C2
Al Ghaydah Yemen **91** C3
Alhama de Murcia Spain **61** C2
Al Ḥammām Egypt **92** A2
Al Ḥanākīyah Saudi Arabia **90** B2
Al Ḥasakah Syria **93** C2
Al Ḥayy Iraq **93** C2
Al Ḥazm al Jawf Yemen **90** B3
Al Ḥibāk *des.* Saudi Arabia **91** C3
Al Ḥillah Saudi Arabia **90** B2
Al Ḥinnāh Saudi Arabia **91** B2
Al Hoceïma Morocco **60** C2
Al Hudaydah Yemen *see* Hodeidah
Al Ḥufūf Saudi Arabia **91** B2
Al Ḥulayq al Kabīr *hills* Libya **101** D2
'Alīābād Iran **93** D3
Aliağa Turkey **65** C3
Aliakmonas *r.* Greece **65** B2
Alicante Spain **61** C2
Alice U.S.A. **141** E3
Alice, Punta *pt* Italy **63** C3
Alice Springs Austr. **114** C2
Aligarh India **87** B2
Aligüdarz Iran **93** C2
Alihe China **81** E1
Alima *r.* Congo **104** B3
Aliova *r.* Turkey **65** C3
Ali Sabieh Djibouti **103** C3
Al Iskandarīyah Egypt *see* Alexandria
Al Ismā'īlīyah Egypt **102** B1
Aliwal North S. Africa **109** C3
Al Jaghbūb Libya **101** E2
Al Jahrah Kuwait **91** B2
Al Jamalīyah Qatar **91** C2
Al Jawf Libya **101** E2
Al Jawf Saudi Arabia **90** A2

Al Jawsh Libya **101** D1
Aljezur Port. **60** B2
Al Jubayl Saudi Arabia **91** B2
Al Junaynah Saudi Arabia **90** B2
Aljustrel Port. **60** B2
Al Kahfah Saudi Arabia **90** B2
Al Kāmil Oman **91** C2
Al Karak Jordan **92** B2
Al Khābūrah Oman **91** C2
Al Khamāsīn Saudi Arabia **90** B2
Al Khārijah Egypt **102** B2
Al Khaşab Oman **91** C2
Al Khawkhah Yemen **90** B3
Al Khawr Qatar **91** C2
Al Khufrah Libya **102** A2
Al Khums Libya **101** D1
Al Khunn Saudi Arabia **91** B2
Al Kir'ānah Qatar **91** C2
Alkmaar Neth. **54** B1
Al Kūt Iraq **93** C2
Al Kuwayt Kuwait *see* Kuwait
Al Lādhiqīyah Syria *see* Latakia
Allahabad India **87** C2
Allakh-Yun' Rus. Fed. **95** L2
'Allāqi, Wādī al *watercourse* Egypt
  90 A2
Allegheny *r.* U.S.A. **137** D3
Allegheny Mountains U.S.A. **137** D3
Allen, Lough *l.* Rep. of Ireland **51** B1
Allende *Coahuila* Mex. **143** B2
Allende *Nuevo León* Mex. **143** B2
Allentown U.S.A. **137** E2
Alleppey India **85** B4
Aller *r.* Ger. **55** D1
Alliance *NE* U.S.A. **136** C2
Alliance *OH* U.S.A. **136** D2
Al Lith Saudi Arabia **90** B2
Alloa U.K. **50** C2
Alma Can. **129** C2
Almada Port. **60** B2
Almadén Spain **60** C2
Al Madīnah Saudi Arabia *see* Medina
Al Maḩwit Yemen **90** B3
Al Majma'ah Saudi Arabia **90** B2
Almanor, Lake U.S.A. **132** B2
Almansa Spain **61** C2
Al Mansūrah Egypt **92** B2
Al Mariyyah U.A.E. **91** C2
Al Marj Libya **101** E1
Almaty Kazakh. **89** D2
Almazán Spain **60** C1
Almeirim Brazil **151** D2
Almelo Neth. **54** C1
Almenara Brazil **155** D1
Almendra, Embalse de *resr* Spain
  60 B1
Almendralejo Spain **60** B2
Almería Spain **60** C2
Almería, Golfo de *b.* Spain **60** C2
Al'met'yevsk Rus. Fed. **41** D2
Al Mindak Saudi Arabia **90** B2
Al Minyā Egypt **102** B2
Al Mish'āb Saudi Arabia **91** B2
Almodôvar Port. **60** B2
Almonte Spain **60** B2
Almora India **87** C2
Al Mubarraz Saudi Arabia **91** B2
Al Muḑaibī Oman **91** C2
Al Mudawwarah Jordan **92** B3
Al Mukallā Yemen *see* Mukalla
Al Mukhā Yemen *see* Mocha
Almuñécar Spain **60** C2
Al Muwaylih Saudi Arabia **90** A2
Almyros Greece **65** B3
Alness U.K. **50** C2
Alnwick U.K. **52** C2
Alofi Niue **113**
Along India **74** A1
Alonnisos *i.* Greece **65** B3
Alor *i.* Indon. **71** C3

Alor, Kepulauan *is* Indon. **71** C3
Alor Setar Malaysia **72** B1
Alozero Rus. Fed. **46** G2
Alpena U.S.A. **136** D1
Alpine U.S.A. **141** D2
Alps *mts* Europe **59** D2
Al Qa'āmīyāt *reg.* Saudi Arabia **91** B3
Al Qaddāḩīyah Libya **101** D1
Al Qāhirah Egypt *see* Cairo
Al Qā'īyah Saudi Arabia **90** B2
Al Qāmishlī Syria **93** C2
Al Qaryatayn Syria **92** B2
Al Qaţn Yemen **91** B3
Al Qunayţirah Syria **92** B2
Al Qunfidhah Saudi Arabia **90** B3
Al Qusayr Egypt **102** B2
Al Quwayyiah Saudi Arabia **90** B2
Alsfeld Ger. **55** D2
Alta Norway **46** E2
Altaelva *r.* Norway **46** E2
Altai Mountains Asia **89** F2
Altamaha *r.* U.S.A. **139** D2
Altamira Brazil **151** D3
Altamura Italy **63** C2
Altay China **89** F2
Altay Mongolia **80** C1
Altdorf Switz. **59** D2
Altea Spain **61** C2
Altenburg Ger. **55** F2
Altenkirchen (Westerwald) Ger. **54** C2
Altentreptow Ger. **55** F1
Altınoluk Turkey **65** C3
Altıntaş Turkey **65** C3
Altiplano *plain* Bol. **152** B2
Alto Araguaia Brazil **154** B1
Alto del Moncayo *mt.* Spain **61** C1
Alto Garças Brazil **154** B1
Alto Molócuè Moz. **107** C1
Altona Can. **127** E3
Altoona U.S.A. **137** E2
Alto Sucuriú Brazil **154** B1
Alto Taquari Brazil **154** B1
Altötting Ger. **56** C3
Altun Shan *mts* China **89** F3
Alturas U.S.A. **132** B2
Altus U.S.A. **141** D2
Alūksne Latvia **42** C2
Al 'Ulā Saudi Arabia **90** A2
Al 'Uqaylah Libya **101** D1
Al Uqşur Egypt *see* Luxor
Alushta Ukr. **45** D3
Alva U.S.A. **141** E1
Alvarado Mex. **143** C2
Älvdalen Sweden **47** C3
Alvdalen *val.* Sweden **47** C3
Älvik Norway **48** E1
Älvsbyn Sweden **46** E2
Al Wajh Saudi Arabia **90** A2
Alwar India **86** B2
Al Widyān *plat.* Iraq/Saudi Arabia
  93 C2
Alxa Youqi China *see* Ehen Hudag
Alyangula Austr. **115** C1
Alytus Lith. **42** B3
Alzada U.S.A. **134** C1
Alzey Ger. **54** D3
Amadeus, Lake *salt flat* Austr. **114** C2
Amadora Port. **60** B2
Amā'ir Saudi Arabia **90** B2
Åmål Sweden **47** C4
Amaliada Greece **65** B3
Amamapare Indon. **71** E3
Amambaí Brazil **154** A2
Amambaí *r.* Brazil **154** B2
Amambaí, Serra de *hills* Brazil/Para.
  154 A2
Amami-Ō-shima *i.* Japan **81** E3
Amami-shotō *is* Japan **81** E3
Amangel'dy Kazakh. **89** D1
Amantea Italy **63** C3

Amanzimtoti S. Africa **109** D3
Amapá Brazil **151** D2
Amareleja Port. **60** B2
Amarillo U.S.A. **141** D1
Amaro, Monte *mt.* Italy **62** B2
Amasya Turkey **92** B1
Amazon *r.* S. America **150** D2
Amazon, Mouths of the Brazil **151** E2
Amazonas *r.* S. America *see* Amazon
Ambala India **86** B1
Ambalavao Madag. **107** [inset] D2
Ambanja Madag. **107** [inset] D1
Ambato Ecuador **150** B3
Ambato Boeny Madag. **107** [inset] D1
Ambato Finandrahana Madag.
  107 [inset] D2
Ambatolampy Madag. **107** [inset] D1
Ambatondrazaka Madag.
  107 [inset] D1
Amberg Ger. **55** E3
Ambergris Cay *i.* Belize **144** B3
Ambikapur India **87** C2
Ambilobe Madag. **107** [inset] D1
Ambleside U.K. **52** B2
Amboasary Madag. **107** [inset] D2
Ambohimahasoa Madag.
  107 [inset] D2
Ambon Indon. **71** C3
Ambon *i.* Indon. **71** C3
Ambositra Madag. **107** [inset] D2
Ambovombe Madag. **107** [inset] D2
Amboy U.S.A. **133** C4
Ambriz Angola **104** B1
Amdo China **87** D1
Amealco Mex. **143** B2
Ameland *i.* Neth. **54** B1
American Falls U.S.A. **132** D2
American Falls Reservoir U.S.A.
  132 D2
American Fork U.S.A. **132** D2
American Samoa *terr.*
  S. Pacific Ocean **113**
Americus U.S.A. **139** D2
Amersfoort Neth. **54** B1
Amery Ice Shelf Antarctica **119** E3
Ames U.S.A. **135** E2
Amfissa Greece **65** B3
Amga Rus. Fed. **95** K2
Amgu Rus. Fed. **78** C1
Amguema *r.* Rus. Fed. **95** L3
Amherst Can. **129** D2
Amiens France **58** C2
Amindivi Islands India **85** B3
Aminuis Namibia **108** A1
Amir Chah Pak. **86** A2
Amisk Lake Can. **127** E2
Amistad Reservoir Mex./U.S.A.
  141 D3
Amlwch U.K. **52** A3
'Ammān Jordan **92** B2
Ammassalik Greenland **125** J2
Am Nābiyah Yemen **90** B3
Amol Iran **93** D2
Amorgos *i.* Greece **65** C3
Amory U.S.A. **138** C2
Amos Can. **128** C2
Amoy China *see* Xiamen
Amparo Brazil **155** C2
Amposta Spain **61** D1
Amqui Can. **137** G1
Amravati India **87** B2
Amritsar India **86** B1
Amstelveen Neth. **54** B1
Amsterdam Neth. **54** B1
Amstetten Austria **56** C3
Am Timan Chad **101** E3
Amudar'ya *r.* Asia **88** C2
Amund Ringnes Island Can. **124** F1

Amundsen Gulf Can. 124 D2
Amuntai Indon. 73 C2
Amur r. China see Heilong Jiang
Amur, Wadi watercourse Sudan 90 A3
Anabanua Indon. 73 D2
Anabar r. Rus. Fed. 95 J2
Anabarskiy Zaliv b. Rus. Fed. 95 J2
Anaconda U.S.A. 132 D1
Anadarko U.S.A. 141 E1
Anadolu Dağları mts Turkey 92 B1
Anadyr' r. Rus. Fed. 95 N2
Anah Iraq 93 C2
Anahuac Mex. 143 B2
Anambas, Kepulauan is Indon. 72 B1
Anamosa U.S.A. 135 E2
Anamur Turkey 92 B2
Anan Japan 79 B4
Anantapur India 85 B3
Anantnag India 86 B1
Anan'yiv Ukr. 44 C2
Anapa Rus. Fed. 45 E3
Anápolis Brazil 154 C1
Anatolia reg. Turkey 66
Añatuya Arg. 152 B3
Ancenis France 58 B2
Anchorage U.S.A. 124 C2
Ancona Italy 62 B2
Ancud Chile 153 A5
Andalsnes Norway 46 B3
Andalucía aut. comm. Spain 60 C2
Andalusia U.S.A. 138 C2
Andaman Islands India 85 D3
Andaman Sea Indian Ocean 75 A2
Andapa Madag. 107 [inset] D1
Andelst Ger. 54 B2
Andenes Norway 46 D2
Andenne Belgium 54 B2
Anderlecht Belgium 54 B2
Anderson r. Can. 124 C2
Anderson AK U.S.A. 124 C2
Anderson IN U.S.A. 136 C2
Anderson SC U.S.A. 139 D2
Andes mts S. America 152 A1
Andijon Uzbek. 89 E2
Andilamena Madag. 107 [inset] D1
Andilanatoby Madag. 107 [inset] D1
Andizhan Uzbek. see Andijon
Andoany Madag. 107 [inset] D1
Andong S. Korea 77 B2
Andorra country Europe 58 C3
Andorra la Vella Andorra 58 C3
Andover U.K. 53 C4
Andradina Brazil 154 B2
Andreapol' Rus. Fed. 43 D2
Andrelândia Brazil 155 D2
Andrews U.S.A. 141 D2
Andria Italy 63 C2
Androka Madag. 107 [inset] D2
Andros i. Bahamas 144 C2
Andros i. Greece 65 B3
Andros Town Bahamas 139 E4
Andrushivka Ukr. 44 C1
Andselv Norway 46 D2
Andújar Spain 60 C2
Andulo Angola 106 A1
Anéfis Mali 100 C3
Aneto mt. Spain 36
Aney Niger 101 D3
Angara r. Rus. Fed. 95 I3
Angarsk Rus. Fed. 80 C1
Ange Sweden 47 D3
Ángel de la Guarda, Isla i. Mex. 142 A2
Angeles Phil. 76 B2
Angelholm Sweden 47 C4
Angermanälven r. Sweden 46 D3
Angermünde Ger. 55 G1
Angers France 58 B2

Angikuni Lake Can. 127 F1
Anglesey i. U.K. 52 A3
Angoche Moz. 107 C1
Angohrän Iran 91 C2
Angola country Africa 104 B4
Angola U.S.A. 136 D2
Angoon U.S.A. 126 B2
Angoulême France 58 C2
Angren Uzbek. 89 E2
Anguilla terr. West Indies 145 D3
Angul India 87 C2
Anhua China 83 B3
Anhui prov. China 82 B2
Anhumas Brazil 154 B1
Anicuns Brazil 154 C1
Aniva, Mys c. Rus. Fed. 78 D1
Aniva, Zaliv b. Rus. Fed. 78 D1
Anjü N. Korea 77 B2
Ankang China 82 A2
Ankara Turkey 92 B2
Anlu China 82 B2
Anna Rus. Fed. 43 F3
Annaba Alg. 100 C1
Annaberg-Buchholtz Ger. 55 F2
An Nafüd des. Saudi Arabia 90 B2
An Najaf Iraq 93 C2
Annan U.K. 50 C3
Annapolis U.S.A. 137 E3
Annapurna I mt. Nepal 87 C2
Ann Arbor U.S.A. 136 D2
Anna Regina Guyana 150 D2
An Näşiriyah Iraq 93 C2
Annecy France 59 D2
An Nimäş Saudi Arabia 90 B3
Anning China 74 B1
Anniston U.S.A. 139 C2
Annonay France 59 C2
An Nu'ayriyah Saudi Arabia 91 B2
Anorontany, Tanjona hd Madag. 107 [inset] D1
Ano Viannos Greece 65 C3
Anpu China 83 B3
Anqing China 82 B2
Ansan S. Korea 77 B2
Ansbach Ger. 55 E3
Anshan China 82 C1
Anshun China 83 A3
An Sirhän, Wädï watercourse Saudi Arabia 90 A1
Ansongo Mali 100 C3
Antabamba Peru 150 B4
Antakya Turkey 92 B2
Antalaha Madag. 107 [inset] E1
Antalya Turkey 92 B2
Antalya Körfezi g. Turkey 92 B2
Antananarivo Madag. 107 [inset] D1
Antarctica 119
Antarctic Peninsula Antarctica 119 K3
An Teallach mt. U.K. 50 B2
Antequera Spain 60 C2
Anthony U.S.A. 140 C2
Anti Atlas mts Morocco 100 B2
Antibes France 59 D3
Anticosti, Île d' i. Can. 129 D2
Antigonish Can. 129 D2
Antigua i. Antigua 145 D3
Antigua and Barbuda country West Indies 145 D3
Antiguo-Morelos Mex. 143 C2
Antikythira i. Greece 65 B3
Antipodes Islands N.Z. 110
Antofagasta Chile 152 A3
Antonina Brazil 154 C3
Antrim U.K. 51 C1
Antrim Hills U.K. 51 C1
Antsalova Madag. 107 [inset] D1
Antsirabe Madag. 107 [inset] D1
Antsirañana Madag. 107 [inset] D1
Antsohihy Madag. 107 [inset] D1

Antwerp Belgium 54 B2
Anupgarh India 86 B2
Anuradhapura Sri Lanka 85 C4
Anxi China 80 C2
Anxious Bay Austr. 116 A2
Anyang China 82 B2
Anzio Italy 62 B2
Aomori Japan 78 D2
Aosta Italy 62 A1
Aoukâr reg. Mali/Maur. 96
Apalachee Bay U.S.A. 139 D3
Apaporis r. Col. 150 C3
Aparecida do Taboado Brazil 154 B2
Aparri Phil. 76 B2
Apatity Rus. Fed. 40 C2
Apatzingán Mex. 142 B3
Apeldoorn Neth. 54 B1
Apen Ger. 54 C1
Apennines mts Italy 62 A2
Apia Samoa 113
Apiaí Brazil 154 C2
Apo, Mount vol. Phil. 76 B3
Apolda Ger. 55 E2
Apollo Bay Austr. 116 C3
Apopka, Lake U.S.A. 139 D3
Aporé Brazil 154 B1
Aporé r. Brazil 154 B1
Apostolos Andreas, Cape Cyprus 92 B2
Appalachian Mountains U.S.A. 131 E3
Appin Austr. 117 C2
Appleton U.S.A. 136 C2
Aprilia Italy 62 B2
Apsheronsk Rus. Fed. 45 E3
Apucarana Brazil 154 B2
Apucarana, Serra da hills Brazil 154 B2
Aqaba, Gulf of Asia 90 A2
Aqqikkol Hu salt l. China 87 C1
Aquidauana Brazil 154 A2
Aquidauana r. Brazil 154 A1
Ara India 87 C2
Arab, Bahr el watercourse Sudan 103 A4
Arabian Peninsula Asia 102 C5
Arabian Sea Indian Ocean 161 G4
Aracaju Brazil 151 F4
Aracati Brazil 151 F3
Araçatuba Brazil 154 B2
Aracruz Brazil 155 D1
Araçuaí Brazil 155 D1
Arad Romania 44 B2
Arada Chad 101 E3
Arafura Sea Austr./Indon. 71 C3
Aragarças Brazil 154 B1
Aragón r. Spain 61 C1
Araguaia r. Brazil 151 E3
Araguaína Brazil 151 E3
Araguari Brazil 154 C1
Arai Japan 79 C3
Arak Alg. 100 C2
Äräk Iran 93 C2
Arakan Yoma mts Myanmar 74 A1
Arak's r. Armenia 93 C1
Aral Sea salt l. Kazakh./Uzbek. 88 D2
Aral'sk Kazakh. 88 D2
Aranda de Duero Spain 60 C1
Arandelovac Serb. and Mont. 64 B2
Aran Islands Rep. of Ireland 51 B2
Aranjuez Spain 60 C1
Aranos Namibia 108 A1
Aransas Pass U.S.A. 141 E3
Arao Japan 79 B4
Araouane Mali 100 B3
Arapiraca Brazil 151 F3
Arapongas Brazil 154 B2
Araquari Brazil 154 C3
'Ar'ar Saudi Arabia 90 B1
Araraquara Brazil 154 C2
Araras Brazil 151 D3

Araras, Serra das *mts* Brazil **154** B3
Ararat, Mount Turkey **93** C2
Araruama, Lago de *lag.* Brazil **155** D2
Arauca Col. **150** B2
Araxá Brazil **154** C1
Arbîl Iraq **93** C2
Arbroath U.K. **50** C2
Arbu Lut, Dasht-e *des.* Afgh. **86** A2
Arcachon France **58** B3
Arcadia U.S.A. **139** D3
Arcata U.S.A. **132** B2
Arcelia Mex. **143** B3
Archangel Rus. Fed. **40** C2
Archer *r.* Austr. **115** D1
Arco U.S.A. **132** D2
Arcos de la Frontera Spain **60** B2
Arctic Bay Can. **125** G2
Arctic Ocean **162**
Ardabîl Iran **93** C2
Ardahan Turkey **93** C1
Ardalstangen Norway **47** B3
Ardennes *plat.* Belgium **54** B3
Ardestân Iran **93** D2
Ardlethan Austr. **117** D2
Ardmore U.S.A. **141** D3
Ardnamurchan, Point of *pt* U.K. **50** A2
Ardrossan France **58** B2
Ardrossan U.K. **50** B3
Arena, Point *pt* U.S.A. **133** B3
Arendal Norway **47** B4
Arendsee (Altmark) Ger. **55** E1
Árès Brazil **151** D3
Arévalo Spain **60** C1
Arezzo Italy **62** B2
Argentan France **58** B2
Argentina *country* S. America **153** B4
Argentino, Lago *l.* Arg. **153** A6
Argenton-sur-Creuse France **58** C2
Argeş *r.* Romania **44** C3
Arghandab *r.* Afgh. **86** A1
Argolikos Kolpos *b.* Greece **65** B3
Argos Greece **65** B3
Argostoli Greece **65** B3
Arguis Spain **61** C1
Argun' *r.* China/Rus. Fed. **81** I1
Argyle, Lake Austr. **114** B1
Ar Horqin Qi China *see* Tianshan
Århus Denmark **47** C4
Ariamsvlei Namibia **108** A2
Ari Atoll Maldives **85** B4
Arica Chile **152** A2
Arinagour U.K. **50** A2
Arinos Brazil **155** C1
Aripuanã Brazil **150** D4
Aripuanã *r.* Brazil **150** D3
Ariquemes Brazil **150** D3
Ariranhá *r.* Brazil **154** D3
Arizona *state* U.S.A. **140** B2
Arizpe Mex. **142** A1
'Arjah Saudi Arabia **90** B2
Arjeplog Sweden **46** D2
Arkadelphia U.S.A. **138** B2
Arkalyk Kazakh. **89** D1
Arkansas *r.* U.S.A. **138** B2
Arkansas *state* U.S.A. **138** B2
Arkansas City U.S.A. **135** D3
Arkhangel'sk Rus. Fed. *see* Archangel
Arklow Rep. of Ireland **51** C2
Arkona, Kap *c.* Ger. **56** C2
Arktícheskogo Instituta, Ostrova *is* Rus. Fed. **94** H1
Arles France **59** C3
Arlit Niger **101** C3
Arlon Belgium **54** B3
Armagh U.K. **51** C1
Armant Egypt **102** B2
Armavir Rus. Fed. **45** F2

Armenia *country* Asia **93** C1
Armenia Col. **150** B2
Armeria Mex. **142** B3
Armidale Austr. **117** E2
Armstrong Can. **128** B1
Armyans'k Ukr. **92** B1
Arnautis, Cape Cyprus **92** B2
Arnaud *r.* Can. **129** D1
Arnhem Neth. **54** B2
Arnhem, Cape Austr. **115** C1
Arnhem Bay Austr. **115** C1
Arnhem Land *reg.* Austr. **115** C1
Arno *r.* Italy **62** B2
Arno Bay Austr. **116** B2
Arnprior Can. **128** C2
Arnsberg Ger. **54** D2
Arnstadt Ger. **55** E2
Aroab Namibia **108** A2
Arolsen Ger. **55** D2
Aroma Sudan **90** A3
Arona Italy **62** A1
Aros *r.* Mex. **142** B2
Ar Ramādī Iraq **93** C2
Arran *i.* U.K. **50** B3
Ar Raqqah Syria **92** B2
Arras France **58** C1
Ar Rass Saudi Arabia **90** B2
Arriagá Mex. **143** C3
Ar Rimāl *reg.* Saudi Arabia **91** C2
Ar Riyāḍ Saudi Arabia *see* Riyadh
Arroyo Seco Mex. **143** C2
Ar Rustāq Oman **91** C2
Ar Ruṭbah Iraq **93** C2
Arsenajān Iran **93** D3
Arsen'yev Rus. Fed. **78** B2
Arta Greece **65** B3
Arteaga Mex. **142** B3
Artem Rus. Fed. **78** B2
Artemivs'k Ukr. **45** E2
Artenay France **58** C2
Artesia U.S.A. **140** D2
Arthur Point *pt* Austr. **115** E2
Arthur's Pass N.Z. **118** B3
Arthur's Town Bahamas **139** E4
Artigas Uru. **152** C4
Artillery Lake Can. **127** E1
Artsyz Ukr. **44** C2
Artux China **89** C3
Artvin Turkey **93** C1
Aru, Kepulauan *is* Indon. **71** C3
Arua Uganda **105** D2
Aruba *terr.* West Indies **145** C3
Arusha Tanz. **105** D3
Arvayheer Mongolia **80** C1
Arvidsjaur Sweden **46** D2
Arvika Sweden **47** C4
Arzamas Rus. Fed. **41** D3
Arzew Alg. **61** C2
Arzfeld Ger. **54** C2
Aš Czech Rep. **55** F2
Asaba Nigeria **101** C4
Asahi-dake *vol.* Japan **78** D2
Asahikawa Japan **78** D2
Asālē *l.* Eth. **90** B3
Asansol India **87** C2
Asbestos Can. **129** C2
Ascea Italy **62** C2
Ascensión Bol. **152** B2
Ascension *i.* S. Atlantic Ocean **97**
Ascensión, Bahía de la *b.* Mex. **143** D3
Aschaffenburg Ger. **55** D3
Ascheberg Ger. **54** C2
Aschersleben Ger. **55** E2
Ascoli Piceno Italy **62** B2
Åsele Sweden **46** D2
Asenovgrad Bulg. **64** B2
Ashburton *watercourse* Austr. **114** A2
Ashburton N.Z. **118** B3

Ashdown U.S.A. **138** B2
Asheville U.S.A. **139** D1
Ashford Austr. **117** E1
Ashford U.K. **53** D4
Ashgabat Turkm. **88** C3
Ashington U.K. **52** C2
Ashizuri-misaki *pt* Japan **79** B4
Ashkhabad Turkm. *see* Ashgabat
Ashland *KS* U.S.A. **134** D3
Ashland *KY* U.S.A. **136** D3
Ashland *OH* U.S.A. **136** D2
Ashland *OR* U.S.A. **132** B2
Ashland *WI* U.S.A. **136** B1
Ashmyany Belarus **42** C3
Ash Sharawrah Saudi Arabia **90** B3
Ash Shāriqah U.A.E. *see* Sharjah
Ash Sharqāṭ Iraq **93** C2
Ash Shaṭrah Iraq **93** C2
Ash Shiḥr Yemen **91** B3
Ash Shināş Oman **91** C2
Ash Shu'bah Saudi Arabia **90** B2
Ash Shumlūl Saudi Arabia **91** B2
Ashtabula U.S.A. **137** D2
Ashuanipi Lake Can. **129** D1
Asilah Morocco **60** B2
Asinara, Golfo dell' *b.* Italy **62** A2
Asino Rus. Fed. **94** H3
Asipovichy Belarus **42** C3
'Asir *reg.* Saudi Arabia **90** B3
Askim Norway **47** C4
Askiz Rus. Fed. **80** C1
Asmara Eritrea **102** B3
Åsnen *l.* Sweden **47** C4
Asoteriba, Jebel *mt.* Sudan **102** B3
Aspang-Markt Austria **57** D3
Aspen U.S.A. **134** B3
Aspiring, Mount N.Z. **118** A3
Assab Eritrea **103** C3
Assal, Lake Djibouti **96**
As Salamiyah Saudi Arabia **91** B2
As Samāwah Iraq **93** C2
Aş Şanām *reg.* Saudi Arabia **91** C2
As Sarīr *reg.* Libya **101** E2
Assen Neth. **54** C1
Assesse Belgium **54** B2
As Sidrah Libya **101** D1
Assiniboia Can. **127** E3
Assis Brazil **154** B2
Assisi Italy **62** E3
Aş Şubayḥiyah Kuwait **91** B2
As Sulaymānīyah Iraq **93** C2
As Sulaymī Saudi Arabia **90** B2
As Sulayyil Saudi Arabia **90** B2
As Sūq Saudi Arabia **90** B2
As Suwaydā' Syria **92** B2
As Suwayq Oman **91** C2
As Suways Egypt *see* Suez
Astakos Greece **65** B3
Astana Kazakh. **89** E1
Astārā Iran **93** C2
Asti Italy **62** A2
Astor Jammu and Kashmir **86** B1
Astorga Spain **60** B1
Astoria U.S.A. **132** B1
Astrakhan' Rus. Fed. **41** D4
Astravyets Belarus **42** C3
Astypalaia *i.* Greece **65** C3
Asunción Para. **152** C3
Aswān Egypt **102** B3
Asyūṭ Egypt **102** B2
Atacama, Desierto de *des.* Chile *see* Atacama Desert
Atacama, Salar de *salt flat* Chile **152** B3
Atacama Desert Chile **152** B3
Atakpamé Togo **100** C4
Atalanti Greece **65** B3
Atalaya Peru **150** B4
Atamyrat Turkm. **89** D3
'Ataq Yemen **90** B3

tår Maur. **100** A2
tascadero U.S.A. **133** B3
tasu Kazakh. **88** C2
tbara Sudan **102** B3
tbara r. Sudan **102** B3
tbasar Kazakh. **89** D1
tchison U.S.A. **135** E2
terno r. Italy **62** B2
tessa Italy **62** B2
th Belgium **54** A2
thabasca Can. **126** D2
thabasca r. Can. **127** D2
thabasca, Lake Can. **127** E2
thens Greece **65** B3
thens GA U.S.A. **139** C2
thens OH U.S.A. **136** D3
thens TN U.S.A. **139** D1
thens TX U.S.A. **141** E2
thies France **54** A3
thina Greece see Athens
thlone Rep. of Ireland **51** C2
thos mt. Greece **65** B2
thy Rep. of Ireland **51** C2
ti Chad **101** D3
tikokan Can. **128** A2
tiu i. Cook Is **111**
tkarsk Rus. Fed. **41** D3
tokai U.S.A. **141** E2
trai r. India **87** C2
Tā'if Saudi Arabia **90** B2
tapu Laos **75** B2
tavyros mt. Greece **65** C3
ttawapiskat Can. **128** B1
ttawapiskat r. Can. **128** B1
ttawapiskat Lake Can. **128** B1
ttendorn Ger. **54** C2
Tūr Egypt **102** B2
t Turbah Yemen **90** B3
tyrau Kazakh. **88** C2
ubenas France **59** C3
uboué France **54** B3
uburn AL U.S.A. **139** C2
uburn CA U.S.A. **133** B3
uburn NE U.S.A. **135** D2
uburn NY U.S.A. **137** E2
ubusson France **58** C2
uch France **58** C2
uckland N.Z. **118** B2
uckland Islands N.Z. **110**
udo Range mts Eth. **105** C2
ue Ger. **55** F2
ugusta Italy **62** C3
ugusta GA U.S.A. **139** D2
ugusta KS U.S.A. **135** D3
ugusta ME U.S.A. **137** G2
ugustus, Mount Austr. **114** A2
ulnoye-Aymeries France
54 A2
unglan Myanmar **74** A2
uob watercourse Namibia/S. Africa
108 B2
urangabad India **86** B3
urich Ger. **54** C1
urilândia Brazil **154** B1
urillac France **58** C3
urora CO U.S.A. **134** C3
urora IL U.S.A. **136** C3
urora NE U.S.A. **135** D2
us Namibia **108** A3

Austin MN U.S.A. **135** E2
Austin NV U.S.A. **133** C3
Austin TX U.S.A. **141** E2
Australes, Îles is Fr. Polynesia see
  Tubuai Islands
Australia country Oceania **114**
Australian Capital Territory
  admin. div. Austr. **117** D3
Austria country Europe **56** C3
Autlán Mex. **142** B3
Autun France **59** C2
Auxerre France **59** C2
Auxonne France **59** D2
Avallon France **59** C2
Avalon Peninsula Can. **129** E2
Avaré Brazil **154** C2
Avarua Cook Is **113**
Avdiyivka Ukr. **45** E12
Aveiro Port. **60** B1
Avellino Italy **62** B2
Avesnes-sur-Helpe France **54** A2
Avesta Sweden **47** D3
Avezzano Italy **62** B2
Aviemore U.K. **50** C2
Avignon France **59** C3
Ávila Spain **60** C1
Avilés Spain **60** B1
Avola Italy **62** C3
Avon r. England U.K. **53** B3
Avon r. England U.K. **53** C4
Avranches France **58** B2
Awanui N.Z. **118** B2
Āwash Eth. **103** C4
Awash r. Eth. **103** C3
Awbārī Libya **101** D2
Aw Dheegle Somalia **103** C4
Awe, Loch l. U.K. **50** B2
Aweil Sudan **103** A4
Awka Nigeria **104** A2
Axel Heiberg Island Can. **124** F1
Axim Ghana **100** B4
Ay France **54** B3
Ayacucho Peru **150** B4
Ayagoz Kazakh. **89** F2
Ayakkum Hu salt l. China **80** B3
Ayamonte Spain **60** B2
Ayan Rus. Fed. **95** L3
Ayaviri Peru **150** B4
Āybak Afgh. **86** A1
Aybas Kazakh. **43** D2
Aydar r. Ukr. **45** E2
Aydarko'li ko'li l. Uzbek. **89** D2
Aydın Turkey **65** C3
Ayeat, Gora n. Kazakh. **89** D2
Ayers Rock h. Austr. see Uluru
Aylesbury U.K. **53** C4
Ayllón Spain **60** C1
Aylmer Lake Can. **127** E1
Ayod Sudan **103** B4
Ayon, Ostrov i. Rus. Fed. **95** N2
'Ayoûn el 'Atroûs Maur. **100** B3
Ayr Austr. **115** D1
Ayr U.K. **50** B3
Ayre, Point of pt Isle of Man **52** A2
Ayteke Bi Kazakh. **88** D2
Aytos Bulg. **64** C2
Ayutla Mex. **143** C3
Ayutthaya Thai. **75** B2
Ayvacık Turkey **65** C3
Ayvalık Turkey **65** C3
Azaouagh, Vallée de watercourse
  Mali/Niger **100** C3
Azerbaijan country Asia **93** C1
Azopol'ye Rus. Fed. **40** D2
Azores terr. N. Atlantic Ocean **38**
Azores aut. reg. Port. **38**
Azov Rus. Fed. **45** E2
Azov, Sea of Rus. Fed./Ukr. **45** E2
Azraq, Bahr el r. Eth./Sudan see
  Blue Nile

Azuaga Spain **60** B2
Azuero, Península de pen. Panama
  144 B4
Azul Arg. **153** C4
Azuero Egypt **92** B2
Az Zaqāzīq Egypt **92** B2
Az Zarqā' Jordan **92** B2
Az Zaydīyah Yemen **90** B3
Azzel Matti, Sebkha salt pan Alg.
  100 C2
Az Zilfī Saudi Arabia **90** B2
Az Zuqur i. Yemen **90** B3

Baardheere Somalia **103** C4
Bābā, Kūh-e mts Afgh. **86** A1
Babadag Romania **44** C3
Babaeski Turkey **65** C2
Bāb al Mandab str. Africa/Asia **90** B3
Babana Indon. **73** C2
Babar i. Indon. **71** C3
Babati Tanz. **105** D3
Babayevo Rus. Fed. **43** E2
Babine r. Can. **126** C2
Babine Lake Can. **126** C2
Babo Indon. **71** C3
Bābol Iran **93** D2
Baboon Point pt S. Africa **108** A3
Babruysk Belarus **42** C3
Babuyan i. Phil. **76** B2
Babuyan Islands Phil. **76** B2
Bacabal Brazil **151** E3
Bacan i. Indon. **71** C3
Bacău Romania **44** C2
Bacchus Marsh Austr. **116** C3
Bachu China **89** E3
Back r. Can. **127** F1
Bačka Palanka Serb. and Mont. **64** A1
Bac Lac Vietnam **74** B1
Bac Liêu Vietnam **75** B3
Bacolod Phil. **76** B2
Bacqueville, Lac l. Can. **128** C1
Badajoz Spain **60** B2
Badarpur India **74** A1
Bad Berka Ger. **55** E2
Bad Berleburg Ger. **55** D2
Bad Bevensen Ger. **55** E1
Bad Ems Ger. **54** C2
Baden Austria **57** D3
Baden-Baden Ger. **56** B3
Bad Freienwalde Ger. **55** G1
Bad Harzburg Ger. **55** E2
Bad Hersfeld Ger. **55** D2
Bad Hofgastein Austria **56** C3
Bad Homburg vor der Höhe Ger.
  55 D2
Badin Pak. **86** A2
Bad Ischl Austria **59** E2
Bādiyat ash Shām des. Asia see
  Syrian Desert
Bad Kissingen Ger. **55** E2
Bad Kreuznach Ger. **54** C2
Bad Lauterberg im Harz Ger. **55** E2
Bad Liebenwerda Ger. **55** F2
Bad Lippspringe Ger. **55** D2
Bad Mergentheim Ger. **55** D3
Bad Nauheim Ger. **55** D2
Bad Neuenahr-Ahrweiler Ger. **54** C2
Bad Neustadt an der Saale Ger.
  55 E2
Bad Oldesloe Ger. **55** E1
Bad Pyrmont Ger. **55** D2
Badr Ḥunayn Saudi Arabia **90** A2
Bad Salzuflen Ger. **55** D1
Bad Salzungen Ger. **55** E2
Bad Schwartau Ger. **56** C2
Bad Segeberg Ger. **56** C2
Badulla Sri Lanka **85** C4

Bad Zwischenahn Ger. **54** D1
Baeza Spain **60** C2
Bafatá Guinea-Bissau **100** A3
Baffin Bay *sea* Can./Greenland **125** H2
Baffin Island Can. **125** H2
Bafia Cameroon **104** B2
Bafing *r.* Guinea/Mali **100** A3
Bafoulabé Mali **100** A3
Bafoussam Cameroon **104** B2
Bāfq Iran **91** D2
Bafra Turkey **92** B1
Bāft Iran **91** C2
Bafwasende Dem. Rep. Congo **105** C2
Bagamoyo Tanz. **105** D3
Bagan Datuk Malaysia **72** B1
Bagani Namibia **106** B1
Bagansiapiapi Indon. **72** B1
Bagdad U.S.A. **140** D2
Bagé Brazil **152** C4
Baghdād Iraq **93** C2
Baghlān Afgh. **86** A1
Bagnères-de-Luchon France **58** C3
Bagrationovsk Rus. Fed. **42** B3
Bagrax China *see* Bohu
Baguio Phil. **76** B2
Bagzane, Monts *mts* Niger **101** C3
Baharampur India **87** C2
Bahau Malaysia **72** B1
Bahawalnagar Pak. **84** B2
Bahawalpur Pak. **86** B2
Bahía, Islas de la *is* Hond. **144** B3
Bahía Blanca Arg. **153** B4
Bahía Kino Mex. **142** A2
Bahía Negra Para. **152** C3
Bahía Tortugas Mex. **142** A2
Bahir Dar Eth. **103** B3
Bahraich India **87** C2
Bahrain *country* Asia **91** C2
Baḥriyah, Wāḥāt al *oasis* Egypt **102** A2
Bāhū Kālāt Iran **91** D2
Baia Mare Romania **44** B2
Baicheng China **81** E1
Baie-Comeau Can. **129** D2
Baie-St-Paul Can. **129** C2
Baihe China **77** B1
Baikal, Lake Rus. Fed. **81** D1
Baile Átha Cliath Rep. of Ireland *see* Dublin
Bāilești Romania **44** B3
Baima China **80** C2
Bainbridge U.S.A. **139** D2
Bairiki Kiribati **112**
Bairin Youqi China *see* Daban
Bairnsdale Austr. **117** D3
Baishan China **77** B1
Baishanzhen China **77** B1
Baiyin China **82** A2
Baiyuda Desert Sudan **102** B3
Baja Hungary **57** D3
Baja California *pen.* Mex. **142** A1
Bajawa Indon. **73** C2
Bājil Yemen **90** B3
Bakel Senegal **100** A3
Baker *CA* U.S.A. **133** C3
Baker *MT* U.S.A. **134** C1
Baker *OR* U.S.A. **132** C2
Baker, Mount *vol.* U.S.A. **132** B1
Baker Foreland *hd* Can. **127** F1
Baker Island *terr.* N. Pacific Ocean **113**
Baker Lake Can. **127** F1
Baker Lake *l.* Can. **127** F1
Bakersfield U.S.A. **133** C3
Bakhchysaray Ukr. **45** D3
Bakherden Turkm. **88** C3
Bakhmach Ukr. **45** D1
Baku Azer. *see* Bakı
Bakırköy Turkey **65** C2
Bakkaflói *b.* Iceland **46** [inset]

Bakouma C.A.R. **104** C2
Baku Azer. **93** C1
Balabac Phil. **76** A3
Balabac *i.* Phil. **76** A3
Balabac Strait Malaysia/Phil. **73** C1
Balaikarkuak Indon. **73** C2
Balakliva Ukr. **45** D3
Balaklava Ukr. **45** D3
Balakliya Ukr. **45** E2
Balakovo Rus. Fed. **41** D3
Bālā Morghāb Afgh. **86** A1
Balancán Mex. **143** C3
Balan Dağı *h.* Turkey **65** C3
Balanga Phil. **76** B2
Balashov Rus. Fed. **41** D3
Balaton, Lake Hungary **57** D3
Balatonboglár Hungary **57** D3
Balbina, Represa de *resr* Brazil **150** D3
Balbriggan Rep. of Ireland **51** C2
Balcanoona Austr. **116** B2
Balchik Bulg. **64** C2
Balclutha N.Z. **118** A4
Baldock Lake Can. **127** F2
Baldy Mountain *h.* Can. **127** E2
Baldy Peak U.S.A. **140** C2
Baleares, Islas *is* Spain *see* Balearic Islands
Balearic Islands *is* Spain **61** D2
Baleia, Ponta da *pt* Brazil **155** E1
Baleine, Grande Rivière de la *r.* Can. **128** C1
Baleine, Rivière à la *r.* Can. **129** D1
Baleshwar India **87** C2
Bali *i.* Indon. **73** C2
Bali, Laut *sea* Indon. **73** C2
Balige Indon. **72** A1
Baliguda India **87** C2
Balıkesir Turkey **65** C3
Balikpapan Indon. **73** C2
Balimo P.N.G. **71** D3
Balingen Ger. **56** B3
Bali Sea Indon. *see* Bali, Laut
Balkanabat Turkm. **88** C3
Balkan Mountains Bulg./Serb. and Mont. **62** E2
Balkhash Kazakh. **89** D2
Balkhash, Lake Kazakh. **89** E2
Balladonia Austr. **114** B3
Ballaghaderreen Rep. of Ireland **51** B2
Ballangen Norway **46** D2
Ballarat Austr. **116** C3
Ballard, Lake *salt flat* Austr. **114** B2
Ballater U.K. **50** C2
Ballé Mali **100** B3
Ballena, Punta *pt* Chile **147**
Ballina Austr. **117** E1
Ballina Rep. of Ireland **51** B1
Ballinasloe Rep. of Ireland **51** B2
Ballinger U.S.A. **141** E2
Ballinrobe Rep. of Ireland **51** B2
Ballycastle Rep. of Ireland **51** B1
Ballycastle U.K. **51** C1
Ballyclare U.K. **51** C1
Ballymena U.K. **51** C1
Ballymoney U.K. **51** C1
Ballynahinch U.K. **51** D1
Ballyshannon Rep. of Ireland **51** B1
Balonne *r.* Austr. **117** D2
Balotra India **86** B2
Balrampur India **87** C2
Balranald Austr. **116** C2
Balş Romania **44** B3
Balsas Brazil **151** E3
Balsas Mex. **143** C3
Balta Ukr. **44** C2
Bălți Moldova **44** C2
Baltic Sea *g.* Europe **47** D4
Baltīm Egypt **92** B2
Baltimore S. Africa **109** C1

Baltimore U.S.A. **137** E3
Baltiysk Rus. Fed. **42** A3
Balu India **74** A1
Balvi Latvia **42** C2
Balya India **42** C2
Balykchy Kyrg. **89** E2
Balykshi Kazakh. **88** C2
Bam Iran **91** C2
Bamaga Austr. **115** D1
Bamaji Lake Can. **128** A1
Bamako Mali **100** B3
Bambari C.A.R. **104** C2
Bamberg Ger. **55** E3
Bambili Dem. Rep. Congo **105** C2
Bambouti C.A.R. **105** C2
Bambuí Brazil **155** C2
Bamenda Cameroon **104** B2
Bāmiān Afgh. **86** A1
Bam Posht, Kūh-e *mts* Iran **86** A2
Bañados del Izozog *swamp* Bol. **152** B2
Banalia Dem. Rep. Congo **105** C2
Bananal, Ilha do *i.* Brazil **151** D4
Banas *r.* India **86** B2
Banaz Turkey **65** C3
Ban Ban Laos **74** B2
Banbridge U.K. **51** C1
Banbury U.K. **53** C3
Bancroft Can. **128** C2
Banda Dem. Rep. Congo **105** C2
Banda India **87** C2
Banda, Kepulauan *is* Indon. **71** C3
Banda, Laut *sea* Indon. **71** C3
Banda Aceh Indon. **72** A1
Bandar-e 'Abbās Iran **91** C2
Bandar-e Anzalī Iran **93** C2
Bandar-e Chārak Iran **91** C2
Bandar-e Emām Khomeynī Iran **93** C2
Bandar-e Lengeh Iran **91** C2
Bandar-e Maqām Iran **91** C2
Bandar Lampung Indon. **72** B2
Bandar Seri Begawan Brunei **73** C1
Banda Sea Indon. *see* Banda, Laut
Bandeiras, Pico de *mt.* Brazil **155** D2
Bandelierkop S. Africa **109** C1
Banderas, Bahía de *b.* Mex. **142** B2
Bandiagara Mali **100** B3
Bandırma Turkey **65** C2
Bandon Rep. of Ireland **51** B3
Bandundu Dem. Rep. Congo **104** B3
Bandung Indon. **72** B2
Banff Can. **126** D2
Banff U.K. **50** C2
Banfora Burkina **100** B3
Banga Phil. **76** B3
Bangalore India **85** B3
Bangassou C.A.R. **104** C2
Banggai Indon. **73** D2
Banggai, Kepulauan *is* Indon. **73** D2
Banggi *i.* Malaysia **73** C1
Bangka *i.* Indon. **72** B2
Bangkalan Indon. **73** C2
Bangkinang Indon. **72** B1
Bangko Indon. **72** B2
Bangkok Thai. **75** C2
Bangladesh *country* Asia **87** C2
Bangor *Northern Ireland* U.K. **51** D1
Bangor Wales U.K. **52** A3
Bangor U.S.A. **137** S2
Bang Saphan Yai Thai. **75** A2
Bangued Phil. **76** B2
Bangui C.A.R. **104** B2
Bangweulu, Lake Zambia **107** B1
Ban Huai Khon Thai. **74** B2
Banī Mazār Egypt **92** B3
Banī Suwayf Egypt **102** B2
Banī Walid Libya **101** D1
Baniyās Syria **92** B2
Banja Luka Bos.-Herz. **63** C2
Banjarmasin Indon. **73** C2
Banjul Gambia **100** A3

Banks Island *B.C.* Can. **126** B2
Banks Island *N.W.T.* Can. **124** D2
Banks Islands Vanuatu **110**
Banks Lake U.S.A. **127** F1
Banks Peninsula N.Z. **118** B3
Bankura India **87** C2
Ban Mouang Laos **74** B2
Bann *r.* U.K. **51** C1
Ban Na San Thai. **75** A3
Bannerman Town Bahamas **139** E4
Bannu Pak. **86** B1
Bannu India **86** B2
Ban Tha Kham Thai. **75** A3
Ban Tha Song Yang Thai. **74** A2
Ban Tôp Laos **75** B2
Bantry Rep. of Ireland **51** B3
Bantry Bay Rep. of Ireland **51** B3
Banyo Cameroon **104** B2
Banyoles Spain **61** D1
Banyuwangi Indon. **73** C2
Baochang China **82** B1
Baoding China **82** B2
Baoji China **82** A2
Bao Lôc Vietnam **75** B2
Baoqing China **78** B1
Baoshan China **74** A1
Baotou China **82** B1
Baotou Shan *mt.* China/N. Korea **77** B1
Bapaume France **54** A2
Ba'qûbah Iraq **93** C2
Bar Serb. and Mont. **64** A2
Baraawe Somalia **103** C4
Baracoa Cuba **145** C2
Baradine Austr. **117** D2
Barahona Dom. Rep. **145** C3
Baraka *watercourse* Eritrea/Sudan **102** B3
Baram *r.* Malaysia **73** C1
Baranavichy Belarus **42** C3
Baranis Egypt **90** A2
Baranivka Ukr. **44** C1
Barankul Kazakh. **88** C2
Baranof Island U.S.A. **126** B2
Barat Daya, Kepulauan *is* Indon. **71** C3
Barbacena Brazil **155** D2
Barbados *country* West Indies **145** E3
Barbastro Spain **61** D1
Barbezieux-St-Hilaire France **58** B2
Barcaldine Austr. **115** D2
Barcelona Spain **61** D1
Barcelona Venez. **150** C1
Barcelonnette France **59** D3
Barcelos Brazil **150** C3
Barcs Hungary **57** D3
Barddhaman India **87** C2
Bardejov Slovakia **57** E3
Bardsīr Iran **91** C2
Bareilly India **87** C2
Barentin France **53** D5
Barents Sea Arctic Ocean **40** D1
Barentu Eritrea **90** A3
Barh India **87** C2
Bar Harbor U.S.A. **137** G2
Bari Italy **63** C2
Barika Alg. **61** E2
Barīkā Afgh. **86** B1
Barinas Venez. **150** B2
Baripada India **87** C2
Barisal Bangl. **87** D2
Barisan, Pegunungan *mts* Indon. **72** B2
Barito *r.* Indon. **73** C2
Barkā Oman **91** C2
Barkava Latvia **42** C2
Barkly Tableland *reg.* Austr. **115** C1
Barkol China **80** C2

Bârlad Romania **44** C2
Bar-le-Duc France **59** D2
Barlee, Lake *salt flat* Austr. **114** A2
Barletta Italy **63** C2
Barmedman Austr. **117** D2
Barmer India **86** B2
Barmouth U.K. **53** A3
Barmstedt Ger. **55** D1
Barnard Castle U.K. **52** C1
Barnato Austr. **117** C2
Barnaul Rus. Fed. **89** F1
Barneveld Neth. **54** B1
Barneville-Carteret France **53** C5
Barnsley U.K. **52** C3
Barnstaple U.K. **53** A4
Barnwell U.S.A. **139** D2
Barquisimeto Venez. **150** C1
Barra *i.* U.K. **50** A2
Barraba Austr. **117** E2
Barra do Corda Brazil **151** E3
Barra do Garças Brazil **154** B1
Barra do São Manuel Brazil **150** D3
Barranca *Lima* Peru **150** B4
Barranca *Loreto* Peru **150** B3
Barranqueras Arg. **152** C3
Barranquilla Col. **150** B1
Barreiras Brazil **151** E4
Barretos Brazil **154** C2
Barrie Can. **128** C2
Barrière Can. **128** C2
Barrier Range *hills* Austr. **116** C2
Barrington, Mount Austr. **117** E2
Barrington Lake Can. **127** E2
Barringun Austr. **117** D1
Barrow *r.* Rep. of Ireland **51** C2
Barrow U.S.A. **124** B2
Barrow, Point *pt* U.S.A. **124** B2
Barrow Creek Austr. **114** C2
Barrow-in-Furness U.K. **52** B2
Barrow Island Austr. **114** A2
Barrow Strait Can. **124** F2
Barry U.K. **53** B4
Barrys Bay Can. **128** C2
Barsalpur India **86** B2
Barstow U.S.A. **133** C4
Bar-sur-Aube France **59** C2
Bartın Turkey **92** B1
Bartle Frere, Mount Austr. **115** D1
Bartlesville U.S.A. **141** E1
Bartoszyce Pol. **57** E2
Barung *i.* Indon. **81** D1
Baruun-Urt Mongolia **81** D1
Barvinkove Ukr. **45** E2
Barwon *r.* Austr. **117** D2
Barysaw Belarus **42** C3
Basarabi Romania **44** C3
Basel Switz. **59** D2
Bashanta Ukr. **45** D2
Basilan *i.* Phil. **76** B3
Basildon U.K. **53** D4
Basingstoke U.K. **53** C4
Başkale Turkey **93** C2
Baskatong, Réservoir *resr* Can. **128** C2
Basle Switz. *see* Basel
Basoko Dem. Rep. Congo **104** C2
Basra Iraq **93** C2
Bassano Can. **127** D2
Bassar Togo **100** C4
Bassein Myanmar **74** A2
Basse-Terre Guadeloupe **145** D3
Basseterre St Kitts and Nevis **145** D3
Bassikounou Maur. **100** B3
Bass Strait Austr. **115** D3
Bastak Iran **91** C2
Bastheim Ger. **55** E2
Basti India **87** C2
Bastia France **59** D3
Bastogne Belgium **54** B2
Bastrop U.S.A. **138** B2

Bata Equat. Guinea **104** A2
Batagay Rus. Fed. **95** K2
Bataguassu Brazil **154** B2
Batalha Port. **60** B2
Batan *i.* Phil. **76** B1
Batangafo C.A.R. **104** B2
Batangas Phil. **76** B2
Batanghari *r.* Indon. **72** B2
Batan Islands Phil. **76** B1
Batavia U.S.A. **137** E2
Bataysk Rus. Fed. **45** E2
Batchawana Mountain *h.* Can. **128** B2
Batchelor Austr. **114** C1
Bătdâmbâng Cambodia **75** B2
Batemans Bay Austr. **117** E3
Batesville U.S.A. **138** B1
Batetskiy Rus. Fed. **43** D2
Bath U.K. **53** B4
Bathinda India **86** B1
Bathsheba Barbados **125** H3
Bathurst Austr. **117** D2
Bathurst Can. **125** D2
Bathurst Inlet Can. **124** E2
Bathurst Inlet *inlet* Can. **124** E2
Bathurst Island Austr. **114** C1
Bathurst Island Can. **124** F1
Bāţin, Wādī al *watercourse* Asia **90** B1
Batman Turkey **93** C2
Batna Alg. **101** C1
Baton Rouge U.S.A. **138** B2
Batopilas Mex. **142** B2
Batouri Cameroon **104** B2
Batovi Brazil **154** B1
Båtsfjord Norway **46** F1
Batticaloa Sri Lanka **85** C4
Battipaglia Italy **62** B2
Battle *r.* Can. **127** E2
Battle Creek U.S.A. **136** C2
Battle Mountain U.S.A. **132** C2
Batu *mt.* Eth. **103** B4
Batu, Pulau-pulau *is* Indon. **72** A2
Batudaka *i.* Indon. **73** D2
Bat'umi Georgia **93** C1
Batu Pahat Malaysia **72** B1
Baubau Indon. **73** D2
Bauchi Nigeria **101** C3
Baugé France **58** B2
Baume-les-Dames France **59** D2
Bauru Brazil **154** C2
Baús Brazil **154** B1
Bauska Latvia **42** B2
Bautzen Ger. **56** C2
Bavispe *r.* Mex. **142** B2
Bavly Rus. Fed. **41** E3
Bawdwin Myanmar **74** A1
Bawean *i.* Indon. **73** C2
Bawku Ghana **100** B3
Bayamo Cuba **145** C2
Bayanhongor Mongolia **80** C1
Bayan Hot China **82** A2
Bayan Obo Kuangqu China **82** B1
Bayan Ul Hot China **82** B1
Bayawan Phil. **76** B3
Bayburt Turkey **92** B1
Bay City *MI* U.S.A. **136** D2
Bay City *TX* U.S.A. **141** E3
Baydaratskaya Guba Rus. Fed. **40** F2
Baydhabo Somalia **103** C4
Bayeux France **53** C5
Bayji Iraq **93** C2
Baykal, Ozero *l.* Rus. Fed. *see* Baikal, Lake
Baykal'skiy Khrebet *mts* Rus. Fed. **95** J3
Baykonyr Kazakh. **88** C2
Baymak Rus. Fed. **41** E3
Bayombong Phil. **76** B2
Bayonne France **58** B3
Bayramic Turkey **65** C3
Bayreuth Ger. **55** E3
Bayt al Faqīh Yemen **90** B3

Baza Spain 60 C2
Baza, Sierra de *mts* Spain 60 C2
Bazaryuzyu, Gora *mt.* Azer./Rus. Fed. 93 C1
Bazas France 58 B3
Bazdar Pak. 86 A2
Bazhong China 82 A2
Bazmän Iran 91 D2
Bazmän, Küh-e *mt.* Iran 91 D2
Bé, Nosy *i.* Madag. 107 [inset] D1
Beachy Head U.K. 53 D4
Beacon Bay S. Africa 109 C3
Beagle Gulf Austr. 114 B1
Bealanana Madag. 107 [inset] D1
Beardmore Can. 128 B2
Bear Paw Mountain U.S.A. 132 E1
Beata, Cabo *c.* Dom. Rep. 145 C3
Beata, Isla *i.* Dom. Rep. 145 C3
Beatrice U.S.A. 135 D2
Beatty U.S.A. 133 C3
Beaudesert Austr. 117 E1
Beaufort Austr. 116 C3
Beaufort Malaysia 73 C1
Beaufort U.S.A. 139 D2
Beaufort West S. Africa 108 B3
Beaufort Sea Can./U.S.A. 124 D2
Beauly *r.* U.K. 50 B2
Beaumont Belgium 54 B2
Beaumont N.Z. 118 A4
Beaumont U.S.A. 141 E3
Beaune France 59 C3
Beauraing Belgium 54 B2
Beauséjour Can. 127 F2
Beauvais France 58 C2
Beauval Can. 127 E2
Beaver *r.* Can. 127 E2
Beaver U.S.A. 133 D3
Beaver Creek Can. 126 A1
Beaver Dam U.S.A. 136 C2
Beaver Hill Lake Can. 127 F2
Beaver Island U.S.A. 136 C1
Beaverlodge Can. 126 D2
Beawar India 86 B2
Bebedouro Brazil 154 C2
Bebra Ger. 55 D2
Becerreá Spain 60 B1
Béchar Alg. 100 B1
Beckley U.S.A. 136 D3
Bedelê Eth. 103 B4
Bedford U.K. 53 C3
Bedford U.S.A. 136 C3
Bedum Neth. 54 C1
Beecroft Peninsula Austr. 117 E2
Beelitz Ger. 55 F1
Beenleigh Austr. 117 E1
Beersheba Israel 92 B2
Beeville U.S.A. 141 E3
Bega Austr. 117 D3
Begur, Cap de *c.* Spain 61 D1
Behshahr Iran 93 D2
Bei'an China 81 E1
Beihai China 83 A3
Beijing China 82 B2
Beilen Neth. 54 C1
Beilngries Ger. 55 E3
Beinn Mhòr *h.* U.K. 50 A2
Beira Moz. 107 C1
Beirut Lebanon 92 B2
Beja Port. 60 B2
Bejaïa Alg. 101 C1
Béjar Spain 60 B1
Beji *r.* Pak. 86 A2
Bekdash Turkm. 88 C2
Békés Hungary 57 E3
Békéscsaba Hungary 57 E3
Bekily Madag. 107 [inset] D2
Bela Pak. 86 A2
Bela-Bela S. Africa 109 C1
Bélabo Cameroon 104 B2
Bela Crkva Serb. and Mont. 64 B2

Belaga Malaysia 73 C1
Belarus *country* Europe 42 C3
Bela Vista Brazil 154 A2
Bela Vista Moz. 109 D2
Belawan Indon. 72 A1
Belaya *r.* Rus. Fed. 95 N2
Belaya Glina Rus. Fed. 45 F2
Belaya Kalitva Rus. Fed. 45 F2
Bełchatów Pol. 57 D2
Belcher Islands Can. 125 G3
Belém Brazil 151 E3
Belen U.S.A. 140 C2
Belev Rus. Fed. 43 E3
Belfast U.K. 51 D1
Belfast U.S.A. 137 G2
Belfort France 59 D2
Belgaum India 85 B3
Belgium *country* Europe 54 B2
Belgorod Rus. Fed. 45 E1
Belgrade Serb. and Mont. 64 B2
Belgrade U.S.A. 132 D1
Beli Nigeria 101 D4
Belinyu Indon. 72 B2
Belitung *i.* Indon. 72 B2
Belize Belize 144 B3
Belize *country* Central America 144 B3
Bel'kovskiy, Ostrov *i.* Rus. Fed. 95 L1
Bella Bella Can. 126 C2
Bellac France 58 C2
Bella Coola Can. 126 C2
Bellata Austr. 117 D1
Belle Fourche U.S.A. 134 C2
Belle Fourche *r.* U.S.A. 134 C2
Belle Glade U.S.A. 139 D3
Belle-Île *i.* France 58 B2
Belle Isle *i.* Can. 129 E1
Belle Isle, Strait of Can. 129 E1
Belleville Can. 128 C2
Belleville *IL* U.S.A. 136 C3
Belleville *KS* U.S.A. 135 D3
Bellevue U.S.A. 132 B1
Bellingham U.S.A. 132 B1
Bellingshausen Sea Antarctica 119 O2
Bellinzona Switz. 59 D2
Belluno Italy 62 B1
Bellville S. Africa 108 A3
Belmonte Brazil 155 E1
Belmopan Belize 144 B3
Belmullet Rep. of Ireland 51 B1
Belogorsk Rus. Fed. 81 E1
Beloha Madag. 107 [inset] D2
Belo Horizonte Brazil 155 D1
Beloit U.S.A. 136 C2
Belomorsk Rus. Fed. 40 C2
Belorechensk Rus. Fed. 45 E3
Beloretsk Rus. Fed. 41 E3
Beloyarskiy Rus. Fed. 40 F2
Beloye, Ozero *l.* Rus. Fed. 43 E1
Beloye More *sea* Rus. Fed. *see* White Sea
Belozersk Rus. Fed. 43 E1
Belukha, Gora *mt.* Kazakh./Rus. Fed. 89 F2
Belush'ye Rus. Fed. 40 D2
Bely Rus. Fed. 43 D2
Belyy, Ostrov *i.* Rus. Fed. 40 G1
Belzig Ger. 55 F1
Bemidji U.S.A. 135 E1
Bena Dibele Dem. Rep. Congo 104 C3
Benalla Austr. 117 D3
Benavente Spain 60 B1
Benbecula *i.* U.K. 50 A2
Bend U.S.A. 132 B2
Bendearg *mt.* S. Africa 109 C3
Bendigo Austr. 116 C3
Bene Moz. 107 C1
Benešov Czech Rep. 56 C3
Benevento Italy 62 B2
Bengal, Bay of *sea* Indian Ocean 85 C3

Bengbu China 82 B2
Benghazi Libya 101 E1
Bengkayang Indon. 72 B1
Bengkulu Indon. 72 B2
Benguela Angola 106 A1
Ben Hope *h.* U.K. 50 B1
Beni *r.* Bol. 152 B2
Beni Dem. Rep. Congo 105 C2
Beni-Abbès Alg. 100 B1
Benidorm Spain 61 C2
Beni Mellal Morocco 100 B1
Benin *country* Africa 100 C4
Benin, Bight of *g.* Africa 100 C4
Benin City Nigeria 101 C4
Beni-Saf Alg. 61 C2
Benito Juárez Arg. 153 C4
Benjamin Constant Brazil 150 C3
Benjamin Hill Mex. 142 A1
Benjina Indon. 71 C3
Ben Lawers *mt.* U.K. 50 B2
Ben Lomond *h.* U.K. 50 B2
Ben Macdui *mt.* U.K. 50 C2
Ben More *h.* U.K. 50 A2
Benmore, Lake N.Z. 118 B3
Ben More Assynt *h.* U.K. 50 B1
Bennett Can. 126 B2
Bennetta, Ostrov *i.* Rus. Fed. 95 L1
Ben Nevis *mt.* U.K. 50 B2
Bennington U.S.A. 137 F2
Benoni S. Africa 109 C2
Bensheim Ger. 55 D3
Benson U.S.A. 140 B2
Benteng Indon. 73 D2
Benton Harbor U.S.A. 136 C2
Bentonville U.S.A. 138 B1
Benue *r.* Nigeria 101 C4
Benwee Head Rep. of Ireland 51 B1
Ben Wyvis *mt.* U.K. 50 B2
Benxi China 82 C1
Beograd Serb. and Mont. *see* Belgrade
Beohari India 87 C2
Beppu Japan 79 B4
Berane Serb. and Mont. 64 A2
Berat Albania 65 A2
Berau, Teluk *b.* Indon. 71 C3
Berber Sudan 102 B3
Berbera Somalia 103 C3
Berbérati C.A.R. 104 B2
Berck France 58 C1
Berdyans'k Ukr. 45 E2
Berdychiv Ukr. 44 C2
Berehove Ukr. 44 B2
Bereina P.N.G. 71 D3
Berens River Can. 127 F2
Berezhany Ukr. 44 B2
Berezivka Ukr. 44 C1
Berezne Ukr. 44 C1
Bereznik Rus. Fed. 40 D2
Berezniki Rus. Fed. 40 E3
Berezovo Rus. Fed. 40 F2
Berga Spain 61 D1
Bergama Turkey 65 C3
Bergamo Italy 62 A1
Bergen *Mecklenburg-Vorpommern* Ger. 56 C2
Bergen *Niedersachsen* Ger. 55 D1
Bergen Norway 47 B3
Bergen op Zoom Neth. 54 B2
Bergerac France 58 C3
Bergheim (Erft) Ger. 54 C2
Bergisch Gladbach Ger. 54 C2
Bergland Namibia 108 A1
Bergsviken Sweden 46 E2
Bergues France 54 A2
Beringen Belgium 54 B2
Bering Sea N. Pacific Ocean 95 N3
Bering Strait Rus. Fed./U.S.A. 95 O2
Berkeley U.S.A. 133 B3
Berkhout Neth. 54 B1
Berkner Island Antarctica 119 A2

Berkovitsa Bulg. 64 B2
Berlevåg Norway 46 F1
Berlin Ger. 55 F1
Berlin U.S.A. 137 F2
Berlingerode Ger. 55 E2
Bermagui Austr. 117 E3
Bermejillo Mex. 142 B2
Bermejo Bol. 152 B3
Bermen, Lac l. Can. 129 D1
Bermuda terr. N. Atlantic Ocean 160 B3
Bern Switz. 59 D2
Bernau Ger. 55 F1
Bernburg (Saale) Ger. 55 E2
Bernkastel-Kues Ger. 54 C3
Beroroha Madag. 107 [inset] D2
Berounka r. Czech Rep. 55 G3
Berri Austr. 116 C2
Berrouaghia Alg. 61 D2
Berry Islands Bahamas 145 C2
Bersenbrück Ger. 54 C1
Bershad' Ukr. 44 C2
Bertoua Cameroon 104 B2
Beru atoll Kiribati 110
Beruri Brazil 150 C3
Berwick-upon-Tweed U.K. 52 B2
Beryslav Ukr. 45 D2
Besalampy Madag. 107 [inset] D1
Besançon France 59 D2
Besnard Lake Can. 127 E2
Bessemer U.S.A. 138 C2
Besshoky, Gora h. Kazakh. 88 C2
Betanzos Spain 60 B1
Bétaré Oya Cameroon 104 B2
Bethanie Namibia 108 A2
Bethlehem S. Africa 109 C2
Bethlehem U.S.A. 137 E2
Béthune France 54 A2
Betioky Madag. 107 [inset] D2
Betpak-Dala plain Kazakh. 89 E2
Betroka Madag. 107 [inset] D2
Betsiamites Can. 129 D2
Betsiboka r. Madag. 107 [inset] D1
Bettendorf U.S.A. 135 E2
Bettiah India 87 C2
Betul India 87 B2
Betwa r. India 87 B2
Betws-y-coed U.K. 52 B3
Beverley U.K. 52 C3
Beverungen Ger. 55 D2
Beverwijk Neth. 54 B1
Bexhill U.K. 53 D4
Beykoz Turkey 65 C2
Beyla Guinea 100 B4
Beyneu Kazakh. 88 C2
Beypazarı Turkey 92 B1
Beyrouth Lebanon see Beirut
Beyşehir Turkey 92 B2
Beyşehir Gölü l. Turkey 92 B2
Beysug r. Rus. Fed. 45 E3
Bezhanitsy Rus. Fed. 42 C2
Bezhetsk Rus. Fed. 43 E2
Béziers France 59 C3
Bhadrak India 87 C2
Bhadravati India 85 B3
Bhagalpur India 87 C2
Bhairab Bazar Bangl. 87 D2
Bhairi Hol mt. Pak. 86 A2
Bhakkar Pak. 86 B1
Bhamo Myanmar 74 A1
Bhanjanagar India 87 C3
Bharatpur India 86 B2
Bharuch India 86 B2
Bhavnagar India 86 B2
Bhawanipatna India 87 C3
Bhekuzulu S. Africa 109 D2
Bhilwara India 86 B2
Bhima r. India 85 B3
Bhiwani India 86 B2
Bhongweni S. Africa 109 C3

Bhopal India 86 B2
Bhubaneshwar India 87 C2
Bhuj India 86 A2
Bhumiphol Dam Thai. 74 A2
Bhusawal India 86 B2
Bhutan country Asia 87 C2
Bia, Phou mt. Laos 74 B2
Biak Indon. 71 D3
Biak i. Indon. 71 D3
Biała Podlaska Pol. 57 E2
Białogard Pol. 57 D2
Białystok Pol. 57 E2
Bianco Italy 63 C3
Biarritz France 58 B3
Biasca Switz. 59 D2
Bibai Japan 78 D2
Bibala Angola 106 A1
Biberach an der Riß Ger. 56 B3
Bida Nigeria 101 C4
Biddeford U.S.A. 137 F2
Bideford U.K. 53 A4
Bideford Bay U.K. 53 A4
Biedenkopf Ger. 55 D2
Biel Switz. 59 D2
Bielefeld Ger. 55 D1
Biella Italy 62 A1
Bielsko-Biała Pol. 57 D3
Biên Hoa Vietnam 75 B2
Bienville, Lac l. Can. 128 C1
Bièvre Belgium 54 B3
Bifoun Gabon 104 B3
Biga Turkey 65 C2
Big Bend Swaziland 109 D2
Biggar Can. 124 C2
Biggar U.K. 50 C2
Big Hole r. U.S.A. 132 D1
Bighorn r. U.S.A. 134 B1
Bighorn Mountains U.S.A. 134 B2
Big Lake U.S.A. 141 D2
Big Rapids U.S.A. 136 C2
Big River Can. 127 E2
Big Sand Lake Can. 127 F2
Big Sioux r. U.S.A. 135 D2
Big Spring U.S.A. 141 D2
Big Timber U.S.A. 132 E1
Big Trout Lake Can. 128 B1
Big Trout Lake l. Can. 128 A1
Bihać Bos.-Herz. 63 C2
Bihar Sharif India 87 C2
Bihor, Vârful mt. Romania 44 B2
Bijagós, Arquipélago dos is Guinea-Bissau 100 A3
Bijār Iran 93 C2
Bijeljina Bos.-Herz. 63 C2
Bijelo Polje Serb. and Mont. 64 A2
Bijie China 83 A3
Bikaner India 86 B2
Bikin Rus. Fed. 78 B1
Bikin r. Rus. Fed. 78 B1
Bikoro Dem. Rep. Congo 104 B3
Bilād Banī Bū 'Alī Oman 91 C2
Bilaspur India 87 C2
Bila Tserkva Ukr. 44 D2
Bilauktaung Range mts Myanmar/Thai. 75 A2
Bilbao Spain 60 C1
Bilecik Turkey 65 C1
Bilgoraj Pol. 57 E2
Bilhorod-Dnistrovs'kyy Ukr. 44 D2
Bili Dem. Rep. Congo 105 C2
Bilibino Rus. Fed. 95 N2
Billings U.S.A. 132 E1
Bill of Portland hd U.K. 53 B4
Bilma Niger 101 D3
Biloela Austr. 115 E2
Bilohirs'k Ukr. 44 D2
Bilohir'ya Ukr. 44 C1
Bilopillya Ukr. 45 D1
Bilovods'k Ukr. 45 E2
Biloxi U.S.A. 138 C2

Bilpa Morea Claypan salt flat Austr. 115 C2
Bilshausen Ger. 55 E2
Biltine Chad 101 E3
Bilyayivka Ukr. 44 D2
Bimini Islands Bahamas 139 E3
Bina-Etawa India 87 B2
Binaija, Gunung mt. Indon. 71 C3
Bindu Dem. Rep. Congo 104 B3
Bindura Zimbabwe 107 C1
Binefar Spain 61 D1
Bingara Austr. 117 E1
Bingen am Rhein Ger. 54 C3
Bingham U.S.A. 137 G1
Binghamton U.S.A. 137 E2
Bingöl Turkey 93 C2
Binjai Indon. 72 A1
Bintuhan Indon. 72 B2
Bintulu Malaysia 73 C1
Binzhou China 82 B2
Bioco i. Equat. Guinea 104 A2
Biograd na Moru Croatia 62 C2
Birao C.A.R. 104 C1
Biratnagar Nepal 87 C2
Birch Mountains Can. 126 D2
Birdsville Austr. 115 C2
Birecik Turkey 92 B2
Bireun Indon. 72 A1
Birganj Nepal 87 C2
Birhan mt. Eth. 103 B3
Birigüi Brazil 154 B2
Birjand Iran 88 C3
Birkenhead U.K. 52 B3
Birmingham U.K. 53 C3
Birmingham U.S.A. 138 C2
Bir Mogrein Maur. 100 A2
Birnin-Kebbi Nigeria 100 C3
Birnin Konni Niger 101 C3
Birobidzhan Rus. Fed. 81 E1
Birr Rep. of Ireland 51 C2
Birsay U.K. 50 C1
Bi'r Shalatayn Egypt 90 A2
Biržai Lith. 42 B2
Bisalpur India 87 B2
Bisbee U.S.A. 140 C2
Biscay, Bay of sea France/Spain 58 A2
Bischofshofen Austria 56 C3
Biscotasi Lake Can. 128 B2
Bishkek Kyrg. 89 E2
Bisho S. Africa 109 C3
Bishop U.S.A. 133 C3
Bishui China 81 E1
Bisinaca Col. 150 C2
Biskra Alg. 101 C1
Bismarck U.S.A. 134 C1
Bismarck Archipelago is P.N.G. 71 D3
Bismarck Sea P.N.G. 110
Bissa, Djebel mt. Alg. 61 D2
Bissamcuttak India 85 C3
Bissau Guinea-Bissau 100 A3
Bissett Can. 127 F2
Bistcho Lake Can. 126 D2
Bistrița Romania 44 B2
Bistrița r. Romania 44 C2
Bitburg Ger. 54 C2
Bitche France 59 D2
Bitkine Chad 101 D3
Bitola Macedonia 65 B2
Bitonto Italy 63 C2
Bitterfontein S. Africa 108 A3
Bitterroot r. U.S.A. 132 D1
Bitterroot Range mts U.S.A. 132 C1
Bityug r. Rus. Fed. 43 E3
Biu Nigeria 101 D3
Biwa-ko l. Japan 79 C3
Biysk Rus. Fed. 89 F1
Bizerte Tunisia 101 C1
Bjargtangar hd Iceland 46 [inset]
Bjästa Sweden 46 D3
Bjerkvik Norway 46 D2

Bjørnøya i. Arctic Ocean **94** D2
Bla Mali **100** D3
Black r. U.S.A. **138** B1
Blackall Austr. **115** D2
Blackburn U.K. **52** B3
Blackfoot U.S.A. **132** D2
Black Forest mts Ger. **56** B3
Black Hills U.S.A. **134** C2
Black Isle pen. U.K. **50** B2
Black Lake Can. **127** E2
Black Lake l. Can. **127** E2
Black Mountains U.K. **53** B4
Blackpool U.K. **52** B3
Black River r. Vietnam **74** B1
Black River Falls U.S.A. **136** B2
Blacksburg U.S.A. **137** D3
Black Sea Asia/Europe **92** B1
Blacksod Bay Rep. of Ireland **51** A1
Blackstairs Mountains Rep. of Ireland **51** C2
Black Volta r. Africa **100** B4
Blackwater r. Rep. of Ireland **51** C2
Blackwater Lake Can. **126** C1
Blackwood r. Austr. **114** A3
Blagoevgrad Bulg. **64** B2
Blagoveshchensk Rus. Fed. **81** E1
Blaine Lake Can. **127** E2
Blair U.S.A. **135** D2
Blair Atholl U.K. **50** C2
Blairgowrie U.K. **50** C2
Blakely U.S.A. **139** C2
Blanc, Mont mt. France/Italy **59** D2
Blanca, Bahía b. Arg. **153** B4
Blanche, Lake salt flat Austr. **116** B1
Blanco r. Bol. **152** B2
Blanco, Cape U.S.A. **120**
Blanc-Sablon Can. **129** E1
Blanda r. Iceland **46** [inset]
Blandford Forum U.K. **53** B4
Blanding U.S.A. **133** E3
Blanes Spain **61** D1
Blangkejeren Indon. **72** A1
Blankenheim Ger. **54** C2
Blankenrath Ger. **54** C2
Blansko Czech Rep. **57** D3
Blantyre Malawi **107** C1
Blaydon U.K. **52** C1
Blayney Austr. **117** D2
Blenheim N.Z. **118** B3
Blida Alg. **100** C1
Blind River Can. **128** B2
Bloemfontein S. Africa **109** C2
Bloemhof S. Africa **109** C2
Bloemhof Dam S. Africa **109** C2
Blönduós Iceland **46** [inset]
Bloody Foreland pt Rep. of Ireland **51** B1
Bloomfield U.S.A. **140** C1
Bloomington IL. U.S.A. **136** C2
Bloomington IN U.S.A. **136** C3
Blosseville Kyst coastal area Greenland **125** K2
Bluefield U.S.A. **136** D3
Bluefields Nic. **144** B3
Blue Mountains Austr. **117** D2
Blue Mountains U.S.A. **132** C1
Blue Nile r. Eth./Sudan **103** B3
Blue Ridge mts U.S.A. **139** D1
Blue Stack Mountains Rep. of Ireland **51** B1
Bluff N.Z. **118** A4
Bluff U.S.A. **133** E3
Blumenau Brazil **154** C3
Blyth Austr. **116** B2
Blyth U.K. **52** C2
Blythe U.S.A. **133** D4
Blytheville U.S.A. **138** C1
Bo Sierra Leone **100** A4
Boac Phil. **76** B2

Boa Esperança, Açude resr Brazil **151** E3
Boa Vista Brazil **150** C2
Bobadah Austr. **117** D2
Bobai China **83** B3
Bobaomby, Tanjona c. Madag. **107** [inset] D1
Bobo-Dioulasso Burkina **100** B3
Bobrov Rus. Fed. **43** F3
Bobrovytsya Ukr. **45** D1
Bobrynets' Ukr. **45** D2
Boby mt. Madag. **107** [inset] D2
Boca do Acre Brazil **150** C3
Bocaiúva Brazil **155** D1
Bocaranga C.A.R. **104** B2
Bochnia Pol. **57** E3
Bocholt Ger. **54** C2
Bochum Ger. **54** C2
Bochum S. Africa **109** C1
Bockenem Ger. **55** E1
Boda C.A.R. **104** B2
Bodaybo Rus. Fed. **95** J3
Bodélé reg. Chad **101** D3
Boden Sweden **46** E2
Bodmin U.K. **53** A4
Bodmin Moor moorland U.K. **53** A4
Bodø Norway **46** C2
Bodrum Turkey **65** C3
Boende Dem. Rep. Congo **104** C3
Bogalusa U.S.A. **138** C2
Bogandé Burkina **100** B3
Bogda Shan mts China **89** F2
Boggabilla Austr. **117** E1
Boggeragh Mountains Rep. of Ireland **51** B2
Bogny-sur-Meuse France **54** B3
Bog of Allen reg. Rep. of Ireland **51** C2
Bogong, Mount Austr. **117** D3
Bogor Indon. **72** B2
Bogoroditsk Rus. Fed. **43** E3
Bogotá Col. **150** B2
Bogotol Rus. Fed. **94** H3
Boguchany Rus. Fed. **95** I3
Boguchar Rus. Fed. **45** F2
Bo Hai g. China **82** B2
Bohain-en-Vermandois France **54** A3
Bohai Wan b. China **82** B2
Bohlokong S. Africa **109** C2
Böhmer Wald mts Ger. **55** F3
Bohodukhiv Ukr. **45** E1
Bohol i. Phil. **76** B3
Bohol Sea Phil. **76** B3
Bohu China **89** D2
Boi, Ponta do pt Brazil **155** C2
Boise U.S.A. **132** C2
Boise City U.S.A. **141** D1
Boitumelong S. Africa **109** C2
Boizenburg Ger. **55** E1
Bojnūrd Iran **93** D2
Bokatola Dem. Rep. Congo **104** B3
Boké Guinea **100** A3
Bokele Dem. Rep. Congo **104** C3
Bokoro Chad **101** D3
Bokovskaya Rus. Fed. **45** F2
Bokpyin Myanmar **75** A2
Boksitogorsk Rus. Fed. **43** D2
Bokspits S. Africa **108** B2
Bolama Guinea-Bissau **100** A3
Bolangir India **87** C2
Bolbec France **58** C2
Bole China **89** D2
Boleko Dem. Rep. Congo **104** B3
Bolgatanga Ghana **100** B3
Bolhrad Ukr. **44** C2
Boli China **78** B1
Bolintin-Vale Romania **44** C3
Bolívar, Pico mt. Venez. **150** B2

Bolivia country S. America **152** B2
Bolkhov Rus. Fed. **43** E3
Bollène France **59** C3
Bollnäs Sweden **47** D3
Bollon Austr. **117** D1
Bolmen l. Sweden **47** C4
Bolobo Dem. Rep. Congo **104** B3
Bologna Italy **62** B2
Bologovo Rus. Fed. **43** D2
Bologoye Rus. Fed. **43** D2
Bolomba Dem. Rep. Congo **104** B2
Bolovens, Phouphieng plat. Laos **75** B2
Bol'shaya Martinovka Rus. Fed. **45** F2
Bol'shevik, Ostrov i. Rus. Fed. **95** I1
Bol'shezemel'skaya Tundra lowland Rus. Fed. **40** E2
Bol'shoy Aluy r. Rus. Fed. **95** M2
Bol'shoy Kamen' Rus. Fed. **78** B2
Bol'shoy Kavkaz mts Asia/Europe see Caucasus
Bol'shoy Lyakhovskiy, Ostrov i. Rus. Fed. **95** L2
Bolsward Neth. **54** B1
Bolton U.K. **52** B3
Bolu Turkey **92** B1
Bolungarvík Iceland **46** [inset]
Bolzano Italy **62** B1
Boma Dem. Rep. Congo **104** B3
Bomaderry Austr. **117** E2
Bombala Austr. **117** D3
Bombay India see Mumbai
Bom Despacho Brazil **155** C1
Bomdila India **87** D2
Bom Jesus da Lapa Brazil **151** E4
Bom Jesus do Itabapoana Brazil **155** D2
Bømlo i. Norway **48** E2
Bon, Cap c. Tunisia **101** D1
Bonaire i. Neth. Antilles **145** D3
Bonaparte Archipelago is Austr. **114** B1
Bonavista Can. **129** E2
Bonavista Bay Can. **129** E2
Bondo Dem. Rep. Congo **104** C2
Bondoukou Côte d'Ivoire **100** B4
Bone, Teluk b. Indon. **73** D2
Bonerate, Kepulauan is Indon. **73** D2
Bonete, Cerro mt. Bol. **152** B3
Bonfinópolis de Minas Brazil **155** C1
Bonga Eth. **103** B4
Bongaigaon India **87** D2
Bongandanga Dem. Rep. Congo **104** C2
Bongo, Massif des mts C.A.R. **104** C2
Bongor Chad **101** D3
Bongouanou Côte d'Ivoire **100** B4
Bông Son Vietnam **75** B2
Bonham U.S.A. **141** E2
Bonifacio France **59** D3
Bonifacio, Strait of France/Italy **62** A2
Bonito Brazil **154** A2
Bonn Ger. **54** C2
Bonners Ferry U.S.A. **132** C1
Bonnie Rock Austr. **114** A3
Bonnyville Can. **127** D2
Bonorva Italy **62** A2
Bontang Indon. **73** C1
Bontoc Phil. **76** B2
Bontosunggu Indon. **73** C2
Bontrug S. Africa **109** C3
Booligal Austr. **116** C2
Boomi Austr. **117** D1
Boonah Austr. **117** E1
Boone IA U.S.A. **135** E2
Boone NC U.S.A. **136** D3
Booneville U.S.A. **138** C2
Boonville U.S.A. **135** E3
Boorowa Austr. **117** D2

oothia, Gulf of Can. **125** G2
oothia Peninsula Can. **124** F2
oppard Ger. **54** C2
oquila, Presa de la *resr* Mex.
 142 B2
or Serb. and Mont. **64** B2
or Sudan **103** B4
or Turkey **92** D3
oraha, Nosy *i.* Madag. **107** [inset]
orås Sweden **47** C4
oräzjän Iran **93** D3
orba Brazil **150** D3
ordeaux France **58** B3
ordertown Austr. **116** C3
ordj Bou Arréridj Alg. **61** D2
ordj Bounaama Alg. **61** D2
ordj Messaouda Alg. **101** C1
ordj Omer Driss Alg. **101** C2
orðoy *i.* Faroe Is **48** B1
orgarnes Iceland **46** [inset]
orgosesia Italy **62** A1
orisoglebsk Rus. Fed. **45** F1
orisoglebskiy Rus. Fed. **43** E2
orisovka Rus. Fed. **45** E1
orisovo-Sudskoye Rus. Fed. **43** E2
orken Ger. **54** C2
orkenes Norway **46** D2
orkum Ger. **54** C1
orkum *i.* Ger. **54** C1
orlänge Sweden **47** D3
orna Ger. **55** F2
orneo *i.* Asia **73** C2
ornholm *i.* Denmark **47** C4
ornova Turkey **65** C3
orodyanka Ukr. **44** C1
orovichi Rus. Fed. **43** E2
orovsk Rus. Fed. **43** E2
orooloola Austr. **115** C1
orşa Romania **44** B2
orshchiv Ukr. **44** B2
orshchovochnyy Khrebet *mts*
 Rus. Fed. **81** D1
orßum Ger. **55** E1
orüjerd Iran **93** C2
oryslav Ukr. **44** B2
oryspil' Ukr. **44** D1
orzna Ukr. **45** D1
orzya Rus. Fed. **81** D1
osanska Dubica Bos.-Herz. **63** C2
osanska Gradiška Bos.-Herz. **63** C1
osanska Krupa Bos.-Herz. **63** C2
osanski Novi Bos.-Herz. **63** C1
osansko Grahovo Bos.-Herz. **63** C2
ose China **83** A3
oshof S. Africa **109** C2
osnia-Herzegovina *country* Europe
 63 C2
osobolo Dem. Rep. Congo **104** B2
osporus *str.* Turkey **65** C2
ossangoa C.A.R. **104** B2
ossembélé C.A.R. **104** B2
osten Hu *i.* China **89** F2
oston U.S.A. **137** F2
oston Mountains U.S.A. **138** B1
otany Bay Austr. **117** E2
otev *mt.* Bulg. **64** B2
otevgrad Bulg. **92** A1
othnia, Gulf of Fin./Sweden **47** D3
otoşani Romania **44** C2
otshabelo S. Africa **109** C2
otswana *country* Africa **106** B2
ottineau U.S.A. **134** C1
ottrop Ger. **54** C2
otucatu Brazil **154** C2
ouaké Côte d'Ivoire **100** B4
ouar C.A.R. **104** B2
ouârfa Morocco **100** B1
ouctouche Can. **129** D2

Bougaa Alg. **61** E2
Bougainville Island P.N.G. **110**
Bougaroûn, Cap *c.* Alg. **61** E2
Bougouni Mali **100** B3
Bouillon Belgium **54** B3
Bouira Alg. **61** D2
Boujdour Western Sahara **100** A2
Boulder U.S.A. **134** B2
Boulder City U.S.A. **133** D3
Boulia Austr. **115** C2
Boulogne-Billancourt France **58** C2
Boulogne-sur-Mer France **53** D4
Boumango Gabon **104** B3
Boumba *r.* Cameroon **104** B3
Boumerdes Alg. **61** D2
Bouna Côte d'Ivoire **100** B4
Boundiali Côte d'Ivoire **100** B4
Bountiful U.S.A. **132** D2
Bourem Mali **100** B3
Bourganeuf France **58** C2
Bourg-en-Bresse France **59** D2
Bourges France **58** C2
Bourke Austr. **117** D2
Bournemouth U.K. **53** C4
Bou Saâda Alg. **101** C1
Bousso Chad **101** D3
Boutilimit Maur. **100** A3
Bouy France **54** B3
Bow *r.* Can. **127** D3
Bowen Austr. **115** D2
Bow Island Can. **127** D3
Bowling Green *KY* U.S.A. **136** C3
Bowling Green *OH* U.S.A. **136** D2
Bowman U.S.A. **134** C1
Boxberg Ger. **55** D3
Boxtel Neth. **54** B2
Boyabat Turkey **92** B1
Boyang China **83** B3
Boyle Rep. of Ireland **51** B2
Boyne *r.* Rep. of Ireland **51** C2
Boysen Reservoir U.S.A. **134** B2
Boyuibe Bol. **152** B3
Bozburun Turkey **65** C3
Bozcaada *i.* Turkey **65** C3
Bozdağ *mt.* Turkey **65** C3
Boz Dağları *mts* Turkey **65** C3
Bozdoğan Turkey **65** C3
Bozeman U.S.A. **132** D1
Bozoum C.A.R. **104** B2
Bozüyük Turkey **65** D3
Brač *i.* Croatia **63** C2
Bracebridge Can. **128** C2
Brachet, Lac au *l.* Can. **129** D2
Bracknell U.K. **53** C4
Bradano *r.* Italy **63** C2
Bradenton U.S.A. **139** D3
Bradford U.K. **52** C3
Bradford U.S.A. **137** E2
Brady U.S.A. **141** E2
Braemar U.K. **50** F1
Braga Port. **60** B1
Bragança Brazil **151** E3
Bragança Port. **60** B1
Bragança Paulista Brazil **155** C2
Brahin Belarus **43** D3
Brahmanbaria Bangl. **74** A1
Brahmapur India **85** C2
Brahmaputra *r.* China/India **74** A1
Brăila Romania **44** C2
Brainerd U.S.A. **135** E1
Braintree U.K. **53** D4
Braives Belgium **54** B2
Brake (Unterweser) Ger. **55** D1
Brakwater Namibia **108** A1
Bramsche Ger. **54** D1
Branco *r.* Brazil **150** C3
Brandenburg Ger. **55** F1
Brandon Can. **127** F3
Brandon Mountain *h.* Rep. of Ireland
 51 A2

Brandvlei S. Africa **108** B3
Braniewo Pol. **57** D2
Brantford Can. **128** C2
Bras d'Or Lake Can. **129** D2
Brasil, Planalto do *plat.* Brazil **155** D1
Brasilândia Brazil **154** C1
Brasília Brazil **154** C1
Brasília de Minas Brazil **155** D1
Braslaw Belarus **42** C2
Braşov Romania **44** C2
Bratislava Slovakia **57** D3
Bratsk Rus. Fed. **95** I3
Braunau am Inn Austria **56** C3
Braunschweig Ger. **55** E1
Braurfarhoit Iceland **46** [inset]
Bráviken *inlet* Sweden **42** C1
Bravo del Norte, Río *r.* Mex./U.S.A. *see*
 Rio Grande
Brawley U.S.A. **133** C4
Bray Rep. of Ireland **51** C2
Brazil *country* S. America **151** D3
Brazilian Highlands *mts* Brazil **146**
Brazos *r.* U.S.A. **141** E3
Brazzaville Congo **104** B3
Brčko Bos.-Herz. **63** C2
Brechin U.K. **50** F1
Brecht Belgium **54** B2
Breckenridge U.S.A. **141** E2
Břeclav Czech Rep. **57** D3
Brecon U.K. **53** B4
Brecon Beacons *reg.* U.K. **53** B4
Breda Neth. **54** B2
Bredasdorp S. Africa **108** B3
Bregenz Austria **56** B3
Breivikbotn Norway **46** E1
Brekstad Norway **46** F3
Bremen Ger. **55** D1
Bremerhaven Ger. **55** D1
Bremerton U.S.A. **132** B1
Bremervörde Ger. **55** D1
Brenham U.S.A. **141** E2
Brennero Italy **56** C3
Brenner Pass Austria/Italy **56** C3
Brentwood U.K. **53** D4
Brescia Italy **62** B1
Bressanone Italy **62** B1
Bressay *i.* U.K. **50** [inset]
Bressuire France **58** B2
Brest Belarus **42** B3
Brest France **58** B2
Breton Sound *b.* U.S.A. **138** C3
Breves Brazil **151** D3
Brewarrina Austr. **117** D1
Brewster U.S.A. **132** C1
Breytovo Rus. Fed. **43** E2
Brezovo Polje *plain* Croatia **63** C1
Bria C.A.R. **104** C2
Briançon France **59** D3
Briceni Moldova **44** C2
Bridgend U.K. **53** B4
Bridgeport *CT* U.S.A. **137** F2
Bridgeport *NE* U.S.A. **134** C2
Bridgetown Barbados **145** E3
Bridgewater Can. **129** D2
Bridgwater U.K. **53** B4
Bridlington U.K. **52** C2
Bridlington Bay U.K. **52** C2
Brig Switz. **59** D2
Brigham City U.S.A. **132** D2
Brighton N.Z. **118** B4
Brighton U.K. **53** C4
Brignoles France **59** D3
Brilon Ger. **55** D2
Brindisi Italy **63** C2
Brisbane Austr. **117** E1
Bristol U.K. **53** B4
Bristol U.S.A. **139** D1
Bristol Bay U.S.A. **95** P3
Bristol Channel *est.* U.K. **53** A4
British Columbia *prov.* Can. **126** C2

British Indian Ocean Territory *terr.* Indian Ocean **69**
Britstown S. Africa **108** B3
Brittany *reg.* France **58** B2
Brive-la-Gaillarde France **58** C2
Briviesca Spain **60** C1
Brno Czech Rep. **57** D3
Broad *r.* U.S.A. **139** D2
Broadback *r.* Can. **128** C1
Broad Law *h.* U.K. **50** C3
Broadus U.S.A. **134** B1
Brochet Can. **127** E2
Brochet, Lac *l.* Can. **127** E2
Bröckel Ger. **55** E1
Brockville Can. **128** C2
Brodeur Peninsula Can. **125** G2
Brodick U.K. **50** B3
Brodnica Pol. **57** D2
Brody Ukr. **44** C1
Broken Arrow U.S.A. **141** E1
Broken Bow U.S.A. **135** D2
Broken Hill Austr. **116** C2
Bromsgrove U.K. **53** B3
Brønderslev Denmark **47** B4
Brønnøysund Norway **46** C2
Brooke's Point Phil. **76** A3
Brookhaven U.S.A. **138** B3
Brookings *OR* U.S.A. **134** B2
Brookings *SD* U.S.A. **135** D2
Brooks Can. **127** D2
Brooks Range *mts* U.S.A. **124** C2
Brooksville U.S.A. **139** D3
Broom, Loch *inlet* U.K. **50** B2
Broome Austr. **114** B1
Brothers U.S.A. **132** B2
Brovary Ukr. **44** D1
Brownfield U.S.A. **141** D2
Browning U.S.A. **126** D3
Brownsville *TN* U.S.A. **138** C1
Brownsville *TX* U.S.A. **141** E3
Brownwood U.S.A. **141** E2
Brú Iceland **46** [inset]
Bruay-la-Buissière France **58** C1
Bruce Crossing U.S.A. **136** C1
Bruchsal Ger. **55** D3
Bruck an der Mur Austria **57** D3
Bruges Belgium *see* Brugge
Brugge Belgium **54** A2
Brühl Ger. **55** D2
Bruint India **74** A1
Brûlé Can. **126** D2
Brumado Brazil **151** E4
Brumunddal Norway **47** C3
Brunei *country* Asia **73** C1
Brunico Italy **56** C3
Brunswick *GA* U.S.A. **139** D2
Brunswick *ME* U.S.A. **137** G2
Brunswick Head Austr. **117** E1
Brush U.S.A. **134** C2
Brussels Belgium **54** B2
Bruxelles Belgium *see* Brussels
Bryan U.S.A. **141** E2
Bryansk Rus. Fed. **43** D3
Bryne Norway **48** E2
Bryn'kovskaya Rus. Fed. **45** E2
Bryukhovetskaya Rus. Fed. **45** E2
Brzeg Pol. **57** D2
Buba Guinea-Bissau **100** A3
Bucak Turkey **92** B2
Bucaramanga Col. **150** B2
Buchan Austr. **117** D3
Buchanan Liberia **100** A4
Bucharest Romania **44** C2
Bucholz in der Nordheide Ger. **55** D1
Buchy France **53** D5
Bucin, Pasul *pass* Romania **44** C2
Bückeburg Ger. **55** D1
Buckey U.S.A. **140** B2
Buckhaven U.K. **50** C2
Buckie U.K. **50** C2

Buckingham Bay Austr. **115** C1
Buckland Tableland *reg.* Austr. **115** D2
Buckleboo Austr. **116** B2
Bucksport U.S.A. **137** G2
Bucureşti Romania *see* Bucharest
Buda-Kashalyova Belarus **43** D3
Budaun India **87** B2
Buddusò Italy **62** A2
Bude U.K. **53** A4
Budennovsk Rus. Fed. **41** D4
Budogoshch' Rus. Fed. **43** D2
Budoni Italy **62** A2
Buea Cameroon **104** A2
Buenaventura Mex. **142** B2
Buendia, Embalse de *resr* Spain **60** C1
Buenópolis Brazil **155** D1
Buenos Aires Arg. **153** C4
Buenos Aires, Lago *l.* Arg./Chile **153** A5
Buffalo *NY* U.S.A. **137** E2
Buffalo *SD* U.S.A. **134** C1
Buffalo *WY* U.S.A. **134** B2
Buffalo Narrows Can. **124** E3
Buffels *watercourse* S. Africa **108** A2
Buftea Romania **44** C2
Bug *r.* Pol. **57** E2
Bugel, Tanjung *pt* Indon. **73** C2
Bugojno Bos.-Herz. **63** C2
Bugsuk *i.* Phil. **76** A3
Buguruslan Rus. Fed. **41** E3
Buhuşi Romania **44** C2
Builth Wells U.K. **53** B3
Buir Nur *l.* Mongolia **81** D1
Buitepos Namibia **108** A1
Bujanovac Serb. and Mont. **64** B2
Bujumbura Burundi **105** C3
Bukachacha Rus. Fed. **81** D1
Bukavu Dem. Rep. Congo **105** C3
Bukhara Uzbek. *see* Buxoro
Bukittinggi Indon. **72** B2
Bukoba Tanz. **105** D3
Bulahdelah Austr. **117** E2
Bulawayo Zimbabwe **107** B2
Buldan Turkey **65** C3
Bulembu Swaziland **109** D2
Bulgan Mongolia **80** C1
Bulgaria *country* Europe **64** B2
Bulloo Downs Austr. **116** C1
Büllsport Namibia **108** A1
Bulukumba Indon. **73** D2
Bulungu Dem. Rep. Congo **104** B3
Bumhkang Myanmar **74** A1
Buna Dem. Rep. Congo **104** B3
Bunbury Austr. **114** A3
Buncrana Rep. of Ireland **51** C1
Bunda Tanz. **105** D3
Bundaberg Austr. **115** E2
Bundarra Austr. **117** E2
Bundi India **86** B2
Bundoran Rep. of Ireland **51** B1
Bungendore Austr. **117** D3
Bungo-suidō *sea chan.* Japan **79** B4
Bunia Dem. Rep. Congo **105** D2
Bunianga Dem. Rep. Congo **104** C3
Buôn Mê Thuôt Vietnam **75** B2
Bura Kenya **105** D3
Buraydah Saudi Arabia **90** B2
Burbach Ger. **54** D2
Burco Somalia **103** C4
Burdaard Neth. **54** B1
Burdur Turkey **92** B2
Burë Eth. **103** B3
Bure *r.* U.K. **53** D3
Burgas Bulg. **64** C2
Burg bei Magdeburg Ger. **55** E1
Burgdorf *Niedersachsen* Ger. **55** E1

Burgdorf *Niedersachsen* Ger. **55** E1
Burgeo Can. **129** E2
Burgersfort S. Africa **109** D1
Burgh-Haamstede Neth. **54** A2
Burglengenfeld Ger. **55** F3
Burgos Mex. **143** C2
Burgos Spain **60** C1
Burhaniye Turkey **65** C3
Burhanpur India **86** B2
Burhave (Butjadingen) Ger. **55** D1
Burin Can. **129** E2
Buriti Bravo Brazil **151** E3
Buritis Brazil **155** C1
Burketown Austr. **115** C1
Burkina *country* Africa **100** B3
Burley U.S.A. **132** D2
Burlington *CO* U.S.A. **134** C3
Burlington *IA* U.S.A. **135** E2
Burlington *NC* U.S.A. **139** E1
Burlington *VT* U.S.A. **137** F2
Burney U.S.A. **132** B2
Burnie Austr. **115** D4
Burnley U.K. **52** B3
Burns U.S.A. **132** C2
Burns Lake Can. **126** C2
Burqin China **89** F2
Burra Austr. **116** B2
Burrel Albania **64** A2
Burren *reg.* Rep. of Ireland **51** B2
Burrendong Reservoir Austr. **117** D2
Burren Junction Austr. **117** D2
Burriana Spain **61** C2
Burrinjuck Reservoir Austr. **117** D2
Burro, Serranías del *mts* Mex. **142** B3
Bursa Turkey **65** C2
Bür Safājah Egypt **102** B2
Bür Sa'īd Egypt *see* Port Said
Burton, Lac *l.* Can. **128** C1
Burtonport Rep. of Ireland **51** B1
Burton upon Trent U.K. **52** C3
Buru *i.* Indon. **71** C3
Burundi *country* Africa **105** D3
Bururi Burundi **105** C3
Burwash Landing Can. **126** B1
Buryn' Ukr. **45** D1
Burynshyk Kazakh. **88** C2
Bury St Edmunds U.K. **53** D3
Busanga Dem. Rep. Congo **104** C3
Büshehr Iran **93** D3
Bushenyi Uganda **105** D3
Businga Dem. Rep. Congo **104** C2
Busselton Austr. **114** A3
Bustamante Mex. **141** D3
Busuanga Phil. **76** A2
Buta Dem. Rep. Congo **104** C2
Butare Rwanda **105** C3
Butha-Buthe Lesotho **109** C2
Butler U.S.A. **137** E2
Buton *i.* Indon. **73** D2
Butte U.S.A. **132** D1
Butterworth Malaysia **72** B1
Butt of Lewis *hd* U.K. **50** A1
Button Bay Can. **127** F2
Butuan Phil. **76** B3
Buturlinovka Rus. Fed. **43** F3
Butwal Nepal **87** C2
Butzbach Ger. **55** D2
Buulobarde Somalia **103** C4
Buur Gaabo Somalia **103** C5
Buurhabaka Somalia **103** C4
Buxoro Uzbek. **88** D3
Buxtehude Ger. **55** D1
Buy Rus. Fed. **43** F2
Buynaksk Rus. Fed. **41** D4
Büyükmenderes *r.* Turkey **65** C3
Buzai Gumbad Afgh. **86** B1
Buzău Romania **44** C2
Búzi Moz. **107** C1
Buzuluk Rus. Fed. **41** E3
Byala Bulg. **64** C2

valynichy Belarus **42** C3
varezina r. Belarus **42** D3
varoza Belarus **42** B3
vdgoszcz Pol. **57** D2
verazino Belarus **42** C3
veshankovichy Belarus **42** C2
rkhaw Belarus **43** D3
vlot Island Can. **125** G2
vrkjelo Norway **48** B3
vrock Austr. **117** D2
vron Bay Austr. **117** E1
vtantay r. Rus. Fed. **95** K2
vtom Pol. **57** D2
vtów Pol. **57** D2

aaguazú, Cordillera de hills Para.
154 A3
aarapó Brazil **154** A3
aazapa Para. **154** A3
abanatuam Phil. **76** B2
abdul Qaadir Somalia **103** C3
abeceira Rio Manso Brazil **154** A1
abeza del Buey Spain **60** B2
aBezaroi Rus. Fed. **152** B2
abimas Venez. **150** B1
abinda Angola **104** B3
abinda prov. Angola **104** B3
abo Frio Brazil **155** D2
abo Frio, Ilha do i. Brazil **155** D2
abonga, Réservoir resr Can. **128** C2
aboolture Austr. **117** E1
abo Pantoja Peru **150** B3
abora Bassa, Lake resr Moz. **107** C1
aborca Mex. **142** A1
abot Strait Can. **129** D2
abral, Serra de mts Brazil **155** D1
abrera i. Spain **61** H2
abrera, Sierra de la mts Spain
60 B1
abri Can. **127** E2
abriel r. Spain **61** C2
açador Brazil **154** B3
accia, Capo c. Italy **62** A2
aceres Brazil **151** D4
aceres Spain **60** B2
acheu Guinea-Bissau **100** A3
achimbo, Serra do hills Brazil
151 D3
achoeira Alta Brazil **154** B1
achoeiro de Itapemirim Brazil
155 D2
acine Guinea-Bissau **100** A3
acolo Angola **104** B4
acu Brazil **154** B1
adca Slovakia **57** D3
adenberge Ger. **55** D1
adereyta Mex. **143** B2
adillac France **58** C3
adillac U.S.A. **136** C2
adiz Spain **60** B2
adiz, Golfo de g. Spain **60** B2
adotte Lake Can. **126** D2
aen France **58** B2
aernarfon U.K. **52** A3
aernarfon Bay U.K. **52** A3
afayate Arg. **152** B3
agli Italy **62** B2
agliari Italy **62** A3
agliari, Golfo di b. Italy **62** A3
aha Mountains Rep. of Ireland **51** B3
ahermore Rep. of Ireland **51** A3
ahersiveen Rep. of Ireland **51** A3
ahir Rep. of Ireland **51** C2
ahore Point pt Rep. of Ireland **51** C2

Cahors France **58** C3
Cahul Moldova **44** D2
Caia Moz. **107** C1
Caiabis, Serra dos hills Brazil **151** D4
Caianda Angola **106** B1
Caiapó, Serra do mts Brazil **154** B1
Caiapônia Brazil **154** B1
Caicos Islands Turks and Caicos Is
145 C2
Cairngorm Mountains U.K. **50** C2
Cairnryan U.K. **50** B3
Cairns Austr. **115** D1
Cairo Egypt **102** B1
Caistor U.K. **52** C3
Caiundo Angola **106** A1
Cajamarca Peru **150** B3
Čakovec Croatia **63** C1
Cala S. Africa **109** C3
Calabar Nigeria **104** A2
Calabozo Venez. **150** C1
Calafat Romania **44** B3
Calafate Arg. **153** A6
Calahorra Spain **61** C1
Calais France **58** C1
Calais U.S.A. **137** G1
Calama Chile **152** B3
Calamian Group is Phil. **76** A2
Calamocha Spain **61** C1
Calandula Angola **104** B3
Calang Indon. **72** A1
Calanscio Sand Sea des. Libya
101 D3
Calapan Phil. **76** B2
Călăraşi Romania **44** C3
Calatayud Spain **61** C1
Calau Ger. **55** F2
Calayan i. Phil. **76** B2
Calbayog Phil. **76** B2
Calcanhar, Ponta do pt Brazil **151** F3
Calçoene Brazil **151** D2
Calcutta India see Kolkata
Caldas da Rainha Port. **60** B2
Caldas Novas Brazil **154** C1
Caldera Chile **152** A3
Caldwell U.S.A. **132** C2
Caledon r. Lesotho/S. Africa **109** C3
Caledon S. Africa **108** A3
Caleta Olivia Arg. **153** B5
Calf of Man i. Isle of Man **52** A2
Calgary Can. **126** D2
Cali Col. **150** B1
Calicut India **85** B3
Caliente U.S.A. **133** D3
California state U.S.A. **132** B2
California, Gulf of Mex. **133** D4
California Aqueduct canal U.S.A.
133 B3
Calitzdorp S. Africa **108** B3
Çalkini Mex. **143** C2
Callabonna, Lake salt flat Austr.
116 C1
Callander U.K. **50** B2
Callao Peru **150** B4
Caltagirone Italy **62** B3
Caltanissetta Italy **62** B3
Caluquembe Angola **106** A1
Caluula Somalia **103** D3
Calvi France **59** D3
Calvià Spain **61** G2
Calvillo Mex. **142** B2
Calvinia S. Africa **108** A3
Calvo, Monte mt. Italy **63** C2
Camacho Mex. **142** B2
Camacupa Angola **106** A1
Camagüey Cuba **144** C2
Camaná Peru **150** B4
Camapuã Brazil **154** B1
Camargo Mex. **143** C2
Ca Mau Vietnam **75** B3
Ca Mau, Mui c. Vietnam **75** B3

Cambodia country Asia **75** B2
Camborne U.K. **53** A4
Cambrai France **59** C1
Cambrian Mountains U.K. **53** B3
Cambridge N.Z. **118** C2
Cambridge U.K. **53** D3
Cambridge MA U.S.A. **137** F2
Cambridge MD U.S.A. **137** E3
Cambridge MN U.S.A. **135** E1
Cambridge OH U.S.A. **136** D2
Cambrien, Lac l. Can. **129** D1
Camden Austr. **117** E2
Camden AR U.S.A. **138** B2
Camden ME U.S.A. **137** G2
Cameroon country Africa **104** B2
Cameroun, Mont vol. Cameroon **96**
Cametá Brazil **151** E3
Camiguin i. Phil. **76** B2
Camiri Bol. **152** B3
Camocim Brazil **151** E3
Camooweal Austr. **115** C1
Camorta i. India **75** A3
Campana, Isla i. Chile **153** A5
Campbell S. Africa **108** B2
Campbell, Cape N.Z. **118** B3
Campbell Island N.Z. **110**
Campbell River Can. **126** C2
Campbellsville U.S.A. **136** C3
Campbellton Can. **137** G1
Campbeltown U.K. **50** B3
Campeche Mex. **143** C3
Campeche, Bahía de g. Mex. **143** C3
Camperdown Austr. **116** C3
Câmpina Romania **44** C2
Campina Grande Brazil **151** F3
Campinas Brazil **154** C2
Campina Verde Brazil **154** C1
Campobasso Italy **62** B2
Campo Belo Brazil **155** C2
Campo Florido Brazil **154** C1
Campo Gallo Arg. **152** B3
Campo Grande Brazil **154** B2
Campo Maior Brazil **151** E3
Campo Maior Port. **60** B2
Campo Mourão Brazil **154** B2
Campos Brazil **155** D2
Campos Altos Brazil **155** C1
Campos do Jordão Brazil **155** C2
Câmpulung Romania **44** C2
Camp Verde U.S.A. **140** B2
Cam Ranh Vietnam **75** B2
Camrose Can. **127** D2
Camsell Portage Can. **127** E2
Çan Turkey **65** C2
Canada country N. America **124** D2
Canadian U.S.A. **141** D1
Canadian r. U.S.A. **141** E1
Canadian Shield reg. Can. **121**
Çanakkale Turkey **65** C2
Cananea Mex. **142** A1
Cananéia Brazil **154** C2
Canary Islands terr. N. Atlantic Ocean
100 A2
Canastra, Serra da mts Brazil **155** C1
Canatlán Mex. **142** B2
Canaveral, Cape U.S.A. **139** D3
Canavieiras Brazil **155** E1
Canberra Austr. **117** D3
Cancún Mex. **143** D2
Çandarlı Turkey **65** C3
Candelaria Mex. **143** C3
Candle Lake Can. **127** E2
Cangamba Angola **106** A1
Cangas del Narcea Spain **60** B1
Canguçu Brazil **152** C4
Cangzhou China **82** B2
Caniapiscau Can. **129** D1
Caniapiscau r. Can. **129** D1
Caniapiscau, Lac l. Can. **129** C1
Canicattì Italy **62** B3

Canindé Brazil 151 F3
Cañitas de Felipe Pescador Mex. 142 B2
Çankırı Turkey 92 B1
Canna i. U.K. 50 A2
Cannanore India 85 B3
Cannes France 59 D3
Cannock U.K. 53 B3
Cann River Austr. 117 D3
Canoas Brazil 152 C3
Canoe Lake Can. 127 E2
Canoinhas Brazil 154 B3
Canon City U.S.A. 134 B3
Canora Can. 124 F3
Canowindra Austr. 117 D2
Cantábrica, Cordillera mts Spain 60 C1
Cantábrico, Mar sea Spain 60 B1
Canterbury U.K. 53 D4
Canterbury Bight b. N.Z. 118 B3
Canterbury Plains N.Z. 118 B3
Cần Thơ Vietnam 75 B2
Canto do Buriti Brazil 151 E3
Canton China see Guangzhou
Canton MS U.S.A. 138 C2
Canton OH U.S.A. 136 C2
Canyon U.S.A. 141 D1
Canyon Ferry Lake U.S.A. 132 D1
Cao Bằng Vietnam 74 B1
Capão Bonito Brazil 155 C2
Caparaó, Serra do mts Brazil 155 D2
Cape Barren Island Austr. 115 D4
Cape Borda Austr. 116 B3
Cape Breton Island Can. 129 D2
Cape Coast Ghana 100 B4
Cape Cod Bay U.S.A. 137 F2
Cape Dorset Can. 125 G2
Cape Fear r. U.S.A. 139 E2
Cape Girardeau U.S.A. 135 F3
Capelinha Brazil 155 D1
Capelle aan de IJssel Neth. 54 B2
Capenda-Camulemba Angola 104 B3
Cape Town S. Africa 108 A3
Cape Verde country
    N. Atlantic Ocean 98
Cape York Peninsula Austr. 115 D1
Cap-Haïtien Haiti 145 C3
Capim r. Brazil 151 E3
Capitol Hill N. Mariana Is 71 D1
Čaplijna Bos.-Herz. 63 C2
Capo d'Orlando Italy 62 B3
Capraia, Isola di i. Italy 62 A2
Caprara, Punta c. Italy 62 A2
Capri, Isola di i. Italy 62 B2
Caprivi Strip reg. Namibia 106 B1
Caquetá r. Col. 150 C3
Caracal Romania 44 B3
Caracas Venez. 150 C1
Caracol Brazil 151 E3
Caraguatatuba Brazil 155 C2
Carahue Chile 153 A4
Caraí Brazil 155 D1
Carangola Brazil 155 D2
Caraquet Can. 129 D2
Caratasca, Laguna de lag. Hond. 144 B3
Caratinga Brazil 155 D1
Carauari Brazil 150 C3
Caravaca de la Cruz Spain 61 C2
Caravelas Brazil 155 E1
Carberry Can. 127 F3
Carbó Mex. 142 A2
Carbonara, Capo c. Italy 62 A3
Carbondale CO U.S.A. 134 B3
Carbondale IL U.S.A. 136 C3
Carbonear Can. 129 E2
Carbonita Brazil 155 D1
Carcaixent Spain 61 C2
Carcassonne France 58 C3

Carcross Can. 126 B1
Cárdenas Mex. 143 C3
Cardiff U.K. 53 B4
Cardigan U.K. 53 A3
Cardigan Bay U.K. 53 A3
Cardston Can. 132 D1
Carei Romania 44 B2
Carentan France 58 B2
Carey, Lake salt flat Austr. 114 B2
Cargados Carajos Islands
    Mauritius 97
Cariacica Brazil 155 D2
Caribbean Sea N. Atlantic Ocean 144 B3
Cariboo r. U.S.A. 137 G1
Caribou Lake Can. 128 B1
Caribou Mountains Can. 126 D2
Carichic Mex. 142 B2
Carignan France 54 B3
Carinda Austr. 117 D2
Cariñena Spain 61 C1
Carleton Place Can. 128 C2
Carletonville S. Africa 109 C2
Carlingford Lough inlet
    Rep. of Ireland/U.K. 51 C1
Carlisle U.K. 52 B2
Carlisle U.S.A. 137 D2
Carlos Chagas Brazil 155 D1
Carlow Rep. of Ireland 51 C2
Carlsbad CA U.S.A. 133 C4
Carlsbad NM U.S.A. 140 D2
Carlyle Can. 134 C1
Carmacks Can. 126 B1
Carman Can. 127 F3
Carmarthen U.K. 53 A4
Carmarthen Bay U.K. 53 A4
Carmaux France 58 C3
Carmelita Guat. 143 C3
Carmen, Isla i. Mex. 142 A2
Carnac France 58 B2
Carnarvon S. Africa 108 B3
Carndonagh Rep. of Ireland 51 C1
Carnegie, Lake salt flat Austr. 114 B2
Carn Eighe mt. U.K. 50 B2
Car Nicobar i. India 75 A3
Carnot C.A.R. 104 B2
Carnsore Point pt Rep. of Ireland 51 C2
Carolina Brazil 151 E3
Caroline Island atoll Kiribati 111
Caroline Islands N. Pacific Ocean 71 D2
Carpathian Mountains Europe 44 A2
Carpaţii Meridionali mts Romania see
    Transylvanian Alps
Carpentaria, Gulf of Austr. 115 C1
Carpentras France 59 D3
Carrantuohill mt. Rep. of Ireland 51 B3
Carrara Italy 59 E3
Carrickmacross Rep. of Ireland 51 C2
Carrick-on-Shannon Rep. of Ireland 51 B2
Carrick-on-Suir Rep. of Ireland 51 C2
Carrington U.S.A. 135 D1
Carrizo Springs U.S.A. 141 E3
Carrizozo U.S.A. 140 C2
Carroll U.S.A. 135 D2
Carrollton U.S.A. 139 C2
Carrot River Can. 127 E2
Carson City U.S.A. 133 C3
Cartagena Col. 150 B1
Cartagena Spain 61 C2
Cartago Costa Rica 144 B4
Carthage MO U.S.A. 135 E3
Carthage TX U.S.A. 141 F2
Cartwright Can. 129 E1
Caruaru Brazil 151 F3
Casablanca Morocco 100 B1
Casa Branca Brazil 154 C2

Casa de Janos Mex. 142 B1
Casa Grande U.S.A. 140 B2
Casale Monferrato Italy 62 A1
Casarano Italy 63 C2
Cascade U.S.A. 132 C2
Cascade Range mts Can./U.S.A. 132 B2
Cascais Port. 60 B2
Cascavel Brazil 154 B2
Caserta Italy 62 B2
Cashel Rep. of Ireland 51 C2
Casino Austr. 117 E1
Caspe Spain 61 C1
Casper U.S.A. 134 B2
Caspian Lowland Kazakh./Rus. Fed. 88 B2
Caspian Sea l. Asia/Europe 88 B2
Cassel France 54 A2
Cássia Brazil 154 C2
Cassiar Can. 126 C2
Cassiar Mountains Can. 126 B2
Cassilândia Brazil 154 B1
Cassino Italy 62 B2
Cassley r. U.K. 50 B2
Castanhal Brazil 151 E3
Castaño r. Arg. 152 B4
Castaños Mex. 142 B2
Casteljaloux France 58 C3
Castelló de la Plana Spain 61 C2
Castelo Branco Port. 60 B2
Castelvetrano Italy 62 B3
Casterton Austr. 116 C3
Castiglione della Pescaia Italy 62 B2
Castlebar Rep. of Ireland 51 B2
Castlebay U.K. 50 A2
Castleblayney Rep. of Ireland 51 C1
Castlederg U.K. 51 C1
Castle Douglas U.K. 50 C3
Castlegar Can. 126 D3
Castleisland Rep. of Ireland 51 B2
Castlemaine Austr. 116 C3
Castle Mountain Can. 126 B1
Castlerea Rep. of Ireland 51 B2
Castlereagh r. Austr. 117 D2
Castle Rock U.S.A. 134 C3
Castor Can. 127 D2
Castres France 58 C3
Castricum Neth. 54 B1
Castries St Lucia 145 D3
Castro Brazil 154 C2
Castro Chile 153 A5
Castro Verde Port. 60 B2
Castrovillari Italy 63 C3
Catacaos Peru 150 A3
Cataguases Brazil 155 D2
Catalão Brazil 154 C1
Cataluña aut. comm. Spain 61 D1
Catamarca Arg. 152 B3
Catanduanes i. Phil. 76 B2
Catanduva Brazil 154 C2
Catania Italy 62 C3
Catanzaro Italy 63 C3
Catarman Phil. 76 B2
Catbalogan Phil. 76 B2
Catemaco Mex. 143 C3
Catherine, Mount Egypt see
    Kātrīnā, Jabal
Cat Island Bahamas 145 C2
Cat Lake Can. 128 A1
Catoche, Cabo c. Mex. 143 D2
Catskill Mountains U.S.A. 137 F2
Cauayan Phil. 76 B3
Caubvick, Mount Can. 129 D1
Cauca r. Col. 150 B2
Caucaia Brazil 151 F3
Caucasus mts Asia/Europe 93 C3
Caudry France 54 A2
Caulonia Italy 63 C3
Causapscal Can. 129 D2

availlon France **59** D3
avalcante Brazil **151** E4
avernoso, Serra de *mts* Brazil **154** B3
axias Brazil **151** E3
axias do Sul Brazil **152** C3
axito Angola **104** B3
ayenne Fr. Guiana **151** D2
ayman Islands *terr.* West Indies **144** B3
aynabo Somalia **103** C4
azombo Angola **106** B1
eballos Mex. **142** B2
ebu Phil. **76** B2
ebu *i.* Phil. **76** B2
ecina Italy **62** B2
edar *r.* U.S.A. **136** D2
edar City U.S.A. **133** D3
edar Falls U.S.A. **135** E2
edar Lake Can. **127** E2
edar Rapids U.S.A. **135** E2
edros, Isla *i.* Mex. **142** A2
eduna Austr. **114** C3
eeldheere Somalia **103** D3
eerigaabo Somalia **103** D3
efalû Italy **62** B3
elaya Mex. **143** D2
elebes *i.* Indon. **73** D2
elebes Sea Indon./Phil. **70** C2
elestún Mex. **143** C2
elle Ger. **55** E1
eltic Sea Rep. of Ireland/U.K. **49** B3
enderawasih, Teluk *b.* Indon. **71** D3
entral, Cordillera *mts* Col. **150** B2
entral, Cordillera *mts* Peru **150** B3
entral, Cordillera *mts* Phil. **76** B2
entral African Republic *country* Africa **104** C2
entral Brahui Range *mts* Pak. **86** A2
entral City U.S.A. **135** D2
entralia *IL* U.S.A. **136** C3
entralia *WA* U.S.A. **132** B1
entral Makran Range *mts* Pak. **86** A2
entral Range *mts* P.N.G. **71** D3
entral Russian Upland *hills* Rus. Fed. **43** E3
entral Siberian Plateau Rus. Fed. **95** J2
ephalonia *i.* Greece **65** B3
ram Sea Indon. *see* Seram, Laut
eres Arg. **152** B3
eres S. Africa **108** A3
eret France **59** C3
erezo de Abajo Spain **60** C1
erignola Italy **62** C2
ernavodă Romania **44** C3
erralvo Mex. **143** C2
erralvo, Isla *i.* Mex. **142** B2
erritos Mex. **143** B2
erro Azul Brazil **154** C2
erro Azul Peru **150** B4
ervione France **59** C3
evo Spain **60** B1
esena Italy **62** B2
esis Latvia **42** C2
eské Budějovice Czech Rep. **56** C3
eský Les *mts* Czech Rep./Ger. **55** F3
eşme Turkey **65** C3
essnock Austr. **117** E2
etinje Serb. and Mont. **64** A2
etraro Italy **63** C3
euta N. Africa **60** B2
evennes *mts* France **59** C3
ěžabhár Iran **91** D2
eyabyêr Caka *salt l.* China **87** C1
achapoyas Peru **150** B3

Chachersk Belarus **43** D3
Chachoengsao Thai. **75** B2
Chad *country* Africa **101** D3
Chadaasan Mongolia **80** C1
Chadan Rus. Fed. **89** G1
Chadron U.S.A. **134** C2
Chaeryŏng N. Korea **77** B2
Chagai Pak. **86** A2
Chaghcharān Afgh. **86** A1
Chagny France **56** A3
Chagoda Rus. Fed. **43** E2
Chagos Archipelago *is* B.I.O.T. **66**
Chagyl Turkm. **88** C2
Chaibasa India **87** C2
Chainat Thai. **75** B2
Chaiyaphum Thai. **75** B2
Chajarí Arg. **152** C4
Chakonipau, Lac *l.* Can. **129** D1
Chala Peru **150** B4
Chalap Dalan *mts* Afgh. **86** A1
Chaleur Bay *inlet* Can. **129** D2
Chalisgaon India **86** B2
Chalki *i.* Greece **65** C3
Chalkida Greece **65** B3
Challans France **58** B2
Challenger Deep *sea feature* N. Pacific Ocean **158** C4
Challis U.S.A. **132** D2
Châlons-en-Champagne France **59** C2
Chalon-sur-Saône France **59** C2
Cham Ger. **55** F3
Chama U.S.A. **140** C1
Chama Zambia **107** C1
Chaman Pak. **86** A1
Chamba India **86** B1
Chambal *r.* India **86** B2
Chamberlain U.S.A. **135** D2
Chambersburg U.S.A. **137** E3
Chambéry France **59** D2
Chambeshi Zambia **107** C1
Champaign U.S.A. **136** C2
Champlain, Lake Can./U.S.A. **128** C2
Champotón Mex. **143** C3
Chañaral Chile **152** A3
Chandalar *r.* U.S.A. **124** C2
Chandeleur Islands U.S.A. **138** C3
Chandigarh India **86** B1
Chandler U.S.A. **140** B2
Chandrapur India **87** B3
Chang, Ko *i.* Thai. **75** B2
Changane *r.* Moz. **107** C2
Changara Moz. **107** C2
Changbai China **77** B1
Changbai Shan *mts* China/N. Korea **77** B1
Changchun China **77** B1
Changde China **83** B3
Ch'angdo N. Korea **77** B2
Changhua Taiwan **83** C3
Changhŭng S. Korea **77** B3
Chang Jiang *r.* China *see* Yangtze
Changjin N. Korea **77** B1
Changjin-gang *r.* N. Korea **77** B1
Changsha China **83** B3
Changsŏng S. Korea **77** B3
Changting China **83** B3
Ch'angwŏn S. Korea **77** B2
Changyuan China **82** B2
Changzhi China **82** B2
Changzhou China **82** B2
Chania Greece **65** B3
Channel Islands English Chan. **53** B5
Channel Islands U.S.A. **133** C4
Channel-Port-aux-Basques Can. **129** E2
Chanthaburi Thai. **75** B2
Chantilly France **58** C2

Chanute U.S.A. **135** D3
Chany, Ozero *salt l.* Rus. Fed. **89** E1
Chaouèn Morocco **60** B2
Chaoyang *Guangdong* China **83** B3
Chaoyang *Liaoning* China **82** C1
Chaozhou China **83** B3
Chapala, Laguna de *l.* Mex. **142** B2
Chapayev Kazakh. **88** C1
Chapecó Brazil **154** B3
Chapel Hill U.S.A. **139** E1
Chapleau Can. **128** B2
Chaplygin Rus. Fed. **43** E3
Chaplynka Ukr. **45** D2
Charcas Mex. **143** B2
Chard U.K. **53** B4
Chardzhev Turkm. *see* Turkmenabat
Charente *r.* France **58** B2
Chārīkār Afgh. **86** A1
Charkayuvom Rus. Fed. **40** E2
Charleroi Belgium **54** E2
Charles, Cape U.S.A. **137** E3
Charles City U.S.A. **135** E2
Charleston *IL* U.S.A. **136** C3
Charleston *SC* U.S.A. **139** E2
Charleston *WV* U.S.A. **136** D3
Charleston Peak U.S.A. **133** C3
Charleville Austr. **115** D2
Charleville-Mézières France **59** C2
Charlotte U.S.A. **139** D1
Charlotte Harbor *b.* U.S.A. **139** D3
Charlottesville U.S.A. **137** E3
Charlottetown Can. **129** D2
Charlton Austr. **116** C3
Charlton Island Can. **128** C1
Charozero Rus. Fed. **43** E1
Charters Towers Austr. **115** D2
Chartres France **58** C2
Chase Can. **126** D2
Chashniki Belarus **42** C3
Chasŏng N. Korea **77** B1
Chassiron, Pointe de *pt* France **58** B2
Châteaubriant France **58** B2
Château-du-Loir France **58** C2
Châteaudun France **58** C2
Châteauneuf-les-Martigues France **59** D3
Châteauneuf-sur-Loire France **58** C2
Château-Thierry France **59** C2
Chateh Can. **126** D2
Châtelet Belgium **54** E2
Châtellerault France **58** C2
Chatham Can. **136** C2
Chatham Islands N.Z. **111**
Châtillon-sur-Seine France **59** C2
Chattahoochee *r.* U.S.A. **139** D2
Chattanooga U.S.A. **139** C1
Châu Đôc Vietnam **75** B2
Chauk Myanmar **74** A1
Chaumont France **59** D2
Chauny France **59** C2
Chaves Brazil **151** E3
Chaves Port. **60** B1
Chavigny, Lac *l.* Can. **128** C1
Chavusy Belarus **43** D3
Chayevo Rus. Fed. **43** E2
Chaykovskiy Rus. Fed. **40** E3
Cheb Czech Rep. **56** C2
Cheboksary Rus. Fed. **41** D3
Chebovgan U.S.A. **136** D1
Chech'ŏn S. Korea **77** B2
Chegga Maur. **100** B2
Chehalis U.S.A. **132** B1
Cheju S. Korea **77** B3
Cheju-do *i.* S. Korea **77** B3
Cheju-haehyŏp *sea chan.* S. Korea **77** B3
Chekhov Rus. Fed. **43** E2
Chelan, Lake U.S.A. **132** B1
Cheleken Turkm. **93** D2

Chelghoum el Aïd Alg. **61** E2
Chélif, Oued r. Alg. **61** D2
Chełm Pol. **57** D2
Chełmno Pol. **57** D2
Chelmsford U.K. **53** D4
Cheltenham U.K. **53** B4
Chelyabinsk Rus. Fed. **41** F3
Chemnitz Ger. **55** F2
Chemachane Alg. **100** B2
Chengde China **82** B1
Chengdu China **82** A2
Chengmai China **83** B4
Chengxian China **82** A2
Chennai India **85** C3
Chenzhou China **83** B3
Chepstow U.K. **53** B4
Cherbourg France **58** B2
Cheremisinovo Rus. Fed. **43** E3
Cheremkhovo Rus. Fed. **80** C1
Cherepovets Rus. Fed. **43** E2
Cherkasy Ukr. **45** D2
Cherkessk Rus. Fed. **41** D4
Chernihiv Ukr. **45** D1
Cherninivka Ukr. **45** E2
Chernivtsi Ukr. **44** C1
Chernyakhiv Ukr. **44** C1
Chernyakhovsk Rus. Fed. **42** B3
Chernyanka Rus. Fed. **43** E3
Chernyshevskiy Rus. Fed. **95** J2
Chernyshkovskiy Rus. Fed. **45** F2
Cherokee U.S.A. **135** D2
Cherskogo, Khrebet mts Rus. Fed. **95** L2
Chertkovo Rus. Fed. **45** F2
Chervonohrad Ukr. **44** B1
Chervyen' Belarus **43** D3
Cherykaw Belarus **43** D3
Chesapeake Bay U.S.A. **137** E3
Cheshskaya Guba b. Rus. Fed. **40** D2
Chester U.K. **53** B3
Chester IL U.S.A. **136** C3
Chester SC U.S.A. **139** D2
Chesterfield U.K. **53** C2
Chesterfield, Îles is New Caledonia **115** E1
Chesterfield Inlet Can. **127** F1
Chesterfield Inlet inlet Can. **127** F1
Chesuncook Lake U.S.A. **137** G1
Chéticamp Can. **129** D2
Chetumal Mex. **143** D3
Chetwynd Can. **126** C2
Cheviot Hills U.K. **52** B2
Cheyenne r. U.S.A. **134** C2
Cheyenne r. U.S.A. **134** C2
Cheyenne Wells U.S.A. **134** C3
Chhapra India **87** C2
Chhatarpur India **87** B2
Chiai Taiwan **83** C3
Chiang Dao Thai. **74** A2
Chiang Mai Thai. **74** A2
Chiang Rai Thai. **74** A2
Chiavenno Italy **62** A1
Chibi China **83** B3
Chiboma Moz. **107** C2
Chibougamau Can. **128** C2
Chibuto Moz. **109** D1
Chicago U.S.A. **136** C2
Chichagof Island U.S.A. **126** B2
Chichester U.K. **53** C4
Chichester Range mts Austr. **114** A2
Chickasha U.S.A. **141** E1
Chiclayo Peru **150** B3
Chico r. Arg. **153** B5
Chico U.S.A. **133** B3
Chicoutimi Can. **129** C2
Chidley, Cape Can. **121**
Chieti Italy **62** B2
Chietla Mex. **143** C3
Chifeng China **82** B1
Chifre, Serra do mts Brazil **155** D1

Chiganak Kazakh. **89** E2
Chignahuapán Mex. **143** C3
Chigubo Moz. **107** C2
Chigu Co l. China **74** D1
Chihuahua Mex. **142** B2
Chikhachevo Rus. Fed. **42** C2
Chikuma-gawa r. Japan **79** C3
Chilanko r. Can. **126** C2
Chilas Jammu and Kashmir **86** B1
Childress U.S.A. **141** D2
Chile country S. America **152** A4
Chilecito Arg. **152** B3
Chilika Lake India **87** C3
Chililabombwe Zambia **106** B1
Chilko r. Can. **126** C2
Chilko Lake Can. **126** C2
Chillán Chile **153** A4
Chillicothe MO U.S.A. **135** E3
Chillicothe OH U.S.A. **136** D3
Chilliwack Can. **126** C3
Chiloé, Isla de i. Chile **153** A5
Chilpancingo Mex. **143** C3
Chiltern Austr. **117** D3
Chilung Taiwan **83** C3
Chimala Tanz. **105** D3
Chimbas Arg. **152** B4
Chimborazo mt. Ecuador **150** B3
Chimbote Peru **150** B3
Chimboy Uzbek. **88** C2
Chimoio Moz. **107** C1
Chimtargha, Qullai mt. Tajik. **89** D3
China country Asia **80** B2
China Mex. **143** C3
Chincha Alta Peru **150** B4
Chinchaga r. Can. **126** C2
Chinchorro, Banco sea feature Mex. **143** D3
Chinde Moz. **107** C1
Chindo S. Korea **77** B3
Chin-do i. S. Korea **77** B3
Chindu China **80** C2
Chindwin r. Myanmar **74** A1
Chinghwa N. Korea **77** B2
Chingola Zambia **106** B1
Chinguar Angola **106** A1
Chinhae S. Korea **77** B2
Chinhoyi Zimbabwe **107** C1
Chiniot Pak. **86** B1
Chinipas Mex. **142** B2
Chinju S. Korea **77** B2
Chinko r. C.A.R. **104** C2
Chinle U.S.A. **140** C1
Chinmen Taiwan **83** B3
Chino Japan **79** C3
Chinon France **58** C2
Chino Valley U.S.A. **140** B2
Chinsali Zambia **105** D4
Chioggia Italy **62** B1
Chios Greece **65** C3
Chios i. Greece **65** C3
Chipata Zambia **107** C1
Chipindo Angola **106** A1
Chipinge Zimbabwe **107** C2
Chiplun India **85** B3
Chippenham U.K. **53** B4
Chipping Norton U.K. **53** C4
Chir r. Rus. Fed. **45** F2
Chirchiq Uzbek. **89** D2
Chiredzi Zimbabwe **107** C2
Chiricahua Peak U.S.A. **140** C2
Chiriquí, Golfo de b. Panama **144** B4
Chiri-san mt. S. Korea **77** B2
Chirripó mt. Costa Rica **144** B4
Chirundu Zimbabwe **107** B1
Chisasibi Can. **128** C1
Chisholm U.S.A. **135** E1
Chişinău Moldova **44** C2
Chistopol' Rus. Fed. **41** E3
Chita Rus. Fed. **81** D1
Chitato Angola **106** A1

Chitambo Zambia **107** C1
Chitato Angola **104** C3
Chitipa Malawi **105** D3
Chitradurga India **85** B3
Chitral Pak. **86** B1
Chitré Panama **144** B4
Chittagong Bangl. **87** D2
Chittaurgarh India **86** B2
Chitungwiza Zimbabwe **107** C1
Chiume Angola **106** B1
Chivhu Zimbabwe **107** C1
Chizhou China **83** A3
Chkalovsk Rus. Fed. **43** F2
Choele Choel Arg. **153** B4
Choiseul i. Solomon Is **110**
Choix Mex. **142** B2
Chojnice Pol. **57** D2
Ch'ok'ē Mountains Eth. **103** B3
Chokurdakh Rus. Fed. **95** L2
Chókwé Moz. **107** C2
Cholet France **58** B2
Chomutov Czech Rep. **56** C2
Chona r. Rus. Fed. **95** J2
Ch'ŏnan S. Korea **77** B2
Chone Ecuador **150** A3
Ch'ŏngjin N. Korea **77** B1
Chŏngju N. Korea **77** B2
Chŏngp'yŏng N. Korea **77** B2
Chongqing China **83** A3
Chongqing mun. China **82** A2
Chŏngŭp S. Korea **77** B2
Chongzuo China **83** A3
Chŏnju S. Korea **77** B2
Chonos, Archipiélago de los is Chile **153** A5
Chopimzinho Brazil **154** B3
Chorley U.K. **52** B3
Chornomors'ke Ukr. **45** D2
Chortkiv Ukr. **44** C2
Ch'ŏrwŏn S. Korea **77** B2
Ch'osan N. Korea **77** B1
Chōshi Japan **79** D3
Choszczno Pol. **57** D2
Choûm Maur. **100** A2
Choybalsan Mongolia **81** D1
Choyr Mongolia **81** D1
Christchurch N.Z. **118** B3
Christchurch U.K. **53** C4
Christian, Cape Can. **125** H2
Christiana S. Africa **109** C2
Christina, Mount N.Z. **118** A3
Christmas Island terr. Indian Ocean **70** B3
Chrysi i. Greece **65** C4
Chubut r. Arg. **153** B5
Chudniv Ukr. **44** C1
Chudovo Rus. Fed. **43** D2
Chugach Mountains U.S.A. **124** C2
Chūgoku-sanchi mts Japan **79** B4
Chuguyevka Rus. Fed. **78** B2
Chuhuyiv Ukr. **45** E2
Chukchi Sea Rus. Fed./U.S.A. **95** O2
Chukhloma Rus. Fed. **43** F2
Chukotskiy Poluostrov pen. Rus. Fed. **95** O2
Chula Vista U.S.A. **133** C4
Chulym Rus. Fed. **94** H3
Chumbicha Arg. **152** B3
Chumikan Rus. Fed. **95** L3
Chumphon Thai. **75** A2
Ch'unch'ŏn S. Korea **77** B2
Chungking China see Chongqing
Chunya r. Rus. Fed. **95** I2
Chuquibamba Peru **150** B4
Chuquicamata Chile **152** B3
Chur Switz. **59** D2
Churachandpur India **74** A1
Churchill Can. **127** F2
Churchill r. Man. Can. **127** F2
Churchill r. Nfld. and Lab. Can. **129** D

Churchill, Cape Can. **127** F2
Churchill Falls Can. **129** D1
Churchill Lake Can. **127** C2
Churu India **86** B2
Chute-des-Passes Can. **129** C2
Chuuk *is* Micronesia **110**
Ciadîr-Lunga Moldova **44** C2
Ciamis Indon. **72** B2
Cianjur Indon. **72** B2
Cianorte Brazil **154** B2
Ciechanów Pol. **57** E2
Ciego de Ávila Cuba **144** C2
Cienfuegos Cuba **144** B2
Cieza Spain **61** C2
Cigüela *r.* Spain **60** C2
Cihanbeyli Turkey **92** B2
Cihuatlán Mex. **142** B3
Cilacap Indon. **72** B2
Cimarron *r.* U.S.A. **141** E1
Cimişlia Moldova **44** C2
Cimone, Monte *mt.* Italy **62** B2
Cincinnati U.S.A. **136** D3
Cine Turkey **65** C3
Ciney Belgium **54** B2
Cintalapa Mex. **143** C3
Circle *AK* U.S.A. **124** C2
Circle *MT* U.S.A. **134** B1
Cirebon Indon. **72** B2
Cirò Marina Italy **63** C3
Čitluk Bos.-Herz. **63** C2
Citrusdal S. Africa **108** A3
Città di Castello Italy **59** E3
Ciudad Acuña Mex. **142** B2
Ciudad Altamirano Mex. **143** B3
Ciudad Bolívar Venez. **150** C2
Ciudad Camargo Mex. **142** B2
Ciudad Constitución Mex. **142** A2
Ciudad del Carmen Mex. **143** C3
Ciudad Delicias Mex. see
Delicias
Ciudad de Valles Mex. **143** C2
Ciudad Guayana Venez. **150** C2
Ciudad Guerrero Mex. **140** C3
Ciudad Guzmán Mex. **142** B3
Ciudad Hidalgo Mex. **143** C3
Ciudad Ixtepec Mex. **143** C3
Ciudad Juárez Mex. **142** B1
Ciudad Mante Mex. **143** C2
Ciudad Mier Mex. **143** C2
Ciudad Obregón Mex. **142** B2
Ciudad Real Spain **60** C2
Ciudad Río Bravo Mex. **143** C2
Ciudad Rodrigo Spain **60** B1
Ciudad Victoria Mex. **143** C2
Ciutadella de Menorca Spain **61** D1
Civan Dağ *mt.* Turkey **65** C3
Cividale del Friuli Italy **62** B1
Civitanova Marche Italy **62** B2
Civitavecchia Italy **62** B2
Civray France **58** C2
Çivril Turkey **65** C3
Cixi China **83** C2
Clacton-on-Sea U.K. **53** D4
Claire, Lake Can. **127** D2
Clamecy France **59** C2
Clanwilliam S. Africa **108** A3
Clare Austr. **116** B2
Clare Island Rep. of Ireland **51** A2
Claremont U.S.A. **137** F2
Claremorris Rep. of Ireland **51** B2
Clarence N.Z. **118** B3
Clarenville Can. **129** E2
Clareshoim Can. **126** D2
Clarinda U.S.A. **135** D2
Clarión, Isla *i.* Mex. **142** A3
Clarkebury S. Africa **109** C3
Clarkebury S. Africa **109** C3

Clark Hill Reservoir U.S.A. **139** D2
Clarksburg U.S.A. **137** D3
Clarksdale U.S.A. **138** B2
Clarksville *AR* U.S.A. **138** B1
Clarksville *TN* U.S.A. **138** C1
Claro *r.* Brazil **154** B1
Clayton U.S.A. **141** D1
Clear, Cape Rep. of Ireland **51** B3
Cleare, Cape U.S.A. **124** C3
Clear Lake U.S.A. **135** E2
Clear Lake *l.* U.S.A. **133** B3
Clearwater Can. **126** D2
Clearwater U.S.A. **139** D3
Clearwater *r.* Can. **127** D2
Clearwater *r.* U.S.A. **132** C1
Cleburne U.S.A. **141** E2
Clermont Austr. **115** D2
Clermont U.S.A. **139** D3
Clermont-en-Argonne France **54** B3
Clermont-Ferrand France **58** C2
Cleve Austr. **116** B2
Cleveland *MS* U.S.A. **138** B2
Cleveland *OH* U.S.A. **136** D2
Cleveland *TN* U.S.A. **138** C1
Cleveland, Mount U.S.A. **132** D1
Clewiston U.S.A. **139** D3
Clifden Rep. of Ireland **51** A2
Clifton Austr. **117** E1
Clifton U.S.A. **140** C2
Clinton Can. **126** C2
Clinton *IA* U.S.A. **135** E2
Clinton *MO* U.S.A. **135** E3
Clinton *OK* U.S.A. **141** E1
Clisham *h.* U.K. **50** A2
Clitheroe U.K. **52** B3
Clonakilty Rep. of Ireland **51** B3
Cloncurry Austr. **115** D2
Clones Rep. of Ireland **51** C1
Clonmel Rep. of Ireland **51** C2
Cloppenburg Ger. **54** D1
Cloud Peak U.S.A. **134** B2
Clovis U.S.A. **141** D2
Cluff Lake Mine Can. **127** E2
Cluj-Napoca Romania **44** B2
Cluny Austr. **115** C2
Cluses France **59** D2
Clutha *r.* N.Z. **118** A4
Clyde *r.* U.K. **50** B3
Clyde, Firth of *est.* U.K. **50** B3
Clydebank U.K. **50** B3
Clyde River Can. **125** H2
Coalcomán Mex. **142** B3
Coaldale U.S.A. **133** C3
Coal River Can. **126** C2
Coari Brazil **150** C3
Coari *r.* Brazil **150** C3
Coastal Plain U.S.A. **138** D2
Coast Mountains Can. **126** C2
Coast Ranges *mts* U.S.A. **132** B2
Coatbridge U.K. **50** B3
Coats Island Can. **127** G1
Coats Land *reg.* Antarctica **119** A2
Coatzacoalcos Mex. **143** C3
Cobán Guat. **144** A3
Cobar Austr. **117** D2
Cóbh Rep. of Ireland **51** B3
Cobija Bol. **152** B2
Cobourg Can. **137** E2
Cobourg Peninsula Austr. **114** C1
Cobram Austr. **117** D3
Coburg Ger. **55** E2
Cochabamba Bol. **152** B2
Cochem Ger. **54** C2
Cochin India **85** B4
Cochrane Can. **128** B2
Cochrane Chile **153** A5
Cockburn Austr. **116** C2
Cockburn Town Turks and Caicos Is
see Grand Turk
Cockermouth U.K. **52** B2
Cockscomb *mt.* S. Africa **108** B3

Coco *r.* Hond./Nic. **144** B3
Cocos Islands *terr.* Indian Ocean **70** A3
Cocula Mex. **142** B2
Cocuy, Sierra Nevada del *mt.* Col. **150** B2
Cod, Cape U.S.A. **137** F2
Codigoro Italy **62** B2
Cod Island Can. **129** D1
Codó Brazil **151** E3
Cody U.S.A. **134** B2
Coen Austr. **115** D1
Coesfeld Ger. **54** C2
Coeur d'Alene U.S.A. **132** C1
Coffee Bay S. Africa **109** C3
Coffeyville U.S.A. **135** D3
Coffs Harbour Austr. **117** E2
Cognac France **58** B2
Cogo Equat. Guinea **104** A2
Cohuna Austr. **116** C3
Coiba, Isla de *i.* Panama **144** B4
Coihaique Chile **153** A5
Coimbatore India **85** B3
Coimbra Port. **60** B1
Colac Austr. **116** C3
Colatina Brazil **155** D1
Colby U.S.A. **134** C3
Colchester U.K. **53** D4
Cold Lake Can. **127** D2
Coldstream U.K. **50** C3
Coleman U.S.A. **141** E2
Coleraine Austr. **116** C3
Coleraine U.K. **51** C1
Coles, Punta de *pt* Peru **146**
Colesberg S. Africa **109** C3
Colima Mex. **142** B3
Colima, Nevado de *vol.* Mex. **142** B3
Coll *i.* U.K. **50** A2
Collarenebri Austr. **117** D1
Collier Bay Austr. **114** B1
Collingwood N.Z. **118** B3
Collo Alg. **61** E2
Collooney Rep. of Ireland **51** B1
Colmar France **59** D2
Cologne Ger. **54** C2
Colômbia Brazil **154** C2
Colombia *country* S. America **150** B2
Colombo Sri Lanka **85** B4
Colomiers France **58** C3
Colón Arg. **152** C4
Colón Panama **144** C4
Colonna, Capo *c.* Italy **63** C3
Colonsay *i.* U.K. **50** A2
Colorado *r.* Arg. **153** B4
Colorado *r.* Mex./U.S.A. **140** A2
Colorado *r.* U.S.A. **141** E3
Colorado *state* U.S.A. **134** B3
Colorado Plateau U.S.A. **134** B3
Colorado Springs U.S.A. **134** C3
Colotlán Mex. **142** B2
Cölpin Ger. **55** F1
Colstrip U.S.A. **134** B1
Columbia *MO* U.S.A. **135** E3
Columbia *SC* U.S.A. **139** D2
Columbia *TN* U.S.A. **138** C1
Columbia *r.* U.S.A. **132** B1
Columbia, Mount U.S.A. **126** D2
Columbia Falls U.S.A. **132** D1
Columbia Mountains Can. **126** C2
Columbia Plateau U.S.A. **132** C1
Columbus *GA* U.S.A. **139** D2
Columbus *IN* U.S.A. **136** C3
Columbus *MS* U.S.A. **138** C2
Columbus *NE* U.S.A. **135** D2
Columbus *NM* U.S.A. **140** C2
Columbus *OH* U.S.A. **136** D3
Colville U.S.A. **132** C1
Colville *r.* U.S.A. **124** B2
Colville Lake Can. **124** C2
Colwyn Bay U.K. **52** B3
Comacchio Italy **62** B2

Comalcalco Mex. **143** C3
Comăneşti Romania **44** C2
Combles France **54** A2
Comencho, Lac *l.* Can. **128** C1
Comeragh Mountains Rep. of Ireland **51** C2
Comilla Bangl. **87** D2
Comines Belgium **54** A2
Comino, Capo *c.* Italy **62** A2
Comitán de Domínguez Mex. **143** C3
Commentry France **58** C2
Commerce U.S.A. **141** E2
Como Italy **62** A1
Como, Lake Italy **62** A1
Comodoro Rivadavia Arg. **153** B5
Comorin, Cape India **67**
Comoro Islands Africa **97**
Comoros *country* Africa **107** C1
Compiègne France **58** C2
Compostela Mex. **142** B2
Comrat Moldova **44** C2
Conakry Guinea **100** A4
Conceição da Barra Brazil **155** E1
Conceição do Araguaia Brazil **151** E3
Conceição do Mato Dentro Brazil **155** D1
Concepción Arg. **152** B3
Concepción Chile **153** A4
Concepción Mex. **142** B2
Conception, Point *pt* U.S.A. **133** B4
Conchas Brazil **154** C2
Conchas Lake U.S.A. **140** D1
Conchos *r.* Nuevo León/Tamaulipas Mex. **143** C2
Conchos *r.* Mex. **142** B2
Concord *CA* U.S.A. **133** B3
Concord *NH* U.S.A. **137** F2
Concordia Arg. **152** C4
Concordia S. Africa **108** A2
Concordia U.S.A. **135** D3
Condobolin Austr. **117** D2
Condom France **58** C3
Condon U.S.A. **132** B1
Conegliano Italy **62** B1
Conflict Group *is* P.N.G. **115** E1
Confolens France **58** C2
Congdü China **87** C2
Congo *country* Africa **104** B3
Congo *r.* Congo/Dem. Rep. Congo **104** C3
Congo *r.* Congo/Dem. Rep. Congo **97**
Congo, Democratic Republic of *country* Africa **104** C3
Congo Basin Dem. Rep. Congo **97**
Conklin Can. **127** D2
Conn, Lough *l.* Rep. of Ireland **51** B1
Connaught *reg.* Rep. of Ireland **51** B2
Connecticut *r.* U.S.A. **137** F2
Connecticut *state* U.S.A. **137** F2
Connemara *reg.* Rep. of Ireland **51** B2
Conrad U.S.A. **132** D1
Conroe U.S.A. **141** E2
Conselheiro Lafaiete Brazil **155** D2
Conselheiro Pena Brazil **155** D1
Consett U.K. **52** C2
Côn Son *i.* Vietnam **75** B3
Constanţa Romania **44** C2
Constantina Spain **60** B2
Constantine Alg. **101** C1
Contact U.S.A. **132** D2
Contamana Peru **150** B3
Contreras, Isla *i.* Chile **153** A6
Contwoyto Lake Can. **127** D1
Conway *AR* U.S.A. **138** B1
Conway *NH* U.S.A. **137** F2
Coober Pedy Austr. **116** A1
Cook, Mount N.Z. **118** B3
Cookeville U.S.A. **139** C1
Cook Inlet *sea chan.* U.S.A. **124** C2
Cook Islands S. Pacific Ocean **111**

Cook Islands *terr.* S. Pacific Ocean **113**
Cook's Harbour Can. **129** E1
Cookstown U.K. **51** C1
Cook Strait N.Z. **118** B3
Cooktown Austr. **115** D1
Coolabah Austr. **117** D2
Coolamon Austr. **117** D2
Coolangatta Austr. **117** E1
Coolgardie Austr. **114** B3
Cooma Austr. **117** D3
Coombah Austr. **116** C2
Coonabarabran Austr. **117** D2
Coonalpyn Austr. **116** B3
Coonamble Austr. **117** D2
Cooper Creek *watercourse* Austr. **116** B1
Coos Bay U.S.A. **132** B2
Cootamundra Austr. **117** D2
Copainalá Mex. **143** C3
Copala Mex. **143** C3
Copenhagen Denmark **47** C4
Copertino Italy **63** C2
Copiapó Chile **152** A3
Copper Harbor U.S.A. **136** C1
Coppermine *r.* Can. *see* Kugluktuk
Coppermine *r.* Can. **124** E2
Copperton S. Africa **108** B2
Coquimbo Chile **152** A3
Corabia Romania **44** B3
Coração de Jesus Brazil **155** D1
Coracora Peru **150** B4
Coraki Austr. **117** E1
Coral Bay Austr. **114** A2
Coral Harbour Can. **125** G2
Coral Sea S. Pacific Ocean **115** E1
Coral Sea Islands Territory *terr.* Austr. **112**
Corangamite, Lake Austr. **116** C3
Corby U.K. **53** C3
Corcovado, Golfo de *sea chan.* Chile **153** A5
Cordele U.S.A. **139** D2
Cordilleras Range *mts* Phil. **76** B3
Córdoba Arg. **152** B4
Córdoba Mex. **143** C3
Córdoba Spain **60** C2
Córdoba, Sierras de *mts* Arg. **152** B4
Cordova U.S.A. **126** A1
Corfu *i.* Greece **65** A3
Coria Spain **60** B2
Corinth Greece **65** B3
Corinth U.S.A. **138** C2
Corinth, Gulf of *sea chan.* Greece **65** B3

Corrib, Lough *l.* Rep. of Ireland **51** B2
Corrientes Arg. **152** C3
Corrientes, Cabo *c.* Arg. **146**
Corrientes, Cabo *c.* Mex. **142** B2
Corryong Austr. **117** D3
Corse *i.* France *see* Corsica
Corse, Cap *c.* France **59** D3
Corsica *i.* France **59** D3
Corsicana U.S.A. **141** E2
Corte France **59** D3
Cortegana Spain **60** B2
Cortez U.S.A. **134** B3
Cortina d'Ampezzo Italy **62** B1
Cortland U.S.A. **137** E2
Cortona Italy **62** B2
Coruche Port. **60** B2
Çoruh Turkey *see* Artvin
Çorum Turkey **92** B1
Corumbá Brazil **154** C2
Corumbá *r.* Brazil **154** C1
Corvallis U.S.A. **132** B2
Corwen U.K. **52** B3
Cosalá Mex. **142** B2
Cosamaloapan Mex. **143** C3
Cosenza Italy **63** C3
Cosne-Cours-sur-Loire France **58** C2
Costa Blanca *coastal area* Spain **61** C2
Costa Brava *coastal area* Spain **61** D1
Costa del Sol *coastal area* Spain **60** B2
Costa de Mosquitos *coastal area* Nic. **144** B3
Costa Rica Brazil **154** C1
Costa Rica *country* Central America **144** B3
Costa Rica Mex. **142** B2
Costeşti Romania **44** B3
Cotabato Phil. **76** B3
Côte d'Ivoire *country* Africa **100** B4
Cotopaxi, Volcán *vol.* Ecuador **150** B3
Cotswold Hills U.K. **53** B4
Cottage Grove U.S.A. **132** B2
Cottbus Ger. **56** C2
Coubre, Pointe de la *pt* France **58** B2
Cöüedic, Cape de Austr. **116** B3
Council Bluffs U.S.A. **135** D2
Courland Lagoon *b.* Lith./Rus. Fed. **42** B2
Courtenay Can. **126** C3
Coutances France **58** B2
Coutras France **58** B2
Couvin Belgium **54** B2
Coventry U.K. **53** C3
Covington U.S.A. **136** D3
Cowan, Lake *salt flat* Austr. **114** B3
Cowdenbeath U.K. **50** C2
Cowes Austr. **117** D3
Cowlitz *r.* U.S.A. **132** B1
Cowra Austr. **117** D2
Coxim Brazil **154** N1
Cox's Bazar Bangl. **87** D2
Coyuca de Benítez Mex. **143** B3
Cozumel Mex. **143** D2
Cozumel, Isla de *i.* Mex. **143** D2
Cradock S. Africa **109** C3
Craig U.S.A. **134** B2
Crailsheim Ger. **55** E3
Craiova Romania **44** B3
Cranberry Portage Can. **127** E2
Cranbourne Austr. **117** D3
Cranbrook Can. **126** D3
Crateús Brazil **151** E3
Crato Brazil **151** F3
Crawford U.S.A. **134** C2
Crawfordsville U.S.A. **136** C2
Crawley U.K. **53** C4
Crazy Mountains U.S.A. **132** D1
Cree *r.* Can. **127** E2
Creel Mex. **142** B2

ree Lake Can. **127** E2
reil Neth. **54** B1
rema Italy **59** D2
remona Italy **59** D2
Crès *i.* Croatia **62** F3
Creston Can. **126** D3
reston U.S.A. **135** E2
Crestview U.S.A. **138** C2
Crete *i.* Greece **65** B3
Creus, Cap de *c.* Spain **61** D1
reutzwald France **54** C3
rewe U.K. **52** B3
rianlarich U.K. **50** B2
riccieth U.K. **50** C2
Crieff U.K. **50** C2
rikvenica Croatia **62** B1
rimea *pen.* Ukr. **45** D2
rimmitschau Ger. **55** F2
rivitz Ger. **55** E1
rnomelj Slovenia **62** C1
roagh Patrick *h.* Rep. of Ireland
51 B2
roatia *country* Europe **63** C1
rocker, Banjaran *mts* Malaysia **73** C1
rockett U.S.A. **141** E2
roker Island Austr. **71** C3
romer U.K. **53** D4
romwell N.Z. **118** A4
rookston U.S.A. **135** D1
rookwell Austr. **117** D2
rosby U.S.A. **134** C1
ross City U.S.A. **139** D3
rossett U.S.A. **138** B2
ross Fell *h.* U.K. **52** B2
ross Lake Can. **127** F2
rossville U.S.A. **139** C1
rotone Italy **63** C3
rowborough U.K. **53** D4
rowley U.S.A. **138** B2
rowsnest Pass Can. **126** D3
ruz, Cabo *c.* Cuba **145** C3
ruz Alta Brazil **152** C3
ruz del Eje Arg. **152** B4
ruzeiro Brazil **155** D2
ruzeiro do Sul Brazil **150** B3
rystal City U.S.A. **141** E3
rystal Falls U.S.A. **136** C1
csongrád Hungary **57** E3
uando *r.* Angola/Zambia **106** B1
uangar Angola **106** A1
uango *r.* Angola/Dem. Rep. Congo
104 B3
uanza *r.* Angola **104** B3
uatro Ciénegas Mex. **141** D3
uauhtémoc Mex. **142** B2
uautla Mex. **143** C2
uba *country* West Indies **144** B2
ubal Angola **106** A1
ubango *r.* Angola/Namibia **106** B1
úcuta Col. **150** B2
uddalore India **85** B3
uddapah India **85** B3
uéllar Spain **60** C1
uemba Angola **106** A1
uenca Ecuador **150** B3
uenca Spain **61** C1
uenca, Serranía de *mts* Spain **61** C1
uernavaca Mex. **143** C3
uero U.S.A. **141** E3
uiabá Brazil **151** A1
uiabá *r.* Brazil **151** D4
uillin Sound *sea chan.* U.K. **50** A2
uilo Angola **104** B3
uito *r.* Angola **106** B1

Cuito Cuanavale Angola **106** A1
Cukai Malaysia **72** B1
Culcairn Austr. **117** D3
Culgoa *r.* Austr. **117** D1
Culiacán Mex. **142** B2
Culion *i.* Phil. **76** A2
Cullera Spain **61** C2
Cullman U.S.A. **138** C2
Cullybackey U.K. **51** C1
Culuene *r.* Brazil **151** D4
Cumaná Venez. **150** C1
Cumberland U.S.A. **137** E3
Cumberland *r.* U.S.A. **136** C3
Cumberland Lake Can. **127** E2
Cumberland Peninsula Can. **125** H2
Cumberland Plateau U.S.A. **139** C1
Cumberland Sound *sea chan.* Can.
125 H2
Cumbernauld U.K. **50** C3
Cumberland U.K. **50** C3
Cumnock U.K. **50** C3
Cumpas Mex. **142** B1
Cunduacán Mex. **143** C3
Cunene *r.* Angola **106** A1
Cuneo Italy **62** A2
Cunnamulla Austr. **117** D1
Cuorgnè Italy **62** A1
Cupar U.K. **50** C2
Curaçao *i.* Neth. Antilles **145** D3
Curaray *r.* Ecuador **150** B3
Curicó Chile **153** A4
Curitiba Brazil **154** D3
Curitibanos Brazil **154** B3
Curnamona Austr. **116** B2
Currie Austr. **115** D2
Curtis Island Austr. **115** E2
Curuá *r.* Brazil **151** D3
Curup Indon. **72** B2
Cururupu Brazil **151** E3
Curvelo Brazil **155** D2
Cusco Peru **150** B4
Cushing U.S.A. **141** E1
Cut Bank U.S.A. **132** D1
Cuttack India **87** C2
Cuxhaven Ger. **55** D1
Cuyo Islands Phil. **76** B2
Cuzco Peru *see* Cusco
Cyangugu Rwanda **105** C3
Cyclades *is* Greece **65** B3
Cypress Hills Can. **127** D3
Cyprus *country* Asia **102** B1
Cyprus *i.* Asia **92** B2
Czech Republic *country* Europe **56** C3
Czersk Pol. **57** D2
Częstochowa Pol. **57** D2

D

Daban China **82** B1
Dabola Guinea **100** A3
Dacca Bangl. *see* Dhaka
Dachau Ger. **54** C3
Dadu Pak. **86** A2
Daegu S. Korea *see* Taegu
Daet Phil. **76** B2
Dagana Senegal **100** A3
Dagupan Phil. **76** B2
Dahanu India **86** B3
Da Hinggan Ling *mts* China **82** B1
Dahlak Archipelago *is* Eritrea **102** C3
Dahlem Ger. **54** C2
Dahm, Ramlat *des.*
Saudi Arabia/Yemen **90** B3
Dahme Ger. **55** F2
Dahn Ger. **54** C3
Daik Indon. **72** B2
Daimiel Spain **60** C2
Dajarra Austr. **115** C2

Dakar Senegal **100** A3
Daketa Shet' *watercourse* Eth. **105** E2
Dākhilah, Wāḥāt al *oasis* Egypt
102 A2
Dakhla Oasis Egypt *see*
Dākhilah, Wāḥāt al
Dakoank India **75** A3
Dakol'ka *r.* Belarus **42** C3
Đakovica Serb. and Mont. **64** B2
Đakovo Croatia **63** C1
Dala Angola **106** B1
Dalain Hob China **80** C2
Dalälven *r.* Sweden **47** D3
Dalaman Turkey **65** C3
Dalaman *r.* Turkey **65** C3
Dalandzadgad Mongolia **80** C2
Đa Lat Vietnam **75** B2
Dalbandin Pak. **86** A2
Dalbeattie U.K. **50** C3
Dalby Austr. **117** E1
Dale *Hordaland* Norway **48** E1
Dale *Sogn og Fjordane* Norway **48** E1
Dale Hollow Lake U.S.A. **139** C1
Dalgety Austr. **117** D3
Dalhart U.S.A. **141** D1
Dalhousie Can. **137** G1
Dali China **74** B1
Dalian China **82** C2
Dalkeith U.K. **50** C3
Dallas U.S.A. **141** E2
Dall Island U.S.A. **126** B2
Dalmatia *reg.* Bos.-Herz./Croatia **63** C2
Dal'negorsk Rus. Fed. **78** C2
Dal'nerechensk Rus. Fed. **78** B1
Daloa Côte d'Ivoire **100** B4
Dalrymple, Mount Austr. **115** D2
Dalsmynni Iceland **46** [inset]
Daltenganj India **87** C2
Dalton U.S.A. **139** D2
Daludalu Indon. **72** B1
Dalvík Iceland **46** [inset]
Daly *r.* Austr. **114** C1
Daly Waters Austr. **114** C1
Daman India **86** B2
Damanhur Egypt **92** B2
Damar *i.* Indon. **71** C3
Damascus Syria **92** B2
Damaturu Nigeria **101** D3
Damghan Iran **93** D2
Dammam Saudi Arabia **91** C2
Damme Ger. **55** D1
Damoh India **87** B2
Damongo Ghana **100** B4
Dampir, Selat *sea chan.* Indon. **71** C3
Damroh India **74** A1
Damxung China **87** D1
Danané Côte d'Ivoire **100** B4
Đa Năng Vietnam **75** B2
Danbury U.S.A. **137** F2
Dandong China **82** C2
Dangriga Belize **144** B3
Dangshan China **82** B2
Danilov Rus. Fed. **43** F2
Danilovskaya Vozvyshennost' *hills*
Rus. Fed. **43** E2
Danjiangkou China **82** B2
Dankov Rus. Fed. **43** E3
Danlí Hond. **144** B3
Dannenberg (Elbe) Ger. **55** E1
Dannevirke N.Z. **118** C3
Dan Sai Thai. **74** B2
Dantu China **82** B2
Danube *r.* Austria/Ger. **56** D3
Danube *r.* Bulg./Croatia/Serb. and
Mont. **64** C2
Danube *r.* Hungary **57** D3
Danube *r.* Romania **44** C2
Danube Delta Romania/Ukr. **44** C2
Danville *Il.* U.S.A. **136** C2
Danville *KY* U.S.A. **136** D3

Danville *VA* U.S.A. **137** E3
Danzhou China **83** A4
Daoxian China **83** B3
Dapaong Togo **100** C3
Da Qaidam Zhen China **80** C2
Daqing China **81** E1
Dar'ā Syria **92** B2
Dārāb Iran **93** D3
Daraj Libya **101** D1
Dārān Iran **93** C2
Đa Răng, Sông *r.* Vietnam **75** B2
Darbhanga India **87** C2
Dar es Salaam Tanz. **105** D3
Dargai Pak. **86** B1
Dargaville N.Z. **118** B2
Dargo Austr. **117** D3
Darhan Mongolia **80** D2
Darién, Golfo del *g.* Col. **150** B2
Darjiling India **87** C2
Darlag China **80** C2
Darling *r.* Austr. **116** C2
Darling Downs *hills* Austr. **117** D1
Darling Range *hills* Austr. **114** A3
Darlington U.K. **52** C2
Darlington Point Austr. **117** D2
Darłowo Pol. **57** D2
Darmstadt Ger. **55** D3
Darnah Libya **101** E1
Darnick Austr. **116** C2
Daroca Spain **61** C1
Dartford U.K. **53** D4
Dartmoor *hills* U.K. **53** A4
Dartmouth Can. **129** D2
Dartmouth U.K. **53** B4
Daru P.N.G. **71** D3
Darvaza Turkm. **88** C2
Darwin Austr. **114** C1
Dashoguz Turkm. **88** C2
Dasht *r.* Pak. **86** A2
Datadian Indon. **73** C1
Datça Turkey **65** C3
Datong China **82** B1
Datu Piang Phil. **76** B3
Daud Khel Pak. **86** B1
Daugava *r.* Latvia **42** B2
Daugavpils Latvia **42** C2
Daun Ger. **54** C2
Dauphin Can. **127** E2
Dauphin Lake Can. **127** F2
Davangere India **85** B3
Davao Phil. **76** B3
Davao Gulf Phil. **76** B3
Davenport U.S.A. **135** E2
Daventry U.K. **53** C3
Daveyton S. Africa **109** C2
David Panama **144** B4
Davidson Can. **127** E2
Davis U.S.A. **133** B3
Davis Inlet Can. **129** D1
Davis Sea Antarctica **119** F3
Davis Strait Can./Greenland **125** I2
Davos Switz. **59** D2
Dawqah Oman **91** C3
Dawson Can. **126** B1
Dawson U.S.A. **139** D2
Dawson Creek Can. **126** C2
Dawsons Landing Can. **126** C2
Dawu China **80** C2
Dax France **58** B3
Da Xueshan *mts* China **80** C2
Dayr az Zawr Syria **92** C2
Dayton U.S.A. **136** D3
Daytona Beach U.S.A. **139** D3
Da Yunhe *canal* China **82** B2
Dazhou China **82** B2
De Aar S. Africa **108** B3
Dead Sea *salt l.* Asia **92** B2
De'an China **82** B2
Deán Funes Arg. **152** B4
Dease Lake Can. **126** C2

Death Valley *depr.* U.S.A. **133** C3
Deauville France **58** C2
Debak Malaysia **73** C1
Debar Macedonia **65** B2
Debrecen Hungary **57** E3
Debre Markos Eth. **103** B3
Debre Tabor Eth. **103** B3
Debre Zeyit Eth. **103** B4
Decatur *AL* U.S.A. **138** C2
Decatur *IL* U.S.A. **136** C3
Deccan *plat.* India **85** B3
Děčín Czech Rep. **56** C2
Decorah U.S.A. **135** E2
Dedovichi Rus. Fed. **42** C2
Dedza Malawi **107** C1
Dee *r.* England/Wales U.K. **52** B3
Dee *r.* Scotland U.K. **50** C2
Deepwater Austr. **117** E1
Deer Lake Can. **129** E2
Deer Lodge U.S.A. **132** D1
Defiance U.S.A. **136** D2
Dêgê China **80** C2
Degeh Bur Eth. **103** C4
Deggendorf Ger. **56** C3
Degtevo Rus. Fed. **45** F2
Dehra Dun India **87** B1
Dehri India **87** C2
Dehui China **81** E2
Deinze Belgium **54** A2
Dej Romania **44** B2
Dekemhare Eritrea **90** A3
Dekese Dem. Rep. Congo **104** C3
Delano U.S.A. **133** C3
Delano Peak U.S.A. **133** D3
Delap-Uliga-Djarrit Marshall Is **112**
Delārām Afgh. **86** A1
Delareyville S. Africa **109** C2
Delaronde Lake Can. **127** E2
Delaware U.S.A. **136** D2
Delaware *r.* U.S.A. **137** E3
Delaware *state* U.S.A. **137** E3
Delegate Austr. **117** D3
Delémont Switz. **59** D2
Delft Neth. **54** A1
Delfzijl Neth. **54** C1
Delgado, Cabo *c.* Moz. **105** E4
Delhi India **86** B2
Deli *i.* Indon. **72** B2
Déline Can. **126** C1
Delitzsch Ger. **55** F2
Dellys Alg. **61** D2
Delmenhorst Ger. **55** D1
Delnice Croatia **62** B1
De-Longa, Ostrova *is* Rus. Fed. **95** M1
Deloraine Can. **127** E3
Delphi *tourist site* Greece **65** B3
Del Rio U.S.A. **141** D3
Delta *CO* U.S.A. **134** B3
Delta *UT* U.S.A. **133** D3
Delta Junction U.S.A. **124** C2
Delvinë Albania **65** B3
Demanda, Sierra de la *mts* Spain **60** C1
Demba Dem. Rep. Congo **104** C3
Dembi Dolo Eth. **103** B4
Demidov Rus. Fed. **43** D2
Deming U.S.A. **140** C2
Demirci Turkey **65** C3
Demirköy Turkey **64** C2
Demmin Ger. **56** C2
Demopolis U.S.A. **138** C2
Dempo, Gunung *vol.* Indon. **72** B2
Demyansk Rus. Fed. **43** D2
De Naawte S. Africa **108** B3
Denakil *reg.* Eritrea/Eth. **103** C3
Den Burg Neth. **54** B1
Dendermonde Belgium **54** B2
Dengkou China **82** A1

Dengzhou China **82** B2
Den Haag Neth. *see* The Hague
Denham Austr. **114** A2
Den Helder Neth. **54** B1
Deniliquin Austr. **116** C3
Denio U.S.A. **132** C2
Denison *IA* U.S.A. **135** D2
Denison *TX* U.S.A. **141** E2
Denizli Turkey **65** C3
Denman Austr. **117** E2
Denmark *country* Europe **47** C4
Denmark Strait Greenland/Iceland **125** K2
Denpasar Indon. **73** C2
Denton U.S.A. **141** E2
D'Entrecasteaux, Point *pt* Austr. **114** A3
Denver U.S.A. **134** B3
Deogarh *Orissa* India **87** C2
Deogarh *Rajasthan* India **86** B2
Deoghar India **87** C2
Deoghar India **87** C2
Deoputatskiy Rus. Fed. **95** L2
Déqên China **74** A1
De Queen U.S.A. **138** B2
Dera Bugti Pak. **86** A2
Dera Ghazi Khan Pak. **86** B1
Dera Ismail Khan Pak. **86** B1
Derbent Rus. Fed. **41** D4
Derby Austr. **114** B1
Derby U.K. **52** C3
Dereham U.K. **53** D3
Derg, Lough *l.* Rep. of Ireland **51** B2
Derhachi Ukr. **45** E1
De Ridder U.S.A. **138** B2
Derkul *r.* Rus. Fed./Ukr. **45** E2
Dêrub China **87** B1
Derudeb Sudan **102** B3
De Rust S. Africa **108** B3
Derventa Bos.-Herz. **63** C2
Derwent *r.* U.K. **52** C3
Derwent Water *l.* U.K. **52** B2
Derzhavinsk Kazakh. **89** D1
Desaguadero *r.* Bol. **152** B2
Désappointement, Îles du *is* Fr. Polynesia **111**
Deschambault Lake Can. **127** E2
Deschutes *r.* U.S.A. **132** B1
Desē Eth. **103** B3
Deseado Arg. **153** B5
Deseado *r.* Arg. **153** B5
Des Moines U.S.A. **135** E2
Des Moines *r.* U.S.A. **135** D1
Desna *r.* Rus. Fed./Ukr. **45** D1
Desnogorsk Rus. Fed. **43** D3
Dessau Ger. **55** F2
Destruction Bay Can. **126** B1
Desventurados, Islas de los *is* S. Pacific Ocean **149**
Detah Can. **126** D1
Detmold Ger. **55** D2
Detroit U.S.A. **136** D2
Detroit Lakes U.S.A. **135** D1
Deurne Neth. **54** B2
Deva Romania **44** B2
Deventer Neth. **54** C1
Deveron *r.* U.K. **50** C2
Devét Skal *h.* Czech Rep. **57** D3
Devil's Lake U.S.A. **135** D1
Devil's Paw *mt.* U.S.A. **126** B2
Devizes U.K. **53** C4
Devli India **86** B2
Devnya Bulg. **64** C2
Devon Can. **126** D2
Devon Island Can. **125** F1
Devonport Austr. **115** D4
Dewas India **86** B2
Dexter U.S.A. **135** F3
Deyang China **82** A2
Deyong, Tanjung *pt* Indon. **71** D3

Dezfūl Iran **93** C2
Dezhou China **82** B2
Dhahran Saudi Arabia **91** C2
Dhaka Bangl. **87** D2
Dhamār Yemen **90** B3
Dhamtari India **87** C2
Dhanbad India **87** C2
Dhankuta Nepal **87** C2
Dharmanagar India **74** A1
Dharmjaygarh India **87** C2
Dharwad India **85** B3
Dhasa India **86** B2
Dhubāb Yemen **90** B3
Dhule India **86** B2
Diablo, Picacho del *mt.* Mex. **143** A1
Diamantina *watercourse* Austr.
    115 C2
Diamantina Brazil **155** D1
Diamantina, Chapada *plat.* Brazil
    151 E4
Diamantino Brazil **151** D4
Dianbai China **83** B3
Dianópolis Brazil **151** E4
Dianra Côte d'Ivoire **100** B4
Dibā al Ḩiṣn U.A.E. **91** C2
Dibrugarh India **84** D2
Dickinson U.S.A. **134** C1
Dickson U.S.A. **138** C1
Dicle *r.* Turkey *see* Tigris
Die France **59** D3
Diefenbaker, Lake Can. **127** E2
Diéma Mali **100** B3
Diepholz Ger. **55** D1
Dieppe France **58** C2
Diffa Niger **101** D3
Digby Can. **129** D2
Digne-les-Bains France **59** D3
Digoin France **59** C2
Digos Phil. **76** B3
Digul *r.* Indon. **71** D3
Dijlah, Nahr *r.* Iraq/Syria **66**
Dijon France **59** D2
Dikili Turkey **65** C3
Diksmuide Belgium **54** A2
Dikwa Nigeria **101** D3
Dīla Eth. **103** B4
Dili East Timor **71** C2
Dillenburg Ger. **55** D2
Dillon U.S.A. **132** D1
Dilolo Dem. Rep. Congo **104** C4
Dimapur India **74** A1
Dimashq Syria *see* Damascus
Dimboola Austr. **116** C3
Dimitrovgrad Bulg. **64** C3
Dimitrovgrad Rus. Fed. **41** D3
Dinagat *i.* Phil. **76** B2
Dinan France **58** B2
Dinant Belgium **54** B2
Dinar Turkey **92** B2
Dīnār, Kūh-e *mt.* Iran **93** D2
Dinaric Alps *mts*
    Bos.-Herz./Croatia **36**
Dindigul India **85** B3
Dindiza Moz. **109** D1
Dingelstädt Ger. **55** E2
Dingle Rep. of Ireland **51** A2
Dingle Bay Rep. of Ireland **51** A2
Dingwall U.K. **50** B2
Dingxi China **82** A2
Dinkelsbühl Ger. **55** E3
Dinngyê China **87** C2
Dionísio Cerqueira Brazil **154** B3
Diourbel Senegal **100** A3
Dipolog Phil. **76** B3
Dir Pak. **86** B1
Direction, Cape Austr. **115** D1

Dirë Dawa Eth. **103** C4
Dirico Angola **106** B1
Dirk Hartog Island Austr. **114** A2
Dirranbandi Austr. **117** D1
Dirs Saudi Arabia **90** B3
Disappointment, Cape S. Georgia
    153 E6
Disappointment, Lake *salt flat* Austr.
    114 B2
Discovery Bay Austr. **116** C3
Dismal Swamp U.S.A. **137** E3
Diss U.K. **53** D3
Dittaino *r.* Italy **62** C3
Diu India **86** B2
Divinópolis Brazil **155** D2
Divnoye Rus. Fed. **41** D4
Divo Côte d'Ivoire **100** B4
Divriği Turkey **92** C2
Dixon U.S.A. **136** C2
Dixon Entrance *sea chan.* Can./U.S.A.
    126 B2
Diyarbakır Turkey **92** C2
Diz Pak. **86** A2
Djado Niger **101** D2
Djado, Plateau du Niger **101** D2
Djamâa Alg. **101** C1
Djambala Congo **104** B3
Djanet Alg. **101** C2
Djelfa Alg. **100** C1
Djéma C.A.R. **105** C2
Djenné Mali **100** B3
Djibo Burkina **100** B3
Djibouti *country* Africa **103** C3
Djibouti Djibouti **103** C3
Djougou Benin **100** C4
Djúpivogur Iceland **46** [inset]
Dmitriyevka Rus. Fed. **43** F3
Dmitriyev-L'govskiy Rus. Fed. **43** E3
Dmitrov Rus. Fed. **43** E2
Dnepr *r.* Rus. Fed. *see* Dnieper
Dnieper *r.* Rus. Fed. **43** D3
Dnieper *r.* Ukr. **45** D2
Dniester *r.* Ukr. **44** C2
Dnipro *r.* Ukr. *see* Dnieper
Dniprodzerzhyns'k Ukr. **45** D2
Dnipropetrovs'k Ukr. **45** E2
Dniprorudne Ukr. **45** D2
Dnister *r.* Ukr. *see* Dniester
Dno Rus. Fed. **42** C2
Doba Chad **101** D4
Dobele Latvia **42** B2
Döbeln Ger. **55** F2
Doberai, Jazirah *pen.* Indon. **71** C3
Dobo Indon. **71** C3
Doboj Bos.-Herz. **63** C2
Dobrich Bulg. **64** C2
Dobrinka Rus. Fed. **43** F3
Dobroye Rus. Fed. **43** E3
Dobrush Belarus **43** D3
Doce *r.* Brazil **155** E1
Doctor Arroyo Mex. **143** B2
Doctor Belisario Domínguez Mex.
    142 B2
Dodecanese *is* Greece **65** C3
Dodekanisos *is* Greece *see*
    Dodecanese
Dodge City U.S.A. **134** C3
Dodoma Tanz. **105** D3
Doetinchem Neth. **54** C2
Dofa Indon. **71** C3
Dogai Coring *salt l.* China **87** C1
Dog Creek Can. **126** C2
Dōgo *i.* Japan **79** B3
Dogondoutchi Niger **100** C3
Doğubeyazıt Turkey **93** C2
Doha Qatar **91** C2
Doi Saket Thai. **74** A2
Dokkum Neth. **54** B1
Dokshytsy Belarus **42** C3
Dokuchayevs'k Ukr. **45** E2
Dolak, Pulau *i.* Indon. **71** D3

Dolbeau Can. **129** C2
Dol-de-Bretagne France **58** B2
Dole France **59** D2
Dolgellau U.K. **53** B3
Dolgorukovo Rus. Fed. **43** E3
Dolgoye Rus. Fed. **43** E3
Dolinsk Rus. Fed. **81** F1
Dolisie Congo *see* Loubomo
Dolomites *mts* Italy **62** B1
Dolo Odo Eth. **103** C4
Dolyna Ukr. **44** B2
Domažlice Czech Rep. **56** C3
Dombås Norway **47** B3
Dombóvár Hungary **57** D3
Dome Creek Can. **126** C2
Dominica *country* West Indies **145** D3
Dominican Republic *country*
    West Indies **145** C3
Domodedovo Rus. Fed. **43** E2
Domokos Greece **65** B3
Dompu Indon. **73** C2
Don *r.* Rus. Fed. **43** E3
Don *r.* U.K. **50** C2
Donaghadee U.K. **51** D1
Donald Austr. **116** C3
Donau *r.* Austria/Ger. *see* Danube
Donauwörth Ger. **56** C3
Don Benito Spain **60** B2
Doncaster U.K. **52** C3
Dondo Angola **104** B3
Dondo Moz. **107** C1
Dondra Head Sri Lanka **85** C4
Donegal Rep. of Ireland **51** B1
Donegal Bay Rep. of Ireland **51** B1
Donets'k Ukr. **45** E2
Donets'kyy Kryazh *hills* Rus. Fed./Ukr.
    45 E2
Dongara Austr. **114** A2
Dongchuan China **83** A3
Dongfang China **83** A4
Dongfanghong China **78** B1
Donggala Indon. **73** C2
Donggang China **77** A2
Dongguan China **83** B3
Đông Ha Vietnam **74** B2
Đông Hôi Vietnam **74** B2
Dongou Congo **104** B3
Dongshan China **83** B3
Dongsheng China *see* Ordos
Dongtai China **82** C2
Dongting Hu *l.* China **83** B3
Dongying China **82** B2
Donnellys Crossing N.Z. **118** B2
Donostia - San Sebastián Spain
    61 C1
Dooxo Nugaaleed *val.* Somalia **103** C4
Dorchester U.K. **53** B4
Dordabis Namibia **108** A1
Dordogne *r.* France **58** B2
Dordrecht Neth. **54** B2
Dordrecht S. Africa **109** C3
Doré Lake Can. **127** E2
Dorfmark Ger. **55** D1
Dori Burkina **100** B3
Doring *r.* S. Africa **108** A3
Dormans France **54** A3
Dornoch U.K. **50** B2
Dornoch Firth *est.* U.K. **50** B2
Dorogobuzh Rus. Fed. **43** D3
Dorohoi Romania **44** C2
Dörgön Nuur *salt l.* Mongolia **80** C1
Dorotea Sweden **46** D3
Dorre Island Austr. **114** A2
Dorrigo Austr. **117** E2
Dorsale Camerounaise *slope*
    Cameroon/Nigeria **104** B2
Dortmund Ger. **54** C2
Dortmund-Ems-Kanal *canal* Ger.
    54 C2
Dos Bahías, Cabo *c.* Arg. **153** B5

Dosse *r.* Ger. **55** F1
Dosso Niger **100** C3
Dothan U.S.A. **139** C2
Döttingen Ger. **55** D1
Douai France **58** C1
Douala Cameroon **104** A2
Douarnenez France **58** B2
Doubtful Sound N.Z. **118** A4
Douentza Mali **100** B3
Douglas Isle of Man **52** A2
Douglas S. Africa **108** B2
Douglas *AK* U.S.A. **126** B2
Douglas *AZ* U.S.A. **140** C2
Douglas *GA* U.S.A. **139** D2
Douglas *WY* U.S.A. **134** B2
Doullens France **58** C1
Dourada, Serra *hills* Brazil **154** B1
Dourados Brazil **154** B2
Dourados, Serra dos *hills* Brazil **154** B2
Douro *r.* Port. **60** B1
Dover U.K. **53** D4
Dover U.S.A. **137** E3
Dover, Strait of France/U.K. **49** D3
Dover-Foxcroft U.S.A. **137** G1
Dowlatābād *Bushehr* Iran **93** D3
Dowlatābād *Kermān* Iran **91** C2
Downpatrick U.K. **51** D1
Dowshi Afgh. **86** A1
Dōzen *is* Japan **79** B3
Dozois, Réservoir *resr* Can. **128** C2
Dracena Brazil **156** D2
Drachten Neth. **54** C1
Drăgănești-Olt Romania **44** B3
Drăgășani Romania **44** B3
Drahichyn Belarus **42** C3
Drakensberg *mts* Lesotho/S. Africa **109** C2
Drakensberg *mts* S. Africa **109** C2
Drake Passage S. Atlantic Ocean **119** L4
Drama Greece **65** B2
Drammen Norway **47** C4
Drau *r.* Austria **62** F1
Drava *r.* Europe **63** C1
Drayton Valley Can. **126** D2
Dreieich Ger. **55** D2
Drepano, Akra *pt* Greece **65** B3
Dresden Ger. **55** F2
Dreux France **58** C2
Driemond Neth. **54** B1
Driffield U.K. **52** C3
Drina *r.* Bos.-Herz./Serb. and Mont. **63** C2
Drniš Croatia **63** C2
Drobeta – Turnu Severin Romania **44** B3
Drochtersen Ger. **55** D1
Drogheda Rep. of Ireland **51** C2
Drohobych Ukr. **44** B2
Dromore U.K. **51** C1
Drosh Pak. **86** B1
Drouin Austr. **117** D3
Drumheller Can. **122** C2
Drummond Island U.S.A. **136** D1
Drummondville Can. **129** C2
Druskininkai Lith. **42** B3
Druzhkivka Ukr. **45** E2
Druzhnaya Gorka Rus. Fed. **42** D2
Dryden Can. **128** A2
Drysdale *r.* Austr. **114** B1
Ḍubā Saudi Arabia **90** A2
Dubai U.A.E. **91** C2
Dubawnt Lake Can. **127** E1
Dubayy U.A.E. *see* Dubai
Dubbāgh, Jabal ad *mt.* Saudi Arabia **90** A2
Dubbo Austr. **117** D2
Dublin Rep. of Ireland **51** C2
Dublin U.S.A. **139** D2
Dubno Ukr. **44** C1

Du Bois U.S.A. **137** E2
Dubréka Guinea **100** A4
Dubrovnik Croatia **63** C2
Dubrovytsya Ukr. **44** C1
Dubuque U.S.A. **135** E2
Ducie Island *atoll* Pitcairn Is **111**
Duck Bay Can. **127** E2
Duderstadt Ger. **55** E2
Dudinka Rus. Fed. **94** H2
Dudley U.K. **53** B3
Duero *r.* Spain **60** B1
Duffreboy, Lac *l.* Can. **129** C1
Dufftown U.K. **50** C2
Dugi Rat Croatia **63** C2
Duisburg Ger. **54** C2
Duiwelskloof S. Africa **109** D1
Dukathole S. Africa **109** C3
Dukhān Qatar **91** C2
Dukhovshchina Rus. Fed. **43** D2
Dūkštas Lith. **42** C2
Dulan China **80** C2
Dulce *r.* Arg. **152** B4
Dülmen Ger. **54** C2
Dulovo Bulg. **64** C2
Duluth U.S.A. **135** E1
Dumaguete Phil. **76** B3
Dumai Indon. **72** B1
Dumaran *i.* Phil. **76** B2
Dumas *AR* U.S.A. **138** B2
Dumas *TX* U.S.A. **141** D1
Dumbarton U.K. **50** B3
Dúmbier *mt.* Slovakia **57** D3
Dumfries U.K. **50** C3
Dumyāţ Egypt **102** B1
Duna *r.* Hungary *see* Danube
Dunakeszi Hungary **57** D2
Dunărea *r.* Romania *see* Danube
Dunaújváros Hungary **57** D2
Dunayivtsi Ukr. **44** C2
Dunbar U.K. **50** C2
Dunbeath U.K. **50** C1
Duncan Can. **126** C3
Duncan U.S.A. **141** E2
Duncansby Head U.K. **50** C1
Dundalk Rep. of Ireland **51** C1
Dundalk Bay Rep. of Ireland **51** C2
Dundas Greenland **125** H1
Dundee S. Africa **109** D2
Dundee U.K. **50** C2
Dundrum Bay U.K. **51** D1
Dunedin N.Z. **118** B4
Dunedin U.S.A. **139** D3
Dunfermline U.K. **50** C2
Dungannon U.K. **51** C1
Dungarpur India **86** B2
Dungarvan Rep. of Ireland **51** C2
Dungeness *hd* U.K. **53** D4
Dungiven U.K. **51** C1
Dungog Austr. **117** E2
Dungu Dem. Rep. Congo **105** C2
Dungun Malaysia **72** B1
Dungunab Sudan **102** B2
Dunhua China **77** B1
Dunhuang China **80** C2
Dunkerque France *see* Dunkirk
Dunkirk France **58** C1
Dunkirk U.S.A. **137** E2
Dún Laoghaire Rep. of Ireland **51** C2
Dunmurry U.K. **51** D1
Dunnet Head U.K. **50** C1
Duns U.K. **50** C3
Dunstable U.K. **53** C4
Dupnitsa Bulg. **64** B2
Dupree U.S.A. **134** C1
Durack *r.* Austr. **114** B1
Durango Mex. **142** B2
Durango Spain **60** C1
Durango U.S.A. **134** B3
Durant U.S.A. **141** E2

Durazno Uru. **153** C4
Durban S. Africa **109** D2
Durban-Corbières France **58** C3
Durbanville S. Africa **108** A3
Durbuy Belgium **54** B2
Düren Ger. **54** C2
Durg India **87** C2
Durham U.K. **52** C2
Durham U.S.A. **139** E1
Duri Indon. **72** B1
Durmitor *mt.* Serb. and Mont. **64** A2
Durness U.K. **50** B1
Durrës Albania **65** A2
Dursey Island Rep. of Ireland **51** A3
Dursunbey Turkey **65** C3
D'Urville, Tanjung *pt* Indon. **71** D3
D'Urville Island N.Z. **118** B3
Dushan China **83** A3
Dushanbe Tajik. **89** D3
Düsseldorf Ger. **54** C2
Duyun China **83** A3
Dvorichna Ukr. **45** E2
Dwarka India **86** A2
Dwarsberg S. Africa **109** C1
Dworshak Reservoir U.S.A. **132** C1
Dyat'kovo Rus. Fed. **43** D3
Dyce U.K. **50** C2
Dyer, Cape Can. **125** H2
Dyersburg U.S.A. **138** C1
Dyfrdwy *r. England/Wales* U.K. *see* Dee
Dyje *r.* Austria/Czech Rep. **57** D3
Dylewska Góra *h.* Pol. **57** D2
Dymytrov Ukr. **45** E2
Dyoki S. Africa **109** C3
Dyurtyuli Rus. Fed. **41** E3
Dzamïn Üüd Mongolia **81** D2
Dzaoudzi Mayotte **107** D1
Dzhanga Turkm. **93** D1
Dzhangala Kazakh. **88** C2
Dzhankoy Ukr. **45** D2
Dzhizak Uzbek. *see* Jizzax
Dzhubga Rus. Fed. **45** E3
Dzhugdzhur, Khrebet *mts* Rus. Fed. **95** L3
Dzhungarskiy Alatau, Khrebet *mts* China/Kazakh. **89** E2
Dzhusaly Kazakh. **88** C2
Działdowo Pol. **57** E2
Dzuunmod Mongolia **80** D1
Dzyarzhynsk Belarus **42** C3
Dzyatlavichy Belarus **42** C3

E

Eagle *r.* Can. **129** E2
Eagle Cap *mt.* U.S.A. **132** C1
Eagle Lake Can. **128** A2
Eagle Lake U.S.A. **132** B2
Eagle Pass U.S.A. **141** D3
Eagle Plain Can. **124** C2
Ear Falls Can. **128** A1
East Antarctica *reg.* Antarctica **119** F
Eastbourne U.K. **53** D4
East China Sea N. Pacific Ocean **81** E2
East Coast Bays N.Z. **118** B2
Eastend Can. **132** E1
Eastern Cape *prov.* S. Africa **109** C3
Eastern Desert Egypt **102** B2
Eastern Ghats *mts* India **85** B3
Easterville Can. **127** F2
East Falkland *i.* Falkland Is **153** C6
East Frisian Islands Ger. **54** C1
East Kilbride U.K. **50** B3
Eastleigh U.K. **53** C4
East Liverpool U.S.A. **137** D2
East London S. Africa **109** C3
Eastmain Can. **128** C1

Eastmain *r.* Can. **128** C1
Eastman U.S.A. **139** D2
East Siberian Sea *see* Japan, Sea of
East Siberian Sea Rus. Fed. **95** L2
East St Louis U.S.A. **136** B3
East Timor *country* Asia **69**
Eau Claire U.S.A. **136** B2
Eau Claire, Lac à l' *l.* Can. **128** C1
Eauripik *atoll* Micronesia **71** D2
Ebano Mex. **143** C2
Ebbw Vale U.K. **53** B4
Eberswalde-Finow Ger. **55** F1
Eboli Italy **62** C2
Ebolowa Cameroon **104** B2
Ebro *r.* Spain **61** D1
Ech Chélif Alg. **100** C1
Echeverria, Pico *mt.* Mex. **142** A2
Eching *r.* Can. **127** F2
Echternach Lux. **54** C3
Echuca Austr. **116** C3
Écija Spain **60** B2
Eckernförde Ger. **56** B2
Ecuador *country* S. America **150** B3
Ed Eritrea **102** C3
Ed Da'ein Sudan **103** A3
Ed Damazin Sudan **103** B3
Ed Damer Sudan **102** B3
Ed Debba Sudan **102** B3
Ed Dueim Sudan **102** B3
Eddystone Point *pt* Austr. **115** D4
Ede Neth. **54** C1
Edéa Cameroon **104** B2
Edéia Brazil **154** C1
Eden Austr. **117** D3
Eden *r.* U.K. **52** B2
Edenburg S. Africa **109** C2
Edenderry Rep. of Ireland **51** C2
Edenhope Austr. **116** C3
Edessa Greece **65** B2
Edgeøya *i.* Svalbard **94** D1
Edinburg U.S.A. **141** E3
Edinburgh U.K. **50** C3
Edirne Turkey **64** C2
Edmonton Can. **137** G1
Edmundston Can. **137** G1
Edremit Turkey **65** C3
Edremit Körfezi *b.* Turkey **65** C3
Edson Can. **126** D2
Edward, Lake Dem. Rep. Congo/Uganda **105** C3
Edward's Creek Austr. **116** B1
Edwards U.S.A. **138** D2
Edwards Plateau U.S.A. **141** D2
Eenrum Neth. **54** C1
Éfaté *i.* Vanuatu **110**
Effingham U.S.A. **136** C3
Egan Range *mts* U.S.A. **133** D3
Eger Hungary **57** E3
Egersund Norway **47** B4
Egilsstaðir Iceland **46** [inset]
Eğirdir Turkey **92** B2
Eğirdir Gölü *l.* Turkey **92** B2
Égletons France **58** C2
Egvekinot Rus. Fed. **95** O2
Egypt *country* Africa **102** A2
E'hen Hudag China **82** A2
Eibergen Neth. **54** C1
Eifel *hills* Ger. **54** C2
Eigg *i.* U.K. **50** A2
Eight Degree Channel India/Maldives **85** B4
Eighty Mile Beach Austr. **114** B1
Eilat Israel **92** B3
Eilenburg Ger. **55** F2
Einbeck Ger. **55** D2
Eindhoven Neth. **54** B2
Eirunepé Brazil **150** C3
Eiseb *watercourse* Namibia **106** B1
Eisenach Ger. **55** E2
Eisenhüttenstadt Ger. **56** C2

Eisenstadt Austria **57** D3
Eisleben Lutherstadt Ger. **55** E2
Eivissa Spain **61** D2
Eivissa *i.* Spain *see* Ibiza
Ejea de los Caballeros Spain **61** C1
Ejeda Madag. **107** [inset] D2
Ekenäs Fin. **47** E4
Ekibastuz Kazakh. **89** E1
Ekostrovskaya Imandra, Ozero *l.* Rus. Fed. **46** G2
Eksjö Sweden **47** C4
Eksteenfontein S. Africa **108** A2
Ekwan *r.* Can. **128** B1
Ela Myanmar **74** A2
Elandsdoorn S. Africa **109** C2
Elassona Greece **65** B3
Elazığ Turkey **92** B2
Elba, Isola d' *i.* Italy **62** B3
El Banco Col. **150** B1
Elbasan Albania **65** B2
El Baúl Venez. **150** C2
El Bayadh Alg. **100** C1
Elbe *r.* Ger. **55** D1
Elberton U.S.A. **139** D2
Elbeuf France **58** C2
Elbistan Turkey **92** B2
Elblag Pol. **57** D2
El'brus *mt.* Rus. Fed. **41** D4
Elburz Mountains Iran **93** C2
El Callao Venez. **150** C2
El Campo U.S.A. **141** E3
El Centro U.S.A. **133** C4
El Cerro Bol. **152** B2
Elche-Elx Spain **61** C2
Elda Spain **61** C2
Eldon U.S.A. **135** E3
Eldorado Arg. **154** B3
El Dorado Mex. **142** B2
El Dorado *AR* U.S.A. **138** B2
El Dorado *KS* U.S.A. **135** D3
El Eglab *plat.* Alg. **100** B2
El Ejido Spain **60** C2
Elektrostal' Rus. Fed. **43** E2
El Encanto Col. **150** B3
El Eulma Alg. **61** E3
Eleuthera *i.* Bahamas **145** C2
El Fasher Sudan **103** A3
El Fuerte Mex. **142** B2
El Geneina Sudan **103** A3
El Geteina Sudan **102** B3
Elgin U.K. **50** C2
Elgin U.S.A. **136** C2
El Goléa Alg. **100** C1
El Golfo de Santa Clara Mex. **142** A1
Elgon, Mount Uganda **105** D2
El Hammâmi *reg.* Maur. **100** A3
El Hierro *i.* Canary Is. **100** A2
El Higo Mex. **143** C2
El Homr Alg. **100** C2
Elim U.S.A. **124** B2
Elista Rus. Fed. **41** D4
Elizabeth U.S.A. **137** F2
Elizabeth City U.S.A. **139** E1
Elizabethtown U.S.A. **136** C3
El Jadida Morocco **100** B1
Elk Pol. **57** E2
Elk City U.S.A. **141** E1
Elkford Can. **126** D2
Elkhart U.S.A. **136** C2
Elkhovo Bulg. **64** C2
Elkins U.S.A. **137** E3
Elko Can. **126** D3
Elko U.S.A. **132** C2
Elk Point Can. **127** D2
Ellef Ringnes Island Can. **124** F1
Ellendale U.S.A. **135** D1
Ellensburg U.S.A. **132** B1
Ellesmere, Lake N.Z. **118** B3
Ellesmere Island Can. **125** G1

Ellesmere Port U.K. **52** B3
Ellice *r.* Can. **124** F2
Elliotdale S. Africa **109** C3
Ellon U.K. **50** C2
Ellsworth U.S.A. **137** G2
Ellsworth Mountains Antarctica **119** K2
Elmalı Turkey **65** C3
El Meghaïer Alg. **101** C1
El Milia Alg. **61** E2
Elmira U.S.A. **137** E2
El Moral Spain **61** C2
Elmshorn Ger. **55** D1
El Muglad Sudan **103** A3
El Nido Phil. **76** A2
El Obeid Sudan **103** B3
El Oro Mex. **142** B2
El Oued Alg. **101** C1
Eloy U.S.A. **140** B2
El Paso U.S.A. **140** C2
El Porvenir Mex. **142** B1
El Prat de Llobregat Spain **61** D1
El Progreso Hond. **143** D3
El Reno U.S.A. **141** E1
Elsa Can. **126** B1
El Salado Mex. **143** B2
El Salto Mex. **142** B2
El Salvador *country* Central America **144** B3
El Salvador Mex. **143** B2
El Sauz Mex. **140** C3
El Socorro Mex. **142** A1
Elsterwerda Ger. **55** F2
El Temascal Mex. **143** C2
El Tigre Venez. **150** C2
El Tocuyo Venez. **145** D4
Elva Estonia **42** C2
Elvas Port. **60** B2
Elverum Norway **47** C3
El Wak Kenya **105** E2
Ely U.K. **53** D3
Ely *MN* U.S.A. **135** E1
Ely *NV* U.S.A. **133** D3
Emāmrūd Iran **93** D2
Emän *r.* Sweden **47** D4
Emba Kazakh. **88** C2
Emba *r.* Kazakh. **88** C2
Embalenhle S. Africa **109** C2
Emborcação, Represa de *resr* Brazil **154** C1
Embu Kenya **105** D3
Emden Ger. **54** C1
Emerald Austr. **115** D2
Emerson Can. **127** F3
Emet Turkey **65** C3
eMgwenya S. Africa **109** D2
eMijindini S. Africa **109** D2
Emi Koussi *mt.* Chad **101** D3
Emine, Nos *pt* Bulg. **64** C2
Emirdağ Turkey **92** B2
Emmaste Estonia **42** B2
Emmeloord Neth. **54** B1
Emmelshausen Ger. **54** C2
Emmen Neth. **54** C1
Emory Peak U.S.A. **141** D3
Empalme Mex. **142** A2
Empangeni S. Africa **109** D2
Empoli Italy **62** B2
Emporia *KS* U.S.A. **135** D3
Emporia *VA* U.S.A. **137** E3
Ems *r.* Ger. **55** C1
Emsdetten Ger. **54** C1
Emzinoni S. Africa **109** C2
Enarotali Indon. **71** D3
Encarnación Mex. **142** B2
Encarnación Para. **152** C2
Encruzilhada Brazil **155** D1
Ende Indon. **73** D2
Endicott Mountains U.S.A. **124** B2
Enerhodar Ukr. **45** D2

Engel's Rus. Fed. **41** D3
Enggano i. Indon. **72** B2
England admin. div. U.K. **52** C3
English r. Can. **128** A1
English Channel France/U.K. **53** C5
Enid U.S.A. **141** E1
Enkhuizen Neth. **54** B1
Enköping Sweden **47** D4
Enna Italy **62** B3
Ennadai Lake Can. **127** I1
En Nahud Sudan **103** A3
Ennedi, Massif mts Chad **101** E3
Enngonia Austr. **117** D1
Ennis Rep. of Ireland **51** B2
Ennis U.S.A. **141** E2
Enniscorthy Rep. of Ireland **51** C2
Enniskillen U.K. **51** C1
Ennistymon Rep. of Ireland **51** B2
Enns r. Austria **56** C3
Enontekiö Fin. **46** E2
Ensay Austr. **117** D3
Enschede Neth. **54** C1
Ensenada Mex. **142** A1
Enshi China **83** C2
Enterprise Can. **126** D1
Enterprise AL U.S.A. **139** C2
Enterprise OR U.S.A. **132** C1
Entre Rios Bol. **152** B3
Entroncamento Port. **60** B2
Enugu Nigeria **101** C4
Envira Brazil **150** B3
Épernay France **54** A3
Ephraim U.S.A. **133** D1
Ephrata U.S.A. **132** C1
Épinal France **59** D2
Epsom U.K. **53** C4
Equatorial Guinea country Africa **104** A2
Erbendorf Ger. **55** F3
Erbeskopf h. Ger. **54** C3
Erciş Turkey **93** C2
Erdao Jiang r. China **77** B1
Erdek Turkey **65** C2
Erdemli Turkey **92** B2
Erechim Brazil **152** C3
Ereentsav Mongolia **81** D1
Ereğli Konya Turkey **92** B2
Ereğli Zonguldak Turkey **92** B1
Erenhot China **82** B1
Erevan Armenia see Yerevan
Erfurt Ger. **55** E2
Ergani Turkey **93** C2
'Erg Chech des. Alg./Mali **100** B2
Ergene r. Turkey **65** C2
Erie U.S.A. **137** D2
Erie, Lake Can./U.S.A. **136** D2
Erimo-misaki c. Japan **78** D2
Eritrea country Africa **102** B3
Erkner Ger. **55** F1
Erlangen Ger. **55** E3
Erldunda Austr. **114** C2
Ermelo S. Africa **109** C2
Ermenek Turkey **92** B2
Ermoupoli Greece **65** B3
Ernakulam India **85** B4
Erode India **85** B3
Erp Neth. **54** B2
Er Rachidia Morocco **100** B1
Er Rahad Sudan **103** B3
Errigal h. Rep. of Ireland **51** B1
Erris Head Rep. of Ireland **51** A1
Erromango i. Vanuatu **110**
Ersekë Albania **65** C2
Ertil' Rus. Fed. **43** F3
Erwitte Ger. **55** D2
Erzgebirge mts Czech Rep./Ger. **56** C2
Erzincan Turkey **92** B2
Erzurum Turkey **41** D5
Esbjerg Denmark **47** B4
Escalante U.S.A. **133** D3

Escalón Mex. **142** B2
Escanaba U.S.A. **136** C1
Escárcega Mex. **143** C3
Escatrón Spain **61** C1
Escaut r. Belgium **54** A2
Eschede Ger. **55** E1
Esch-sur-Alzette Lux. **54** B3
Eschwege Ger. **55** E2
Eschweiler Ger. **54** C2
Escondido U.S.A. **133** C4
Escuinapa Mex. **142** B2
Escuintla Guat. **144** B3
Eşen Turkey **65** C3
Eşfahān Iran **93** D2
Esikhawini S. Africa **109** D2
Esk r. U.K. **52** B2
Esker Can. **129** D1
Eskifjörður Iceland **46** [inset]
Eskilstuna Sweden **47** D4
Eskişehir Turkey **92** B2
Eslāmābād-e Gharb Iran **93** C2
Esler Dağı mt. Turkey **65** C3
Eşme Turkey **65** C3
Esmeraldas Ecuador **150** B2
Espakeh Iran **91** D2
Espalion France **58** C3
Espanola Can. **128** B2
Espanola U.S.A. **140** C1
Esperance Austr. **114** B3
Esperanza Mex. **142** B2
Espichel, Cabo c. Port. **60** B2
Espinhaço, Serra do mts Brazil **155** D1
Espinosa Brazil **151** E4
Espíritu Santo i. Vanuatu **158** D6
Espíritu Santo, Isla i. Mex. **142** A2
Espoo Fin. **47** E3
Esquel Arg. **153** A5
Essaouira Morocco **100** B1
Es Semara Western Sahara **100** A2
Essen Ger. **54** C2
Essequibo r. Guyana **150** D2
Esso Rus. Fed. **95** M3
Estados, Isla de los i. Arg. **153** B6
Eşţahbān Iran **93** D3
Estância Brazil **151** F4
Estcourt S. Africa **109** C2
Estella Spain **61** C1
Estepona Spain **60** B2
Esteras de Medinaceli Spain **60** C1
Esterhazy Can. **127** E2
Esteros Para. **152** B3
Estes Park U.S.A. **134** B2
Estevan Can. **134** C1
Estherville U.S.A. **135** E2
Eston Can. **127** E2
Estonia country Europe **42** C2
Estrela, Serra da mts Port. **60** B1
Estremoz Port. **60** B2
Etadunna Austr. **116** B1
Étain France **54** B3
Étampes France **58** C2
Étaples France **58** C1
Etawah India **87** B2
eThandakukhanya S. Africa **109** D2
Ethiopia country Africa **103** B4
Ethiopian Highlands plat. Eth. **96**
Etna, Monte vol. Italy **62** C3
Etne Norway **42** E2
Etolin Island U.S.A. **126** B2
Etosha salt pan Namibia **106** A1
Ettelbruck Lux. **54** B3
Etten-Leur Neth. **54** B2
Etxarri-Aranatz Spain **61** C1
Eu France **53** D4
Euabalong Austr. **117** D2
Euboea i. Greece see Evvoia
Eucla Austr. **114** B3
Eufaula U.S.A. **139** C2
Eufaula Lake resr U.S.A. **141** E1
Eugene U.S.A. **132** B2

Eugenia, Punta pt Mex. **142** A2
Eulo Austr. **117** D1
Eumungerie Austr. **117** D2
Eunice U.S.A. **141** D2
Euphrates r. Asia **92** C2
Eureka CA U.S.A. **132** B2
Eureka MT U.S.A. **132** C1
Eureka NV U.S.A. **133** C3
Euriowie Austr. **116** C2
Euroa Austr. **117** D3
Europa Point pt Gibraltar **60** B2
Eutsuk Lake Can. **126** C2
Evans, Lac l. Can. **128** C1
Evans Head Austr. **117** E1
Evans Strait Can. **127** G1
Evanston U.S.A. **134** D2
Evansville U.S.A. **136** C3
Evaton S. Africa **109** C2
Evaz Iran **91** D2
Evensk Rus. Fed. **95** M2
Everard, Lake salt flat Austr. **116** B2
Everest, Mount China/Nepal **87** C2
Everett U.S.A. **132** B1
Evergem Belgium **54** A2
Everglades swamp U.S.A. **139** D3
Evinayong Equat. Guinea **104** B2
Evje Norway **47** B4
Évora Port. **60** B2
Évreux France **58** C2
Evros r. Greece/Turkey **65** C2
Evrotas r. Greece **65** B3
Evrychou Cyprus **92** B2
Evvoia i. Greece **65** B3
Ewaso Ngiro r. Kenya **105** D2
Exaltación Bol. **152** B2
Exe r. U.K. **53** B4
Exeter U.K. **53** B4
Exmoor hills U.K. **53** B4
Exmouth U.K. **53** B4
Exmouth Gulf Austr. **114** A2
Exuma Cays is Bahamas **145** C2
Eya r. Rus. Fed. **45** E2
Eyl Somalia **103** C4
Eyre, Lake salt flat S.A. Austr. **116** B1
Eyre Peninsula Austr. **116** B2
Eysturoy i. Faroe Is **48** B1
Ezakheni S. Africa **109** D2
Ezenzeleni S. Africa **109** C2
Ezhou China **83** B2
Ezhva Rus. Fed. **40** E2
Ezine Turkey **65** C3

Fabens U.S.A. **140** C2
Fåborg Denmark **56** C1
Fabriano Italy **62** C2
Fachi Niger **101** D3
Fada-N'Gourma Burkina **100** C3
Faenza Italy **62** B2
Fafanlap Indon. **71** C3
Făgăraș Romania **44** B3
Fagatogo American Samoa **113**
Fagernes Norway **47** B3
Fagersta Sweden **47** D4
Fagnano, Lago l. Arg./Chile **153** B6
Faguibine, Lac l. Mali **100** B3
Fagurhólsmýri Iceland **46** [inset]
Fairbanks U.S.A. **124** C2
Fairbury U.S.A. **135** D2
Fairfield U.S.A. **133** D2
Fair Isle i. U.K. **50** [inset]
Fairmont MN U.S.A. **135** E2
Fairmont WV U.S.A. **137** D3
Fairview Can. **126** D2
Fairweather, Mount Can./U.S.A. **126** B2
Fais i. Micronesia **71** D2

...aisalabad Pak. **86** B1
...aith U.S.A. **134** C1
...aizabad India **87** C2
...akarava *atoll* Fr. Polynesia **111**
...akfak Indon. **71** C3
...aku China **77** A1
...alaba Sierra Leone **100** A4
...alcon Lake Mex./U.S.A. **141** E3
...alher Can. **126** D2
...alkenberg Ger. **55** B2
...alkenberg Sweden **47** C4
...alkensee Ger. **55** F1
...alkirk U.K. **50** C2
alkland Islands *terr.* S. Atlantic Ocean **153** C6
...alköping Sweden **47** C4
...allon U.S.A. **133** C3
...all River U.S.A. **137** F2
...alls City U.S.A. **135** D2
...almouth U.K. **53** A4
...alse Bay S. Africa **108** A3
...also, Cabo *c.* Mex. **120**
...alster *i.* Denmark **47** C5
...alticoni Romania **44** C2
...alun Sweden **47** D3
...ameck France **54** C2
...angchenggang China **83** A3
...angshan Taiwan **83** C3
...angzheng China **81** E1
...ano Italy **62** B2
...an Si Pan *mt.* Vietnam **74** B1
...aradje Dem. Rep. Congo **105** C2
...arafangana Madag. **107** [inset] D2
...aräfīrah, Wāḥāt al *oasis* Egypt **102** A2
...arāh Afgh. **86** A1
...arah Rūd *watercourse* Afgh. **86** A1
...aranah Guinea **100** A3
...arasān, Jazā'īr *is* Saudi Arabia **90** B3
...arewell, Cape Greenland **125** J2
...arewell, Cape N.Z. **118** B3
...argo U.S.A. **135** D2
...aribault, La *l.* Can. **129** C1
...armington *ME* U.S.A. **137** F2
...armington *NM* U.S.A. **140** C1
...armville U.S.A. **137** E3
...arnborough U.K. **53** C4
...arnham, Mount Can. **126** D2
...aro Can. **126** B1
...aro Port. **60** B2
...ärö *i.* Sweden **42** A2
aroe Islands *terr.* N. Atlantic Ocean **48** B1
...arräshband Iran **93** D3
...arwell U.S.A. **141** D2
...äryāb Iran **91** D2
...asā Iran **93** D3
...asano Italy **63** C2
...astiv Ukr. **44** C1
...atehgarh India **87** B2
...atehpur India **87** B2
...aulquemont France **54** C3
...auske Norway **46** D2
...axäflói *b.* Iceland **46** [inset]
...axälven *r.* Sweden **46** D3
...aya Chad **101** D3
...ayetteville *AR* U.S.A. **138** D1
...ayetteville *NC* U.S.A. **139** D1
...ayetteville *TN* U.S.A. **138** C1
...azilka India **86** B1
...éarik Maur. **100** A2
...ear, Cape U.S.A. **139** E2
...eatherston N.Z. **118** C3
...écamp France **58** C2
...ehmann *i.* Ger. **56** C2
...ehrbellin Ger. **55** F1
...eia, Lagoa *lag.* Brazil **155** D2

Feijó Brazil **150** B3
Feilding N.Z. **118** C3
Feira de Santana Brazil **151** F4
Felanitx Spain **61** D2
Feldberg Ger. **55** F1
Felipe C. Puerto Mex. **143** D3
Felixlândia Brazil **155** D1
Felixstowe U.K. **53** D4
Felsberg Ger. **55** D2
Feltre Italy **62** B1
Femunden *l.* Norway **47** C3
Fengcheng *Jiangxi* China **83** B3
Fengcheng *Liaoning* China **77** A1
Fengqing China **74** A1
Fengxian China **82** B2
Fengyüan Taiwan **83** C3
Fenzhen China **82** B1
Feno, Capo di *c.* France **59** D3
Fenoarivo Atsinanana Madag. **107** [inset] D1
Fer, Cap de *c.* Alg. **62** A3
Fergus Falls U.S.A. **135** D2
Ferkessédougou Côte d'Ivoire **100** B4
Fermo Italy **62** B2
Fermont Can. **129** C1
Fermoselle Spain **60** B1
Fermoy Rep. of Ireland **51** B2
Fernandina Beach U.S.A. **139** D2
Fernandópolis Brazil **154** B2
Fernie Can. **126** D3
Ferrara Italy **62** B2
Ferreiros Brazil **154** B2
Ferro, Capo *c.* Italy **62** A2
Ferrol Spain **60** B1
Ferwert Neth. **54** B1
Fès Morocco **100** B1
Feshi Dem. Rep. Congo **104** B3
Festus U.S.A. **135** E3
Fethiye Turkey **65** C3
Fetlar *i.* U.K. **50** [inset]
Feucht Ger. **55** E3
Feuilles, Rivière aux *r.* Can. **128** C1
Feyzābād Afgh. **86** B1
Fez Morocco *see* Fès
Fianarantsoa Madag. **107** [inset] D2
Fichè Eth. **103** B4
Fier Albania **65** A4
Fife Ness *pt* U.K. **50** C2
Figeac France **58** C3
Figueira da Foz Port. **60** B1
Figueres Spain **61** D1
Figuig Morocco **100** B1
Fiji *country* S. Pacific Ocean **112**
Fik' Eth. **105** E2
Filadélfia Para. **152** B3
Filey U.K. **52** C2
Filippiada Greece **65** B3
Filipstad Sweden **47** C4
Findhorn *r.* U.K. **50** C2
Findlay U.S.A. **136** D2
Fingal Austr. **115** D4
Finger Lakes U.S.A. **137** E2
Finisterre, Cape Spain **60** B1
Finland *country* Europe **46** F3
Finland, Gulf of Europe **47** E4
Finlay *r.* Can. **126** C2
Finley Austr. **117** D3
Finne *ridge* Ger. **55** E2
Finnmarksvidda *reg.* Norway **46** E2
Finnsnes Norway **46** D2
Finspång Sweden **47** D4
Finsterwalde Ger. **55** F2
Fionnphort U.K. **50** A2
Firenze Italy *see* Florence
Firminy France **59** C2
Firozabad India **87** B2
Firozpur India **86** B1

Firūzābād Iran **93** D3
Fish *watercourse* Namibia **108** A2
Fish *r.* S. Africa **108** B3
Fisher Strait Can. **127** G1
Fishguard U.K. **53** A4
Fismes France **59** C2
Fisterra, Cabo *c.* Spain *see* Finisterre, Cape
Fitchburg U.S.A. **137** F2
Fitzgerald Can. **127** D2
Fitzroy Crossing Austr. **114** B1
Fivizzano Italy **62** B2
Fizi Dem. Rep. Congo **105** C3
Fjällbäcka S. Africa **109** C3
Fjällsjöälven *r.* Sweden **46** D3
Flagstaff S. Africa **109** C3
Flagstaff U.S.A. **140** B1
Flaherty Island Can. **128** C1
Flamborough Head U.K. **52** C2
Fläming *hills* Ger. **55** F1
Flaming Gorge Reservoir U.S.A. **134** B2
Flathead *r.* U.S.A. **132** D1
Flathead Lake U.S.A. **132** D1
Flattery, Cape Austr. **115** D1
Flattery, Cape U.S.A. **132** B1
Fleetwood U.K. **52** B3
Flekkefjord Norway **47** A4
Flen Sweden **42** A2
Flensburg Ger. **56** D2
Flers France **58** B2
Flinders *r.* Austr. **115** D1
Flinders Bay Austr. **114** A3
Flinders Island Austr. **115** D3
Flinders Ranges *mts* Austr. **116** B2
Flint U.S.A. **136** D2
Flint *i.* Kiribati **109** E1
Flora France **61** D1
Florence Italy **62** B2
Florence *AL* U.S.A. **138** C2
Florence *AZ* U.S.A. **140** C2
Florence *OR* U.S.A. **132** B2
Florence *SC* U.S.A. **139** E2
Florencia Col. **150** B2
Flores Guat. **144** B3
Flores *i.* Indon. **73** D2
Flores, Laut *sea* Indon. **73** C2
Flores Sea Indon. *see* Flores, Laut
Floresta Brazil **151** F3
Floresville U.S.A. **141** E3
Floriano Brazil **151** E3
Florianópolis Brazil **154** C3
Florida Uru. **153** C4
Florida *state* U.S.A. **139** D2
Florida, Straits of Bahamas/U.S.A. **144** B2
Florida Keys *is* U.S.A. **139** D4
Florina Greece **65** B2
Florø Norway **47** B3
Foam Lake Can. **127** E2
Foča Bos.-Herz. **63** C2
Focşani Romania **44** C2
Fogang China **83** B3
Foggia Italy **62** C2
Fogo Island Can. **129** E2
Foix France **58** C3
Fokino Rus. Fed. **43** D3
Foleyet Can. **128** B2
Foligno Italy **62** B2
Folkestone U.K. **53** D4
Folkston U.S.A. **139** D2
Follonica Italy **62** B2
Fond-du-Lac Can. **124** E3
Fond du Lac *r.* Can. **127** E2
Fond du Lac U.S.A. **136** C2
Fondevila Spain **60** B1
Fondi Italy **62** B2
Fonseca, Golfo do *b.* Central America **144** B3
Fonte Boa Brazil **150** C3
Fontenay-le-Comte France **58** B2

Fontur *pt* Iceland **46** [inset]
Forbes Austr. **117** D2
Forchheim Ger. **55** E3
Førde Norway **47** B3
Fords Bridge Austr. **117** D1
Fordyce U.S.A. **138** B2
Forest U.S.A. **138** C2
Forest Hill Austr. **117** D3
Forestville Can. **129** D2
Forfar U.K. **50** C2
Forks U.S.A. **132** B1
Forlì Italy **62** B2
Formentera *i.* Spain **61** D2
Formento, Cap de *c.* Spain **61** D2
Formiga Brazil **155** C2
Formosa Arg. **152** C3
Formosa Brazil **154** C1
Forres U.K. **50** C2
Forrest Austr. **114** C3
Forrest City U.S.A. **138** B1
Forsayth Austr. **115** D1
Forssa Fin. **47** E3
Forster Austr. **117** E2
Forsyth U.S.A. **132** E1
Fort Abbas Pak. **86** B2
Fort Albany Can. **128** B1
Fortaleza Brazil **151** F3
Fort Assiniboine Can. **126** D2
Fort Augustus U.K. **50** B2
Fort Benton U.S.A. **132** D1
Fort Bragg U.S.A. **133** B3
Fort Chimo Can. *see* Kuujjuaq
Fort Chipewyan Can. **127** D2
Fort Collins U.S.A. **134** B2
Fort-de-France Martinique **145** D3
Fort Dodge U.S.A. **135** E2
Fort Frances Can. **128** A2
Fort George Can. *see* Chisasibi
Fort Good Hope Can. **124** D2
Forth *r.* U.K. **50** C2
Forth, Firth of *est.* U.K. **50** C2
Fortin Madrejón Para. **152** C2
Fort Lauderdale U.S.A. **139** D3
Fort Liard Can. **126** C1
Fort Mackay Can. **127** D2
Fort McMurray Can. **127** D2
Fort McPherson Can. **124** D2
Fort Morgan U.S.A. **134** C2
Fort Myers U.S.A. **139** D3
Fort Nelson Can. **126** C2
Fort Nelson *r.* Can. **126** C2
Fort Payne U.S.A. **139** C2
Fort Peck U.S.A. **134** B1
Fort Peck Reservoir U.S.A. **134** B1
Fort Pierce U.S.A. **139** D3
Fort Providence Can. **126** D1
Fort Qu'Appelle Can. **127** E2
Fort Resolution Can. **126** D1
Fort Rupert Can. *see* Waskaganish
Fort Saskatchewan Can. **126** D2
Fort Scott U.S.A. **135** E3
Fort Severn Can. **128** B1
Fort-Shevchenko Kazakh. **88** C2
Fort Simpson Can. **126** C1
Fort Smith Can. **127** D1
Fort Smith U.S.A. **138** B1
Fort St James Can. **126** C2
Fort St John Can. **126** C2
Fort Stockton U.S.A. **141** D2
Fort Sumner U.S.A. **140** D2
Fort Vermilion Can. **126** D2
Fort Walton Beach U.S.A. **138** C2
Fort Wayne U.S.A. **136** C2
Fort William U.K. **50** B2
Fort Worth U.S.A. **141** E2
Fort Yukon U.S.A. **124** C2
Foshan China **83** B3
Fosna *pen.* Norway **46** C3
Fosnavåg Norway **47** B3
Foss Iceland **46** [inset]

Fossá Iceland **46** [inset]
Fossano Italy **62** A2
Foster Austr. **117** D3
Fougères France **58** B2
Foula *i.* U.K. **50** [inset]
Fournoi *i.* Greece **65** C3
Fouta Djallon *reg.* Guinea **100** A3
Foveaux Strait N.Z. **118** A4
Fowler U.S.A. **134** C3
Fowlers Bay Austr. **114** C3
Fox Creek Can. **126** D2
Foxe Basin *g.* Can. **125** G2
Foxe Channel Can. **125** G2
Foxe Peninsula Can. **125** G2
Fox Glacier N.Z. **118** B3
Fox Lake Can. **126** D2
Fox Mountain Can. **126** B1
Foxton N.Z. **118** C3
Fox Valley Can. **127** E2
Foyle, Lough *b.* Rep. of Ireland/U.K. **51** C1
Foz de Areia, Represa de *resr* Brazil **154** B3
Foz do Cunene Angola **106** A1
Foz do Iguaçu Brazil **154** B3
Fraga Spain **61** D1
Franca Brazil **154** C2
Francavilla Fontana Italy **63** C2
France *country* Europe **58** C2
Franceville Gabon **104** B3
Francis Case, Lake U.S.A. **135** D2
Francisco Sá Brazil **155** D1
Francistown Botswana **106** B2
François Lake Can. **126** C2
Frankenberg (Eder) Ger. **55** D2
Frankenhöhe *hills* Ger. **55** E3
Frankenthal (Pfalz) Ger. **55** D3
Frankenwald *mts* Ger. **55** E2
Frankfort U.S.A. **136** D3
Frankfurt am Main Ger. **55** D2
Frankfurt an der Oder Ger. **56** C2
Fränkische Alb *hills* Ger. **56** C2
Fränkische Schweiz *reg.* Ger. **55** E3
Franklin U.S.A. **137** E2
Franklin D. Roosevelt Lake *resr* U.S.A. **132** C1
Franklin Mountains Can. **126** C1
Frantsa-Iosifa, Zemlya *is* Rus. Fed. **94** F1
Franz Josef Glacier N.Z. **118** B3
Frasca, Capo della *c.* Italy **62** A3
Frascati Italy **59** E3
Fraser *r.* B.C. Can. **126** C3
Fraser *r.* Nfld. and Lab. Can. **129** D1
Fraserburg S. Africa **108** B3
Fraserburgh U.K. **50** C2
Fraserdale Can. **128** B2
Fraser Island Austr. **115** E2
Fraser Lake Can. **126** C2
Fray Bentos Uru. **153** C4
Fredericia Denmark **47** B4
Frederick *TX* U.S.A. **141** E2
Fredericksburg *TX* U.S.A. **141** E2
Fredericksburg *VA* U.S.A. **137** E3
Frederick Sound *sea chan.* U.S.A. **126** B2
Fredericton Can. **125** H3
Frederikshavn Denmark **47** C4
Fredrikstad Norway **47** C4
Freeport *IL* U.S.A. **136** C2
Freeport *TX* U.S.A. **141** E3
Freeport City Bahamas **144** C2
Freer U.S.A. **141** E3
Free State *prov.* S. Africa **109** C2
Freetown Sierra Leone **100** A4
Fregenal de la Sierra Spain **60** B2
Fréhel, Cap *c.* France **58** B2
Freiberg Ger. **55** F2
Freiburg im Breisgau Ger. **56** B3
Freising Ger. **56** C3

Freistadt Austria **56** C3
Freital Ger. **55** F2
Fréjus France **59** D3
Fremantle Austr. **114** A3
Fremont *NE* U.S.A. **135** D2
Fremont *OH* U.S.A. **136** D2
French Guiana *terr.* S. America **151** D2
Frenchman *r.* U.S.A. **132** E1
French Polynesia *terr.* S. Pacific Ocean **113**
Frenda Alg. **61** D2
Fresnillo Mex. **142** B2
Fresno U.S.A. **133** C3
Freu, Cap des *c.* Spain **61** D2
Freyming-Merlebach France **59** D2
Fria Guinea **100** A3
Frías Arg. **152** B3
Friedland Ger. **55** F1
Friedrichshafen Ger. **56** B3
Friesack Ger. **55** F1
Friesoythe Ger. **54** C1
Frobisher Bay Can. *see* Iqaluit
Frobisher Bay *b.* Can. **125** H2
Frohburg Ger. **55** F2
Frolovo Rus. Fed. **41** D4
Frome, Lake *salt flat* Austr. **116** B2
Frome Downs Austr. **116** B2
Fröndenberg Ger. **54** C2
Frontera Mex. **143** C3
Fronteras Mex. **142** B1
Frosinone Italy **62** B2
Frøya *i.* Norway **46** B3
Frutigen Switz. **59** D2
Frýdek-Místek Czech Rep. **57** D3
Fu'an China **83** B3
Fuenlabrada Spain **60** C1
Fuerte Olimpo Para. **152** C3
Fuerteventura *i.* Canary Is **100** A2
Fuga *i.* Phil. **76** B2
Fujairah U.A.E. **91** C2
Fuji Japan **79** C3
Fujian *prov.* China **83** B3
Fujinomiya Japan **79** C3
Fuji-san *vol.* Japan **79** C3
Fukui Japan **79** C3
Fukuoka Japan **79** B4
Fukushima Japan **79** D3
Fulda Ger. **55** D2
Fulda *r.* Ger. **55** D2
Fuling China **83** A3
Fulton U.S.A. **135** E3
Fumay France **59** C2
Funabashi Japan **79** D3
Funafuti *atoll* Tuvalu **110**
Funchal Madeira **100** A1
Fundão Port. **60** B1
Fundy, Bay of *g.* Can. **129** D2
Funhalouro Moz. **109** D1
Funing *Jiangsu* China **82** B2
Funing *Yunnan* China **83** A3
Funtua Nigeria **101** C3
Fürgun, Küh-e *mt.* Iran **91** C2
Furmanov Rus. Fed. **43** F2
Furnas, Represa *resr* Brazil **155** C2
Furneaux Group *is* Austr. **115** D4
Fürstenau Ger. **54** C1
Fürstenwalde Ger. **56** C1
Fürth Ger. **55** E3
Furth im Wald Ger. **55** F3
Furukawa Japan **78** D3
Fushun China **82** C1
Fusong China **77** B1
Fuwayriṭ Qatar **91** C2
Fuxin China **82** C1
Fuyang China **82** B2
Fuyu China **81** E1
Fuyun China **89** F2
Fuzhou *Fujian* China **83** B3
Fuzhou *Jiangxi* China **83** B3
Fyn *i.* Denmark **47** C4

aalkacyo Somalia **103** C4
aabela Angola **106** A1
aabès Tunisia **101** D1
aabès, Golfe de *g.* Tunisia **101** D1
aadag India **85** B3
aadchiroli India **87** C2
aadebusch Ger. **55** E1
aadsden U.S.A. **139** C2
aaeşti Romania **44** C3
aaeta Italy **62** B2
aaborne Botswana **109** C1
aabrovo Bulg. **66** C2
aabù Guinea-Bissau **100** A3
aachon *country* Africa **104** B3
aafertut U. Micronesia **110**
aaffney U.S.A. **139** D1
aafsa Tunisia **101** C1
aagarin Rus. Fed. **43** E2
aagnoa Côte d'Ivoire **100** B4
aagnon India **87** C2
aagra Georgia **93** C1
aaiab *watercourse* Namibia **108** A2
aaillac France **58** C3
aainesville *FL* U.S.A. **139** D3
aainesville *GA* U.S.A. **139** D2
aainesville *TX* U.S.A. **141** E2
aainsborough U.K. **52** C3
aairdner, Lake *salt flat* Austr. **116** B2
aairloch U.K. **50** B2
aalana *r.* Kenya **105** E3
aalashiels U.K. **50** C3
aalaţi Romania **44** C2
aaldhøpiggen *mt.* Norway **47** B3
aaleana Mex. **143** B2
aalena Bay Can. **126** D2
aalera, Punta *pt* Chile **147**
aalesburg U.S.A. **136** B2
aalesheve S. Africa **108** B2
aalich Rus. Fed. **43** F2
aalichskaya Vozvyshennost' *hills*
Rus. Fed. **43** F2
aalicia *aut. comm.* Spain **60** B1
aalilee, Sea of *l.* Israel **92** B2
aalilee Sri Lanka **85** C4
aallatin U.S.A. **139** C1
aallinas, Punta *pt* Col. **150** B1
aallipoli Italy **63** C2
aallipoli Turkey **65** C2
aallup U.S.A. **140** C1
aaltat Zemmour Western Sahara
100 A2
aaltymore *h.* Rep. of Ireland **51** B2
aalveston U.S.A. **141** F3
aalveston Bay U.S.A. **141** F3
aalway Rep. of Ireland **51** B2
aalway Bay Rep. of Ireland **51** B2
aamá Brazil **154** C1
aamalakhe S. Africa **109** D3
aambia, The *country* Africa **100** A3
aambier, Îles *is* Fr. Polynesia **111**
aambier Islands Austr. **116** B3
aambo Can. **129** C2
aamboma Congo **104** B3
aanado U.S.A. **140** C1
aanäveh Iran **91** C2
aancã Azer. **93** C1
aandaiwata, Bukit *mt.* Indon. **73** C2
aandajika Dem. Rep. Congo **104** C3
aander Can. **129** C2
aander *r.* Can. **129** E2
aanderkesee Ger. **55** D1

Gandesa Spain **61** D1
Gandhidham India **86** B2
Gandhinagar India **86** B2
Gandhi Sagar *resr* India **86** B2
Gandía Spain **61** C2
Ganga *r.* Bangl./India **87** D2
Gangán Arg. **153** B5
Ganganagar India **86** B2
Gangdisê Shan *mts* China **87** C1
Ganges France **59** C3
Ganges, Mouths of the Bangl./India
87 C2
Gangtok India **87** C2
Gannat France **59** C2
Gannett Peak U.S.A. **134** B2
Gansbaai S. Africa **108** A3
Gansu *prov.* China **82** A2
Ganzhou China **83** B3
Gao Mali **100** B3
Gaoual Guinea **100** A3
Gaoyou China **82** B2
Gaoyou Hu *l.* China **82** B2
Gap France **59** D3
Gap Carbon *hd* Alg. **61** C2
Gar China **87** C1
Garah Austr. **117** D1
Garanhuns Brazil **151** F3
Garbahaarrey Somalia **105** E2
Garberville U.S.A. **132** B2
Garbsen Ger. **55** D1
Garça Brazil **154** C2
Garda, Lake Italy **62** B1
Gardelegen Ger. **55** E1
Garden City U.S.A. **134** C3
Garden Hill Can. **127** F2
Gardēz Afgh. **86** A1
Gargždai Lith. **42** B2
Gariep Dam *resr* S. Africa **109** C3
Garies S. Africa **108** A3
Garissa Kenya **105** D3
Garmisch-Partenkirchen Ger. **56** C3
Garnpung Lake *imp. l.* Austr. **116** C2
Garonne *r.* France **58** B3
Garoowe Somalia **103** C4
Garoth India **86** B2
Garoua Cameroon **104** B3
Garry *r.* U.K. **50** B2
Garry Lake Can. **127** E1
Garsen Kenya **105** E3
Garut Indon. **72** B2
Gary U.S.A. **136** C2
Garza García Mex. **143** B2
Garzê China **80** C2
Gascony, Gulf of France **58** B3
Gascoyne *r.* Austr. **114** A2
Gashua Nigeria **101** D3
Gaspé Can. **129** D2
Gaspé, Péninsule de *pen.* Can.
129 D2
Gaston, Lake U.S.A. **139** E1
Gastonia U.S.A. **139** D1
Gata, Cabo de *c.* Spain **61** C2
Gatchina Rus. Fed. **42** D2
Gateshead U.K. **52** C2
Gatesville U.S.A. **141** E2
Gatineau *r.* Can. **128** C2
Gatton Austr. **117** E1
Gauer Lake Can. **127** F2
Gausta *mt.* Norway **47** B4
Gauteng *prov.* S. Africa **109** C2
Gâvbandī Iran **91** C2
Gavdos *i.* Greece **65** B4
Gävle Sweden **47** D3
Gavrilov Posad Rus. Fed. **43** F2
Gavrilov-Yam Rus. Fed. **43** F2
Gawai Myanmar **74** A1
Gawler Austr. **116** B2
Gawler Ranges *hills* Austr. **116** B2
Gaya India **87** C2

Gaya Niger **100** C3
Gaylord U.S.A. **136** D1
Gayny Rus. Fed. **40** E2
Gaza *terr.* Asia **92** B2
Gaza China **92** B2
Gaz-Achak Turkm. **88** D2
Gazandzhyk Turkm. **88** C2
Gaziantep Turkey **102** B1
Gbarnga Liberia **100** B4
Gdańsk Pol. **57** D2
Gdańsk, Gulf of Pol./Rus. Fed. **57** D2
Gdov Rus. Fed. **42** C2
Gdynia Pol. **57** D2
Gedaref Sudan **102** B3
Gedern Ger. **55** D2
Gediz *r.* Turkey **65** C3
Gedser Denmark **56** C2
Geel Belgium **54** B2
Geelong Austr. **116** C3
Geesthacht Ger. **55** E1
Gê'gyai China **87** C1
Geikie *r.* Can. **124** F3
Geilo Norway **47** B3
Gejiu China **83** A3
Gela Italy **62** B3
Gelendzhik Rus. Fed. **45** E3
Gelibolu Turkey *see* Gallipoli
Gelsenkirchen Ger. **54** C2
Gemena Dem. Rep. Congo **104** B2
Gemlik Turkey **65** C2
Gemona del Friuli Italy **59** E2
Genalē Wenz *r.* Eth. **103** C4
General Acha Arg. **153** B4
General Alvear Arg. **153** B4
General Belgrano Arg. **153** C4
General Cepeda Mex. **142** B2
General Pico Arg. **153** B4
General Roca Arg. **153** B4
General Santos Phil. **76** B3
Genesee *r.* U.S.A. **137** C2
Geneseo U.S.A. **137** E2
Geneva Switz. **59** D2
Geneva U.S.A. **137** E2
Geneva, Lake France/Switz. **59** D2
Genève Switz. *see* Geneva
Genil *r.* Spain **60** B2
Genk Belgium **54** B2
Genoa Italy **62** A2
Genova Italy *see* Genoa
Gent Belgium *see* Ghent
Genthin Ger. **55** F1
Geographe Bay Austr. **114** A3
George *r.* Can. **129** D1
George S. Africa **108** B3
George, Lake *FL* U.S.A. **139** D3
George, Lake *NY* U.S.A. **137** F2
Georgetown Gambia **100** A3
George Town Malaysia **72** B1
Georgetown *SC* U.S.A. **139** E2
Georgetown *TX* U.S.A. **141** E2
George V Land *reg.* Antarctica **119** H3
Georgia *country* Asia **93** C1
Georgia *state* U.S.A. **139** D2
Georgian Bay Can. **137** D1
Georgina *watercourse* Austr. **115** C2
Georgiyevka Kazakh. **89** F2
Georgiyevsk Rus. Fed. **41** D4
Gera Ger. **55** F2
Geral, Serra *mts* Brazil **154** C3
Geraldine N.Z. **118** B3
Geraldton Austr. **114** A2
Gerede Turkey **92** B1
Gereshk Afgh. **86** A1
Gerlach U.S.A. **132** C2
Gerlachovský štít *mt.* Slovakia **57** E3
Germany *country* Europe **56** B2
Gerolstein Ger. **54** C2
Gerolzhofen Ger. **55** E3
Gersfeld (Rhön) Ger. **55** D2

Gêrzê China **87** C1
Gettysburg *PA* U.S.A. **137** E3
Gettysburg *SD* U.S.A. **134** D1
Gevgelija Macedonia **65** B2
Geyikli Turkey **65** C3
Ghaap Plateau S. Africa **108** B2
Ghadāmis Libya **101** C1
Ghaghara *r.* India **87** C2
Ghana *country* Africa **100** B4
Ghanzi Botswana **108** B2
Ghardaïa Alg. **100** C1
Gharyān Libya **101** D1
Ghatal India **87** B2
Ghazaouet Alg. **61** F2
Ghaziabad India **87** B2
Ghazipur India **87** B2
Ghaznī Afgh. **86** A1
Ghent Belgium **54** A2
Gherla Romania **44** B2
Ghisonaccia France **59** D3
Ghotaru India **86** B2
Ghotki Pak. **86** A2
Giaginskaya Rus. Fed. **45** F3
Giant's Causeway *lava field* U.K.
51 C1
Gianyar Indon. **73** C2
Giarre Italy **62** C3
Giaveno Italy **62** A1
Gibeon Namibia **108** A2
Gibraltar Gibraltar **60** B2
Gibraltar, Strait of Morocco/Spain
60 B2
Gibson Desert Austr. **114** B2
Gichgeniyn Nuruu *mts* Mongolia
80 C1
Gīdolē Eth. **103** B4
Gien France **58** C2
Gießen Ger. **55** E1
Gifhorn Ger. **55** D1
Gift Lake Can. **126** D2
Gifu Japan **79** C3
Gigha *i.* U.K. **50** B3
Gijón-Xixón Spain **60** B1
Gila *r.* U.S.A. **140** B2
Gila Bend U.S.A. **140** B2
Gilbert *r.* Austr. **115** D1
Gilbert Islands Kiribati **110**
Gildford U.S.A. **132** D1
Gilgandra Austr. **117** D2
Gilgit Jammu and Kashmir **86** B1
Gilgit *r.* Jammu and Kashmir **86** B1
Gilgunnia Austr. **117** D2
Gillam Can. **127** F2
Gillette U.S.A. **134** B2
Gillingham U.K. **53** D4
Gilmour Island Can. **128** C1
Gimli Can. **127** F2
Gīnīr Eth. **103** C4
Ginosa Italy **62** C2
Gippsland *reg.* Austr. **117** D3
Girdi Iran **91** D1
Giresun Turkey **92** B1
Girona Spain **61** D1
Girvan U.K. **50** B3
Gisborne N.Z. **118** C2
Gislaved Sweden **47** C4
Gitarama Rwanda **105** C3
Giulianova Italy **62** B2
Giurgiu Romania **44** C3
Giuvala, Pasul *pass* Romania **44** C2
Givors France **59** C2
Giyani S. Africa **109** D1
Giza Egypt **102** B2
Gjirokastër Albania **65** B2
Gjoa Haven Can. **124** F2
Gjøvik Norway **47** C3
Glace Bay Can. **129** E2
Glacier Peak *vol.* U.S.A. **132** B1
Gladstone Austr. **115** E2

Gláma *mts* Iceland **46** [inset]
Glamoč Bos.-Herz. **63** C2
Glan *r.* Ger. **54** C3
Glanaruddery Mountains
Rep. of Ireland **51** B2
Glasgow U.K. **50** B3
Glasgow *KY* U.S.A. **136** C3
Glasgow *MT* U.S.A. **132** E1
Glastonbury U.K. **53** B4
Glauchau Ger. **55** F2
Glazov Rus. Fed. **40** E3
Glazunovka Rus. Fed. **43** E3
Glen Coe *val.* U.K. **50** B2
Glendale U.S.A. **140** B2
Glen Davis Austr. **117** E2
Glendive U.S.A. **134** C1
Glenelg *r.* Austr. **116** C3
Glen Innes Austr. **117** E1
Glenmorgan Austr. **117** D1
Glennallen U.S.A. **124** C2
Glenrothes U.K. **50** C2
Glens Falls U.S.A. **137** F2
Glen Shee *val.* U.K. **50** C2
Glenties Rep. of Ireland **51** B1
Glenwood U.S.A. **140** C2
Glenwood Springs U.S.A. **134** B3
Gliwice Pol. **57** D2
Globe U.S.A. **140** B2
Głogów Pol. **57** D2
Glomfjord Norway **46** C2
Glomma *r.* Norway **47** C4
Gloucester Austr. **117** E2
Gloucester U.K. **53** B4
Glöwen Ger. **55** F1
Glubokoye Kazakh. **89** F1
Glückstadt Ger. **55** D1
Gmünd Austria **56** C3
Gmunden Austria **56** C3
Gnarrenburg Ger. **55** D1
Gniezno Pol. **57** D2
Gnjilane Serb. and Mont. **64** B2
Goalpara India **87** D2
Goat Fell *h.* U.K. **50** B3
Goba Eth. **103** C4
Gobabis Namibia **108** A1
Gobernador Gregores Arg. **153** A3
Gobi *des.* China/Mongolia **82** A1
Goch Ger. **54** C2
Gochas Namibia **108** A1
Godavari *r.* India **85** C3
Goderich Can. **128** B2
Godhra India **86** B2
Gods *r.* Can. **127** F2
Gods Lake Can. **127** F2
Godthåb Greenland *see* Nuuk
Godwin Austen *mt.*
China/Jammu and Kashmir *see* K2
Goéland, Lac au l. Can. **128** C2
Goélands, Lac aux l. Can. **129** D1
Goiandira Brazil **154** C1
Goiânia Brazil **154** C1
Goiás Brazil **154** B1
Goio-Erê Brazil **154** B2
Gökçeada *i.* Turkey **65** C2
Gökçedağ Turkey **65** C3
Gokwe Zimbabwe **107** B1
Gol Norway **47** B3
Golaghat India **74** A1
Gol'chikha Rus. Fed. **40** H1
Gölcük Turkey **65** C2
Gołdap Pol. **57** E2
Goldberg Ger. **55** F1
Gold Coast Austr. **117** E1
Gold Coast *coastal area* Ghana **100** B4
Golden Can. **126** D2
Golden Bay N.Z. **118** B3
Golden Hinde *mt.* Can. **126** C3
Golden Vale *lowland* Rep. of Ireland
51 B2

Goldfield U.S.A. **133** C3
Gold River Can. **126** C3
Goldsboro U.S.A. **139** E1
Goleta U.S.A. **133** C4
Golmud China **80** C2
Golpāyegān Iran **93** D2
Golspie U.K. **50** C2
Goma Dem. Rep. Congo **105** C3
Gomati *r.* India **87** C2
Gombe Nigeria **101** D3
Gombi Nigeria **101** D3
Gómez Palacio Mex. **142** B2
Gonaïves Haiti **145** C3
Gonâve, Île de la *i.* Haiti **145** C3
Gonbad-e Kavus Iran **93** D2
Gonder Eth. **103** B3
Gondia India **87** C2
Gönen Turkey **65** C2
Gongola *r.* Nigeria **101** D4
Gongogxon Austr. **117** D2
Gongzhuling China **77** A1
Gonzáles Mex. **143** C2
Gonzales U.S.A. **141** E3
Good Hope, Cape of S. Africa **108** A3
Gooding U.S.A. **132** D2
Goodland U.S.A. **134** C3
Goodooga Austr. **117** D1
Goole U.K. **52** C3
Goolgowi Austr. **117** D2
Goolwa Austr. **116** B3
Goondiwindi Austr. **117** E1
Goose Lake U.S.A. **132** B2
Göppingen Ger. **56** B3
Gorakhpur India **87** C2
Goražde Bos.-Herz. **63** C2
Gördes Turkey **65** C3
Gordeyevka Rus. Fed. **43** D3
Goré Chad **101** D4
Gorē Eth. **103** B4
Gore N.Z. **118** A4
Gorey Rep. of Ireland **51** C2
Gorgān Iran **93** D2
Gori Georgia **93** C1
Gorizia Italy **62** B1
Gorlice Pol. **57** E3
Görlitz Ger. **56** C2
Gornji Milanovac Serb. and Mont.
64 B2
Gornji Vakuf Bos.-Herz. **63** C2
Gorno-Altaysk Rus. Fed. **89** F1
Gornotrakiyska Nizina *lowland* Bulg.
64 C2
Gornyak Rus. Fed. **89** F1
Goroka P.N.G. **71** D3
Gorokhovets Rus. Fed. **43** F2
Gorom Gorom Burkina **100** B3
Gorontalo Indon. **73** C1
Gorshechnoye Rus. Fed. **43** E3
Gorumna Island Rep. of Ireland **51** B2
Goryachiy Klyuch Rus. Fed. **45** E3
Gorzów Wielkopolski Pol. **56** D2
Gosford Austr. **117** E2
Goshogawara Japan **78** D2
Goslar Ger. **55** E2
Gospić Croatia **62** C2
Gosport U.K. **53** C4
Gostivar Macedonia **64** B2
Göteborg Sweden *see* Gothenburg
Gotha Ger. **55** E2
Gothenburg Sweden **47** C4
Gothenburg U.S.A. **134** C2
Gotland *i.* Sweden **47** D4
Gotse Delchev Bulg. **65** B2
Gotska Sandön *i.* Sweden **47** D4
Gōtsu Japan **79** B4
Göttingen Ger. **55** D2
Gott Peak Can. **126** C3
Gouda Neth. **54** B1
Goudiri Senegal **100** A3
Goudoumaria Niger **101** D3

ouin, Réservoir resr Can. **128** C2
oulburn Austr. **117** D2
oulburn r. N.S.W. Austr. **117** C3
oulburn r. Vic. Austr. **117** C3
oundam Mali **100** B3
ouraya Alg. **61** D2
ourdon France **58** C3
ouré Niger **101** D3
ourits r. S. Africa **108** B3
ourma-Rharous Mali **100** B3
overnador Valadares Brazil **155** D1
overnor's Harbour Bahamas **139** E3
ovi Altayn Nuruu mts Mongolia
80 C2
ower pen. U.K. **53** A4
oya Arg. **152** C3
öyçay Azer. **93** C1
ozha Co salt l. China **87** C1
abow Ger. **55** E1
ačac Croatia **63** C2
ačachevka Rus. Fed. **41** E3
äfenhainichen Ger. **55** F2
rafton Austr. **117** E1
rafton U.S.A. **135** D1
raham U.S.A. **141** D3
raham Island Can. **126** B2
raham Land reg. Antarctica **119** K3
rahamstown S. Africa **109** C3
rajaú Brazil **151** E3
rammos mt. Greece **65** B2
rampian Mountains U.K. **50** D3
ranada Nic. **144** B3
ranada Spain **60** C2
ranby Can. **137** F1
ran Canaria i. Canary Is **100** A2
ran Chaco reg. Arg./Para. **152** B3
rand r. U.S.A. **134** F2
rand Bahama i. Bahamas **144** C2
rand Bank Can. **129** E2
rand Canal China see Da Yunhe
rand Canyon U.S.A. **140** B1
rand Canyon gorge U.S.A. **140** B1
rand Cayman i. Cayman Is **144** B3
rand Centre Can. **127** D2
rand Coulee U.S.A. **132** C1
rande r. Bol. **152** B2
rande r. Brazil **155** D2
rande, Bahía b. Arg. **153** B6
rande, Ilha i. Brazil **155** D2
rande Cache Can. **126** D2
rande Comore i. Comoros see
Njazidja
rande Prairie Can. **126** D2
rand Erg de Bilma des. Niger **101** D3
rand Erg Occidental des. Alg.
100 B1
rand Erg Oriental des. Alg. **101** C2
rande-Rivière Can. **129** D2
randes, Salinas salt marsh Arg.
152 B2
rand Falls N.B. Can. **137** D3
rand Falls Nfld. and Lab. Can. **129** E2
rand Forks Can. **126** D3
rand Forks U.S.A. **135** D1
rand Island U.S.A. **138** B3
rand Isle U.S.A. **138** B3
rand Junction U.S.A. **134** B3
rand Lake N.B. Can. **129** D2
rand Lake Nfld. and Lab. Can. **129** E2
rand Marais U.S.A. **135** E1
rândola Port. **60** B2
rand Rapids Can. **127** E2
rand Rapids MI U.S.A. **136** C2
rand Rapids MN U.S.A. **135** E1

Grand Teton mt. U.S.A. **134** A2
Grand Turk Turks and Caicos Is
145 C2
Grangeville U.S.A. **132** C1
Granisle Can. **126** C2
Granite Peak U.S.A. **132** E1
Granitola, Capo c. Italy **62** B3
Gränna Sweden **47** C4
Gransee Ger. **55** F1
Grantham U.K. **52** C3
Grantown-on-Spey U.K. **50** C2
Grants U.S.A. **140** C1
Grants Pass U.S.A. **132** B2
Granville France **58** B2
Granville Lake Can. **127** E2
Grão Mogol Brazil **155** D1
Grarem Alg. **61** E2
Graskop S. Africa **109** D1
Grasse France **59** D3
Graus Spain **61** D1
Gravdal Norway **46** H2
Grave, Pointe de pt France **58** B2
Gravelbourg Can. **127** E3
Gravenhurst Can. **128** C2
Gravesend U.K. **53** D4
Gravesend Austr. **117** E1
Gray France **59** D2
Graz Austria **57** D3
Great Abaco i. Bahamas **145** C2
Great Australian Bight g. Austr.
114 F3
Great Barrier Island N.Z. **118** C3
Great Barrier Reef Austr. **115** D1
Great Basin U.S.A. **133** C3
Great Bear Lake Can. **126** D1
Great Belt sea chan. Denmark **47** C4
Great Bend U.S.A. **138** D3
Great Coco Island Cocos Is **75** A2
Great Dividing Range mts Austr.
117 C3
Greater Antilles is Caribbean Sea
144 B2
Great Falls U.S.A. **132** D1
Great Fish r. S. Africa **109** C3
Great Fish Point pt S. Africa **109** C3
Great Inagua i. Bahamas **145** C2
Great Karoo plat. S. Africa **108** B3
Great Kei r. S. Africa **109** C3
Great Malvern U.K. **53** B3
Great Namaqualand reg. Namibia
108 A2
Great Nicobar i. India **75** A3
Great Ouse r. U.K. **53** D3
Great Plains reg. U.S.A. **121**
Great Rift Valley Africa **105** D3
Great Ruaha r. Tanz. **105** D3
Great Salt Lake U.S.A. **132** D2
Great Salt Lake Desert U.S.A. **132** D2
Great Sand Sea des. Egypt/Libya
102 A2
Great Sandy Desert Austr. **114** B2
Great Slave Lake Can. **126** D1
Great Smoky Mountains U.S.A.
139 D1
Great Victoria Desert Austr. **114** B2
Great Yarmouth U.K. **53** D3
Gredos, Sierra de mts Spain **60** D2
Greece country Europe **65** B3
Greeley U.S.A. **134** C2
Greem-Bell, Ostrov i. Rus. Fed. **94** G1
Green r. Can. **136** G1
Green r. KY U.S.A. **139** C1
Green r. WY U.S.A. **134** B3
Green Bay U.S.A. **136** C2
Green Bay b. U.S.A. **136** C1
Greenbrier r. U.S.A. **137** D3
Greencastle U.S.A. **136** C3
Greeneville U.S.A. **139** D1
Greenfield U.S.A. **137** F2
Green Lake Can. **127** E2

Greenland terr. N. America **125** J2
Greenland Sea Greenland/Svalbard
94 B1
Greenock U.K. **50** B3
Green River UT U.S.A. **133** D3
Green River WY U.S.A. **134** B2
Greensburg IN U.S.A. **136** C3
Greensburg PA U.S.A. **137** E2
Green Swamp U.S.A. **139** E2
Green Valley U.S.A. **140** B2
Greenville Liberia **100** B4
Greenville AL U.S.A. **138** C2
Greenville MS U.S.A. **138** B2
Greenville NC U.S.A. **139** E1
Greenville SC U.S.A. **139** D2
Greenville TX U.S.A. **141** E2
Greenwell Point Austr. **117** E2
Greenwood U.S.A. **139** D2
Gregory, Lake salt flat Austr. **114** B2
Gregory Range hills Austr. **115** D1
Greifswald Ger. **56** C2
Greiz Ger. **55** F2
Grená Denmark **47** C4
Grenada U.S.A. **138** C2
Grenada country West Indies **145** D3
Grenade France **58** C3
Grenfell Austr. **117** D2
Grenfell Can. **127** E2
Grenoble France **59** D2
Grenville, Cape Austr. **115** D1
Gresham U.S.A. **132** B1
Greven Ger. **54** C1
Grevena Greece **65** B2
Grevenbroich Ger. **54** C2
Greybull U.S.A. **134** B2
Grey Hunter Peak Can. **126** B1
Grey Islands Can. **129** E1
Greymouth N.Z. **118** B3
Grey Range hills Austr. **116** C1
Greystones Rep. of Ireland **51** C2
Gribanovskiy Rus. Fed. **45** F1
Griffin U.S.A. **139** D2
Griffith Austr. **117** D2
Grimma Ger. **55** F2
Grimmen Ger. **56** C2
Grimsby U.K. **52** C3
Grimshaw Can. **126** D2
Grímsstaðir Iceland **46** [inset]
Grimstad Norway **47** B4
Grinnell U.S.A. **135** E2
Griquland East reg. S. Africa **109** C3
Griquland West reg. S. Africa **108** B2
Grise Fiord Can. **125** G1
Gritley U.K. **50** C1
Groblersdal S. Africa **109** C2
Groblershoop S. Africa **108** B2
Groix, Île de i. France **58** B2
Gronau (Westfalen) Ger. **54** C1
Grong Norway **46** C3
Groningen Neth. **54** C1
Grootdrink S. Africa **108** B2
Groote Eylandt i. Austr. **115** C1
Grootfontein Namibia **106** A1
Groot Karas Berg plat. Namibia
108 A2
Groot Swartberge mts S. Africa
108 B3
Groot Winterberg mts. S. Africa **109** C3
Großenlüder Ger. **55** D2
Großer Rachel mt. Ger. **55** F3
Grosser Speikkogel mt. Austria **56** C3
Grosseto Italy **62** B2
Groß-Gerau Ger. **55** D3
Großglockner mt. Austria **56** C3
Groß-Hesepe Ger. **54** C1
Großlohra Ger. **55** E2
Groß Schönebeck Ger. **55** F1
Gross Ums Namibia **108** A1
Groswater Bay Can. **129** E1
Groundhog r. Can. **128** B2

Grover Beach U.S.A. **133** B3
Groveton U.S.A. **137** F2
Grozny Rus. Fed. **41** D4
Grubišno Polje Croatia **63** C1
Grudziądz Pol. **57** D2
Grünau Namibia **108** A2
Grundarfjörður Iceland **46** [inset]
Gryazi Rus. Fed. **43** E3
Gryazovets Rus. Fed. **43** F2
Gryfice Pol. **56** C2
Gryfino Pol. **56** C2
Grytviken S. Georgia **153** E6
Guacanayabo, Golfo de b. Cuba
   144 C2
Guadalajara Mex. **142** B2
Guadalcanal i. Solomon Is **110**
Guadalope r. Spain **61** C1
Guadalquivir r. Spain **60** B2
Guadalupe i. Mex. **130** B4
Guadalupe, Sierra de mts Spain
   60 B2
Guadalupe Peak U.S.A. **140** D2
Guadalupe Victoria Mex. **142** B2
Guadalupe y Calvo Mex. **142** B2
Guadarrama, Sierra de mts Spain
   60 C1
Guadeloupe terr. West Indies **145** C2
Guadiana r. Port./Spain **60** B2
Guadix Spain **60** C2
Guaíra Brazil **154** B2
Guajira, Península de la pen. Col.
   145 C3
Gualaceo Ecuador **150** B3
Guam terr. N. Pacific Ocean **71** D2
Guamúchil Mex. **142** B2
Guanacevi Mex. **142** B2
Guanambi Brazil **151** E4
Guanare Venez. **150** C2
Guane Cuba **144** B2
Guang'an China **83** A2
Guangchang China **83** B3
Guangdong prov. China **83** B3
Guangxi Zhuangzu Zizhiqu aut. reg.
   China **83** A3
Guangyuan China **82** A2
Guangzhou China **83** B3
Guanhães Brazil **155** D1
Guanipa r. Venez. **145** D4
Guanling China **83** A3
Guanshui China **77** A1
Guantánamo Cuba **145** C2
Guaporé r. Bol./Brazil **152** B2
Guarapuava Brazil **154** C3
Guaraqueçaba Brazil **154** C3
Guaratinguetá Brazil **155** C3
Guarda Port. **60** B1
Guarda Mor Brazil **154** C1
Guardo Spain **60** C1
Guarujá Brazil **155** C2
Guasave Mex. **142** B2
Guatemala country Central America
   144 A3
Guatemala City Guat. **144** A3
Guaviare r. Col. **150** C2
Guaxupé Brazil **155** C2
Guayaquil Ecuador **150** B3
Guayaquil, Golfo de g. Ecuador **146**
Guayaramerín Bol. **152** B2
Guaymas Mex. **142** A2
Guba Eth. **103** B3
Guba Dolgaya Rus. Fed. **40** E1
Gubbio Italy **59** E3
Gubkin Rus. Fed. **43** E3
Guelma Alg. **101** C1
Guelph Can. **128** B2
Guémez Mex. **143** C2
Guénange France **54** C3
Guéret France **58** C2
Guernsey i. Channel Is **53** B5

Guerrero Negro Mex. **142** A2
Guers, Lac l. Can. **129** D1
Guiana Highlands mts Guyana/Venez.
   150 C2
Guider Cameroon **104** B2
Guidonia-Montecelio Italy **62** B2
Guigang China **83** A3
Guignicourt France **54** A3
Guija Moz. **109** D1
Guildford U.K. **53** C4
Guilin China **83** B3
Guillaume-Delisle, Lac l. Can. **128** C1
Guimarães Port. **60** B1
Guinea country Africa **100** A3
Guinea, Gulf of Africa **100** C4
Guinea-Bissau country Africa **100** A3
Guingamp France **58** B2
Guipavas France **58** B2
Guiratinga Brazil **154** B1
Güiria Venez. **150** C1
Guise France **54** A3
Guiuan Phil. **76** B3
Guiyang China **83** A3
Guizhou prov. China **83** A3
Gujranwala Pak. **86** B1
Gujrat Pak. **86** B1
Gukovo Rus. Fed. **45** E2
Gulang China **82** A2
Gulargambone Austr. **117** D2
Gulbarga India **85** B3
Gulbene Latvia **42** C2
Gulfport U.S.A. **138** C2
Gulian China **81** E1
Guliston Uzbek. **89** D2
Gul'kevichi Rus. Fed. **45** F2
Gull Lake Can. **127** C2
Güllük Turkey **65** C3
Gulu Uganda **105** D2
Gumare Botswana **106** B1
Gumdag Turkm. **88** B3
Gumla India **87** C2
Gummersbach Ger. **54** C2
Guna India **86** B2
Gundagai Austr. **117** D3
Güney Turkey **65** C3
Gungu Dem. Rep. Congo **104** B3
Gunisao r. Can. **127** F2
Gunnedah Austr. **117** E2
Gunnison CO U.S.A. **134** B3
Gunnison UT U.S.A. **133** D3
Gunnison r. U.S.A. **134** B3
Guntakal India **85** B3
Gunungsitoli Indon. **72** A1
Gunungtua Indon. **72** A1
Günzburg Ger. **56** C3
Gunzenhausen Ger. **55** E3
Guojiaba China **82** B2
Gurgaon India **86** B2
Gurgueia r. Brazil **151** E3
Gurinhatã Brazil **154** C1
Gurupi r. Brazil **151** E3
Guru Sikhar mt. India **86** B2
Gusau Nigeria **101** C3
Gushan China **77** A2
Gushgy Turkm. **86** A1
Gushi China **82** B2
Gusinoozersk Rus. Fed. **95** J3
Gus'-Khrustal'nyy Rus. Fed. **43** F2
Guspini Italy **62** A3
Gustavus U.S.A. **126** B2
Güstrow Ger. **55** F1
Gütersloh Ger. **55** D2
Gutu Zimbabwe **107** C1
Guwahati India **87** D2
Guyana country S. America **150** D2
Guymon U.S.A. **141** D1
Guyra Austr. **117** E2
Guyuan China **82** A2
Guzmán Mex. **142** B1

Guzmán, Lago de l. Mex. **142** B1

Haapsalu Estonia **42** B2
Haarlem Neth. **54** B1
Haarstrang ridge Ger. **55** C2
Haast N.Z. **118** A3
Habban Yemen **90** B3
Habbānīyah, Hawr al l. Iraq **93** C2
Hachijō-jima i. Japan **79** C4
Hachinohe Japan **78** D2
Hacufera Moz. **107** C2
Ḥadd, Ra's al pt Oman **91** C2
Haddington U.K. **50** C3
Hadejia Nigeria **101** D3
Haderslev Denmark **47** B4
Hadyach Ukr. **45** D1
Haeju N. Korea **77** B2
Haeju-man b. N. Korea **77** B2
Haenam S. Korea **77** B3
Ḥafar al Bāṭin Saudi Arabia **90** B2
Haflong India **74** A1
Hafnarfjörður Iceland **46** [inset]
Hagar Nish Plateau Eritrea **90** A3
Hagåtña Guam **71** D2
Hagen Ger. **54** C2
Hagenow Ger. **55** E1
Hagensborg Can. **126** C2
Hagerstown U.S.A. **137** E3
Hagfors Sweden **47** C3
Hagi Japan **79** B4
Ha Giang Vietnam **74** B1
Hag's Head Rep. of Ireland **51** B2
Hague, Cap de la c. France **58** B2
Hai Tanz. **105** D3
Haicheng China **77** A1
Hai Duong Vietnam **74** B1
Haifa Israel **92** B3
Haifeng China **83** B3
Haikou China **83** B3
Ḥā'il Saudi Arabia **90** B2
Hailar China see Hulun Buir
Hailuoto i. Fin. **46** E2
Hainan i. China **81** D3
Hainan prov. China **83** A4
Haines U.S.A. **126** B2
Haines Junction Can. **126** B1
Hainich ridge Ger. **55** E2
Hainleite ridge Ger. **55** E2
Hai Phong Vietnam **74** B1
Haiti country West Indies **145** C3
Haiya Sudan **102** B3
Hajdúböszörmény Hungary **57** E3

ajhir *mt.* Yemen **91** C3
ajjah Yemen **90** B3
ijjābād Iran **93** D3
ajmā' Oman **91** C3
aka Myanmar **74** A1
akkārī Turkey **93** C2
akodate Japan **78** D2
alab Syria *see* Aleppo
alabān Saudi Arabia **90** B2
alabja Iraq **93** C2
alaib Sudan **102** B2
alāniyāt, Juzur al *is* Oman **91** C3
alban Mongolia **80** C1
alberstadt Ger. **55** E2
alcon, Mount Phil. **76** B2
alden Norway **47** C4
aldensleben Ger. **55** E1
aldwani India **87** B2
aleh Iran **91** C2
alfmoen Bay N.Z. **118** A4
alifax Can. **129** D2
alifax U.K. **52** C3
alifax U.S.A. **137** E3
alla-san *mt.* S. Korea **77** B3
all Beach Can. **125** G2
alle Belgium **54** B2
allein Austria **56** C3
alle (Saale) Ger. **55** E2
allock U.S.A. **135** D1
alls Creek Austr. **114** B1
almahera *i.* Indon. **71** C2
almstad Sweden **47** C4
am France **54** A3
amada Japan **79** B4
amadan Iran **93** C2
amāh Syria **92** B2
amamatsu Japan **79** C4
amar Norway **47** C3
amātah, Jabal *mt.* Egypt **102** B2
ambantota Sri Lanka **85** C4
amburg Ger. **55** D1
amḏ, Wādī al *watercourse*
Saudi Arabia **90** A2
amedah Saudi Arabia **90** B3
ameenlinna Fin. **47** E3
ameln Ger. **55** D1
amersley Range *mts* Austr. **114** A2
amhŭng N. Korea **77** B2
ami China **80** C2
amid Sudan **102** B2
amilton Austr. **116** C3
amilton Can. **128** C2
amilton N.Z. **118** C2
amilton U.K. **50** B3
amilton *AL* U.S.A. **138** C2
amilton *MT* U.S.A. **132** D1
amilton *OH* U.S.A. **136** D3
amina Fin. **47** F3
amm Ger. **54** C2
ammada du Drâa *plat.* Alg. **100** B2
ammār, Hawr al *imp. l.* Iraq **93** C2
ammelburg Ger. **55** D2
ammerdale Sweden **46** C3
ammerfest Norway **46** E1
ammond U.S.A. **138** B2
ammonton U.S.A. **137** F3
amūn-e Jaz Mūriān *salt marsh* Iran
91 C2
amūn-i-Lora *dry lake* Afgh./Pak.
86 A2
amūn-i Mashkel *salt flat* Iran **91** C2
amūn-i-Mashkel *salt flat* Pak. **86** A2
anak Saudi Arabia **90** A2
anamaki Japan **78** D3
anau Ger. **55** D2
ancheng China **82** B2
ancock U.S.A. **136** C1
andan China **82** B2
anford U.S.A. **133** C3

Hangayn Nuruu *mts* Mongolia **80** C1
Hangzhou China **83** C2
Hangzhou Wan *b.* China **82** C2
Hanko Fin. **47** E4
Hanksville U.S.A. **133** D3
Hanmer Springs N.Z. **118** B3
Hanna Can. **127** D2
Hannibal U.S.A. **135** E3
Hannover Ger. **55** D1
Hannoversch Münden Ger. **55** D2
Hanöbukten *b.* Sweden **47** C4
Ha Nôi Vietnam **74** B1
Hanover Can. **128** B2
Hanover S. Africa **108** B3
Hanstholm Denmark **47** B4
Hantsavichy Belarus **42** C3
Hanumana India **87** C2
Hanumangarh India **86** B2
Hanzhong China **82** A2
Hao *atoll* Fr. Polynesia **111**
Haparanda Sweden **46** E2
Hapert Neth. **54** B2
Happy Valley - Goose Bay Can.
129 D1
Haql Saudi Arabia **90** A2
Haradh Saudi Arabia **91** B2
Haradok Belarus **42** C3
Harajā Saudi Arabia **90** B3
Harare Zimbabwe **107** C1
Harāsis, Jiddat al *des.* Oman **91** C3
Har-Ayrag Mongolia **81** D1
Harbin China **81** E1
Harbour Breton Can. **129** E2
Harda India **86** B2
Hardenberg Neth. **54** C1
Harderwijk Neth. **54** B1
Hardeveld *mts* S. Africa **108** A3
Hardin U.S.A. **132** E1
Hardisty Lake Can. **126** D1
Haren Ger. **54** C1
Härer Eth. **103** C4
Hargeysa Somalia **103** C4
Harghita-Mădăraş, Vârful *mt.* Romania
44 C2
Har Hu *l.* China **80** C2
Haripur Pak. **86** B1
Hari Rūd *r.* Afgh./Iran **86** A1
Harlingen Neth. **54** B1
Harlingen U.S.A. **141** D3
Harlow U.K. **53** D4
Harlowton U.S.A. **132** E1
Harnes France **54** A2
Harney Basin U.S.A. **132** C2
Harney Lake U.S.A. **132** C2
Härnösand Sweden **47** D3
Har Nur China **81** C1
Har Nuur *l.* Mongolia **80** C1
Harper Liberia **100** B4
Harpstedt Ger. **55** D1
Harricanaw *r.* Can. **128** C1
Harrington Austr. **117** E2
Harrington Harbour Can. **129** E1
Harris *pen.* U.K. **50** A2
Harris, Lake *salt flat* Austr. **116** B2
Harris, Sound of *sea chan.* U.K. **50** A2
Harrisburg *IL* U.S.A. **136** C3
Harrisburg *PA* U.S.A. **137** E2
Harrismith S. Africa **109** C2
Harrison U.S.A. **138** B1
Harrison, Cape Can. **129** E1
Harrison Bay U.S.A. **124** B2
Harrisonville U.S.A. **137** E3
Harrogate U.K. **52** C3
Hârşova Romania **44** C3
Harstad Norway **46** C2
Hartbees *watercourse* S. Africa **108** B2

Hartberg Austria **57** D3
Hartford U.S.A. **137** F2
Hartland Point *pt* U.K. **53** A4
Hartlepool U.K. **52** C2
Hartley Bay Can. **126** C2
Harts *r.* S. Africa **109** B2
Hartwell Reservoir U.S.A. **139** D2
Har Us Nuur *l.* Mongolia **80** C1
Harvey U.S.A. **134** C1
Harwich U.K. **53** D4
Harz *hills* Ger. **55** E2
Hassan India **85** B3
Hasselt Belgium **54** B2
Hassi Messaoud Alg. **101** C1
Hässleholm Sweden **47** C4
Hastière-Lavaux Belgium **54** B2
Hastings Austr. **117** D3
Hastings N.Z. **118** C2
Hastings U.K. **53** D4
Hastings *MN* U.S.A. **135** E2
Hastings *NE* U.S.A. **135** D2
Hatay Turkey *see* Antakya
Hatchet Lake Can. **127** E2
Hatfield Austr. **116** C2
Hatgal Mongolia **80** C1
Ha Tinh Vietnam **74** B2
Hatteras, Cape U.S.A. **139** E1
Hattiesburg U.S.A. **138** C2
Hattingen Ger. **54** C2
Hat Yai Thai. **75** B3
Haud *reg.* Eth. **103** C4
Haugesund Norway **47** B4
Haukeligrend Norway **47** B4
Haukipudas Fin. **46** F2
Hauraki Gulf N.Z. **118** C2
Haut Atlas *mts* Morocco **100** B1
Hauterive Can. **129** D2
Hauts Plateaux Alg. **100** B1
Havana Cuba **144** B2
Havant U.K. **53** C4
Havel *r.* Ger. **55** F1
Havelberg Ger. **55** F1
Havelock Norway **47** B4
Havelock North N.Z. **118** C2
Haverfordwest U.K. **53** A4
Havlíčkův Brod Czech Rep. **57** D3
Havøysund Norway **46** E1
Havran Turkey **65** C3
Havre U.S.A. **132** E1
Havre Aubert Can. **129** D2
Havre-St-Pierre Can. **129** D1
Hawaii *i.* U.S.A. **120**
Hawaiian Islands N. Pacific Ocean
158 E3
Hawarden U.K. **52** B3
Hawea, Lake N.Z. **118** A3
Hawera N.Z. **118** B2
Hawes U.K. **52** B2
Hawick U.K. **50** C3
Hawke Bay N.Z. **118** C2
Hawker Austr. **116** B2
Hawkers Gate Austr. **116** C2
Hawthorne U.S.A. **133** C3
Hay Austr. **116** C2
Hay *r.* Can. **126** D1
Hayden U.S.A. **132** C3
Hayes *r. Man.* Can. **127** F2
Hayes *r. Nunavut* Can. **125** F2
Hayotboshi tog'i *mt.* Uzbek. **89** D2
Hayrabolu Turkey **65** C2
Hay River Can. **126** D1
Hays U.S.A. **135** D3
Hays Yemen **90** B3
Haysyn Ukr. **44** C2
Haywards Heath U.K. **53** C4
Hazarajat *reg.* Afgh. **86** A1
Hazard U.S.A. **136** D3
Hazaribagh India **87** C2
Hazaribagh Range *mts* India **87** C2
Hazebrouck France **54** A2

Hazelton Can. **126** C2
Healesville Austr. **117** D3
Hearst Can. **128** B2
Hebei *prov.* China **82** B2
Hebel Austr. **117** D1
Heber Springs U.S.A. **138** B1
Hebi China **82** B2
Hebron Can. **129** D1
Hecate Strait Can. **126** B2
Hechi China **83** A3
Hede Sweden **47** C3
Heerenveen Neth. **54** B1
Heerhugowaard Neth. **54** B1
Heerlen Neth. **54** B2
Ḥefa Israel *see* Haifa
Hefei China **82** B2
Hefeng China **83** B3
Hegang China **81** C1
Heide Ger. **56** B2
Heide Namibia **108** A1
Heidelberg Ger. **55** D3
Heidelberg S. Africa **108** B3
Heilbronn Ger. **55** D3
Heilongjiang *prov.* China **78** B1
Heilong Jiang *r.* China **81** E1
Heinola Fin. **47** F3
Helagsfjället *mt.* Sweden **46** C3
Helena *AR* U.S.A. **138** B2
Helena *MT* U.S.A. **132** D1
Helensburgh U.K. **50** B2
Helgoland *i.* Ger. **56** B2
Helgoländer Bucht *g.* Ger. **56** B2
Hella Iceland **46** [inset]
Hellevoetsluis Neth. **54** B2
Hellín Spain **61** C2
Helmand *r.* Afgh. **86** A1
Helmbrechts Ger. **55** E2
Helmeringhausen Namibia **108** A2
Helmond Neth. **54** B2
Helmsdale U.K. **50** C1
Helmsdale *r.* U.K. **50** C1
Helmstedt Ger. **55** E1
Helong China **77** B1
Helsingborg Sweden **47** C4
Helsingfors Fin. *see* Helsinki
Helsingør Denmark **47** C4
Helsinki Fin. **47** F3
Helvick Head Rep. of Ireland **51** C2
Hemel Hempstead U.K. **53** C4
Hemmoor Ger. **55** D1
Hemnesberget Norway **46** C2
Henan *prov.* China **82** B2
Henderson *KY* U.S.A. **136** C3
Henderson *NC* U.S.A. **139** E1
Henderson *NV* U.S.A. **133** D3
Henderson *TX* U.S.A. **141** F2
Hendersonville U.S.A. **139** D1
Hendon U.K. **53** C4
Hengduan Shan *mts* China **74** A1
Hengelo Neth. **54** C1
Hengshui China **82** B2
Hengxian China **83** A3
Hengyang China **83** B3
Heniches'k Ukr. **45** D2
Hennef (Sieg) Ger. **54** C2
Henrietta Maria, Cape Can. **128** B1
Henryetta U.S.A. **141** E1
Henry Kater, Cape Can. **125** H2
Henstedt-Ulzburg Ger. **55** D1
Hentiesbaai Namibia **106** A2
Hepu China **83** A3
Herāt Afgh. **86** A1
Herbert Can. **127** E2
Herbstein Ger. **55** D2
Hereford U.K. **53** B3
Hereford U.S.A. **141** D2
Herford Ger. **55** D1
Herkenbosch Neth. **54** C2
Herma Ness *hd* U.K. **50** [inset]
Hermanus S. Africa **108** A3

Hermidale Austr. **117** D2
Hermiston U.S.A. **132** C1
Hermit Islands P.N.G. **71** D3
Hermosillo Mex. **142** A2
Hernandarias Para. **154** B3
Herne Ger. **54** C2
Herning Denmark **47** B4
Herrieden Ger. **55** E3
Hertford U.K. **53** C4
Hertzogville S. Africa **109** C2
Hervey Bay Austr. **115** E2
Herzberg Ger. **55** F2
Herzogenaurach Ger. **55** E3
Heshan China **83** A3
Hess *r.* Can. **126** B1
Hesselberg *h.* Ger. **55** E3
Hessisch Lichtenau Ger. **55** D2
Hettinger U.S.A. **134** C1
Hettstedt Ger. **55** E2
Hexham U.K. **52** B2
Heyuan China **83** B3
Heywood Austr. **116** C3
Heze China **82** B2
Hezhou China **83** B3
Hiawatha U.S.A. **135** D3
Hibbing U.S.A. **135** E1
Hicks Bay N.Z. **118** C2
Hidaka-sanmyaku *mts* Japan **78** D2
Hidalgo Mex. **143** C2
Hidalgo del Parral Mex. **142** B2
Hidrolândia Brazil **154** C1
High Atlas *mts* Morocco *see* Haut Atlas
High Desert U.S.A. **132** B2
High Level Can. **126** D2
High Point U.S.A. **139** E1
High Prairie Can. **126** D2
High River Can. **126** D2
Highrock Lake Can. **127** E2
High Wycombe U.K. **53** C4
Hiiumaa *i.* Estonia **42** B2
Hijaz *reg.* Saudi Arabia **90** A2
Hikurangi *mt.* N.Z. **118** C2
Hildburghausen Ger. **55** E2
Hilders Ger. **55** E2
Hildesheim Ger. **55** D1
Hillah Iraq **93** C2
Hillesheim Ger. **54** C2
Hillsboro *OH* U.S.A. **136** D3
Hillsboro *TX* U.S.A. **141** E2
Hillston Austr. **117** D2
Hilton Head Island U.S.A. **139** D2
Hilversum Neth. **54** B1
Himalaya *mts* Asia **87** B1
Himeji Japan **79** B4
Himeville S. Africa **109** C2
Hinchinbrook Island Austr. **115** D1
Hindu Kush *mts* Afgh./Pak. **86** A1
Hinesville U.S.A. **139** D2
Hinganghat India **87** B2
Hınıs Turkey **93** C2
Hinnøya *i.* Norway **46** D2
Hinojosa del Duque Spain **60** B2
Hinthada Myanmar **74** A2
Hinton Can. **126** D2
Hirakud Reservoir India **87** C2
Hirosaki Japan **78** D2
Hiroshima Japan **79** B4
Hirschaid Ger. **55** E3
Hirschberg Ger. **55** E2
Hirson France **59** C2
Hirtshals Denmark **47** B4
Hisar India **86** B2
Hispaniola *i.* Caribbean Sea **145** C2
Ḥīt Iraq **93** C2
Hitachi Japan **79** D3
Hitachinaka Japan **79** D3
Hitra *i.* Norway **46** B3
Hiva Oa *i.* Fr. Polynesia **111**
Hjälmaren *l.* Sweden **47** D4
Hjalmar Lake Can. **127** E1

Hjørring Denmark **47** C4
Hlabisa S. Africa **109** D2
Hlíð Iceland **46** [inset]
Hlobyne Ukr. **45** D2
Hlohlowane S. Africa **109** C2
Hlotse Lesotho **109** C2
Hlukhiv Ukr. **45** D1
Hlybokaye Belarus **42** C2
Ho Ghana **100** C2
Hoachanas Namibia **108** A1
Hobart Austr. **115** D4
Hobart U.S.A. **141** E1
Hobbs U.S.A. **141** D2
Hobro Denmark **47** B4
Hobyo Somalia **103** C4
Hoceïma, Baie d'Al *b.* Morocco **60** C2
Hồ Chí Minh City Vietnam **75** B2
Hồd *reg.* Maur. **100** B3
Hodeidah Yemen **90** B3
Hódmezővásárhely Hungary **57** D3
Hodna, Chott el *salt l.* Alg. **61** D2
Hoek van Holland Neth. *see*
    Hook of Holland
Hoeyang N. Korea **77** B2
Hof Ger. **55** F2
Hofheim in Unterfranken Ger. **55** E2
Höfn *Austurland* Iceland **46** [inset]
Höfn *Vestfirðir* Iceland **46** [inset]
Hofsjökull *ice cap* Iceland **46** [inset]
Hōfu Japan **79** B4
Hoggar *plat.* Alg. **101** C2
Högsby Sweden **47** D4
Høgste Breakulen *mt.* Norway **47** B3
Hohe Rhön *mts* Ger. **55** D2
Hohe Venn *moorland* Belgium **54** C2
Hohhot China **82** B1
Hoh Xil Shan *mts* China **87** C1
Hôi An Vietnam **75** B2
Hojai India **74** A1
Hokitika N.Z. **118** B3
Hokkaidō *i.* Japan **78** D2
Holberg Can. **126** C2
Holbrook U.S.A. **140** B2
Holdrege U.S.A. **135** D2
Holguín Cuba **145** C2
Hóll Iceland **46** [inset]
Holland U.S.A. **136** C2
Hollum Neth. **54** B1
Holly Springs U.S.A. **138** C2
Hollywood *CA* U.S.A. **133** C4
Hollywood *FL* U.S.A. **139** D3
Holm Norway **46** C2
Holman Can. **124** E2
Holmsund Sweden **46** E3
Holoog Namibia **108** A2
Holstebro Denmark **47** B4
Holston *r.* U.S.A. **139** D1
Holyhead U.K. **52** A3
Holy Island *England* U.K. **52** C2
Holy Island *Wales* U.K. **52** A3
Holyoke U.S.A. **134** C2
Holzminden Ger. **55** D2
Homalin Myanmar **74** A1
Homberg (Efze) Ger. **55** D2
Hombori Mali **100** B3
Homburg Ger. **54** C3
Home Bay Can. **125** H2
Homestead U.S.A. **139** D3
Hommelvik Norway **46** C3
Homs Syria **92** B2
Homyel' Belarus **43** D3
Hondeklipbaai S. Africa **108** A3
Hondo *r.* Belize/Mex. **143** D3
Hondo U.S.A. **141** E3
Honduras *country* Central America
    144 B3
Hønefoss Norway **47** C3
Honey Lake *salt l.* U.S.A. **132** B2
Honfleur France **58** C2
Hồng Gai Vietnam **74** B1

onghu China 83 B3
ongjiang China 83 A3
ong Kong China 83 B3
ong Kong aut. reg. China 83 B3
ongwŏn N. Korea 77 B1
ongze Hu i. China 82 B2
oniara Solomon Is 112
onjō Japan 78 D3
onshū i. Japan 79 B3
onningsvåg Norway 46 F1
ood, Mount vol. U.S.A. 132 B1
ood River U.S.A. 132 B1
oogeveen Neth. 54 C1
oogezand-Sappemeer Neth. 54 C1
oog-Keppel Neth. 54 B2
ook of Holland Neth. 54 B2
oonah U.S.A. 126 B2
oorn Neth. 54 B2
oorn, Îles de is Wallis and Futuna Is
  111
ope Can. 126 C3
ope U.S.A. 138 B2
ope, Point pt U.S.A. 95 O2
opedale Can. 129 D1
ope Mountains Can. 129 D1
opetoun Austr. 116 C3
opetown S. Africa 108 B2
opewell U.S.A. 137 E3
opewell Islands Can. 128 C1
opkins, Lake salt flat Austr. 114 B2
opkinsville U.S.A. 136 C3
oquiam U.S.A. 132 B1
orasan Turkey 93 C1
oražďovice Czech Rep. 55 F3
örby Sweden 47 C4
orki Belarus 43 F5
orlivka Ukr. 45 E2
ormak Iran 91 D2
ormuz, Strait of Iran/Oman 91 C2
orn Austria 57 D3
orn c. Iceland 46 [inset]
orn, Cape Chile 153 B6
ornell U.S.A. 137 E2
ornepayne Can. 128 B2
ornsea U.K. 52 C3
orodenka Ukr. 44 C2
orodnya Ukr. 45 D1
orodok Khmel'nyts'ka Oblast' Ukr.
  44 C2
orodok L'vivs'ka Oblast' Ukr. 44 B2
orokhiv Ukr. 44 B1
orse Islands Can. 129 E1
orsham Austr. 116 C3
osa'ina Eth. 103 B4
oshab Pak. 86 A2
oshiarpur India 86 B1
otan China 87 C1
otazel S. Africa 108 B2
ot Springs AR U.S.A. 138 B2
ot Springs SD U.S.A. 134 C2
ottah Lake Can. 126 D1
ouffalize Belgium 54 B2
ouma China 82 B2
ouma U.S.A. 138 B3
ouston Can. 126 C2
ouston U.S.A. 141 E3
ouwater S. Africa 108 B3
ove U.K. 53 C4
övsgöl Nuur l. Mongolia 80 C1
övüün Mongolia 80 C1
owar, Wadi watercourse Sudan
  102 A3
owe, Cape Austr. 117 D3
owland Island terr. N. Pacific Ocean
  113
owlong Austr. 117 D3
öxter Ger. 55 D2

Hoy i. U.K. 50 C1
Høyanger Norway 47 B3
Hoyerswerda Ger. 56 C2
Hpapun Myanmar 74 A2
Hradec Králové Czech Rep. 57 D2
Hrasnica Bos.-Herz. 63 C2
Hrebinka Ukr. 45 D1
Hrodna Belarus 42 B3
Hsi-hseng Myanmar 74 A1
Hsinchu Taiwan 83 C3
Hsinying Taiwan 83 C3
Hsipaw Myanmar 74 A1
Huachi China 82 A2
Huacho Peru 150 B4
Huade China 82 B1
Huadian China 77 B1
Huai'an China 82 B2
Huaibei China 82 B2
Huaihua China 83 A3
Huainan China 82 B2
Huaiyang China 82 B2
Huaiyin China see Huai'an
Huajuápan de León Mex. 143 C3
Huaki Indon. 71 C3
Hualien Taiwan 83 C3
Huallaga r. Peru 150 B3
Huambo Angola 106 A1
Huancavelica Peru 150 B4
Huancayo Peru 150 B4
Huangchuan China 82 B2
Huang Hai sea N. Pacific Ocean see
  Yellow Sea
Huang He r. China see Yellow River
Huangliu China 83 A4
Huangnihe China 77 B1
Huangshan China 83 B3
Huangshi China 83 B2
Huangtu Gaoyuan plat. China 82 A2
Huangyan China 83 C3
Huanren China 77 B1
Huánuco Peru 150 B3
Huanuni Bol. 152 B2
Huaráz Peru 150 B3
Huarmey Peru 150 B3
Huascarán, Nevado de mt. Peru 146
Huasco Chile 152 A3
Huasco r. Chile 152 A3
Huatabampo Mex. 142 B2
Huatusco Mex. 143 C3
Huayuan China 83 A3
Huayxay Laos 74 B1
Hubei prov. China 82 B2
Hubli India 85 B3
Hückelhoven Ger. 54 C2
Hucknall U.K. 52 C3
Huddersfield U.K. 52 C3
Hudiksvall Sweden 47 D3
Hudson r. U.S.A. 137 F2
Hudson Bay Can. 127 E2
Hudson Bay sea Can. 125 G3
Hudson's Hope Can. 126 C2
Hudson Strait Can. 125 H2
Huê Vietnam 74 B2
Huehuetenango Guat. 144 A3
Huehueto, Cerro mt. Mex. 142 B2
Huejutla Mex. 143 C2
Huelva Spain 60 B2
Huércal-Overa Spain 61 C2
Huesca Spain 61 C1
Huéscar Spain 60 C2
Hughes Austr. 114 C3
Hugo U.S.A. 141 E2
Huhudi S. Africa 108 B2
Huib-Hoch Plateau Namibia
  108 A2
Huichang China 83 B3
Huich'ŏn N. Korea 77 B1
Huilai China 83 B3
Huila Plateau Angola 106 A1
Huili China 74 B1

Huinan China 77 B1
Huittinen Fin. 47 E3
Huixtla Mex. 143 C3
Huize China 83 A3
Huizhou China 83 B3
Hujirt Mongolia 80 C1
Hujr Saudi Arabia 90 B2
Hukuntsi Botswana 108 B1
Hulin China 78 B1
Hull Can. 128 C2
Hulun Buir China 81 D1
Hulun Nur l. China 81 D1
Hulyaypole Ukr. 45 E2
Huma China 81 E1
Humaitá Brazil 150 C3
Humansdorp S. Africa 108 B3
Humber est. U.K. 52 C3
Humboldt Can. 124 E3
Humboldt U.S.A. 138 C1
Humboldt r. U.S.A. 132 C2
Humenné Slovakia 57 E3
Hume Reservoir Austr. 117 D3
Humphreys Peak U.S.A. 140 B1
Húnaflói b. Iceland 46 [inset]
Hunan prov. China 83 B3
Hunchun China 77 C1
Hunedoara Romania 44 B2
Hünfeld Ger. 55 D2
Hungary country Europe 57 D3
Hungerford Austr. 116 C1
Hŭngnam N. Korea 77 B2
Hun He r. China 77 A1
Hunstanton U.K. 52 D3
Hunte r. Ger. 55 D1
Hunter Island
  S. Pacific Ocean 110
Hunter Islands Austr. 115 D4
Huntingdon U.K. 53 C3
Huntington IN U.S.A. 136 C3
Huntington WV U.S.A. 136 D3
Huntly N.Z. 118 C1
Huntly U.K. 50 C2
Huntsville Can. 128 C2
Huntsville AL U.S.A. 138 C2
Huntsville TX U.S.A. 141 E2
Huon Peninsula P.N.G. 71 D3
Huozhou China 82 B2
Huron U.S.A. 135 D2
Huron, Lake Can./U.S.A. 136 D2
Hurricane U.S.A. 133 D3
Húsavík Iceland 46 [inset]
Huşi Romania 44 C2
Huslia U.S.A. 124 B2
Husn Āl 'Abr Yemen 90 B3
Husnes Norway 48 E2
Husum Ger. 56 B2
Hutag Mongolia 80 C1
Hutanopan Indon. 72 A1
Hutchinson U.S.A. 135 D3
Huzhou China 82 C2
Hvalnes Iceland 46 [inset]
Hvannadalshnúkur vol. Iceland
  46 [inset]
Hvar i. Croatia 60 C2
Hwange Zimbabwe 106 B1
Hyannis U.S.A. 134 C2
Hyargas Nuur salt l. Mongolia
  80 C1
Hyden Austr. 114 A3
Hyderabad India 85 B3
Hyderabad Pak. 86 A2
Hyères France 59 D3
Hyères, Îles d' is France 59 D3
Hyesan N. Korea 77 B1
Hyland Post Can. 126 C2
Hyllestad Norway 48 E1
Hyōno-sen mt. Japan 79 B3
Hythe U.K. 53 D4
Hyvinkää Fin. 47 E3

I

Iaco r. Brazil **150** C3
Ialomița r. Romania **44** C3
Ianca Romania **44** C2
Iași Romania **44** C2
Iba Phil. **76** A2
Ibadan Nigeria **100** C4
Ibagué Col. **150** B2
Ibarra Ecuador **150** B2
Ibb Yemen **90** B3
Ibi Nigeria **101** C4
Ibiá Brazil **155** C1
Ibiraçu Brazil **155** D1
Ibiza i. Spain **61** D2
Ibotirama Brazil **151** E4
Ibrā' Oman **91** C2
Ibri Oman **91** C2
Ica Peru **150** B4
İçel Turkey see Mersin
Iceland country Europe **46** [inset]
Ichinoseki Japan **78** D3
Ichnya Ukr. **45** D1
Ich'ŏn N. Korea **77** D2
Idabel U.S.A. **141** F2
Idaho state U.S.A. **132** D2
Idaho Falls U.S.A. **132** D2
Idar-Oberstein Ger. **54** C3
Idfū Egypt **102** B2
Iepê Brazil **154** B2
Ieper Belgium **54** A2
Ifakara Tanz. **105** D3
Ifanadiana Madag. **107** [inset] D2
Ife Nigeria **100** C4
Ifôghas, Adrar des hills Mali **100** C3
Igan Malaysia **73** C1
Igarapava Brazil **155** C2
Igarka Rus. Fed. **94** H2
Iggdurt India **86** B3
Iğdır Turkey **93** C2
Iglesias Italy **62** C3
Igloolik Can. **125** G2
Ignace Can. **128** A2
Ignalina Lith. **42** C2
Iğneada Turkey **64** C2
Igoumenitsa Greece **65** B3
Igra Rus. Fed. **40** E3
Igrim Rus. Fed. **40** F2
Iguaçu r. Brazil **154** B3
Iguaçu Falls r./Brazil **154** B3
Iguala Mex. **143** C3
Igualada Spain **61** D1
Iguape Brazil **154** C2
Iguatemi Brazil **154** B2
Iguatemi r. Brazil **154** B2
Iguatu Brazil **151** F3
Iguéla Gabon **104** A3
Igunga Tanz. **105** D3
Ihbulag Mongolia **81** D2
Ihosy Madag. **107** [inset] D2
Iisalmi Fin. **46** F3
Ijebu-Ode Nigeria **100** C4
IJmuiden Neth. **54** B1
IJssel r. Neth. **54** B1
IJsselmeer l. Neth. **54** B1
Ikageng S. Africa **109** C2
Ikaria i. Greece **65** C3
Ikela Dem. Rep. Congo **104** C3
Ikhtiman Bulg. **64** B2
Iki i. Japan **79** A4
Ikongo Madag. **107** [inset] D2
Iksan S. Korea **77** D2
Ilagan Phil. **76** B2

Ilām Iran **93** C2
Ilam Nepal **87** C2
Iława Pol. **57** D2
Ilazārān, Kūh-e mt. Iran **91** C2
Île-à-la-Crosse Can. **127** E2
Île-à-la-Crosse, Lac l. Can. **127** E2
Ilebo Dem. Rep. Congo **104** C3
Ileret Kenya **105** D2
Ilford U.K. **53** D4
Ilfracombe U.K. **53** A4
Ilha Grande, Baía da b. Brazil **155** D2
Ilha Grande, Represa resr Brazil
  154 B2
Ilha Solteira, Represa resr Brazil
  154 B2
Ílhavo Port. **60** B1
Ilhéus Brazil **151** F4
Iligan Phil. **76** B3
Illapel Chile **152** A4
Illichivs'k Ukr. **44** D2
Illinois r. U.S.A. **136** B3
Illinois state U.S.A. **136** C3
Illintsi Ukr. **44** C2
Illizi Alg. **101** C2
Il'men', Ozero l. Rus. Fed. **43** D2
Ilmenau Ger. **55** E2
Ilo Peru **150** B4
Iloilo Phil. **76** B2
Ilomantsi Fin. **46** G3
Ilorin Nigeria **100** C4
Iluka Austr. **117** E1
Ilulissat Greenland **125** I2
Imari Japan **79** A4
Imi Eth. **103** C4
Imola Italy **62** B2
Imperatriz Brazil **151** E3
Imperial U.S.A. **134** C2
Impfondo Congo **104** B2
Imphal India **74** A1
İmroz Turkey **65** C2
Inambari r. Peru **150** C4
In Aménas Alg. **101** C2
Inanwatan Indon. **71** C3
Inari Fin. **46** F2
Inarijärvi l. Fin. **46** F2
Inawashiro-ko l. Japan **79** D3
İnce Burun pt Turkey **92** B1
Inch'ŏn S. Korea **77** D2
Incomati r. Moz. **109** D2
Indalstø Norway **48** E1
Inda Silasē Eth. **90** A3
Indé Mex. **142** B2
Independence CA U.S.A. **133** C3
Independence IA U.S.A. **135** E2
Independence KS U.S.A. **135** D3
Independence MO U.S.A. **135** E3
Independence Mountains U.S.A.
  132 C2
Inderborskiy Kazakh. **88** C2
India country Asia **84** B2
Indiana U.S.A. **137** C2
Indiana state U.S.A. **136** C2
Indianapolis U.S.A. **136** C3
Indian Head Can. **127** E2
Indian Ocean **161**
Indianola IA U.S.A. **135** E2
Indianola MS U.S.A. **138** B2
Indian Springs U.S.A. **133** C3
Indiga Rus. Fed. **40** D2
Indigirka r. Rus. Fed. **95** L2
Indija Serb. and Mont. **64** B1
Indio U.S.A. **133** C4
Indonesia country Asia **72** B3
Indore India **86** B2
Indramayu, Tanjung pt Indon. **72** B2
Indre r. France **58** C2
Indus r. China/Pakistan **86** A2
Indus, Mouths of the Pak. **86** A2
İnebolu Turkey **92** B1

İnegöl Turkey **65** C2
Infiernillo, Presa resr Mex. **142** B3
Inglewood Austr. **117** E1
Ingolstadt Ger. **56** C5
Ingomar Austr. **116** A1
Ingraj Bazar India **87** C2
Inhaca Moz. **109** D2
Inhambane Moz. **107** C2
Inishbofin i. Rep. of Ireland **51** A2
Inishmore i. Rep. of Ireland **51** B2
Inishowen pen. Rep. of Ireland **51** C1
Inland Kaikoura Range mts N.Z.
  118 B3
Inn r. Europe **56** C3
Innaanganeq c. Greenland **125** H1
Inner Mongolia aut. reg. China see
  Nei Mongol Zizhiqu
Inner Sound sea chan. U.K. **50** B2
Innisfail Austr. **115** D1
Innsbruck Austria **56** C3
Inocência Brazil **154** B1
Inongo Dem. Rep. Congo **104** B3
Inowrocław Pol. **57** D2
In Salah Alg. **100** C2
Insein Myanmar **74** A2
Inta Rus. Fed. **40** F2
International Falls U.S.A. **135** E1
Inukjuak Can. **128** C1
Inuvik Can. **124** D2
Inveraray U.K. **50** B2
Invercargill N.Z. **118** A4
Inverell Austr. **117** E1
Invergordon U.K. **50** B2
Invermere Can. **126** D2
Inverness Can. **129** D2
Inverness U.K. **50** B2
Inverurie U.K. **50** C2
Investigator Strait Austr. **116** B3
Inya Rus. Fed. **89** F1
Inyonga Tanz. **105** D3
Inza Rus. Fed. **41** D3
Inzhavino Rus. Fed. **45** F1
Ioannina Greece **65** B3
Iola U.S.A. **135** D3
Iona i. U.K. **50** A2
Ionian Islands admin. reg. Greece
  65 A3
Ionian Sea Greece/Italy **65** A3
Ionioi Nisoi admin. reg. Greece see
  Ionian Islands
Ios i. Greece **65** C3
Iowa state U.S.A. **135** E2
Iowa City U.S.A. **135** E2
Ipameri Brazil **154** C1
Ipatinga Brazil **155** D1
Ipatovo Rus. Fed. **93** C1
Ipelegeng S. Africa **109** C2
Ipiales Col. **150** B2
Ipiranga Brazil **154** B3
Ipoh Malaysia **72** B1
Iporá Brazil **154** B1
Ippy C.A.R. **104** C2
Ipsala Turkey **65** C2
Ipswich Austr. **117** E1
Ipswich U.K. **53** D3
Iqaluit Can. **125** H2
Iquique Chile **152** A3
Iquitos Peru **150** B3
Irai Brazil **154** B3
Irakleio Greece see Iraklion
Iraklion Greece **65** C3
Iran country Asia **93** D2
Iran, Pegunungan mts Indon. **73** C1
Īrānshahr Iran **91** D2
Irapuato Mex. **142** B2
Iraq country Asia **93** C2
Irati Brazil **154** B3
Irbid Jordan **92** B2
Irbit Rus. Fed. **40** F3
Irecê Brazil **151** E4

...eland i. Rep. of Ireland/U.K. **36**
...eland, Republic of country Europe **51** B2
...ema Dem. Rep. Congo **104** C3
...giz Kazakh. **88** D2
...igui reg. Mali/Maur. **100** B3
...inga Tanz. **105** D3
...iri r. Brazil **151** D3
...ish Sea Rep. of Ireland/U.K. **49** B3
...kutsk Rus. Fed. **80** C1
...on Knob Austr. **116** B2
...on Mountain U.S.A. **136** C1
...onwood U.S.A. **136** B1
...osin Phil. **76** B2
...ō-zaki pt Japan **79** C4
...oin' Ukr. **44** D1
...rawaddy r. Myanmar **74** A2
...rawaddy, Mouths of the Myanmar **75** A2
...tysh r. Kazakh./Rus. Fed. **89** E1
...ún Spain **61** C1
...vine U.K. **50** B3
...abela Phil. **76** B3
...abela, Cordillera mts Nic. **144** B3
...safjörður Iceland **46** [inset]
...safjörður r. Japan **79** B4
...ar r. Ger. **59** E2
...bister U.K. **50** [inset]
...chia, Isola d' i. Italy **62** B2
...e Japan **79** C4
...engi Dem. Rep. Congo **104** C2
...ère, Pointe pt Fr. Guiana **146**
...erlohn Ger. **54** C2
...ernhagen Ger. **55** D1
...e-wan b. Japan **78** D2
...eyin Nigeria **100** C4
...hikari-wan b. Japan **78** D2
...him r. Kazakh./Rus. Fed. **89** E1
...hinomaki Japan **78** D3
...hioka Japan **79** D3
...hpeming U.S.A. **136** C1
...iklar Dağı mts Turkey **65** C2
...iklı Turkey **65** C3
...il'kul' Rus. Fed. **89** E1
...ipingo S. Africa **109** D2
...ro Dem. Rep. Congo **105** C2
...kenderun Turkey **92** B2
...kitim Rus. Fed. **94** H3
...kür r. Bulg. **64** B2
...kut r. Can. **126** B2
...lamabad Pak. **86** C1
...land Lagoon salt flat Austr. **116** B2
...land Lake Can. **127** F2
...lands, Bay of N.Z. **118** B2
...lay i. U.K. **50** A3
...le of Man i. Irish Sea **52** A2
...moili Somoni, Qullai mt. Tajik. **89** E3
...na Egypt **90** A2
...ola di Capo Rizzuto Italy **63** C3
...perikh Bulg. **64** C2
...rael country Asia **92** B2
...soire France **59** C2
...tanbul Turkey **65** C2
...tanbul Boğazı str. Turkey see Bosporus
...tiaia Greece **65** B3
...tres France **59** C3
...tria pen. Croatia **62** B1
...aberaba Brazil **151** E4
...abira Brazil **155** D1
...abirito Brazil **155** D2
...abuna Brazil **151** F4
...acoatiara Brazil **150** D3
...aguajé Brazil **154** B2
...ai Brazil **154** C2
...aipu, Represa de resr Brazil **154** B3
...aituba Brazil **151** D3
...ajaí Brazil **154** C3
...ajubá Brazil **155** C2

Italy country Europe **62** B2
Itamarandiba Brazil **155** D1
Itambacuri Brazil **155** D1
Itambé, Pico de mt. Brazil **155** D1
Itanagar India **74** A1
Itanhaém Brazil **154** C2
Itanhém Brazil **155** D1
Itaobim Brazil **155** D1
Itapajipe Brazil **154** C1
Itapebi Brazil **155** E1
Itapemirim Brazil **155** D2
Itaperuna Brazil **155** D2
Itapetinga Brazil **151** E4
Itapetininga Brazil **154** C2
Itapeva Brazil **154** C2
Itapicuru r. Brazil **151** F4
Itapicuru Mirim Brazil **151** E3
Itapuranga Brazil **154** C1
Itararé Brazil **154** C2
Itarsi India **87** B2
Itarumã Brazil **154** B1
Itaúna Brazil **155** D2
Itbayat i. Phil. **76** B1
Ithaca U.S.A. **137** E2
Ith Hils ridge Ger. **55** D1
Itimbiri r. Dem. Rep. Congo **104** C2
Itinga Brazil **155** D1
Itiquira Brazil **154** B1
Itiquira r. Brazil **154** A1
Itō Japan **79** C4
Ittoqqortoormiit Greenland **125** K2
Itu Brazil **154** C2
Itui r. Brazil **150** B3
Ituiutaba Brazil **154** C1
Itula Dem. Rep. Congo **105** C2
Itumbiara Brazil **154** C1
Iturama Brazil **154** B1
Itzehoe Ger. **56** B2
Iul'tin Rus. Fed. **95** O2
Ivai r. Brazil **154** B2
Ivalo Fin. **46** F2
Ivanava Belarus **42** C3
Ivanhoe Austr. **116** C2
Ivankiv Ukr. **44** C1
Ivano-Frankivs'k Ukr. **44** B2
Ivanovo Rus. Fed. **43** F2
Ivatsevichy Belarus **42** C3
Ivaylovgrad Bulg. **65** C2
Ivdel' Rus. Fed. **40** F2
Ivinheima Brazil **154** B2
Ivinheima r. Brazil **154** B2
Ivittuut Greenland **125** I2
Ivrea Italy **62** A1
İvrindi Turkey **65** C3
Ivujivik Can. **125** G2
Iwaki Japan **79** D3
Iwakuni Japan **79** B4
Iwamizawa Japan **78** D2
Iwanai Japan **78** D2
Iwye Belarus **42** C3
Ixopo S. Africa **109** D3
Ixtlán Mex. **142** B2
Izabal, Lago de l. Guat. **143** D3
Izamal Mex. **143** D2
Izberbash Rus. Fed. **93** C1
Izhma Rus. Fed. **40** E2
Izhevsk Rus. Fed. **40** F2
Izmalkovo Rus. Fed. **43** E3
Izmayil Ukr. **44** C2
İzmir Turkey **65** C3
İznik Gölü l. Turkey **65** C2
Izumo Japan **79** B3
Izyaslav Ukr. **44** C1
Izyum Ukr. **45** E2

J

Jabalón r. Spain **60** C2

Jabalpur India **87** B2
Jabiru Austr. **114** C1
Jablanica Bos.-Herz. **63** C2
Jaboatão Brazil **151** F4
Jaboticabal Brazil **154** C2
Jaca Spain **61** C1
Jacala Mex. **143** C2
Jacareacanga Brazil **151** D3
Jacareí Brazil **155** C2
Jacinto Brazil **155** D1
Jackman U.S.A. **137** F1
Jackson AL U.S.A. **138** C2
Jackson MI U.S.A. **136** D2
Jackson MS U.S.A. **138** B2
Jackson TN U.S.A. **138** C1
Jackson WY U.S.A. **134** A2
Jackson Head N.Z. **118** A3
Jacksonville AR U.S.A. **138** B2
Jacksonville FL U.S.A. **139** D2
Jacksonville IL U.S.A. **136** B3
Jacksonville NC U.S.A. **139** E2
Jacksonville TX U.S.A. **141** E2
Jacmel Haiti **145** C3
Jacobabad Pak. **86** A2
Jacobina Brazil **151** E4
Jacques Cartier, Mont mt. Can. **129** D2
Jacunda Brazil **151** E3
Jacupiranga Brazil **154** C2
Jadovnik mt. Bos.-Herz. **63** C2
Jaén Peru **150** B3
Jaén Spain **60** C2
Jaffa, Cape Austr. **116** B3
Jaffna Sri Lanka **85** B4
Jagdalpur India **85** C3
Jagersfontein S. Africa **109** C2
Jaghin Iran **91** C2
Jaguariaíva Brazil **154** C2
Jahrom Iran **93** D3
Jaipur India **86** B2
Jaisalmer India **86** B2
Jajarkot Nepal **87** C2
Jajce Bos.-Herz. **63** C2
Jakarta Indon. **72** B2
Jakes Corner Can. **126** B1
Jäkkvik Sweden **46** E3
Jakobstad Fin. **46** E3
Jalālābād Afgh. **86** B1
Jalal-Abad Kyrg. **89** E2
Jalandhar India **86** B1
Jalapa Mex. **143** C3
Jales Brazil **154** B2
Jalgaon India **86** B2
Jalingo Nigeria **101** D4
Jalna India **86** B3
Jalpa Mex. **142** B2
Jalpaiguri India **87** C2
Jalpan Mex. **143** C2
Jālū Libya **101** E2
Jamaica country West Indies **144** C3
Jamalpur Bangl. **87** C2
Jambi Indon. **72** B2
James r. N. Dakota/S. Dakota U.S.A. **135** D2
James r. VA U.S.A. **137** E3
James Bay Can. **125** G3
Jameson Land reg. Greenland **125** K2
Jamestown Austr. **116** B2
Jamestown ND U.S.A. **135** D1
Jamestown NY U.S.A. **137** E2
Jammu India **86** B1
Jammu and Kashmir terr. Asia **86** B1
Jamnagar India **86** B2
Jämsä Fin. **47** F3
Jamshedpur India **87** C2
Jamuna r. Bangl. **87** C2
Janakpur Nepal **87** C2
Janaúba Brazil **155** D1
Jandaq Iran **93** D2
Janesville U.S.A. **136** C2

Jan Mayen *terr.* Arctic Ocean **94** B2
Jansenville S. Africa **108** B3
Januária Brazil **151** E4
Jaora India **86** B2
Japan *country* Asia **79** C3
Japan, Sea of N. Pacific Ocean **81** E2
Japurá *r.* Brazil **150** C3
Jaraguá Brazil **154** C1
Jaraguari Brazil **154** B2
Jardim Brazil **154** A2
Jargalant Mongolia **81** D1
Jarocin Pol. **57** D2
Jarosław Pol. **57** E2
Järpen Sweden **46** C3
Jartai China **82** A2
Jarú Brazil **150** C4
Jarud China *see* Lubei
Järvenpää Fin. **42** C1
Jarvis Island *terr.* S. Pacific Ocean **113**
Jäsk Iran **91** C2
Jasło Pol. **57** E3
Jasper Can. **126** D2
Jasper *IN* U.S.A. **136** C3
Jasper *TX* U.S.A. **141** F2
Jastrzębie-Zdrój Pol. **57** D3
Jászberény Hungary **57** D3
Jataí Brazil **154** B1
Jati Pak. **86** A2
Jaú Brazil **154** C2
Jaú *r.* Brazil **150** C3
Jaumave Mex. **143** C2
Jaunpur India **87** C2
Jauru Brazil **184** B1
Java *i.* Indon. **72** D2
Javarthushuu Mongolia **81** D1
Java Sea Indon. *see* Jawa, Laut
Java Trench *sea feature* Indian Ocean **161** H6
Jawa *i.* Indon. *see* Java
Jawa, Laut *sea* Indon. **72** C2
Jawhar Somalia **103** C4
Jawor Pol. **57** D2
Jaworzno Pol. **57** D2
Jaya, Puncak *mt.* Indon. **71** D3
Jayapura Indon. **71** D3
Jean Marie River Can. **126** F2
Jeannin, Lac *l.* Can. **129** D1
Jebel, Bahr el *r.* Sudan/Uganda *see* White Nile
Jebel Abyad Plateau Sudan **102** A3
Jedburgh U.K. **50** G5
Jeddah Saudi Arabia **90** A2
Jeetze *r.* Ger. **55** E1
Jefferson, Mount U.S.A. **133** C3
Jefferson City U.S.A. **135** E3
Jejui Guazú *r.* Para. **154** A3
Jêkabpils Latvia **42** C2
Jelenia Góra Pol. **57** D2
Jelgava Latvia **42** C2
Jember Indon. **73** C2
Jena Ger. **55** E2
Jengish Chokusu *mt.* China/Kyrg. *see* Pobeda Peak
Jenin West Bank **92** B2
Jennings U.S.A. **138** B2
Jequié Brazil **151** E4
Jequitaí Brazil **155** D2
Jequitinhonha Brazil **155** D1
Jequitinhonha *r.* Brazil **155** E1
Jérémie Haiti **145** C3
Jerez Mex. **142** B2
Jerez de la Frontera Spain **60** B2
Jergucat Albania **65** B3
Jerid, Chott el *salt l.* Tunisia **101** C1
Jerome U.S.A. **132** D2
Jersey *i.* Channel Is **53** B5
Jerumenha Brazil **151** E3
Jerusalem Israel/West Bank **92** B2

Jervis Bay Territory *admin. div.* Austr. **117** E3
Jesenice Slovenia **62** B1
Jesi Italy **62** E2
Jessen Ger. **55** F2
Jessore Bangl. **87** C2
Jesup U.S.A. **139** D2
Jesús Carranza Mex. **143** C3
Jhalawar India **86** B2
Jhang Pak. **86** B1
Jhansi India **87** B2
Jharsuguda India **87** C2
Jhelum Pak. **86** B1
Jiading China **82** C2
Jiamusi China **78** B1
Ji'an *Jiangxi* China **83** B3
Ji'an *Jilin* China **77** B1
Jianchuan China **74** A1
Jiangsu *prov.* China **82** B2
Jiangxi *prov.* China **83** B3
Jiangyou China **82** A2
Jianli China **83** B3
Jianqiao China **82** B2
Jianyang *Fujian* China **83** B3
Jianyang *Sichuan* China **82** A2
Jiaohe China **77** B1
Jiaozhou China **82** C2
Jiaozuo China **82** B2
Jiaxing China **82** C2
Jiayuguan China **80** C2
Jiddah Saudi Arabia *see* Jeddah
Jiehkkevárri *mt.* Norway **46** D2
Jiexiu China **82** B2
Jigzhi China **80** C2
Jihlava Czech Rep. **57** D3
Jijel Alg. **61** E2
Jijiga Eth. **103** C4
Jilf al Kabīr, Haḍabat al *plat.* Egypt **102** A2
Jilib Somalia **103** C4
Jilin China **77** B1
Jilin *prov.* China **82** C1
Jilin Hada ling *mts* China **77** A1
Jīma Eth. **103** B4
Jiménez *Chihuahua* Mex. **142** B2
Jiménez *Tamaulipas* Mex. **143** C2
Jinan China **82** B2
Jinchang China **82** A2
Jincheng China **82** B2
Jindabyne Austr. **117** D3
Jindřichův Hradec Czech Rep. **56** D3
Jingdezhen China **83** B3
Jinggangshan China **83** B3
Jinghong China **74** B1
Jingmen China **82** B2
Jingning China **82** A2
Jingtai China **82** A2
Jingxi China **83** A3
Jingyu China **77** B1
Jingyuan China **82** A2
Jingzhou *Hubei* China **83** B2
Jingzhou *Hubei* China **83** B2
Jinhua China **83** B3
Jining *Nei Mongol* China **82** B1
Jining *Shandong* China **82** B2
Jinja Uganda **105** D2
Jinka Eth. **103** B4
Jinotepe Nic. **144** B3
Jinping China **83** A3
Jinsha Jiang *r.* China *see* Yangtze
Jinshi China **83** B2
Jinzhong China **82** B2
Jinzhou China **82** C1
Jiparaná *r.* Brazil **150** C3
Jirang China **87** C1
Jirkov Czech Rep. **55** F2
Jiroft Iran **91** C2
Jishou China **83** A3
Jiu *r.* Romania **44** B3
Jiuding Shan *mt.* China **82** A2

Jiujiang China **83** B3
Jiwani Pak. **91** D2
Jixi China **78** B1
Jīzān Saudi Arabia **90** B3
Jizzax Uzbek. **89** D2
Joaçaba Brazil **154** B3
João Pessoa Brazil **151** F3
João Pinheiro Brazil **155** C1
Jodhpur India **86** B2
Joensuu Fin. **46** F3
Jõetsu Japan **79** C3
Jofane Moz. **107** C2
Jõgeva Estonia **42** C2
Johannesburg S. Africa **109** C2
John Day U.S.A. **132** C2
John Day *r.* U.S.A. **132** B2
John d'Or Prairie Can. **126** D2
John H. Kerr Reservoir U.S.A. **137** E3
John o'Groats U.K. **50** C1
Johnson City U.S.A. **139** D1
Johnson's Crossing Can. **126** B1
Johnstone U.K. **50** B3
Johnstown U.S.A. **137** E2
Johor Bahru Malaysia **72** B1
Jõhvi Estonia **42** C2
Joinville Brazil **154** C3
Joinville France **59** D2
Jokkmokk Sweden **46** D2
Jökulsá á Fjöllum *r.* Iceland **46** [inset]
Joliet U.S.A. **136** C2
Joliette Can. **128** C2
Jolo Phil. **76** B3
Jolo *i.* Phil. **76** B3
Jombang Indon. **73** C2
Jomsom Nepal **87** C2
Jonava Lith. **42** B2
Jonesboro *AR* U.S.A. **138** B1
Jonesboro *LA* U.S.A. **138** B2
Jones Sound *sea chan.* Can. **125** G1
Jönköping Sweden **47** C4
Jonquière Can. **129** C2
Jonuta Mex. **143** C3
Joplin U.S.A. **135** E3
Jordan *country* Asia **92** B2
Jordan *r.* Asia **92** B2
Jordan U.S.A. **132** E1
Jordan Valley U.S.A. **132** C2
Jorhat India **74** A1
Jørpeland Norway **47** B4
Jos Nigeria **100** C4
José Cardel Mex. **143** C3
Joseph, Lac *l.* Can. **129** D1
Joseph Bonaparte Gulf Austr. **114** B1
Jos Plateau Nigeria **101** C4
Jotunheimen *mts* Norway **47** B3
Joubertina S. Africa **108** B3
Jouberton S. Africa **109** C2
Joutseno Fin. **47** F3
Juan de Fuca Strait Can./U.S.A. **132** B1
Juan Fernández, Archipiélago *is* S. Pacific Ocean **149**
Juaréz Mex. **143** B2
Juàzeiro Brazil **151** E3
Juàzeiro do Norte Brazil **151** F3
Juba Sudan **103** D4
Jubba *r.* Somalia **103** C5
Jubbah Saudi Arabia **90** B2
Júcar *r.* Spain **61** C2
Juchitán Mex. **143** C3
Judenburg Austria **56** C2
Jühnde Ger. **55** D2
Juigalpa Nic. **144** B3
Juist *i.* Ger. **54** C1
Juiz de Fora Brazil **155** D2
Juliaca Peru **150** B4
Jumla Nepal **87** C2
Junagadh India **86** B2
Junction U.S.A. **141** E2
Junction City U.S.A. **135** D3

undiaí Brazil **154** C2
uneau U.S.A. **126** B2
unee Austr. **117** D2
ungfrau mt. Switz. **59** D2
uniata r. U.S.A. **137** E2
unsele Sweden **46** D3
untura U.S.A. **132** C2
uquiá Brazil **154** C2
ur r. Sudan **103** A4
ura mts France/Switz. **59** D2
ura i. U.K. **50** B2
ura, Sound of sea chan. U.K. **50** B3
urbarkas Lith. **42** B2
úrmala Latvia **42** B2
uruá r. Brazil **150** D3
uruena r. Brazil **150** D3
utaí r. Brazil **150** C2
üterbog Ger. **55** F2
utland pen. Denmark **36**
uventud, Isla de la i. Cuba **144** B2
uxian China **82** B2
ũyom Iran **93** D3
waneng Botswana **108** B1
yväskylä Fin. **47** F3

K

2 mt. China/Jammu and Kashmir
  86 B1
aarina Fin. **42** B1
abaena i. Indon. **73** D2
abalo Dem. Rep. Congo **105** C3
abare Dem. Rep. Congo **105** C3
abinakagami Lake Can. **128** D3
abinda Dem. Rep. Congo **104** C3
abo C.A.R. **104** B2
abompo Zambia **106** B1
abongo Dem. Rep. Congo **105** C3
ābul Afgh. **86** A1
aburuang i. Indon. **76** B3
abwe Zambia **107** B1
achchh, Gulf of India **86** A2
achchh, Rann of marsh India **86** B2
achug Rus. Fed. **95** J3
adavu i. Fiji **110**
adıköy Turkey **65** C2
adiolo Mali **100** B3
admat atoll India **85** B3
adom Rus. Fed. **43** F3
adonkani Myanmar **75** A2
adugli Sudan **103** A3
aduna Nigeria **101** C3
aduy Rus. Fed. **43** E2
adzherom Rus. Fed. **40** E2
aédi Maur. **100** A3
aélé Cameroon **104** B1
aesŏng N. Korea **77** B2
afireas, Akra pt Greece **65** B3
afue Zambia **107** B1
agoshima Japan **79** B4
aharlyk Ukr. **44** D2
ahayan r. Indon. **73** C2
ahemba Dem. Rep. Congo **104** B3
ahla Ger. **55** E2
ahnūj Iran **91** C2
aherusvaarat mts Fin. **46** E2
ahramanmaraş Turkey **92** B2
ahūrak Iran **91** C2
ai, Kepulauan is Indon. **71** C3
aiama Nigeria **100** C4
aiapoi N.Z. **118** B3
ai Besar i. Indon. **71** C3

Kaifeng China **82** B2
Kaiingveld reg. S. Africa **108** B2
Kai Kecil i. Indon. **71** C3
Kaikoura N.Z. **118** B3
Kaili China **83** A3
Kailahun Sierra Leone **100** A4
Kaimana Indon. **71** C3
Kaimanawa Mountains N.Z. **118** C2
Kainan Japan **79** C4
Kainji Reservoir Nigeria **100** C3
Kaipara Harbour N.Z. **118** B2
Kairana India **86** B2
Kairouan Tunisia **101** D1
Kaitaia N.Z. **118** B2
Kaitawa N.Z. **118** C2
Kaiyuan Liaoning China **77** A1
Kaiyuan Yunnan China **83** A3
Kajaani Fin. **46** F2
Kajabbi Austr. **115** D2
Kakamas S. Africa **108** B2
Kakamega Kenya **105** D2
Kakhovka Ukr. **45** D2
Kakhovs'ke Vodoskhovyshche resr
  Ukr. **45** D2
Kakinada India **85** C3
Kakisa Can. **126** B1
Kakoswa Dem. Rep. Congo **105** C3
Kaktovik U.S.A. **124** C2
Kalabahi Indon. **71** C3
Kalabo Zambia **106** B1
Kalach Rus. Fed. **45** F1
Kalacha Dida Kenya **105** D2
Kaladan r. India/Myanmar **74** A1
Kalahari Desert Africa **106** B2
Kalajoki Fin. **46** E3
Kalamare Botswana **109** C1
Kalamaria Greece **65** B2
Kalamata Greece **65** B3
Kalamazoo U.S.A. **136** C2
Kalampaka Greece **65** B3
Kalanchak Ukr. **45** D2
Kalao i. Indon. **73** D2
Kalaotoa i. Indon. **73** D2
Kalasin Thai. **74** B2
Kalāt Afgh. **86** A1
Kalāt Iran **91** C2
Kalat Pak. **86** A2
Kalbarri Austr. **114** A2
Kale Turkey **65** C3
Kalecik Turkey **92** B1
Kalema Dem. Rep. Congo **104** C3
Kalemie Dem. Rep. Congo **105** C3
Kalemyo Myanmar **74** A1
Kalevala Rus. Fed. **46** G2
Kalgoorlie Austr. **114** B3
Kali Croatia **62** C2
Kaliakra, Nos pt Bulg. **64** C2
Kalima Dem. Rep. Congo **105** C3
Kalimantan reg. Indon. **73** C2
Kaliningrad Rus. Fed. **42** B3
Kalininskaya Rus. Fed. **45** E2
Kalinkavichy Belarus **42** C3
Kalispell U.S.A. **132** D1
Kalisz Pol. **57** D2
Kalitva r. Rus. Fed. **45** F2
Kalix Sweden **46** E2
Kälixälven r. Sweden **46** E2
Kalkan Turkey **65** C3
Kalkfeld Namibia **106** A2
Kallavesi l. Fin. **46** F3
Kallsjön l. Sweden **46** E3
Kalmar Sweden **47** D4
Kalmarsund sea chan. Sweden **47** D4
Kalomo Zambia **106** B1
Kalone Peak Can. **126** C2
Kalpa India **87** B1
Kalpeni atoll India **85** B3
Kalpi India **87** B2
Kaltag U.S.A. **124** B2

Kaltenkirchen Ger. **55** D1
Kaluga Rus. Fed. **43** E3
Kalundborg Denmark **47** C4
Kalush Ukr. **44** B2
Kalyazin Rus. Fed. **43** E2
Kalymnos i. Greece **65** C3
Kama Dem. Rep. Congo **105** C3
Kama Myanmar **74** A2
Kama r. Rus. Fed. **40** E3
Kamaishi Japan **78** D3
Kaman Turkey **92** B2
Kamanjab Namibia **106** A1
Kamarān i. Yemen **90** B3
Kamarod Pak. **86** A2
Kambaida Austr. **114** B3
Kambove Dem. Rep. Congo **105** C4
Kamchatka Peninsula Rus. Fed. **67**
Kamchiya r. Bulg. **64** C2
Kamenitsa mt. Bulg. **64** B2
Kamenjak, Rt pt Croatia **62** B2
Kamenka Kazakh. **88** C1
Kamenka Rus. Fed. **45** E1
Kamen'-na-Obi Rus. Fed. **89** F1
Kamennomostskiy Rus. Fed. **45** F3
Kamennolomni Rus. Fed. **45** F2
Kamenskoye Rus. Fed. **95** N2
Kamensk-Shakhtinskiy Rus. Fed.
  45 F2
Kamensk-Ural'skiy Rus. Fed. **40** F3
Kamiesberge mts S. Africa **108** A3
Kamieskroon S. Africa **108** A3
Kamilukuak Lake Can. **127** E1
Kamina Dem. Rep. Congo **105** C3
Kaminak Lake Can. **127** F1
Kamin'-Kashyrs'kyy Ukr. **44** B1
Kamloops Can. **126** C2
Kamonia Dem. Rep. Congo **104** C3
Kampala Uganda **105** D2
Kampar r. Indon. **72** B1
Kampar Malaysia **72** B1
Kampen Neth. **54** B1
Kampene Dem. Rep. Congo **105** C3
Kamphaeng Phet Thai. **74** A2
Kâmpóng Cham Cambodia **75** B2
Kâmpóng Chhnǎng Cambodia **75** B2
Kâmpóng Spœ Cambodia **75** B2
Kâmpôt Cambodia **75** B2
Kamsack Can. **127** E2
Kamskoye Vodokhranilishche resr
  Rus. Fed. **40** E3
Kamsuuma Somalia **103** C4
Kam"yanets'-Podil's'kyy Ukr. **44** C2
Kamyanyets Belarus **42** B3
Kamyshevatskaya Rus. Fed. **45** E2
Kamyshin Rus. Fed. **41** D3
Kanab U.S.A. **133** D3
Kananga Dem. Rep. Congo **104** C3
Kanash Rus. Fed. **41** D3
Kanawha r. U.S.A. **137** D3
Kanazawa Japan **79** C3
Kanbalu Myanmar **74** A1
Kanchanaburi Thai. **75** A2
Kanchipuram India **85** B3
Kandahār Afgh. **86** A1
Kandalaksha Rus. Fed. **46** G2
Kandangan Indon. **73** C2
Kandhkot Pak. **86** A2
Kandi Benin **100** C3
Kandla India **86** B2
Kandos Austr. **117** D2
Kandreho Madag. **107** [inset] D1
Kandy Sri Lanka **85** C4
Kandyagash Kazakh. **88** C2
Kanevskaya Rus. Fed. **45** E2
Kang Botswana **108** B1
Kangaatsiaq Greenland **125** I2
Kangaba Mali **100** B3
Kangal Turkey **92** B2
Kangān Iran **91** C2

Kangar Malaysia **72** B1
Kangaroo Island Austr. **116** B3
Kangchenjunga *mt.* India/Nepal **87** C2
Kangdong N. Korea **77** B2
Kangean, Kepulauan *is* Indon. **73** C2
Kangeq *c.* Greenland **125** J2
Kangersuatsiaq Greenland **125** I2
Kanggye N. Korea **77** B1
Kangiqsualujjuaq Can. **129** D1
Kangiqsujuaq Can. **125** H2
Kangirsuk Can. **125** H2
Kangmar China **87** C2
Kangnŭng S. Korea **77** B2
Kangping China **77** A1
Kangto *mt.* China/India **87** D2
Kani Myanmar **74** A1
Kanin, Poluostrov *pen.* Rus. Fed. **40** D2
Kanin Nos Rus. Fed. **40** D2
Kaniv Ukr. **45** D2
Kankaanpää Fin. **47** E3
Kankakee U.S.A. **136** C3
Kankan Guinea **100** B3
Kanker India **87** C2
Kano Nigeria **101** C3
Kanonpunt *pt* S. Africa **108** B3
Kanoya Japan **79** B4
Kanpur India **87** C2
Kansas *r.* U.S.A. **134** E3
Kansas *state* U.S.A. **135** D3
Kansas City U.S.A. **135** E3
Kansk Rus. Fed. **95** I3
Kantchari Burkina **100** C3
Kantemirovka Rus. Fed. **45** E2
Kanton *atoll* Kiribati **111**
Kanturk Rep. of Ireland **51** B2
KaNyamazane S. Africa **109** D2
Kanye Botswana **109** C1
Kaohsiung Taiwan **83** C3
Kaokoveld *plat.* Namibia **106** A1
Kaolack Senegal **100** A3
Kaoma Zambia **106** C2
Kapanga Dem. Rep. Congo **104** C3
Kapchagay Kazakh. **89** E2
Kapchagayskoye Vodokhranilishche *resr* Kazakh. **89** E2
Kapellen Belgium **54** B2
Kapiri Mposhi Zambia **107** B1
Kapisillit Greenland **125** I3
Kapiskau *r.* Can. **128** B1
Kapit Malaysia **73** C1
Kapoe Thai. **75** A1
Kapoeta Sudan **103** B4
Kaposvár Hungary **57** D3
Kapuas *r.* Indon. **73** B2
Kapunda Austr. **116** B2
Kapuskasing Can. **128** B2
Kapyl' Belarus **42** C3
Kapyl' Belarus **42** C3
Kara Togo **100** C4
Kara Ada *i.* Turkey **65** C3
Karabalyk Kazakh. **88** D2
Karabaur, Uval *hills* Kazakh./Uzbek. **93** D3
Karabogazkel' Turkm. **88** C2
Karabük Turkey **92** B1
Karabutak Kazakh. **88** D2
Karacaköy Turkey **64** C2
Karachev Rus. Fed. **43** D3
Karachi Pak. **86** A2
Karaganda Kazakh. **89** E2
Karagayly Kazakh. **89** E2
Karaginskiy Zaliv *b.* Rus. Fed. **95** M3
Karaj Iran **93** D2
Karakelong *i.* Indon. **76** B3
Kara-Köl Kyrg. **89** E2
Karakol Kyrg. **89** E2
Karakoram Range *mts* Asia **89** E3

Karakum, Peski *des.* Kazakh. *see* Karakum Desert
Karakum Desert Kazakh. **88** C2
Karakum Desert Turkm. *see* Karakum Desert
Karakumy, Peski *des.* Turkm. **88** D3
Karaman Turkey **102** B1
Karamay China **89** F2
Karamea N.Z. **118** B3
Karamea Bight *b.* N.Z. **118** B3
Karapınar Turkey **92** B1
Karasburg Namibia **108** A2
Kárášjohka Norway *see* Karasjok
Karasjok Norway **46** F2
Karasuk Rus. Fed. **89** E1
Karatau Kazakh. **89** E2
Karatau, Khrebet *mts* Kazakh. **89** D2
Karatayka Rus. Fed. **40** F2
Karatsu Japan **79** A4
Karawang Indon. **72** B2
Karbalā' Iraq **93** C2
Karcag Hungary **57** E3
Karditsa Greece **65** B3
Kärdla Estonia **42** B2
Kareeberge *mts* S. Africa **108** B3
Kareli India **87** B2
Kargil India **86** B1
Kariba Zimbabwe **107** B1
Kariba, Lake *resr* Zambia/Zimbabwe **107** B1
Karimata, Pulau-pulau *is* Indon. **72** B2
Karimata, Selat *str.* Indon. **72** B2
Karimnagar India **85** B3
Karimunjawa, Pulau-pulau *is* Indon. **72** C2
Karkinits'ka Zatoka *g.* Ukr. **45** D2
Karkinits'ka Zatoka *b.* Ukr. **37**
Karlivka Ukr. **45** E2
Karl Marks, Qullai *mt.* Tajik. **86** B1
Karlovac Croatia **62** C1
Karlovy Vary Czech Rep. **56** C2
Karlshamn Sweden **47** C4
Karlskrona Sweden **47** C4
Karlsruhe Ger. **55** D3
Karlstad Sweden **47** C4
Karlstadt Ger. **55** D3
Karma Belarus **43** D3
Karmøy *i.* Norway **47** B4
Karnafuli Reservoir Bangl. **87** D2
Karnal India **86** B2
Karnobat Bulg. **64** C2
Karodi Pak. **86** A2
Karoi Zimbabwe **107** B1
Karonga Malawi **105** D3
Karora Eritrea **102** B3
Karpenisi Greece **65** B3
Karpogory Rus. Fed. **40** D2
Karratha Austr. **114** A2
Kars Turkey **93** C1
Kārsava Latvia **42** C2
Karshi Turkm. **41** E4
Karshi Uzbek. *see* Qarshi
Karskiye Vorota, Proliv *str.* Rus. Fed. **40** F2
Karskoye More *sea* Rus. Fed. *see* Kara Sea
Karstädt Ger. **55** E1
Kartal Turkey **65** C2
Kartaly Rus. Fed. **41** F3
Karwar India **85** B3
Karymskoye Rus. Fed. **95** J3
Karystos Greece **65** B3
Kaş Turkey **92** B1
Kasabonika Lake Can. **128** B1
Kasaji Dem. Rep. Congo **104** C4
Kasama Zambia **105** D3
Kasangulu Dem. Rep. Congo **104** B3

Kasaragod India **85** B3
Kasba Lake Can. **127** E1
Kasempa Zambia **106** B1
Kasese Dem. Rep. Congo **105** C4
Kasese Uganda **105** D2
Kāshān Iran **93** D2
Kashary Rus. Fed. **45** F2
Kashi China **89** E3
Kashima-nada *b.* Japan **79** D3
Kashin Rus. Fed. **43** E2
Kashira Rus. Fed. **43** E3
Kashirskoye Rus. Fed. **43** E3
Kashiwazaki Japan **79** C3
Kashmar Iran **88** C3
Kashmir *terr.* Asia *see* Jammu and Kashmir
Kashmor Pak. **86** A2
Kashyukulu Dem. Rep. Congo **105** C3
Kasimov Rus. Fed. **43** F3
Kaskinen Fin. **47** E3
Kasongo Dem. Rep. Congo **105** C3
Kasongo-Lunda Dem. Rep. Congo **104** B3
Kasos *i.* Greece **65** C3
Kassala Sudan **102** B3
Kassel Ger. **55** D2
Kastamonu Turkey **92** B1
Kastelli Greece **65** B3
Kastoria Greece **65** B2
Kastsyukovichy Belarus **43** D3
Kasulu Tanz. **105** D3
Kasungu Malawi **107** C1
Katahdin, Mount U.S.A. **137** G1
Katako-Kombe Dem. Rep. Congo **104** C3
Katanning Austr. **114** A3
Katchall *i.* India **75** A3
Katerini Greece **65** B2
Kate's Needle *mt.* Can./U.S.A. **126** B2
Katete Zambia **107** C1
Katha Myanmar **74** A1
Katherine *r.* Austr. **114** C1
Kathiawar *pen.* India **86** B2
Kathlehong S. Africa **109** C2
Kathmandu Nepal **87** C2
Kathu S. Africa **108** B2
Kathua India **86** B1
Kati Mali **100** B3
Katihar India **87** C2
Katikati N.Z. **118** C2
Kati-Kati S. Africa **109** C3
Katima Mulilo Namibia **106** B1
Kato Achaïa Greece **65** B3
Katoomba Austr. **117** E2
Katowice Pol. **57** D2
Kātrīnā, Jabal *mt.* Egypt **92** B3
Katrineholm Sweden **47** D4
Katsina Nigeria **101** C3
Katsina-Ala Nigeria **101** C4
Kattaqo'rg'on Uzbek. **89** D3
Kattegat *str.* Denmark/Sweden **47** C4
Katwijk aan Zee Neth. **54** B1
Kauai *i.* U.S.A. **120**
Kauhajoki Fin. **47** E3
Kaunas Lith. **42** B3
Kaura-Namoda Nigeria **101** C3
Kautokeino Norway **46** E2
Kavala Greece **65** C2
Kavalerovo Rus. Fed. **78** C2
Kavali India **85** C3
Kavaratti *atoll* India **85** B3
Kavarna Bulg. **64** C2
Kavīr, Dasht-e *des.* Iran **93** D2
Kawagoe Japan **79** C3
Kawakawa N.Z. **118** B2
Kawanishi Japan **79** C3
Kawartha Lakes Can. **128** C2
Kawasaki Japan **79** C3
Kawerau N.Z. **118** C2

Lawkareik Myanmar **74** A2
Lawlin Myanmar **74** A1
Lawmapyin Myanmar **75** A2
Lawn Umbu Egypt **80** A2
Lawthaung Myanmar **75** A2
Laxgar He r. China **89** E3
Laya Burkina **100** B3
Layan r. China **73** C1
Laycee U.S.A. **134** D4
Layenta U.S.A. **140** B1
Layes Mali **100** A3
Laynar Kazakh. **89** E2
Layseri Turkey **92** B2
Lazakhskiy Melkosopochnik *plain*
  Kazakh. **89** E1
Lea i. Greece **68** B3
Leady U.K. **51** C1
Learney U.S.A. **135** D2
Learny U.S.A. **140** B2
Lebkabiya Sudan **102** A3
Lebnekaise *mt.* Sweden **46** D2
Lebumen Indon. **73** B2
Lechika r. Can. **126** C2
Lecskemét Hungary **57** D3
Lédainiai Lith. **42** B2
Leele r. Can. **126** C1
Leele Peak Can. **126** B1
Leele Taiwan *see* Chilung
Leene U.S.A. **137** F2
Leetmanshoop Namibia **108** A2
Leewatin Can. **127** F3
Lefallonia *i.* Greece *see* Cephalonia
Lefamenanu Indon. **71** C3
Leflavik Iceland **46** [inset]
Leg River Can. **126** D2
Leighley U.K. **52** C3
Lehsi Mansam Myanmar **74** A1
Leila Estonia **42** B2
Leimoes S. Africa **108** B2
Leitele *i.* Fin. **46** F3
Lellogg U.S.A. **132** C1
Lelloselkä Fin. **46** F2
Lells Rep. of Ireland **51** C2
Lelmê Lith. **42** B2
Lelo Chad **101** D4
Lelowna Can. **126** D3
Lelso U.K. **50** C3
Lelso U.S.A. **132** B1
Leluang Malaysia **72** B1
Lelvington Can. **127** E2
Lem' Rus. Fed. **40** C2
Lemano Can. **126** C2
Lemer Turkey **65** C3
Lemerovo Rus. Fed. **94** H3
Lemi Fin. **46** E2
Lemijärvi Fin. **46** F2
Lemijoki r. Fin. **46** F2
Lemmerer U.S.A. **134** A2
Lempele Fin. **46** F3
Lempsey Austr. **117** E2

Kempt, Lac *l.* Can. **128** C2
Kempten (Allgäu) Ger. **56** C3
Kempton Park S. Africa **109** C2
Kemujan *i.* Indon. **73** C2
Kenai U.S.A. **124** D2
Kenaston Can. **127** E2
Kendal U.K. **52** B2
Kendari Indon. **73** D2
Kendawangan Indon. **73** C2
Kendégué Chad **101** D3
Kenema Sierra Leone **100** A4
Kenge Dem. Rep. Congo **104** B3
Kenhardt S. Africa **108** B2
Kénitra Morocco **100** B1
Kenmare Rep. of Ireland **51** B3
Kenmare U.S.A. **134** C1
Kenmare River *inlet* Rep. of Ireland
  51 A3
Kenn Ger. **54** C3
Kennett U.S.A. **135** E3
Kennewick U.S.A. **132** C1
Kenora Can. **127** F3
Kenosha U.S.A. **136** C2
Kentau Kazakh. **89** D2
Kentucky *r.* U.S.A. **136** C3
Kentucky *state* U.S.A. **136** C3
Kentucky Lake U.S.A. **136** C3
Kenya *country* Africa **105** D2
Kenya, Mount Kenya **105** D3
Keokuk U.S.A. **135** E2
Keonjhar India **87** F1
Kepsut Turkey **65** A3
Kerang Austr. **116** C3
Kerava Fin. **42** C1
Kerch Ukr. **45** E2
Kerema P.N.G. **71** D3
Keremeos Can. **126** D3
Keren Eritrea **102** B3
Kerend Iran **93** C2
Kericho Kenya **105** D3
Kerikeri N.Z. **118** B2
Kerkyra Greece **65** A3
Kerkyra *i.* Greece *see* Corfu
Kerma Sudan **102** B3
Kermadec Islands
  S. Pacific Ocean **111**
Kermān Iran **91** C1
Kermānshāh Iran **93** C2
Kermit U.S.A. **141** D2
Kern *r.* U.S.A. **133** C3
Kerpen Ger. **54** C2
Kerrobert Can. **127** E2
Kerrville U.S.A. **141** E2
Keryneia Cyprus *see* Kyrenia
Kesagami Lake Can. **128** B1
Keşan Turkey **65** C2
Kesennuma Japan **78** D3
Keshod India **86** B2
Kessel Neth. **54** C2
Keswick U.K. **52** B2
Keszthely Hungary **57** D3
Ket' r. Rus. Fed. **94** H3
Ketapang Indon. **73** C2
Ketchikan U.S.A. **126** B2
Ketchum U.S.A. **132** D2
Kettering U.K. **53** C3
Keuruu Fin. **47** E3
Kevelaer Ger. **54** C2
Kewanee U.S.A. **136** C2
Keweenaw Bay U.S.A. **136** C1
Keweenaw Peninsula U.S.A. **136** C1
Key Largo U.S.A. **139** D3
Keyser U.S.A. **137** E3
Key West U.S.A. **139** D4
Kgotsong S. Africa **109** C2
Khabarovsk Rus. Fed. **81** F1
Khadyzhensk Rus. Fed. **92** B1

Khagrachari Bangl. **74** A1
Khairpur Pak. **86** A2
Khakhea Botswana **108** B1
Khamar-Daban, Khrebet *mts* Rus. Fed.
  80 C1
Khambhat India **86** B2
Khambhat, Gulf of India **86** B3
Khamgaon India **86** B2
Khamir Yemen **90** B3
Khamis Mushayt Saudi Arabia **90** B3
Khammam India **85** C3
Khānābād Afgh. **86** A1
Khandwa India **86** B2
Khandyga Rus. Fed. **95** L2
Khanewal Pak. **86** B1
Khanka, Lake China/Rus. Fed. **78** B2
Khanpur Pak. **86** B2
Khantau Kazakh. **89** E2
Khantayskoye, Ozero *l.* Rus. Fed.
  95 I2
Khanty-Mansiysk Rus. Fed. **40** F2
Khao Chum Thong Thai. **75** A3
Khao Laem Reservoir Thai. **75** A2
Kharabali Rus. Fed. **41** D4
Kharagpur India **87** C2
Khārān r. Iran **91** C2
Khārijah, Wāḥāt al *oasis* Egypt
  102 B2
Kharkiv Ukr. **45** E2
Khar'kov Ukr. *see* Kharkiv
Kharmanli Bulg. **64** C2
Kharovsk Rus. Fed. **43** F2
Khartoum Sudan **102** B3
Khasav'yurt Rus. Fed. **41** D4
Khash Iran **91** D2
Khashm el Girba Sudan **90** A3
Khashm el Girba Dam Sudan **90** A3
Khasi Hills India **87** D2
Khaskovo Bulg. **64** C2
Khayamnandi S. Africa **109** C3
Khaybar Saudi Arabia **90** A2
Khayelitsha S. Africa **108** A3
Khê Bo Vietnam **74** B2
Khemis Miliana Alg. **61** D2
Khemmarat Thai. **75** B2
Khenchela Alg. **101** C1
Khorrāmeh Iran **93** C3
Kherson Ukr. **45** D2
Kheta r. Rus. Fed. **95** I2
Khilok Rus. Fed. **81** D1
Khimki Rus. Fed. **43** E2
Khlevnoye Rus. Fed. **43** E3
Khmel'nyts'kyy Ukr. **44** C2
Khobda Kazakh. **88** C1
Khokhol'skiy Rus. Fed. **43** E3
Khokhropar Pak. **86** B2
Kholm Afgh. **86** A1
Kholm Rus. Fed. **43** D2
Kholmsk Rus. Fed. **78** D1
Kholm-Zhirkovskiy Rus. Fed. **43** D2
Khomas Highland *hills* Namibia
  108 A1
Khonj Iran **91** C2
Khon Kaen Thai. **74** B2
Khonsa India **74** A1
Khonuu Rus. Fed. **95** L2
Khoper r. Rus. Fed. **45** F1
Khorixas Rus. Fed. **40** E2
Khorinsk Rus. Fed. **81** D1
Khorol Ukr. **45** D2
Khorramābād Iran **93** C2
Khorramshahr Iran **93** C2
Khorugh Tajik. **89** E3
Khowst Afgh. **86** A1
Khreum Myanmar **74** A1
Khromtau Kazakh. **88** C1
Khrystynivka Ukr. **44** C2
Khūjand Tajik. **89** D2
Khu Khan Thai. **75** B2
Khulays Saudi Arabia **90** A2

Khulna Bangl. **87** C2
Khunsar Iran **93** D2
Khurays Saudi Arabia **91** B2
Khushab Pak. **86** B1
Khust Ukr. **44** A2
Khutsong S. Africa **109** C2
Khuzdar Pak. **86** A2
Khvormūj Iran **93** D3
Khvoy Iran **93** C2
Khvoynaya Rus. Fed. **43** D2
Khyber Pass Afgh./Pak. **86** B1
Kiama Austr. **117** E2
Kiambi Dem. Rep. Congo **105** C3
Kibiti Tanz. **105** D3
Kičevo Macedonia **65** B2
Kidal Mali **100** C3
Kidderminster U.K. **53** B3
Kidira Senegal **100** A3
Kidnappers, Cape N.Z. **118** C2
Kiel Ger. **56** C2
Kielce Pol. **57** E2
Kielder Water *resr* U.K. **52** B2
Kieler Bucht *b.* Ger. **47** C5
Kiev Ukr. **44** D1
Kiffa Maur. **100** A3
Kigali Rwanda **105** D3
Kigoma Tanz. **105** C3
Kihnu *i.* Estonia **42** B2
Kiiminki Fin. **46** F2
Kii-suidō *sea chan.* Japan **79** B4
Kikinda Serb. and Mont. **64** B1
Kikondja Dem. Rep. Congo **105** C3
Kikori *r.* P.N.G. **71** D3
Kikwit Dem. Rep. Congo **104** B3
Kilembe Dem. Rep. Congo **104** B3
Kilgore U.S.A. **141** F2
Kilimanjaro *vol.* Tanz. **105** D3
Kilis Turkey **92** B2
Kiliya Ukr. **44** C2
Kilkee Rep. of Ireland **51** B2
Kilkeel U.K. **51** D1
Kilkenny Rep. of Ireland **51** C2
Kilkis Greece **65** B2
Killala Bay Rep. of Ireland **51** B1
Killaloe Rep. of Ireland **51** B2
Killam Can. **127** D2
Killarney Rep. of Ireland **51** B2
Killeen U.S.A. **141** E2
Killin U.K. **50** B2
Killybegs Rep. of Ireland **51** B1
Kilmarnock U.K. **50** B3
Kilmore Austr. **117** C3
Kilosa Tanz. **105** D3
Kilrush Rep. of Ireland **51** B2
Kilwa Dem. Rep. Congo **105** C3
Kilwa Masoko Tanz. **105** D3
Kimambi Tanz. **105** D3
Kimba Austr. **116** B2
Kimball U.S.A. **134** C2
Kimberley Can. **126** D3
Kimberley S. Africa **108** B2
Kimberley Plateau Austr. **114** B1
Kimch'aek N. Korea **77** B1
Kimch'ŏn S. Korea **77** B2
Kimmirut Can. **125** H2
Kimovsk Rus. Fed. **43** E3
Kimpese Dem. Rep. Congo **104** B3
Kimry Rus. Fed. **43** E2
Kinabalu, Gunung *mt.* Malaysia **73** C1
Kinbasket Lake Can. **126** D2
Kincardine Can. **128** B2
Kinchang Myanmar **74** A1
Kinda Dem. Rep. Congo **105** C3
Kinder Scout *h.* U.K. **52** C3
Kindersley Can. **124** E3
Kindia Guinea **100** A3
Kindu Dem. Rep. Congo **105** C3
Kineshma Rus. Fed. **43** F2
Kingaroy Austr. **115** E2

King City U.S.A. **133** B3
King George Islands Can. **128** C1
Kingisepp Rus. Fed. **42** C2
King Island Austr. **115** D3
King Leopold Ranges *hills* Austr. **114** B1
Kingman U.S.A. **140** B1
Kings *r.* U.S.A. **133** B3
Kingscote Austr. **116** B3
King's Lynn U.K. **53** D3
Kingsmill Group *is* Kiribati **110**
King Sound *b.* Austr. **114** B1
Kings Peak U.S.A. **132** D2
Kingsport U.S.A. **139** D1
Kingston Can. **128** C2
Kingston Jamaica **145** C3
Kingston U.S.A. **137** F2
Kingston South East Austr. **116** B3
Kingston upon Hull U.K. **52** C3
Kingstown St Vincent **145** D3
Kingsville U.S.A. **141** E3
Kingswood U.K. **53** B4
Kingussie U.K. **50** B2
King William Island Can. **124** F2
King William's Town S. Africa **109** C3
Kinka-san *i.* Japan **78** D3
Kinna Sweden **47** C4
Kinsale Rep. of Ireland **51** B3
Kinshasa Dem. Rep. Congo **104** B3
Kinston U.S.A. **139** E1
Kintai Lith. **42** B2
Kintampo Ghana **100** B4
Kintyre *pen.* U.K. **50** B3
Kipawa, Lac *l.* Can. **128** C2
Kirensk Rus. Fed. **95** J3
Kireyevsk Rus. Fed. **43** E3
Kiribati *country* Pacific Ocean **113**
Kırıkkale Turkey **92** B2
Kirillov Rus. Fed. **43** E2
Kirinyaga *mt.* Kenya *see* Kenya, Mount
Kirishi Rus. Fed. **43** D2
Kiritimati *atoll* Kiribati **111**
Krkağaç Turkey **65** C3
Kirkcaldy U.K. **50** C2
Kirkcudbright U.K. **50** B3
Kirkenes Norway **46** G2
Kirkkonummi Fin. **42** B1
Kirkland Lake Can. **128** C2
Kirksville U.S.A. **135** E2
Kirkūk Iraq **93** C2
Kirkwall U.K. **50** C1
Kirov *Kaluzhskaya Oblast'* Rus. Fed. **43** D3
Kirov *Kirovskaya Oblast'* Rus. Fed. **40** D3
Kirovo-Chepetsk Rus. Fed. **40** E3
Kirovohrad Ukr. **45** D2
Kirovsk Rus. Fed. **46** G2
Kirovs'ke Ukr. **45** E2
Kirriemuir U.K. **50** C2
Kirs Rus. Fed. **40** E3
Kirsanov Rus. Fed. **45** F1
Kirthar Range *mts* Pak. **86** A2
Kiruna Sweden **46** E2
Kiryū Japan **79** C3
Kirzhach Rus. Fed. **43** E2
Kisangani Dem. Rep. Congo **105** C2
Kisantu Dem. Rep. Congo **104** B3
Kisaran Indon. **72** A1
Kiselevsk Rus. Fed. **94** H3
Kishanganj India **87** C2
Kishi Nigeria **100** C4
Kishinev Moldova *see* Chişinău
Kishkenekol' Kazakh. **89** E1
Kishorganj Bangl. **74** A1
Kishtwar Jammu and Kashmir **86** B1
Kisii Kenya **105** D3
Kiskunfélegyháza Hungary **57** D3
Kiskunhalas Hungary **57** D3
Kislovodsk Rus. Fed. **41** D4

Kismaayo Somalia **103** C5
Kisoro Uganda **105** C3
Kissidougou Guinea **100** A4
Kissimmee U.S.A. **139** D3
Kissimmee, Lake U.S.A. **139** D3
Kississing Lake Can. **127** E2
Kisumu Kenya **105** D3
Kita Mali **100** B3
Kitakami Japan **78** D3
Kitakami-gawa *r.* Japan **78** D3
Kita-Kyūshū Japan **79** B4
Kitale Kenya **105** D2
Kitami Japan **78** D2
Kitchener Can. **128** B2
Kitee Fin. **47** G3
Kitgum Uganda **105** D2
Kitimat Can. **126** C2
Kitona Dem. Rep. Congo **104** B3
Kitunda Tanz. **105** D3
Kitwanga Can. **126** C2
Kitwe Zambia **107** B1
Kitzingen Ger. **55** E3
Kiuruvesi Fin. **46** F3
Kivu, Lake Dem. Rep. Congo/Rwanda **105** C3
Kıyıköy Turkey **64** C2
Kizel Rus. Fed. **40** E3
Kızılca Dağ *mt.* Turkey **65** C3
Kizlyar Rus. Fed. **41** D4
Kjøllefjord Norway **46** F1
Kjøpsvik Norway **46** C2
Kladno Czech Rep. **56** C2
Klagenfurt Austria **56** C3
Klaipėda Lith. **42** B2
Klaksvík Faroe Is **48** B1
Klamath *r.* U.S.A. **132** B2
Klamath Falls U.S.A. **132** B2
Klamath Mountains U.S.A. **132** B2
Klang Malaysia **72** B1
Klatovy Czech Rep. **56** C3
Klawer S. Africa **108** A3
Klawock U.S.A. **126** B2
Kleena Kleene Can. **126** C2
Kleinbegin S. Africa **108** B2
Kleinsee S. Africa **108** A2
Klerksdorp S. Africa **109** C2
Kletnya Rus. Fed. **43** D3
Kleve Ger. **54** C2
Klimavichy Belarus **43** D3
Klimovo Rus. Fed. **43** D3
Klimovsk Rus. Fed. **43** E2
Klin Rus. Fed. **43** E2
Klinovec *mt.* Czech Rep. **55** F2
Klintehamn Sweden **47** D4
Klintsy Rus. Fed. **43** D3
Ključ Bos.-Herz. **63** C2
Kłodzko Pol. **57** D2
Kloosterhaar Neth. **54** C1
Klosterneuburg Austria **57** D3
Klötze (Altmark) Ger. **55** E1
Kluane Lake Can. **126** B1
Kluczbork Pol. **57** D2
Klukwan U.S.A. **126** B2
Klupro Pak. **86** A2
Klyaz'ma *r.* Rus. Fed. **43** F2
Klyetsk Belarus **42** C3
Knaresborough U.K. **52** C2
Knästen *h.* Sweden **47** C3
Knee Lake Can. **127** F2
Knesebeck Ger. **55** E1
Knetzgau Ger. **55** E3
Knin Croatia **63** C2
Knittelfeld Austria **56** C3
Knjaževac Serb. and Mont. **64** B2
Knokke-Heist Belgium **54** A2
Knoxville U.S.A. **139** D1
Knysna S. Africa **108** B3
Kōbe Japan **79** C4
København Denmark *see* Copenhagen
Koblenz Ger. **54** C2

obroör *i.* Indon. **71** C3
obryn Belarus **42** B3
očani Macedonia **64** B2
ocasu *r.* Turkey **65** C2
och Bihar India **87** C2
ōchi Japan **79** B4
ochubey Rus. Fed. **41** D4
odarma India **87** C2
odiak Island U.S.A. **124** B3
odok Sudan **103** B4
odyma Ukr. **44** C2
odzhaele *mt.* Bulg./Greece **65** C3
oës Namibia **108** A2
offiefontein S. Africa **108** C2
oforidua Ghana **100** B4
ōfu Japan **79** B4
ogaluk *r.* Can. **129** D1
ohat Pak. **86** B1
ohima India **74** A1
ohtla-Järve Estonia **42** C2
okand Uzbek. *see* Qo'qon
okkola Fin. **46** E3
okomo U.S.A. **136** C2
okpekti Kazakh. **89** F2
okshetau Kazakh. **89** F1
oksoak *r.* Can. **129** D1
okstad S. Africa **109** C3
oktokay China *see* Fuyun
olaka Indon. **73** D2
ola Peninsula Rus. Fed. **40** C2
olari Fin. **46** E2
olda Senegal **100** A3
olding Denmark **47** B4
oléa Alg. **61** D2
olguyev, Ostrov *i.* Rus. Fed. **40** D2
olhapur India **86** B3
olkasrags *pt* Latvia **42** B2
olkata India **87** C2
ôln Ger. *see* Cologne
olobrzeg Pol. **57** D2
olokani Mali **100** B3
olomna Rus. Fed. **43** E2
olonedale Indon. **73** D2
olonkwaneng Botswana **108** B2
olpashevo Rus. Fed. **94** H3
olpny Rus. Fed. **43** F2
ol'skiy Poluostrov *pen.* Rus. Fed. *see*
  Kola Peninsula
oluli Eritrea **90** D1
olwezi Dem. Rep. Congo **105** C4
olyma *r.* Rus. Fed. **95** M2
olymskaya Nizmennost' *lowland*
  Rus. Fed. **95** M2
olymskiy, Khrebet *mts* Rus. Fed.
  95 N2
omaki Japan **79** C4
omandorskiye Ostrova *is* Rus. Fed.
  95 N3
omárno Slovakia **57** D3
omati *r.* Swaziland **109** D2
omatsu Japan **79** C3
ombe Dem. Rep. Congo **105** C3
ominternivs'ke Ukr. **44** D2
omizla Croatia **63** C2
omló Hungary **57** D3
omono Congo **104** B3
omotini Greece **65** C2
omsberg *mt.* S. Africa **108** B3
omsomolets, Ostrov *i.* Rus. Fed.
  95 I1
omsomol'sk Rus. Fed. **43** F2
omsomol's'k Ukr. **45** D2
omsomol'skiy Rus. Fed. **41** D4
omsomol'sk-na-Amure Rus. Fed.
  81 F1
onakovo Rus. Fed. **43** E2
ondagaon India **87** C3
ondinskoye Rus. Fed. **40** C2

Kondoa Tanz. **105** D3
Kondopoga Rus. Fed. **40** C2
Kondrovo Rus. Fed. **43** E3
Kong Christian IX Land *reg.* Greenland
  125 J3
Kong Frederik VI Kyst *coastal area*
  Greenland **125** J2
Kongju S. Korea **77** B2
Kongolo Dem. Rep. Congo **105** C3
Kongsberg Norway **47** B4
Kongsvinger Norway **47** C3
Kongur Shan *mt.* China **89** E3
Königswinter Ger. **54** C2
Königs Wusterhausen Ger. **55** F1
Konin Pol. **57** D2
Konjic Bos.-Herz. **63** C2
Konkiep *watercourse* Namibia **108** A2
Konotop Ukr. **45** D1
Konstantinovsk Rus. Fed. **45** F2
Konstanz Ger. **56** B3
Kontagora Nigeria **101** C3
Kon Tum Vietnam **75** D2
Kon Tum, Cao Nguyên *plat.* Vietnam
  75 B2
Konya Turkey **92** B3
Konz Ger. **54** C3
Konzhakovskiy Kamen', Gora *mt.*
  Rus. Fed. **40** F3
Kooskia U.S.A. **132** C1
Kootenay Lake Can. **126** D3
Kootjieskolk S. Africa **108** B3
Kópasker Iceland **46** [inset]
Koper Slovenia **62** B1
Kopparberg Sweden **47** D4
Koprivnica Croatia **63** C1
Korablino Rus. Fed. **43** F3
Koraput India **85** C3
Korbach Ger. **55** D2
Korçë Albania **65** C2
Korčula Croatia **63** C2
Korčula *i.* Croatia **63** C2
Korea, North *country* Asia **77** B1
Korea, South *country* Asia **77** B2
Korea Bay *g.* China/N. Korea **77** A2
Korea Strait Japan/S. Korea **77** B3
Korenovsk Rus. Fed. **45** E2
Korets' Ukr. **44** C1
Körfez Turkey **65** M4
Korhogo Côte d'Ivoire **100** B4
Korinthos Greece *see* Corinth
Kőris-hegy *h.* Hungary **57** D3
Koritnik *mt.* Albania **64** B2
Kōriyama Japan **79** D3
Korkuteli Turkey **92** B2
Korla China **89** F2
Körmend Hungary **57** D3
Koro Mali **100** B3
Koroc *r.* Can. **129** D1
Korocha Rus. Fed. **45** E1
Korogwe Tanz. **105** D3
Koror Palau **71** C2
Korosten' Ukr. **44** C1
Korostyshiv Ukr. **44** C1
Koro Toro Chad **101** D3
Korsakov Rus. Fed. **78** D1
Korsør Denmark **47** B4
Korsun'-Shevchenkivs'kyy Ukr. **45** D2
Korsze Pol. **57** E2
Kortrijk Belgium **54** A2
Koryakskaya, Sopka *vol.* Rus. Fed.
  95 M3
Koryakskiy Khrebet *mts* Rus. Fed.
  95 N2
Koryazhma Rus. Fed. **40** D2
Koryŏng S. Korea **77** B2
Koryukivka Ukr. **45** D1
Kos *i.* Greece **65** C3
Kos *i.* Greece **65** C3
Kosan N. Korea **77** B2
Kościan Pol. **57** D2

Kosciuszko, Mount Austr. **117** D3
Kosh-Agach Rus. Fed. **89** F2
Košice Slovakia **57** E3
Koskullskulle Sweden **46** E2
Kosŏng N. Korea **77** B2
Kosovo *prov.* Serb. and Mont. **64** B2
Kosovska Mitrovica Serb. and Mont.
  64 B2
Kosrae *atoll* Micronesia **110**
Kossou, Lac de *l.* Côte d'Ivoire **100** B4
Kostanay Kazakh. **88** D1
Kostenets Bulg. **64** B2
Koster S. Africa **109** C2
Kosti Sudan **103** B3
Kostomuksha Rus. Fed. **46** G3
Kostopil' Ukr. **44** C1
Kostroma Rus. Fed. **43** F2
Kostroma *r.* Rus. Fed. **43** F2
Kostrzyn Pol. **56** C2
Koszalin Pol. **57** D2
Kőszeg Hungary **57** D3
Kota India **86** B2
Kotaagung Indon. **72** B2
Kotabaru Indon. **73** C2
Kota Belud Malaysia **73** C1
Kota Bharu Malaysia **72** B1
Kotabumi Indon. **72** B2
Kota Kinabalu Malaysia **73** C1
Kotel'nich Rus. Fed. **40** D3
Kotel'nikovo Rus. Fed. **41** D4
Kotel'nyy, Ostrov *i.* Rus. Fed. **95** L1
Köthen (Anhalt) Ger. **55** E2
Kotka Fin. **47** F3
Kotlas Rus. Fed. **40** D2
Kotlik U.S.A. **124** B2
Kotor Varoš Bos.-Herz. **63** C2
Kotovo Rus. Fed. **41** D3
Kotovsk Rus. Fed. **43** F3
Kotovs'k Ukr. **44** C2
Kotuy *r.* Rus. Fed. **95** I2
Kotzebue U.S.A. **124** B2
Kotzebue Sound *sea chan.* U.S.A.
  124 B2
Kötzting Ger. **55** F3
Koudekerke Neth. **54** A2
Koudougou Burkina **100** B3
Kougaberge *mts* S. Africa **108** B3
Koulamoutou Gabon **104** B3
Koulikoro Mali **100** B3
Koundâra Guinea **100** A3
Kourou Fr. Guiana **151** D2
Kouroussa Guinea **100** B3
Kousséri Cameroon **104** B1
Koutiala Mali **100** B3
Kouvola Fin. **47** F3
Kovdor Rus. Fed. **46** G2
Kovel' Ukr. **44** B1
Kovrov Rus. Fed. **43** F2
Kowhitirangi N.Z. **118** F4
Köyceğiz Turkey **65** C3
Koyda Rus. Fed. **40** D2
Koyukuk *r.* U.S.A. **124** B2
Kozani Greece **65** B2
Kozelets' Ukr. **44** D1
Kozel'sk Rus. Fed. **43** E3
Kozyatyn Ukr. **44** C2
Krabi Thai. **75** A3
Kra Buri Thai. **75** A2
Krâchéh Cambodia **75** B2
Kragerø Norway **47** B4
Kraggenburg Neth. **54** B1
Kragujevac Serb. and Mont. **64** B2
Krakatau *i.* Indon. **72** B2
Kraków Pol. **57** D2
Kralovice Czech Rep. **55** F3
Kramators'k Ukr. **45** E2
Kramfors Sweden **46** F3
Kranidi Greece **65** B3
Krasino Rus. Fed. **40** E1

Krāslava Latvia **42** C2
Kraslice Czech Rep. **55** F2
Krasnapollye Belarus **43** D3
Krasnaya Gora Rus. Fed. **43** D3
Krasnaya Gorbatka Rus. Fed. **43** F2
Krasnoarmeysk Rus. Fed. **41** D3
Krasnoarmiys'k Ukr. **45** E2
Krasnoborsk Rus. Fed. **40** D2
Krasnodar Rus. Fed. **45** E2
Krasnodon Ukr. **45** F2
Krasnogorodskoye Rus. Fed. **42** C2
Krasnogvardeyskoye *Belgorodskaya Oblast'* Rus. Fed. **45** E1
Krasnogvardeyskoye *Stavropol'skiy Kray* Rus. Fed. **45** F2
Krasnohrad Ukr. **45** E2
Krasnohvardiys'ke Ukr. **45** D2
Krasnokamsk Rus. Fed. **40** D2
Krasnomayskiy Rus. Fed. **43** D2
Krasnoperekops'k Ukr. **45** D2
Krasnoslobodsk Rus. Fed. **41** D3
Krasnoufimsk Rus. Fed. **40** D3
Krasnoyarsk Rus. Fed. **95** I3
Krasnoye-na-Volge Rus. Fed. **43** F2
Krasnyy Rus. Fed. **43** D3
Krasnyy Kholm Rus. Fed. **43** E2
Krasnyy Luch Ukr. **45** F2
Krasnyy Sulin Rus. Fed. **45** F2
Krasyliv Ukr. **44** C2
Krefeld Ger. **54** C2
Kremenchuk Ukr. **45** D2
Kremenchuts'ka Vodoskhovyshche *resr* Ukr. **45** D2
Křemešník *h.* Czech Rep. **57** D3
Kreminna Ukr. **45** E2
Krems an der Donau Austria **57** D3
Kresttsy Rus. Fed. **43** D2
Kretinga Lith. **42** B2
Kreuzau Ger. **54** C2
Kreuztal Ger. **54** C2
Kribi Cameroon **104** A2
Krikellos Greece **65** B3
Kril'on, Mys *c.* Rus. Fed. **78** D1
Krishna *r.* India **85** C3
Krishnanagar India **87** C2
Kristiansand Norway **47** B4
Kristianstad Sweden **47** C4
Kristiansund Norway **46** B3
Kristinehamn Sweden **47** C4
Kriti *i.* Greece *see* Crete
Križevci Croatia **63** C1
Krk *i.* Croatia **62** B1
Krokom Sweden **46** C3
Krolevets' Ukr. **45** D1
Kronach Ger. **55** E2
Krông Kaôh Kông Cambodia **75** B2
Kronprins Frederik Bjerge *nunataks* Greenland **125** J2
Kroonstad S. Africa **109** C2
Kropotkin Rus. Fed. **45** F2
Krosno Pol. **57** E3
Krotoszyn Pol. **57** D2
Krui Indon. **72** B2
Krujë Albania **64** A2
Krumovgrad Bulg. **65** C2
Krung Thep Thai. *see* Bangkok
Krupki Belarus **42** C3
Kruševac Serb. and Mont. **64** B2
Krušné hory *mts* Czech Rep. **55** F2
Kruzof Island U.S.A. **126** B3
Krychaw Belarus **43** D3
Krymsk Rus. Fed. **45** E3
Krytiko Pelagos *sea* Greece **65** C3
Kryvyy Rih Ukr. **45** D2
Ksabi Alg. **100** B2
Ksar Chellala Alg. **61** D2
Ksar el Boukhari Alg. **61** D2
Ksar el Kebir Morocco **100** B1
Kshensky Rus. Fed. **43** E3
Kŭ', Jabal al *h.* Saudi Arabia **90** B2

Kuala Belait Brunei **73** C1
Kuala Kerai Malaysia **72** B1
Kuala Lipis Malaysia **72** B1
Kuala Lumpur Malaysia **72** B1
Kualapembuang Indon. **73** C2
Kuala Terengganu Malaysia **72** B1
Kualatungal Indon. **72** B2
Kuamut Malaysia **73** C1
Kuandian China **77** A1
Kuantan Malaysia **72** B1
Kuban' *r.* Rus. Fed. **45** E2
Kubenskoye, Ozero *l.* Rus. Fed. **43** E2
Kubrat Bulg. **64** C2
Kubuang Indon. **73** C1
Kuching Malaysia **73** C1
Kuçovë Albania **65** A2
Kudat Malaysia **73** C1
Kudus Indon. **73** C2
Kufstein Austria **56** C3
Kugaaruk Can. **125** H2
Kugluktuk Can. **124** E2
Kuhmo Fin. **46** F3
Kührān, Kūh-e *mt.* Iran **91** C2
Kuiseb *watercourse* Namibia **108** A1
Kuito Angola **106** A1
Kuivaniemi Fin. **46** F2
Kujzing N. Korea **77** B2
Kükës Albania **64** B2
Kula Turkey **65** C3
Kula Kangri *mt.* Bhutan/China **87** D2
Kulandy Kazakh. **88** C2
Kuldiga Latvia **42** B2
Kule Botswana **108** B1
Kulebaki Rus. Fed. **43** F2
Kulmbach Ger. **55** E2
Külob Tajik. **89** D3
Kul'sary Kazakh. **88** C2
Kulunda Rus. Fed. **89** E1
Kulundinskoye, Ozero *salt l.* Rus. Fed. **89** E1
Kulusuk Greenland **125** J2
Kumagaya Japan **79** C3
Kumamoto Japan **79** B4
Kumanovo Macedonia **64** B2
Kumasi Ghana **100** B4
Kumba Cameroon **104** A2
Kumdah Saudi Arabia **90** B2
Kumertau Rus. Fed. **41** E3
Kumi S. Korea **77** B2
Kumla Sweden **47** D4
Kumo Nigeria **101** D3
Kumon Range *mts* Myanmar **74** A1
Kumphawapi Thai. **74** B2
Kumylzhenskiy Rus. Fed. **45** F2
Kunashir, Ostrov *i.* Rus. Fed. **78** E2
Kunene *r.* Angola/Namibia **106** A1
Kungei Alatau *mts* Kazakh./Kyrg. **89** E2
Kungsbacka Sweden **47** C4
Kungu Dem. Rep. Congo **104** B2
Kungur Rus. Fed. **40** E3
Kunhing Myanmar **74** A1
Kunlun Shan *mts* China **87** B1
Kunming China **83** A3
Kunsan S. Korea **77** B2
Kununurra Austr. **114** B1
Künzelsau Ger. **55** D3
Kuopio Fin. **46** F3
Kupa *r.* Croatia/Slovenia **62** C1
Kupang Indon. **71** C3
Kupiškis Lith. **42** B2
Küplü Turkey **65** C2
Kupreanof Island U.S.A. **126** B3
Kup"yans'k Ukr. **45** E2
Kuqa China **89** F2
Kurashiki Japan **79** B4
Kurayoshi Japan **79** B3
Kurchatov Rus. Fed. **43** E3
Kürdzhali Bulg. **64** C2
Kure Japan **79** B4

Kuressaare Estonia **42** B2
Kurgan Rus. Fed. **41** F3
Kurganinsk Rus. Fed. **45** F3
Kurikka Fin. **47** E3
Kuril Islands Rus. Fed. **95** L3
Kuril'sk Rus. Fed. **95** L3
Kurkino Rus. Fed. **43** E3
Kurmuk Sudan **103** B3
Kurnool India **85** B3
Kuroiso Japan **79** D3
Kurri Kurri Austr. **117** E2
Kursk Rus. Fed. **43** E3
Kuruman S. Africa **108** B2
Kuruman *watercourse* S. Africa **108** B2
Kurume Japan **79** B4
Kurumkan Rus. Fed. **95** J3
Kurunegala Sri Lanka **85** C4
Kuşadası Turkey **65** C3
Kuşadası Körfezi *b.* Turkey **65** C3
Kuş Gölü *l.* Turkey **65** C2
Kushchevskaya Rus. Fed. **45** E2
Kushiro Japan **78** D2
Kushmurun Kazakh. **88** D1
Kushtia Bangl. **87** C2
Kuskokwim *r.* U.S.A. **95** P2
Kuskokwim Mountains U.S.A. **124** B2
Kussharo-ko *l.* Japan **78** D2
Kütahya Turkey **65** C3
K'ut'aisi Georgia **93** C1
Kutjevo Croatia **63** C1
Kutno Pol. **57** D2
Kutu Dem. Rep. Congo **104** B3
Kuujjua *r.* Can. **124** E2
Kuujjuaq Can. **129** D1
Kuujjuarapik Can. **128** C1
Kuusamo Fin. **46** F2
Kuvango Angola **106** A1
Kuvshinovo Rus. Fed. **43** D2
Kuwait *country* Asia **91** B2
Kuwait Kuwait **91** B2
Kuybyshev Ukr. **45** D2
Kuybyshevskoye Vodokhranilishche *resr* Rus. Fed. **41** D3
Kuytun China **89** F2
Kuyucak Turkey **65** C3
Kuznetsk Rus. Fed. **41** D3
Kuznetsovs'k Ukr. **44** C1
Kvalsund Norway **46** E1
Kwajalein *atoll* Marshall Is **110**
KwaMashu S. Africa **109** D2
Kwandang Indon. **73** D1
Kwangju S. Korea **77** B2
Kwanmo-bong *mt.* N. Korea **77** B1
Kwanobuhle S. Africa **109** C3
Kwanonzame S. Africa **108** B3
Kwatinidubu S. Africa **109** C3
KwaZamokhule S. Africa **109** C2
Kwazulu-Natal *prov.* S. Africa **109** D2
Kwekwe Zimbabwe **107** B1
Kwenge *r.* Dem. Rep. Congo **104** B3
Kwidzyn Pol. **57** D2
Kwilu *r.* Angola/Dem. Rep. Congo **104** B3
Kwoka *mt.* Indon. **71** C3
Kyabram Austr. **117** D3
Kyaikto Myanmar **74** A2
Kyakhta Rus. Fed. **80** D1
Kyancutta Austr. **116** B2
Kyaukpadaung Myanmar **74** A1
Kyaukpyu Myanmar **74** A2
Kybartai Lith. **42** B3
Kyebogyi Myanmar **74** A2
Kyeintali Myanmar **74** A2
Kyelang India **86** B1
Kyiv Ukr. *see* Kiev
Kyklades *is* Greece *see* Cyclades
Kyle Can. **127** E2
Kyle of Lochalsh U.K. **50** B2
Kyll *r.* Ger. **54** C3
Kyllini *mt.* Greece **65** B3

ymi Greece **65** B3
yneton Austr. **116** C3
yoga, Lake Uganda **105** D2
yogle Austr. **117** E1
yŏnggi-man *b.* S. Korea **77** B2
yŏngju S. Korea **77** B2
yōto Japan **79** C4
yparissia Greece **65** B3
ypshak, Ozero *salt l.* Kazakh. **89** D1
yra Panagia *i.* Greece **65** B3
yrenia Cyprus **92** B2
yrgyzstan *country* Asia **89** E2
yritz Ger. **55** F1
yrönjoki *r.* Fin. **46** E3
yrta Rus. Fed. **40** E2
yssa Rus. Fed. **40** F2
ythira *i.* Greece **65** B3
ythnos *i.* Greece **65** B3
yuquot Can. **126** D2
yūshū *i.* Japan **79** B4
yustendil Bulg. **64** B2
yyivs'ke Vodoskhovyshche *resr* Ukr. **44** D1
yyjärvi Fin. **46** E3
yzyl Rus. Fed. **80** C1
yzylkum Desert Kazakh./Uzbek. **88** D2
yzyl-Mazhalyk Rus. Fed. **89** G1
yzylorda Kazakh. **89** D2

L

a Angostura, Presa de *resr* Mex. **143** C3
ascaanood Somalia **103** C4
aáyoune Western Sahara **100** A2
aba *r.* Rus. Fed. **45** F2
a Babia Mex. **142** B2
a Banda Arg. **152** B3
abé Guinea **100** A3
aberge, Lake Can. **126** B1
a Biche, Lac *l.* Can. **127** D2
abinsk Rus. Fed. **45** F3
abo Phil. **76** B2
abouheyre France **58** B3
abrador *reg.* Can. **129** D1
abrador City Can. **129** D1
abrador Sea Can./Greenland **125** I2
abrea Brazil **150** C3
abuan Malaysia **73** C1
abuhanbajo Indon. **73** C2
abuhanbilik Indon. **72** B1
abuna Indon. **71** C3
abutta Myanmar **74** A2
abytnangi Rus. Fed. **40** F2
a Capelle France **59** C2
accadive Islands India **85** B3
ac Albania **64** A2
achlan *r.* Austr. **117** C2
achute Can. **137** F1
a Ciotat France **59** D3
a La Biche Can. **127** D2
ac-Mégantic Can. **129** C2
acombe Can. **126** D2
Concepción Panama **144** B4
Concordia Mex. **143** C3
aconia U.S.A. **137** F2
a Crete Can. **126** D2
a Crosse U.S.A. **136** B3
a Cruz Mex. **142** B2
a Cuesta Mex. **142** B2
adakh Range *mts* India **87** B2
adismith S. Africa **108** B3

Lādīz Iran **91** D2
Ladozhskoye Ozero *l.* Rus. Fed. *see* Lagoda, Lake
Ladysmith Can. **126** C3
Ladysmith S. Africa **109** C4
Lae P.N.G. **71** D3
La Esmeralda Bol. **152** B3
Læsø *i.* Denmark **47** C4
La Fayette U.S.A. **139** C2
Lafayette *IN* U.S.A. **136** C2
Lafayette *LA* U.S.A. **138** C2
La-Ferté-Milon France **54** A3
Lafia Nigeria **101** C4
La Flèche France **58** B2
La Follette U.S.A. **139** D1
Laforge Can. **129** C1
Läft Iran **91** C2
La Galite *i.* Tunisia **62** A3
Lagan' Rus. Fed. **41** D4
Lagdo, Lac de Cameroon **104** B2
Laghouat Alg. **100** C1
Lagoa Santa Brazil **155** D1
Lagoda, Lake Rus. Fed. **43** D1
La Gomera *i.* Canary Is **100** A2
Lagos Nigeria **100** C4
Lagos Port. **60** B2
La Grande Can. **132** C1
a Grande 2, Réservoir *resr* Can. **128** C1
La Grande 3, Réservoir *resr* Can. **128** C1
LLa Grande 4, Réservoir *resr* Can. **129** C1
Lagrange Austr. **114** B1
La Grange U.S.A. **139** C2
La Gran Sabana *plat.* Venez. **150** C2
Laguna Brazil **152** D3
Laguna, Picacho de la *mt.* Mex. **142** A1
Lagunas Peru **150** B3
La Habana Cuba *see* Havana
Lahad Datu Malaysia **73** C1
Lahat Indon. **72** B2
Lahij Yemen **90** B3
Lahijān Iran **91** C2
Lahnstein Ger. **54** C2
Lahore Pak. **86** A2
Lahri Pak. **86** A2
Lahti Fin. **47** F3
Laï Chad **101** D4
Laidley Austr. **117** E1
L'Aigle France **58** B2
Laingsburg S. Africa **108** B3
Lainioälven *r.* Sweden **46** E2
Lairg U.K. **50** B1
Laives Italy **62** B1
Laiwu China **82** B2
Laiyang China **82** C2
Laizhou China **82** B2
Laizhou Wan *b.* China **82** B2
Lajamanu Austr. **114** C1
Lajes Brazil **152** C3
La Junta Mex. **142** B2
La Junta U.S.A. **134** C3
La Cargelligo Austr. **117** D2
Lake Cathie Austr. **117** E2
Lake Charles U.S.A. **138** B2
Lake City *FL* U.S.A. **139** D2
Lake City *SC* U.S.A. **139** D2
Lake Cowichan Can. **126** B3
Lakeland U.S.A. **139** D3
Lake Louise Can. **126** D2
Lake Oswego U.S.A. **132** B1
Lake Paringa N.Z. **118** A3
Lake Providence U.S.A. **138** B2
Lakes Entrance Austr. **117** D3
Lakeview U.S.A. **132** B2
Lakewood *CO* U.S.A. **134** B3
Lakewood *NJ* U.S.A. **137** F2

Lake Worth U.S.A. **139** D3
Lakhpat India **86** A2
Lakki Pak. **86** B1
Lakonikos Kolpos *b.* Greece **65** B3
Lakselv Norway **46** E1
La Libertad Guat. **143** C3
Lalín Spain **60** B1
Lalitpur India **87** B2
La Loche Can. **124** E3
La Louvière Belgium **54** B2
La Maddalena Italy **62** A2
Lamag Malaysia **73** C1
La Manche *str.* France/U.K. *see* English Channel
Lamar U.S.A. **134** C3
Lamard Iran **91** C2
La Marmora, Punta *mt.* Italy **62** A3
La Martre, Lac *l.* Can. **126** D1
Lambaréné Gabon **104** B3
Lambert's Bay S. Africa **108** A3
Lambeyri Iceland **46** [inset]
Lamego Port. **60** B1
La Merced Peru **150** B4
Lameroo Austr. **116** C3
Lamesa U.S.A. **141** D2
Lamia Greece **65** B3
Lamoni U.S.A. **135** E2
Lampang Thai. **74** A2
Lampasas U.S.A. **141** E2
Lampazos Mex. **143** B2
Lampeter U.K. **53** A3
Lamphun Thai. **74** A2
Lamu Kenya **105** E3
Lanark U.K. **50** C3
Lanbi Kyun *i.* Myanmar **75** A2
Lancang Jiang *r.* China *see* Mekong
Lancaster U.K. **52** B2
Lancaster *CA* U.S.A. **133** C4
Lancaster *OH* U.S.A. **136** D3
Lancaster *PA* U.S.A. **137** E2
Lancaster *SC* U.S.A. **139** D2
Lancaster Sound *str.* Can. **125** G2
Landau in der Pfalz Ger. **54** D3
Landeck Austria **56** C3
Lander U.S.A. **134** B2
Land's End *pt* U.K. **53** A4
Landshut Ger. **56** C3
Landskrona Sweden **47** C4
Landstuhl Ger. **54** C3
Lanett U.S.A. **139** C2
Langberg *mts* S. Africa **108** B2
Langdon U.S.A. **135** D1
Langeland *i.* Denmark **47** C4
Langen Ger. **55** D1
Langeoog Ger. **54** C1
Langeoog *i.* Ger. **54** C1
Langgöns Ger. **55** D2
Langjökull *ice cap* Iceland **46** [inset]
Langogne France **59** C3
Langon France **58** B3
Langres France **59** D2
Langsa Indon. **72** A1
Lang Son Vietnam **74** B1
Langwedel Ger. **55** D1
Lanigan Can. **127** E2
Lanín, Volcán *vol.* Arg./Chile **153** A4
Länkäran Azer. **93** C2
Lannion France **58** B2
Lansing U.S.A. **136** D2
Lanxi China **83** B3
Lanya Sudan **103** B4
Lanzarote *i.* Canary Is **100** A2
Lanzhou China **82** A2
Laoag Phil. **76** B2
Lao Cai Vietnam **74** B1
Laohekou China **82** B2
Laoling China **77** B1
Lao Ling *mts* China **77** B1
Laon France **59** C2

Laos *country* Asia **74** B2
Laotougou China **77** B1
Lapa Brazil **154** C3
La Palma *i.* Canary Is **100** A2
La Palma Panama **144** C4
La Paragua Venez. **150** C2
La Paz Bol. **152** B2
La Paz Hond. **143** D3
La Paz Mex. **142** A2
La Pedrera Col. **150** C2
La Pérouse Strait Japan/Rus. Fed.
   78 D1
La Pesca Mex. **143** C2
La Piedad Mex. **142** B2
La Plata Arg. **153** C4
La Plata, Río de *sea chan.* Arg./Uru.
   153 C4
La Potherie, Lac *l.* Can. **129** E1
Lappeenranta Fin. **47** F3
Lappersdorf Ger. **55** F3
Lappland *reg.* Europe **46** D2
Låpseki Turkey **65** C2
Laptev Sea Rus. Fed. **95** K1
Laptevykh, More *sea* Rus. Fed. *see*
   Laptev Sea
Lapua Fin. **46** E3
La Quiaca Arg. **152** B3
Lär Iran **91** C2
Larache Morocco **100** B1
Laramie U.S.A. **134** B2
Laramie Mountains U.S.A. **134** B2
Laranda Turkey *see* Karaman
Laranjeiras do Sul Brazil **154** B3
Larantuka Indon. **73** D2
Larat *i.* Indon. **71** C3
Larba Alg. **61** D2
Laredo Spain **60** C1
Laredo U.S.A. **141** D3
Largs U.K. **50** B3
La Rioja Arg. **152** B3
Larisa Greece **65** B3
Larkana Pak. **86** A2
Larnaca Cyprus **92** B2
Larne U.K. **51** D1
La Roche-en-Ardenne Belgium **54** B2
La Rochelle France **58** B2
La Roche-sur-Yon France **58** B2
La Roda Spain **61** C2
La Romana Dom. Rep. **145** D3
La Ronge Can. **124** E3
La Ronge, Lac *l.* Can. **124** F3
Larrimah Austr. **114** C1
Larsen Ice Shelf Antarctica **119** K3
Larvik Norway **47** C4
La Sarre Can. **128** C2
Las Cruces U.S.A. **140** C2
La Serena Chile **152** A3
Las Flores Arg. **153** C4
Las Heras Arg. **153** B4
Lashio Myanmar **74** A1
Lashkar Gāh Afgh. **86** A1
La Sila *reg.* Italy **63** C3
Las Lomitas Arg. **152** B3
Las Nieves Mex. **142** B2
Las Palmas de Gran Canaria
   Canary Is **100** A2
La Spezia Italy **62** A2
Las Plumas Arg. **153** B5
Last Mountain Lake Can. **127** E2
Las Tórtolas, Cerro *mt.* Chile **152** B3
Lastoursville Gabon **104** B3
Lastovo *i.* Croatia **63** C2
Las Tres Vírgenes, Volcán *vol.* Mex.
   142 A2
Las Tunas Cuba **145** C2
Las Varas Chihuahua Mex. **142** B2
Las Varas Nayarit Mex. **142** B2
Las Vegas NM U.S.A. **140** C1
Las Vegas NV U.S.A. **133** C3
La Tabatière Can. **129** E1

Latakia Syria **92** B2
La Teste-de-Buch France **58** B3
Latina Italy **62** B2
La Tortuga, Isla *i.* Venez. **145** D3
La Trinidad Phil. **76** B2
Latskoye Rus. Fed. **43** E2
La Tuque Can. **129** C2
Latvia *country* Europe **42** B2
Lauchhammer Ger. **55** F2
Lauf an der Pegnitz Ger. **55** E3
Laufen Switz. **59** D2
Launceston Austr. **115** D4
Launceston U.K. **53** A4
Launggyaung Myanmar **74** A1
Laura Austr. **115** D1
Laurel MS U.S.A. **138** C2
Laurel MT U.S.A. **132** E1
Lauria Italy **63** C2
Laurinburg U.S.A. **139** E2
Lausanne Switz. **59** D2
Laut *i.* Indon. **73** C2
Lautersbach (Hessen) Ger. **55** D2
Laut Kecil, Kepulauan *is* Indon. **73** C2
Lauwersmeer *l.* Neth. **54** C1
Laval France **58** B2
Lavapié, Punta *pt* Chile **147**
Laverton Austr. **114** B3
Lavras Brazil **155** D2
Lavumisa Swaziland **109** D2
Lawas Malaysia **73** C1
Lawksawk Myanmar **74** A1
Lawra Ghana **100** B3
Lawrence U.S.A. **135** D3
Lawrenceburg U.S.A. **138** C1
Lawton U.S.A. **141** E2
Lawz, Jabal al *mt.* Saudi Arabia **90** A2
Laxå Sweden **47** C4
Lazarev Rus. Fed. **95** J2
Lazarevac Serb. and Mont. **64** B2
Lázaro Cárdenas Baja California Mex.
   142 A1
Lázaro Cárdenas Michoacán Mex.
   142 B3
Lazdijai Lith. **42** B3
Lead U.S.A. **134** C2
Leader Can. **127** E2
Leadville U.S.A. **134** B3
Leaf Rapids Can. **127** E2
Leane, Lough *l.* Rep. of Ireland **51** B2
Leavenworth U.S.A. **135** E3
Lebach Ger. **54** C3
Lebanon *country* Asia **92** B2
Lebanon MO U.S.A. **135** E3
Lebanon NH U.S.A. **137** F2
Lebanon OR U.S.A. **132** B2
Lebanon PA U.S.A. **137** E2
Lebedyan' Rus. Fed. **43** E3
Lebedyn Ukr. **45** D1
Le Blanc France **58** C2
Lębork Pol. **57** D2
Lebowakgomo S. Africa **109** C1
Lebrija Spain **60** B2
Lebu Chile **153** A4
Le Bugue France **58** C3
Le Catelet France **54** A2
Lecce Italy **63** D2
Lecco Italy **62** A1
Lech *r.* Austria/Ger. **56** C3
Lechaina Greece **65** B3
Lechang China **83** B3
Leck Ger. **56** B2
Lectoure France **58** C3
Ledesma Spain **60** B1
Le Dorat France **58** C2
Leduc Can. **126** D2
Leech Lake U.S.A. **135** E1
Leeds U.K. **52** C3
Leek U.K. **52** B3
Leer (Ostfriesland) Ger. **54** C1
Leesburg U.S.A. **139** D3
Leesville U.S.A. **138** B2

Leeton Austr. **117** D2
Leeu-Gamka S. Africa **108** B3
Leeuwarden Neth. **54** B1
Leeuwin, Cape Austr. **114** A3
Leeward Islands Caribbean Sea
   145 D3
Lefkada Greece **65** B3
Lefkada *i.* Greece **65** B3
Lefkosia Cyprus *see* Nicosia
Legaspi Phil. **76** B2
Legnago Italy **62** B1
Legnica Pol. **57** D2
Leh India **87** B1
Le Havre France **58** C2
Lehututu Botswana **108** B1
Leiah Pak. **86** B1
Leibnitz Austria **57** D3
Leicester U.K. **53** C3
Leichhardt *r.* Austr. **115** C1
Leiden Neth. **54** B1
Leie *r.* Belgium **54** A2
Leigh Creek Austr. **116** B2
Leikanger Norway **47** B3
Leimen Ger. **55** D3
Leine *r.* Ger. **55** D2
Leinster *reg.* Rep. of Ireland **51** C2
Leipzig Ger. **55** F2
Leiranger Norway **46** C2
Leiria Port. **60** B2
Leirvik Norway **47** B4
Leixlip Rep. of Ireland **51** C2
Leiyang China **83** B3
Leizhou China **83** B3
Leizhou Bandao *pen.* China **83** A3
Lékana Congo **104** B3
Lejystad Neth. **54** B1
Le Maire, Estrecho de *sea chan.* Arg.
   153 B6
Léman, Lac *l.* France/Switz. *see*
   Geneva, Lake
Le Mans France **58** C2
Le Mars U.S.A. **135** D2
Leme Brazil **154** C2
Lemesos Cyprus *see* Limassol
Lemförde Ger. **55** D1
Lemieux Islands Can. **125** H2
Lemmon U.S.A. **134** C1
Lemoore U.S.A. **133** C3
Le Moyne, Lac *l.* Can. **129** D1
Lemro *r.* Myanmar **74** A1
Le Murge *hills* Italy **63** C2
Lena *r.* Rus. Fed. **95** K2
Lendery Rus. Fed. **46** D3
Lengerich Ger. **54** C1
Lengshuijiang China **83** B3
Lengshuitan China **83** B3
Lenine Ukr. **45** E2
Leningradskaya Rus. Fed. **45** E2
Lenin Peak Kyrg./Tajik. **89** E3
Leninskiy Rus. Fed. **43** E3
Lens Belgium **54** A2
Lens France **58** C1
Lensk Rus. Fed. **95** J2
Lenti Hungary **57** D3
Lentini Italy **62** C3
Léo Burkina **100** B3
Leoben Austria **56** D3
Leominster U.K. **53** B3
León Mex. **142** B2
León Nic. **144** B3
León Spain **60** B1
Leonardville Namibia **108** A1
Leonora Austr. **114** B3
Leopoldina Brazil **155** D2
Lephalale S. Africa **109** C1
Lephepe Botswana **109** C1
Lephoi S. Africa **109** C3
Leping China **83** B3
Le Puy-en-Velay France **59** C2
Lerala Botswana **109** C1

érida Col. 150 B3
erma China 81 B2
eros i. Greece 65 C3
e Roy, Lac l. Can. 128 C1
erum Sweden 47 C4
erwick U.K. 50 [inset]
esbos i. Greece 65 C3
es Cayes Haiti 145 C3
eshan China 80 C3
eshukonskoye Rus. Fed. 40 D2
eskovac Serb. and Mont. 64 B2
esneven France 58 B2
esnoye Rus. Fed. 40 D2
esosibirsk Rus. Fed. 95 I3
esotho country Africa 109 C2
esozavodsk Rus. Fed. 78 E1
esser Antilles is Caribbean Sea
   145 D3
esser Caucasus mts Asia 93 C1
esser Slave Lake Can. 126 D2
es Vans France 59 C3
esvos i. Greece see Lesbos
eszno Pol. 57 D2
etchworth U.K. 53 C4
ethbridge Can. 127 D3
ethem Guyana 150 D2
eticia Col. 150 C3
etihakeng Botswana 109 C1
e Touquet-Paris-Plage France 58 C1
e Tréport France 53 D4
etsok-aw Kyun i. Myanmar 75 A2
etsopa S. Africa 109 C2
euca China 127 D3
eucate, Étang de l. France 58 D3
euser, Gunung mt. Indon. 72 A1
euven Belgium 54 B2
evadeia Greece 65 B3
evelland U.S.A. 141 D2
evêque, Cape Austr. 114 B1
everkusen Ger. 54 C2
evice Slovakia 57 D3
evin N.Z. 118 C3
évis Can. 129 C2
ev Tolstoy Rus. Fed. 43 E3
ewes U.K. 53 D4
ewis, Isle of i. U.K. 50 A1
ewisburg U.S.A. 137 D3
ewis Range mts U.S.A. 132 D1
ewiston ID U.S.A. 132 C1
ewiston ME U.S.A. 137 F2
ewistown U.S.A. 132 E1
exington KY U.S.A. 136 D3
exington NE U.S.A. 134 D3
exington VA U.S.A. 137 E3
eyte i. Phil. 76 B2
ezhë Albania 64 A2
gov Rus. Fed. 43 F2
hagoi Kangri mt. China 87 C2
hasa China 87 D2
hazê China 87 C2
anhua China 83 B3
anjiang China 83 B3
 anshan China 82 C1
anyungang China 82 B2
anzhou China 83 B3
aocheng China 82 B2
aodong Bandao pen. China 82 C1
aodong Wan b. China 82 C1
ao He r. China 77 A1
aoning prov. China 82 C1
aoyang China 82 C1
aoyuan China 77 B1

Libby U.S.A. 132 C1
Libenge Dem. Rep. Congo 104 B2
Liberal U.S.A. 134 C3
Liberec Czech Rep. 56 D2
Liberia country Africa 100 B4
Liberia Costa Rica 144 B3
Libertad Venez. 145 D4
Libin China 81 B2
Libourne France 58 B3
Libreville Gabon 104 A2
Libya country Africa 101 D2
Libyan Desert Egypt/Libya 101 E2
Libyan Plateau Egypt 102 A1
Licata Italy 62 B3
Lichinga Moz. 107 C1
Lichte Ger. 55 E2
Lichtenburg S. Africa 109 C2
Lichtenfels Ger. 55 E2
Lida Belarus 42 C3
Lidköping Sweden 47 C4
Liebenwalde Ger. 55 F1
Liebig, Mount Austr. 114 C2
Liechtenstein country Europe 59 D2
Liège Belgium 54 B2
Lieksa Fin. 46 G3
Lienart Dem. Rep. Congo 105 C2
Lienz Austria 56 C3
Liepāja Latvia 42 B2
Liévin France 54 A2
Liezen Austria 56 C3
Liffey r. Rep. of Ireland 51 C2
Lifford Rep. of Ireland 51 C1
Lightning Ridge Austr. 117 D1
Ligonha r. Moz. 107 C1
Ligurian Sea France/Italy 62 A2
Likasi Dem. Rep. Congo 105 C4
Likely Can. 126 C2
Likhoslavl' Rus. Fed. 43 E2
Liku Indon. 72 B1
L'Île-Rousse France 59 D3
Liling China 83 B3
Lilla Edet Sweden 47 C4
Lille Belgium 54 B2
Lille France 58 C1
Lille Bælt sea chan. Denmark see
   Little Belt
Lillehammer Norway 47 C3
Lillestrøm Norway 47 C4
Lillooet Can. 126 C2
Lilongwe Malawi 107 C1
Liloy Phil. 76 B3
Lima Peru 150 B4
Lima U.S.A. 136 D2
Limassol Cyprus 92 B2
Limavady U.K. 51 C1
Limay r. Arg. 153 B4
Limbach-Oberfrohna Ger. 55 F2
Limbaži Latvia 42 B2
Limbe Cameroon 104 A2
Limburg an der Lahn Ger. 54 D2
Lime Acres S. Africa 108 B2
Limeira Brazil 154 C2
Limerick Rep. of Ireland 51 B2
Limfjorden sea chan. Denmark 47 B4
Limnos i. Greece 65 C3
Limoges France 58 C2
Limon U.S.A. 134 C3
Limoux France 58 C3
Limpopo prov. S. Africa 109 C1
Limpopo r. S. Africa/Zimbabwe 109 D2
Linapacan i. Phil. 76 A2
Linares Chile 153 A4
Linares Mex. 143 C2
Linares Spain 60 C2
Lincang China 74 B1
Lincoln U.K. 52 C3
Lincoln IL U.S.A. 136 C2
Lincoln ME U.S.A. 137 G1
Lincoln NE U.S.A. 135 D2
Linden Guyana 151 D2

Linden U.S.A. 138 C1
Lindi r. Dem. Rep. Congo 105 C2
Lindi Tanz. 105 D3
Lindisfarne i. U.K. see Holy Island
Lindos Greece 92 A2
Lindsay Can. 137 E2
Line Islands Kiribati 159 E4
Linfen China 82 B2
Lingayen Phil. 76 B2
Lingbao China 82 B2
Lingelethu S. Africa 109 C3
Lingelihle S. Africa 109 C3
Lingen (Ems) Ger. 54 C1
Lingga, Kepulauan is Indon. 72 B2
Lingshan China 83 A4
Lingshui China 83 A4
Linguère Senegal 100 A3
Linhares Brazil 155 D1
Linhe China 82 A1
Linköping Sweden 47 D4
Linkou China 78 B1
Linnhe, Loch inlet U.K. 50 B2
Linqing China 82 B2
Lins Brazil 154 C2
Linton U.S.A. 134 C1
Linxi China 82 B1
Linxia China 82 A2
Linyi Shandong China 82 B2
Linyi Shandong China 82 B2
Linying China 82 B2
Linz Austria 56 C3
Lion, Golfe du g. France 59 C3
Lipari Italy 62 B3
Lipari, Isole is Italy 62 B3
Lipetsk Rus. Fed. 43 E3
Lipin Bor Rus. Fed. 43 E1
Lipova Romania 44 B2
Lippstadt Ger. 55 D2
Lipu China 83 B3
Lisakovsk Kazakh. 88 D1
Lisala Dem. Rep. Congo 104 C2
Lisboa Port. see Lisbon
Lisbon Port. 60 B2
Lisburn U.K. 51 C1
Liscannor Bay Rep. of Ireland 51 B2
Lisieux France 58 C2
Liskeard U.K. 53 A4
Liski Rus. Fed. 43 E3
Lismore Austr. 117 E1
Lisnaskea U.K. 51 C1
Listowel Rep. of Ireland 51 B2
Litang Guangxi China 83 A3
Litang Sichuan China 80 C2
Litchfield IL U.S.A. 136 C3
Litchfield MN U.S.A. 135 E1
Lithgow Austr. 117 E2
Lithino, Akra pt Greece 65 B4
Lithuania country Europe 42 B2
Litoměřice Czech Rep. 56 C2
Little Abaco i. Bahamas 145 C2
Little Andaman i. India 75 A2
Little Belt sea chan. Denmark 47 B4
Little Falls U.S.A. 135 E1
Littlefield U.S.A. 141 D2
Littlehampton U.K. 53 C4
Little Karas Berg plat. Namibia
   108 A2
Little Karoo plat. S. Africa 108 B3
Little Minch sea chan. U.K. 50 A2
Little Missouri r. U.S.A. 134 C1
Little Nicobar i. India 75 A3
Little Rock U.S.A. 138 B2
Littleton U.S.A. 137 F2
Liujiachang China 83 B2
Liuzhou China 83 A3
Līvāni Latvia 42 C2
Liveringa Austr. 114 B1
Livermore, Mount U.S.A. 140 D2
Liverpool Can. 129 D2
Liverpool U.K. 52 B3

ard r. Can. 124 D2
ancourt Rocks i. N. Pacific Ocean
   77 C2
hokseumawe Indon. 72 A1

Liverpool Range *mts* Austr. **117** D2
Livingston *MT* U.S.A. **132** D1
Livingston *TX* U.S.A. **141** F2
Livingstone, Lake U.S.A. **141** E2
Livingstone Zambia **106** D3
Livno Bos.-Herz. **62** C2
Livny Rus. Fed. **43** E3
Livonia U.S.A. **136** D2
Livorno Italy **62** B2
Liwale Tanz. **105** D3
Lizard Point *pt* U.K. **53** A5
Lizy-sur-Ourcq France **54** A3
Ljubljana Slovenia **62** B1
Ljungan *r.* Sweden **47** D3
Ljungby Sweden **47** C4
Ljusdal Sweden **47** D3
Ljusnan *r.* Sweden **47** D3
Llandeilo U.K. **53** B4
Llandovery U.K. **53** B4
Llandrindod Wells U.K. **53** B3
Llandudno U.K. **52** B3
Llanelli U.K. **53** A4
Llangefni U.K. **52** A3
Llano Estacado *plain* U.S.A. **141** D2
Llanos *reg.* Col./Venez. **150** C2
Lleida Spain **61** C1
Lliria Spain **61** C2
Llodio Spain **60** C1
Lloyd George, Mount Can. **126** C2
Lloyd Lake Can. **127** E2
Lloydminster Can. **127** D2
Llullaillaco, Volcán *vol.* Chile **152** B3
Lobatse Botswana **109** C3
Lobito Angola **106** A1
Loburg Ger. **55** F1
Lochaber *reg.* U.K. **50** A2
Lochboisdale U.K. **50** A2
Loches France **58** C2
Lochgilphead U.K. **50** A2
Lochinver U.K. **50** B1
Lochmaddy U.K. **50** A2
Lochnagar *mt.* U.K. **50** C1
Lock Austr. **116** B2
Lockerbie U.K. **50** C3
Lockhart U.S.A. **141** E3
Lock Haven U.S.A. **137** E2
Lockport U.S.A. **137** E2
Lôc Ninh Vietnam **75** B2
Lodève France **59** C3
Lodeynoye Pole Rus. Fed. **40** C2
Løding Norway **46** C2
Lodwar Kenya **105** D2
Łódź Pol. **57** D2
Loei Thai. **74** B2
Loeriesfontein S. Africa **108** A3
Lofoten *is* Norway **46** C2
Logan U.S.A. **132** D2
Logan, Mount Can. **126** A1
Logansport U.S.A. **136** C2
Logatec Slovenia **62** B1
Logroño Spain **60** C1
Löhne Ger. **55** D1
Lohne (Oldenburg) Ger. **55** D1
Loikaw Myanmar **74** A2
Loi Lan *mt.* Myanmar/Thai. **74** A2
Loire *r.* France **58** B2
Loja Ecuador **150** B3
Loja Spain **60** C2
Lokan tekojärvi *l.* Fin. **46** F2
Lokeren Belgium **54** B2
Lokgwabe Botswana **108** B1
Lokichar Kenya **105** D2
Lokichokio Kenya **105** D2
Loknya Rus. Fed. **43** D2
Lokoja Nigeria **101** C4
Lokot' Rus. Fed. **43** D3
Loksa Estonia **42** C2
Loks Land *i.* Can. **125** H2
Lolland *i.* Denmark **47** C5
Lollondo Tanz. **105** D3

Lolwane S. Africa **108** B2
Lom Bulg. **64** B2
Lom Norway **47** B3
Lomami *r.* Dem. Rep. Congo **105** C2
Lomas de Zamora Arg. **153** C4
Lombok *i.* Indon. **73** C2
Lombok, Selat *sea chan.* Indon. **73** C2
Lomé Togo **100** C4
Lomela *r.* Dem. Rep. Congo **104** C3
Lomme France **54** A2
Lommel Belgium **54** B2
Lomonosov Rus. Fed. **42** C2
Lompobattang, Gunung *mt.* Indon. **73** C2
Lompoc U.S.A. **133** B4
Lom Sak Thai. **74** B2
Łomża Pol. **57** E2
London Can. **128** B2
London U.K. **53** C4
Londonderry U.K. **51** C1
Londonderry, Cape Austr. **114** B1
Londrina Brazil **154** B2
Longa, Proliv *sea chan.* Rus. Fed. **95** N2
Long Akah Malaysia **73** C1
Long Bay U.S.A. **139** E2
Long Beach U.S.A. **133** C4
Longford Rep. of Ireland **51** C2
Longiram Indon. **73** C2
Long Island Bahamas **145** C2
Long Island Can. **128** C1
Long Island P.N.G. **71** D3
Long Island U.S.A. **137** F2
Longjiang China **82** A2
Long Lake Can. **128** B2
Longmont U.S.A. **134** B2
Long Point *pt* Can. **137** D2
Longquan China **83** B3
Long Xuyên Vietnam **75** B2
Longyan China **83** B3
Longyearbyen Svalbard **94** C1
Lons-le-Saunier France **56** B3
Lookout, Cape U.S.A. **139** E2
Loop Head Rep. of Ireland **51** B2
Lop Buri Thai. **75** B2
Lopez Phil. **76** B2
Lop Nur *salt flat* China **80** C2
Lopori *r.* Dem. Rep. Congo **104** B2
Lora del Rio Spain **60** B2
Lorain U.S.A. **136** D2
Loralai Pak. **86** A1
Lorca Spain **61** C2
Lord Howe Island Austr. **115** E3
Lordsburg U.S.A. **140** C2
Lorena Brazil **155** C2
Loreto Bol. **152** B2
Loreto Mex. **142** A2
Lorient France **58** B2
Lorn, Firth of *est.* U.K. **50** B2
Lorne Austr. **116** C3
Los Alamos U.S.A. **140** C1
Los Aldamas Mex. **141** E3
Los Ángeles Chile **153** A4
Los Angeles U.S.A. **133** C4
Los Banos U.S.A. **133** B3
Los Blancos Arg. **152** B3
Losevo Rus. Fed. **45** F1
Lošinj *i.* Croatia **62** B2
Los Mochis Mex. **142** B2

Losombo Dem. Rep. Congo **104** B2
Los Roques, Islas *is* Venez. **145** D3
Lossiemouth U.K. **50** C2
Los Teques Venez. **150** C1
Los Vilos Chile **152** A4
Lot *r.* France **58** C3
Loth U.K. **50** C1
Lotikipi Plain Kenya **105** D2
Loto Dem. Rep. Congo **104** C3
Lotoshino Rus. Fed. **43** E2
Louangnamtha Laos **74** B1
Louangphabang Laos **74** B2
Loudomo Congo **104** B3
Loudéac France **58** B2
Loudi China **83** B3
Louga Senegal **100** A3
Loughborough U.K. **53** C3
Loughrea Rep. of Ireland **51** B2
Louhans France **59** D2
Louisburgh Rep. of Ireland **51** B2
Louisiade Archipelago *is* P.N.G. **115** E1
Louisiana *state* U.S.A. **138** B2
Louisville *KY* U.S.A. **136** C3
Louisville *MS* U.S.A. **138** C2
Loukhi Rus. Fed. **46** G2
Louny Czech Rep. **55** F2
Loups Marins, Lacs des *lakes* Can. **128** C1
Lourdes France **58** B3
Lourenço Brazil **151** D2
Lousã Port. **60** B1
Louth Austr. **117** D2
Louth U.K. **52** C3
Lovat' *r.* Rus. Fed. **43** D2
Lovech Bulg. **64** B2
Loveland U.S.A. **134** B2
Lovelock U.S.A. **132** C2
Loviisa Fin. **42** C1
Lovington U.S.A. **141** D2
Lowa Dem. Rep. Congo **105** C3
Lowell U.S.A. **137** F2
Lower Arrow Lake Can. **126** D3
Lower Hutt N.Z. **118** B3
Lower Lough Erne *l.* U.K. **51** C1
Lower Post Can. **126** C2
Lowestoft U.K. **53** D3
Łowicz Pol. **57** D2
Lowville U.S.A. **137** E2
Loxton Austr. **116** C2
Loyauté, Îles *is* New Caledonia **110**
Loyew Belarus **43** D3
Leypshtardinden *mt.* Norway **46** C2
Loznica Serb. and Mont. **64** A2
Lozova Ukr. **45** E2
Luacano Angola **106** C1
Lu'an China **82** B2
Luanda Angola **104** B3
Luangwa *r.* Zambia **107** C1
Luanshya Zambia **107** C1
Luarca Spain **60** B1
Luau Angola **106** C1
Lubaczów Pol. **57** E2
Lubango Angola **106** A1
Lubao Dem. Rep. Congo **105** C3
Lubartów Pol. **57** E2
Lübbecke Ger. **55** D1
Lübben Ger. **55** F2
Lübbenau Ger. **55** F2
Lubbock U.S.A. **141** D2
Lübeck Ger. **55** E1
Lubei China **82** C1
Lubenka Kazakh. **88** C1
Lubin Pol. **57** D2
Lublin Pol. **57** E2
Lubny Ukr. **45** D1
Lubok Antu Malaysia **73** C1
Lübtheen Ger. **55** E1
Lubudi Dem. Rep. Congo **105** C3
Lubuklinggau Indon. **72** B2

bumbashi Dem. Rep. Congo 105 C4
bungu Zambia 106 C3
butu Dem. Rep. Congo 105 C3
cala Angola 106 A3
icapa Angola 104 C3
ce Bay U.K. 50 B3
célia Brazil 154 B2
cena Phil. 76 B2
cena Spain 60 C2
čenec Slovakia 57 D3
cera Italy 62 C2
cerne Switz. 59 D2
chow Ger. 55 E1
cira Angola 106 A1
ckau Ger. 55 F2
ckenwalde Ger. 55 F1
ckhoff S. Africa 108 B2
cknow India 87 C2
cusse Angola 106 B1
denscheid Ger. 54 C2
der Ger. 55 E1
deritz Namibia 108 A2
dhiana India 86 B1
dington U.S.A. 136 C3
dlow U.K. 53 B3
dlow U.S.A. 133 C4
dogorie reg. Bulg. 64 C2
dvika Sweden 47 D3
dwigsburg Ger. 56 B3
dwigsfelde Ger. 55 F1
dwigshafen am Rhein Ger. 55 D3
dwigslust Ger. 55 E1
dza Latvia 42 C2
ebo Dem. Rep. Congo 104 C3
ena Angola 106 A1
eyang China 82 A2
feng China 83 B3
kin U.S.A. 141 F3
ga Rus. Fed. 42 C2
ga r. Rus. Fed. 42 C2
gano Switz. 59 D2
genda r. Moz. 107 C1
goj Romania 44 B2
hans'k Ukr. 45 E2
hombero Tanz. 105 D3
hyny Ukr. 44 C1
iana Angola 106 B1
laka r. Dem. Rep. Congo 104 C3
no Italy 56 B3
ro r. Fin. 46 F2
za Dem. Rep. Congo 104 C3
iang China 82 B2
kavac Bos.-Herz. 63 C2
kenie r. Dem. Rep. Congo 104 B3
keville U.S.A. 140 B2
kh r. Rus. Fed. 43 F2
khovitsy Rus. Fed. 43 E3
ków Pol. 57 E2
kulu Zambia 106 B1
eä Sweden 46 E2
eälven r. Sweden 46 E2
eburgaz Turkey 64 C2
iang Shan mts China 82 B2
najang Indon. 73 C2
najangdong Co salt l. China
7 C1
nbala Kaquengue Angola
06 B1
nbala N'guimbo Angola 106 B1
nbis Indon. 73 C1
nbrales Spain 60 B1
nphát Cambodia 75 B2
nsden Can. 127 E2
nsden N.Z. 118 A4
d Sweden 47 C4
dazi Zambia 107 C1
dy i. U.K. 53 A4

Lüneburg Ger. 55 E1
Lüneburger Heide reg. Ger. 55 E1
Lünen Ger. 54 C2
Lunéville France 59 D2
Lunga r. Zambia 106 B1
Lungi Sierra Leone 100 A4
Lunglei India 74 A1
Lungnaquilla Mountain h.
  Rep. of Ireland 51 C2
Lungwebungu r. Zambia 106 B1
Luni r. India 86 B2
Luninyets Belarus 42 C3
Lunsar Sierra Leone 100 A4
Luntai China 89 F2
Luodian China 83 A3
Luoding China 83 B3
Luohe China 82 B2
Luoyang China 82 B2
Lupane Zimbabwe 106 B1
Lupanshui China 83 A3
Lupeni Romania 44 B2
Lupilichi Moz. 107 C1
Luppa Ger. 55 F2
Lúrio Moz. 107 D1
Lurio r. Moz. 107 D1
Lusaka Zambia 107 B1
Lusambo Dem. Rep. Congo 104 C3
Lushnjë Albania 65 A2
Lusk U.S.A. 135 D2
Lut, Dasht-e des. Iran 88 C3
Lutherstadt Wittenberg Ger. 55 F2
Luton U.K. 53 C4
Lutong Malaysia 73 C1
Łutselk'e Can. 127 D1
Luts'k Ukr. 44 C1
Lutzputs S. Africa 108 B2
Lutzville S. Africa 108 A3
Luuq Somalia 103 C4
Luverne U.S.A. 135 D2
Luvua r. Dem. Rep. Congo 105 C3
Luvuvhu r. S. Africa 109 D1
Luwero Uganda 105 D3
Luwuk Indon. 73 D2
Luxembourg Lux. 54 C3
Luxembourg country Europe
  54 C3
Luxeuil-les-Bains France 59 D2
Luxolweni S. Africa 109 C3
Luxor Egypt 102 D2
Luyksgestel Neth. 54 B2
Luza Rus. Fed. 40 D2
Luzern Switz. see Lucerne
Luzhou China 83 A3
Luziânia Brazil 154 C1
Luzilândia Brazil 151 E3
Luzon i. Phil. 76 B2
Luzon Strait Phil. 76 B1
L'viv Ukr. 44 B2
L'vov Ukr. see L'viv
Lyakhavichy Belarus 42 C3
Lycksele Sweden 46 D3
Lydenburg S. Africa 109 D2
Lyel'chytsy Belarus 42 C3
Lyepyel' Belarus 42 C3
Lyme Bay U.K. 53 B4
Lynchburg U.S.A. 137 E3
Lynn Lake Can. 127 E1
Lynx Lake Can. 127 E1
Lyon France 59 C2
Lyozna Belarus 42 C3
Lys'va Rus. Fed. 40 E3
Lysychans'k Ukr. 45 E2
Lytham St Anne's U.K. 52 B3
Lyuban' Belarus 42 C3
Lyubertsy Rus. Fed. 43 E2
Lyubeshiv Ukr. 44 C1
Lyubim Rus. Fed. 43 F2
Lyubotyn Ukr. 45 E2
Lyubytino Rus. Fed. 43 D2
Lyudinovo Rus. Fed. 43 D3

M

Ma'ān Jordan 92 B2
Maardu Estonia 42 C2
Maas r. Neth. 54 B2
Maaseik Belgium 54 B2
Maasin Phil. 76 B2
Maastricht Neth. 54 B2
Mabalane Moz. 107 C2
Mabaruma Guyana 150 D2
Mabote Moz. 107 C2
Mabule Botswana 108 B2
Mabutsane Botswana 108 B1
Macaé Brazil 155 D2
Macalope Moz. 107 C1
Macapá Brazil 151 D2
Macará Ecuador 150 B3
Macarani Brazil 155 D1
Macassar Strait Indon. see
  Makassar, Selat
Macau China 81 D3
Macau aut. reg. China 83 B3
Maccaretane Moz. 109 D1
Macclesfield U.K. 52 B3
Macdonald, Lake salt flat Austr.
  114 B2
Macdonnell Ranges mts Austr. 114 C2
MacDowell Lake Can. 128 A1
Macedo de Cavaleiros Port. 60 B1
Macedon mt. Austr. 116 C3
Macedonia country Europe 64 B2
Maceió Brazil 151 F3
Macerata Italy 62 B2
Macfarlane, Lake salt flat Austr.
  116 B2
Macgillycuddy's Reeks mts
  Rep. of Ireland 51 B3
Mach Pak. 86 A2
Machado Brazil 155 C2
Machaila Moz. 107 C2
Machakos Kenya 105 D3
Machala Ecuador 150 B3
Machanga Moz. 107 C2
Machault France 54 B3
Macheng China 82 B2
Machias U.S.A. 137 G2
Machiques Venez. 150 B1
Macia Moz. 109 D2
Măcin Romania 44 D2
Macintyre r. Austr. 117 E1
Mackay Austr. 115 D2
Mackay, Lake salt flat Austr. 114 B2
MacKay Lake Can. 127 D1
Mackenzie Can. 126 C2
Mackenzie r. Can. 126 B1
Mackenzie Bay Can. 124 E1
Mackenzie King Island Can. 124 E1
Mackenzie Mountains Can. 126 B1
Macklin Can. 127 E2
Macksville Austr. 117 E2
Maclean Austr. 117 E1
MacLeod, Lake imp. l. Austr. 114 A2
Macomb U.S.A. 136 B2
Macomer Italy 62 A2
Mâcon France 59 C2
Macon GA U.S.A. 139 D2
Macon MO U.S.A. 135 E3
Macquarie r. Austr. 117 D2
Macquarie Island
  S. Pacific Ocean 110
Macquarie Marshes Austr. 117 D2
Macroom Rep. of Ireland 51 B3
Macumba watercourse Austr. 116 B1
Macuspana Mex. 143 C3
Macuzari, Presa resr Mex. 142 B2
Madadeni S. Africa 109 D2
Madagascar country Africa
  107 [inset] D2

Madama Niger 101 D2
Madan Bulg. 65 B2
Madeira P.N.G. 71 D3
Madeira r. Brazil 150 D3
Madeira terr. N. Atlantic Ocean 100 A1
Madeleine, Îles de la is Can. 129 D2
Madera Mex. 142 B2
Madera U.S.A. 133 B3
Madgaon India 85 B3
Madingou Congo 104 B3
Madison IN U.S.A. 136 C3
Madison SD U.S.A. 135 D2
Madison WI U.S.A. 136 C2
Madison WV U.S.A. 136 C3
Madison r. U.S.A. 132 D1
Madisonville U.S.A. 136 C3
Madiun Indon. 73 C2
Mado Gashi Kenya 105 D2
Madoi China 80 C2
Madona Latvia 42 C2
Madrakah Saudi Arabia 90 A2
Madras India see Chennai
Madras U.S.A. 132 B2
Madre, Laguna lag. Mex. 143 C2
Madre de Dios r. Peru 150 C4
Madre del Sur, Sierra mts Mex. 143 B3
Madre Occidental, Sierra mts Mex. 142 B2
Madre Oriental, Sierra mts Mex. 143 B2
Madrid Spain 60 C1
Madridejos Spain 60 C2
Madura i. Indon. 73 C2
Madura, Selat sea chan. Indon. 73 C2
Madurai India 85 B4
Maebashi Japan 79 C3
Mae Hong Son Thai. 74 A2
Mae Sai Thai. 74 A1
Mae Sariang Thai. 74 A2
Mae Suai Thai. 74 A2
Mafeteng Lesotho 109 C2
Mafia Island Tanz. 105 D3
Mafikeng S. Africa 109 C2
Mafinga Tanz. 105 D3
Mafra Brazil 154 C3
Magadan Rus. Fed. 95 M3
Magangue Col. 145 C4
Magdalena Mex. 142 A1
Magdalena r. Col. 148
Magdalena U.S.A. 140 C2
Magdalena, Bahía b. Mex. 142 A2
Magdeburg Ger. 55 E1
Magellan, Strait of Chile 153 A6
Magherafelt U.K. 51 C1
Magnitogorsk Rus. Fed. 41 E3
Magnolia U.S.A. 138 B2
Magpie, Lac l. Can. 129 D1
Magta' Lahjar Maur. 100 A3
Maguarinho, Cabo c. Brazil 151 E3
Magude Moz. 109 D2
Magwe Myanmar 74 A1
Mahābād Iran 93 C2
Mahajan India 86 B2
Mahajanga Madag. 107 [inset] D1
Mahakam r. Indon. 73 C2
Mahalapye Botswana 109 C1
Mahalevona Madag. 107 [inset] D1
Mahanadi r. India 87 C2
Mahanoro Madag. 107 [inset] D1
Maha Sarakham Thai. 75 B2
Mahavavy r. Madag. 107 [inset] D1
Mahbubnagar India 85 B3
Mahd adh Dhahab Saudi Arabia 90 B2
Mahdia Alg. 61 D2
Mahdia Guyana 150 D2
Mahesana India 86 B2
Mahi r. India 86 B2
Mahia Peninsula N.Z. 118 C2
Mahilyow Belarus 43 D3

Mahón Spain 61 D2
Mahony Lake Can. 126 C1
Mahuva India 86 B2
Mahya Dağı mt. Turkey 64 C2
Maidstone Can. 127 E2
Maidstone U.K. 53 D4
Maiduguri Nigeria 101 D3
Mailani India 87 C2
Main r. Ger. 55 D2
Mai-Ndombe, Lac l. Dem. Rep. Congo 104 B3
Main-Donau-Kanal canal Ger. 55 E3
Maine state U.S.A. 137 G1
Maingkwan Myanmar 74 A1
Mainland i. Scotland U.K. 50 C1
Mainland i. Scotland U.K. 50 [inset]
Maintirano Madag. 107 [inset] D1
Mainz Ger. 55 D2
Maiquetía Venez. 145 D3
Maitland N.S.W. Austr. 117 E2
Maitland S.A. Austr. 116 B2
Maíz, Islas del is Nic. 144 B3
Maizuru Japan 79 C3
Maja Jezërcë mt. Albania 64 A2
Majene Indon. 73 C2
Majorca i. Spain 61 D2
Majuro atoll Marshall Is 110
Majwemasweu S. Africa 109 C2
Makabana Congo 104 B3
Makale Indon. 73 C2
Makanchi Kazakh. 89 F2
Makarska Croatia 63 C2
Makassar Indon. 73 C2
Makassar, Selat str. Indon. 73 C2
Makat Kazakh. 88 C2
Makatini Flats lowland S. Africa 109 D2
Makeni Sierra Leone 100 A4
Makgadikgadi salt pan Botswana 106 B2
Makhachkala Rus. Fed. 41 D4
Makhado S. Africa 109 C1
Makhambet Kazakh. 88 C2
Makhazine, Barrage El dam Morocco 60 B3
Makindu Kenya 105 D3
Makinsk Kazakh. 89 E1
Makiyivka Ukr. 45 E2
Makkah Saudi Arabia see Mecca
Makkovik Can. 129 E1
Makó Hungary 57 E2
Makokou Gabon 104 B2
Makongolosi Tanz. 105 D3
Makopong Botswana 108 B2
Makran reg. Iran/Pak. 89 F3
Makran Coast Range mts Pak. 86 A2
Maksatikha Rus. Fed. 43 E2
Mākū Iran 93 C2
Makum India 74 A1
Makurazaki Japan 79 B4
Makurdi Nigeria 101 C4
Malā Sweden 46 H2
Mala, Punta pt Panama 144 B4
Malabo Equat. Guinea 104 A2
Malacca, Strait of Indon./Malaysia 72 A1
Malad City U.S.A. 132 D2
Maladzyechna Belarus 42 C3
Málaga Spain 60 C2
Malaita i. Solomon Is 110
Malakal Sudan 103 B4
Malakula i. Vanuatu 110
Malamala Indon. 73 C2
Malang Indon. 73 C2
Malanje Angola 104 B3
Mälaren l. Sweden 47 D4
Malargüe Arg. 153 B4
Malatya Turkey 92 B2
Malawi country Africa 107 C1
Malawi, Lake Africa see Nyasa, Lake

Malaya Vishera Rus. Fed. 43 D2
Malaybalay Phil. 76 B3
Malāyer Iran 93 C2
Malaysia country Asia 72 B1
Malazgirt Turkey 93 C2
Malbork Pol. 57 D2
Malchin Ger. 55 F1
Maldegem Belgium 54 A2
Malden Island Kiribati 111
Maldives country Indian Ocean 85 B4
Male Maldives 85 B4
Maleas, Akra c. Greece 65 B3
Male Atoll Maldives 85 B4
Malé Karpaty hills Slovakia 57 D3
Malheur Lake U.S.A. 132 C2
Mali country Africa 100 B3
Mali Guinea 100 A3
Malili Indon. 73 C2
Malin Head Rep. of Ireland 51 C1
Malin More Rep. of Ireland 51 B1
Malkara Turkey 65 C2
Mal'kavichy Belarus 42 C3
Malko Tŭrnovo Bulg. 64 C2
Mallacoota Austr. 117 D3
Mallacoota Inlet b. Austr. 117 D3
Mallaig U.K. 50 B2
Mallery Lake Can. 127 F1
Mallorca i. Spain see Majorca
Mallow Rep. of Ireland 51 B2
Malmberget Sweden 46 E2
Malmédy Belgium 54 C2
Malmesbury S. Africa 108 A3
Malmö Sweden 47 C4
Malong China 83 A3
Malonga Dem. Rep. Congo 104 C4
Måløy Norway 47 B3
Maloyaroslavets Rus. Fed. 43 E2
Maloye Borisovo Rus. Fed. 43 E2
Malta country Europe 101 D1
Malta Latvia 42 C2
Malta i. Malta 36
Malta U.S.A. 132 E1
Maltahöhe Namibia 108 A1
Malton U.K. 52 C2
Maluku is Indon. see Moluccas
Maluku, Laut sea Indon. 71 C3
Malung Sweden 47 C3
Maluti Mountains Lesotho 109 C2
Malvan India 85 B3
Malvern U.K. 53 B3
Malyn Ukr. 44 C1
Malyy Anyuy r. Rus. Fed. 95 M2
Malyy Lyakhovskiy, Ostrov i. Rus. Fed. 95 L2
Mamafubedu S. Africa 109 C2
Mambasa Dem. Rep. Congo 105 C2
Mambéré r. C.A.R. 104 B2
Mamelodi S. Africa 109 C2
Mamoré r. Bol./Brazil 152 B2
Mamou Guinea 100 A3
Mamuju Indon. 73 C2
Man Côte d'Ivoire 100 B4
Man, Isle of i. Irish Sea 52 A2
Manacapuru Brazil 150 C3
Manacor Spain 61 D2
Manado Indon. 71 C2
Managua Nic. 144 B3
Manakara Madag. 107 [inset] D2
Manākhah Yemen 90 B3
Manama Bahrain 91 C2
Manam Island P.N.G. 71 D3
Mananara r. Madag. 107 [inset] D1
Mananara Avaratra Madag. 107 [inset] D1
Mananjary Madag. 107 [inset] D2
Manantali, Lac de l. Mali 100 A3
Manas Hu l. China 89 F2
Manatuto East Timor 71 C3
Man-aung Kyun i. Myanmar 74 A2

anaus Brazil **150** C3
anavgat Turkey **92** B2
anchester U.K. **52** B3
anchester U.S.A. **137** F2
andabe Madag. **107** [inset] D2
andal Norway **47** B4
andala, Puncak *mt.* Indon. **71** D3
andalay Myanmar **74** A1
andalgovi Mongolia **80** D1
andan U.S.A. **134** C1
andara Mountains Cameroon/Nigeria
104 B1
andas Italy **62** A3
anderscheid Ger. **54** C2
andi India **86** B1
andiana Guinea **100** B3
andi Burewala Pak. **86** B1
andla India **87** C2
andritsaria Madag. **107** [inset] D1
andsaur India **86** B2
andurah Austr. **114** A3
andya India **85** B3
anerbio Italy **62** B1
anevychi Ukr. **44** C1
anfredonia Italy **63** C2
anga Burkina **100** B3
angochi Malawi **107** C1
angalia Romania **44** C3
angalore India **85** B3
angaung S. Africa **109** C2
anggar Indon. **72** B2
angnai China **80** C2
angole *i.* Indon. **71** C3
angueirinha Brazil **154** B3
angui China **81** E1
angystau Kazakh. **88** C2
anhattan U.S.A. **135** D3
anhica Moz. **107** C2
anhuaçu Brazil **155** D2
ania *r.* Madag. **107** [inset] D1
aniago Italy **62** B1
anicoré Brazil **150** C3
anicouagan *r.* Can. **129** D2
anicouagan, Petit Lac *l.* Can.
129 D1
anicouagan, Réservoir *resr* Can.
29 D1
anifah Saudi Arabia **91** B2
aning Can. **126** D2
annum Austr. **116** B3
anville Can. **127** D2
anokwari Indon. **71** C3
anono Dem. Rep. Congo **105** C3
anoron Myanmar **75** A2
anosque France **59** D3
anouane, Lac *l.* Can. **129** C1
ansa Zambia **107** B1
ansel Island Can. **125** G2

Mansel'kya *ridge* Fin./Rus. Fed. **46** F2
Mansfield Austr. **117** D3
Mansfield U.K. **52** B3
Mansfield *LA* U.S.A. **138** B2
Mansfield *OH* U.S.A. **136** D2
Mansfield *PA* U.S.A. **137** E2
Manta Ecuador **150** A3
Manteo U.S.A. **139** E1
Mantes-la-Jolie France **58** C2
Mantiqueira, Serra da *mts* Brazil
155 C2
Mantova Italy *see* Mantua
Mantua Italy **62** B1
Manuelzinho Brazil **151** D3
Manui *i.* Indon. **73** D2
Manukau N.Z. **118** B2
Manus Island P.N.G. **71** D3
Many U.S.A. **138** B2
Manych-Gudilo, Ozero *l.* Rus. Fed.
41 D4
Manyoni Tanz. **105** D3
Manzanares Spain **60** C2
Manzanillo Mex. **142** B3
Manzhouli China **81** D1
Manzini Swaziland **109** D2
Mao Chad **101** D3
Maoke, Pegunungan *mts* Indon. **71** D3
Maokui Shan *mt.* China **77** A1
Maoming China **83** B3
Mapai Moz. **107** C2
Mapam Yumco *l.* China **87** C1
Mapane Indon. **73** D2
Mapastepec Mex. **143** C3
Mapimí Mex. **142** B2
Mapimí, Bolsón de *des.* Mex. **142** B2
Mapin *i.* Phil. **76** A3
Mapinhane Moz. **107** C2
Maple Creek Can. **127** E3
Maputo Moz. **107** C2
Maputo *r.* Moz./S. Africa **109** D2
Maquan He *r.* China **87** C2
Maquela do Zombo Angola **104** B3
Maquinchao Arg. **153** B5
Maquoketa U.S.A. **135** E2
Mar, Serra do *mts* Brazil **147**
Maraã Brazil **150** C3
Maracá, Ilha de *i.* Brazil **151** D2
Maracaibo Venez. **150** B1
Maracaibo, Lake Venez. **150** B2
Maracaju Brazil **154** A2
Maracaju, Serra de *hills* Brazil **154** A2
Maracay Venez. **150** C1
Marādah Libya **101** D2
Maradi Niger **101** C3
Marāgheh Iran **93** C2
Marajó, Baía de *est.* Brazil **151** E3
Marajó, Ilha de *i.* Brazil **151** D3
Marākī Iran **91** C2
Maralal Kenya **105** D2
Maralinga Austr. **114** C3
Marand Iran **93** C2
Maranoa *r.* Austr. **117** D1
Marañón *r.* Peru **150** B3
Marathon Can. **128** C2
Marathon U.S.A. **139** D4
Marbella Spain **60** C2
Marble Bar Austr. **114** A2
Marble Hall S. Africa **109** C1
Marburg S. Africa **109** C3
Marburg an der Lahn Ger. **55** D2
March U.K. **53** D3
Marche-en-Famenne Belgium **54** B2
Marchena Spain **60** B2
Mar Chiquita, Lago *l.* Arg. **152** B4
Marchtrenk Austria **59** E2
Marcoing France **54** A2
Marcy, Mount U.S.A. **137** F2
Mardan Pak. **86** B1

Mar del Plata Arg. **153** C4
Mardin Turkey **93** C2
Maree, Loch *l.* U.K. **50** B2
Marettimo, Isola *i.* Italy **62** B3
Marevo Rus. Fed. **43** D2
Marfa U.S.A. **140** D2
Margaret River Austr. **114** A3
Margarita, Isla de *i.* Venez. **145** D3
Margate S. Africa **109** D3
Margate U.K. **53** D4
Margherita Peak Dem. Rep. Congo/
Uganda **105** C2
Mārgow, Dasht-e *des.* Afgh. **86** A1
Marhanets' Ukr. **45** D2
Mari Myanmar **74** A1
María Elena Chile **152** B3
Mariana Trench *sea feature*
N. Pacific Ocean **158** C4
Marianna *AR* U.S.A. **138** B2
Marianna *FL* U.S.A. **139** C2
Mariánské Lázně Czech Rep. **56** C3
Marías, Islas *is* Mex. **142** B2
Mariato, Punta *pt* Panama **150** A2
Ma'rib Yemen **90** B3
Maribor Slovenia **62** C1
Maridi *watercourse* Sudan **103** A4
Marie Byrd Land *reg.* Antarctica
119 I2
Marie-Galante *i.* Guadeloupe **145** D3
Mariehamn Fin. **47** D3
Mariental Namibia **108** A1
Mariestad Sweden **47** C4
Marietta *GA* U.S.A. **139** C2
Marietta *OH* U.S.A. **136** D3
Marignane France **59** D3
Marii, Mys *pt* Rus. Fed. **95** L3
Marijampolė Lith. **42** B3
Marília Brazil **154** C2
Marín Spain **60** B1
Marina di Gioiosa Ionica Italy **63** C3
Mar"ina Horka Belarus **42** C3
Marinette U.S.A. **136** C1
Maringá Brazil **154** B2
Marinha Grande Port. **60** B2
Marion *IN* U.S.A. **136** C2
Marion *OH* U.S.A. **136** D2
Marion *SC* U.S.A. **139** E2
Marion *VA* U.S.A. **136** D3
Marion, Lake U.S.A. **139** D2
Marion Bay Austr. **116** B3
Mariscal Estigarribia Para. **152** B3
Maritsa *r.* Bulg. **64** C2
Mariupol' Ukr. **45** E2
Marka Somalia **103** C4
Marken S. Africa **109** C1
Markermeer *l.* Neth. **54** B1
Markha *r.* Rus. Fed. **95** J2
Markivka Ukr. **45** E2
Marksville U.S.A. **138** B2
Marktheidenfeld Ger. **55** D3
Marktredwitz Ger. **55** F2
Marl Ger. **54** C2
Marle France **54** A3
Marlin U.S.A. **141** E2
Marmande France **58** C3
Marmara, Sea of *g.* Turkey **65** C2
Marmara Denizi *g.* Turkey *see*
Marmara, Sea of
Marmaris Turkey **65** C3
Marne *r.* France **54** A3
Marne-la-Vallée France **58** C2
Maroantsetra Madag. **107** [inset] D1
Maroldsweisach Ger. **55** E2
Maromokotro *mt.* Madag.
107 [inset] D1
Marondera Zimbabwe **107** C1
Maroni *r.* Fr. Guiana **151** D2
Marotiri *i.* Fr. Polynesia **111**
Maroua Cameroon **104** D3
Marovoay Madag. **107** [inset] D1

Marquesas Islands Fr. Polynesia **111**
Marquette U.S.A. **136** C1
Marquion France **54** A2
Marra, Jebel mt. Sudan **103** A3
Marracuene Moz. **109** D2
Marrakech Morocco **100** B1
Marra Plateau Sudan **103** A3
Marree Austr. **116** B1
Marresale Rus. Fed. **40** F2
Marromeu Moz. **107** C1
Marrupa Moz. **107** C1
Marsá al'Alam Egypt **102** B2
Marsa al Burayqah Libya **101** D1
Marsabit Kenya **105** D2
Marsala Italy **62** B3
Marsá Maṭrūḥ Egypt **102** A1
Marsberg Ger. **55** D2
Marsciano Italy **62** B2
Marsden Austr. **117** D2
Marseille France **59** D3
Marshall MN U.S.A. **135** D2
Marshall MO U.S.A. **135** E3
Marshall TX U.S.A. **141** F2
Marshall Islands country
  N. Pacific Ocean **112**
Marshalltown U.S.A. **135** E2
Marshfield U.S.A. **136** B2
Marsh Harbour Bahamas **139** E3
Marsh Island U.S.A. **138** B3
Märsta Sweden **42** A2
Martapura Kalimantan Selatan Indon.
  73 C2
Martapura Sumatera Selatan Indon.
  72 B2
Martha's Vineyard i. U.S.A. **137** F2
Martigny Switz. **59** D2
Martin Slovakia **57** D3
Martin U.S.A. **134** C2
Martinez Mex. **143** C2
Martinique terr. West Indies **145** D3
Martinsburg U.S.A. **137** E3
Martinsville U.S.A. **137** E3
Marton N.Z. **118** C3
Martorell Spain **61** D1
Martos Spain **60** C2
Martuk Kazakh. **88** C1
Marvejols France **59** C3
Mary Turkm. **88** D3
Maryborough Austr. **115** E2
Marydale S. Africa **108** B2
Maryland state U.S.A. **137** E3
Marysville U.S.A. **135** D3
Maryville MO U.S.A. **135** E2
Maryville TN U.S.A. **139** D1
Masai Steppe plain Tanz. **105** D3
Masaka Uganda **105** D3
Masamba Indon. **73** C2
Masan S. Korea **77** B2
Masasi Tanz. **105** D4
Masbate i. Phil. **76** B2
Masbate i. Phil. **76** B2
Mascara Alg. **61** D2
Maseru Lesotho **109** C2
Mashhad Iran **88** C3
Masilah, Wādī al watercourse Yemen
  91 C3
Masilo S. Africa **109** C2
Masindi Uganda **105** D2
Maşīrah, Jazīrat i. Oman **91** C2
Maşīrah, Khalīj b. Oman **91** C3
Masjed Soleymān Iran **93** C2
Mask, Lough i. Rep. of Ireland **51** B2
Masoala, Tanjona c. Madag.
  107 [inset] E1
Mason City U.S.A. **135** E2
Masqaţ Oman see Muscat
Massa Italy **62** B2
Massachusetts state U.S.A. **137** F2
Massachusetts Bay U.S.A. **137** F2

Massangena Moz. **107** C2
Massango Angola **104** B3
Massawa Eritrea **102** B3
Massena U.S.A. **137** F2
Masset Can. **126** B2
Massif Central mts France **58** C2
Massif de l'Aïr mts Niger **101** C3
Massillon U.S.A. **136** D2
Massina Mali **100** B3
Massinga Moz. **107** C2
Massingir Moz. **109** D1
Mastābah Saudi Arabia **90** A2
Masterton N.Z. **118** C3
Mastung Pak. **86** A2
Mastūrah Saudi Arabia **90** A2
Masty Belarus **42** B3
Masuda Japan **79** B4
Masvingo Zimbabwe **107** C2
Matadi Dem. Rep. Congo **104** B3
Matagalpa Nic. **144** B3
Matagami Can. **128** C2
Matagami, Lac i. Can. **128** C2
Matagorda Island U.S.A. **141** E3
Matala Angola **106** A1
Matam Senegal **100** A3
Matamoros Coahuila Mex. **142** B2
Matamoros Tamaulipas Mex. **143** C2
Matandu r. Tanz. **105** D3
Matane Can. **128** C2
Matanzas Cuba **144** B2
Matara Sri Lanka **85** C4
Mataram Indon. **73** C2
Mataró Spain **61** D1
Matatiele S. Africa **109** C3
Mataura N.Z. **118** A4
Matā'utu Wallis and Futuna Is **113**
Matawai N.Z. **118** C2
Mategua Bol. **152** B2
Matehuala Mex. **143** B2
Matera Italy **63** C2
Mathis U.S.A. **141** E3
Mathura India **87** B2
Mati Phil. **76** B3
Matías Romero Mex. **144** A3
Matlock U.K. **52** C3
Mato Grosso Brazil **150** D4
Mato Grosso, Planalto do plat. Brazil
  154 B1
Matola Moz. **109** D2
Matsue Japan **79** B3
Matsumae Japan **78** D2
Matsusaka Japan **79** C4
Matsu Tao i. Taiwan **80** C3
Matsuyama Japan **79** B4
Mattagami r. Can. **128** B1
Matterhorn mt. Italy/Switz. **62** A1
Matterhorn mt. U.S.A. **132** C2
Mattoon U.S.A. **136** C3
Maturín Venez. **150** C2
Matwabeng S. Africa **109** C2
Maubeuge France **54** A2
Maubourguet France **58** C3
Maui i. U.S.A. **120**
Maumee r. U.S.A. **136** D2
Maumere Indon. **73** C2
Maun Botswana **106** B1
Maunatlala Botswana **109** C1
Maungdaw Myanmar **74** A1
Maurice, Lake salt flat Austr. **114** C2
Mauritania country Africa **100** A3
Mauritius country Indian Ocean **99**
Māwān, Khashm h. Saudi Arabia
  90 B2
Mawanga Dem. Rep. Congo **104** B3
Mawei China **83** B3
Mawkmai Myanmar **74** A1
Mawlaik Myanmar **74** A1
Mawlamyaing Myanmar **74** A2
Mawqaq Saudi Arabia **90** B2

Mawza Yemen **90** B3
Maxia, Punta mt. Italy **62** A3
Maya r. Rus. Fed. **95** K2
Mayaguana i. Bahamas **145** C2
Mayamey Iran **93** D2
Maybole U.K. **50** B3
Mayenne France **58** B2
Mayenne r. France **58** B2
Mayerthorpe Can. **126** D2
Mayfield U.S.A. **136** C3
Maykop Rus. Fed. **45** F3
Mayo Can. **126** B1
Mayoko Congo **104** B3
Mayotte terr. Africa **107** D1
Mayskiy Rus. Fed. **95** K3
Maysville U.S.A. **136** D3
Mayumba Gabon **104** B3
Mayville U.S.A. **135** D1
Mazagão Brazil **151** D3
Mazamet France **58** C3
Mazar China **81** A1
Mazara del Vallo Italy **62** B3
Mazār-e Sharīf Afgh. **86** A1
Mazatán Mex. **142** A2
Mazatenango Guat. **144** A3
Mazatlán Mex. **142** B2
Mažeikiai Lith. **42** B2
Mazirbe Latvia **42** B2
Mazunga Zimbabwe **107** B2
Mazyr Belarus **42** C3
Mbabane Swaziland **109** D2
Mbaïki C.A.R. **104** B2
Mbala Zambia **105** D3
Mbale Uganda **105** D2
Mbalmayo Cameroon **104** B2
Mbandaka Dem. Rep. Congo **104** B3
Mbanga Cameroon **104** A2
M'banza Congo Angola **104** B3
Mbeya Tanz. **105** D3
Mbinga Tanz. **105** D4
Mbomo Congo **104** B2
Mbouda Cameroon **104** B2
Mbour Senegal **100** A3
Mbout Maur. **100** A3
Mbuji-Mayi Dem. Rep. Congo **104** C3
Mbuyuni Tanz. **105** D3
McAlester U.S.A. **141** E2
McAllen U.S.A. **141** E3
McBride Can. **126** C2
McCall U.S.A. **132** C2
McClintock Channel Can. **124** E2
McClure Strait Can. **124** E2
McComb U.S.A. **138** B2
McConaughy, Lake U.S.A. **134** C2
McCook U.S.A. **134** C2
McDermitt U.S.A. **132** C2
McDonald Peak U.S.A. **132** D1
McGrath U.S.A. **124** B2
McGuire, Mount U.S.A. **132** D1
M'Chounèche Alg. **61** E2
McKinley, Mount U.S.A. **124** B2
McLennan Can. **126** D2
McLeod Lake Can. **126** C2
McMinnville OR U.S.A. **132** B1
McMinnville TN U.S.A. **139** C1
McPherson U.S.A. **135** D3
McTavish Arm b. Can. **126** D1
Mdantsane S. Africa **109** C3
Mead, Lake resr U.S.A. **133** D3
Meadow Lake Can. **127** E2
Meadville U.S.A. **137** D2
Meaken-dake vol. Japan **78** D2
Mealhada Port. **60** B1
Mealy Mountains Can. **129** E1
Meander River Can. **126** D2
Meaux France **54** A3
Mecca Saudi Arabia **90** A2
Mechelen Belgium **54** B2
Mechelen Neth. **54** B2
Mechernich Ger. **54** C2

eckenheim Ger. **54** C2
ecklenburger Bucht *b.* Ger. **47** C5
eda Port. **60** B1
edan Indon. **73** A2
edanosa, Punta *pt* Arg. **153** B5
edawachchiya Sri Lanka **85** C4
edéa Alg. **61** D2
edellín Col. **150** B2
edenine Tunisia **101** D1
edford U.S.A. **132** B2
edgidia Romania **44** C3
edias Romania **44** B2
edicine Bow Mountains U.S.A.
134 B2
edicine Bow Peak U.S.A. **134** B2
edicine Hat Can. **127** D2
edicine Lodge U.S.A. **135** D3
edina Brazil **155** D1
edina Saudi Arabia **90** A2
edina del Campo Spain **60** C1
edina de Rioseco Spain **60** B1
editerranean Sea **61** C2
edjedel Alg. **61** D2
edley Can. **127** D2
ednogorsk Rus. Fed. **41** E3
edvezh'i, Ostrova *is* Rus. Fed. **95** M2
edvezh'yegorsk Rus. Fed. **40** C2
eekatharra Austr. **114** A2
eeker U.S.A. **134** B2
eerut India **87** B2
eetkerke Belgium **54** A2
egalopoli Greece **65** B3
eghasani *mt.* India **87** C2
egisti *i.* Greece **65** C3
ehamn Norway **46** F1
eharry, Mount Austr. **114** A2
eia Ponte *r.* Brazil **154** C1
eiganga Cameroon **104** B3
eihekou China **77** B1
eiktila Myanmar **74** A1
einingen Ger. **55** E2
eißen Ger. **55** F2
eizhou China **83** B3
ejicana *mt.* Arg. **152** B3
ejillones Chile **152** A3
ek'elê Eth. **103** B3
eknès Morocco **100** B1
ekong *r.* Asia **75** B2
ekong *r.* China **74** B1
ekong, Mouths of the Vietnam
75 B3
elaka Malaysia **72** B1
elanesia *is* Pacific Ocean **158** D5
elbourne Austr. **117** C3
elbourne U.S.A. **139** D3
elenki Rus. Fed. **43** F2
elfi Chad **101** D3
elfort Can. **127** E2
elhus Norway **46** C3
elide Spain **60** B1
elilla N. Africa **60** C2
elle Ger. **55** D1
ellerud Sweden **47** C4
ellrichstadt Ger. **55** E2
ellum *i.* Ger. **54** D1
elo Uru. **152** C4
elrhir, Chott *salt l.* Alg. **101** C1
elton Mowbray U.K. **53** C3
elun France **58** C2
elville Can. **124** F3
elville, Cape Austr. **115** D1
elville, Lake Can. **129** E1

Melville Island Austr. **114** C1
Melville Island Can. **124** E1
Melville Peninsula Can. **125** G2
Memboro Indon. **73** C2
Memmingen Ger. **56** C3
Mempawah Indon. **72** B1
Memphis *tourist site* Egypt **92** B3
Memphis *TN* U.S.A. **138** B1
Memphis *TX* U.S.A. **141** C2
Mena Ukr. **45** D1
Mena U.S.A. **138** B2
Ménaka Mali **100** C3
Mènam Khong *r.* Asia *see* Mekong
Mende France **59** C3
Mendefera Eritrea **102** B3
Méndez Mex. **143** C2
Mendi Eth. **105** D2
Mendi P.N.G. **71** D3
Mendip Hills U.K. **53** C3
Mendoza Arg. **153** B4
Menemen Turkey **65** C3
Menggala Indon. **72** B2
Mengzi China **83** A3
Menihek Can. **129** D1
Meningie Austr. **116** C3
Menindee Austr. **116** C2
Menindee, Lake Austr. **116** C2
Mennecy France **58** C2
Menominee U.S.A. **136** C1
Menongue Angola **106** A1
Menorca *i.* Spain *see* Minorca
Mentawai, Kepulauan *is* Indon.
72 A2
Mentok Indon. **72** B2
Menzies Austr. **114** B2
Meppel Neth. **54** C1
Meppen Ger. **54** C1
Mepuze Moz. **109** D1
Meqheleng S. Africa **109** C2
Merano Italy **62** B1
Merauke Indon. **71** D3
Merbein Austr. **116** C2
Merced U.S.A. **133** B3
Mercedes Arg. **152** C3
Mercy, Cape Can. **125** H2
Meredith, Lake U.S.A. **141** C1
Merefa Ukr. **45** E2
Merga Oasis Sudan **102** A3
Mergui Archipelago *is* Myanmar **75** A2
Meriç *r.* Greece/Turkey **65** C2
Mérida Mex. **143** D2
Mérida Spain **60** B2
Mérida Venez. **150** B2
Meridian U.S.A. **138** C2
Mérignac France **58** B3
Merimbula Austr. **117** D3
Merouana Alg. **61** B2
Merowe Sudan **102** B3
Merredin Austr. **114** A3
Merrick *h.* U.K. **50** B3
Merrill U.S.A. **136** C1
Merrillville U.S.A. **136** C2
Merritt Can. **126** C2
Merrygoen Austr. **117** D2
Mersa Fatma Eritrea **102** C3
Mersch Lux. **54** C1
Merseburg (Saale) Ger. **55** E2
Mersey *r.* U.K. **52** B3
Mersin Turkey **92** B2
Mersing Malaysia **72** B1
Mers-les-Bains France **53** D4
Merta India **86** B2
Merthyr Tydfil U.K. **53** B4
Mértola Port. **60** B2
Mertvyg Kultuk, Sor *dry lake* Kazakh.
88 C2
Meru *vol.* Tanz. **105** D3
Merzig Ger. **54** C3
Mesa U.S.A. **140** B2
Mesagne Italy **63** C2

Meschede Ger. **55** D2
Meshchovsk Rus. Fed. **43** E3
Meshkovskaya Rus. Fed. **45** F2
Mesimeri Greece **65** B2
Mesolongi Greece **65** B3
Messalo *r.* Moz. **107** D1
Messina Italy **62** C3
Messina, Stretta di *str.* Italy **63** C3
Messiniakos Kolpos *b.* Greece **65** B3
Mesta *r.* Bulg. **64** B2
Meta *r.* Col./Venez. **150** C2
Metán Arg. **152** B3
Methoni Greece **65** B3
Metkovic Croatia **63** C2
Metro Indon. **72** B2
Metu Eth. **103** B4
Metz France **59** D2
Meuse *r.* Belgium/France **54** B2
Mexia U.S.A. **141** E2
Mexicali Mex. **142** A1
Mexico *country* Central America
142 B2
Mexico U.S.A. **135** E3
Mexico, Gulf of Mex./U.S.A. **144** A2
Mexico City U.S.A. **143** C3
Meyerburg Ger. **55** F1
Meymaneh Afgh. **86** A1
Mezen' Rus. Fed. **40** D2
Mezen' *r.* Rus. Fed. **40** D2
Mezhdusharskiy, Ostrov *i.* Rus. Fed.
40 E1
Mezőtúr Hungary **57** E3
Mezquitic Mex. **142** B2
Mežvidi Latvia **42** C2
Mfuwe Zambia **107** C1
Mhlume Swaziland **109** D2
Mhow India **86** B2
Miahuatlán Mex. **143** C3
Miajadas Spain **60** B2
Miami *FL* U.S.A. **139** D3
Miami *OK* U.S.A. **141** F1
Miami Beach U.S.A. **139** D3
Miandowāb Iran **93** C2
Miandrivazo Madag. **107** [inset] D1
Miáneh Iran **93** C2
Mianwali Pak. **86** B1
Mianyang China **82** A2
Miarinarivo Madag. **107** [inset] D1
Miass Rus. Fed. **41** F3
Mica Creek Can. **126** C2
Michalovce Slovakia **57** E3
Michigan *state* U.S.A. **136** C1
Michigan, Lake U.S.A. **136** C2
Michigan City U.S.A. **136** C2
Michipicoten Island Can. **128** B2
Michipicoten River Can. **128** B2
Michurinsk Rus. Fed. **43** F3
Micronesia *is* Pacific Ocean **158** D4
Micronesia, Federated States of
country N. Pacific Ocean **71** D2
Middelburg Neth. **54** A2
Middelburg *E. Cape* S. Africa **109** C3
Middelburg *Mpumalanga* S. Africa
109 C2
Middelharnis Neth. **54** B2
Middle Alkali Lake U.S.A. **132** B2
Middle Andaman *i.* India **75** A2
Middle Loup *r.* U.S.A. **134** D2
Middlesboro U.S.A. **136** D3
Middlesbrough U.K. **52** C2
Middletown *NY* U.S.A. **137** F2
Middletown *OH* U.S.A. **136** D3
Midī Yemen **90** B3
Midland Can. **128** C2
Midland *MI* U.S.A. **136** D2
Midland *TX* U.S.A. **141** C2
Midleton Rep. of Ireland **51** B3
Miðvágur Faroe Is **48** A1
Midzhur *mt.* Bulg./Serb. and Mont.
64 B2

Mielec Pol. **57** E2
Miercurea-Ciuc Romania **44** C2
Mieres Spain **60** B1
Mieste Ger. **55** E2
Migriggyangzham Co *l.* China **87** D1
Miguel Alemán, Presa *resr* Mex. **143** C3
Miguel Auza Mex. **142** B2
Miguel Hidalgo, Presa *resr* Mex. **142** B2
Migyaunglaung Myanmar **75** A2
Mikhaylov Rus. Fed. **43** E3
Mikhaylovka Rus. Fed. **78** B2
Mikhaylovskiy Rus. Fed. **89** E1
Mikkeli Fin. **47** F3
Mikun' Rus. Fed. **40** E2
Mikuni-sanmyaku *mts* Japan **79** C3
Mila Alg. **61** E2
Miladhunmadulu Atoll Maldives **85** B4
Milan Italy **62** A1
Milange Moz. **107** C1
Milano Italy *see* Milan
Milas Turkey **65** C3
Milbank U.S.A. **135** D1
Mildenhall U.K. **53** D3
Mildura Austr. **116** C2
Mile China **83** A3
Miles City U.S.A. **134** B1
Milford *DE* U.S.A. **137** E3
Milford *UT* U.S.A. **133** D3
Milford Haven U.K. **53** A4
Milford Sound N.Z. **118** A4
Miliana Alg. **61** D2
Milk, Wadi el *watercourse* Sudan **102** B3
Mil'kovo Rus. Fed. **95** M3
Milk River Can. **127** D3
Millau France **58** C3
Milledgeville U.S.A. **139** D2
Mille Lacs *lakes* U.S.A. **135** E1
Mille Lacs, Lac des *l.* Can. **128** A2
Millennium Island *atoll* Kiribati *see*
  Caroline Island
Miller U.S.A. **135** D2
Millerovo Rus. Fed. **45** F2
Millers Creek Austr. **116** B2
Millicent Austr. **116** C3
Millinocket U.S.A. **137** G1
Milmerran Austr. **117** E1
Millom U.K. **52** B2
Mills Lake Can. **126** D2
Milos *i.* Greece **65** B3
Miloslavskoye Rus. Fed. **43** E5
Milove Ukr. **45** F2
Milparinka Austr. **116** C1
Milton N.Z. **118** A4
Milton Keynes U.K. **53** C3
Milwaukee U.S.A. **136** C2
Milwaukee Deep *sea feature*
  Caribbean Sea **160** B4
Mimizan France **58** B3
Mimongo Gabon **104** B3
Mīnāb Iran **91** C2
Minahasa, Semenanjung *pen.* Indon.
  73 D1
Mina Jebel Ali U.A.E. **91** C2
Minas Indon. **72** B1
Minas Uru. **153** C4
Minas Novas Brazil **155** D1
Minatitlán Mex. **143** C3
Minbu Myanmar **74** A1
Mindanao *i.* Phil. **76** B3
Minden Ger. **55** D1
Minden *LA* U.S.A. **138** B2
Minden *NE* U.S.A. **135** D2
Mindoro *i.* Phil. **76** B2
Mindoro Strait Phil. **76** A2
Minehead U.K. **53** B4
Mineiros Brazil **154** B1
Mineral Wells U.S.A. **141** E2

Minfeng China **87** C1
Minga Dem. Rep. Congo **105** C4
Mingäçevir Azer. **93** C1
Mingan Can. **129** D1
Mingary Austr. **116** C2
Mingguang China **82** B2
Mingin Myanmar **74** A1
Minglanilla Spain **61** C2
Mingoyo Tanz. **105** D2
Mingshui China **81** E1
Mingxi China **83** B3
Minhe China **82** A2
Minicoy *atoll* India **85** B4
Minilya Austr. **114** A2
Minipi Lake Can. **129** D1
Minius *r.* Spain *see* Miño
Minna Nigeria **101** C4
Minneapolis U.S.A. **135** E2
Minnedosa Can. **127** F2
Minnesota *r.* U.S.A. **135** E2
Minnesota *state* U.S.A. **135** E1
Miño *r.* Port./Spain **60** B1
Minorca *i.* Spain **61** D1
Minot U.S.A. **134** C1
Minsk Belarus **42** C1
Mińsk Mazowiecki Pol. **57** E2
Minto Can. **129** D2
Minto, Lac *l.* Can. **128** C1
Minutang India **74** A1
Minxian China **82** A2
Mirabela Brazil **155** D1
Miralta Brazil **155** D1
Miramichi Can. **129** D2
Mirampelou, Kolpos *b.* Greece **65** C3
Miranda Brazil **154** A2
Miranda *r.* Brazil **154** A1
Miranda de Ebro Spain **60** C1
Mirandela Port. **60** B1
Mirandópolis Brazil **154** B2
Mirbāṭ Oman **91** C3
Miri Malaysia **73** C1
Mirim, Lagoa *l.* Brazil **153** C4
Mīrjāveh Iran **91** D2
Mirnyy Rus. Fed. **95** J2
Mirow Ger. **55** F1
Mirpur Khas Pak. **86** A2
Mirtoö Pelagos *sea* Greece **65** B3
Miryang S. Korea **77** B2
Mirzapur India **87** C2
Mishan China **78** D1
Miskitos, Cayos *is* Nic. **144** B3
Miskolc Hungary **57** E3
Misoöl *i.* Indon. **71** C3
Miṣrātah Libya **101** D1
Missinaibi *r.* Can. **128** B1
Missinaibi Lake Can. **128** B2
Mission Can. **126** C3
Missisa Lake Can. **128** B1
Mississippi *r.* U.S.A. **138** C3
Mississippi *state* U.S.A. **138** C2
Mississippi Delta U.S.A. **138** C3
Missoula U.S.A. **132** D1
Missouri *r.* U.S.A. **135** E3
Missouri *state* U.S.A. **135** E3
Mistassini, Lac *l.* Can. **129** C2
Mistastin Lake Can. **129** D1
Mistelbach Austria **57** D3
Mistinibi, Lac *l.* Can. **129** D1
Mistissini Can. **128** C2
Mitchell Austr. **115** D2
Mitchell *r.* Austr. **115** D1
Mitchell U.S.A. **135** D2
Mitchelstown Rep. of Ireland **51** B2
Mithi Pak. **86** A2
Mito Japan **79** D3
Mitole Tanz. **105** D3
Mittagong Austr. **117** E2
Mittelhausen Ger. **55** E2
Mittellandkanal *canal* Ger. **55** D1

Mitterteich Ger. **55** F3
Mitú Col. **150** B2
Mitumba, Chaîne des *mts*
  Dem. Rep. Congo **105** C4
Mitumba, Monts *mts* Dem. Rep. Congo
  105 C3
Mitzic Gabon **104** B2
Miyah, Wādī al *watercourse*
  Saudi Arabia **90** B2
Miyake-jima *i.* Japan **79** C4
Miyako Japan **78** D3
Miyakonojō Japan **79** B4
Miyaly Kazakh. **88** C2
Miyazaki Japan **79** B4
Mizdah Libya **101** D1
Mizen Head Rep. of Ireland **51** B3
Mizhhir''ya Ukr. **44** B2
Mjölby Sweden **47** D4
Mjøsa *l.* Norway **47** C3
Mkomazi Tanz. **105** D3
Mladá Boleslav Czech Rep. **56** C2
Mladenovac Serb. and Mont. **64** B2
Mława Pol. **57** E2
Mlungisi S. Africa **109** C3
Mlyniv Ukr. **44** C1
Mmabatho S. Africa **109** C2
Mmathethe Botswana **109** C2
Mo Norway **48** E1
Moab U.S.A. **133** E3
Moamba Moz. **109** D2
Moba Dem. Rep. Congo **105** C3
Mobayi-Mbongo Dem. Rep. Congo
  104 C2
Moberly U.S.A. **135** E3
Mobile U.S.A. **138** C2
Mobile Bay U.S.A. **138** C2
Mobridge U.S.A. **134** C1
Moçambique Moz. **107** D1
Môc Châu Vietnam **74** B1
Mocha Yemen **90** B3
Mochudi Botswana **109** C1
Mocímboa da Praia Moz. **107** D1
Möckmühl Ger. **55** D3
Mocoa Col. **150** B2
Mococa Brazil **154** C2
Mocorito Mex. **142** B2
Moctezuma *Chihuahua* Mex. **142** B1
Moctezuma *San Luis Potosí* Mex.
  143 C2
Moctezuma *Sonora* Mex. **142** B2
Mocuba Moz. **107** C1
Modane France **59** D2
Modder *r.* S. Africa **108** B2
Modena Italy **62** B2
Modesto U.S.A. **133** B3
Modimolle S. Africa **109** C1
Moe Austr. **117** D3
Moers Ger. **54** C2
Moffat U.K. **50** C3
Mogadishu Somalia **103** C4
Mogalakwena *r.* S. Africa **109** C1
Mogaung Myanmar **74** A1
Mogi-Mirim Brazil **154** C2
Mogocha Rus. Fed. **95** J3
Mogok Myanmar **74** A1
Mohács Hungary **57** D3
Mohale's Hoek Lesotho **109** C3
Mohammadia Alg. **61** D2
Mohawk *r.* U.S.A. **137** E2
Mohoro Tanz. **105** D3
Mohyliv Podil's'kyy Ukr. **44** C2
Moijabana Botswana **109** C1
Moineşti Romania **44** C2
Mo i Rana Norway **46** C2
Moissac France **58** C3
Mojave U.S.A. **133** C3
Mojave Desert U.S.A. **133** C3
Mojiang China **74** B1
Moji das Cruzes Brazil **155** C2
Moji-Guaçu *r.* Brazil **154** C2

okau N.Z. **118** B2
okhotlong Lesotho **109** C2
okopane S. Africa **109** C1
okp'o S. Korea **77** B3
olango Mex. **143** C2
olde Norway **46** B3
oldova country Europe **44** C2
oldoveanu, Vârful mt. Romania **44** B2
Moldova **44** C2
oldovei Centrale, Podişul plat. Moldova **44** C2
olepolole Botswana **109** C1
olétai Lith. **42** C2
olfetta Italy **63** C2
olina de Aragón Spain **61** C1
ollenbeck Ger. **55** F1
ollendo Peru **150** B4
olong Austr. **117** D2
olopo watercourse Botswana/S. Africa **108** B2
oloundou Cameroon **104** B2
omba Austr. **116** C2
ombasa Kenya **105** D3
ombasa, Sierra da hills Brazil **154** B1
omi, Ra's pt Yemen **91** C3
en i. Denmark **47** C4
onaco country Europe **59** D3
onadhliath Mountains U.K. **50** B2
onaghan Rep. of Ireland **51** C1
onastyrshchina Rus. Fed. **43** D3
onastyrshchina Ukr. **44** C2
onbetsu Japan **78** D2
oncalieri Italy **62** A1
onchegorsk Rus. Fed. **46** G2
önchengladbach Ger. **54** C2
onclova Mex. **142** B2
oncouche, Lac l. Can. **137** F1
oncton Can. **129** D2
ondego r. Port. **60** B1
ondlo S. Africa **109** D2
ondovi Italy **62** A2
onemvasia Greece **65** B3
oneron, Ostrov i. Rus. Fed.
78 D1
onett U.S.A. **135** E3
onfalcone Italy **62** B1
onforte Spain **60** B1
ong Cai Vietnam **74** B1
ông Lin Myanmar **74** B1
ongolia country Asia **80** C2
ong Pawk Myanmar **74** A1
ong Ping Myanmar **74** A1
ongu Zambia **106** B1
onitor Range mts U.S.A. **133** C3
ono r. Togo **100** C4
ono Lake U.S.A. **133** C3
onopoli Italy **63** C2
onreal del Campo Spain **61** C1
onroe LA U.S.A. **138** B2
onroe WI U.S.A. **136** C2
onroeville U.S.A. **138** C2
onrovia Liberia **100** A4
ons Belgium **54** A2
ontagu S. Africa **108** B3
ontalto mt. Italy **63** C3
ontana Bulg. **64** B2
ontana state U.S.A. **130** C2
ontargis France **58** C2
ontauban France **58** C3
ontauk Point pt U.S.A. **137** F2
ontbard France **59** C2
ont Blanc mt. France/Italy **59** D2
ontbrison France **59** C2
ontcornet France **54** B3
ont-de-Marsan France **58** B3
ontdidier France **58** C2

Monte Alegre Brazil **151** D3
Monte-Carlo Monaco **59** D3
Monte Caseros Arg. **152** C4
Montego Bay Jamaica **144** C3
Montélimar France **59** C3
Montella Italy **62** C2
Montemorelos Mex. **143** C2
Montendre France **58** B2
Montenegro aut. rep. Serb. and Mont. see Crna Gora
Montepuez Moz. **107** C1
Montepulciano Italy **62** B2
Monterey U.S.A. **133** B3
Monterey Bay U.S.A. **133** B3
Montería Col. **150** B2
Montero Bol. **152** B2
Monterrey Mex. **143** B2
Montesano sulla Marcellana Italy **63** C2
Monte Sant'Angelo Italy **63** C2
Monte Santo Brazil **151** E4
Monte Santu, Capo di c. Italy **62** A2
Montes Claros Brazil **155** D1
Montevideo Uru. **153** C4
Montevideo U.S.A. **135** D2
Monte Vista U.S.A. **134** B3
Montgomery U.S.A. **139** C2
Monthey Switz. **59** D2
Monticello AR U.S.A. **138** B2
Monticello UT U.S.A. **133** E3
Montignac France **58** C2
Montilla Spain **60** C2
Mont-Joli Can. **129** D2
Mont-Laurier Can. **128** C2
Montluçon France **58** C2
Montmagny Can. **129** C2
Montmorillon France **58** C2
Monto Austr. **115** E2
Montpelier ID U.S.A. **132** D2
Montpelier VT U.S.A. **137** F2
Montpellier France **59** C3
Montréal Can. **128** C2
Montreal Lake Can. **127** E2
Montreal Lake l. Can. **127** E2
Montreux Switz. **59** D2
Montrose U.K. **50** C2
Montrose U.S.A. **134** B3
Montserrat terr. West Indies **145** D3
Monywa Myanmar **74** A1
Monza Italy **62** A1
Monzón Spain **61** D1
Mookane Botswana **109** C1
Moonie Austr. **117** E1
Moonie r. Austr. **117** D1
Moonta Austr. **116** B2
Moore, Lake salt flat Austr. **114** A2
Moorhead U.S.A. **135** D1
Mooreesburg S. Africa **108** A3
Moose r. Can. **128** B1
Moose Factory Can. **128** B1
Moosehead Lake U.S.A. **137** G1
Moose Jaw Can. **124** E3
Moose Lake U.S.A. **135** E1
Moosomin Can. **124** F3
Moosonee Can. **128** B1
Mootwingee Austr. **116** C2
M'Oukal Alg. **61** E2
Mopane S. Africa **109** C1
Mopti Mali **100** B3
Moquegua Peru **150** B4
Mora Sweden **47** C3
Mora U.S.A. **135** E1
Moradabad India **87** B2
Moramanga Madag. **107** [inset] D1
Morava r. Europe **64** A1
Moray Firth b. U.K. **50** B2
Morbach Ger. **54** C3
Morbi India **86** B2
Morcenx France **58** B3
Mordaga China **81** D1

Morden Can. **127** F3
Mordovo Rus. Fed. **43** F3
Morecambe U.K. **52** B2
Morecambe Bay U.K. **52** B2
Moree Austr. **117** D1
Morehead P.N.G. **71** D3
Morehead U.S.A. **136** D3
Morehead City U.S.A. **139** E2
Morelia Mex. **143** B3
Morella Spain **61** C1
Morena, Sierra mts Spain **60** B2
Moreni Romania **44** C3
Moresby, Mount Can. **126** B2
Moresby Island Can. **126** B2
Moreton Island Austr. **117** E1
Morgan City U.S.A. **138** B3
Morganton U.S.A. **139** D1
Morgantown U.S.A. **137** E3
Morges Switz. **59** D2
Mori Japan **78** D2
Morice Lake Can. **126** C2
Morioka Japan **78** D3
Morisset Austr. **117** E2
Morlaix France **58** B2
Mornington Island Austr. **115** C1
Morobe P.N.G. **71** D3
Morocco country Africa **100** B1
Morogoro Tanz. **105** D3
Moro Gulf Phil. **76** B3
Morokweng S. Africa **108** B2
Morombe Madag. **107** [inset] D2
Mörön Mongolia **80** C1
Morondava Madag. **107** [inset] D2
Moroni Comoros **107** D1
Morotai i. Indon. **71** C2
Moroto Uganda **105** D2
Morozovsk Rus. Fed. **45** F2
Morpeth U.K. **52** C2
Morrinhos Brazil **154** C1
Morris Can. **127** F3
Morris U.S.A. **135** D1
Morristown U.S.A. **139** D1
Morshanka Rus. Fed. **43** F3
Mortes, Rio das r. Brazil **151** D4
Mortlake Austr. **116** C3
Moruya Austr. **117** E3
Morvern reg. U.K. **50** B2
Morwell Austr. **117** D3
Mosbach Ger. **55** D3
Moscow Rus. Fed. **43** E2
Moscow U.S.A. **132** C1
Mosel r. Ger. **54** C2
Moselle r. France **59** D2
Moses Lake U.S.A. **132** C1
Mosfellsbær Iceland **46** [inset]
Mosgiel N.Z. **118** B4
Moshenskoye Rus. Fed. **43** D2
Moshi Tanz. **105** D3
Mosjøen Norway **46** C2
Moskva Rus. Fed. see Moscow
Mosonmagyaróvár Hungary **57** D2
Mosquitos, Golfo de los b. Panama **144** B4
Moss Norway **47** C4
Mossel Bay S. Africa **108** B3
Mossendjo Congo **104** B3
Mossgiel Austr. **116** C2
Mossman Austr. **115** D1
Mossoró Brazil **151** F3
Moss Vale Austr. **117** E2
Most Czech Rep. **56** C2
Mostaganem Alg. **100** C1
Mostar Bos.-Herz. **63** C2
Mostardas Brazil **152** C4
Mostovskoy Rus. Fed. **45** F3
Mosul Iraq **93** C2
Motala Sweden **47** D4
Motherwell U.K. **50** C3
Motilla del Palancar Spain **61** C2
Motokwe Botswana **108** B1

Motril Spain **60** C2
Motru Romania **44** B2
Mottama, Gulf of Myanmar **74** A2
Motul Mex. **143** D2
Motu One *atoll* Fr. Polynesia **111**
Moudros Greece **65** C3
Mouila Gabon **104** B3
Moulamein Austr. **116** C3
Moulins France **59** C2
Moultrie U.S.A. **139** D2
Moultrie, Lake U.S.A. **139** E2
Mound City U.S.A. **136** C3
Moundou Chad **101** D4
Mountain Grove U.S.A. **135** E3
Mountain Home *AR* U.S.A. **138** B1
Mountain Home *ID* U.S.A. **132** C2
Mount Airy U.S.A. **139** D1
Mount Barker Austr. **116** B3
Mount Beauty Austr. **117** C3
Mount Darwin Zimbabwe **107** C1
Mount Desert Island U.S.A. **137** G2
Mount Fletcher S. Africa **109** C3
Mount Frere S. Africa **109** C3
Mount Gambier Austr. **116** C3
Mount Hagen P.N.G. **71** B3
Mount Hope Austr. **117** D2
Mount Isa Austr. **115** C2
Mount Magnet Austr. **114** A2
Mount Manara Austr. **116** C2
Mount Maunganui N.Z. **118** C2
Mount Pleasant *IA* U.S.A. **135** E2
Mount Pleasant *MI* U.S.A. **136** C2
Mount Pleasant *TX* U.S.A. **141** F2
Mount's Bay U.K. **53** A4
Mount Shasta U.S.A. **132** B2
Mount Vernon *IL* U.S.A. **136** C3
Mount Vernon *OH* U.S.A. **136** D2
Mount Vernon *WA* U.S.A. **132** B1
Moura Austr. **115** D2
Mourdi, Dépression du *depr.* Chad
101 E3
Mourne Mountains U.K. **51** C1
Mouscron Belgium **54** A2
Moussoro Chad **101** D3
Moutong Indon. **73** D1
Mouydir, Monts du *plat.* Alg. **100** C3
Mouzon France **54** B3
Moy *r.* Rep. of Ireland **51** B1
Moyale Eth. **103** B4
Moyeni Lesotho **109** C3
Mo'ynoq Uzbek. **88** C2
Moyynty Kazakh. **89** C2
Mozambique *country* Africa **107** C2
Mozambique Channel Africa **107** D2
Mozhaysk Rus. Fed. **43** E2
Mpanda Tanz. **105** D3
Mpika Zambia **107** C1
Mporokoso Zambia **105** D3
Mpumalanga *prov.* S. Africa **109** C2
Mrauk-U Myanmar **74** A1
Mrkonjić-Grad Bos.-Herz. **64** A2
Mshinskaya Rus. Fed. **42** C2
M'Sila Alg. **61** D2
Msta *r.* Rus. Fed. **43** D2
Mstinskiy Most Rus. Fed. **43** D2
Mstsislaw Belarus **43** D3
Mtsensk Rus. Fed. **43** E3
Mtwara Tanz. **105** E4
Muanda Dem. Rep. Congo **104** B3
Muang Hinboun Laos **83** A4
Muang Không Laos **75** D2
Muang Ngoy Laos **74** B1
Muang Pakbeng Laos **74** B2
Muang Sing Laos **74** B1
Muang Vangviang Laos **74** B2
Muar Malaysia **72** B1
Muarabungo Indon. **72** B2
Muaradua Indon. **72** B2
Muaralaung Indon. **73** C2
Muarasiberut Indon. **72** A2

Muaratembesi Indon. **72** B2
Muarateweh Indon. **73** C2
Mubende Uganda **105** D2
Mubi Nigeria **101** D3
Muchkapskiy Rus. Fed. **45** F1
Muconda Angola **104** C4
Mucuri Brazil **155** E1
Mucuri *r.* Brazil **155** E1
Mudanjiang China **78** A3
Mudan Jiang *r.* China **78** A1
Mudanya Turkey **65** C2
Müden (Örtze) Ger. **55** E1
Mudgee Austr. **117** D2
Mudon Myanmar **74** A2
Mudurnu Turkey **92** B1
Mueda Moz. **107** C1
Mufulira Zambia **107** B1
Mufumbwe Zambia **106** B1
Muğla Turkey **65** C3
Muhammad Qol Sudan **102** B2
Mühlberg Ger. **55** F2
Mühlhausen (Thüringen) Ger. **55** E2
Muine Bheag Rep. of Ireland **51** C2
Muite Moz. **107** C1
Muju S. Korea **77** B2
Mukacheve Ukr. **44** B2
Mukah Malaysia **73** C1
Mukalla Yemen **91** B3
Mukdahan Thai. **74** B2
Mukinbudin Austr. **114** A3
Mukomuko Indon. **72** B2
Mulanje, Mount Malawi **107** C1
Mulde *r.* Ger. **55** F2
Mulegé Mex. **142** A2
Muleshoe U.S.A. **141** D2
Mulhacén *mt.* Spain **60** C2
Mülheim an der Ruhr Ger. **54** C2
Mulhouse France **59** D2
Muling China **78** B1
Muling He *r.* China **78** B1
Mull *i.* U.K. **50** B2
Mullaley Austr. **117** D2
Mullen U.S.A. **134** C2
Muller, Pegunungan *mts* Indon. **73** C1
Mullewa Austr. **114** A2
Mullingar Rep. of Ireland **51** C2
Mull of Galloway *c.* U.K. **50** B3
Mull of Kintyre *hd* U.K. **50** B3
Mull of Oa *hd* U.K. **50** A3
Mulobezi Zambia **106** B1
Multan Pak. **86** B1
Mumbai India **85** B3
Mumbwa Zambia **106** B1
Muna *i.* Indon. **73** D2
Muna Mex. **143** D2
Münchberg Ger. **55** E2
München Ger. *see* Munich
Mundrabilla Austr. **114** B3
Mungbere Dem. Rep. Congo **105** C2
Munger India **87** C2
Mungeranie Austr. **116** B1
Mungindi Austr. **117** D1
Munich Ger. **56** C3
Muniz Freire Brazil **155** D2
Münster *Niedersachsen* Ger. **55** E1
Münster *Nordrhein-Westfalen* Ger.
54 C2
Munster *reg.* Rep. of Ireland **51** B2
Münsterland *reg.* Ger. **54** C2
Mương Nhie Vietnam **74** B1
Muonio Fin. **46** E2
Muonioälven *r.* Fin./Sweden **46** E2
Muqdisho Somalia *see* Mogadishu
Mur *r.* Austria **57** D3
Muramvya Burundi **105** C3
Murang'a Kenya **105** D3
Murat *r.* Turkey **93** D2
Muratlı Turkey **65** C2
Murchison *watercourse* Austr. **114** A2

Murcia Spain **61** C2
Mürefte Turkey **65** C2
Mureşul *r.* Romania **44** B2
Muret France **58** C3
Murfreesboro U.S.A. **139** C1
Murghab *r.* Afgh. **86** A1
Murghob Tajik. **89** D3
Muriaé Brazil **155** D2
Muriege Angola **104** C3
Müritz *l.* Ger. **55** F1
Murmansk Rus. Fed. **46** G2
Murom Rus. Fed. **43** F2
Muroran Japan **78** D2
Muros Spain **60** B1
Muroto Japan **79** B4
Muroto-zaki *pt* Japan **79** B4
Murphy U.S.A. **139** D1
Murra Murra Austr. **117** D1
Murray *r.* Austr. **117** B3
Murray *r.* Can. **126** C2
Murray U.S.A. **136** C3
Murray, Lake U.S.A. **139** D2
Murray Bridge Austr. **116** B3
Murraysburg S. Africa **108** B3
Murrayville Austr. **116** C3
Murrumbidgee *r.* Austr. **116** C2
Murrupula Moz. **107** C1
Murrurundi Austr. **117** E2
Murska Sobota Slovenia **63** C1
Murupara N.Z. **118** C2
Mururoa *atoll* Fr. Polynesia **111**
Murwara India **87** C2
Murwillumbah Austr. **117** E1
Murzechirla Turkm. **41** F5
Murzūq Libya **101** D2
Muş Turkey **93** C2
Musala *mt.* Bulg. **64** B2
Musan N. Korea **77** B1
Musaymir Yemen **90** B3
Muscat Oman **91** C2
Muscatine U.S.A. **135** E2
Musgrave Ranges *mts* Austr. **114** C2
Mushie Dem. Rep. Congo **104** B3
Musi *r.* Indon. **72** B2
Musina S. Africa **109** C1
Muskegon U.S.A. **136** C2
Muskegee U.S.A. **141** E1
Muskwa *r.* Can. **126** C2
Muslimbagh Pak. **86** A1
Musmar Sudan **90** A3
Musoma Tanz. **105** D3
Musselburgh U.K. **50** C3
Mustjala Estonia **42** B2
Muswellbrook Austr. **117** E2
Mūṭ Egypt **102** A2
Mutare Zimbabwe **107** C1
Mutsu Japan **78** D2
Mutuali Moz. **107** C1
Muurola Fin. **46** F2
Mu Us Shamo *des.* China **82** A2
Muxaluando Angola **104** B3
Muyezerskiy Rus. Fed. **46** G3
Muyinga Burundi **105** D3
Muzaffargarh Pak. **86** B1
Muzaffarpur India **87** C2
Muzamane Moz. **109** D1
Múzquiz Mex. **142** B2
Muz Tag *mt.* China **87** C1
Muz Tag *mt.* China **82** B1
Mwanza Dem. Rep. Congo **105** C3
Mwanza Tanz. **105** D3
Mweka Dem. Rep. Congo **104** C3
Mwenda Zambia **105** C4
Mwene-Ditu Dem. Rep. Congo **104** C3
Mwenezi Zimbabwe **107** C2
Mweru, Lake Dem. Rep. Congo/Zambia
105 C3
Mwimba Dem. Rep. Congo **104** C3
Mwinilunga Zambia **106** B1
Myadzyel Belarus **42** C3

Myanaung Myanmar **74** A2
Myanmar country Asia **74** A1
Myaungmya Myanmar **74** A2
Myeik Myanmar **75** A2
Myingyan Myanmar **74** A1
Myitkyina Myanmar **74** A1
Mykolayiv Ukr. **45** D2
Mykonos Greece **65** C3
Myla Rus. Fed. **40** E2
Mymensingh Bangl. **87** D2
Myŏnggan N. Korea **77** B1
Myory Belarus **42** C2
Myrhorod Ukr. **45** D2
Myronivka Ukr. **45** D2
Mýrdalsjökull *ice cap* Iceland **46** [inset]
Myrtle Beach U.S.A. **139** E2
Myrtleford Austr. **117** D3
Myrtle Point U.S.A. **132** B2
Myshkin Rus. Fed. **43** E2
Myślibórz Pol. **56** C2
Mysore India **85** B3
Mys Shmidta Rus. Fed. **95** O2
My Tho Vietnam **75** B2
Mytilini Greece **65** C3
Mytishchi Rus. Fed. **43** E2
Mzimba Malawi **107** C1
Mzamomhle S. Africa **109** C3
Mzuzu Malawi **107** C1

N

aas Rep. of Ireland **51** C2
ababeep S. Africa **108** A2
aberezhnyye Chelny Rus. Fed. **41** E3
abire Indon. **71** E2
ablus West Bank **92** B2
aboomspruit S. Africa **109** C1
acala Mex. **107** D1
achuge India **75** A2
acogdoches U.S.A. **141** F2
acozari de García Mex. **142** B1
adiad India **86** B2
ador Morocco **60** C2
advirna Ukr. **44** B2
advoitsy Rus. Fed. **40** C2
adym Rus. Fed. **40** G2
æstved Denmark **47** C4
afpaktos Greece **65** B3
afplio Greece **65** B3
afy Saudi Arabia **90** B2
aga Phil. **76** B2
agagami r. Can. **128** B1
agano Japan **79** C3
agaoka Japan **79** C3
agaon India **87** D2
agar India **86** B1
agar Parkar Pak. **86** B2
agasaki Japan **79** A4
agato Japan **79** B4
agaur India **86** B2
agercoil India **85** B4
agha Kalat Pak. **86** A2
ag' Ḥammādī Egypt **90** A2
agina India **87** B2
agoya Japan **79** C3
agpur India **87** B2
agqu China **87** D1
agyatád Hungary **57** D2
agykanizsa Hungary **57** D3
ahanni Butte Can. **126** C1
ahāvand Iran **93** C2
ahrendorf Ger. **55** E1
ahuel Huapí, Lago l. Arg. **153** A5
ain Can. **129** D1
a'in Iran **93** D2
airn U.K. **50** C2
airobi Kenya **105** D3

Naivasha Kenya **105** D3
Najafābād Iran **93** D2
Najd reg. Saudi Arabia **90** B2
Nájera Spain **60** C1
Najin N. Korea **77** C1
Najrān Saudi Arabia **90** B2
Nakatsugawa Japan **79** C3
Nakfa Eritrea **90** A3
Nakhodka Rus. Fed. **78** B2
Nakhon Pathom Thai. **75** B2
Nakhon Ratchasima Thai. **75** B2
Nakhon Sawan Thai. **75** B2
Nakhon Si Thammarat Thai. **75** A3
Nakina Can. **128** B1
Nakonde Zambia **105** D3
Nakskov Denmark **47** C5
Nakuru Kenya **105** D3
Nakusp Can. **126** D2
Nalbari India **87** D2
Nal'chik Rus. Fed. **41** D4
Nālūt Libya **101** D1
Namahadi S. Africa **109** C2
Namakzar-e Shadad salt flat Iran **91** C1
Namangan Uzbek. **89** E2
Namaqualand reg. S. Africa **108** A2
Nambour Austr. **115** E2
Nambucca Heads Austr. **117** E2
Nam Co salt l. China **87** D1
Nam Đinh Vietnam **74** B1
Namib Desert Namibia **106** A2
Namibe Angola **106** A1
Namibia country Africa **108** A1
Namjagbarwa Feng mt. China **84** D2
Namlea Indon. **71** C3
Namoi r. Austr. **117** D2
Nampa U.S.A. **132** C2
Nampala Mali **100** B3
Namp'o N. Korea **77** B2
Nampula Moz. **107** C1
Namrup India **74** A1
Namsang Myanmar **74** A1
Namsos Norway **46** C3
Nam Tok Thai. **75** A2
Namtsy Rus. Fed. **95** K2
Namtu Myanmar **74** A1
Namur Belgium **54** B2
Namwala Zambia **106** B1
Namwŏn S. Korea **77** B2
Namya Ra Myanmar **74** A1
Nan Thai. **74** B2
Nanaimo Can. **126** C3
Nan'an China **83** B3
Nananib Plateau Namibia **108** A1
Nanao Japan **79** C3
Nanchang Jiangxi China **83** B3
Nanchang Jiangxi China **83** B3
Nanchong China **82** A2
Nancowry i. India **75** A3
Nancy France **59** D2
Nanda Devi mt. India **87** C1
Nandan China **83** A3
Nanded India **85** B3
Nandurbar India **86** B2
Nandyal India **85** B3
Nanfeng China **83** B3
Nanga Eboko Cameroon **104** B2
Nangahpinoh Indon. **73** C2
Nanga Parbat mt. Jammu and Kashmir **86** B1
Nangatayap Indon. **73** C2
Nangong China **82** B2
Nangulangwa Tanz. **105** D3
Nanjing China **82** B2
Nanking China see Nanjing
Nankova Angola **106** A1
Nan Ling mts China **83** B3
Nanning China **83** A3
Nanortalik Greenland **125** I2
Nanpan Jiang r. China **83** A3

Nanpara India **87** C2
Nanping China **83** B3
Nansei-shotō is Japan see
Ryukyu Islands
Nantes France **58** B2
Nantong China **82** C2
Nantucket Island U.S.A. **137** G2
Nanumea atoll Tuvalu **110**
Nanuque Brazil **155** D1
Nanusa, Kepulauan is Indon. **76** B3
Nanxiong China **83** B3
Nanyang China **82** B2
Nanzhang China **82** B2
Nao, Cabo de la c. Spain **61** D2
Naococane, Lac l. Can. **129** C1
Naokot Pak. **86** A2
Napa U.S.A. **133** B3
Napaktulik Lake Can. **127** D1
Napasoq Greenland **125** I2
Napier N.Z. **118** C2
Naples Italy **62** B2
Naples U.S.A. **139** D3
Napo r. Ecuador **150** B3
Napoli Italy see Naples
Nara Mali **100** B3
Narach Belarus **42** C3
Naracoorte Austr. **116** C3
Naranjos Mex. **143** C2
Narathiwat Thai. **75** B3
Narbonne France **58** C3
Narcondam Island India **75** A2
Nares Strait Can./Greenland **125** H1
Narib Namibia **108** A1
Narimanov Rus. Fed. **41** D4
Narita Japan **79** D3
Narmada r. India **86** B2
Narnaul India **86** B2
Narni Italy **62** B2
Narodychi Ukr. **44** C1
Naro-Fominsk Rus. Fed. **43** E2
Narooma Austr. **117** E3
Narowlya Belarus **42** C3
Narrabri Austr. **117** D2
Narrandera Austr. **117** D2
Narromine Austr. **117** D2
Narva Estonia **42** C2
Narva Bay Estonia/Rus. Fed. **42** C2
Narvik Norway **46** D2
Narvskoye Vodokhranilishche resr Estonia/Rus. Fed. **42** C2
Nar'yan-Mar Rus. Fed. **40** E2
Naryn Kyrg. **89** E2
Nashik India **86** B2
Nashua U.S.A. **137** F2
Nashville U.S.A. **138** C1
Nasir Sudan **103** B4
Nass r. Can. **126** C2
Nassau Bahamas **145** C2
Nasser, Lake resr Egypt **102** B2
Nässjö Sweden **47** C4
Nastapoca r. Can. **128** C1
Nastapoka Islands Can. **128** C1
Nata Botswana **106** B2
Natal Brazil **151** F3
Natal prov. S. Africa see Kwazulu-Natal
Natashquan Can. **129** D1
Natashquan r. Can. **129** D1
Natchez U.S.A. **138** B2
Natchitoches U.S.A. **138** B2
Nathalia Austr. **117** D3
Nati, Punta pt Spain **61** D1
Natitingou Benin **100** C3
Natividade Brazil **151** E4
Natori Japan **78** D3
Natuashish Can. **129** D1
Natuna, Kepulauan is Indon. **72** B1
Natuna Besar i. Indon. **72** B1
Nauchas Namibia **108** A1
Nauen Ger. **55** F1
Naujoji Akmenė Lith. **42** B2

Naumburg (Saale) Ger. **55** E2
Nauru country S. Pacific Ocean **112**
Naustdal Norway **48** E1
Nautla Mex. **143** C2
Navahrudak Belarus **42** C3
Navalmoral de la Mata Spain **60** B2
Navalvillar de Pela Spain **60** B2
Navan Rep. of Ireland **51** C2
Navapolatsk Belarus **42** C2
Navarin, Mys c. Rus. Fed. **95** N2
Navarino, Isla i. Chile **153** B6
Navashino Rus. Fed. **43** F2
Naver r. U.K. **50** E1
Navlya Rus. Fed. **43** D3
Năvodari Romania **44** C3
Navoiy Uzbek. **89** D2
Navojoa Mex. **142** B2
Navolato Mex. **142** B2
Nawabshah Pak. **86** A2
Nawnghkio Myanmar **74** A1
Nawngleng Myanmar **74** A1
Naxçivan Azer. **93** C2
Naxos i. Greece **65** C3
Nayar Mex. **142** B2
Nayoro Japan **78** D2
Nazareth Israel **92** B2
Nazas Mex. **142** B2
Nazas r. Mex. **142** B2
Nazca Peru **150** B4
Nazilli Turkey **65** C3
Nazrēt Eth. **103** B4
Nazwá Oman **91** C2
Nchelenge Zambia **105** C3
Ncojane Botswana **108** B1
N'dalatando Angola **104** B3
Ndélé C.A.R. **104** C3
Ndendé Gabon **104** B3
Ndjamena Chad **101** D3
Ndola Zambia **107** B1
Neagh, Lough l. U.K. **51** C1
Neale, Lake salt flat Austr. **114** C2
Nea Roda Greece **65** B2
Neath U.K. **53** B4
Nebine Creek r. Austr. **117** D1
Neblina, Pico da mt. Brazil **150** C2
Nebolchi Rus. Fed. **43** D2
Nebraska state U.S.A. **134** C2
Nebraska City U.S.A. **135** D2
Nebrodi, Monti mts Italy **62** B3
Necochea Arg. **153** C4
Nedlouc, Lac l. Can. **129** C1
Nédroma Alg. **61** C2
Needles U.S.A. **133** D4
Neemuch India **86** B2
Neepawa Can. **127** F2
Neftekamsk Rus. Fed. **41** E3
Nefteyugansk Rus. Fed. **40** G2
Negage Angola **104** B3
Negēlē Eth. **103** B4
Negra, Punta pt Peru **150** A3
Negrais, Cape Myanmar **75** A2
Negro r. Arg. **153** B5
Negro r. Brazil **154** A1
Negro r. S. America **150** D3
Negro r. Uru. **152** C4
Negro, Cabo c. Morocco **60** B2
Negros i. Phil. **76** B3
Nehbandān Iran **91** D1
Nehe China **81** E1
Neijiang China **83** A3
Neilburg Can. **127** E2
Nei Mongol Zizhiqu aut. reg. China **82** A1
Neiva Col. **150** B2
Nejanilini Lake Can. **127** F2
Nek'emtē Eth. **103** B4
Nekrasovskoye Rus. Fed. **43** F2
Nelidovo Rus. Fed. **43** D2
Nellore India **85** B3
Nelson Can. **126** D3

Nelson r. Can. **127** F2
Nelson N.Z. **118** B3
Nelson, Cape Austr. **116** C3
Nelson Bay Austr. **117** E2
Nelson House Can. **127** F2
Nelson Reservoir U.S.A. **132** E1
Nelspruit S. Africa **109** D2
Néma Maur. **100** B3
Neman Rus. Fed. **42** B3
Nemda r. Rus. Fed. **43** F2
Nemours France **58** C2
Nemuro Japan **78** E2
Nemyriv Ukr. **44** C2
Nenagh Rep. of Ireland **51** B2
Nene r. U.K. **53** D3
Nenjiang China **81** E1
Neosho U.S.A. **135** E3
Nepal country Asia **87** C2
Nepalganj Nepal **87** C2
Nephi U.S.A. **133** D3
Nephin h. Rep. of Ireland **51** B1
Nephin Beg Range hills Rep. of Ireland **51** B1
Nepisiguit r. Can. **129** D2
Nepoko r. Dem. Rep. Congo **105** C2
Nepomuk Czech Rep. **55** F3
Nérac France **58** C3
Nerang Austr. **117** E1
Nerchinsk Rus. Fed. **81** D1
Nerekhta Rus. Fed. **43** F2
Neretva r. Bos.-Herz./Croatia **63** C2
Neriquinha Angola **106** B1
Neris r. Lith. **42** B3
Nerl' r. Rus. Fed. **43** F2
Nerokhi Rus. Fed. **40** F2
Nerópolis Brazil **154** C1
Neryungri Rus. Fed. **95** K3
Neskaupstaður Iceland **46** [inset]
Ness, Loch l. U.K. **50** B2
Ness City U.S.A. **134** D3
Nestos r. Greece **65** B2
Netherlands country Europe **54** B1
Netherlands Antilles terr. West Indies **145** D3
Neubrandenburg Ger. **55** F1
Neuchâtel Switz. **59** D2
Neuenhagen Berlin Ger. **55** F1
Neuerburg Ger. **54** C2
Neufchâteau Belgium **54** B3
Neufchâteau France **59** D2
Neufchâtel-en-Bray France **58** C2
Neuhof Ger. **55** D2
Neu Lübbenau Ger. **55** F1
Neumarkt in der Oberpfalz Ger. **55** E3
Neumünster Ger. **56** B2
Neunkirchen Ger. **54** C2
Neuquén Arg. **153** B4
Neuquén r. Arg. **153** B4
Neuruppin Ger. **55** F1
Neuss Ger. **54** C2
Neustadt am Rübenberge Ger. **55** D1
Neustadt an der Aisch Ger. **55** E3
Neustadt an der Weinstraße Ger. **54** D3
Neustrelitz Ger. **55** F1
Neutraubling Ger. **55** F3
Neuwied Ger. **54** C2
Nevada U.S.A. **135** E3
Nevada state U.S.A. **133** C3
Nevada, Sierra mts Spain **60** C2
Nevada, Sierra mts U.S.A. **133** B2
Nevel' Rus. Fed. **42** C2
Nevers France **59** C2
Nevertire Austr. **117** D2
Nevesinje Bos.-Herz. **63** C2
Nevinnomyssk Rus. Fed. **41** D4
New Aiyansh Can. **126** C2
New Albany U.S.A. **136** C3
New Amsterdam Guyana **151** D2
Newark NJ U.S.A. **137** F2

Newark OH U.S.A. **136** D2
Newark-on-Trent U.K. **52** C3
New Bedford U.S.A. **137** F2
New Bern U.S.A. **139** E1
Newberry U.S.A. **139** D2
New Boston U.S.A. **141** F2
New Braunfels U.S.A. **141** E3
Newbridge Rep. of Ireland **51** C2
New Britain i. P.N.G. **158** D5
New Brunswick prov. Can. **129** D2
Newbury U.K. **53** C4
New Caledonia terr. S. Pacific Ocean **112**
Newcastle Austr. **117** E2
Newcastle S. Africa **109** C2
Newcastle U.K. **51** D1
New Castle U.S.A. **137** D2
Newcastle U.S.A. **134** C2
Newcastle-under-Lyme U.K. **52** B3
Newcastle upon Tyne U.K. **52** C2
Newcastle West Rep. of Ireland **51** B2
New Delhi India **86** B2
New Denver Can. **126** D3
New England Range mts Austr. **117** E2
Newfoundland i. Can. **129** E2
Newfoundland and Labrador prov. Can. **129** E1
New Glasgow Can. **129** D2
New Guinea i. Indon./P.N.G. **71** D3
New Halfa Sudan **90** A3
New Hampshire state U.S.A. **137** F2
New Haven U.S.A. **137** F2
New Hazelton Can. **126** C2
New Iberia U.S.A. **138** B2
New Ireland i. P.N.G. **112**
New Jersey state U.S.A. **137** F3
New Liskeard Can. **128** C2
Newman Austr. **114** A2
New Mexico state U.S.A. **140** C2
New Orleans U.S.A. **138** B3
New Philadelphia U.S.A. **136** D2
New Plymouth N.Z. **118** B2
Newport England U.K. **53** C4
Newport Wales U.K. **53** B4
Newport AR U.S.A. **138** B1
Newport OR U.S.A. **132** B2
Newport RI U.S.A. **137** F2
Newport VT U.S.A. **137** F2
Newport WA U.S.A. **132** C1
Newport News U.S.A. **137** E3
New Providence i. Bahamas **139** E3
Newquay U.K. **53** A4
New Roads U.S.A. **138** B2
New Ross Rep. of Ireland **51** C2
Newry U.K. **51** C1
New Siberia Islands Rus. Fed. **95** L1
New South Wales state Austr. **117** D2
Newton IA U.S.A. **135** E2
Newton KS U.S.A. **135** D3
Newton Abbot U.K. **53** B4
Newton Stewart U.K. **50** B3
Newtown Rep. of Ireland **51** B2
Newtown U.K. **53** B3
New Town U.S.A. **134** C1
Newtownabbey U.K. **51** D1
Newtownards U.K. **51** D1
Newtown St Boswells U.K. **50** C3
Newtownstewart U.K. **51** C1
New Ulm U.S.A. **135** E2
New York U.S.A. **137** F2
New York state U.S.A. **137** E2
New Zealand country Oceania **118**
Neya Rus. Fed. **43** F2
Neya r. Rus. Fed. **43** F2
Neyrīz Iran **93** D3
Neyshābūr Iran **88** C3
Nezahualcóyotl Mex. **143** C3
Nezahualcóyotl, Presa resr Mex. **143** C3

Ngabang Indon. **73** B1
Ngamring China **87** C2
Ngangla Ringco salt l. China **87** C1
Nganglong Kangri mt. China **87** C1
Nganglong Kangri mts China **87** C1
Ngao Thai. **74** A2
Ngaoundéré Cameroon **104** B2
Ngaruawahia N.Z. **118** C2
Ngathaingyaung Myanmar **74** A2
Ngo Congo **104** B3
Ngoc Linh mt. Vietnam **75** B2
Ngol Bembo Nigeria **101** D4
Ngoring Hu l. China **80** C2
Ngourti Niger **101** D3
Nguigmi Niger **101** D3
Ngulu atoll Micronesia **71** D2
Nguru Nigeria **101** D3
Ngwelezana S. Africa **109** D2
Nhamalabué Moz. **107** C1
Nha Trang Vietnam **75** B2
Nhill Austr. **116** C3
Nhlangano Swaziland **109** D2
Nhulunbuy Austr. **115** C1
Niagara Falls Can. **137** E2
Niamey Niger **100** C3
Niangara Dem. Rep. Congo **105** C2
Niangxé, Lac l. Mali **100** B3
Nias i. Indon. **72** A1
Nicaragua country Central America **144** B3
Nicaragua, Lake Nic. **144** B3
Nice France **59** D3
Nicobar Islands India **85** D4
Nicosia Cyprus **92** B2
Nicoya, Golfo de b. Costa Rica **144** B4
Nida Lith. **42** B2
Nidzica Pol. **57** E2
Niebüll Ger. **56** B2
Niederaula Ger. **55** D2
Niefang Equat. Guinea **104** B2
Niemegk Ger. **55** F1
Nienburg (Weser) Ger. **55** D1
Nieuwe-Niedorp Neth. **54** B1
Nieuw Nickerie Suriname **151** C2
Nieuwoudtville S. Africa **108** A3
Nieuwpoort Belgium **54** A2
Niğde Turkey **92** B2
Niger country Africa **101** D3
Niger r. Africa **101** C4
Niger, Mouths of the Nigeria **101** C4
Nigeria country Africa **101** C4
Nighthawk Lake Can. **128** C2
Nigrita Greece **65** B2
Niigata Japan **79** C3
Niihama Japan **79** B4
Nijmegen Neth. **54** B2
Nii-jima i. Japan **79** C4
Niitsu Japan **79** C3
Nikel' Rus. Fed. **46** G2
Nikol'skoye Rus. Fed. **95** N3
Nikopol' Ukr. **45** D2
Niksar Turkey **92** B1
Nikshahr Iran **91** D2
Nikšić Serb. and Mont. **64** A2
Nile r. Africa **102** B1
Niles U.S.A. **136** C2
Nîmes France **59** C3
Nimmitabel Austr. **117** D3
Nimule Sudan **103** B4
Nindigully Austr. **117** D1
Nine Degree Channel India **85** B4
Ninety Mile Beach Austr. **117** D3
Ninety Mile Beach N.Z. **118** B1
Ningbo China **83** C3
Ningde China **83** B3
Ningdu China **83** B3
Ningguo China **83** B2
Ninghai China **83** C3

Ninging India **74** A1
Ningjing Shan mts China **80** C2
Ningxia Huizu Zizhiqu aut. reg. China **82** A2
Ningyang China **82** B2
Ninh Binh Vietnam **74** B2
Ninh Hoa Vietnam **75** B2
Ninohe Japan **78** D2
Niobrara r. U.S.A. **135** D2
Niono Mali **100** B3
Nioro Mali **100** B3
Niort France **58** B2
Nipawin Can. **124** F3
Nipigon Can. **128** B2
Nipigon, Lake Can. **128** B2
Nipishish Lake Can. **129** D1
Nipissing, Lake Can. **128** C2
Nipton U.S.A. **133** C3
Niquelândia Brazil **151** E4
Nirmal India **85** B3
Niš Serb. and Mont. **64** B2
Nišava r. Serb. and Mont. **64** B2
Niscemi Italy **62** B3
Nishino-omote Japan **79** B4
Niterói Brazil **155** D2
Nith r. U.K. **50** C3
Nitra Slovakia **57** D3
Niue terr. S. Pacific Ocean **113**
Nivala Fin. **46** E3
Nivelles Belgium **54** B2
Nizamabad India **85** B3
Nizhnekamsk Rus. Fed. **41** E3
Nizhneudinsk Rus. Fed. **95** I3
Nizhnevartovsk Rus. Fed. **94** H2
Nizhniy Kislyay Rus. Fed. **43** F3
Nizhniy Lomov Rus. Fed. **41** D3
Nizhniy Novgorod Rus. Fed. **41** D3
Nizhniy Odes Rus. Fed. **40** E2
Nizhniy Tagil Rus. Fed. **41** E3
Nizhnyaya Tunguska r. Rus. Fed. **95** H2
Nizhyn Ukr. **45** D1
Njazidja i. Comoros **107** C1
Njinjo Tanz. **105** D3
Njombe Tanz. **105** D3
Nkhotakota Malawi **107** C1
Nkongsamba Cameroon **104** A2
Nkululeko S. Africa **109** C3
Nkwenkwezi S. Africa **109** C3
Nobeoka Japan **79** B4
Noccundra Austr. **116** C1
Nogales Mex. **142** A1
Nogales U.S.A. **140** B2
Nogent-le-Rotrou France **58** C2
Noginsk Rus. Fed. **43** E2
Nohar India **86** B2
Nohfelden Ger. **54** C3
Noirmoutier, Île de i. France **58** B2
Noirmoutier-en-l'Île France **58** B2
Noisseville France **54** C3
Nojima-zaki c. Japan **79** C4
Nokha India **86** B2
Nokia Fin. **47** E3
Nok Kundi Pak. **86** A2
Nola C.A.R. **104** B2
Nolinsk Rus. Fed. **40** D3
Nomonde S. Africa **109** C3
Nondweni S. Africa **109** D2
Nong Khai Thai. **74** B2
Nonning Austr. **116** B2
Nonoava Mex. **142** B2
Nonsan S. Korea **77** B2
Nonthaburi Thai. **75** B2
Nonzwakazi S. Africa **108** B3
Noordoewer Namibia **108** A2
Noranda Can. **137** E1
Nordaustlandet i. Svalbard **94** D1
Nordegg Can. **126** D2
Norden Ger. **54** C1
Nordenshel'da, Arkhipelag is Rus. Fed. **95** I1

Norderney Ger. **54** C1
Norderney i. Ger. **54** C1
Norderstedt Ger. **55** E1
Nordfjordeid Norway **47** B3
Nordhausen Ger. **55** E2
Nordholz Ger. **55** D1
Nordhorn Ger. **54** C1
Nordkapp c. Norway see **North Cape**
Nordli Norway **46** C3
Nördlingen Ger. **56** C3
Nordmaling Sweden **46** D3
Norðoyar i. Faroe Is **48** B1
Nore r. Rep. of Ireland **51** C2
Norfolk NE U.S.A. **135** D2
Norfolk VA U.S.A. **137** E3
Norfolk Island terr.
   S. Pacific Ocean **112**
Norheimsund Norway **47** B3
Noril'sk Rus. Fed. **94** H2
Norkyung China **87** C2
Norman U.S.A. **141** E1
Normandes, Îles is English Chan. see
   Channel Islands
Normandy reg. France **58** B2
Normanton Austr. **115** C1
Norman Wells Can. **126** C1
Norrköping Sweden **47** D4
Norrtälje Sweden **47** D4
Norseman Austr. **114** B3
Norsjö Sweden **46** D3
Norte, Punta pt Arg. **147**
Northallerton U.K. **52** C2
Northampton Austr. **114** A2
Northampton U.K. **53** C3
North Andaman i. India **75** A2
North Battleford Can. **124** E3
North Bay Can. **128** C2
North Belcher Islands Can. **128** C1
North Berwick U.K. **50** C2
North Cape Norway **46** F1
North Cape N.Z. **118** B1
North Caribou Lake Can. **128** A1
North Carolina state U.S.A. **139** E1
North Channel lake channel Can. **128** B2
North Channel U.K. **51** C1
North Cowichan Can. **126** C3
North Dakota state U.S.A. **134** C1
North Downs hills U.K. **53** C3
Northeim Ger. **55** D2
Northern Cape prov. S. Africa **108** A2
Northern Indian Lake Can. **127** F2
Northern Ireland prov. U.K. **51** C1
Northern Mariana Islands terr.
   N. Pacific Ocean **71** D1
Northern Territory admin. div. Austr. **114** C1
North Esk r. U.K. **50** C2
Northfield U.S.A. **135** E2
North Foreland c. U.K. **53** D4
North Frisian Islands Ger. **56** B2
North Geomagnetic Pole **162** J2
North Island N.Z. **118** B2
North Knife Lake Can. **127** F2
North Korea country Asia **77** B1
North Lakhimpur India **74** A1
North Magnetic Pole Can. **162** K1
North Nahanni r. Can. **126** C1
North Platte U.S.A. **134** C2
North Platte r. U.S.A. **134** C2
North Pole Arctic Ocean **162**
North Ronaldsay i. U.K. **50** C1
North Sea Europe **48** D2
North Spirit Lake Can. **128** A1
North Stradbroke Island Austr. **117** E1
North Taranaki Bight b. N.Z. **118** B2
North Twin Island Can. **128** C1
North Tyne r. U.K. **52** B2

North Uist *i.* U.K. **50** A2
Northumberland Strait Can. **129** D2
North West *prov.* S. Africa **108** B2
North West Lake Austr. **114** A2
North West River Can. **129** E1
Northwest Territories *admin. div.* Can.
124 E2
North York Moors *moorland* U.K.
52 C2
Norton U.S.A. **136** D3
Norton Zimbabwe **107** C1
Norton Sound *sea chan.* U.S.A. **124** B2
Norwalk U.S.A. **136** D2
Norway *country* Europe **47** C3
Norway House Can. **127** F2
Norwegian Sea N. Atlantic Ocean
46 B2
Norwich U.K. **53** D3
Norwich *CT* U.S.A. **137** F2
Norwich *NY* U.S.A. **137** E2
Noshiro Japan **78** D2
Nosivka Ukr. **45** D1
Nosop *watercourse* Africa **108** B2
Nosovaya Rus. Fed. **40** E2
Noşratābād Iran **91** C2
Nossen Ger. **55** F2
Noteć *r.* Pol. **57** D2
Notodden Norway **47** B4
Noto-hantō *pen.* Japan **79** C3
Notre Dame, Monts *mts* Can. **129** D2
Notre Dame Bay Can. **129** E2
Nottaway *r.* Can. **128** C1
Nottingham U.K. **52** C3
Nouâdhibou Maur. **100** A2
Nouakchott Maur. **100** A3
Nouâmghâr Maur. **100** A3
Nouméa New Caledonia **112**
Nouna Burkina **100** B3
Nouvelle Calédonie *i.*
S. Pacific Ocean **110**
Nova Esperança Brazil **154** B2
Nova Friburgo Brazil **155** D2
Nova Gradiška Croatia **63** C1
Nova Granada Brazil **154** C2
Nova Iguaçu Brazil **155** D2
Nova Kakhovka Ukr. **45** D2
Nova Lima Brazil **155** D1
Nova Londrina Brazil **154** B2
Nova Odesa Ukr. **45** D2
Nova Paraíso Brazil **150** C2
Nova Scotia *prov.* Can. **129** D2
Nova Venécia Brazil **155** D1
Novaya Sibir', Ostrov *i.* Rus. Fed.
95 L1
Novaya Zemlya *i.* Rus. Fed. **40** E1
Nové Zámky Slovakia **57** D3
Novhorod-Sivers'kyy Ukr. **45** D1
Novi Iskŭr Bulg. **64** B3
Novi Ligure Italy **62** A2
Novi Pazar Serb. and Mont. **64** B2
Novi Sad Serb. and Mont. **64** A1
Novoaleksandrovsk Rus. Fed. **45** F2
Novoanninskiy Rus. Fed. **45** F1
Novo Aripuanã Brazil **150** C3
Novoazovs'k Ukr. **45** E2
Novocherkassk Rus. Fed. **45** F2
Novodvinsk Rus. Fed. **40** D2
Novo Hamburgo Brazil **152** C3
Novo Horizonte Brazil **154** C2
Novohrad-Volyns'kyy Ukr. **45** C1
Novokhopersk Rus. Fed. **43** F1
Novokubansk Rus. Fed. **45** F2
Novokuznetsk Rus. Fed. **89** F1
Novo Mesto Slovenia **59** C1
Novomikhaylovskiy Rus. Fed. **45** E3
Novomoskovsk Rus. Fed. **43** E3
Novomoskovs'k Ukr. **45** D2
Novomyrhorod Ukr. **45** D2
Novonikolayevskiy Rus. Fed. **45** F1
Novooleksiyivka Ukr. **45** D2

Novopokrovskaya Rus. Fed. **45** F2
Novopskov Ukr. **45** E2
Novorossiysk Rus. Fed. **45** E3
Novorzhev Rus. Fed. **42** C2
Novosergiyevka Rus. Fed. **41** E3
Novoshakhtinsk Rus. Fed. **45** E2
Novosibirsk Rus. Fed. **94** H3
Novosibirskiye Ostrova *is* Rus. Fed.
see New Siberia Islands
Novosil' Rus. Fed. **43** E3
Novosokol'niki Rus. Fed. **43** D2
Novotroyits'ke Ukr. **45** D2
Novoukrayinka Ukr. **45** D2
Novovolyns'k Ukr. **44** B1
Novozybkov Rus. Fed. **43** D3
Nový Jičín Czech Rep. **57** D3
Novyy Bor Rus. Fed. **40** E2
Novyy Oskol Rus. Fed. **45** E1
Novyy Port Rus. Fed. **40** G2
Novyy Urengoy Rus. Fed. **40** G2
Novyy Urgal Rus. Fed. **81** E1
Nowogard Pol. **56** D2
Nowra Austr. **117** E2
Now Shahr Iran **93** D2
Nowshera Pak. **86** B1
Nowy Sącz Pol. **57** E3
Nowy Targ Pol. **57** E3
Noyabr'sk Rus. Fed. **41** G2
Noyon France **58** C2
Nsanje Malawi **107** C1
Ntandembele Dem. Rep. Congo
104 B3
Ntungamo Uganda **105** D3
Nu'aym *reg.* Oman **91** C2
Nubian Desert Sudan **102** B2
Nudo Coropuna *mt.* Peru **150** B4
Nueltin Lake Can. **127** F1
Nueva Lubecka Arg. **153** A5
Nueva Rosita Mex. **143** B2
Nuevo Casas Grandes Mex.
142 B1
Nuevo Ideal Mex. **142** B2
Nuevo Laredo Mex. **143** C2
Nugaal *watercourse* Somalia **103** C4
Nuits-St-Georges France **59** C2
Nu Jiang *r.* China/Myanmar *see*
Salween
Nuku'alofa Tonga **113**
Nuku Hiva *i.* Fr. Polynesia **111**
Nukulaelae *atoll* Tuvalu **110**
Nukunonu *atoll* Tokelau **111**
Nukus Uzbek. **88** C2
Nulagine Austr. **114** B2
Nullarbor Plain Austr. **114** B3
Numan Nigeria **101** D4
Numazu Japan **79** C3
Numedal *val.* Norway **47** B3
Numfoor *i.* Indon. **71** C3
Numurkah Austr. **117** D3
Nunap Isua *c.* Greenland *see*
Farewell, Cape
Nunavik Can. **125** H3
Nunavut *admin. div.* Can. **124** G2
Nuneaton U.K. **53** C3
Nunivak Island U.S.A. **95** O3
Nuñomoral Spain **60** B1
Nuoro Italy **62** A2
Nuqrah Saudi Arabia **90** B2
Nuremberg Ger. **55** E3
Nuriootpa Austr. **116** B2
Nurmes Fin. **46** F3
Nürnberg Ger. *see* Nuremberg
Nu Shan *mts* China **74** A1
Nushki Pak. **86** A2
Nuuk Greenland **125** I2
Nuussuaq Greenland **125** I2
Nuussuaq *pen.* Greenland **125** I2
Nuwaybi' al Muzayyinah Egypt **92** B3
Nuweveldberge *mts* S. Africa **108** B3
Nyagan' Rus. Fed. **40** F2

Nyainqêntanglha Feng *mt.* China
87 D1
Nyainqêntanglha Shan *mts* China
87 D2
Nyala Sudan **103** A3
Nyandoma Rus. Fed. **40** D2
Nyanga *r.* Gabon **104** B3
Nyanga Zimbabwe **107** C1
Nyasa, Lake Africa **107** C1
Nyborg Denmark **47** C4
Nyborg Norway **46** F1
Nybro Sweden **47** D4
Nyeri Kenya **105** D3
Nyima China **87** C1
Nyingchi China **80** C2
Nyíregyháza Hungary **57** E3
Nykøbing Denmark **47** C5
Nyköping Sweden **47** D4
Nymagee Austr. **117** D2
Nynäshamn Sweden **47** D4
Nyngan Austr. **117** D2
Nyoman *r.* Belarus/Lith. **42** B3
Nyons France **59** D3
Nýřany Czech Rep. **55** F3
Nyrob Rus. Fed. **40** E2
Nyssa U.S.A. **132** C2
Nyunzu Dem. Rep. Congo **105** C3
Nyzhn'ohirs'kyy Ukr. **45** D2
Nzega Tanz. **105** D3
Nzérékoré Guinea **100** B4
N'zeto Angola **104** B3

Oahe, Lake U.S.A. **134** C2
Oahu *i.* U.S.A. **120**
Oakbank Austr. **116** C2
Oakdale U.S.A. **138** B2
Oakey Austr. **117** E1
Oak Harbor U.S.A. **132** B1
Oak Hill U.S.A. **136** D3
Oakland U.S.A. **133** B3
Oakover *r.* Austr. **114** B2
Oakridge U.S.A. **132** B2
Oak Ridge U.S.A. **139** D1
Oamaru N.Z. **118** B4
Oas Phil. **76** B2
Oaxaca Mex. **143** C3
Ob' *r.* Rus. Fed. **40** F2
Obala Cameroon **104** B2
Oban U.K. **50** B2
O Barco Spain **60** B1
Oberá Arg. **154** A3
Oberon Austr. **117** D2
Oberpfälzer Wald *mts* Ger. **55** F3
Oberviechtach Ger. **55** F3
Obi *i.* Indon. **71** C3
Óbidos Brazil **151** D3
Obihiro Japan **78** D2
Obluch'ye Rus. Fed. **81** E1
Obninsk Rus. Fed. **43** E2
Obo C.A.R. **105** C2
Obock Djibouti **103** C3
Obouya Congo **104** B3
Oboyan' Rus. Fed. **43** E3
Obregón, Presa *resr* Mex. **142** B2
Obrenovac Serb. and Mont. **64** B2
Obshchiy Syrt *hills* Rus. Fed. **41** E3
Obskaya Guba *sea chan.* Rus. Fed.
40 G2
Obuasi Ghana **100** B4
Obukhiv Ukr. **44** D1
Ob"yachevo Rus. Fed. **40** D2
Ocala U.S.A. **139** D3
Ocampo Mex. **142** B2
Ocaña Spain **60** C2
Occidental, Cordillera *mts* Col.
150 B2

ccidental, Cordillera *mts* Peru **150** B4
cean City U.S.A. **137** E3
cean Falls Can. **126** C2
ceanside U.S.A. **133** C4
chakiv Ukr. **45** D2
cher Rus. Fed. **40** E3
chsenfurt Ger. **55** E3
conee r. U.S.A. **139** D2
cosingo Mex. **143** C3
cussi *enclave* East Timor **71** C3
da, Jebel *mt.* Sudan **102** B2
date Japan **79** C7
dawara Japan **79** C3
dda Norway **47** B3
demira Port. **60** B2
demiş Turkey **65** D3
dense Denmark **47** C4
denwald *reg.* Ger. **55** D3
derbucht b. Ger. **56** C2
desa Ukr. **44** D2
dessa U.S.A. **141** C2
dienné Côte d'Ivoire **100** B4
dra r. Ger./Pol. **57** D3
eiras Brazil **151** E3
elde Ger. **54** D2
elrichs U.S.A. **134** C2
elsnitz Ger. **55** F2
enkerk Neth. **54** B1
fanto r. Italy **63** C2
fenbach am Main Ger. **55** D2
ffenburg Ger. **58** B3
gadën *reg.* Eth. **103** C4
ga-hantô *pen.* Japan **78** C3
gaki Japan **79** C3
gallala U.S.A. **134** C2
gbomosho Nigeria **100** C4
gden U.S.A. **132** D2
gdensburg U.S.A. **137** E2
gilvie r. Can. **124** C2
gilvie Mountains Can. **124** C2
gilvie, Mount U.S.A. **139** D2
glethorpe, Mount U.S.A. **139** D2
goki r. Can. **128** B1
goki Reservoir Can. **128** B1
gre Latvia **42** B2
gulin Croatia **62** C1
hio r. U.S.A. **137** C3
hio *state* U.S.A. **136** D2
hrdruf Ger. **55** E2
hrid *Macedonia* **65** B2
hringen Ger. **55** D3
iapoque Brazil **151** D2
il City U.S.A. **137** E2
se r. France **54** A3
ta Japan **79** B4
inaga Mex. **142** B2
os del Salado, Nevado *mt.*
Arg./Chile **152** B3
ta r. Rus. Fed. **43** F2
iahandja Namibia **106** A2
iakarara Namibia **106** A2
ianagan Falls Can. **126** D3
ianagan Lake Can. **126** D3
ianogan U.S.A. **132** C1
ianogan r. U.S.A. **132** C1
iara Pak. **86** B1
iavango r. Botswana/Namibia **106** B1
iavango Delta *swamp* Botswana
106 B1
iayama Japan **79** C4
iazaki Japan **79** B4
ieechobee, Lake U.S.A. **139** D3
iefenokee Swamp U.S.A. **139** D2
iehampton U.K. **53** A4
iha India **86** A2
iha Rus. Fed. **95** L3
ihaldhunga Nepal **87** C2
ihotka r. Rus. Fed. **95** L3
ihotsk Rus. Fed. **95** L3

Okhotsk, Sea of Japan/Rus. Fed.
95 L4
Okhtyrka Ukr. **45** D1
Okinawa i. Japan **81** E3
Oki-shotō *is* Japan **79** B3
Oklahoma *state* U.S.A. **141** E1
Oklahoma U.S.A. **141** E1
Okmulgee U.S.A. **141** E1
Oko, Wadi *watercourse* Sudan **90** A2
Okondja Gabon **104** B3
Okotoks Can. **126** D2
Okovskiy Les Rus. Fed. **43** D3
Okoyo Congo **104** B4
Øksfjord Norway **46** F1
Oktwin Myanmar **74** A2
Oktyabr'skiy *Arkhangel'skaya Oblast'*
Rus. Fed. **40** D2
Oktyabr'skiy *Kamchatskaya Oblast'*
Rus. Fed. **95** M3
Oktyabr'skiy *Respublika Bashkortostan*
Rus. Fed. **41** F3
Oktyabr'skoye Rus. Fed. **40** F2
Oktyabr'skoy Revolyutsii, Ostrov i.
Rus. Fed. **95** I1
Okulovka Rus. Fed. **43** D2
Okushiri-tō i. Japan **78** C2
Ólafsvík Iceland **46** [inset]
Öland i. Sweden **47** D4
Olary Austr. **116** C2
Olavarría Arg. **153** B4
Oława Pol. **57** D2
Olbernhau Ger. **55** F2
Olbia Italy **62** A2
Old Crow Can. **124** C2
Oldenburg Ger. **56** D1
Oldenburg in Holstein Ger. **56** C2
Oldenzaal Neth. **54** C1
Old Head of Kinsale *hd* Rep. of Ireland
51 B3
Olds Can. **126** D2
Old Wives Lake Can. **127** E2
Olean U.S.A. **137** E2
Olecko Pol. **57** E2
Olekminsk Rus. Fed. **95** K2
Oleksandriya Ukr. **45** D2
Ølen Norway **48** E2
Olenegorsk Rus. Fed. **46** G2
Olenek Rus. Fed. **95** J2
Olenek r. Rus. Fed. **95** J2
Olenino Rus. Fed. **43** D2
Olevs'k Ukr. **44** C1
Olhão Port. **60** B2
Olifants r. Moz./S. Africa **109** D1
Olifants S. Africa **109** D1
Olifants *watercourse* Namibia **108** A2
Olifants S. Africa **109** C1
Olifants r. S. Africa **108** A3
Olifantshoek S. Africa **108** B2
Olímpia Brazil **154** C2
Olinda Brazil **151** F3
Oliphants Drift S. Africa **109** C1
Oliva Spain **61** C2
Oliveira Brazil **155** C2
Olivenza Spain **60** B2
Ollagüe Chile **152** B3
Olmos Peru **150** B3
Olney U.S.A. **136** C3
Olomouc Czech Rep. **57** D3
Olongapo Phil. **76** B2
Oloron-Ste-Marie France **58** B3
Olot Spain **61** D1
Olovyannaya Rus. Fed. **81** D1
Olpe Ger. **54** C2
Olsztyn Pol. **57** E2
Olt r. Romania **44** B3
Oltu Turkey **93** C1
Olympia *tourist site* Greece **65** B3
Olympia U.S.A. **132** B1
Olympus, Mount Greece **65** B2
Olympus, Mount U.S.A. **132** B1
Olyutorskiy, Mys c. Rus. Fed. **95** N3

Omagh U.K. **51** C1
Omaha U.S.A. **135** D2
Oman *country* Asia **91** C2
Oman, Gulf of Asia **91** C2
Omaruru Namibia **106** A2
Omatako *watercourse* Namibia **106** B1
Omdurman Sudan **102** B3
Omeo Austr. **117** D3
Ometepec Mex. **143** C3
Om Hajër Eritrea **90** A3
Omineca Mountains Can. **126** C2
Ōmiya Japan **79** C3
Ommen Neth. **54** C1
Omolon r. Rus. Fed. **95** M2
Omont France **54** B3
Omsk Rus. Fed. **89** E1
Omsukchan Rus. Fed. **95** M2
Ōmu, Vârful mt. Romania **44** C2
Ōmura Japan **79** A4
Onancock U.S.A. **137** E3
Onaping Lake Can. **136** D1
Onatchiway, Lac l. Can. **129** C2
Oncócua Angola **106** A1
Onderstedorings S. Africa **108** B3
Ondjiva Angola **106** A1
Onega Rus. Fed. **40** C2
Onega r. Rus. Fed. **40** C2
Onega, Lake Rus. Fed. **40** C2
Oneida Lake U.S.A. **137** E2
O'Neill U.S.A. **135** D2
Oneonta U.S.A. **137** E2
Oneşti Romania **44** C2
Onezhskoye Ozero l. Rus. Fed. *see*
Onega, Lake
Ongers *watercourse* S. Africa **108** B2
Ongjin N. Korea **77** B2
Ongole India **85** C3
Onilahy r. Madag. **107** [inset] D2
Onitsha Nigeria **101** C4
Onotoa *atoll* Kiribati **110**
Onseepkans S. Africa **108** A2
Onslow Austr. **114** A2
Onslow Bay U.S.A. **139** E2
Ontario *prov.* Can. **128** A1
Ontario U.S.A. **132** C2
Ontario, Lake Can./U.S.A. **137** E2
Oodnadatta Austr. **116** B1
Oostende Belgium *see* Ostend
Oosterhout Neth. **54** B2
Oosterschelde *est.* Neth. **54** A2
Oost-Vlieland Neth. **54** B1
Ootsa Lake Can. **126** C2
Ootsa Lake l. Can. **126** C2
Opala Dem. Rep. Congo **104** C3
Opataca, Lac l. Can. **128** C1
Opava Czech Rep. **57** D3
Opelika U.S.A. **139** C2
Opelousas U.S.A. **138** B2
Opinaca, Réservoir resr Can. **128** C1
Opiscotéo, Lac l. Can. **129** C1
Opochka Rus. Fed. **42** C2
Opodepe Mex. **142** A2
Opole Pol. **57** D2
Oporto Port. **60** B1
Opotiki N.Z. **118** C1
Oppdal Norway **47** B3
Opunake N.Z. **118** B1
Opuwo Namibia **106** A1
Oradea Romania **44** B2
Orahovac Serb. and Mont. **64** B2
Oran Alg. **100** B1
Orán Arg. **152** B3
Örang N. Korea **77** B1
Orange France **59** C3
Orange r. Namibia/S. Africa **108** A2
Orange U.S.A. **141** F2
Orange, Cabo c. Brazil **146**
Orangeburg U.S.A. **139** D2
Orangeville Can. **137** D2

Orange Walk Belize **143** D3
Oranienburg Ger. **55** F1
Oranjemund Namibia **108** A2
Orapa Botswana **106** B2
Orăştie Romania **44** B2
Orbetello Italy **62** B2
Orbost Austr. **117** D3
Ord, Mount Austr. **114** B1
Ordes Spain **60** B1
Ordos China **82** B2
Ordu Turkey **92** B1
Ordzhonikidze Ukr. **45** D2
Örebro Sweden **47** D4
Oregon state U.S.A. **132** B2
Oregon City U.S.A. **132** B1
Orekhovo-Zuyevo Rus. Fed. **41** C3
Orel Rus. Fed. **43** E3
Orem U.S.A. **132** D2
Ören Turkey **65** C3
Orenburg Rus. Fed. **41** E3
Orepuki N.Z. **118** A4
Öresund str. Denmark/Sweden **47** C4
Orford Ness hd U.K. **53** D3
Orhaneli Turkey **65** C3
Orhangazi Turkey **65** C2
Orhon Gol r. Mongolia **95** J3
Oriental, Cordillera mts Bol. **152** B2
Oriental, Cordillera mts Col. **150** B2
Oriental, Cordillera mts Peru **150** B4
Orihuela Spain **61** C2
Orikhiv Ukr. **45** E2
Orillia Can. **128** C2
Orinoco r. Col./Venez. **150** C2
Orinoco Delta Venez. **150** C2
Orissaare Estonia **42** B2
Oristano Italy **62** A3
Orivesi l. Fin. **46** F3
Oriximiná Brazil **151** D3
Orizaba Mex. **143** C3
Orizaba, Pico de vol. Mex. **143** C3
Orkanger Norway **46** B3
Örkelljunga Sweden **47** C4
Orkla r. Norway **46** B3
Orkney Islands Scotland U.K. **50** C1
Orlândia Brazil **154** C2
Orlando U.S.A. **139** D3
Orléans France **58** C2
Ormara Pak. **86** A2
Ormoc Phil. **76** B2
Ormskirk U.K. **52** B3
Örnsköldsvik Sweden **46** D3
Orodara Burkina **100** B3
Orofino U.S.A. **132** C1
Orona atoll Kiribati **111**
Oroquieta Phil. **76** B3
Orosei Italy **62** A2
Orosei, Golfo di b. Italy **62** A2
Orosháza Hungary **57** E3
Oroville U.S.A. **133** B3
Orroroo Austr. **116** B2
Orsha Belarus **43** D3
Orsk Rus. Fed. **41** E3
Ørsta Norway **47** B3
Ortegal, Cabo c. Spain **60** B1
Orthez France **58** B3
Ortigueira Spain **60** B1
Ortonville U.S.A. **135** D1
Orulgan, Khrebet mts Rus. Fed. **95** K2
Orūmīyeh, Daryācheh-ye salt l. Iran see Urmia, Lake
Oruro Bol. **152** B2
Orvieto Italy **62** B2
Osa, Península de pen. Costa Rica **144** B4
Osage r. U.S.A. **135** E3
Ōsaka Japan **79** C4
Oschersleben (Bode) Ger. **55** E1
Oschiri Italy **62** A2

Osetr r. Rus. Fed. **43** E3
Osh Kyrg. **89** E2
Oshakati Namibia **106** A1
Oshawa Can. **128** C2
Ō-shima i. Japan **78** C2
Ō-shima i. Japan **79** C4
Oshkosh U.S.A. **136** C2
Oshnovīyeh Iran **93** C2
Oshogbo Nigeria **100** C4
Oshwe Dem. Rep. Congo **104** B3
Osijek Croatia **63** C1
Osilinka r. Can. **126** C2
Osimo Italy **62** B2
Osizweni S. Africa **109** D2
Oskaloosa U.S.A. **135** E2
Oskarshamn Sweden **47** D4
Oskol r. Rus. Fed. **43** E3
Oslo Norway **47** C4
Oslofjorden sea chan. Norway **47** C4
Osmancık Turkey **92** B1
Osmaneli Turkey **65** C2
Osmaniye Turkey **92** B2
Os'mino Rus. Fed. **42** C2
Osnabrück Ger. **54** T1
Osorno Chile **153** A5
Osorno Spain **60** C1
Osoyoos Can. **126** D3
Osøyri Norway **48** E1
Oss Neth. **54** B2
Ossa, Mount Austr. **115** D4
Ossora Rus. Fed. **95** M3
Ostashkov Rus. Fed. **43** D2
Oste r. Ger. **55** D1
Ostend Belgium **54** A2
Osterburg (Altmark) Ger. **55** E1
Österdalälven l. Sweden **47** D3
Osterholz-Scharmbeck Ger. **55** D1
Osterode am Harz Ger. **55** E2
Östersund Sweden **46** C3
Ostfriesland reg. Ger. **54** C1
Östhammar Sweden **47** D3
Ostrava Czech Rep. **57** D3
Ostróda Pol. **57** D2
Ostrogozhsk Rus. Fed. **43** E3
Ostrołęka Pol. **57** E2
Ostrov Czech Rep. **55** F2
Ostrov Rus. Fed. **42** C2
Ostrovskoye Rus. Fed. **43** F2
Ostrowiec Świętokrzyski Pol. **57** E2
Ostrów Mazowiecka Pol. **57** E2
Ostrów Wielkopolski Pol. **57** D2
Osūm r. Bulg. **64** B2
Ōsumi-kaikyō sea chan. Japan **79** B4
Ōsumi-shotō is Japan **79** B4
Osuna Spain **60** B2
Oswego U.S.A. **137** E2
Oswestry U.K. **52** B3
Ōta Japan **79** C3
Otago Peninsula N.Z. **118** B3
Otaki N.Z. **118** C3
Otaru Japan **78** D2
Otavi Namibia **106** A1
Othello U.S.A. **132** C1
Otjiwarongo Namibia **106** A1
Otoro, Jebel mt. Sudan **103** B3
Otra r. Norway **47** B4
Otranto, Strait of Albania/Italy **65** C2
Ōtsu Japan **79** C3
Otta Norway **47** B3
Ottawa Can. **128** C2
Ottawa r. Can. **128** C2
Ottawa r. U.S.A. **135** C2
Ottawa KS U.S.A. **135** D3
Ottawa Islands Can. **128** B1
Otter Rapids Can. **128** B2
Ottignies Belgium **54** B2
Ottumwa U.S.A. **135** E2

Otuzco Peru **150** B3
Otway, Cape Austr. **116** C3
Ouachita r. U.S.A. **138** B2
Ouachita, Lake U.S.A. **138** B2
Ouachita Mountains U.S.A. **138** B2
Ouadda C.A.R. **104** C2
Ouaddaï reg. Chad **101** D3
Ouagadougou Burkina **100** B3
Ouahigouya Burkina **100** B3
Oualâta Maur. **100** B3
Ouanda-Djallé C.A.R. **104** C2
Ouarâne reg. Maur. **100** B2
Ouargla Alg. **101** C1
Ouarzazate Morocco **100** B1
Oudenaarde Belgium **54** A2
Oudtshoorn S. Africa **108** B3
Oued Tlélat Alg. **61** C2
Ouessa Burkina **100** B3
Ouessant, Île d' i. France **58** A2
Ouesso Congo **104** B3
Ouistreham France **53** C5
Oujda Morocco **100** B1
Ouled Farès Alg. **61** D2
Oulu Fin. **46** F2
Oulujärvi l. Fin. **46** F3
Oulx Italy **62** A1
Oum-Chalouba Chad **101** E3
Oum-Hadjer Chad **101** D3
Ounianga Kébir Chad **101** E3
Oupeye Belgium **54** B2
Our r. Lux. **54** C3
Ourense Spain **60** B1
Ourinhos Brazil **154** C2
Ouro Preto Brazil **155** D2
Ourthe r. Belgium **54** B2
Ouse r. U.K. **52** C3
Outardes r. Can. **129** D2
Outardes Quatre, Réservoir resr Can. **129** D1
Outer Hebrides is U.K. **50** A2
Outjo Namibia **106** A2
Outlook Can. **127** E2
Outokumpu Fin. **46** F3
Ouyen Austr. **116** C3
Ovar Port. **60** B1
Överkalix Sweden **46** E2
Overton U.S.A. **133** D3
Övertorneå Sweden **46** E2
Oviedo Spain **60** B1
Øvre Årdal Norway **47** B3
Øvre Rendal Norway **47** C3
Ovruch Ukr. **44** C1
Owando Congo **104** B3
Owase Japan **79** C4
Owatonna U.S.A. **135** E2
Owensboro U.S.A. **136** C3
Owens Lake U.S.A. **133** C3
Owen Sound Can. **128** B2
Owerri Nigeria **101** C4
Owosso U.S.A. **136** D2
Owyhee U.S.A. **132** C2
Owyhee r. U.S.A. **132** C2
Oxelösund Sweden **42** A2
Oxford N.Z. **118** B3
Oxford U.K. **53** C4
Oxford U.S.A. **138** C2
Oxford Lake Can. **127** F2
Oxley Austr. **116** C2
Oxnard U.S.A. **133** C4
Oyama Japan **79** C3
Oyem Gabon **104** B2
Oyen Can. **127** D2
Oyonnax France **59** D2
Ozamiz Phil. **76** B3
Ozark U.S.A. **139** C2
Ozark Plateau U.S.A. **135** E3
Ozarks, Lake of the U.S.A. **135** E3
Ozernovskiy Rus. Fed. **95** M3
Ozersk Rus. Fed. **42** B3
Ozery Rus. Fed. **43** E3
Ozinki Rus. Fed. **41** D3

amiut Greenland **125** I2
arl S. Africa **108** A3
bianice Pol. **57** D2
bna Bangl. **87** C2
chino Italy **62** C3
chuca Mex. **143** C2
cific Ocean **158**
czków Pol. **57** D2
dang Indon. **72** B2
dang Endau Malaysia **72** B1
dangpanjang Indon. **72** B2
dangsidimpuan Indon. **72** A1
derborn Ger. **55** D2
dova Italy *see* Padua
dre Island U.S.A. **141** E3
dthaway Austr. **116** C3
dua Italy **62** B1
ducah *KY* U.S.A. **136** C3
ducah *TX* U.S.A. **141** D2
egam N. Korea **77** B1
engnyŏng-do *i.* S. Korea **77** A2
eroa N.Z. **118** C2
fos Cyprus *see* Paphos
gadian Phil. **76** B3
gai Selatan *i.* Indon. **72** B2
gai Utara *i.* Indon. **72** B2
gan *i.* N. Mariana Is **71** D1
gatan Indon. **73** C2
ge U.S.A. **140** B1
gégiai Lith. **42** B2
gosa Springs U.S.A. **134** B3
de Estonia **42** C2
jänne *l.* Fin. **47** F3
kü Co *l.* China **87** C2
mio Fin. **47** F3
nted Desert U.S.A. **140** B1
isley U.K. **50** B3
ala Sweden **46** E2
karaima Mountains
S. America **146**
kistan *country* Asia **86** A2
kokku Myanmar **74** A1
kruojis Lith. **42** B2
ks Laos **74** B2
kwash Lake Can. **128** A1
kxé Laos **75** D2
na Chad **101** D4
labuhanratu, Teluk *b.* Indon. **72** B2
laikastro Greece **65** C3
laiochora Greece **65** C3
lamakoloi Botswana **108** B1
lamós Spain **61** D1
lana Rus. Fed. **95** M3
langaraya Indon. **73** C2
lanpur India **86** B2
lapye Botswana **109** C1
lau Islands Palau **67**
lau country N. Pacific Ocean **71** C2
law Myanmar **75** A2
lawan *i.* Phil. **76** A3
ldiski Estonia **42** B2
lelh Rus. Fed. **43** F2
lembang Indon. **72** B2
lepon Gabon **100** C1
lenque Mex. **143** C3
lermo Italy **62** B3
lestine U.S.A. **141** E2
letwa Myanmar **74** A1
li India **86** B2
likir Micronesia **112**

Palinuro, Capo *c.* Italy **62** C2
Paliouri, Akra *pt* Greece **65** B3
Paliseul Belgium **54** B3
Paljakka *h.* Fin. **46** F3
Palkino Rus. Fed. **42** C2
Palk Strait India/Sri Lanka **85** B4
Palma del Río Spain **60** B2
Palma de Mallorca Spain **61** D2
Palmas *Paraná* Brazil **154** B3
Palmas Brazil **151** E4
Palmas, Cape Liberia **100** B4
Palmeira Brazil **154** C3
Palmeirais Brazil **151** E3
Palmer U.S.A. **124** C2
Palmer Land *reg.* Antarctica
119 K3
Palmerston North N.Z. **118** C3
Palmi Italy **63** C3
Palmillas Mex. **143** C2
Palmira Col. **150** B3
Palm Springs U.S.A. **133** C4
Palmyra Atoll *terr.*
N. Pacific Ocean **113**
Paloich Sudan **103** B3
Palomares Mex. **143** C3
Palopo Indon. **73** D2
Palos, Cabo de *c.* Spain **61** C2
Paltamo Fin. **46** F3
Palu *i.* Indon. **72** B2
Palyavaam *r.* Rus. Fed. **95** N2
Pamiers France **58** C3
Pamir *mts* Asia **89** B3
Pamlico Sound *sea chan.* U.S.A.
139 E1
Pampa Grande Bol. **152** B2
Pampas *reg.* Arg. **153** B4
Pamplona *l.* Fin. **47** F3
Pamplona Spain **61** C1
Pamukova Turkey **65** D2
Panaitan *i.* Indon. **72** B2
Panaji India **85** B2
Panama *country* Central America
144 B4
Panama, Gulf of Panama **144** C4
Panama Canal Panama **144** C4
Panama City Panama **144** C4
Panama City U.S.A. **139** C2
Panamint Range *mts* U.S.A. **133** C3
Panarik Indon. **72** B1
Panay *i.* Phil. **76** B2
Pančevo Serb. and Mont. **64** B2
Panda Moz. **109** D1
Pandan Phil. **76** B2
Pandaria India **87** C1
Pandharpur India **85** B3
Panevėžys Lith. **42** B2
Pangkalanbuun Indon. **73** C2
Pangkalansusu Indon. **72** A1
Pangkalpinang Indon. **72** B2
Pangnirtung Can. **125** H2
Pangody Rus. Fed. **40** G2
Panino Rus. Fed. **43** F3
Panipat India **86** B2
Panjgur Pak. **86** A2
Pan Ling *mts* China **77** C1
Panna India **87** C2
Pannawonica Austr. **114** A2
Panorama Brazil **154** B2
Panshi China **77** B1
Pantanal *reg.* Brazil **152** C2
Pánuco Mex. **143** C2
Panxian China **83** A3
Panzhihua China **74** B1
Paola Italy **63** C3
Paôy Pêt Cambodia **75** B2
Pápa Hungary **57** D3
Papakura N.Z. **118** B2
Papantla Mex. **143** C2

Papeete Fr. Polynesia **113**
Papenburg Ger. **54** C1
Paphos Cyprus **92** B2
Papua, Gulf of P.N.G. **71** D3
Papua New Guinea *country* Oceania
71 D3
Para *r.* Rus. Fed. **43** F3
Paraburdoo Austr. **114** A2
Paracatu Brazil **154** C1
Paracatu *r.* Brazil **155** C1
Parachilna Austr. **116** B2
Paracín Serb. and Mont. **64** B2
Pará de Minas Brazil **155** D1
Paradise U.S.A. **133** B3
Paragould U.S.A. **138** B1
Paraguai *r.* Brazil **151** D4
Paraguay *r.* Arg./Para. **152** C3
Paraguay *country* S. America **152** B3
Paraíba do Sul *r.* Brazil **155** D2
Paraíso Mex. **143** C3
Parakou Benin **100** C4
Paramaribo Suriname **151** D2
Paraná Arg. **152** B4
Paraná *r.* S. America **154** B2
Paranaguá Brazil **154** C3
Paranaíba Brazil **154** B1
Paranaíba *r.* Brazil **154** B2
Paranapanema *r.* Brazil **154** B2
Paranapiacaba, Serra *mts* Brazil
154 B2
Paranavaí Brazil **154** B2
Paraparaumu N.Z. **118** B3
Paratí Brazil **155** D2
Paraúna Brazil **154** B1
Paray-le-Monial France **59** C2
Parbhani India **85** B3
Parchim Ger. **55** E1
Pardo *r.* Bahia Brazil **155** E1
Pardo *r.* Mato Grosso do Sul Brazil
154 B2
Pardo *r.* São Paulo Brazil **154** C2
Pardubice Czech Rep. **57** E2
Parecis, Serra dos *hills* Brazil **150** C4
Parent, Lac *l.* Can. **128** C2
Parepare Indon. **73** C2
Parga Greece **65** B3
Pargas Fin. **42** B3
Parghelia Italy **63** C3
Paria, Gulf of Trin. and Tob./Venez.
145 D3
Parima, Serra *mts* Brazil **150** C2
Parintins Brazil **151** D3
Paris France **58** C2
Paris *TN* U.S.A. **138** C1
Paris *TX* U.S.A. **141** E2
Parkano Fin. **47** E3
Parker U.S.A. **140** B2
Parkersburg U.S.A. **136** D3
Parkes Austr. **117** D2
Park Falls U.S.A. **136** B1
Park Rapids U.S.A. **135** D1
Parma Italy **62** B2
Parnaíba Brazil **151** E3
Parnaíba *r.* Brazil **151** E3
Parnassos *mt.* Greece **65** B3
Parnassus N.Z. **118** B3
Parnon *mts* Greece **65** B3
Pärnu Estonia **42** B2
P'aro-ho *l.* S. Korea **77** B2
Paroo *watercourse* Austr. **116** C2
Paropamisus *mts* Afgh. **86** A1
Paros *i.* Greece **65** C3
Parras Mex. **142** B2
Parry, Cape Can. **124** D2
Parry Channel Can. **140**
Parry Islands Can. **124** E1
Parry Sound Can. **128** B2
Parsons U.S.A. **135** D3

Partenstein Ger. **55** D2
Parthenay France **58** B2
Partry Mountains Rep. of Ireland **51** B2
Paru r. Brazil **151** D3
Pasadena U.S.A. **133** C4
Pascagoula U.S.A. **138** C2
Paşcani Romania **44** C2
Pasco U.S.A. **132** C1
Pasewalk Ger. **56** C2
Pasfield Lake Can. **127** E2
Pasha Rus. Fed. **43** D1
Pasir Putih Malaysia **72** B1
Pasni Pak. **86** A2
Paso Río Mayo Arg. **153** A5
Paso Robles U.S.A. **133** B3
Passa Tempo Brazil **155** C3
Passau Ger. **56** C3
Passo Fundo Brazil **152** C3
Passos Brazil **155** C2
Pastavy Belarus **42** C2
Pastaza r. Peru **150** B3
Pasto Col. **150** B2
Pasuruan Indon. **73** C2
Pasvalys Lith. **42** B2
Patagonia reg. Arg. **153** A6
Patan Nepal **87** C2
Patea N.Z. **118** E4
Paterson U.S.A. **137** F2
Pathfinder Reservoir U.S.A. **134** B2
Pati Indon. **73** C2
Patkai Bum mts India/Myanmar **74** A1
Patmos i. Greece **65** C3
Patna India **87** C2
Patnos Turkey **93** C2
Pato Branco Brazil **154** B3
Patos, Lagoa dos l. Brazil **152** C4
Patos de Minas Brazil **155** C1
Patquía Arg. **152** B4
Patras Greece **65** B3
Patratu India **87** C2
Patrocínio Brazil **154** C1
Pattani Thai. **75** B3
Pattaya Thai. **75** B2
Patterson, Mount Can. **126** B1
Pattullo, Mount Can. **126** C2
Patuanak Can. **127** E2
Pátzcuaro Mex. **142** B3
Pau France **58** B3
Pauillac France **58** B2
Pauk Myanmar **74** A1
Paulistana Brazil **151** E3
Paulo Afonso Brazil **151** F3
Paulpietersburg S. Africa **109** D2
Pauls Valley U.S.A. **141** E2
Paungde Myanmar **74** A2
Pavão Brazil **155** D1
Pavia Italy **62** A1
Pāvilosta Latvia **42** B2
Pavlikeni Bulg. **64** C3
Pavlodar Kazakh. **89** E1
Pavlohrad Ukr. **45** E2
Pavlovo Rus. Fed. **43** F2
Pavlovsk Rus. Fed. **45** F1
Pavlovskaya Rus. Fed. **45** E2
Payakumbuh Indon. **72** B2
Payette U.S.A. **132** C2
Payette r. U.S.A. **132** C2
Pay-Khoy, Khrebet hills Rus. Fed. **40** F2
Payne, Lac l. Can. **128** C1
Paysandú Uru. **152** C4
Pazar Turkey **93** C1
Pazardzhik Bulg. **64** B2
Pazarköy Turkey **65** C3
Pazin Croatia **62** E1
Pe Myanmar **75** A2
Peace r. Can. **126** D2
Peace River Can. **126** D2

Peale, Mount U.S.A. **133** E3
Pearl r. U.S.A. **138** C2
Pearsall U.S.A. **141** E3
Pebane Moz. **107** C1
Peć Serb. and Mont. **64** C3
Peçanha Brazil **155** D1
Pechora r. Rus. Fed. **40** E2
Pechora r. Rus. Fed. **40** E2
Pechory Rus. Fed. **42** C2
Pecos U.S.A. **141** D2
Pecos r. U.S.A. **141** D3
Pécs Hungary **57** D3
Pedra Azul Brazil **155** D1
Pedregulho Brazil **154** C2
Pedreiras Brazil **151** E3
Pedro, Point pt Sri Lanka **85** C4
Pedro Afonso Brazil **151** E3
Pedro Gomes Brazil **154** B1
Pedro Juan Caballero Para. **152** C3
Peebles U.K. **50** C3
Dee Dee r. U.S.A. **139** E2
Peel r. Can. **124** D2
Peel Isle of Man **52** A2
Peerless Lake Can. **126** D2
Pegasus Bay N.Z. **118** D3
Pegnitz Ger. **55** E3
Pegu Myanmar **74** A2
Pegu Yoma mts Myanmar **74** A2
Pehuajó Arg. **153** B4
Peine Ger. **55** F1
Peipus, Lake Estonia/Rus. Fed. **42** C2
Peixe r. Brazil **154** B2
Peixoto de Azevedo Brazil **152** C2
Pekalongan Indon. **73** B2
Pekan Malaysia **72** B1
Pekanbaru Indon. **72** B1
Peking China see Beijing
Pelee Island Can. **128** B2
Peleng i. Indon. **73** D2
Pelkosenniemi Fin. **46** F2
Pella S. Africa **108** A2
Pelleluhu Islands P.N.G. **71** D3
Pello Fin. **46** E2
Pelly r. Can. **126** B1
Pelly Mountains Can. **126** B1
Pelotas Brazil **152** C3
Pelotas, Rio das r. Brazil **152** C3
Pemadumcook Lake U.S.A. **137** G1
Pemangkat Indon. **72** B1
Pematangsiantar Indon. **72** A1
Pemba Moz. **107** D1
Pemba Zambia **106** B1
Pemba Island Tanz. **105** D3
Pemberton Can. **126** C3
Pembina r. Can. **135** D1
Pembroke Can. **128** C2
Pembroke U.K. **53** A4
Peña Nevada, Cerro mt. Mex. **143** C2
Penápolis Brazil **154** B2
Peñaranda de Bracamonte Spain **60** B1
Peñarroya mt. Spain **61** C1
Peñarroya-Pueblonuevo Spain **60** B2
Peñas, Cabo de c. Spain **60** B1
Penas, Golfo de g. Chile **153** A5
Peña Ubiña mt. Spain **60** B1
Pendleton U.S.A. **132** C1
Pendleton Bay Can. **126** C2
Pend Oreille Lake U.S.A. **132** C1
Penganga r. India **86** B3
Penge S. Africa **109** D1
Penglai China **83** A3
Pengshui China **83** A3
Peniche Port. **60** B2
Penicuik U.K. **50** C3
Peninsular Malaysia Malaysia **72** B1
Penne Italy **62** B2
Pennines hills U.K. **52** B2
Pennsylvania state U.S.A. **137** E2
Penobscot r. U.S.A. **137** G2

Penola Austr. **116** C3
Penong Austr. **114** C3
Penrhyn atoll Cook Is **111**
Penrith U.K. **52** B2
Pensacola U.S.A. **138** C2
Pensacola Mountains Antarctica **119** K1
Pensiangan Malaysia **73** C1
Penticton Can. **126** D3
Pentland Firth sea chan. U.K. **50** C1
Penygadair h. U.K. **53** B3
Penza Rus. Fed. **43** D1
Penzance U.S.A. **53** A4
Peoria U.S.A. **136** C2
Perales del Alfambra Spain **61** C1
Percy Isles Austr. **115** E2
Peregrebnoye Rus. Fed. **40** F2
Pereira Col. **150** B2
Pereira Barreto Brazil **154** B2
Peremyshlyany Ukr. **44** B2
Pereslavl'-Zalesskiy Rus. Fed. **43** E2
Pereyaslav-Khmel'nyts'kyy Ukr. **45** D2
Pergamino Arg. **153** B4
Perhonjoki r. Fin. **46** E3
Péribonka, Lac l. Can. **129** C1
Perico Arg. **152** B3
Pericos Mex. **142** B2
Périgueux France **58** C2
Perija, Sierra de mts Venez. **145** C3
Perito Moreno Arg. **153** A5
Perleberg Ger. **55** E1
Perm' Rus. Fed. **40** E3
Pernatty Lagoon salt flat Austr. **116** B2
Pernik Bulg. **64** A1
Péronne France **58** C2
Perote Mex. **143** C3
Perpignan France **58** C3
Perranporth U.K. **53** A4
Perry FL U.S.A. **139** D2
Perry GA U.S.A. **139** D2
Perry IA U.S.A. **135** E2
Perryton U.S.A. **141** D1
Perryville U.S.A. **135** F3
Pershore U.K. **53** B3
Pershotravens'k Ukr. **45** E2
Perth Austr. **114** A3
Perth U.K. **50** C2
Pertuis France **59** D3
Pertusato, Capo c. France **62** A2
Peru country S. America **150** B3
Perugia Italy **62** B2
Peruíbe Brazil **154** C2
Péruwelz Belgium **54** A2
Pervomays'k Ukr. **44** D2
Pervomays'ke Ukr. **45** D2
Pervomayskiy Rus. Fed. **43** F3
Pervomays'kyy Ukr. **45** E2
Pesaro Italy **62** B2
Pescara Italy **62** B2
Pescara r. Italy **62** B2
Peschanokopskoye Rus. Fed. **45** E2
Peshawar Pak. **86** B1
Peshkopi Albania **64** B2
Pesnica Slovenia **62** C1
Pessac France **58** B3
Pestovo Rus. Fed. **43** E2
Pestyaki Rus. Fed. **43** F2
Petatlán Mex. **142** B3
Petenwell Lake U.S.A. **136** C2
Peterborough Austr. **116** B2
Peterborough Can. **128** C2
Peterborough U.K. **53** C3
Peterhead U.K. **50** D2
Petermann Ranges mts Austr. **114** C2
Peter Pond Lake Can. **127** E2
Petersburg U.S.A. **126** B2
Petersburg VA U.S.A. **137** E3
Petershagen Ger. **55** D1
Petit Mécatina r. Can. **129** E2
Peto Mex. **143** D2

etoskey U.S.A. **136** D1
etra tourist site Jordan **92** B2
etra Velikogo, Zaliv b. Rus. Fed. **78** B2
etrich Bulg. **65** B2
etrolina Brazil **151** E3
etropavlovsk Kazakh. **89** D1
etropavlovsk-Kamchatskiy Rus. Fed. **95** M3
etroşani Romania **44** B2
etrovskaya Rus. Fed. **43** F3
etrovskoye Rus. Fed. **43** F3
etrozavodsk Rus. Fed. **40** C2
etrusburg S. Africa **109** C2
etrus Steyn S. Africa **109** C2
etrusville S. Africa **108** B3
etukhovo Rus. Fed. **41** F3
etushki Rus. Fed. **43** E2
eureula Indon. **72** A1
evek Rus. Fed. **95** N2
forzheim Ger. **56** B3
funds Austria **56** C3
ungstadt Ger. **55** D3
ahameng S. Africa **109** C2
halaborwa S. Africa **109** D1
halodi India **86** B2
hang Hoei, San Khao mts Thai. **75** B2
hangnga Thai. **75** A3
han Rang Vietnam **75** D3
han Thiêt Vietnam **75** B2
aatthalung Thai. **75** B3
aayao Thai. **74** A2
elps Lake Can. **127** E2
enix City U.S.A. **139** C2
et Buri Thai. **75** A2
ichit Thai. **74** B2
iladelphia U.S.A. **137** E3
ilip U.S.A. **134** C2
ilippeville Belgium **54** B2
ilippine Neth. **54** A2
ilippines country Asia **76** B2
ilippine Sea N. Pacific Ocean **71** C1
ilippsburg Ger. **55** D3
ilip Smith Mountains U.S.A. **124** C2
illipstown S. Africa **108** B3
illipsburg U.S.A. **135** D3
iritona S. Africa **109** C2
itsanulok Thai. **74** B2
nom Penh Cambodia **75** B2
oenix U.S.A. **140** B2
oenix Islands Kiribati **111**
on Thai. **75** B2
ôngsali Laos **74** B1
rae Thai. **74** B2
uket Thai. **75** A3
umi Sâmraông Cambodia **75** B2
uthaditjhaba S. Africa **109** C2
yu Myanmar **74** A2
acenza Italy **62** A1
anosa, Isola i. Italy **59** E3
atra Neamţ Romania **44** C2
aui r. Brazil **151** E3
ave r. Italy **62** B1
por r. Sudan **103** B4
por Post Sudan **103** B4
cayune U.S.A. **138** C2
chanal Arg. **152** B3
chilingue Mex. **142** A2
ckering U.K. **52** C2
ckle Lake Can. **128** A1
ctos Brazil **151** E3
cton Austr. **117** E2
ston N.Z. **118** B3
dras Negras Guat. **143** C3
dras Negras Mex. **143** D2
dräsämäki Fin. **46** F3
hainen r. Fin. **46** F3
erre U.S.A. **134** C2

Pierrelatte France **59** C3
Pietermaritzburg S. Africa **109** D2
Pietersburg S. Africa see Polokwane
Pietrosa mt. Romania **44** B2
Pigeon Lake Can. **126** D2
Pigüé Arg. **153** B4
Pihtipudas Fin. **46** F3
Pijijiapan Mex. **143** C3
Pikes Peak U.S.A. **134** C3
Piketberg S. Africa **108** A3
Pikeville U.S.A. **136** D3
Piła Pol. **57** D2
Pilar Arg. **153** C4
Pilar Para. **152** C3
Pilliga Austr. **117** D2
Piloes, Serra dos mts Brazil **154** C1
Pimenta Bueno Brazil **150** C4
Pinamar Arg. **153** C4
Pınarbaşı Turkey **92** B2
Pinar del Rio Cuba **144** B2
Pińczów Pol. **57** E2
Pindaré r. Brazil **151** E3
Pindos mts Greece see Pindus Mountains
Pine Bluff U.S.A. **138** B2
Pine Creek Austr. **114** C1
Pinedale U.S.A. **134** B2
Pinega Rus. Fed. **40** D2
Pinehouse Lake Can. **127** E2
Pineios r. Greece **65** B3
Pine Point Can. **126** D1
Pine Ridge U.S.A. **134** C2
Pinetown S. Africa **109** D2
Pingdingshan China **82** B2
Pingguo China **83** A3
Pingjiang China **83** B3
Pingliang China **82** A2
P'ingtung Taiwan **83** C3
Pingxiang Guangxi China **83** A3
Pingxiang Jiangxi China **83** B3
Pingyin China **82** B2
Pinheiro Brazil **151** E3
Pinneberg Ger. **55** D1
Pinotepa Nacional Mex. **143** C3
Pinsk Belarus **42** C3
Pioche U.S.A. **133** D3
Piodi Dem. Rep. Congo **105** C3
Pionki Pol. **57** E2
Piotrków Trybunalski Pol. **57** D2
Pipestone U.S.A. **135** D2
Pipmuacan, Réservoir resr Can. **129** C2
Piquiri r. Brazil **154** C1
Piracanjuba Brazil **154** C1
Piracicaba Brazil **154** C2
Piracicaba r. Brazil **155** D1
Piraçununga Brazil **154** C2
Piraeus Greece **65** B3
Piraí do Sul Brazil **154** C2
Pirajuí Brazil **154** C2
Piranhas Brazil **151** E3
Piranhas r. Brazil **151** E3
Pirapora Brazil **155** D1
Pires do Rio Brazil **154** C1
Piripiri Brazil **151** E3
Pirmasens Ger. **54** C3
Pirna Ger. **55** F2
Piru Indon. **71** C3
Pisa Italy **62** B2
Pisagua Chile **152** A2
Pisco Peru **150** B4
Písek Czech Rep. **56** C3
Pishin Iran **91** D2
Pisté Mex. **143** D2
Pisticci Italy **63** C2
Pistoia Italy **62** B2
Pisuerga r. Spain **60** C1
Pit r. U.S.A. **132** B2

Pitanga Brazil **154** B2
Pitangui Brazil **155** D1
Pitcairn Island Pitcairn Is **111**
Pitcairn Islands terr. S. Pacific Ocean **113**
Piteå Sweden **46** E2
Piteålven r. Sweden **46** E2
Piteşti Romania **44** B3
Pithoragarh India **87** C2
Pitlochry U.K. **50** C2
Pitt Island Can. **126** B2
Pittsburg U.S.A. **135** E3
Pittsburgh U.S.A. **137** E2
Pittsfield U.S.A. **137** F2
Pittsworth Austr. **117** E1
Piumhi Brazil **155** C2
Piura Peru **150** A3
Pivdennyy Buh r. Ukr. **44** D2
Placentia Can. **129** E2
Placerville U.S.A. **133** B3
Placetas Cuba **144** C2
Plainview U.S.A. **141** D2
Planaltina Brazil **154** C1
Plaquemine U.S.A. **138** B2
Plasencia Spain **60** B1
Plasy Czech Rep. **55** F3
Plato Col. **145** C4
Platte r. U.S.A. **135** D2
Plattsburgh U.S.A. **137** F2
Plau Ger. **55** F1
Plauen Ger. **55** F2
Plauer See l. Ger. **55** F1
Plavsk Rus. Fed. **43** E3
Plây Cu Vietnam **75** B2
Playgreen Lake Can. **127** F2
Plaza Huincul Arg. **153** B4
Pleasanton U.S.A. **141** E3
Pleasant Point N.Z. **118** B3
Pléaux France **58** C2
Pledger Lake Can. **128** B1
Pleinfeld Ger. **55** E3
Plenty, Bay of g. N.Z. **118** C2
Plentywood U.S.A. **134** C1
Plesetsk Rus. Fed. **40** D2
Plétipi, Lac l. Can. **129** C1
Plettenberg Ger. **54** C2
Plettenberg Bay S. Africa **108** B3
Pleven Bulg. **64** B2
Pljevlja Serb. and Mont. **64** C2
Ploče Croatia **63** C2
Płock Pol. **57** D2
Pločno mt. Bos.-Herz. **63** C2
Ploemeur France **58** B2
Ploieşti Romania **44** C3
Ploskoye Rus. Fed. **43** F2
Plouzané France **58** B2
Plovdiv Bulg. **64** B2
Plungė Lith. **42** B2
Plyeshchanitsy Belarus **42** C3
Plymouth Montserrat **145** D3
Plymouth U.K. **53** A4
Plymouth U.S.A. **136** C2
Plyussa Rus. Fed. **42** C2
Plzeň Czech Rep. **56** C3
Pô Burkina **100** B3
Po r. Italy **62** B1
Pobeda Peak China/Kyrg. **89** E3
Pocahontas U.S.A. **138** B1
Pocatello U.S.A. **132** D2
Pochayiv Ukr. **44** C1
Pochep Rus. Fed. **43** D3
Pochinok Rus. Fed. **43** D3
Pochutla Mex. **143** C3
Pocomoke City U.S.A. **137** E3
Poços de Caldas Brazil **155** C2
Podbořany Czech Rep. **55** F2
Poddor'ye Rus. Fed. **43** D2
Podgorenskiy Rus. Fed. **45** E1
Podgorica Serb. and Mont. **64** A2
Podgornoye Rus. Fed. **94** H3

Podkamennaya Tunguska *r.* Rus. Fed. **95** I2
Podol'sk Rus. Fed. **43** E2
Podujevo Serb. and Mont. **64** B2
Pofadder S. Africa **108** A2
Pogar Rus. Fed. **43** D3
Pogradec Albania **65** B2
P'ohang S. Korea **77** B2
Pohnpei *atoll* Micronesia **110**
Poiana Mare Romania **44** B3
Poie Dem. Rep. Congo **104** C3
Pointe-Noire Congo **104** B3
Point Lake Can. **127** D1
Point Pleasant U.S.A. **136** D3
Poitiers France **58** C2
Pokaran India **86** B2
Pokhara Nepal **87** C2
Pokrovsk Rus. Fed. **95** K2
Pokrovskoye Rus. Fed. **45** E2
Polacca U.S.A. **140** B1
Pola de Lena Spain **60** B1
Poland *country* Europe **57** D2
Polatsk Belarus **42** C2
Pol-e Khomri Afgh. **86** A1
Polewali Indon. **73** C2
Poli Cameroon **104** B2
Police Pol. **56** C2
Policoro Italy **63** C2
Poligny France **59** D2
Polillo Islands Phil. **76** B2
Polis'ke Ukr. **44** C1
Polkowice Pol. **57** D2
Pollino, Monte *mt.* Italy **63** C3
Polohy Ukr. **45** E2
Polokwane S. Africa **109** C1
Polonne Ukr. **44** C1
Polson U.S.A. **132** D1
Poltava Ukr. **45** D2
Poltavka Rus. Fed. **78** B2
Poltavskaya Rus. Fed. **45** E2
Põlva Estonia **42** C2
Polyarnyy Rus. Fed. **46** G2
Polyarnyye Zori Rus. Fed. **46** G2
Polygyros Greece **65** B2
Polykastro Greece **92** A1
Polynesia *is* Pacific Ocean **158** E5
Pombal Port. **60** B2
Pomezia Italy **62** B2
Pomokaira *reg.* Fin. **46** F2
Pomorie Bulg. **64** C2
Pomorska, Zatoka *b.* Pol. **56** C2
Pompéu Brazil **155** D1
Ponca City U.S.A. **141** E1
Ponce Puerto Rico **145** D3
Pondicherry India **85** B3
Pond Inlet Can. **125** G2
Ponferrada Spain **60** B1
Pongo *watercourse* Sudan **103** A4
Pongola *r.* S. Africa **109** D2
Ponoka Can. **126** D2
Ponta Grossa Brazil **154** B3
Pontalina Brazil **154** C1
Pont-à-Mousson France **59** D2
Ponta Porã Brazil **154** A2
Pontarlier France **59** D2
Pontcharra France **56** B3
Pontchartrain, Lake U.S.A. **138** B2
Ponte de Sor Port. **60** B2
Ponteix Can. **127** D3
Pontes-e-Lacerda Brazil **150** D4
Pontevedra Spain **60** B1
Pontiac *IL* U.S.A. **136** C2
Pontiac *MI* U.S.A. **136** D2
Pontianak Indon. **72** B2
Pontivy France **58** B2
Pontoetoe Suriname **151** D2
Pontoise France **49** D4
Ponton Can. **127** E2
Pontypool U.K. **53** B4
Ponziane, Isole *is* Italy **62** B2

Poochera Austr. **116** A2
Poole U.K. **53** C4
Poona India *see* Pune
Pooncarie Austr. **116** C2
Poopó, Lago de *l.* Bol. **152** B2
Popayán Col. **150** B2
Popigay *r.* Rus. Fed. **95** J2
Popiltah Austr. **116** C2
Poplar *r.* Can. **127** F2
Poplar Bluff U.S.A. **135** E3
Popocatépetl, Volcán *vol.* Mex. **137**
Popokabaka Dem. Rep. Congo **104** B3
Popovo Bulg. **64** C2
Poprad Slovakia **57** E3
Porangatu Brazil **151** E4
Porbandar India **86** A2
Porcupine *r.* Can./U.S.A. **124** C2
Poreč Croatia **62** B1
Pori Fin. **47** E3
Porirua N.Z. **118** B3
Porkhov Rus. Fed. **42** C2
Pornic France **58** B2
Poronaysk Rus. Fed. **81** F1
Poros Greece **65** B3
Porsgrunn Norway **47** B4
Portadown U.K. **51** C1
Portaferry U.K. **51** D1
Portage U.S.A. **136** C2
Portage la Prairie Can. **127** F3
Port Alberni Can. **126** C3
Portalegre Port. **60** B2
Portales U.S.A. **141** D2
Port Alexander U.S.A. **126** B2
Port Alice Can. **126** C2
Port Angeles U.S.A. **132** B1
Port Arthur Austr. **115** D4
Port Arthur U.S.A. **141** F3
Port Askaig U.K. **50** A3
Port Augusta Austr. **116** B2
Port-au-Prince Haiti **145** C3
Port aux Choix Can. **129** E1
Port Blair India **75** A2
Port Campbell Austr. **116** C3
Port Chalmers N.Z. **118** B4
Port Charlotte U.S.A. **139** D3
Port-de-Paix Haiti **145** C3
Port Edward Can. **126** C2
Porteirinha Brazil **155** D1
Portel Brazil **151** D3
Port Elgin Can. **128** B2
Port Elizabeth S. Africa **109** C3
Port Ellen U.K. **50** A3
Port Erin Isle of Man **52** A2
Porterville S. Africa **108** A3
Porterville U.S.A. **133** C3
Port Fairy Austr. **116** C3
Port Fitzroy N.Z. **118** C2
Port-Gentil Gabon **104** A3
Port Harcourt Nigeria **101** C4
Port Hardy Can. **126** C2
Port Hawkesbury Can. **129** D2
Port Hedland Austr. **114** A2
Porthmadog U.K. **52** A3
Port Hope Simpson Can. **129** E1
Port Huron U.S.A. **136** D2
Portimão Port. **60** B2
Portland *N.S.W.* Austr. **117** D2
Portland *Vic.* Austr. **116** C3
Portland *ME* U.S.A. **137** F2
Portland *OR* U.S.A. **132** B1
Portland Canal *inlet* Can. **126** B2
Portlaoise Rep. of Ireland **51** C2
Port Lavaca U.S.A. **141** E3
Port Lincoln Austr. **116** B2
Port Loko Sierra Leone **100** A4
Port Louis Mauritius **99**
Port Macquarie Austr. **117** E2
Port McNeill Can. **126** C2
Port-Menier Can. **129** D2

Port Moresby P.N.G. **71** D3
Port Ness U.K. **50** A1
Port Nolloth S. Africa **108** A2
Porto Port. *see* Oporto
Porto Acre Brazil **150** C3
Porto Alegre Brazil **152** C4
Porto Artur Brazil **151** D4
Porto dos Gaúchos Óbidos Brazil **151** D4
Porto Esperidião Brazil **150** D4
Portoferraio Italy **62** B2
Porto Franco Brazil **151** E3
Port of Spain Trin. and Tob. **145** D3
Portogruaro Italy **62** B1
Portomaggiore Italy **62** B2
Porto Mendes Brazil **154** B2
Porto Murtinho Brazil **152** C3
Porto Nacional Brazil **151** E4
Porto-Novo Benin **100** C4
Porto Primavera, Represa *resr* Brazil **154** B2
Porto Santana Brazil **151** D3
Porto Seguro Brazil **155** E1
Porto Tolle Italy **62** B2
Porto Torres Italy **62** A2
Porto-Vecchio France **59** D3
Porto Velho Brazil **150** C3
Portoviejo Ecuador **150** A2
Port Phillip Bay Austr. **116** C3
Port Pirie Austr. **116** B2
Portree U.K. **50** A2
Port Renfrew Can. **126** C3
Portrush U.K. **51** C1
Port Said Egypt **102** B1
Port Shepstone S. Africa **109** D3
Portsmouth U.K. **53** C4
Portsmouth *NH* U.S.A. **137** F2
Portsmouth *OH* U.S.A. **136** D3
Portsmouth *VA* U.S.A. **137** E3
Portstewart U.K. **51** C1
Port St Joe U.S.A. **139** C3
Port St Johns S. Africa **109** C3
Port Sudan Sudan **102** B3
Port Sulphur U.S.A. **138** C3
Port Talbot U.K. **53** B4
Portugal *country* Europe **60** B2
Portumna Rep. of Ireland **51** B2
Port-Vendres France **59** C3
Port Vila Vanuatu **112**
Porvoo Fin. **47** F3
Poryŏng S. Korea **77** B2
Posadas Arg. **152** C3
Poshekhon'ye Rus. Fed. **43** E2
Posio Fin. **46** F2
Poso Indon. **73** D2
Posse Brazil **151** E4
Pößneck Ger. **55** E2
Post U.S.A. **141** D2
Poste-de-la-Baleine Can. *see* Kuujjuarapik
Postmasburg S. Africa **108** B2
Posušje Bos.-Herz. **63** C2
Poteau U.S.A. **141** F1
Potenza Italy **63** C2
Poti *r.* Brazil **151** E3
P'ot'i Georgia **93** C1
Potiskum Nigeria **101** D3
Potomac, South Branch *r.* U.S.A. **137** E3
Potosí Bol. **152** B2
Pototan Phil. **76** B2
Potrero del Llano Mex. **140** D3
Potsdam Ger. **55** F1
Potsdam U.S.A. **137** E2
Pottstown U.S.A. **137** E2
Pottsville U.S.A. **137** E2
Pouch Cove Can. **129** E2
Poughkeepsie U.S.A. **137** F2
Poulton-le-Fylde U.K. **52** B3
Pouso Alegre Brazil **155** C2

oûthïsăt Cambodia **75** B2
ovažská Bystrica Slovakia **57** D3
ovlen *mt.* Serb. and Mont. **64** A2
óvoa de Varzim Port. **60** B1
ovorino Rus. Fed. **45** F1
owell U.S.A. **134** B2
owell River Can. **126** C3
oxoréu Brazil **154** B1
oyang Hu *l.* China **83** B3
ožarevac Serb. and Mont. **64** B2
oza Rica Mex. **143** C2
ožega Croatia **63** C1
ožega Serb. and Mont. **64** B2
ozm Tiâb Iran **91** D2
oznań Pol. **57** D2
ozoblanco Spain **60** C2
ozzuoli Italy **62** B2
rabumulih Indon. **72** B2
rachatice Czech Rep. **56** C3
rachuap Khiri Khan Thai. **75** A2
rado Brazil **155** E1
rague Czech Rep. **56** C2
raha Czech Rep. *see* Prague
aia Cape Verde **98**
rairie Dog Town Fork *r.* U.S.A.
  141 D2
rapat Indon. **72** A1
rata Brazil **154** C1
rato Italy **59** E3
ratt U.S.A. **133** D3
raya Indon. **73** C2
reăh Vihear Cambodia **75** B2
rechistoye Rus. Fed. **43** F2
reeceville Can. **127** C2
reili Latvia **42** C2
rémery France **59** C2
remnica Slovakia **57** D3
remnitz Ger. **55** F1
reparis Island Cocos Is **75** A2
reparis North Channel Cocos Is
  75 A2
reparis South Channel Cocos Is
  75 A2
rerov Czech Rep. **57** D3
rescott U.S.A. **140** B2
reševo Serb. and Mont. **64** B2
rešov Slovakia **57** E3
resque Isle U.S.A. **137** G1
ressel Ger. **55** F2
reštice Czech Rep. **55** F3
reston U.K. **52** B3
reston U.S.A. **132** D2
restwick U.K. **50** B3
reto *r.* Brazil **155** C1
retoria S. Africa **109** C2
reveza Greece **65** B3
rey Vêng Cambodia **75** B2
rice U.S.A. **133** D3
riboj Serb. and Mont. **64** A2
rienai Lith. **42** B3
rieska S. Africa **108** B2
rievidza Slovakia **57** D3
rijedor Bos.-Herz. **63** C2
rikaspiýskaya Nizmennost' *lowland*
  Kazakh./Rus. Fed. *see*
  Caspian Lowland
rilep Macedonia **65** B2
rimorsk Rus. Fed. **42** C1
rimorsko-Akhtarsk Rus. Fed. **45** E2
rimrose Lake Can. **127** E2
rince Albert Can. **124** E3

Prince Albert S. Africa **108** B3
Prince Albert Peninsula Can. **124** E2
Prince Albert Road S. Africa **108** B3
Prince Alfred, Cape Can. **124** D2
Prince Alfred Hamlet S. Africa **108** A3
Prince Charles Island Can. **125** G2
Prince Charles Mountains Antarctica
  119 E2
Prince Edward Island *prov.* Can.
  129 D2
Prince George Can. **126** C2
Prince of Wales Island Can. **124** F2
Prince of Wales Island U.S.A. **126** B3
Prince Patrick Island Can. **124** E1
Prince Regent Inlet *sea chan.* Can.
  125 F2
Prince Rupert Can. **126** B2
Princess Charlotte Bay Austr. **115** D1
Princess Royal Island Can. **126** C2
Princeton Can. **126** C3
Principe *i.* São Tomé and Principe
  104 A2
Prineville U.S.A. **132** B2
Priozersk Rus. Fed. **47** Q3
Pripet *r.* Belarus *see* Prypyats'
Pripet Marshes Belarus/Ukr. **42** B3
Priština Serb. and Mont. **64** B2
Pritzwalk Ger. **55** F1
Privlaka Croatia **62** C2
Privolzhsk Rus. Fed. **43** F2
Prizren Serb. and Mont. **64** B2
Professor van Blommestein Meer *resr*
  Suriname **151** D2
Progreso Mex. **143** D2
Prokhladnyy Rus. Fed. **93** C1
Prokuplje Serb. and Mont. **64** B2
Proletarsk Rus. Fed. **45** F2
Prophet *r.* Can. **124** D3
Prophet River Can. **126** C2
Proserpine Austr. **115** D2
Protvino Rus. Fed. **43** E3
Provadiya Bulg. **64** C2
Providence U.S.A. **137** F2
Providencia, Isla de *i.* Caribbean Sea
  144 B3
Provideniya Rus. Fed. **95** O2
Provo U.S.A. **132** D2
Provost Can. **127** D2
Prüm Ger. **54** C2
Prunelli-di-Fiumorbo France **59** D3
Pruszków Pol. **57** E2
Prut *r.* Europe **44** C2
Pryluky Ukr. **45** D1
Prymors'k Ukr. **45** E2
Pryor U.S.A. **141** E1
Prypyats' *r.* Belarus **42** C3
Przemyśl Pol. **57** E3
Psara *i.* Greece **65** C3
Psebay Rus. Fed. **93** C1
Pshekha *r.* Rus. Fed. **45** E3
Pskov Rus. Fed. **42** C2
Pskov, Lake Estonia/Rus. Fed. **42** C2
Ptolemaïda Greece **65** B2
Ptuj Slovenia **63** C1
Pucallpa Peru **150** B3
Pucheng China **83** B3
Puchezh Rus. Fed. **43** F2
Puch'ŏn S. Korea **77** B2
Puck Pol. **57** D2
Pudasjärvi Fin. **46** F2
Pudong China **82** C2
Pudozh Rus. Fed. **40** C2
Puebla Mex. **143** C3
Pueblo U.S.A. **134** C3
Puelén Arg. **153** B4
Puente-Genil Spain **60** C2
Puerto Aisén Chile **153** A5

Puerto Alegre Bol. **152** B2
Puerto Ángel Mex. **143** C3
Puerto Armuelles Panama **144** B4
Puerto Ayacucho Venez. **150** C2
Puerto Barrios Guat. **143** D3
Puerto Cabezas Nic. **144** B3
Puerto Carreño Venez. **150** C2
Puerto Cisnes Chile **153** A5
Puerto Cortés Mex. **142** B2
Puerto Escondido Mex. **143** C3
Puerto Frey Bol. **152** B2
Puerto Inírida Col. **150** C2
Puerto Isabel Bol. **152** C2
Puerto Leguizamo Col. **150** B3
Puerto Libertad Mex. **142** A2
Puerto Limón Costa Rica **144** B3
Puertollano Spain **60** C2
Puerto Madryn Arg. **153** B5
Puerto Maldonado Peru **150** C4
Puerto Montt Chile **153** A5
Puerto Natales Chile **153** A6
Puerto Nuevo Col. **150** C2
Puerto Peñasco Mex. **142** A1
Puerto Pinasco Para. **152** C3
Puerto Plata Dom. Rep. **145** C3
Puerto Portillo Peru **150** B3
Puerto Princesa Phil. **76** A3
Puerto Rico Arg. **154** A3
Puerto Rico *terr.* West Indies **145** D3
Puerto Rico Trench *sea feature*
  Caribbean Sea **160** B4
Puerto San José Guat. **144** A3
Puerto Santa Cruz Arg. **153** B6
Puerto Vallarta Mex. **142** B2
Pugachev Rus. Fed. **41** D3
Pugal India **86** B2
Pukaki, Lake N.Z. **118** B3
Pukatawagan Can. **127** E2
Pukchin N. Korea **77** B1
Pukch'ŏng N. Korea **77** B1
Pukekohe N.Z. **118** B2
Puksubaek-san *mt.* N. Korea **77** B1
Pula Croatia **62** B2
Pula Italy **62** A3
Pulkkila Fin. **46** F3
Pullman U.S.A. **132** C1
Pulog, Mount Phil. **76** B2
Puná, Isla *i.* Ecuador **150** A3
Punakaiki N.Z. **118** B3
Punda Maria S. Africa **109** D1
Pune India **85** B3
P'ungsan N. Korea **77** B1
Púnguè *r.* Moz. **107** C1
Punta Alta Arg. **153** B4
Punta Arenas Chile **153** A6
Punta Balestrieri *mt.* Italy **62** A2
Punta del Este Uru. **153** C4
Punta Gorda Belize **143** D3
Puntarenas Costa Rica **144** B3
Punto Fijo Venez. **150** B1
Puolanka Fin. **46** F3
Pur *r.* Rus. Fed. **40** G2
Puri India **87** C2
Purmerend Neth. **54** B1
Purnia India **87** C2
Puruliya India **87** C2
Purus *r.* Peru **150** C3
Purwakarta Indon. **72** B2
Puryŏng N. Korea **77** B1
Pusan S. Korea **77** B2
Pushkinskiye Gory Rus. Fed. **42** C2
Pustoshka Rus. Fed. **42** C2
Putao Myanmar **74** A1
Putian China **83** B3
Putília, Tanjung *pt* Indon. **73** C2
Putlitz Ger. **55** F1
Putrajaya Malaysia **72** B1
Puttgarden Ger. **56** C2
Putumayo *r.* Col. **150** B3

Putusibau Indon. **73** C1
Putyvl' Ukr. **45** D1
Puvurnituq Can. **128** C1
Puyang China **82** B2
Puylaurens France **58** C3
Pwllheli U.K. **52** A3
Pyapon Myanmar **74** A2
Pyasina *r.* Rus. Fed. **94** H2
Pyatigorsk Rus. Fed. **41** D4
P''yatykhatky Ukr. **45** D2
Pyè Myanmar **74** A2
Pyetrykaw Belarus **42** C3
Pyhäjärvi *l.* Fin. **47** E3
Pyhäjoki *r.* Fin. **46** E3
Pyhäsalmi Fin. **46** E3
Pyinmana Myanmar **74** A2
Pyōksŏng N. Korea **77** B2
P'yŏnggang N. Korea **77** B2
P'yŏngsan N. Korea **77** B2
P'yŏngyang N. Korea **77** B2
Pyramid Lake U.S.A. **132** C2
Pyramids of Giza *tourist site* Egypt
  92 B3
Pyrenees *mts* Europe **61** D1
Pyrgos Greece **65** B3
Pyryatyn Ukr. **45** D1
Pyrzyce Pol. **56** C2
Pytalovo Rus. Fed. **42** C2
Pyxaria *mt.* Greece **65** B3

Q

Qaanaaq Greenland *see* Thule
Qacha's Nek Lesotho **109** C3
Qādub Yemen **91** C3
Qagan Nur China **82** B1
Qaidam Pendi *basin* China **80** C2
Qalansiyah Yemen **91** C3
Qal'at Bīshah Saudi Arabia **90** B2
Qamanirjuaq Lake Can. **127** F1
Qamar, Ghubbat al *b.* Yemen **91** C3
Qam Hadīl Saudi Arabia **90** B3
Qarshi Uzbek. **89** C2
Qaryat al Ulyā Saudi Arabia **91** B2
Qasigiannguit Greenland **125** I2
Qaşr-e Qand Iran **91** D2
Qaşr-e Shīrīn Iran **93** C2
Qassimiut Greenland **125** I2
Qa'ţabah Yemen **90** B3
Qatar *country* Asia **91** C2
Qattara Depression Egypt **102** A2
Qausuittuq Can. *see* Resolute
Qazax Azer. **93** C1
Qazimämmäd Azer. **93** C1
Qazvīn Iran **93** C2
Qeqertarsuaq *i.* Greenland **125** I2
Qeqertarsuatsiaat Greenland **125** I2
Qeqertarsuup Tunua *b.* Greenland
  125 I2
Qeshm Iran **91** C2
Qianjiang *Chongqing* China **83** A3
Qianjiang *Hubei* China **83** B2
Qian Shan *mts* China **77** A1
Qidong China **82** C2
Qiemo China **80** F3
Qijiang China **83** A3
Qijiaojing China **80** C2
Qikiqtarjuaq Can. **125** H2
Qila Ladgasht Pak. **86** A2
Qilian Shan *mts* China **80** C2
Qillak *i.* Greenland **125** J2
Qimen China **83** B2
Qimusseriarsuaq *b.* Greenland **125** H1
Qinā Egypt **102** B2
Qingdao China **82** C2
Qinghai *prov.* China **87** D1
Qinghai Hu *salt l.* China **80** C2
Qinghai Nanshan *mts* China **80** C2

Qingyuan *Guangdong* China **83** B3
Qingyuan *Liaoning* China **77** A1
Qingzang Gaoyuan *plat.* China *see*
  Tibet, Plateau of
Qingzhou China **82** B2
Qinhuangdao China **82** B2
Qin Ling *mts* China **82** A2
Qinyang China **82** B2
Qinzhou China **83** A3
Qionghai China **83** B4
Qionglai Shan *mts* China **82** A2
Qiongshan China **83** B4
Qiqihar China **81** E1
Qir Iran **93** D3
Qitaihe China **78** B1
Qixian China **82** B2
Qogir Feng *mt.*
  China/Jammu and Kashmir *see* K2
Qom Iran **93** D2
Qomolangma Feng *mt.* China/Nepal
  see Everest, Mount
Qo'ng'irot Uzbek. **88** C2
Qo'qon Uzbek. **89** C2
Qoraqalpog'iston Uzbek. **88** C2
Quang Ngai Vietnam **75** B2
Quang Tri Vietnam **74** B2
Quanzhou *Fujian* China **83** B3
Quanzhou *Guangxi* China **83** B3
Quartu Sant'Elena Italy **62** A3
Quartzsite U.S.A. **140** A2
Quba Azer. **93** C1

Queanbeyan Austr. **117** D3
Québec Can. **129** C2
Québec *prov.* Can. **128** C1
Quedlinburg Ger. **55** E2
Queen Charlotte Can. **126** B2
Queen Charlotte Islands Can. **126** B2
Queen Charlotte Sound *sea chan.*
  Can. **126** B2
Queen Charlotte Strait Can. **126** C2
Queen Elizabeth Islands Can. **124** E1
Queen Maud Gulf Can. **124** F2
Queen Maud Land *reg.* Antarctica
  119 C2
Queen Maud Mountains Antarctica
  119 I1
Queensland *state* Austr. **115** D2
Queenstown Austr. **115** D4
Queenstown N.Z. **118** A4
Queenstown S. Africa **109** C3
Quelimane Moz. **107** C1
Quemado U.S.A. **140** C2
Querência do Norte Brazil **154** B2
Querétaro Mex. **143** B2
Querfurt Ger. **55** E2
Quesnel Can. **126** C2
Quesnel Lake Can. **126** C2
Quetta Pak. **86** A1
Quezaltenango Guat. **143** C3
Quezon Phil. **76** A3
Quezon City Phil. **76** B2
Quibala Angola **106** A1
Quibdó Col. **150** B1
Quiberon France **58** B2
Quillan France **58** C3
Quilmes Arg. **153** C4
Quilon India **85** B4
Quilpie Austr. **115** D2
Quilpué Chile **153** A4
Quimbele Angola **104** B3
Quimilí Arg. **152** B3
Quimper France **58** B2
Quimperlé France **58** B2
Quincy *IL* U.S.A. **136** B3
Quincy *MA* U.S.A. **137** F2
Qui Nhơn Vietnam **75** B2
Quinto Spain **61** C1
Quionga Moz. **105** E4
Quirindi Austr. **117** E2

Quissico Moz. **107** C2
Quitapa Angola **104** B4
Quito Ecuador **150** B3
Quixadá Brazil **151** F3
Qujing China **83** A3
Qumar He *r.* China **87** D1
Quoich *r.* Can. **127** F1
Quorn Austr. **116** B2
Qurayat Oman **91** C2
Qŭrghonteppa Tajik. **89** D3
Quzhou China **83** B3

R

Raab *r.* Austria **57** C3
Raahe Fin. **46** E3
Raalte Neth. **54** C1
Raas *i.* Indon. **73** C2
Raba Indon. **73** C2
Rabat Morocco **100** B1
Rābigh Saudi Arabia **90** A2
Race, Cape Can. **129** E2
Raceland U.S.A. **138** B3
Rach Gia Vietnam **75** B3
Racine U.S.A. **136** C2
Radā' Yemen **90** B3
Rădăuţi Romania **44** C2
Radcliff U.S.A. **136** C3
Radebeul Ger. **55** F2
Radhanpur India **86** B2
Radisson Can. **128** C1
Radom Pol. **57** E2
Radomsko Pol. **57** D2
Radomyshl' Ukr. **44** C1
Radoviš Macedonia **63** D2
Radviliškis Lith. **42** B2
Raḍwā, Jabal *mt.* Saudi Arabia **90** A2
Radyvyliv Ukr. **44** C1
Rae Bareli India **87** C2
Rae-Edzo Can. **126** D1
Rae Lakes Can. **126** D1
Raeren Belgium **54** C2
Raetihi N.Z. **118** C2
Rafaela Arg. **152** B4
Rafai C.A.R. **104** C2
Rafḥā' Saudi Arabia **90** B2
Rafsanjān Iran **93** D2
Ragang, Mount *vol.* Phil. **76** B3
Ragusa Italy **62** B3
Raha Indon. **73** C2
Rahachow Belarus **42** D3
Rahimyar Khan Pak. **86** B2
Raichur India **85** B3
Raigarh India **87** C2
Rainbow Lake Can. **126** D2
Rainier, Mount *vol.* U.S.A. **132** B1
Rainy Lake Can./U.S.A. **127** F3
Rainy River Can. **127** F3
Raipur India **87** C2
Raisio Fin. **47** E3
Rajahmundry India **85** C3
Rajang *r.* Malaysia **73** C1
Rajanpur Pak. **86** B2
Rajapalaiyam India **85** B4
Rajasthan Canal India **86** B2
Rajgarh India **86** B2
Rajkot India **86** B2
Rajpur India **86** B2
Rajshahi Bangl. **87** C2
Rakaia *r.* N.Z. **118** B3
Rakhiv Ukr. **44** B2
Rakitnoye Rus. Fed. **45** E1
Rakke Estonia **42** C2
Rakovník Czech Rep. **55** F2
Rakvere Estonia **42** C2
Raleigh U.S.A. **139** C1
Ralik Chain *is* Marshall Is **110**
Rambutyo Island P.N.G. **71** D3

...amgarh India 86 B2
...tâmhormoz Iran 93 C2
...tâmnicu Sârat Romania 44 C2
...tâmnicu Vâlcea Romania 44 B2
...amon' Rus. Fed. 43 E3
...amotswa Botswana 109 C1
...ampur India 87 B2
...amree Island Myanmar 74 A2
...amsey Isle of Man 52 A2
...amsgate U.K. 53 D4
...amsing India 74 A1
...anaghat India 87 C2
...anau Malaysia 73 C1
...ancagua Chile 153 A4
...anchi India 87 C2
...anders Denmark 47 C4
...angiora N.Z. 118 B3
...angitaiki r. N.Z. 118 C2
...angoon Myanmar 74 A2
...angpur Bangl. 87 C2
...anua Fin. 46 F2
...anyah, Wādī watercourse
  Saudi Arabia 90 B2
...aoul Island Kermadec Is 111
...apa i. Fr. Polynesia 111
...apid City U.S.A. 134 C2
...apla Estonia 42 B2
...apur India 86 A2
...arotonga i. Cook Is 111
...asa, Punta pt Arg. 153 B5
...a's al Khaymah U.A.E. 91 C2
...as Dejen mt. Eth. 103 B3
...aseiniai Lith. 42 B2
...asht Iran 93 C2
...as Koh mt. Pak. 86 A2
...asony Belarus 42 C2
...asskazovo Rus. Fed. 43 F3
...as Tannūrah Saudi Arabia 91 C2
...astede Ger. 55 D1
...aton U.S.A. 140 D1
...attray Head U.K. 50 D2
...atzeburg Ger. 55 E1
...aufarhöfn Iceland 46 [inset]
...aukumara Range mts N.Z. 118 C2
...auma Fin. 47 E3
...aung, Gunung vol. Indon. 73 C2
...aurkela India 87 C2
...avalli U.S.A. 132 D1
...avānsar Iran 93 C2
...avenna Italy 62 B2
...avensburg Ger. 56 B3
...avi r. Pak. 86 B1
...awalpindi Pak. 86 B1
...awicz Pol. 57 D2
...awlinna Austr. 114 B3
...awlins U.S.A. 134 B2
...awson Arg. 153 B5
...ayagada India 85 C3
...ychikhinsk Rus. Fed. 81 E1

Raydah Yemen 90 B3
Rayevskiy Rus. Fed. 41 E3
Raymond Can. 132 D1
Raymond U.S.A. 132 B1
Raymond Terrace Austr. 117 E2
Raymondville U.S.A. 141 E3
Rayón Mex. 143 C2
Rayong Thai. 75 B2
Rayyis Saudi Arabia 90 A2
Raz, Pointe du pt France 58 B2
Razāzah, Buḥayrat ar l. Iraq 93 C2
Razgrad Bulg. 64 C2
Razim, Lacul lag. Romania 44 C3
Razlog Bulg. 64 B2
Ré, Île de i. France 58 B2
Reading U.K. 53 C4
Reading U.S.A. 137 E2
Rebiana Sand Sea des. Libya 101 E2
Rebun-tō i. Japan 78 D1
Recherche, Archipelago of the is
  Austr. 114 B3
Rechytsa Belarus 43 D3
Recife Brazil 151 F3
Recife, Cape S. Africa 109 C3
Recklinghausen Ger. 54 C2
Reconquista Arg. 152 C3
Red r. U.S.A. 141 F2
Red Bay Can. 129 E1
Red Bluff U.S.A. 132 B2
Redcar U.K. 52 C2
Redcliff Can. 127 D2
Red Cliffs Austr. 116 C2
Red Deer Can. 126 D2
Red Deer r. Can. 124 E3
Red Deer Lake Can. 127 E2
Redding U.S.A. 132 B2
Redditch U.K. 53 C3
Redfield U.S.A. 135 D2
Red Lake Can. 128 A1
Red Lakes U.S.A. 135 E1
Red Lodge U.S.A. 132 E1
Redmond U.S.A. 132 B2
Red Oak U.S.A. 135 D2
Redondo Port. 60 B2
Red Sea Africa/Asia 90 A2
Redstone r. Can. 126 C1
Reduzum Neth. 54 B1
Red Wing U.S.A. 135 E2
Redwood Falls U.S.A. 135 D2
Ree, Lough l. Rep. of Ireland 51 C2
Reedsport U.S.A. 132 B2
Reefton N.Z. 118 B3
Regen Ger. 55 F3
Regência Brazil 155 E1
Regensburg Ger. 55 F3
Regenstauf Ger. 55 F3
Reggane Alg. 100 C2
Reggio di Calabria Italy 63 C3
Reggio nell'Emilia Italy 62 B2
Reghin Romania 44 B2
Regina Can. 124 F3
Rehoboth Namibia 108 A1
Reichenbach Ger. 55 F2
Reidsville U.S.A. 139 E1
Reigate U.K. 53 C4
Reims France 59 C2
Reina Adelaida, Archipiélago de la is
  Chile 153 A6
Reinbek Ger. 55 E1
Reindeer r. Can. 127 E2
Reindeer Island Can. 127 F2
Reindeer Lake Can. 127 E2
Reine Norway 46 C2
Reinsfeld Ger. 54 C3
Reitz S. Africa 109 C2
Reivilo S. Africa 108 B2
Reliance Can. 127 E1
Relizane Alg. 61 D2
Remeshk Iran 91 C2
Remiremont France 59 D2

Remscheid Ger. 54 C2
Rendsburg Ger. 56 B2
Renfrew Can. 137 E1
Rengat Indon. 72 B2
Reni Ukr. 44 C2
Renmark Austr. 116 C2
Rennell i. Solomon Is 110
Rennerod Ger. 54 D2
Rennes France 58 B2
Rennie Lake Can. 127 E1
Reno r. Italy 62 B2
Reno U.S.A. 133 C3
Renshou China 83 A3
Rensselaer U.S.A. 136 C2
Renukut India 87 C2
Renwick N.Z. 118 B3
Reo Indon. 73 D2
Republican r. U.S.A. 134 D3
Repulse Bay Can. 125 G2
Requena Peru 150 B3
Requena Spain 61 C2
Reserva Brazil 154 B2
Resistencia Arg. 152 C3
Reșița Romania 44 B2
Resolute Can. 124 F2
Resolution Island Can. 125 H2
Rethel France 59 C2
Rethymno Greece 65 B3
Réunion terr. Indian Ocean 99
Reus Spain 61 D1
Reutlingen Ger. 56 B3
Revelstoke Can. 126 D2
Revillagigedo, Islas is Mex. 142 A3
Revillagigedo Island U.S.A. 126 B2
Rewa India 87 C2
Rexburg U.S.A. 132 D2
Reykjanestá pt Iceland 46 [inset]
Reykjavík Iceland 46 [inset]
Reynosa Mex. 143 C2
Rēzekne Latvia 42 C2
Rhein r. Ger. see Rhine
Rheine Ger. 54 C1
Rheinsberg Ger. 55 F1
Rhin r. France see Rhine
Rhine r. France 56 B3
Rhine r. Ger. 54 C2
Rhinelander U.S.A. 136 C1
Rhinluch marsh Ger. 55 F1
Rhinow Ger. 55 F1
Rhode Island state U.S.A. 137 F2
Rhodes Greece 65 C3
Rhodes i. Greece 65 C3
Rhodope Mountains Bulg./Greece
  64 B2
Rhône r. France/Switz. 59 C3
Rhoufi Alg. 61 E2
Rhyl U.K. 52 B3
Rianópolis Brazil 154 C1
Riau, Kepulauan is Indon. 72 B1
Ribadeo Spain 60 B1
Ribadesella Spain 60 B1
Ribas do Rio Pardo Brazil 154 B2
Ribáuè Moz. 107 C1
Ribble r. U.K. 52 B3
Ribécourt-Dreslincourt France 54 A3
Ribeira r. Brazil 154 C2
Ribeirão Preto Brazil 154 C2
Riberac France 58 C2
Riberalta Bol. 152 B2
Ribnița Moldova 44 C2
Ribnitz-Damgarten Ger. 56 C2
Rice Lake U.S.A. 136 B1
Richards Bay S. Africa 109 D2
Richardson Mountains Can. 124 C2
Richfield U.S.A. 133 D3
Richland U.S.A. 132 C1
Richland Center U.S.A. 136 B2
Richmond N.S.W. Austr. 117 E2
Richmond Qld Austr. 115 D2
Richmond N.Z. 118 B3

Richmond S. Africa **108** B3
Richmond *IN* U.K. **52** C2
Richmond *IN* U.S.A. **136** D3
Richmond *KY* U.S.A. **136** D3
Richmond *VA* U.S.A. **137** E3
Rideau Lakes Can. **128** C2
Ridgecrest U.S.A. **133** C3
Riesa Ger. **55** F2
Rieste Ger. **54** D1
Riet *r.* S. Africa **109** B2
Rietberg Ger. **55** D2
Rieti Italy **62** B2
Rifle U.S.A. **134** B3
Riga Latvia **42** B2
Riga, Gulf of Estonia/Latvia **47** E4
Rīgān Iran **91** C2
Rigby U.S.A. **132** D2
Rigolet Can. **129** E1
Riihimäki Fin. **47** E3
Rijeka Croatia **62** B1
Riley U.S.A. **132** C2
Rimah, Wādī al *watercourse*
    Saudi Arabia **90** B2
Rimavská Sobota Slovakia **57** E3
Rimini Italy **62** B2
Rimouski Can. **129** D2
Ringebu Norway **47** F3
Ringkøbing Denmark **47** B4
Ringvassøya *i.* Norway **46** D2
Rinteln Ger. **55** D1
Riobamba Ecuador **150** B3
Rio Branco Brazil **150** C4
Rio Branco do Sul Brazil **154** C3
Rio Brilhante Brazil **154** B2
Rio Claro Brazil **156** C2
Río Colorado Arg. **153** B4
Río Cuarto Arg. **153** B4
Rio de Janeiro Brazil **155** D2
Rio do Sul Brazil **154** C3
Río Gallegos Arg. **153** B6
Río Grande Arg. **153** B6
Rio Grande Brazil **152** C4
Río Grande Mex. **142** B2
Río Grande *r.* Mex./U.S.A. **142** C2
Rio Grande City U.S.A. **141** D3
Riohacha Col. **150** D1
Rioja Peru **150** B3
Río Lagartos Mex. **143** D2
Riom France **59** C2
Río Mulatos Bol. **152** B2
Río Negro Brazil **154** C3
Rio Rancho U.S.A. **140** C1
Río Tigre Ecuador **150** B3
Rio Verde Brazil **154** B1
Río Verde Mex. **143** C2
Rio Verde de Mato Grosso Brazil
    154 B1
Ripky Ukr. **44** D1
Ripley U.K. **52** C3
Ripoll Spain **61** D1
Ripon U.K. **52** C2
Rishiri-tō *i.* Japan **78** D1
Risør Norway **47** B4
Ritchie S. Africa **108** B2
Ritchie's Archipelago *is* India **75** A2
Ritzville U.S.A. **132** C1
Rivadavia Arg. **152** B3
Riva del Garda Italy **62** B1
Rivas Nic. **144** B3
Rivera Uru. **152** C4
Riverhurst Can. **127** E2
Riverina *reg.* Austr. **117** D2
Riversdale S. Africa **108** B3
Riverside U.S.A. **133** C4
Riverton Can. **134** B2
Riverview Can. **129** D2
Rivesaltes France **58** C3
Rivière-du-Loup Can. **129** D2
Rivne Ukr. **44** C1

Riwaka N.Z. **118** B3
Riyadh Saudi Arabia **90** B2
Rize Turkey **93** C1
Rizhao China **82** B2
Roanne France **59** C2
Roanoke U.S.A. **137** E3
Roanoke *r.* U.S.A. **139** E1
Roanoke Rapids U.S.A. **139** E1
Robe Austr. **116** B3
Röbel Ger. **55** F1
Robertsfors Sweden **46** E3
Robertson S. Africa **108** A3
Robertsport Liberia **100** A4
Roberval Can. **129** C2
Robinson Range *hills* Austr. **114** A2
Robinvale Austr. **116** C2
Roblin Can. **127** E2
Robson, Mount Can. **126** D2
Rocca Busambra *mt.* Italy **62** B3
Rocha Uru. **153** C4
Rochdale U.K. **52** B3
Rochedo Brazil **154** B1
Rochefort Belgium **54** B2
Rochefort France **58** B2
Rochester *MN* U.S.A. **135** E2
Rochester *NH* U.S.A. **137** F2
Rochester *NY* U.S.A. **137** E2
Rockford U.S.A. **136** C2
Rockhampton Austr. **115** E2
Rock Hill U.S.A. **139** D2
Rockingham Austr. **114** A3
Rock Island U.S.A. **136** B2
Rock Springs *MT* U.S.A. **134** B1
Rocksprings U.S.A. **141** D3
Rock Springs *WY* U.S.A. **134** B2
Rocky Ford U.S.A. **134** C3
Rocky Mount U.S.A. **139** E1
Rocky Mountains Can./U.S.A. **130** C2
Rocourt-St-Martin France **54** A3
Rocroi France **54** B3
Rødbyhavn Denmark **56** C2
Roddickton Can. **129** E1
Rodez France **58** C3
Roding Ger. **55** F3
Rodniki Rus. Fed. **43** F2
Rodos Greece *see* Rhodes
Rodos *i.* Greece *see* Rhodes
Roebourne Austr. **114** A2
Roebuck Bay Austr. **114** B1
Roedtan S. Africa **109** C1
Roermond Neth. **54** B2
Roeselare Belgium **54** A2
Rogers U.S.A. **138** B1
Roggeveldberge *esc.* S. Africa **108** B3
Rognan Norway **46** D2
Rogue *r.* U.S.A. **132** B2
Roja Latvia **42** B2
Rokan *r.* Indon. **72** B1
Rokiškis Lith. **42** C2
Rokycany Czech Rep. **55** F3
Rokytne Ukr. **44** C1
Rolândia Brazil **154** B2
Rolla U.S.A. **135** E3
Roma Austr. **115** D2
Roma *i.* Indon. **71** C2
Roma Italy *see* Rome
Roma Lesotho **109** C2
Roma U.S.A. **141** E3
Romain, Cape U.S.A. **139** E2
Roman Romania **44** C2
Roman-Kosh *mt.* Ukr. **45** D3
Romanovka *Respublika Buryatiya*
    Rus. Fed. **81** D1
Romanovka *Saratovskaya Oblast'*
    Rus. Fed. **45** F1
Rombas France **59** D2
Romblon Phil. **76** B2
Rome Italy **62** B2
Rome *GA* U.S.A. **139** C2

Rome *NY* U.S.A. **137** E2
Romford U.K. **53** D4
Romilly-sur-Seine France **59** C2
Romny Ukr. **45** D1
Romorantin-Lanthenay France **58** C2
Romsey U.K. **53** C4
Roncador, Serra do *hills* Brazil **151** D4
Ronda Spain **60** B2
Rondon Brazil **154** B2
Rondonópolis Brazil **154** B1
Rondu Jammu and Kashmir **86** B1
Rong'an China **83** A3
Rongjiang China **83** A3
Rongklang Range *mts* Myanmar **74** A1
Rønne Denmark **47** C4
Ronne Ice Shelf Antarctica **119** K2
Ronnenberg Ger. **55** D1
Ronse Belgium **54** A2
Roorkee India **87** B2
Roosendaal Neth. **54** B2
Roosevelt U.S.A. **132** E2
Roosevelt, Mount Can. **126** D2
Roosevelt Island Antarctica **119** I2
Roquefort France **58** B3
Roraima, Mount Guyana **150** C2
Røros Norway **47** C3
Rosario Arg. **153** B4
Rosario *Baja California* Mex. **142** A1
Rosario *Sinaloa* Mex. **142** B2
Rosario *Sonora* Mex. **142** B2
Rosário Oeste Brazil **151** D4
Rosarito Mex. **142** A2
Rosarno Italy **63** C3
Roscoff France **58** B2
Roscommon Rep. of Ireland **51** B2
Roscrea Rep. of Ireland **51** C2
Roseau Dominica **145** D3
Roseau U.S.A. **135** D1
Roseburg U.S.A. **132** B2
Rosenberg U.S.A. **141** E3
Rosendal Norway **48** E2
Rosengarten Ger. **55** D1
Rosenheim Ger. **56** C3
Rosetown Can. **127** E2
Roshchino Rus. Fed. **42** C1
Rosh Pinah Namibia **108** A2
Roșiori de Vede Romania **44** C3
Roskilde Denmark **47** C4
Roslavl' Rus. Fed. **43** D3
Rossano Italy **63** C3
Rossan Point *pt* Rep. of Ireland **51** B1
Ross Ice Shelf Antarctica **119** H1
Rossignol, Lake Can. **129** D2
Rossland Can. **126** D3
Rosslare Rep. of Ireland **51** C2
Rosso Maur. **100** A3
Rosso, Capo *c.* France **59** D3
Ross-on-Wye U.K. **53** B4
Rossosh' Rus. Fed. **45** E1
Ross River Can. **126** B1
Røssvatnet *l.* Norway **46** C2
Rostāq Iran **93** D3
Rosthern Can. **124** E3
Rostock Ger. **56** C2
Rostov Rus. Fed. **43** E2
Rostov-na-Donu Rus. Fed. **45** E2
Roswik Sweden **46** E2
Roswell U.S.A. **140** D2
Rota *i.* N. Mariana Is **71** D2
Rot am See Ger. **55** E3
Rote *i.* Indon. **71** C3
Rotenburg (Wümme) Ger. **55** D1
Roth Ger. **55** E3
Rothbury U.K. **52** C2
Rothenburg ob der Tauber Ger. **55** E3
Rotherham U.K. **52** C3
Rothesay U.K. **50** B3
Roto Austr. **117** D2
Rotondo, Monte *mt.* France **59** D3
Rotorua N.Z. **118** C2

Rotorua, Lake N.Z. **118** C2
Rottenbach Ger. **55** F2
Rottenmann Austria **56** C3
Rotterdam Neth. **54** B2
Rottweil Ger. **56** B3
Rotuma *i.* Fiji **110**
Roubaix France **59** C1
Rouen France **58** C2
Round Mountain Austr. **117** E2
Round Pond *l.* Can. **129** E2
Round Rock U.S.A. **141** E2
Roundup U.S.A. **132** E1
Rousay *i.* U.K. **50** C1
Rouyn-Noranda Can. **128** C2
Rovaniemi Fin. **46** F2
Roven'ki Rus. Fed. **45** E2
Roven'ky Ukr. **45** E2
Rovereto Italy **62** B1
Rovigo Italy **62** B1
Rovinj Croatia **62** B1
Rowena Austr. **117** D1
Roxas Phil. **76** B2
Roxas Phil. **76** B2
Roxas Phil. **76** A2
Roxas Phil. **76** B3
Roxby Downs Austr. **116** B2
Roy U.S.A. **140** D1
Royale, Isle *i.* U.S.A. **136** C1
Royan France **58** B2
Roye France **54** A3
Royston U.K. **53** C3
Rozdil'na Ukr. **44** D2
Rozdol'ne Ukr. **45** D2
Rozoy-sur-Serre France **54** B3
Ruapehu, Mount *vol.* N.Z. **118** C2
Ruapuke Island N.Z. **118** A4
Rub' al Khālī *des.* Saudi Arabia **90** B3
Rubizhne Ukr. **45** E2
Rubtsovsk Rus. Fed. **89** F1
Ruby U.S.A. **124** B3
Ruby Mountains U.S.A. **132** C2
Rudnaya Pristan' Rus. Fed. **78** C2
Rudnya Rus. Fed. **43** D3
Rudnyy Kazakh. **88** F1
Rudol'fa, Ostrov *i.* Rus. Fed. **94** F1
Rudolstadt Ger. **55** E2
Rufiji *r.* Tanz. **105** D3
Rufino Arg. **153** B4
Rufunsa Zambia **107** B1
Rugao China **82** C2
Rugby U.K. **53** C3
Rugby U.S.A. **134** C1
Rügen *i.* Ger. **56** C2
Ruhla Ger. **55** E2
Ruhnu *i.* Estonia **42** B2
Ruhr *r.* Ger. **54** C2
Rui'an China **83** C3
Ruidoso U.S.A. **140** C2
Ruiz Mex. **142** B2
Rukwa, Lake Tanz. **105** D3
Rum *i.* U.K. **50** A2
Ruma Serb. and Mont. **64** A1
Rumāh Saudi Arabia **90** B2
Rumbek Sudan **103** A4
Rumilly France **59** D2
Rum Jungle Austr. **114** C1
Runanga N.Z. **118** B3
Runcorn U.K. **52** B3
Rundu Namibia **106** A1
Ruoqiang China **89** F3
Rupert *r.* Can. **128** C1
Rupert Bay Can. **128** C1
Rusape Zimbabwe **107** C1
Ruse Bulg. **64** C2
Rushon Tajik. **89** E3
Rushville U.S.A. **134** C2
Rushworth Austr. **117** D3
Russell Can. **127** E2

Russell N.Z. **118** B2
Russellville *AL* U.S.A. **138** C2
Russellville *AR* U.S.A. **138** B1
Russellville *KY* U.S.A. **136** C3
Rüsselsheim Ger. **55** D2
Russian Federation *country*
  Asia/Europe **94** G2
Ruston U.S.A. **138** B2
Ruteng Indon. **73** C2
Ruthin U.K. **52** B3
Rutland U.S.A. **137** F2
Ruvuma *r.* Moz./Tanz. **105** E4
Ruweis U.A.E. **91** C2
Ruzayevka Kazakh. **89** D1
Ruzayevka Rus. Fed. **41** D3
Rwanda *country* Africa **105** C3
Ryazan' Rus. Fed. **43** E3
Ryazhsk Rus. Fed. **43** F3
Rybachiy, Poluostrov *pen.* Rus. Fed.
  46 G1
Rybinsk Rus. Fed. **43** E2
Rybinskoye Vodokhranilishche *resr*
  Rus. Fed. **43** E2
Rybnik Pol. **57** D2
Rybnoye Rus. Fed. **43** E3
Rye U.K. **53** D4
Ryl'sk Rus. Fed. **43** D3
Ryōtsu Japan **78** C3
Ryukyu Islands Japan **81** E3
Rzeszów Pol. **57** E2
Rzhaksa Rus. Fed. **43** F3
Rzhev Rus. Fed. **43** D2

Sa'ādatābād Iran **93** D3
Saale *r.* Ger. **55** E2
Saalfeld Ger. **55** E2
Saarbrücken Ger. **54** C3
Saaremaa *i.* Estonia **42** B2
Saarenkylä Fin. **46** F2
Saarijärvi Fin. **46** F3
Saarlouis Ger. **54** C3
Sab' Ābār Syria **92** B2
Sabadell Spain **61** D1
Sabah *state* Malaysia **73** C1
Sabalana *i.* Indon. **73** C2
Sabará Brazil **155** D1
Sabaudia Italy **62** B2
Sabhā Libya **101** D2
Sabie *r.* Moz./S. Africa **109** D2
Sabinas Mex. **143** B2
Sabinas Hidalgo Mex. **143** B2
Sable, Cape Can. **129** D2
Sable, Cape U.S.A. **139** D3
Sable Island Can. **129** E2
Sabugal Port. **60** B1
Ṣabyā Saudi Arabia **90** B3
Sabzevār Iran **88** C3
Sachanga Angola **106** A1
Sachigo Lake Can. **128** A1
Sach'on S. Korea **77** B3
Sachs Harbour Can. **124** D2
Sacramento U.S.A. **133** B3
Sacramento Mountains U.S.A. **140** C2
Sacramento Valley U.S.A. **132** B2
Sada S. Africa **109** C3
Sádaba Spain **61** C1
Ṣa'dah Yemen **90** B3
Sadiya India **74** A1
Sadoga-shima *i.* Japan **78** C3
Sa Dragonera *i.* Spain **61** D2
Säffle Sweden **47** C4
Safford U.S.A. **140** C2
Saffron Walden U.K. **53** D3
Safi Morocco **100** B1
Safonovo *Arkhangel'skaya Oblast'*
  Rus. Fed. **40** D2

Safonovo *Smolenskaya Oblast'*
  Rus. Fed. **43** D2
Safrā' as Sark *esc.* Saudi Arabia **90** B2
Saga China **87** C2
Saga Japan **79** B4
Sagaing Myanmar **74** A1
Sagamihara Japan **79** C3
Sagar India **87** B2
Saginaw U.S.A. **136** D2
Saginaw Bay U.S.A. **136** D2
Sagres Port. **60** B2
Sagua la Grande Cuba **144** B2
Saguenay *r.* Can. **137** G1
Sagunto Spain **61** C2
Sagyndyk, Mys *pt* Kazakh. **88** C2
Sahagún Spain **60** B1
Sahara *des.* Africa **100** C3
Saharan Atlas *mts* Alg. *see*
  Atlas Saharien
Saharanpur India **87** B2
Saharsa India **87** C2
Sahel *reg.* Africa **100** B3
Sahuayo Mex. **142** B2
Ṣāḥūq *reg.* Saudi Arabia **90** B2
Saïdia Morocco **61** C2
Saidpur Bangl. **87** C2
Saigon Vietnam *see* Hồ Chí Minh City
Saiha India **74** A1
Saihan Tal China **82** B1
Saiki Japan **79** B4
Saimaa *l.* Fin. **47** F3
Sain Alto Mex. **142** B2
St Abb's Head U.K. **50** C3
St Albans U.K. **53** C4
St Alban's Head U.K. **53** B4
St Aldhelm's Head U.K.
  see St Alban's Head
St Andrews U.K. **50** C2
St Anthony Can. **129** E1
St Anthony U.S.A. **132** D2
St Arnaud Austr. **116** C3
St-Augustin Can. **129** E1
St Augustin *r.* Can. **129** E1
St Augustine U.S.A. **139** D3
St Austell U.K. **53** A4
St-Avertin France **58** C2
St-Avold France **54** C2
St Bees Head U.K. **52** B2
St-Bonnet-en-Champsaur France
  59 D3
St Bride's Bay U.K. **53** A4
St-Brieuc France **58** B2
St Catharines Can. **128** C2
St Catherine's Point *pt* U.K. **53** C4
St Charles U.S.A. **135** E3
St Clair, Lake Can./U.S.A. **128** C2
St-Claude France **59** D2
St Cloud U.S.A. **135** E1
St Croix *r.* U.S.A. **137** B2
St Croix *i.* Virgin Is (U.S.A.)
  145 D3
St David's Head U.K. **53** A4
St-Denis Réunion **99**
St-Dizier France **59** D2
Ste-Anne-des-Monts Can. **129** D2
St-Égrève France **59** D2
St Elias Mountains Can. **124** C2
Ste-Marguerite *r.* Can. **129** D1
Sainte Rose du Lac Can. **127** F2
Saintes France **58** B2
St-Étienne France **59** C2
St-Florent France **62** A2
St-Flour France **58** C2
St Francis U.S.A. **134** C3
St-Gaudens France **58** C3
St George Austr. **117** D1
St George U.S.A. **133** D3
St George Island U.S.A. **139** D3
St-Georges Can. **129** C2
St George's Grenada **145** D3

St George's Channel
Rep. of Ireland/U.K. **51** C3
St Gotthard Pass Switz. **59** D2
St Helena i. S. Atlantic Ocean **99**
St Helena and Dependencies terr.
S. Atlantic Ocean **99**
St Helena Bay S. Africa **108** A3
St Helena Bay b. S. Africa **108** A3
St Helens U.K. **52** B3
St Helens, Mount vol. U.S.A. **132** B1
St Helier Channel Is **53** B5
St-Hubert Belgium **54** B2
St-Hyacinthe Can. **137** F1
St Ignace U.S.A. **136** D1
St Ignace Island Can. **128** B2
St Ives U.K. **53** A4
St James, Cape Can. **126** B2
St-Jean, Lac l. Can. **129** C2
St-Jean-d'Angély France **58** B2
St-Jean-de-Monts France **58** B2
St-Jean-sur-Richelieu Can. **128** C2
St-Jérôme Can. **137** F1
St Joe r. U.S.A. **132** C1
Saint John Can. **125** H3
St John r. U.S.A. **137** G1
St John's Antigua **145** D3
St John's Can. **129** E2
St Johns U.S.A. **140** C2
St Johnsbury U.S.A. **137** F2
St Joseph U.S.A. **135** E3
St Joseph, Lake Can. **128** A1
St Joseph Island Can. **128** B2
St-Junien France **58** C2
St Kilda i. U.K. **50** B2
St Kitts and Nevis country West Indies
145 D3
St-Laurent, Golfe du g. Can. see
St Lawrence, Gulf of
St-Laurent-du-Maroni Fr. Guiana
151 D2
St Lawrence inlet Can. **129** D2
St Lawrence, Gulf of Can. **129** D2
St Lawrence Island U.S.A. **124** A2
St-Lô France **58** B2
St Louis Senegal **100** A3
St Louis U.S.A. **135** E3
St Louis r. U.S.A. **135** E1
St Lucia country West Indies **145** D3
St Lucia Estuary S. Africa **109** D3
St-Malo France **58** B2
St-Malo, Golfe de g. France **58** B2
St-Martin i. West Indies **145** D3
St Martin, Cape S. Africa **108** A3
St Marys U.S.A. **137** E2
St Matthias Group is P.N.G. **71** D3
St-Maurice r. Can. **128** C2
St-Nazaire France **58** B2
St-Omer France **58** C1
St Paul Can. **127** D2
St Paul U.S.A. **135** E2
St Peter U.S.A. **135** E2
St Peter Port Channel Is **53** B5
St Petersburg Rus. Fed. **43** D2
St Petersburg U.S.A. **139** D3
St Pierre St Pierre and Miquelon
129 E2
St Pierre and Miquelon terr.
N. America **129** E2
St-Pierre-d'Oléron France **58** B2
St-Pourçain-sur-Sioule France **59** C2
St Quentin Can. **137** G1
St-Quentin France **59** C2
St-Siméon Can. **129** D2
St Theresa Point Can. **127** F2
St Thomas Can. **128** C2
St-Tropez France **59** D3
St-Tropez, Cap de c. France **59** D3
St-Vaast-la-Hougue France **53** C5
St-Valery-en-Caux France **53** D5
St Vincent, Gulf Austr. **116** B3

St Vincent and the Grenadines
country West Indies **145** D3
St-Vith Belgium **54** C2
St Walburg Can. **127** E2
St-Yrieix-la-Perche France **58** C2
Saipan i. N. Mariana Is **71** D1
Sajama, Nevado mt. Bol. **152** B2
Sak watercourse S. Africa **108** B2
Sakai Japan **79** C4
Sakaide Japan **79** B4
Sakākah Saudi Arabia **90** B2
Sakakawea, Lake U.S.A. **134** C1
Sakarya Turkey see **Adapazarı**
Sakarya r. Turkey **65** D2
Sakata Japan **78** C3
Sakchu N. Korea **77** B1
Sakhalin i. Rus. Fed. **78** D1
Sakhile S. Africa **109** C2
Şäki Azer. **93** C1
Šakiai Lith. **42** B3
Sakishima-shotō is Japan **81** E3
Sakon Nakhon Thai. **74** B2
Sakrivier S. Africa **108** B3
Sakura Japan **79** D3
Saky Ukr. **45** D2
Sal r. Rus. Fed. **45** F2
Sala Sweden **47** D4
Salaberry-de-Valleyfield Can. **128** C2
Salacgrīva Latvia **42** B2
Sala Consilina Italy **62** C2
Salada, Laguna l. Mex. **140** A2
Salado r. Arg. **152** B4
Salado r. Mex. **143** C2
Salaga Ghana **100** B4
Salajwe Botswana **108** B1
Salal Chad **101** D3
Salālah Sudan **90** A2
Şalālah Oman **91** C3
Salamanca Mex. **143** B2
Salamanca Spain **60** B1
Salas Spain **60** B1
Salavan Laos **75** B2
Salawati i. Indon. **71** C3
Salayar i. Indon. **73** D2
Salbris France **58** C2
Šalčininkai Lith. **42** C3
Saldaña Spain **60** C1
Saldanha S. Africa **108** A3
Saldus Latvia **42** B2
Sale Austr. **117** D3
Salekhard Rus. Fed. **40** F2
Salem India **85** B3
Salem MO U.S.A. **135** E3
Salem OR U.S.A. **132** B2
Salem U.K. **50** B2
Salerno Italy **62** B2
Salford U.K. **52** B3
Salgado r. Brazil **151** F3
Salgótarján Hungary **57** D3
Salgueiro Brazil **151** F3
Salida U.S.A. **134** B3
Salihli Turkey **65** C3
Salihorsk Belarus **42** C1
Salima Malawi **107** C1
Salimo Moz. **107** C1
Salina U.S.A. **135** D3
Salina, Isola i. Italy **62** B3
Salina Cruz Mex. **143** C3
Salinas Brazil **155** D1
Salinas Mex. **142** B2
Salinas U.S.A. **133** B3
Salines, Cap de ses c. Spain **61** D2
Salinópolis Brazil **151** E3
Salisbury U.K. **53** C4
Salisbury MD U.S.A. **137** E3
Salisbury NC U.S.A. **139** D1
Salisbury Plain U.K. **53** B4
Salitre r. Brazil **151** E3
Salla Fin. **46** F2
Salluit Can. **125** G2

Sallyana Nepal **87** C2
Salmās Iran **93** C2
Salmon U.S.A. **132** D1
Salmon r. U.S.A. **132** D1
Salmon Arm Can. **126** D2
Salmon River Mountains U.S.A.
132 C2
Salmtal Ger. **54** C3
Salo Fin. **47** E3
Sal'sk Rus. Fed. **45** F2
Salt watercourse S. Africa **108** B3
Salt r. U.S.A. **140** B2
Salta Arg. **152** B3
Saltillo Mex. **143** B2
Salt Lake City U.S.A. **132** D2
Salto Brazil **154** C2
Salto Uru. **152** C4
Salto da Divisa Brazil **155** E1
Salto del Guairá Para. **154** B2
Salton Sea salt l. U.S.A. **133** C4
Saluda U.S.A. **139** D2
Saluzzo Italy **62** A2
Salvador Brazil **151** F4
Salwah Saudi Arabia **91** C2
Salween r. China/Myanmar **74** A1
Salween r. China/Myanmar **80** C3
Salyan Azer. **93** C2
Salzburg Austria **56** C3
Salzgitter Ger. **55** E1
Salzkotten Ger. **55** D2
Salzwedel Ger. **55** E1
Samalayuca Mex. **142** B1
Samani Japan **78** D2
Samar i. Phil. **76** B2
Samara Rus. Fed. **41** E3
Samarinda Indon. **73** C2
Samarqand Uzbek. **89** D3
Sāmarrā' Iraq **93** C2
Şamaxı Azer. **93** C1
Samba Dem. Rep. Congo **105** C3
Sambaliung mts Indon. **73** C1
Sambalpur India **87** C2
Sambar, Tanjung pt Indon. **73** C2
Sambas Indon. **72** B1
Sambava Madag. **107** [inset] E1
Sambir Ukr. **44** B2
Samborombón, Bahía b. Arg. **153** C4
Samch'ŏk S. Korea **77** B2
Samdi Dag mt. Turkey **93** C2
Same Tanz. **105** D3
Samirah Saudi Arabia **90** B2
Samjiyŏn N. Korea **77** B1
Samoa country S. Pacific Ocean **113**
Samoan Islands is
S. Pacific Ocean **111**
Samobor Croatia **62** C1
Samos i. Greece **65** C3
Samothraki Greece **65** C2
Samothraki i. Greece **65** C2
Sampit Indon. **73** C2
Sampwe Dem. Rep. Congo **105** C3
Sam Rayburn Reservoir U.S.A. **141** F2
Samsun Turkey **92** B1
Samtredia Georgia **93** C1
Samui, Ko i. Thai. **75** B3
Samut Songkhram Thai. **75** B2
San Mali **100** B3
Şan'ā' Yemen **90** B3
Sanaga r. Cameroon **104** A2
San Ambrosio, Isla i.
S. Pacific Ocean **149**
Sanandaj Iran **93** C2
San Andrés, Isla de i. Caribbean Sea
144 B3
San Andres Mountains U.S.A. **140** C2
San Andrés Tuxtla Mex. **143** C3
San Angelo U.S.A. **141** D2
San Antonio U.S.A. **141** E3
San Antonio, Mount U.S.A. **133** C4
San Antonio Abad Spain **61** D2

an Antonio de los Cobres Arg. 152 B3
an Antonio Oeste Arg. 153 B5
an Benedetto del Tronto Italy 62 B2
an Benedicto, Isla i. Mex. 142 A3
an Bernardino U.S.A. 133 C4
an Bernardino Mountains U.S.A. 133 C4
an Blas, Cape U.S.A. 139 C3
an Borja Bol. 152 B2
an Buenaventura Mex. 142 B2
an Carlos Phil. 76 B2
an Carlos Venez. 145 D4
an Carlos de Bariloche Arg. 153 A5
an Carlos del Zulia Venez. 145 C2
an Clemente Island U.S.A. 133 C4
ancoins France 58 C2
an Cristobal i. Solomon Is 110
an Cristóbal Venez. 150 B2
an Cristóbal de las Casas Mex. 143 C3
ancti Spiritus Cuba 144 C2
andak S. Africa 109 D1
andakan Malaysia 73 C1
andane Norway 47 B3
andanski Bulg. 65 B2
anday i. U.K. 50 C1
anderson U.S.A. 141 D2
andia Peru 150 C4
an Diego U.S.A. 133 C4
andikli Turkey 92 B3
andnessjøen Norway 46 C2
andoa Dem. Rep. Congo 104 C3
andomierz Pol. 57 E2
andovo Rus. Fed. 43 E2
andoy i. Faroe Is 48 B1
andpoint U.S.A. 132 C1
andu China 83 B3
andusky U.S.A. 136 D2
andveld mts S. Africa 108 A3
andvika Norway 47 C4
andviken Sweden 47 D3
andwich Bay Can. 129 E1
andy Bay Can. 127 E2
andy Cape Austr. 115 E2
andy Lake Can. 128 A1
andy Lake i. Can. 128 A1
an Estanislao Para. 154 A2
an Felipe Baja California Mex. 142 A1
an Felipe Guanajuato Mex. 143 B2
an Felipe Venez. 150 C1
an Félix Chile 149
an Fernando Baja California Mex. 142 A2
an Fernando Tamaulipas Mex. 143 C2
an Fernando Phil. 76 B2
an Fernando Phil. 76 B2
an Fernando Spain 60 B2
an Fernando Trin. and Tob. 145 D3
an Fernando de Apure Venez. 150 C2
anford FL U.S.A. 139 C3
anford ME U.S.A. 137 F2
an Francisco Arg. 152 B4
an Francisco U.S.A. 133 B3
an Francisco Javier Spain 61 D2
angamner India 86 B3
angar Rus. Fed. 95 K2
an Gavino Monreale Italy 62 A3
angerhausen Ger. 55 E2
anggau Indon. 73 C1
angha r. Congo 104 B3
an Giovanni in Fiore Italy 63 C3
angir i. Indon. 76 B3
angir, Kepulauan is Indon. 71 C2
angju S. Korea 77 B3
angkulirang Indon. 73 C1
angli India 85 B3

Sangmélima Cameroon 104 B2
Sango Zimbabwe 107 C2
Sangre de Cristo Range mts U.S.A. 134 B3
Sangsang China 87 C2
San Hipólito, Punta pt Mex. 142 A2
San Ignacio Mex. 142 A2
Sanikiluaq Can. 128 C1
Sanjiang China 83 A3
San Joaquin r. U.S.A. 133 B3
San Jorge, Golfo de g. Arg. 153 B5
San Jose Phil. 76 B2
San Jose Phil. 76 B2
San Jose U.S.A. 133 B3
San José, Isla i. Mex. 142 A2
San José de Bavicora Mex. 142 B2
San Jose de Buenavista Phil. 76 B2
San José de Comondú Mex. 142 A2
San José del Cabo Mex. 142 B2
San José del Guaviare Col. 150 B2
San Juan Arg. 152 B4
San Juan r. Costa Rica/Nic. 144 B3
San Juan r. Puerto Rico 145 D3
San Juan r. U.S.A. 133 D3
San Juan Bautista Spain 61 D2
San Juan Bautista Tuxtepec Mex. 143 C3
San Juan Islands U.S.A. 132 B1
San Juanito Mex. 142 B2
San Juan Mountains U.S.A. 134 B3
San Julián Arg. 153 B5
Sankh r. India 87 C2
Sankt Gallen Switz. 59 D2
Sankt Moritz Switz. 59 D2
Sankt-Peterburg Rus. Fed. see St Petersburg
Sankt Veit an der Glan Austria 56 C3
Sankt Wendel Ger. 54 C3
San Lorenzo Mex. 140 C3
Sanlúcar de Barrameda Spain 60 B2
San Lucas Mex. 142 B2
San Luis Arg. 153 B4
San Luis de la Paz Mex. 143 B2
San Luis Obispo U.S.A. 133 B3
San Luis Potosí Mex. 143 B2
San Luis Río Colorado Mex. 142 A1
San Marcos U.S.A. 141 E3
San Marino country Europe 62 B2
San Marino San Marino 62 B2
San Martín de Bolaños Mex. 142 B2
San Martin de los Andes Arg. 153 A5
San Matías, Golfo g. Arg. 153 B5
Sanmenxia China 82 B2
Sanming China 83 B3
San Nicolás de los Arroyos Arg. 153 B4
San Nicolas Island U.S.A. 133 C4
Sannieshof S. Africa 109 C2
Sanok Pol. 57 E3
San Pablo Phil. 76 B2
San Pablo Balleza Mex. 142 B2
San Pedro Bol. 152 B2
San-Pédro Côte d'Ivoire 100 B3
San Pedro Mex. 142 A2
San Pedro watercourse U.S.A. 140 C3
San Pedro, Sierra de mts Spain 60 B2
San Pedro de las Colonias Mex. 142 B2
San Pedro Sula Hond. 144 B3
San Pietro, Isola di i. Italy 62 A3
San Quintín, Cabo c. Mex. 142 A1
San Rafael Arg. 153 B4

San Remo Italy 62 A2
San Salvador El Salvador 144 B3
San Salvador de Jujuy Arg. 152 B3
San Severo Italy 62 C2
Sanski Most Bos.-Herz. 63 C2
Santa Ana Bol. 152 B2
Santa Ana El Salvador 144 B3
Santa Ana Mex. 142 A1
Santa Ana U.S.A. 133 C4
Santa Bárbara Mex. 142 B2
Santa Barbara U.S.A. 133 C4
Santa Bárbara, Serra de hills Brazil 154 B2
Santa Catalina Chile 152 B3
Santa Clara Col. 150 C3
Santa Clara Cuba 144 C2
Santa Clarita U.S.A. 133 C4
Santa Croce, Capo c. Italy 62 C3
Santa Cruz r. Arg. 153 B6
Santa Cruz Bol. 152 B2
Santa Cruz Phil. 76 B2
Santa Cruz U.S.A. 133 B3
Santa Cruz Barillas Guat. 143 C3
Santa Cruz Cabrália Brazil 155 E1
Santa Cruz de Moya Spain 61 C2
Santa Cruz de Tenerife Canary Is 100 A3
Santa Cruz Island U.S.A. 133 C4
Santa Cruz Islands Solomon Is 110
Santa Elena, Punta pt Ecuador 146
Santa Fé Arg. 152 B4
Santa Fe U.S.A. 140 C1
Santa Helena de Goiás Brazil 154 B1
Santa Isabel Arg. 153 B4
Santa Isabel i. Solomon Is 110
Santa Luisa, Serra de hills Brazil 154 B1
Santa Maria Brazil 152 C3
Santa María r. Mex. 142 B1
Santa Maria U.S.A. 133 B4
Santa Maria, Cabo de c. Moz. 109 D2
Santa Maria, Cabo de c. Port. 60 B2
Santa Maria das Barreiras Brazil 151 E3
Santa Maria de Leuca, Capo c. Italy 63 C3
Santa Marta Col. 150 B1
Santa Monica U.S.A. 133 C4
Santana Brazil 151 E4
Santander Spain 60 C1
Sant'Antioco Italy 62 A3
Sant'Antioco, Isola di i. Italy 62 A3
Santarém Brazil 151 D3
Santarém Port. 60 B2
Santa Rita do Araguaia Brazil 154 B1
Santa Rosa Arg. 153 B4
Santa Rosa Brazil 152 C3
Santa Rosa CA U.S.A. 133 B3
Santa Rosa NM U.S.A. 140 D2
Santa Rosa de Copán Hond. 144 B3
Santa Rosa Island U.S.A. 133 B4
Santa Rosalía Mex. 142 A2
Santiago Brazil 152 C3
Santiago Chile 153 A4
Santiago Dom. Rep. 145 C3
Santiago Mex. 142 B2
Santiago Panama 144 B4
Santiago Phil. 76 B2
Santiago de Compostela Spain 60 B1
Santiago Ixcuintla Mex. 142 B2
Santiago Papasquiaro Mex. 142 B2
Sant Jordi, Golf de g. Spain 61 D1
Santo Amaro de Campos Brazil 155 D2
Santo André Brazil 155 C2
Santo Ângelo Brazil 152 C3
Santo Antônio, Cabo c. Brazil 151 F4
Santo Antônio da Platina Brazil 154 B2
Santo Antônio de Jesus Brazil 151 F4

Santo Antônio do Içá Brazil **150** C3
Santo Antônio do Monte Brazil
155 C2
Santo Domingo Dom. Rep. **145** D3
Santo Domingo Pueblo U.S.A. **140** C1
Santoríni *i. Greece see* Thíra
Santos Brazil **155** C2
Santo Tomé Arg. **152** C3
San Valentín, Cerro *mt.* Chile **153** A5
San Vicente El Salvador **144** B3
San Vicente Mex. **142** A1
San Vicente de Cañete Peru **150** B4
San Vincenzo Italy **62** B2
San Vito, Capo *c.* Italy **62** B3
Sanya China **83** A4
São Bernardo do Campo Brazil
155 C2
São Borja Brazil **152** C3
São Carlos Brazil **154** C2
São Félix *Mato Grosso* Brazil **151** D4
São Félix *Pará* Brazil **151** D3
São Fidélis Brazil **155** D2
São Francisco Brazil **155** D1
São Francisco *r.* Brazil **151** E4
São Francisco, Ilha de *i.* Brazil
154 C3
São Francisco do Sul Brazil **154** C3
São Gabriel Brazil **152** C4
São Gonçalo Brazil **155** D2
São Gotardo Brazil **155** C1
São João da Barra Brazil **155** D2
São João da Boa Vista Brazil **155** C2
São João da Madeira Port. **60** B1
São João Nepomuceno Brazil **155** D2
São Joaquim da Barra Brazil **154** C2
São José do Rio Preto Brazil **154** C2
São José dos Campos Brazil **155** C2
São José dos Pinhais Brazil **154** C3
São Lourenço Brazil **155** C2
São Lourenço, Pantanal de *marsh*
Brazil **154** A1
São Luís Brazil **151** E3
São Manuel Brazil **154** C2
São Marcos *r.* Brazil **154** C1
São Mateus Brazil **155** E1
São Paulo Brazil **155** C2
São Raimundo Nonato Brazil **151** E3
São Romão Brazil **155** C1
São Roque, Cabo de *c.* Brazil **146**
São Sebastião, Ilha do *i.* Brazil
155 C2
São Sebastião do Paraíso Brazil
154 C2
São Simão Brazil **154** C2
São Simão, Barragem de *resr* Brazil
154 B1
Sao-Siu Indon. **71** C2
São Tomé São Tomé and Príncipe
104 A2
São Tomé *i.* São Tomé and Príncipe
104 A2
São Tomé, Cabo de *c.* Brazil **155** D2
São Tomé and Príncipe *country* Africa
104 A2
São Vicente Brazil **155** C2
São Vicente, Cabo de *c.* Port. **60** B2
Saparua Indon. **71** C3
Sapozhok Rus. Fed. **43** F3
Sapporo Japan **78** D2
Sapri Italy **62** C2
Saqqez Iran **93** C2
Saráb Iran **93** C2
Sara Buri Thai. **75** C2
Sarai Rus. Fed. **43** F3
Sarajevo Bos.-Herz. **63** C2
Saraktash Rus. Fed. **94** F3
Saranac Lake U.S.A. **137** F2
Sarandë Albania **65** B3
Sarangani Islands Phil. **76** B3
Saransk Rus. Fed. **41** D3

Sarapul Rus. Fed. **41** E3
Sarasota U.S.A. **139** D3
Sarata Ukr. **44** C2
Saratoga U.S.A. **134** B2
Saratoga Springs U.S.A. **137** F2
Saratok Malaysia **73** C1
Saratov Rus. Fed. **41** D3
Sarawak *state* Malaysia **73** C1
Saray Turkey **64** C2
Sarayköy Turkey **65** C3
Sarbāz Iran **91** D2
Sardarshahr India **86** B2
Sardegna *i.* Italy *see* Sardinia
Sardinia *i.* Italy **62** A2
Sarektjåkkå *mt.* Sweden **46** D2
Sar-e Pol Afgh. **86** A1
Sargasso Sea N. Atlantic Ocean
160 B4
Sargodha Pak. **86** B1
Sarh Chad **101** D4
Sārī Iran **93** D2
Sarıgöl Turkey **65** C3
Sarıkamış Turkey **93** C1
Sarikei Malaysia **73** C1
Sarina Austr. **115** D2
Sarir Tibesti *des.* Libya **101** D2
Sariwŏn N. Korea **77** B2
Sarıyer Turkey **65** C2
Sarkand Kazakh. **89** E2
Şarköy Turkey **65** C2
Sarmi Indon. **71** D3
Sarnia Can. **136** D2
Sarny Ukr. **44** C1
Sarolangun Indon. **72** B2
Saronikos Kolpos *g.* Greece **65** B3
Saros Körfezi *b.* Turkey **65** C2
Sarova Rus. Fed. **41** D3
Sarrebourg France **59** D2
Sarria Spain **60** B1
Sarrión Spain **61** C1
Sartène France **59** D3
Sárvár Hungary **57** D3
Sarykamyshskoye Ozero *salt l.*
Turkm./Uzbek. **88** C2
Saryshagan Kazakh. **89** E2
Sarysu *watercourse* Kazakh. **94** G3
Sary-Tash Kyrg. **89** E3
Sasaram India **87** C2
Sasebo Japan **79** A4
Saskatchewan *prov.* Can. **127** E2
Saskatchewan *r.* Can. **127** E2
Saskatoon Can. **124** E3
Saskylakh Rus. Fed. **95** J2
Sasolburg S. Africa **109** C2
Sasovo Rus. Fed. **43** F3
Sassandra Côte d'Ivoire **100** B4
Sassari Italy **62** A2
Sassnitz Ger. **56** C2
Satadougou Mali **100** A3
Satara S. Africa **109** D1
Satna India **87** C2
Satpura Range *mts* India **86** B2
Sattahip Thai. **75** B2
Satu Mare Romania **44** B2
Satun Thai. **75** B3
Saucillo Mex. **142** B2
Sauda Norway **47** B4
Sauðárkrókur Iceland **46** [inset]
Saudi Arabia *country* Asia **90** B2
Saugues France **59** C3
Saulieu France **59** C2
Sault Sainte Marie Can. **128** B2
Sault Sainte Marie U.S.A. **136** D1
Saumalkol' Kazakh. **89** D1
Saumlakki Indon. **71** C3
Saumur France **58** B2
Saurimo Angola **104** C3

Sava *r.* Europe **62** D2
Savai'i *i.* Samoa **111**
Savala *r.* Rus. Fed. **43** F3
Savannah *GA* U.S.A. **139** D2
Savannah *TN* U.S.A. **138** C1
Savannah *r.* U.S.A. **139** D2
Savannakhét Laos **74** B2
Savant Lake Can. **128** A1
Savaştepe Turkey **65** C3
Savino Rus. Fed. **43** F2
Savinskiy Rus. Fed. **40** D2
Savona Italy **62** A2
Savonlinna Fin. **47** F3
Savu *i.* Indon. **73** D2
Savukoski Fin. **46** F2
Savu Sea Indon. *see* Sawu, Laut
Sawai Madhopur India **86** B2
Sawankhalok Thai. **74** A2
Sawatch Range *mts* U.S.A. **134** B3
Sawhāj Egypt **102** B2
Sawtell Austr. **117** E2
Sawu, Laut *sea* Indon. **73** D3
Sayhūt Yemen **91** C3
Saynshand Mongolia **81** D2
Sayre U.S.A. **137** E2
Sayula *Jalisco* Mex. **142** B3
Sayula *Veracruz* Mex. **143** C3
Sayward Can. **126** C2
Sazonovo Rus. Fed. **43** E2
Sbaa Alg. **100** B2
Scafell Pike *h.* U.K. **52** B2
Scalea Italy **63** C3
Scapa Flow *inlet* U.K. **50** C1
Scarborough Can. **128** C2
Scarborough Trin. and Tob. **145** D3
Scarborough U.K. **52** C2
Scarborough Shoal *sea feature*
S. China Sea **76** A2
Scarinish U.K. **50** A2
Scarpanto *i.* Greece *see* Karpathos
Schaffhausen Switz. **59** D2
Schagen Neth. **54** A2
Schärding Austria **56** C3
Scharendijke Neth. **54** A2
Scheeßel Ger. **55** D1
Schefferville Can. **129** D1
Schell Creek Range *mts* U.S.A.
133 D3
Schenectady U.S.A. **137** F2
Scheßlitz Ger. **55** E3
Schiermonnikoog *i.* Neth. **54** C1
Schio Italy **62** B1
Schkeuditz Ger. **55** F2
Schladen Ger. **55** E1
Schleiz Ger. **55** F2
Schleswig Ger. **56** B2
Schloss Holte-Stukenbrock Ger.
55 D2
Schlüchtern Ger. **55** D2
Schlüsselfeld Ger. **55** E3
Schmallenberg Ger. **55** D2
Schneverdingen Ger. **55** D1
Schönebeck (Elbe) Ger. **55** E1
Schöningen Ger. **55** E1
Schöntal Ger. **55** D3
Schoonhoven Neth. **54** B2
Schouten Islands P.N.G. **71** D3
Schwabach Ger. **55** E3
Schwäbische Alb *mts* Ger. **56** B3
Schwandorf Ger. **55** F3
Schwaner, Pegunungan *mts* Indon.
73 C2
Schwarzenbek Ger. **55** E1
Schwarzenberg Ger. **55** F2
Schwarzrand *mts* Namibia **108** A2
Schwarzwald *mts* Ger. *see*
Black Forest
Schwaz Austria **56** C3
Schwedt an der Oder Ger. **56** C2
Schweinfurt Ger. **55** E2

chwerin Ger. **55** E1
chweriner See *l.* Ger. **55** E1
chwyz Switz. **59** D2
ciacca Italy **62** B3
cilly, Isles of U.K. **49** B4
cioto *r.* U.S.A. **136** D3
cobey U.S.A. **134** B1
cone Austr. **117** E2
cotia Sea *S. Atlantic Ocean* **119** A4
cotland *admin. div.* U.K. **50** C2
cott, Cape Can. **126** C2
cott City U.S.A. **134** C3
cottsbluff U.S.A. **134** C2
cottsboro U.S.A. **139** C2
courie U.K. **50** B1
cranton U.S.A. **137** E2
cunthorpe U.K. **52** C3
cuol Switz. **59** E2
eal *r.* Can. **127** F2
eal, Cape S. Africa **108** B3
ea Lake Austr. **116** C3
ealy U.S.A. **141** E3
earcy U.S.A. **138** B1
eascale U.K. **52** D2
eattle U.S.A. **132** B1
ebago Lake U.S.A. **137** F2
ebastián Vizcaíno, Bahía *b.* Mex.
  142 A2
ebeş Romania **44** B2
ebesi *i.* Indon. **72** B2
ebezh Rus. Fed. **42** C2
ebinkarahisar Turkey **92** B1
ebring U.S.A. **139** D3
echelt Can. **126** C3
echura Peru **150** A3
ecunderabad India **85** B3
edalia U.S.A. **135** E3
edan France **59** C2
eddon N.Z. **118** B3
edona U.S.A. **140** B2
eeburg Ger. **55** E2
eehausen (Altmark) Ger. **55** E1
eeheim Namibia **108** A2
ées France **58** B2
eesen Ger. **55** E2
eevetal Ger. **55** E1
efadu Sierra Leone **100** A4
efare Botswana **109** C1
egamat Malaysia **72** B1
egezha Rus. Fed. **40** C2
égou Mali **100** B3
egovia Spain **60** C1
eguédine Niger **101** D2
eguéla Côte d'Ivoire **100** B4
eguin U.S.A. **141** E3
egura *r.* Spain **61** C2
egura, Sierra de *mts* Spain **60** C2
ehithwa Botswana **106** B2
einäjoki Fin. **46** E3
eine *r.* France **59** C2
eine, Baie de *b.* France **58** B2
ejny Pol. **57** E2
ekayu Indon. **72** B2
ekondi Ghana **100** B4
elaru *i.* Indon. **71** C3
elatan, Tanjung *pt* Indon. **73** C2
elawik U.S.A. **124** B2
elby U.K. **52** C3
elebi-Phikwe Botswana **106** B2
elenga *r.* Rus. Fed. **67**
elestat France **59** D2
elfoss Iceland **46** [inset]
elibabi Maur. **100** A3
eligman U.S.A. **140** B1
elima Oasis Sudan **102** A2
elimiye Turkey **65** C3
elingué, Lac de *l.* Mali **100** B3
elizharovo Rus. Fed. **42** D2
eljord Norway **47** B4

Selkirk Can. **127** F2
Selkirk U.K. **50** C3
Selkirk Mountains Can. **126** D2
Selma *AL* U.S.A. **138** C2
Selma *CA* U.S.A. **133** C3
Sel'tso Rus. Fed. **43** D3
Selvas *reg.* Brazil **150** B3
Selway *r.* U.S.A. **132** C1
Selwyn Lake Can. **127** E1
Selwyn Mountains Can. **126** B1
Selwyn Range *hills* Austr. **115** C3
Semangka, Teluk *b.* Indon. **72** B2
Semarang Indon. **73** C2
Sematan Malaysia **73** B1
Sembé Congo **104** B2
Semdinli Turkey **93** C2
Semenivka Ukr. **45** D1
Semeru, Gunung *vol.* Indon. **73** C2
Semikarakorsk Rus. Fed. **45** F2
Semiluki Rus. Fed. **43** E3
Seminoe Reservoir U.S.A. **134** B2
Seminole U.S.A. **141** D2
Seminole, Lake U.S.A. **139** C2
Semipalatinsk Kazakh. **89** F1
Semitau Indon. **73** C1
Semnän Iran **93** D2
Semporna Malaysia **73** C1
Semur-en-Auxois France **59** C2
Sena Madureira Brazil **150** C3
Senanga Zambia **106** B1
Sendai *Kagoshima* Japan **79** B4
Sendai *Miyagi* Japan **78** D3
Senegal *country* Africa **100** A3
Sénégal *r.* Maur./Senegal **100** A3
Senftenberg Ger. **55** G2
Sengerema Tanz. **105** D3
Senhor do Bonfim Brazil **151** E4
Senigallia Italy **62** B2
Senj Croatia **62** B2
Senja *i.* Norway **46** D2
Senlac S. Africa **108** B2
Senlis France **58** C2
Senmonorom Cambodia **75** B2
Sennar Sudan **103** B3
Senneterre Can. **128** C2
Senqu *r.* Lesotho **109** C3
Sens France **59** C2
Senta Serb. and Mont. **64** B1
Sentinel Peak Can. **126** C2
Seoni India **87** B2
Seoul S. Korea **77** B2
Sepetiba, Baía de *b.* Brazil **155** D2
Sepik *r.* P.N.G. **71** D3
Sepinang Indon. **73** C1
Sept-Îles Can. **129** D1
Seram *i.* Indon. **71** C3
Seram, Laut *sea* Indon. **71** C3
Serang Indon. **72** B2
Serbia *aut. rep.* Serb. and Mont.
  see Srbija
Serbia and Montenegro *country*
Europe **64** B2
Serebryanyye Prudy Rus. Fed. **43** E3
Seremban Malaysia **72** B1
Serengeti Plain Tanz. **105** D3
Sergach Rus. Fed. **41** D3
Sergiyev Posad Rus. Fed. **43** E2
Seria Brunei **73** C1
Serian Malaysia **73** C1
Serifos *i.* Greece **65** B3
Serik Turkey **65** C3
Sermata, Kepulauan *is* Indon. **71** C3
Serov Rus. Fed. **40** F3
Serowe Botswana **109** C1
Serpa Port. **60** B2
Serpukhov Rus. Fed. **43** E3
Serra da Mesa, Represa *resr* Brazil
  151 E4
Serre *r.* France **54** A3

Serres Greece **65** B2
Serrinha Brazil **151** F4
Sêrro Brazil **155** D1
Sertãozinho Brazil **154** C2
Sertolovo Rus. Fed. **43** D1
Seruyan *r.* Indon. **73** C2
Sêrxü China **80** C2
Sesfontein Namibia **106** A1
Sessa Aurunca Italy **62** B2
Sestri Levante Italy **62** A2
Sestroretsk Rus. Fed. **42** C1
Sète France **59** C3
Sete Lagoas Brazil **155** D1
Setermoen Norway **46** D2
Setesdal *val.* Norway **47** B4
Sétif Alg. **101** C1
Seto-naikai *sea* Japan **79** B4
Settat Morocco **100** B1
Settle U.K. **52** B2
Setúbal Port. **60** B2
Setúbal, Baía de *b.* Port. **60** B2
Seul, Lac *l.* Can. **128** A1
Sevan Armenia **41** D4
Sevan, Lake Armenia **88** B2
Sevastopol' Ukr. **45** D3
Seven Islands Bay Can. **129** D1
Sévérac-le-Château France **58** C3
Severn *r.* Can. **128** B1
Severn S. Africa **108** B2
Severn *r.* U.K. **53** B4
Severnaya Dvina *r.* Rus. Fed. **40** D2
Severnaya Zemlya *is* Rus. Fed. **95** I1
Severnyy *Nenetskiy Avtonomnyy Okrug*
  Rus. Fed. **40** D2
Severnyy *Respublika Komi* Rus. Fed.
  40 F2
Severodvinsk Rus. Fed. **40** C2
Severomorsk Rus. Fed. **46** G2
Severskaya Rus. Fed. **45** E3
Sevier *r.* U.S.A. **133** D3
Sevier Lake U.S.A. **133** D3
Sevilla Spain *see* Seville
Seville Spain **60** B2
Seward U.S.A. **124** C2
Seward Peninsula U.S.A. **124** B2
Sewell Inlet Can. **126** B2
Sexsmith Can. **126** D2
Sextín *r.* Mex. **142** B2
Seyakha Rus. Fed. **40** G1
Seychelles *country* Indian Ocean **99**
Seyðisfjörður Iceland **46** [inset]
Seym *r.* Rus. Fed./Ukr. **45** D1
Seymchan Rus. Fed. **95** M2
Seymour Austr. **117** D3
Seymour *IN* U.S.A. **136** C3
Seymour *TX* U.S.A. **141** E2
Sézanne France **59** C2
Sfakia Greece **65** B3
Sfântu Gheorghe Romania **44** C2
Sfax Tunisia **101** D1
's-Gravenhage Neth. *see* The Hague
Sgurr Alasdair *h.* U.K. **50** A2
Shaanxi *prov.* China **82** A2
Shabel'sk Rus. Fed. **45** E3
Shache China **89** E3
Shackleton Range *mts* Antarctica
  119 A1
Shaftesbury U.K. **53** B4
Shageluk U.S.A. **124** B2
Shahdol India **87** C2
Shah Fuladi *mt.* Afgh. **86** A1
Shahjahanpur India **87** B2
Shahr-e Kord Iran **93** C2
Shahrezā Iran **93** D2
Shahrisabz Uzbek. **89** D3
Shakhovskaya Rus. Fed. **43** E2
Shakhty Rus. Fed. **45** F2
Shakhun'ya Rus. Fed. **40** D3
Shakotan-misaki *c.* Japan **78** D2
Shalkar Kazakh. **88** C2

Shaluli Shan *mts* China **80** C2
Shamattawa Can. **127** F2
Shamrock U.S.A. **141** D1
Shandan China **80** C2
Shandong *prov.* China **82** B2
Shandong Bandao *pen.* China **82** C2
Shangani *r.* Zimbabwe **107** C3
Shanghai China **82** C2
Shanghai *mun.* China **82** C2
Shanghang China **83** B3
Shangluo China **82** A2
Shangrao China **83** B3
Shangshui China **82** B2
Shangyu China **83** C2
Shangzhi China **81** E1
Shangzhou China *see* Shangluo
Shannon *r.* Rep. of Ireland **51** B2
Shannon, Mouth of the Rep. of Ireland **51** B2
Shantou China **83** B3
Shanxi *prov.* China **82** B2
Shaoguan China **83** B3
Shaowu China **83** B3
Shaoxing China **83** C2
Shaoyang China **83** B3
Shaqrā' Saudi Arabia **102** C2
Sharhorod Ukr. **44** C2
Sharjah U.A.E. **91** C2
Sharkawshchyna Belarus **42** C2
Shark Bay Austr. **114** A2
Sharm ash Shaykh Egypt **90** A2
Sharon U.S.A. **137** D2
Shar'ya Rus. Fed. **40** D3
Shashe *r.* Botswana/Zimbabwe **107** B2
Shashemenē Eth. **103** B4
Shasta, Mount *vol.* U.S.A. **132** B2
Shasta Lake U.S.A. **132** B2
Shatsk Rus. Fed. **43** F3
Shatura Rus. Fed. **43** E2
Shaunavon Can. **127** E3
Shawano U.S.A. **136** C2
Shawinigan Can. **129** C2
Shawnee U.S.A. **141** E1
Shay Gap Austr. **114** B2
Shchekino Rus. Fed. **43** E3
Shchelkovo Rus. Fed. **43** E2
Shchigry Rus. Fed. **43** E3
Shchors Ukr. **45** D1
Shchuchyn Belarus **42** C3
Shebekino Rus. Fed. **45** E1
Sheberghān Afgh. **86** A1
Sheboygan U.S.A. **136** C2
Shebsh *r.* Rus. Fed. **45** E3
Sheelin, Lough *l.* Rep. of Ireland **51** C2
Sheffield U.K. **52** C3
Sheksna Rus. Fed. **43** E2
Sheksninskoye Vodokhranilishche *resr* Rus. Fed. **43** E2
Shelagskiy, Mys *pt* Rus. Fed. **95** N2
Shelburne Can. **129** D2
Shelby U.S.A. **132** D1
Shelbyville *IN* U.S.A. **136** C3
Shelbyville *TN* U.S.A. **139** C1
Shelikhova, Zaliv *g.* Rus. Fed. **95** M2
Shellbrook Can. **127** E2
Shelton U.S.A. **132** B1
Shenandoah U.S.A. **135** D2
Shenandoah *r.* U.S.A. **137** E3
Shendam Nigeria **104** A2
Shendi Sudan **90** A3
Shenkursk Rus. Fed. **40** D2
Shenyang China **82** C1
Shenzhen China **83** B3
Shepetivka Ukr. **44** C1
Shepparton Austr. **117** D3
Sheppey, Isle of *i.* U.K. **53** D4
Sherbro Island Sierra Leone **100** A4
Sherbrooke *N.S.* Can. **129** D2
Sherbrooke *Que.* Can. **129** C2
Shereiq Sudan **102** B3
Sheridan U.S.A. **134** B2

Sherman U.S.A. **141** E2
's-Hertogenbosch Neth. **54** B2
Shetland Islands *Scotland* U.K. **50** [inset]
Shetpe Kazakh. **88** C2
Sheyenne *r.* U.S.A. **135** D1
Shibām Yemen **91** B3
Shibetsu Japan **78** E2
Shicheng China **83** B3
Shiel, Loch *l.* U.K. **50** B2
Shihezi China **89** F2
Shijiazhuang China **82** B2
Shikarpur Pak. **86** A2
Shikoku *i.* Japan **79** B4
Shikotsu-ko *l.* Japan **78** D2
Shilega Rus. Fed. **40** D2
Shiliguri India **87** C2
Shillong India **87** D2
Shilovo Rus. Fed. **43** F3
Shimbiris *mt.* Somalia **103** C3
Shimizu Japan **79** C3
Shimla India **87** B1
Shimoga India **85** B3
Shimonoseki Japan **79** B4
Shin, Loch *l.* U.K. **50** B1
Shindand Afgh. **86** A1
Shingū Japan **79** C4
Shingwedzi S. Africa **109** D1
Shingwedzi *r.* S. Africa **109** D1
Shinyanga Tanz. **105** D3
Shiono-misaki *c.* Japan **79** C4
Shiprock U.S.A. **140** C1
Shiqian China **83** A3
Shiquan China **82** A2
Shirane-san *mt.* Japan **79** C3
Shīrāz Iran **93** D3
Shiretoko-misaki *c.* Japan **78** E2
Shiriya-zaki *c.* Japan **78** D2
Shiv India **86** B2
Shivpuri India **87** B2
Shiyan China **82** B2
Shizuishan China **82** A2
Shizuoka Japan **79** C4
Shklow Belarus **43** D3
Shkodër Albania **63** C2
Shmidta, Ostrov *i.* Rus. Fed. **95** I1
Shor Barsa-Kel'mes *salt marsh* Uzbek. **93** D1
Shoshone U.S.A. **133** C3
Shoshone Mountains U.S.A. **133** C3
Shoshong Botswana **109** C1
Shostka Ukr. **45** D1
Shouxian China **82** B2
Shpola Ukr. **45** D2
Shreveport U.S.A. **142** B2
Shrewsbury U.K. **53** B3
Shu'ab, Ra's *pt* Yemen **91** C3
Shuangcheng China **74** A1
Shuangliao China **77** A1
Shuangyang China **77** B1
Shuangyashan China **78** B1
Shubarkuduk Kazakh. **88** C2
Shubrā al Khaymah Egypt **102** B1
Shugozero Rus. Fed. **43** D2
Shumba Zimbabwe **106** B1
Shumen Bulg. **64** C2
Shumilina Belarus **42** C2
Shumyachi Rus. Fed. **43** D3
Shungnak U.S.A. **124** C2
Shuqrah Yemen **90** B3
Shushkodom Rus. Fed. **43** F2
Shushtar Iran **93** C2
Shuswap Lake Can. **126** D2
Shuya Rus. Fed. **43** F2
Shuyskoye Rus. Fed. **43** F2
Shwebo Myanmar **74** A1
Shwedwin Myanmar **74** A1
Shwegyin Myanmar **74** A2

Shymkent Kazakh. **89** D2
Shyroke Ukr. **45** D2
Sia Indon. **71** C3
Siahan Range *mts* Pak. **86** A2
Sialkot Pak. **86** B1
Siargao *i.* Phil. **76** B3
Šiauliai Lith. **42** B2
Šibenik Croatia **63** C2
Siberia *reg.* Rus. Fed. **95** J2
Siberut *i.* Indon. **72** A2
Sibi Pak. **86** A2
Sibiu Romania **44** B2
Sibolga Indon. **72** A1
Sibsagar India **74** A1
Sibu Malaysia **73** C1
Sibut C.A.R. **104** B2
Sibuyan *i.* Phil. **76** B2
Sibuyan Sea Phil. **76** B2
Sicamous Can. **126** D2
Sichon Thai. **75** A3
Sichuan *prov.* China **82** A2
Sichuan Pendi *basin* China **83** A3
Sicié, Cap *c.* France **59** D3
Sicilia *i.* Italy *see* Sicily
Sicilian Channel Italy/Tunisia **62** B3
Sicily *i.* Italy **62** B3
Sicuani Peru **150** B4
Siddhapur India **86** B2
Sideros, Akra *pt* Greece **65** C3
Sidi Aïssa Alg. **61** D2
Sidi Ali Alg. **61** D2
Sidi Bel Abbès Alg. **100** B1
Sidi Ifni Morocco **100** A2
Sidikalang Indon. **72** A1
Sidi Okba Alg. **61** E3
Sidlaw Hills U.K. **50** C2
Sidmouth U.K. **53** B4
Sidney Can. **132** B1
Sidney *MT* U.S.A. **134** C1
Sidney *NE* U.S.A. **134** C2
Sidney *OH* U.S.A. **136** D2
Sidney Lanier, Lake U.S.A. **139** D2
Sidoan Indon. **73** D1
Sidon Lebanon **92** B2
Sidrolândia Brazil **154** B2
Siedlce Pol. **57** E2
Sieg *r.* Ger. **54** C2
Siegen Ger. **54** D2
Siĕmréab Cambodia **75** B2
Siena Italy **62** B2
Sieradz Pol. **57** D2
Sierra Grande Arg. **153** B5
Sierra Leone *country* Africa **100** A4
Sierra Mojada Mex. **142** B2
Sierra Vista U.S.A. **140** B2
Sierre Switz. **59** D2
Sifnos *i.* Greece **65** B3
Sig Alg. **61** C2
Sigguup Nunaa *pen.* Greenland **125** [?]
Sighetu Marmaţiei Romania **44** B2
Sighişoara Romania **44** B2
Sigli Indon. **72** A1
Siglufjörður Iceland **46** [inset]
Sigmaringen Ger. **56** B3
Signy-l'Abbaye France **54** B3
Sigüenza Spain **60** C1
Sigüiri Guinea **100** B3
Sigulda Latvia **42** B2
Sihanoukville Cambodia **75** B2
Siilinjärvi Fin. **46** F3
Siirt Turkey **93** C2
Sijunjung Indon. **72** B2
Sikar India **86** B2
Sikasso Mali **100** B3
Sikeston U.S.A. **135** F3
Sikhote-Alin' *mts* Rus. Fed. **78** B2
Sikinos *i.* Greece **65** C3
Silao Mex. **142** B2
Silchar India **74** A1
Siletiteniz, Ozero *salt l.* Kazakh. **89** [?]

ilgarhi Nepal **87** C2
ilifke Turkey **92** B2
iling Co *salt l.* China **87** C1
ilistra Bulg. **64** C2
ilivri Turkey **92** A1
iljan I. Sweden **47** C2
ilkeborg Denmark **47** B4
illamãe Estonia **42** C2
iloam Springs U.S.A. **138** B1
ilobela S. Africa **109** D2
ilutē Lith. **42** B2
ilvan Turkey **93** C2
ilver City U.S.A. **140** C2
ilverton U.S.A. **134** B3
imao China **74** B1
imav Turkey **65** C3
imav Dağları *mts* Turkey **65** C3
imcoe, Lake Can. **137** C2
imba Dem. Rep. Congo **107** D4
imcoe, Lake Can. **137** C2
imeulue *i.* Indon. **72** A1
imferopol' Ukr. **45** D3
imleu Silvaniei Romania **44** B2
immern (Hunsrück) Ger. **54** C3
imonhouse Can. **127** C2
impson Desert Austr. **115** C2
imrishamn Sweden **47** C4
inabang Indon. **72** A1
inai *pen.* Egypt **102** B2
inadogo Asia **72** B1
ingahi India **87** C2
inga Sudan **90** A3
ingapore Asia **72** B1
ingapore *country* Asia **72** B1
ingaraja Indon. **73** C2
ingida Tanz. **105** D3
ingkaling Hkamti Myanmar **74** A1
ingkang Indon. **73** D2
ingkawang Indon. **72** B1
ingkil Indon. **72** A1
ingleton Austr. **117** E2
inh Myanmar **74** A1
iniscola Italy **62** A2
inj Croatia **63** C2
injai Indon. **73** D2
inkat Sudan **102** B3
inkiang Aut. reg. China see
inop Turkey **92** B1
inp'o N. Korea **77** B1
insheim Ger. **55** D3
intang China **73** C1
int Anthonis Neth. **54** B2
int-Laureins Belgium **54** A2
int-Niklaas Belgium **54** B2
inton U.S.A. **141** E3
inŭiju N. Korea **77** A1
iofok Hungary **57** D3
ion Switz. **59** D2
iux Center U.S.A. **135** D2
iux City U.S.A. **135** D2
iux Falls U.S.A. **135** D2
iux Lookout Can. **128** A1
iping China **77** A1
iowsk Lake Can. **127** C2
iura *i.* Indon. **72** A2
ia *r.* Norway **47** B4
Edward Pellew Group *is* Austr.
  15 C1
iik Iran **91** C2
i Kit Dam Thai. **74** B2

Sir James MacBrien, Mount Can.
  126 C1
Sirjan Iran **93** D3
Şırnak Turkey **93** C2
Sirohi India **86** B2
Sirsa India **86** B2
Sirte Libya **101** D1
Sirte, Gulf of Libya **101** D1
Širvintos Lith. **42** C2
Sisal Mex. **143** C2
Sishen S. Africa **108** B2
Sisian Armenia **93** C2
Sisipuk Lake Can. **127** E2
Sisophon Cambodia **75** B2
Sisteron France **59** D3
Sitapur India **87** C2
Siteki Swaziland **109** D2
Sitka U.S.A. **126** B2
Sittard Neth. **54** B2
Sittaung *r.* Myanmar **74** A2
Sittwe Myanmar **74** A1
Situbondo Indon. **73** C2
Sivas Turkey **92** B2
Sivasli Turkey **65** C3
Siverek Turkey **92** B2
Sivrihisar Turkey **92** B2
Sīwah Egypt **102** A2
Sīwah, Wāḩāt *oasis* Egypt **92** A3
Siwalik Range *mts* India/Nepal **86** B1
Siwa Oasis Egypt *see* Sīwah, Wāḩāt
Six-Fours-les-Plages France **59** D3
Sixian China **82** B2
Siyabuswa S. Africa **109** C2
Sjenica Serb. and Mont. **64** B2
Sjøvegan Norway **46** D2
Skadovs'k Ukr. **45** D2
Skagen Denmark **47** C4
Skagerrak *str.* Denmark/Norway **47** B4
Skagit *r.* U.S.A. **132** B1
Skagway U.S.A. **126** B2
Skardu Jammu and Kashmir **86** B1
Skarżysko-Kamienna Pol. **57** E2
Skawina Pol. **57** D3
Skeena *r.* Can. **126** C2
Skeena Mountains Can. **126** C2
Skegness U.K. **52** D3
Skellefteå Sweden **46** E3
Skellefteälven *r.* Sweden **46** E3
Skerries Rep. of Ireland **51** C2
Skiathos *i.* Greece **65** B3
Skibbereen Rep. of Ireland **51** B3
Skiðadals-jökull *glacier* Iceland
  46 [inset]
Skiddaw *h.* U.K. **52** B2
Skien Norway **47** B4
Skierniewice Pol. **57** E2
Skikda Alg. **101** C1
Skipton U.K. **116** C3
Skipton U.K. **52** B3
Skive Denmark **47** B4
Skjervøy Norway **46** E1
Skodje Norway **48** E1
Skopelos *i.* Greece **65** B3
Skopin Rus. Fed. **43** E3
Skopje Macedonia **64** B2
Skövde Sweden **47** C4
Skowhegan U.S.A. **137** G2
Skrunda Latvia **42** B2
Skukum, Mount Can. **126** B1
Skukuza S. Africa **109** D1
Skuodas Lith. **42** B2
Skye *i.* U.K. **50** A2
Skyros Greece **65** B3
Skyros *i.* Greece **65** B3
Slagelse Denmark **47** C4
Slaney *r.* Rep. of Ireland **51** C2
Slantsy Rus. Fed. **42** C2
Slatina Croatia **63** C1
Slatina Romania **44** B3
Slave *r.* Can. **127** D1

Slave Coast Africa **100** C4
Slave Lake Can. **126** D2
Slavgorod Rus. Fed. **89** E1
Slavonski Brod Croatia **63** C1
Slavuta Ukr. **44** C1
Slavutych Ukr. **44** D1
Slavyanka Rus. Fed. **78** B2
Slavyansk-na-Kubani Rus. Fed. **45** E2
Slawharad Belarus **43** D3
Sławno Pol. **57** D2
Slea Head Rep. of Ireland **51** A2
Sleeper Islands Can. **128** C1
Slieve Donard *h.* U.K. **51** D1
Slieve Gamph *hills* Rep. of Ireland
  51 B2
Sligo Rep. of Ireland **51** B1
Sligo Bay Rep. of Ireland **51** B1
Slite Sweden **47** D4
Sliven Bulg. **64** C2
Slobozia Romania **44** C3
Slocan Can. **126** D3
Slonim Belarus **42** C3
Sloten Neth. **54** B1
Slough U.K. **53** C4
Slovakia *country* Europe **57** D3
Slovenia *country* Europe **62** B1
Slov"yans'k Ukr. **45** E2
Sluch *r.* Ukr. **44** C1
Słupsk Pol. **57** D2
Slutsk Belarus **42** C3
Slyne Head Rep. of Ireland **51** A2
Smallwood Reservoir Can. **129** D1
Smalyavichy Belarus **42** C3
Smarhon' Belarus **42** C3
Smeaton Can. **127** E2
Smederevo Serb. and Mont. **64** B2
Smederevska Palanka Serb. and Mont.
  64 B2
Smila Ukr. **45** D2
Smiltene Latvia **42** C2
Smithers Can. **126** C2
Smithfield U.S.A. **139** E1
Smith Mountain Lake U.S.A. **137** D3
Smiths Falls Can. **128** C2
Smoky Hills U.S.A. **135** D3
Smøla *i.* Norway **46** E3
Smolensk Rus. Fed. **43** D3
Smolyan Bulg. **64** B2
Smooth Rock Falls Can. **128** B2
Smyrna Turkey *see* İzmir
Snæfell *mt.* Iceland **46** [inset]
Snaefell *h.* Isle of Man **52** A2
Snake *r.* U.S.A. **132** C1
Snake River Plain U.S.A. **132** D2
Sneek Neth. **54** B1
Sneem Rep. of Ireland **51** B3
Sneeuberge *mts* S. Africa **108** B3
Snežnik *mt.* Slovenia **62** B1
Snihurivka Ukr. **45** D2
Snøhetta *mt.* Norway **47** B3
Snowbird Lake Can. **127** E1
Snowdon *mt.* U.K. **52** A3
Snowdrift *r.* Can. **127** D1
Snowdrift Can. **127** D1
Snowflake U.S.A. **140** B2
Snow Lake Can. **127** E2
Snowtown Austr. **116** B2
Snowy *r.* Austr. **117** D3
Snowy Mountains Austr. **117** D3
Snyder U.S.A. **141** D2
Soalala Madag. **107** [inset] D1
Sobat *r.* Sudan **103** B4
Sobernheim Ger. **54** C3
Sobinka Rus. Fed. **43** F2
Sobradinho, Barragem de *resr* Brazil
  151 E4
Sobral Brazil **151** E3
Sochi Rus. Fed. **45** E3
Sŏch'ŏn S. Korea **77** B2
Society Islands Fr. Polynesia **159** E6
Socorro Col. **150** B2

Socorro U.S.A. **140** C2
Socorro, Isla i. Mex. **142** A3
Socotra i. Yemen **91** C3
Soc Trăng Vietnam **75** B3
Socuéllamos Spain **60** C2
Sodankylä Fin. **46** E3
Soda Springs U.S.A. **132** D2
Söderhamn Sweden **47** D3
Söderköping Sweden **42** A2
Södertälje Sweden **47** D4
Sodiri Sudan **102** A3
Sodo Eth. **103** B4
Södra Kvarken str. Fin./Sweden **47** D3
Soest Ger. **54** D2
Sofia Bulg. **64** D2
Sofiya Bulg. see Sofia
Sofporog Rus. Fed. **46** G2
Sōfu-gan i. Japan **79** D5
Sog China **80** C2
Sognefjorden inlet Norway **47** B3
Söğüt Turkey **65** D2
Soignies Belgium **54** B2
Soissons France **59** C2
Sokal' Ukr. **44** B1
Söke Turkey **65** C3
Sokhumi Georgia **93** C1
Sokodé Togo **100** C4
Sokol Rus. Fed. **43** F2
Sokolov Czech Rep. **55** F2
Sokol'skoye Rus. Fed. **43** F2
Sokoto Nigeria **101** C3
Sokoto r. Nigeria **100** C3
Sokyryany Ukr. **44** C2
Solapur India **85** B3
Soledad U.S.A. **133** B3
Soligalich Rus. Fed. **43** F2
Solihull U.K. **53** C3
Solikamsk Rus. Fed. **40** E3
Sol'-Iletsk Rus. Fed. **41** E3
Solingen Ger. **54** C2
Solitaire Namibia **108** A1
Sollefteå Sweden **46** D3
Sollentuna Sweden **47** D4
Solling hills Ger. **55** D2
Solnechnogorsk Rus. Fed. **43** E2
Solok Indon. **72** B2
Solomon Islands country
S. Pacific Ocean **112**
Solomon Sea S. Pacific Ocean **158** D3
Solothurn Switz. **59** D2
Soltau Ger. **55** D1
Sol'tsy Rus. Fed. **43** D2
Solway Firth est. U.K. **50** C3
Solwezi Zambia **106** B1
Soma Turkey **65** C2
Somalia country Africa **103** C4
Sombo Angola **104** C3
Sombor Serb. and Mont. **64** A1
Sombrerete Mex. **142** B2
Somerset U.S.A. **136** D3
Somerset East S. Africa **109** C3
Somerset Island Can. **124** C1
Somerset West S. Africa **108** A3
Sömmerda Ger. **55** E2
Son r. India **87** C2
Sønderborg Denmark **47** B5
Sondershausen Ger. **55** E2
Sông Đa r. Vietnam see Black River
Sông Da, Hồ resr Vietnam **74** B1
Sông Dà, Hồ resr Vietnam **105** D4
Sŏngan N. Korea **77** B3
Sŏnghua Hu resr China **77** B1
Songkhla Thai. **75** B3
Sŏngnam S. Korea **77** B2
Sŏngnim N. Korea **77** B2
Songo Angola **104** B3
Songo Moz. **107** C1
Songyuan China **81** E1
Sonkovo Rus. Fed. **43** E2
Son La Vietnam **74** B1

Sonmiani Pak. **86** A2
Sonneberg Ger. **55** E2
Sonora r. Mex. **142** A2
Sonora CA U.S.A. **133** B3
Sonora TX U.S.A. **141** D2
Sopo watercourse Sudan **103** A4
Sopron Hungary **57** D3
Sora Italy **62** B2
Sorel Can. **128** C2
Sorell Austr. **115** D4
Soria Spain **60** C1
Soroca Moldova **44** C2
Sorocaba Brazil **154** C2
Sorochinsk Rus. Fed. **41** E3
Sorol atoll Micronesia **71** D2
Sorong Indon. **71** C3
Soroti Uganda **105** D2
Sørøya i. Norway **46** E1
Sorsele Sweden **46** D2
Sorsogon Phil. **76** B2
Sortavala Rus. Fed. **47** G3
Sortland Norway **46** D2
Sŏsan S. Korea **77** B2
Soshanguve S. Africa **109** C2
Sosna r. Rus. Fed. **43** E3
Sosneado mt. Arg. **153** B4
Sosnogorsk Rus. Fed. **40** E2
Sosnovka Murmanskaya Oblast'
Rus. Fed. **40** D2
Sosnovka Tambovskaya Oblast'
Rus. Fed. **43** F3
Sosnovo Rus. Fed. **43** D1
Sosnovyy Bor Rus. Fed. **42** C2
Sosnowiec Pol. **57** D2
Sosyka r. Rus. Fed. **45** E2
Sotea la Marina Mex. **143** C2
Souanké Congo **104** B2
Sougueur Alg. **61** D2
Souillac France **58** C3
Souilly France **54** B3
Sŏul S. Korea see Seoul
Soulac-sur-Mer France **58** B2
Soulom France **58** B3
Sour el Ghozlane Alg. **61** D2
Souris Man. Can. **127** E3
Souris P.E.I. Can. **129** D2
Souris r. Can. **134** D1
Sousa Brazil **151** F3
Sousse Tunisia **101** D1
Soustons France **58** B3
South Africa, Republic of country
Africa **108** B3
Southampton U.K. **53** C4
Southampton, Cape Can. **127** G1
Southampton Island Can. **127** G1
South Andaman i. India **75** A2
South Australia state Austr. **116** A2
South Baymouth Can. **128** B2
South Bend U.S.A. **136** C2
South Carolina state U.S.A. **139** D2
South China Sea N. Pacific Ocean
70 B2
South Dakota state U.S.A. **134** C2
South Downs hills U.K. **53** C4
South East Cape Austr. **110**
Southend Can. **127** E2
Southend-on-Sea U.K. **53** D4
Southern Alps mts N.Z. **118** B3
Southern Cross Austr. **114** A3
Southern Indian Lake Can. **127** F2
Southern Pines U.S.A. **139** E1
Southern Uplands hills U.K. **50** B3
South Geomagnetic Pole Antarctica
119 F1
South Georgia i. S. Atlantic Ocean
153 E6
South Georgia and South Sandwich
Islands terr. S. Atlantic Ocean **149**
South Henik Lake Can. **127** F1

South Korea country Asia **77** B2
South Lake Tahoe U.S.A. **133** B3
South Magnetic Pole Antarctica
119 G3
South Orkney Islands
S. Atlantic Ocean **119** A3
South Platte r. U.S.A. **134** C2
South Pole Antarctica **119**
Southport U.K. **52** B3
Southport U.S.A. **139** E2
South Ronaldsay i. U.K. **50** C1
South Sandwich Islands
S. Atlantic Ocean **147**
South Saskatchewan r. Can. **127** E2
South Seal r. Can. **127** F2
South Shetland Islands Antarctica
119 A3
South Shields U.K. **52** C2
South Taranaki Bight b. N.Z. **118** B3
South Twin Island Can. **128** C1
South Uist i. U.K. **50** A2
South West Rocks Austr. **117** E2
Southwold U.K. **53** D3
Soverato Italy **63** C3
Sovetsk Rus. Fed. **42** B2
Sovetskiy Khanty-Mansiyskiy
Avtonomnyy Okrug Rus. Fed. **40** F2
Sovetskiy Leningradskaya Oblast'
Rus. Fed. **42** C1
Sovyets'kyy Ukr. **45** D2
Soweto S. Africa **109** C2
Sōya-misaki c. Japan **78** D1
Sozh r. Europe **44** D1
Sozopol Bulg. **64** C2
Spain country Europe **60** C1
Spalding U.K. **52** C3
Spanish Fork U.S.A. **132** D2
Spanish Point Rep. of Ireland **51** B2
Sparagio, Monte mt. Italy **62** B3
Sparks U.S.A. **133** C3
Sparta U.S.A. **136** B2
Spartanburg U.S.A. **139** D2
Sparti Greece **65** B3
Spartivento, Capo c. Italy **63** C3
Spas-Demensk Rus. Fed. **43** D3
Spas-Klepiki Rus. Fed. **43** F2
Spassk-Dal'niy Rus. Fed. **78** B2
Spassk-Ryazanskiy Rus. Fed. **43** F3
Spatha, Akra pt Greece **65** B3
Spearfish U.S.A. **134** C2
Spearman U.S.A. **141** D1
Spencer U.S.A. **135** D2
Spencer Gulf est. Austr. **116** B2
Spennymoor U.K. **52** C2
Spenser Mountains N.Z. **118** B3
Spessart reg. Ger. **55** D3
Spey r. U.K. **50** C2
Speyer Ger. **55** D3
Spiekeroog i. Ger. **54** C1
Spijkenisse Neth. **54** B2
Spirit River Can. **126** C2
Spišská Nová Ves Slovakia **57** D3
Spitsbergen i. Svalbard **94** A2
Spittal an der Drau Austria **56** C3
Split Croatia **63** C2
Split Lake Can. **127** F2
Split Lake l. Can. **127** F2
Spokane U.S.A. **132** C1
Spoleto Italy **59** E3
Spooner U.S.A. **136** B1
Spratly Islands S. China Sea **72** C1
Spree r. Ger. **56** C2
Springbok S. Africa **108** A2
Springdale Can. **129** E2
Springdale U.S.A. **138** B1
Springe Ger. **55** D1
Springer U.S.A. **140** D1
Springerville U.S.A. **140** C2
Springfield CO U.S.A. **134** C3
Springfield IL U.S.A. **136** C3
Springfield MA U.S.A. **137** F2

Springfield *MO* U.S.A. **135** E3
Springfield *OH* U.S.A. **136** D3
Springfield *OR* U.S.A. **132** B2
Springfontein S. Africa **109** C3
Springhill Can. **129** D2
Spring Hill U.S.A. **139** D3
Springs Junction N.Z. **118** B3
Spurn Head U.K. **52** D3
Squamish Can. **126** C3
Squillace, Golfo di *g.* Italy **63** C3
Srbija *aut. rep.* Serb. and Mont. **64** B2
Srebrenica Bos.-Herz. **63** C2
Sredets Bulg. **64** C2
Srednyy Khrebet *mts* Rus. Fed.
95 M3
Srednekolymsk Rus. Fed. **95** M2
Sredne-Russkaya Vozvyshennost'
hills Rus. Fed. *see*
Central Russian Upland
Srednogorie Bulg. **64** D2
Sretensk Rus. Fed. **81** D1
Sri Aman Malaysia **73** C1
Sri Kakulam India **85** C3
Sri Lanka *country* Asia **85** C4
Sri Pada *mt.* Sri Lanka **85** C4
Srinagar India **86** B1
Sri Jawardenepura Kotte Sri Lanka
85 B4
Srivardhan India **85** B3
Stade Ger. **55** D1
Stadensen Ger. **55** E1
Stadskanaal Neth. **54** C1
Stadtlendorf Ger. **55** D2
Stadthagen Ger. **55** D1
Staffelstein Ger. **55** E2
Stafford U.K. **52** B3
Staines U.K. **53** C4
Stakhanov Ukr. **45** E2
Stalingrad Rus. Fed. *see* Volgograd
Stalowa Wola Pol. **57** E2
Stamford U.K. **53** C3
Stamford *CT* U.S.A. **137** F2
Stamford *TX* U.S.A. **141** E2
Stampriet Namibia **108** A1
Stamsund Norway **46** C2
Standerton S. Africa **109** C2
Standish U.S.A. **136** D2
Stanger S. Africa **109** D2
Stanikov Czech Rep. **55** F3
Stanley Falkland Is **153** C6
Stanley U.S.A. **134** C1
Stanovoye Nagor'ye *mts* Rus. Fed.
95 J3
Stanovoy Khrebet *mts* Rus. Fed.
95 K3
Stanthorpe Austr. **117** E1
Starachowice Pol. **57** E2
Stara Planina *mts* Bulg./Serb. and
Mont. *see* Balkan Mountains
Staraya Russa Rus. Fed. **43** D2
Staraya Toropa Rus. Fed. **43** D2
Stara Zagora Bulg. **64** C2
Stargard Szczeciński Pol. **57** D2
Starkville U.S.A. **138** C2
Starobil's'k Ukr. **45** E2
Starodub Rus. Fed. **43** D3
Starogard Gdański Pol. **57** D2
Starokostyantyniv Ukr. **44** C2
Starominskaya Rus. Fed. **45** E2
Staroshcherbinovskaya Rus. Fed.
45 E2
Starotitarovskaya Rus. Fed. **45** E2
Staroyur'yevo Rus. Fed. **43** F3
Start Point *pt* U.K. **53** B4
Starya Darohi Belarus **42** C3
Staryy Oskol Rus. Fed. **43** E3
Stforf Ger. **55** E2
State College U.S.A. **137** E2
Statesboro U.S.A. **139** D2
Statesville U.S.A. **139** D1

Stavanger Norway **47** B4
Stavropol' Rus. Fed. **41** D4
Stavropol'skaya Vozvyshennost' *hills*
Rus. Fed. **41** D4
Stawell Austr. **116** C3
Steadville S. Africa **109** C2
Steamboat Springs U.S.A. **134** B2
Stedten Ger. **55** E2
Steen River Can. **126** D2
Steens Mountain U.S.A. **132** C2
Steenwijk Neth. **54** C1
Stefansson Island Can. **124** C2
Steigerwald *mts* Ger. **55** E3
Steinbach Can. **127** F3
Steinfurt Ger. **54** C1
Steinhausen Namibia **106** A2
Steinkjer Norway **46** C2
Steinkopf S. Africa **108** A2
Stella S. Africa **108** B2
Stenay France **59** D2
Stendal Ger. **55** E1
Stephenville Can. **129** E2
Stephenville U.S.A. **141** E2
Sterling S. Africa **108** B3
Sterling *CO* U.S.A. **134** C2
Sterling *IL* U.S.A. **136** C2
Sterlitamak Rus. Fed. **41** E3
Sternberg Ger. **55** E1
Stettler Can. **127** D2
Steubenville U.S.A. **137** D2
Stevenage U.K. **53** C4
Stevenson Lake Can. **127** F2
Stevens Village U.S.A. **124** C2
Stewart Can. **126** C2
Stewart *r.* Can. **126** B1
Stewart Island N.Z. **118** A4
Steyr Austria **56** C3
Steytlerville S. Africa **108** B3
Stikine *r.* Can. **126** B2
Stikine Plateau Can. **126** B2
Stilbaai S. Africa **108** B3
Stillwater U.S.A. **141** E1
Štip Macedonia **63** D2
Stirling U.K. **50** C2
Stjørdalshalsen Norway **46** C3
Stockerau Austria **57** D3
Stockholm Sweden **47** D4
Stockport U.K. **52** B3
Stockton U.S.A. **133** B3
Stockton-on-Tees U.K. **52** C2
Stod Czech Rep. **55** F3
Stœng Trêng Cambodia **75** B2
Stoer, Point of *pt* U.K. **50** B1
Stoke-on-Trent U.K. **52** B3
Stol *mt.* Serb. and Mont. **64** B2
Stolac Bos.-Herz. **63** C2
Stolberg (Rheinland) Ger. **54** C2
Stolbovoy Rus. Fed. **40** F1
Stolin Belarus **42** C3
Stollberg Ger. **55** F2
Stolzenau Ger. **55** D1
Stonehaven U.K. **50** C2
Stonewall Can. **127** F2
Stony Rapids Can. **124** C3
Storavan *l.* Sweden **46** D2
Store Bælt *sea chan.* Denmark *see*
Great Belt
Støren Norway **46** C3
Storforshei Norway **46** C2
Storkerson Peninsula Can. **124** E2
Storm Lake U.S.A. **135** D2
Stornoway U.K. **50** A1
Storozhevsk Rus. Fed. **40** E2
Storozhynets' Ukr. **44** C2
Storsjön *l.* Sweden **46** C3
Storslett Norway **46** E2
Storuman Sweden **46** D2
Stour *r.* England U.K. **53** C3
Stour *r.* England U.K. **53** C4
Stout Lake Can. **128** A1

Stowbtsy Belarus **42** C3
Strabane U.K. **51** C1
Strakonice Czech Rep. **56** C3
Stralsund Ger. **56** C2
Strand S. Africa **108** A3
Stranda Norway **47** B3
Strangford Lough *inlet* U.K. **51** D1
Stranraer U.K. **50** B3
Strasbourg France **59** D2
Strasburg Ger. **55** F1
Stratford Can. **137** D2
Stratford N.Z. **118** B2
Stratford U.S.A. **141** D1
Stratford-upon-Avon U.K. **53** C3
Strathspey *val.* U.K. **50** C2
Straubing Ger. **56** C3
Strausberg Ger. **55** F1
Streaky Bay Austr. **116** A2
Streator U.S.A. **136** C2
Strehaia Romania **44** B3
Stroeder Arg. **153** B5
Ströhen Ger. **55** D1
Stromboli, Isola *i.* Italy **62** C3
Stromness U.K. **50** C1
Strömsund Sweden **46** D3
Stronsay *i.* U.K. **50** C1
Stroud U.K. **53** B4
Stroud Lake Can. **128** A1
Strücklingen (Saterland) Ger. **54** C1
Struga Macedonia **65** B2
Strugi-Krasnyye Rus. Fed. **42** C2
Struis Bay S. Africa **108** B3
Strumica Macedonia **65** B2
Strydenburg S. Africa **108** B2
Stryy Ukr. **44** B2
Stuart Can. **126** C2
Stull Lake Can. **127** F2
Stupino Rus. Fed. **43** E3
Sturgeon Bay U.S.A. **136** C2
Sturgeon Falls Can. **128** C2
Sturgeon Lake Can. **128** A2
Sturgis *MI* U.S.A. **136** C2
Sturgis *SD* U.S.A. **134** C2
Sturt Creek *watercourse* Austr. **114** B1
Sturt Stony Desert Austr. **116** C1
Stutterheim S. Africa **109** C3
Stuttgart Ger. **56** B3
Stuttgart U.S.A. **138** B2
Stykkishólmur Iceland **46** [inset]
Styr *r.* Belarus/Ukr. **44** C1
Suaçuí Grande *r.* Brazil **155** D1
Suakin Sudan **102** B3
Suara, Mount Eritrea **90** A3
Subotica Serb. and Mont. **64** A1
Suceava Romania **44** C2
Suck *r.* Rep. of Ireland **51** B2
Sucre Bol. **152** B2
Sucuriú *r.* Brazil **154** B2
Suda Rus. Fed. **43** E2
Sudak Ukr. **45** D3
Sudan *country* Africa **103** A3
Sudbury Can. **128** C2
Sudd *swamp* Sudan **103** A4
Sudety *mts* Czech Rep./Pol. **36**
Sudislavl' Rus. Fed. **43** F2
Sudogda Rus. Fed. **43** F2
Suðuroy *i.* Faroe Is **48** B1
Sueca Spain **61** C2
Suez Egypt **102** B2
Suez, Gulf of Egypt **102** B2
Suez Canal Egypt **92** B2
Suffolk U.S.A. **137** E3
Şuḩār Oman **91** C2
Sühbaatar Mongolia **80** D1
Suhl Ger. **55** E2
Suhopolje Croatia **63** C1
Suide China **82** B2
Suifenhe China **78** B2
Suihua China **81** E1
Suining China **82** A2

Suiping China **82** B2
Suippes France **54** B3
Suiyang China **82** B2
Suizhou China **82** B2
Sujangarh India **86** D2
Sujanpur India **86** B1
Sujawal Pak. **86** A2
Sukabumi Indon. **72** B2
Sukadana Indon. **73** B2
Sukaraja Indon. **73** C2
Sukhinichi Rus. Fed. **43** E3
Sukhona *r.* Rus. Fed. **43** F2
Sukhothai Thai. **74** A2
Sukkur Pak. **86** A2
Sukromny Rus. Fed. **43** E3
Sula *i.* Norway **48** D1
Sula, Kepulauan *is* Indon. **71** C3
Sulaiman Range *mts* Pak. **86** A1
Sulawesi *i.* Indon. *see* Celebes
Sullana Peru **150** A3
Sullivan U.S.A. **135** E3
Sulphur Springs U.S.A. **141** E2
Sulu Archipelago *is* Phil. **76** B3
Sulu Sea N. Pacific Ocean **76** A3
Sulzbach-Rosenberg Ger. **55** E2
Sumāil Oman **91** C2
Sumatera *i.* Indon. *see* Sumatra
Sumatra *i.* Indon. **72** A1
Šumava *mts* Czech Rep. **55** F3
Sumba *i.* Indon. **73** C2
Sumba, Selat *sea chan.* Indon. **73** C2
Sumbawa *i.* Indon. **73** C2
Sumbawabesar Indon. **73** C2
Sumbawanga Tanz. **105** D3
Sumbe Angola **106** A1
Sumburgh U.K. **50** [inset]
Sumburgh Head U.K. **50** [inset]
Sumenep Indon. **73** C2
Sumisu-jima *i.* Japan **79** D4
Summerside Can. **129** D2
Summersville U.S.A. **136** D3
Summit Lake Can. **126** C2
Šumperk Czech Rep. **57** D3
Sumqayıt Azer. **93** C1
Sumter U.S.A. **139** D2
Sumy Ukr. **45** D1
Sunamganj Bangl. **87** D2
Sunan N. Korea **77** B2
Sunaynah Oman **91** C2
Sunbury Austr. **116** C3
Sunbury U.S.A. **137** E2
Sunch'ŏn N. Korea **77** B2
Sunch'ŏn S. Korea **77** B3
Sun City S. Africa **109** C2
Sunda, Selat *str.* Indon. **72** B2
Sundance U.S.A. **134** C2
Sundarbans *coastal area* Bangl./India **87** C2
Sunderland U.K. **52** C2
Sundre Can. **126** C2
Sundsvall Sweden **47** D3
Sundumbili S. Africa **109** D2
Sungailiat Indon. **72** B2
Sungaipenuh Indon. **72** B2
Sungai Petani Malaysia **72** B1
Sungurlu Turkey **92** B1
Sunndal Norway **46** B3
Sunndalsøra Norway **46** B3
Sunnyside U.S.A. **132** C1
Sunnyvale U.S.A. **133** B3
Suntar Rus. Fed. **95** J2
Suntsar Pak. **86** A2
Sunyani Ghana **100** B4
Suoyarvi Rus. Fed. **43** D3
Superior *AZ* U.S.A. **140** B2
Superior *NE* U.S.A. **135** D2
Superior *WI* U.S.A. **136** B1
Superior, Lake Can./U.S.A. **136** C1
Suponevo Rus. Fed. **43** D3
Sūq ash Shuyūkh Iraq **93** C2

Suqian China **82** B2
Sūq Suwayq Saudi Arabia **90** A2
Suqutrā *i.* Yemen *see* Socotra
Şūr Oman **91** C2
Şur, Punta *pt* Arg. **147**
Şūr Oman **91** C2
Surab Pak. **86** A2
Surabaya Indon. **73** C2
Surakarta Indon. **73** C2
Surat India **86** B2
Suratgarh India **86** B2
Surat Thani Thai. **75** A3
Surazh Rus. Fed. **43** D3
Surdulica Serb. and Mont. **64** B2
Surendranagar India **86** B2
Surgut Rus. Fed. **40** G2
Surigao Phil. **76** B3
Surin Thai. **75** B2
Suriname *country* S. America **151** D2
Surulangun Indon. **72** B2
Susanino Rus. Fed. **43** F2
Susanville U.S.A. **132** B2
Suşehri Turkey **92** B1
Sušice Czech Rep. **55** F3
Sussex Can. **129** D2
Süstedt Ger. **55** D1
Sustrum Ger. **54** C1
Susuman Rus. Fed. **95** L2
Susurluk Turkey **65** C3
Sutak Jammu and Kashmir **87** B1
Sutherland S. Africa **108** B3
Sutton Coldfield U.K. **53** C3
Suttsu Japan **78** D2
Suva Fiji **112**
Suvorov Rus. Fed. **43** E3
Suwałki Pol. **57** E2
Suwannaphum Thai. **75** B2
Suwannee *r.* U.S.A. **139** D3
Suwarrow *atoll* Cook Is. **111**
Suways, Qanāt as *canal* Egypt *see*
  Suez Canal
Suwŏn S. Korea **77** B2
Süzä Iran **91** C2
Suzdal' Rus. Fed. **43** F2
Suzhou *Anhui* China **82** B2
Suzhou *Jiangsu* China **82** C2
Suzu Japan **79** C3
Suzu-misaki *pt* Japan **79** C3
Svalbard *terr.* Arctic Ocean **94** C1
Svatove Ukr. **45** E2
Svay Riĕng Cambodia **75** B2
Sveg Sweden **47** C3
Svelgen Norway **48** E1
Svendborg Denmark **47** C4
Sverdlovsk Rus. Fed. *see*
  Yekaterinburg
Sveti Nikole Macedonia **64** B2
Svetlaya Rus. Fed. **78** C1
Svetlogorsk Rus. Fed. **42** B3
Svetlyy Rus. Fed. **42** B3
Svetogorsk Rus. Fed. **47** F3
Svilengrad Bulg. **64** C2
Svinecea Mare, Vârful *mt.* Romania **44** B3
Svir' *r.* Rus. Fed. **43** D3
Svishtov Bulg. **64** C2
Svitavy Czech Rep. **57** D3
Svitlovods'k Ukr. **45** D2
Svobodnyy Rus. Fed. **81** E1
Svolvær Norway **46** C2
Svyetlahorsk Belarus **42** C3
Swainsboro U.S.A. **139** D2
Swakop *watercourse* Namibia **108** A1
Swakopmund Namibia **106** A2
Swan Hill Austr. **116** C3
Swan Hills Can. **126** D2
Swan Lake Can. **127** E2
Swan River Can. **127** E2
Swansea Austr. **117** E2
Swansea U.K. **53** B4

Swartruggens S. Africa **109** C2
Swatow China *see* Shantou
Swaziland *country* Africa **109** D2
Sweden *country* Europe **47** D3
Sweetwater U.S.A. **141** D2
Sweetwater *r.* U.S.A. **134** B2
Swellendam S. Africa **108** B3
Świdnica Pol. **57** D2
Świdwin Pol. **57** D2
Świebodzin Pol. **57** D2
Świecie Pol. **57** D2
Swift Current Can. **124** E3
Swilly, Lough *inlet* Rep. of Ireland **51** C1
Swindon U.K. **53** C4
Świnoujście Pol. **56** C2
Switzerland *country* Europe **59** D2
Swords Rep. of Ireland **51** C2
Syanno Belarus **42** C3
Sychevka Rus. Fed. **43** D2
Sydney Austr. **117** E2
Sydney Can. **129** D2
Sydney Mines Can. **129** D2
Syeverodonets'k Ukr. **45** E2
Syktyvkar Rus. Fed. **40** E2
Sylacauga U.S.A. **139** C2
Sylhet Bangl. **87** D2
Sylt *i.* Ger. **56** B2
Symi *i.* Greece **65** C3
Synel'nykove Ukr. **45** E2
Syracuse Italy **62** C3
Syracuse *KS* U.S.A. **134** C3
Syracuse *NY* U.S.A. **137** E2
Syrdar'ya *r.* Asia **89** D2
Syria *country* Asia **92** B2
Syrian Desert Asia **92** B2
Syros *i.* Greece **65** B3
Syzran' Rus. Fed. **41** D3
Szczecin Pol. **56** C2
Szczecinek Pol. **57** D2
Szczytno Pol. **57** E2
Szeged Hungary **57** E3
Székesfehérvár Hungary **57** D3
Szekszárd Hungary **57** D3
Szentes Hungary **57** E3
Szentgotthárd Hungary **57** D3
Szigetvár Hungary **57** D3
Szolnok Hungary **57** E3
Szombathely Hungary **57** D3

Tābah Saudi Arabia **90** B2
Tabas Iran **93** D2
Tābask, Kūh-e *mt.* Iran **93** D3
Tabatinga Brazil **150** C3
Tabelbala Alg. **100** B2
Taber Can. **127** D3
Tábor Czech Rep. **56** C3
Tabora Tanz. **105** D3
Tabou Côte d'Ivoire **100** B4
Tabrīz Iran **93** C2
Tabūk Saudi Arabia **90** A2
Täby Sweden **42** A2
Tacheng China **89** F2
Tachov Czech Rep. **56** C3
Tacloban Phil. **76** B2
Tacna Peru **150** B4
Tacoma U.S.A. **132** B1
Tacuarembó Uru. **152** C4
Tacupeto Mex. **140** C2
Tadjoura Djibouti **103** C3
Tadmur Syria **92** B2
Tadoule Lake Can. **127** F2
Taegu S. Korea **77** B2
Taejŏn S. Korea **77** B2
Taejŏng S. Korea **77** B3
T'aepaek S. Korea **77** B2

'erqi China **81** E1
falla Spain **61** C1
rí Viejo Arg. **152** B3
ftän, Kühr-e *mt.* Iran **91** D2
ganrog Rus. Fed. **45** E2
ganrog, Gulf of Rus. Fed./Ukr. **45** E2
gaung Myanmar **74** A1
gaytay City Phil. **76** B2
gbilaran Phil. **76** B3
gudin Phil. **76** B2
gum Phil. **76** B3
gus *r.* Port. **60** B2
gus *r.* Spain **60** B2
han, Gunung *mt.* Malaysia **72** B1
hat, Mont *mt.* Alg. **101** C2
he China **81** E1
hiti *i.* Fr. Polynesia **111**
hlequah U.S.A. **141** F1
hoe, Lake U.S.A. **133** B3
hoe City U.S.A. **133** B3
houa Niger **101** C3
hsis Can. **126** C3
i'an China **82** D2
aichung Taiwan **83** C3
hape N.Z. **118** C1
   Hu *i.* China **82** C2
ilem Bend Austr. **116** B3
iobeiras Brazil **155** D1
ishan China **83** C3
iping Malaysia **72** B1
izhou *Jiangsu* China **82** B2
izhou *Zhejiang* China **83** C3
yuan China **82** B2
izz Yemen **90** B3
amulco, Volcán de *vol.* Guat.
143 C3
iikistan *country* Asia **89** E3
i Mahal *tourist site* India **87** B2
io *r.* Spain *see* Tagus
k Thai. **74** A2
kaka N.Z. **118** B3
kamatsu Japan **79** B4
kaoka Japan **79** C3
kapuna N.Z. **118** B2
kasaki Japan **79** C1
kayama Japan **79** C3
kengon Indon. **72** A1
kev Cambodia **75** B2
khemaret Alg. **61** D2
Khmau Cambodia **75** B2
kikawa Japan **78** D2
kla Lake Can. **126** C2
kla Landing Can. **126** C2
klimakan Desert China **89** F3
klimakan Shamo *des.* China *see*
Taklimakan Desert
ku *r.* Can./U.S.A. **126** B2
kua Pa Thai. **75** A3
kum Nigeria **101** C4
achyn Belarus **42** C3
agang Pak. **86** B1
au, Kepulauan *is* Indon. **71** C2
avera de la Reina Spain **60** C2
ca Chile **153** A4
cahuano Chile **153** A4

Taldom Rus. Fed. **43** E2
Taldykorgan Kazakh. **89** E2
Talia Austr. **116** A2
Taliabu *i.* Indon. **71** C3
Talisay Phil. **76** B2
Taliwang Indon. **73** B3
Tall 'Afar Iraq **93** C2
Tallahassee U.S.A. **139** D2
Tallinn Estonia **42** B2
Tallulah U.S.A. **138** B2
Talmont-St-Hilaire France **58** B2
Tal'ne Ukr. **44** D2
Talodi Sudan **103** B3
Tálogán Afgh. **86** A1
Talovaya Rus. Fed. **43** F3
Taloyoak Can. **124** F2
Talsi Latvia **42** B2
Taltal Chile **152** A3
Taltson *r.* Can. **127** D1
Talu Indon. **72** A1
Talwood Austr. **117** D1
Tamala Rus. Fed. **45** F1
Tamale Ghana **100** B4
Tamanrasset Alg. **101** C2
Tamar *r.* U.K. **53** A4
Tamazunchale Mex. **143** C2
Tambacounda Senegal **100** A3
Tambelan, Kepulauan *is* Indon. **72** B1
Tambey Rus. Fed. **40** G1
Tambov Rus. Fed. **43** F3
Tamiahua, Laguna *de lag.* Mex.
143 C2
Tampa U.S.A. **139** D3
Tampa Bay U.S.A. **139** D3
Tampere Fin. **47** E3
Tampico Mex. **143** C2
Tamsagbulag Mongolia **81** D1
Tamsweg Austria **56** C3
Tamworth Austr. **117** E2
Tamworth U.K. **53** C3
Tana *r.* Kenya **105** E3
Tana, Lake Eth. **103** D3
Tanabe Japan **79** C4
Tana Bru Norway **46** F1
Tanafjorden Indon. **73** C2
Tanahjampea *i.* Indon. **73** D2
Tanami Desert Austr. **114** C1
Tanana U.S.A. **124** B2
Tanaro *r.* Italy **62** A2
Tanch'ŏn N. Korea **77** B1
Tandag Phil. **76** B3
Tândărei Romania **44** C2
Tandil Arg. **153** E3
Tando Adam Pak. **86** A2
Tando Muhammad Khan Pak. **86** A2
Tanezrouft *reg.* Alg./Mali **100** B2
Tanga Tanz. **105** D3
Tanganyika, Lake Africa **105** C3
Tanger Morocco *see* Tangier
Tangermünde Ger. **55** E1
Tanggula Shan *mt.* China **87** C1
Tanggula Shan *mts* China **87** C1
Tangier Morocco **100** B1
Tangra Yumco *salt l.* China **87** C1
Tangshan China **82** B2
Taniantaweng Shan *mts* China **80** C2
Tanimbar, Kepulauan *is* Indon. **71** C3
Tanjay Phil. **76** B3
Tanjungbalai Indon. **72** A1
Tanjungpandan Indon. **72** B2
Tanjungpinang Indon. **72** B1
Tanjungredeb Indon. **73** C1
Tanjungselor Indon. **73** C1
Tank Pak. **86** B1
Tanna *i.* Vanuatu **110**
Tanout Niger **101** C3
Tansen Nepal **87** C2
Tanṭā Egypt **102** B1
Tanzania *country* Africa **105** D3
Taonan China **81** E1

Taos U.S.A. **140** C1
Taoudenni Mali **100** B2
Tapa Estonia **42** C2
Tapachula Mex. **143** C3
Tapajós *r.* Brazil **151** D3
Tapaktuan Indon. **72** A1
Tapanatepec Mex. **143** C3
Tapauá Brazil **150** C3
Tapeta Liberia **100** B4
Tapi *r.* India **86** B2
Tappahannock U.S.A. **137** E3
Tapurucuara Brazil **150** C3
Taquari *r.* Brazil **154** A1
Taquari, Pantanal do *marsh* Brazil
154 A1
Taquari, Serra do *hills* Brazil **154** B1
Taquaritinga Brazil **154** C2
Taraba *r.* Nigeria **101** D4
Ṭarābulus Libya *see* Tripoli
Tarakan Indon. **73** C1
Taran, Mys *pt* Rus. Fed. **42** A3
Taranaki, Mount *vol.* N.Z. **118** B2
Tarancón Spain **60** C1
Taranto Italy **63** C2
Taranto, Golfo di *g.* Italy **63** C2
Tarapoto Peru **150** B3
Tarasovskiy Rus. Fed. **45** F2
Tarauacá Brazil **150** B3
Tarauacá *r.* Brazil **150** C3
Tarawa *atoll* Kiribati **110**
Taraz Kazakh. **89** E2
Tarazona Spain **61** C1
Tarbagatay, Khrebet *mts* Kazakh.
89 F2
Tarbert *Scotland* U.K. **50** B3
Tarbert *Scotland* U.K. **50** A3
Tarbes France **58** C3
Tarbet U.K. **50** B2
Tarcoola Austr. **116** A2
Taree Austr. **117** E2
Târgovişte Romania **44** C3
Targuist Morocco **60** C3
Târgu Jiu Romania **44** B2
Târgu Mureş Romania **44** B2
Târgu Neamţ Romania **44** C2
Tarif U.A.E. **91** C2
Tarija Bol. **152** B3
Tarim Yemen **91** B3
Tarim Basin China **89** F3
Tarim He *r.* China **89** F2
Tarim Pendi *basin* China *see*
Tarim Basin
Taritatu *r.* Indon. **71** D3
Tarko-Sale Rus. Fed. **40** G2
Tarkwa Ghana **100** B4
Tarlac Phil. **76** B2
Tárnaby Sweden **46** D2
Tarnak *r.* Afgh. **86** A1
Târnăveni Romania **44** B2
Tarnobrzeg Pol. **57** E2
Tarnów Pol. **57** E2
Taroudannt Morocco **100** B1
Tarquinia Italy **62** B2
Tarragona Spain **61** D1
Tàrrega Spain **61** D1
Tarsus Turkey **92** B2
Tartagal Arg. **152** B3
Tartas France **58** B3
Tartu Estonia **42** C2
Ṭarṭūs Syria **92** B2
Tarumirim Brazil **155** D1
Tarusa Rus. Fed. **43** E3
Tarvisio Italy **62** B1
Tashk, Daryācheh-ye *l.* Iran **93** D3
Tashkent Uzbek. **89** D2
Tasiilaq Greenland see
Tasialujjuaq, Lac *l.* Can. **129** C1
Tasiat, Lac *l.* Can. **128** C1
Tasiujaq Can. **129** D1
Taskesken Kazakh. **89** F2
Tasman Bay N.Z. **118** B3

Tasmania *i.* Austr. **110**
Tasmania *state* Austr. **115** D4
Tasman Mountains N.Z. **118** B3
Tasman Sea S. Pacific Ocean **115** E3
Tassili du Hoggar *plat.* Alg. **101** C2
Tassili n'Ajjer *plat.* Alg. **101** C2
Tataba Indon. **73** D2
Tatabánya Hungary **57** D3
Tatarbunary Ukr. **44** C2
Tatarskiy Proliv *str.* Rus. Fed. **81** F1
Tateyama Japan **79** C4
Tathlina Lake Can. **126** D1
Tathlīth Saudi Arabia **90** B3
Tathlīth, Wādī *watercourse*
    Saudi Arabia **90** B2
Tathra Austr. **117** D3
Tatkon Myanmar **74** A1
Tatla Lake Can. **126** E5
Tatra Mountains Pol. **57** D3
Tatta Pak. **86** A2
Tatuí Brazil **155** C2
Tatum U.S.A. **141** D2
Tatvan Turkey **93** C2
Taua Brazil **151** D2
Taubaté Brazil **155** C2
Tauberbischofsheim Ger. **55** D3
Taumarunui N.Z. **118** C2
Taunggyi Myanmar **74** A1
Taung-ngu Myanmar **74** A2
Taungup Myanmar **74** A2
Taunton U.K. **53** B4
Taunus *hills* Ger. **54** C2
Taupo N.Z. **118** C2
Taupo, Lake N.Z. **118** C2
Tauragė Lith. **42** B2
Tauranga N.Z. **118** C2
Taurus Mountains Turkey **92** B2
Tavas Turkey **65** C3
Tavda Rus. Fed. **40** F3
Tavira Port. **60** B2
Tavistock U.K. **53** A4
Tavoy Myanmar **75** A4
Tavşanlı Turkey **65** C3
Taw *r.* U.K. **53** A4
Tawas City U.S.A. **136** D2
Tawau Malaysia **73** C1
Tawitawi *i.* Phil. **76** A3
Taxco Mex. **143** C3
Taxiatosh Uzbek. **88** C2
Taxkorgan China **89** E3
Tay *r.* U.K. **50** C2
Tay, Firth of *est.* U.K. **50** C2
Tay, Loch *l.* U.K. **50** B2
Taylor Can. **126** C2
Taylor U.S.A. **141** E2
Taylorville U.S.A. **136** C3
Taymā' Saudi Arabia **90** A2
Taymura *r.* Rus. Fed. **95** I2
Taymyr, Ozero *l.* Rus. Fed. **95** I2
Taymyr, Poluostrov *pen.* Rus. Fed. *see*
    Taymyr Peninsula
Taymyr Peninsula Rus. Fed. **95** H2
Tây Ninh Vietnam **75** B2
Taytay Phil. **76** A2
Taz *r.* Rus. Fed. **40** G2
Taza Morocco **100** B1
Tazin Lake Can. **127** E2
Tazoult Lambèse Alg. **61** D2
Tazovskaya Guba *sea chan.* Rus. Fed.
    40 G2
T'bilisi Georgia **93** C1
Tbilisskaya Rus. Fed. **45** F2
Tchibanga Gabon **104** B3
Tchollíré Cameroon **104** B2
Tczew Pol. **57** D2
Teacapán Mex. **142** B2
Te Anau N.Z. **118** A4
Te Anau, Lake N.Z. **118** A4
Teapa Mex. **143** C3

Te Awamutu N.Z. **118** C2
Tébessa Alg. **101** C1
Tebingtinggi *Sumatera Selatan* Indon.
    72 B2
Tebingtinggi *Sumatera Utara* Indon.
    72 A1
Techiman Ghana **100** B4
Tecomán Mex. **142** B3
Tecoripa Mex. **142** B2
Técpan Mex. **143** B3
Tecuala Mex. **142** B2
Tecuci Romania **44** C2
Tedzhen Turkm. **88** D3
Teeli Rus. Fed. **89** G1
Tees *r.* U.K. **52** C2
Tefenni Turkey **65** C3
Tegal Indon. **72** B2
Tegucigalpa Hond. **144** B3
Teguidda-n-Tessoumt Niger **101** C3
Tehek Lake Can. **127** F1
Téhini Côte d'Ivoire **100** B4
Tehrān Iran **93** D2
Tehuacán Mex. **143** C3
Tehuantepec, Golfo de *g.* Mex.
    143 C3
Tehuantepec, Istmo de *isth.* Mex.
    143 C3
Teifi *r.* U.K. **53** A3
Tejo *r.* Port. *see* Tagus
Tejupilco Mex. **143** B3
Tekapo, Lake N.Z. **118** B3
Tekax Mex. **143** D2
Tekezê Wenz *r.* Eritrea/Eth. **102** B3
Tekirdağ Turkey **65** C2
Te Kuiti N.Z. **118** C2
Tel *r.* India **87** C2
T'elavi Georgia **93** C1
Tel Aviv-Yafo Israel **92** B2
Telchac Puerto Mex. **143** D2
Telegraph Creek Can. **126** B2
Telêmaco Borba Brazil **154** B2
Telford U.K. **53** B3
Telo Indon. **72** A2
Tel'pos-Iz, Gora *mt.* Rus. Fed. **40** E2
Telšiai Lith. **42** B2
Telukbatang Indon. **73** B2
Telukdalam Indon. **72** A1
Teluk Intan Malaysia **72** B1
Temagami Lake Can. **128** C2
Temanggung Indon. **73** C2
Temba S. Africa **109** C2
Tembilahan Indon. **72** B2
Tembo Aluma Angola **104** B3
Teme *r.* U.K. **53** B3
Temerluh Malaysia **72** B1
Temirtau Kazakh. **89** E1
Temora Austr. **117** D2
Temple U.S.A. **141** E2
Templemore Rep. of Ireland **51** C2
Templin Ger. **55** F1
Tempoal Mex. **143** C2
Temryuk Rus. Fed. **45** E2
Temuco Chile **153** A4
Temuka N.Z. **118** B3
Tenabo Mex. **143** C2
Tenali India **85** C3
Tenasserim Myanmar **75** A2
Tenby U.K. **53** A4
Tendaho Eth. **103** C3
Tende France **59** D3
Tende, Col de *pass* France/Italy **59** D3
Tendō Japan **78** D3
Ténenkou Mali **100** B3
Ténéré, Erg du *des.* Niger **101** D3
Ténéré du Tafassâsset *des.* Niger
    101 D2
Tenerife *i.* Canary Is **100** A2
Ténès Alg. **61** D2

Tengah, Kepulauan *is* Indon. **73** C2
Tengchong China **74** A1
Tenggarong Indon. **73** C2
Tengger Shamo *des.* China **82** A2
Tengxian China **83** B3
Tenke Dem. Rep. Congo **105** C4
Tenkodogo Burkina **100** B3
Tennant Creek Austr. **114** C1
Tennessee *r.* U.S.A. **138** C1
Tennessee *state* U.S.A. **138** C1
Tenosique Mex. **143** C3
Tenteno Indon. **73** D2
Tenterfield Austr. **117** E1
Teodoro Sampaio Brazil **154** B2
Teófilo Otôni Brazil **155** D1
Teopisca Mex. **143** C3
Tepache Mex. **142** B2
Te Paki N.Z. **118** B1
Tepalcatepec Mex. **142** B3
Tepatitlán Mex. **142** B2
Tepehuanes Mex. **142** B2
Tepic Mex. **142** B2
Teplice Czech Rep. **56** C2
Teploye Rus. Fed. **43** E3
Tequila Mex. **142** B2
Teramo Italy **62** B2
Terbuny Rus. Fed. **43** E3
Terek *r.* Rus. Fed. **41** D4
Teresina Brazil **151** D2
Teresópolis Brazil **155** D2
Teressa Island India **75** A3
Tergnier France **54** A3
Terme Turkey **92** B1
Termini Imerese Italy **62** B3
Términos, Laguna de *lag.* Mex.
    143 C3
Termiz Uzbek. **89** D3
Termoli Italy **62** B2
Ternate Indon. **71** C2
Terneuzen Neth. **54** A2
Terni Italy **62** B2
Ternopil' Ukr. **44** C2
Terpeniya, Mys *c.* Rus. Fed. **81** F1
Terpeniya, Zaliv *g.* Rus. Fed. **81** F1
Terrace Can. **126** C2
Terrace Bay Can. **128** B2
Terra Firma S. Africa **108** C2
Terre Haute U.S.A. **136** C3
Terrenceville Can. **129** E2
Terschelling *i.* Neth. **54** B1
Tertenia Italy **62** A3
Teruel Spain **61** C1
Tervola Fin. **46** E2
Tešanj Bos.-Herz. **63** C2
Teseney Eritrea **102** B3
Teshio-gawa *r.* Japan **78** D2
Teslin Can. **126** B1
Teslin Lake Can. **126** B1
Tesouro Brazil **154** B1
Tessaoua Niger **101** C3
Tetas, Punta *pt* Chile **152** A3
Tete Moz. **107** C1
Teterev *r.* Ukr. **44** D1
Teterow Ger. **55** F1
Tetiyiv Ukr. **44** C2
Tétouan Morocco **100** B1
Tetovo Macedonia **64** B2
Teuco *r.* Arg. **152** B3
Teul de González Ortega Mex. **142**
Teutoburger Wald *hills* Ger. **55** D1
Tevere *r.* Italy *see* Tiber
Teviot N.Z. **118** A4
Tewantin Austr. **115** E2
Te Waihau N.Z. **118** C3
Texarkana U.S.A. **141** F2
Texas Austr. **117** C1
Texas *state* U.S.A. **141** E2
Texas City U.S.A. **141** F3

exel i. Neth. 54 B1
exoma, Lake U.S.A. 141 E2
eyateyaneng Lesotho 109 C2
eykovo Rus. Fed. 43 F2
eza r. Rus. Fed. 43 F2
ezpur India 87 D2
ezu India 74 A1
na-anne r. Can. 127 F1
habana-Ntlenyana mt. Lesotho 109 C2
haba Putsoa mt. Lesotho 109 C2
habazimbi S. Africa 109 C1
habong S. Africa 109 C2
hagyettaw Myanmar 75 A2
hai Binh Vietnam 74 B1
hailand country Asia 75 B2
hailand, Gulf of Asia 75 B2
hai Nguyên Vietnam 74 B1
hakèk Laos 74 B2
halang Thai. 75 A3
ha Li Thai. 74 B2
hamaga Botswana 109 C1
hamarit Oman 91 C3
hames r. Can. 128 B2
hames r. U.K. 53 D4
hames est. U.K. 53 D4
hanbyuzayat Myanmar 75 A2
handwe Myanmar 74 A2
hanh Hoa Vietnam 74 B2
hanjavur India 85 B3
hanlyin Myanmar 74 A2
hano Bula Khan Pak. 86 A2
haan Uyen Vietnam 74 B1
har Desert India/Pak. 86 A2
hargomindah Austr. 116 C1
harthār, Buḩayrat ath l. Iraq 93 C2
hasos i. Greece 65 B3
hât Khê Vietnam 74 B1
haton Myanmar 74 A2
haungdut Myanmar 74 A1
hayawadi r. Myanmar 74 A2
hayetmyo Myanmar 74 A2
hazi Myanmar 74 A1
he Bahamas country West Indies 145 C2
he Cheviot h. U.K. 52 B2
he Dalles U.S.A. 132 B1
he Fens reg. U.K. 53 C3
he Gambia country Africa 100 A3
he Great Oasis Egypt see
  Khārijah, Wāḩāt al
he Gulf Asia 91 C2
he Hague Neth. 54 B1
helon r. Can. 127 F1
hemar Ger. 55 E2
he Minch sea chan. U.K. 50 A1
heodore Roosevelt r. Brazil 150 C3
he Pas Can. 127 E2
hermaïkos Kolpos g. Greece 65 B2
hermopolis U.S.A. 134 B2
he Rock Austr. 117 D3
hessalon Can. 128 B2
hessaloniki Greece 65 B2
hetford U.K. 53 D3
hetford Mines Can. 129 C2
he Triangle mts Myanmar 74 A1
hévenet, Lac l. Can. 129 D1
he Wash b. U.K. 52 D3
he Woodlands U.S.A. 141 E2
hibodaux U.S.A. 138 B3
hief River Falls U.S.A. 135 D1
hiers France 59 C2
hika Kenya 105 D3
hiladhunmathi Atoll Maldives 85 B4

Thimphu Bhutan 87 C2
Thionville France 59 D2
Thira i. Greece 65 C3
Thirsk U.K. 52 C2
Thisted Denmark 47 B4
Thlewiaza r. Can. 127 F1
Thoen Thai. 74 A2
Thohoyandou S. Africa 109 D1
Thomasburg Ger. 55 E1
Thomastown Rep. of Ireland 51 C2
Thomasville U.S.A. 139 D2
Thommen Belgium 54 C2
Thompson Can. 127 F2
Thompson r. U.S.A. 126 D2
Thompson Falls U.S.A. 132 C1
Thompson Sound Can. 126 C2
Thornhill U.K. 50 C3
Thorshavnheiane reg. Antarctica 119 C2
Thouars France 58 B2
Three Hills Can. 126 D2
Three Pagodas Pass Myanmar/Thai. 75 A2
Three Points, Cape Ghana 100 B4
Thu Dâu Một Vietnam 75 B2
Thuin Belgium 54 B2
Thule Greenland 125 H1
Thuli Zimbabwe 107 B2
Thunder Bay Can. 128 B2
Thung Song Thai. 75 A3
Thüringer Becken reg. Ger. 55 E2
Thüringer Wald mts Ger. 55 E2
Thurles Rep. of Ireland 51 C2
Thurso U.K. 50 C1
Thurso r. U.K. 50 C1
Tianguá Brazil 151 E3
Tianjin China 82 B2
Tianjin mun. China 82 B2
Tianlin China 83 A3
Tianmen China 82 B2
Tianshan China 82 A1
Tianshui China 82 A2
Tianzhu China 82 A2
Tiaret Alg. 61 D2
Tibagi r. Brazil 154 B2
Tibati Cameroon 104 B2
Tiber r. Italy 62 B2
Tiberias, Lake Israel see
  Galilee, Sea of
Tibesti mts Chad 101 D2
Tibet aut. reg. China see Xizang Zizhiqu
Tibet, Plateau of China 87 C1
Tibooburra Austr. 116 C1
Tiburón, Isla i. Mex. 142 A2
Tichît Maur. 100 B3
Tichla Western Sahara 100 A2
Ticul Mex. 143 D2
Tidjikja Maur. 100 A3
Tiel Neth. 54 B2
Tieling China 82 C1
Tielt Belgium 54 A2
Tienen Belgium 54 B2
Tien Shan mts China/Kyrg. 80 B2
Tientsin China see Tianjin
Tierp Sweden 47 D3
Tierra Blanca Mex. 143 C3
Tierra Colorada Mex. 143 C3
Tierra del Fuego, Isla Grande de i.
  Arg./Chile 153 B6
Tietê Brazil 154 C2
Tietê r. Brazil 154 B2
Tiflis Georgia see T'bilisi
Tifton U.S.A. 139 D2
Tighina Moldova 44 C2
Tignish Can. 129 D2
Tigre r. Ecuador/Peru 150 B3
Tigris r. Asia 102 C3
Tigris r. Turkey 93 C2
Tihuatlán Mex. 143 C2
Tijuana Mex. 142 A1

Tikhoretsk Rus. Fed. 45 F2
Tikhvin Rus. Fed. 43 D2
Tikhvinskaya Gryada ridge Rus. Fed.
  43 D2
Tikokino N.Z. 118 C2
Tikrit Iraq 93 C2
Tiksi Rus. Fed. 95 K2
Tilburg Neth. 54 B2
Tilcara Arg. 152 B3
Tilcha Austr. 116 C1
Tillabéri Niger 100 C3
Tillamook U.S.A. 132 B1
Tillanchong Island India 75 A3
Tilos i. Greece 65 C3
Tilpa Austr. 116 C2
Til'tim Rus. Fed. 40 F2
Timanskiy Kryazh ridge Rus. Fed.
  40 D2
Timaru N.Z. 118 B3
Timashevsk Rus. Fed. 45 E2
Timbedgha Maur. 100 B3
Timber Creek Austr. 114 C1
Timbuktu Mali 100 B3
Timimoun Alg. 100 C2
Timiş r. Romania 44 B2
Timişoara Romania 44 B2
Timmins Can. 128 B2
Timokhino Rus. Fed. 43 E2
Timon Brazil 151 E3
Timor i. East Timor/Indonesia 71 C3
Timor Sea Austr./Indon. 70 C3
Timrå Sweden 47 D3
Tindouf Alg. 100 B2
Tingri China 87 C2
Tingsryd Sweden 47 C4
Tinian i. N. Mariana Is 71 D2
Tinogasta Arg. 152 B3
Tinos Greece 65 C3
Tinos i. Greece 65 C3
Tinqueux France 54 A3
Tinrhert, Plateau du Alg. 101 C2
Tinsukia India 74 A1
Tipasa Alg. 61 D2
Tipperary Rep. of Ireland 51 B2
Tirana Albania 65 A2
Tiranë Albania see Tirana
Tirano Italy 62 B1
Tiraspol Moldova 44 C2
Tire Turkey 65 C3
Tiree i. U.K. 50 A2
Tirich Mir mt. Pak. 86 B1
Tiruchchirappalli India 85 B3
Tirunelveli India 85 B4
Tirupati India 85 B3
Tiruppattur India 85 B3
Tiruppur India 85 B3
Tisa r. Serb. and Mont. 64 B1
Tisdale Can. 127 E2
Tissemsilt Alg. 61 D2
Titicaca, Lake Bol./Peru 152 B2
Titlagarh India 87 C2
Titu Romania 44 C3
Titusville U.S.A. 139 D3
Tiverton U.K. 53 B4
Tivoli Italy 62 B2
Tīwī Oman 91 C2
Tizimín Mex. 143 D2
Tizi Ouzou Alg. 61 D1
Tiznit Morocco 100 B2
Tlacotalpán Mex. 143 C3
Tlahualilo Mex. 142 B2
Tlapa Mex. 143 C3
Tlaxcala Mex. 143 C3
Tlaxiaco Mex. 143 C3
Tlemcen Alg. 100 B1
Tlokweng Botswana 109 C1
Toad River Can. 126 C2
Toamasina Madag. 107 [inset] D1
Toba, Danau l. Indon. 72 A1

Toba and Kakar Ranges mts Pak. 86 A1
Tobago i. Trin. and Tob. 145 D3
Tobelo Indon. 71 C2
Tobermory Can. 128 B2
Tobermory U.K. 50 A2
Tobin Lake Can. 127 E2
Toboali Indon. 72 D2
Tobol r. Kazakh./Rus. Fed. 88 D1
Tobol'sk Rus. Fed. 40 F3
Tocantinópolis Brazil 151 E3
Tocantins r. Brazil 151 E3
Toccoa U.S.A. 139 D2
Toce r. Italy 62 A1
Tocopilla Chile 152 A3
Todos Santos Mex. 142 A2
Tofino Can. 126 C3
Toft U.K. 50 [inset]
Tofua i. Tonga 111
Togian i. Indon. 73 D2
Togian, Kepulauan is Indon. 73 D2
Togo country Africa 100 C4
Tohana India 86 B1
Tok U.S.A. 126 A1
Tokar Sudan 102 E3
Tokara-rettō is Japan 81 E3
Tokarevka Rus. Fed. 43 F3
Tokelau terr. S. Pacific Ocean 113
Tokelau is Tokelau 111
Tokmak Ukr. 45 E2
Tokmok Kyrg. 89 E2
Tokoroa N.Z. 118 C2
Toksun China 89 F2
Tokushima Japan 79 B4
Tōkyō Japan 79 C3
Tôlañaro Madag. 107 [inset] D2
Toledo Brazil 154 B2
Toledo Spain 60 C2
Toledo U.S.A. 136 D2
Toledo, Montes de mts Spain 60 C2
Toledo Bend Reservoir U.S.A. 138 B2
Toliara Madag. 107 [inset] D2
Tolitoli Indon. 73 D1
Tolmezzo Italy 62 B1
Tolosa Spain 58 B3
Toluca Mex. 143 C3
Tol'yatti Rus. Fed. 41 C3
Tomah U.S.A. 134 B2
Tomakomai Japan 78 D2
Tomar Port. 60 B2
Tomaszów Lubelski Pol. 57 E2
Tomaszów Mazowiecki Pol. 57 E2
Tomatlán Mex. 142 B3
Tombigbee r. U.S.A. 138 C2
Tombos Brazil 155 D2
Tombouctou Mali see Timbuktu
Tombua Angola 109 C1
Tom Burke S. Africa 109 C1
Tomingley Austr. 117 D2
Tomini, Teluk g. Indon. 73 D2
Tomislavgrad Bos.-Herz. 63 C2
Tom Price Austr. 114 A2
Tomsk Rus. Fed. 94 H3
Tomtabacken h. Sweden 47 C4
Tonalá Mex. 143 C3
Tonantins Brazil 150 C3
Tondano Indon. 71 C2
Tønder Denmark 56 B2
Tonga country S. Pacific Ocean 113
Tongatapu Group is Tonga 113
Tongcheng China 83 B3
Tongchuan China 82 B2
Tongdao China 83 A3
Tongduch'ŏn S. Korea 77 B2
Tongeren Belgium 54 B2
Tonghae S. Korea 77 B2
Tonghai China 83 A3
Tonghua China 77 B1
Tongjosŏn-man b. N. Korea 77 B2

Tongking, Gulf of China/Vietnam 83 A3
Tongliao China 82 C1
Tongling China 82 B2
Tongo Austr. 116 C2
Tongren China 83 A3
Tongshan China 82 B2
Tongshi China see Wuzhishan
Tongtian He r. China see Yangtze
Tongue U.K. 50 B1
Tongyu China 81 A1
Tongyuanpu China 77 A1
Tonk India 86 B2
Tonle Sap l. Cambodia 75 B2
Tooele U.S.A. 132 D2
Toonsberg Norway 47 C4
Toowoomba Austr. 117 E1
Topeka U.S.A. 135 D3
Topia Mex. 142 B2
Topolobampo Mex. 142 B2
Topozero, Ozero l. Rus. Fed. 46 G2
Toppenish U.S.A. 132 B1
Torbalı Turkey 65 C3
Torbat-e Heydariyeh Iran 88 C3
Torbat-e Jām Iran 88 D3
Tordesillas Spain 60 C1
Tordesilos Spain 61 C1
Torelló Spain 61 D1
Torgau Ger. 55 F2
Torgelow Ger. 55 G1
Torhout Belgium 54 A2
Torino Italy see Turin
Tori-shima i. Japan 79 D4
Torixoréu Brazil 154 B1
Tor'kovskoye Vodokhranilishche resr Rus. Fed. 43 F2
Tormes r. Spain 60 B1
Torneälven r. Sweden 46 E2
Torngat Mountains Can. 129 D1
Tornio Fin. 46 E2
Toro Spain 60 B1
Toronto Can. 128 C2
Tororo Uganda 105 D2
Toros Dağları mts Turkey see Taurus Mountains
Torquay U.K. 53 B4
Torrão Port. 60 B2
Torre mt. Port. 60 B1
Torreblanca Spain 61 C1
Torrecerredo mt. Spain 60 C1
Torre de Moncorvo Port. 60 B1
Torrelavega Spain 60 C1
Torremolinos Spain 60 C2
Torrens, Lake salt flat Austr. 116 B2
Torrent Spain 61 C2
Torreón Mex. 142 B2
Torres Novas Port. 60 B2
Torres Strait Austr. 110
Torres Vedras Port. 60 B2
Torrevieja Spain 61 C2
Torridon U.K. 50 B2
Torrijos Spain 60 C2
Torrington CT U.S.A. 137 E2
Torrington WY U.S.A. 134 C2
Torroella de Montgrí Spain 61 D1
Tórshavn Faroe Is 48 B1
Tortolì Italy 62 A3
Tortosa Spain 61 D1
Toruń Pol. 57 D2
Tory Island Rep. of Ireland 51 B1
Torzhok Rus. Fed. 43 D2
Tosca S. Africa 108 B2
Toscano, Arcipelago is Italy 62 A2
Tosno Rus. Fed. 43 D2
Tostado Arg. 152 B3
Tostedt Ger. 55 D1
Tosya Turkey 92 B1

Tot'ma Rus. Fed. 43 F2
Tottori Japan 79 B3
Touba Côte d'Ivoire 100 B4
Toubkal, Jbel mt. Morocco 100 B1
Tougan Burkina 100 B3
Touggourt Alg. 101 C1
Toul France 59 D2
Touliu Taiwan 83 C3
Toulon France 59 D3
Toulouse France 58 C3
Tourcoing France 54 A2
Tournai Belgium 54 A2
Tournus France 59 C2
Touros Brazil 151 F3
Tours France 58 C2
Tousside, Pic mt. Chad 101 D2
Touwsrivier S. Africa 108 B3
Towada Japan 78 D2
Townsend U.S.A. 132 D1
Townsville Austr. 115 D1
Towori, Teluk b. Indon. 73 D2
Toxkan He r. China 89 F2
Tōya-ko l. Japan 78 D2
Toyama Japan 79 C3
Toyota Japan 79 C3
Tozeur Tunisia 101 C1
Tqvarch'eli Georgia 93 C1
Trâblous Lebanon see Tripoli
Trabzon Turkey 92 B1
Trafalgar, Cabo c. Spain 60 B2
Trail Can. 126 D3
Trakai Lith. 42 B3
Tralee Rep. of Ireland 51 B2
Tramore Rep. of Ireland 51 C2
Trang Thai. 75 A3
Trangan i. Indon. 71 C3
Transantarctic Mountains Antarctica 119 H2
Transylvanian Alps mts Romania 44 B2
Trapani Italy 62 B3
Traralgon Austr. 117 D3
Trat Thai. 75 B2
Traunstein Ger. 56 C3
Traverse City U.S.A. 136 C2
Třebíč Czech Rep. 57 D3
Trebinje Bos.-Herz. 63 C2
Trebišov Slovakia 57 E3
Trebnje Slovenia 62 C1
Treinta y Tres Uru. 153 C4
Trelew Arg. 153 B5
Trelleborg Sweden 47 C4
Tremblant, Mont h. Can. 128 C2
Tremiti, Isole is Italy 62 C2
Tremonton U.S.A. 132 D2
Třemošná Czech Rep. 55 F3
Tremp Spain 61 D1
Trenčín Slovakia 57 D3
Trenque Lauquén Arg. 153 B4
Trent r. U.K. 52 C3
Trento Italy 62 B1
Trenton Can. 137 E2
Trenton MO U.S.A. 135 E2
Trenton NJ U.S.A. 137 F2
Trepassey Can. 129 E2
Tres Arroyos Arg. 153 B4
Três Corações Brazil 155 C2
Três Lagoas Brazil 154 B2
Tres Lagos Arg. 153 A5
Três Marias, Represa resr Brazil 155 C1
Três Pontas Brazil 155 C2
Tres Puntas, Cabo c. Arg. 153 B5
Três Rios Brazil 155 D2
Treuenbrietzen Ger. 55 F1
Treviglio Italy 62 A1
Treviso Italy 62 B1
Trevose Head U.K. 53 A4
Tricase Italy 63 C3
Trichur India 85 B3

rida Austr. **117** D2
rier Ger. **54** C3
rieste Italy **62** B1
riglav *mt.* Slovenia **62** B1
rikora, Puncak *mt.* Indon. **71** D3
rim Rep. of Ireland **51** C2
rincomalee Sri Lanka **85** C4
rindade Brazil **154** C1
rinidad *i.* Trin. and Tob. **145** D3
rinidad U.S.A. **134** C3
rinidad and Tobago *country*
  West Indies **145** D3
rinity Bay Can. **129** E2
ripoli Greece **65** B3
ripoli Lebanon **92** B2
ripoli Libya **101** D1
ristan da Cunha *i.* S. Atlantic Ocean
  160 D8
rivandrum India **85** B4
rivento Italy **62** F4
rnava Slovakia **57** D3
rogir Croatia **63** C2
roia Italy **62** C2
roisdorf Ger. **54** C2
rois Fourches, Cap des *c.* Morocco
  60 D2
rois-Rivières Can. **129** C2
roitsko-Pechorsk Rus. Fed. **40** E2
rombetas *r.* Brazil **151** D3
rompsburg S. Africa **109** C3
romsø Norway **46** D2
rondheim Norway **46** C3
rout Lake Can. **126** D2
rout Lake *l. N.W.T.* Can. **126** C1
rout Lake *l. Ont.* Can. **128** A1
rowbridge U.K. **53** B4
roy *AL* U.S.A. **139** C2
roy *NY* U.S.A. **137** F2
royes France **59** C2
rstenik Serb. and Mont. **64** B2
rubchevsk Rus. Fed. **43** D3
ruchas Spain **61** C2
rucial Coast U.A.E. **91** C2
rujillo Hond. **144** B3
rujillo Peru **150** B3
rujillo Spain **60** B2
rujillo Venez. **145** C4
rulben Ger. **54** C2
rumann U.S.A. **138** B1
ruro Can. **129** D2
ruro U.K. **53** A4
ruth or Consequences U.S.A.
  140 C2
rutnov Czech Rep. **57** D2
rysil Norway **47** C3
rzebiatow Pol. **56** D2
saagaannur Mongolia **80** B1
saratanana, Massif du *mts* Madag.
  107 [inset] D1
sarevo Bulg. **64** C2
selina Rus. Fed. **45** F2
ses Namibia **108** A2
setseng Botswana **108** B1
setserleg Mongolia **80** C1
shabong Botswana **108** B2
shane Botswana **108** B1
shchikaskoye Vodokhranilishche *resr*
  Rus. Fed. **45** E2
shela Dem. Rep. Congo **104** B3
shikapa Dem. Rep. Congo **104** C3
shikapa *r.* Dem. Rep. Congo **104** C3
shipise S. Africa **109** D1
shitanzu Dem. Rep. Congo
  104 C3
shuapa *r.* Dem. Rep. Congo **104** C3
shwane S. Africa *see* Pretoria
simlyanskoye Vodokhranilishche
  resr Rus. Fed. **41** D4
singtao China *see* Qingdao

Tsiroanomandidy Madag.
  107 [inset] D1
Tsna *r.* Rus. Fed. **43** F3
Tsomo S. Africa **109** C3
Tsu Japan **79** C4
Tsuchiura Japan **79** D3
Tsugarū-kaikyō *str.* Japan **78** D2
Tsumeb Namibia **106** A1
Tsumis Park Namibia **108** A1
Tsumkwe Namibia **106** B1
Tsuruga Japan **79** C3
Tsuruoka Japan **78** C3
Tsushima *is* Japan **79** A4
Tsuyama Japan **79** B3
Tsweelelang S. Africa **109** C2
Tsyurupyns'k Ukr. **45** D2
Tual Indon. **71** C3
Tuam Rep. of Ireland **51** B2
Tuamotu Archipelago *is* Fr. Polynesia
  159 F6
Tuapse Rus. Fed. **45** E3
Tuatapere N.Z. **118** A4
Tuath, Loch a' *b.* U.K. **50** A1
Tuba City U.S.A. **140** B1
Tuban Indon. **73** C2
Tubarão Brazil **152** D3
Tübingen Ger. **56** B3
Tubruq Libya **101** E1
Tubuai Islands Fr. Polynesia **111**
Tubutama Mex. **142** A1
Tucavaca Bol. **152** C2
Tuchitua Can. **126** C1
Tucson U.S.A. **140** B2
Tucumcari U.S.A. **141** D1
Tucupita Venez. **150** C1
Tucuruí Brazil **151** E3
Tucuruí, Represa *resr* Brazil **151** E3
Tudela Spain **61** C1
Tuela *r.* Port. **60** B1
Tuensang India **74** A1
Tugela *r.* S. Africa **109** D2
Tuguegarao Phil. **76** B2
Tui Spain **60** B1
Tukangbesi, Kepulauan *is* Indon.
  71 C3
Tuktoyaktuk Can. **124** D2
Tukums Latvia **42** B2
Tula Mex. **143** C2
Tula Rus. Fed. **43** E3
Tulancingo Mex. **143** C2
Tulare U.S.A. **133** C3
Tularosa U.S.A. **140** C2
Tulcán Col. **150** B2
Tulcea Romania **44** B2
Tul'chyn Ukr. **44** C2
Tulemalu Lake Can. **127** F1
Tulia U.S.A. **141** D2
Tulit'a Can. **126** C1
Tullahoma U.S.A. **139** C1
Tullamore Rep. of Ireland **51** C2
Tulle France **58** C2
Tully Austr. **115** D1
Tulsa U.S.A. **141** E1
Tuluksak U.S.A. **124** B2
Tumaco Col. **150** B2
Tumahole S. Africa **109** C2
Tumba Sweden **47** D4
Tumba, Lac *l.* Dem. Rep. Congo
  104 B3
Tumbarumba Austr. **117** D3
Tumbes Peru **150** A3
Tumbler Ridge Can. **126** C2
Tumby Bay Austr. **116** B2
Tumen China **77** B1
Tumereng Guyana **150** C2
Tumindao *i.* Phil. **76** A3
Tumkur India **85** B3
Tumnin *r.* Rus. Fed. **81** F1
Tump Pak. **86** A2
Tumucumaque, Serra *hills* Brazil
  151 D2

Tumut Austr. **117** D3
Tunbridge Wells, Royal U.K. **53** D4
Tunceli Turkey **92** B2
Tuncurry Austr. **117** E2
Tunduru Tanz. **105** D4
Tundzha *r.* Bulg. **64** C2
Tungsten Can. **126** C1
Tunis Tunisia **101** D1
Tunisia *country* Africa **101** C1
Tunja Col. **150** B2
Tunnsjøen *l.* Norway **46** C3
Tupã Brazil **154** B2
Tupaciguara Brazil **154** C1
Tupelo U.S.A. **138** C2
Tupiza Bol. **152** B3
Tura Rus. Fed. **95** I3
Tura *r.* Rus. Fed. **40** F3
Turabah Saudi Arabia **90** B2
Turana, Khrebet *mts* Rus. Fed. **95** K3
Turangi N.Z. **118** C2
Turan Lowland Asia **88** C3
Ţurayf Saudi Arabia **90** A1
Turba Estonia **42** B2
Turbat Pak. **86** A2
Turbo Col. **150** B2
Turda Romania **44** B2
Turfan China *see* Turpan
Turgay Kazakh. **88** D2
Turgutlu Turkey **65** C3
Turhal Turkey **92** B1
Turia *r.* Spain **61** C2
Turin Italy **62** A1
Turinsk Rus. Fed. **40** F3
Turiys'k Ukr. **44** B1
Turkana, Lake *salt l.* Eth./Kenya
  103 B4
Turkestan Kazakh. **89** D2
Turkey *country* Asia/Europe **92** B2
Turkmenabat Turkm. **88** D3
Turkmenbashi Turkm. **88** C2
Turkmenistan *country* Asia **88** C2
Turks and Caicos Islands *terr.*
  West Indies **145** C2
Turku Fin. **47** E3
Turlock U.S.A. **133** B3
Turnagain, Cape N.Z. **118** C3
Turneffe Islands *atoll* Belize **143** D3
Turnhout Belgium **54** B2
Turnor Lake Can. **127** E2
Turnu Măgurele Romania **64** B2
Turpan China **89** F2
Turugart Pass China/Kyrg. **89** E2
Tuscaloosa U.S.A. **138** C2
Tuskegee U.S.A. **139** C2
Tuticorin India **85** B4
Tutume Botswana **106** B2
Tuvalu *country* S. Pacific Ocean **112**
Tuwayq, Jabal *hills* Saudi Arabia **90** B2
Tuwayq, Jabal *mts* Saudi Arabia **90** B2
Tuwwal Saudi Arabia **90** A2
Tuxpan *Nayarit* Mex. **142** B2
Tuxpan *Veracruz* Mex. **143** C2
Tuxtla Gutiérrez Mex. **143** C3
Tuyên Quang Vietnam **74** B1
Tuy Hoa Vietnam **75** B2
Tuz, Lake *salt l.* Turkey *see* Tuz, Lake
Tuz Gölü *salt l.* Turkey *see* Tuz, Lake
Tuz Khurmātū Iraq **93** C2
Tuzla Bos.-Herz. **63** C2
Tuzlov *r.* Rus. Fed. **45** F2
Tver' Rus. Fed. **43** E2
Tweed *r.* U.K. **52** B2
Twee Rivier Namibia **108** A2
Twentynine Palms U.S.A. **133** C4
Twillingate Can. **129** E2
Twin Falls U.S.A. **132** D2
Twizel N.Z. **118** B3
Two Harbors U.S.A. **135** E1
Two Hills Can. **127** D2
Tyler U.S.A. **141** E2

Tynda Rus. Fed. **95** K3
Tynset Norway **47** C3
Tyre Lebanon **92** B2
Tyrnavos Greece **65** B3
Tyrrell, Lake *dry lake* Austr. **116** C3
Tyrrhenian Sea France/Italy **62** B2
Tyub-Karagan, Mys *pt* Kazakh. **88** C2
Tyul'gan Rus. Fed. **41** E3
Tyumen' Rus. Fed. **40** F3
Tyung *r.* Rus. Fed. **95** K2
Tywi *r.* U.K. **53** A4
Tzaneen S. Africa **109** D1

Uamanda Angola **106** B1
Uaupés Brazil **150** C3
Ubá Brazil **155** D2
Ubaí Brazil **155** D1
Ubaitaba Brazil **151** F4
Ubangi *r.* C.A.R./Dem. Rep. Congo **104** B3
Ube Japan **79** B4
Úbeda Spain **60** C2
Uberaba Brazil **154** C1
Uberlândia Brazil **154** C1
Ubombo S. Africa **109** D2
Ubon Ratchathani Thai. **75** B2
Ubstadt-Weiher Ger. **55** I3
Ubundu Dem. Rep. Congo **105** C3
Ucayali *r.* Peru **150** B3
Uch Pak. **86** B2
Ucharal Kazakh. **89** F2
Uchiura-wan *b.* Japan **78** D2
Uchur *r.* Rus. Fed. **95** K3
Ucluelet Can. **126** C3
Udaipur India **86** B2
Uday *r.* Ukr. **45** D1
Uddevalla Sweden **47** C4
Uddjaure *l.* Sweden **46** D2
Uden Neth. **54** B2
Udhampur India **86** B1
Udine Italy **62** B1
Udomlya Rus. Fed. **43** E2
Udon Thani Thai. **74** B2
Udupi India **85** B3
Ueda Japan **79** C3
Uekuli Indon. **73** D2
Uele *r.* Dem. Rep. Congo **104** C3
Uelen Rus. Fed. **124** A2
Uelzen Ger. **55** E1
Uere *r.* Dem. Rep. Congo **105** C3
Ufa Rus. Fed. **41** E3
Uganda *country* Africa **105** D2
Uglegorsk Rus. Fed. **81** F1
Uglich Rus. Fed. **43** E2
Uglovka Rus. Fed. **43** D2
Ugra Rus. Fed. **43** D3
Uherské Hradiště Czech Rep. **57** D3
Úhlava *r.* Czech Rep. **55** F3
Uichteritz Ger. **55** E2
Uig U.K. **50** A2
Uíge Angola **104** B3
Uijŏngbu S. Korea **77** B2
Uinta Mountains U.S.A. **132** D2
Uis Mine Namibia **106** A2
Úisŏng S. Korea **77** B2
Uitenhage S. Africa **109** C3
Uithuizen Neth. **54** C1
Uivak, Cape Can. **129** D1
Ujjain India **86** B2
Ukholovo Rus. Fed. **43** F3
Ukhrul India **74** A1
Ukhta Rus. Fed. **40** E2
Ukiah U.S.A. **133** B3
Ukkusissat Greenland **125** I2
Ukmergė Lith. **42** B2

Ukraine *country* Europe **44** D2
Ulaanbaatar Mongolia *see* Ulan Bator
Ulaangom Mongolia **80** C1
Ulan Bator Mongolia **80** D1
Ulanhad China *see* Chifeng
Ulanhot China **81** E1
Ulan-Khol Rus. Fed. **41** D4
Ulan-Ude Rus. Fed. **80** D1
Ulan Ul Hu *l.* China **87** D1
Ulchin S. Korea **77** B2
Ülenurme Estonia **42** C2
Ulhasnagar India **85** B3
Uliastai China **81** D1
Uliastay Mongolia **80** C1
Ulithi *atoll* Micronesia **71** D2
Uljadulla Austr. **117** E3
Ullapool U.K. **50** B2
Ullswater *l.* U.K. **52** B2
Ullŭng-do *i.* S. Korea **77** C2
Ulm Ger. **56** B3
Ulsan S. Korea **77** B2
Ulsta U.K. **50** [inset]
Ultima Austr. **116** C3
Ulua *r.* Hond. **143** D3
Ulubey Turkey **65** C3
Uludağ *mt.* Turkey **65** C2
Ulundi S. Africa **109** D2
Ulungur Hu *l.* China **89** F2
Uluru *h.* Austr. **114** C2
Ulverston U.K. **52** B2
Ul'yanovsk Rus. Fed. **41** D3
Ulysses U.S.A. **134** C3
Uman' Ukr. **44** D2
Umba Rus. Fed. **40** C2
Umboi *i.* P.N.G. **71** D3
Umeå Sweden **46** E3
Umeälven *r.* Sweden **46** E3
Umet Rus. Fed. **45** F1
Umingmaktok Can. **124** D1
Umlazi S. Africa **109** D2
Umm Keddada Sudan **103** A3
Umm Lajj Saudi Arabia **90** A2
Umm Ruwaba Sudan **103** B3
Umm Sa'ad Libya **101** E1
Umpqua *r.* U.S.A. **132** B2
Umpulo Angola **106** A1
Umtata S. Africa **109** C3
Umuarama Brazil **154** B2
Una *r.* Bos.-Herz./Croatia **63** C1
Una Brazil **151** F4
Unaí Brazil **154** C1
Unalakleet U.S.A. **124** B2
'Unayzah Saudi Arabia **90** B2
Underwood U.S.A. **134** C1
Unecha Rus. Fed. **43** D3
Ungarie Austr. **117** D2
Ungarra Austr. **116** B2
Ungava, Péninsule d' *pen.* Can. **125** H2
Ungava Bay Can. **129** D1
Unggi N. Korea **77** C1
Ungheni Moldova **44** C2
Unguja *i.* Tanz. *see* Zanzibar Island
União da Vitória Brazil **154** B3
Unini *r.* Brazil **150** C3
Union City U.S.A. **138** C1
Uniondale S. Africa **108** B3
Uniontown U.S.A. **137** C3
United Arab Emirates *country* Asia **91** C2
United Kingdom *country* Europe **48** C2
United States of America *country* N. America **130** D3
Unity Can. **124** E3
Unst *i.* U.K. **50** [inset]
Unstrut *r.* Ger. **55** E2
Upa *r.* Rus. Fed. **43** E3
Upemba, Lac *l.* Dem. Rep. Congo **105** C3

Upington S. Africa **108** B2
Upolu *i.* Samoa **111**
Upper Alkali Lake U.S.A. **132** C3
Upper Arrow Lake Can. **126** D2
Upper Klamath Lake U.S.A. **132** B2
Upper Liard Can. **126** C1
Upper Lough Erne *l.* U.K. **51** C1
Uppsala Sweden **47** D4
'Uqlat aş Şuqūr Saudi Arabia **90** B2
Ural *r.* Kazakh./Rus. Fed. **88** C2
Uralla Austr. **117** E2
Ural Mountains Rus. Fed. **41** F2
Ural'sk Kazakh. **88** C1
Ural'skiy Khrebet *mts* Rus. Fed. *see* Ural Mountains
Urambo Tanz. **105** D3
Urana Austr. **117** D3
Uranium City Can. **124** E3
Uray Rus. Fed. **40** F2
Ure *r.* U.K. **52** C2
Uren' Rus. Fed. **40** D3
Urengoy Rus. Fed. **40** G2
Ures Mex. **142** A2
Urganch Uzbek. **88** D2
Urk Neth. **54** B1
Urla Turkey **65** C3
Urmia, Lake *salt l.* Iran **93** C2
Uroševac Serb. and Mont. **64** B2
Uruáchic Mex. **142** B3
Uruaçu Brazil **151** E4
Uruapan Mex. **142** B3
Urubamba *r.* Peru **150** B4
Urucara Brazil **151** D3
Uruçuí Brazil **151** E3
Urucurituba Brazil **151** D3
Uruguai *r.* Brazil **154** B3
Uruguaiana Brazil **152** C3
Uruguay *r.* Arg./Uru. **149**
Uruguay *country* S. America **153** C4
Ürümqi China **89** F2
Urunga Austr. **117** E2
Urup *r.* Rus. Fed. **45** F3
Uryupinsk Rus. Fed. **45** F1
Urziceni Romania **44** C3
Usa Japan **79** B4
Usa *r.* Rus. Fed. **40** F2
Uşa *r.* Rus. Fed. **37**
Uşak Turkey **65** C3
Usakos Namibia **108** A1
Ushakova, Ostrov *i.* Rus. Fed. **94** H1
Ushtobe Kazakh. **89** E2
Ushuaia Arg. **153** B6
Usinsk Rus. Fed. **40** E2
Uskhodni Belarus **42** C2
Usman' Rus. Fed. **43** E3
Usogorsk Rus. Fed. **40** D2
Ussel France **58** C2
Ussuriysk Rus. Fed. **78** B2
Ust'-Donetskiy Rus. Fed. **45** F2
Ust'-Ilimsk Rus. Fed. **95** I3
Ust'-Ilych Rus. Fed. **40** E2
Ustka Pol. **57** D2
Ust'-Kamchatsk Rus. Fed. **95** M3
Ust'-Kamenogorsk Kazakh. **89** F2
Ust'-Kara Rus. Fed. **40** F2
Ust'-Kulom Rus. Fed. **40** E2
Ust'-Kut Rus. Fed. **95** J3
Ust'-Labinsk Rus. Fed. **45** E2
Ust'-Luga Rus. Fed. **42** C2
Ust'-Nem Rus. Fed. **40** E2
Ust'-Nera Rus. Fed. **95** L2
Ust'-Omchug Rus. Fed. **95** L2
Ust'-Ordynskiy Rus. Fed. **95** I3
Ust'-Port Rus. Fed. **40** H2
Ust'-Tsil'ma Rus. Fed. **40** E2
Ust'-Ura Rus. Fed. **40** D2
Ustyurt Plateau Kazakh./Uzbek. **88** C2
Ustyuzhna Rus. Fed. **43** E2

Usvyaty Rus. Fed. **43** D2
Utah state U.S.A. **133** D3
Utah Lake U.S.A. **132** D2
Utena Lith. **42** C2
Utica U.S.A. **137** E2
Utiel Spain **61** C2
Utikuma Lake Can. **126** D2
Utrecht Neth. **54** B1
Utsjoki Fin. **46** F2
Utsunomiya Japan **79** C3
Utsjoki Fin. **41** D4
Uttaradit Thai. **74** B2
Jummannaq Greenland see Dundas
Jummannaq Fjord inlet Greenland
    125 I2
Jusikaupunki Fin. **47** E3
Jvalde U.S.A. **141** E3
Jvarovo Rus. Fed. **45** F1
Jvinza Tanz. **105** D3
Jyuni Bol. **152** B3
Jyuni, Salar de salt flat Bol. **152** B3
Jzbekistan country Asia **88** D2
Jzerche France **58** C2
Jzès France **59** C3
Jzh r. Ukr. **44** D1
Jzhhorod Ukr. **44** B2
Jžice Serb. and Mont. **64** A2
Jzlovaya Rus. Fed. **43** E3
Jzümlü Turkey **65** C2
Jzunköprü Turkey **65** C2

V

Vaal r. S. Africa **109** B2
Vaal Dam S. Africa **109** C2
Vaalwater S. Africa **109** C1
Vaasa Fin. **46** E3
Vác Hungary **57** D3
Vacaria Brazil **152** C3
Vacaria, Serra hills Brazil **154** B2
Vacaville U.S.A. **133** B3
Vacha Rus. Fed. **43** F2
Vadodara India **86** B2
Vadsø Norway **46** F1
Vaduz Liechtenstein **59** D2
Vaeldaskaya Vozvyshennost' hills
    Rus. Fed. **43** D2
Valdecañas, Embalse de resr Spain
    60 B2
Valdemarsvik Sweden **47** D4
Val-de-Meuse France **59** D2
Valdepeñas Spain **60** C2
Val-de-Reuil France **53** D5
Valdés, Península pen. Arg. **153** B5
Valdez U.S.A. **126** A1
Valdivia Chile **153** A4
Val-d'Or Can. **128** C2
Valdosta U.S.A. **139** D2
Valemount Can. **126** D2
Valence France **59** C3
Valencia Spain **61** C2

Valencia Venez. **150** C1
Valencia, Golfo de g. Spain **61** D2
Valenciennes France **54** A2
Valentine U.S.A. **134** C2
Valenzuela Phil. **76** B2
Valera Venez. **150** B2
Valjevo Serb. and Mont. **64** A2
Valka Latvia **42** C2
Valkeakoski Fin. **47** E3
Valkenswaard Neth. **54** B2
Valky Ukr. **45** E2
Valkyrie Dome ice feature Antarctica
    159 D2
Valladolid Mex. **143** D2
Valladolid Spain **60** C1
Vall de Uxó Spain **61** C2
Valle Norway **47** B4
Vallecillos Mex. **143** C2
Valle de la Pascua Venez. **150** C2
Valledupar Col. **150** B1
Valle Hermoso Mex. **143** C2
Vallejo U.S.A. **133** B3
Vallenar Chile **152** A3
Valletta Malta **101** C1
Valley City U.S.A. **135** D1
Valley Falls U.S.A. **132** B2
Valleyview Can. **126** D2
Valls Spain **61** D1
Val Marie Can. **134** B2
Valmiera Latvia **42** C2
Valognes France **53** C5
Valozhyn Belarus **42** C3
Valparaíso Brazil **154** B2
Valparaíso Chile **153** A4
Valréas France **59** C3
Vals, Tanjung c. Indon. **71** D3
Valsad India **86** B2
Valspan S. Africa **108** B2
Valuyki Rus. Fed. **45** E1
Valverde del Camino Spain **60** B2
Van Turkey **93** C2
Van, Lake salt l. Turkey **93** C2
Van Buren U.S.A. **137** G1
Vancouver Can. **126** D3
Vancouver U.S.A. **132** B1
Vancouver Island Can. **126** C3
Vandalia U.S.A. **136** C3
Vanderbijlpark S. Africa **109** C2
Vanderhoof Can. **126** D2
Van Diemen Gulf Austr. **71** C3
Vändra Estonia **42** C2
Vänern l. Sweden **47** C4
Vänersborg Sweden **47** C4
Vangaindrano Madag. **107** [inset] D2
Van Gölü salt l. Turkey see Van, Lake
Van Horn U.S.A. **140** D2
Vanimo P.N.G. **71** D3
Vanino Rus. Fed. **81** F1
Vannes France **58** B2
Van Rees, Pegunungan mts Indon.
    71 D3
Vanrhynsdorp S. Africa **108** A3
Vantaa Fin. **47** E3
Vanua Levu i. Fiji **158** E6
Vanuatu country S. Pacific Ocean **112**
Van Wert U.S.A. **136** D2
Vanwyksvlei S. Africa **108** B3
Van Zylsrus S. Africa **108** B2
Varanasi India **87** C2
Varangerfjorden sea chan. Norway
    46 F1
Varangerhalvøya pen. Norway **46** F1
Varaždin Croatia **63** C1
Varberg Sweden **47** C4
Vardar r. Macedonia **65** B2
Varde Denmark **47** B4
Vardø Norway **46** G1
Varel Ger. **54** D1
Varéna Lith. **42** B3
Varese Italy **62** A1

Varginha Brazil **155** C2
Varkaus Fin. **47** F3
Varna Bulg. **64** C2
Värnamo Sweden **47** C4
Várzea da Palma Brazil **155** D1
Varzino Rus. Fed. **40** C2
Vasknarva Estonia **42** C2
Vaslui Romania **44** C2
Västerås Sweden **47** D4
Västerdalälven r. Sweden **47** D3
Västerhaninge Sweden **42** A2
Västervik Sweden **47** D4
Vasto Italy **62** B2
Vasyl'kiv Ukr. **44** D1
Vatan France **58** C2
Vatican City Europe **62** B2
Vatnajökull ice cap Iceland **46** [inset]
Vatra Dornei Romania **44** C2
Vättern l. Sweden **47** C4
Vaughn U.S.A. **140** C2
Vauvert France **59** C3
Vava'u Group is Tonga **111**
Vawkavysk Belarus **42** B3
Växjö Sweden **47** C4
Vaygach, Ostrov i. Rus. Fed. **40** E1
Vechta Ger. **55** D1
Vedea r. Romania **44** C3
Veendam Neth. **54** C1
Veenendaal Neth. **54** B1
Vegreville Can. **127** D2
Vejer de la Frontera Spain **60** B2
Vejle Denmark **47** B4
Velbüzhdki Prokhod pass
    Bulg./Macedonia **64** B2
Veldhoven Neth. **54** B2
Velebit mts Croatia **62** B2
Velen Ger. **54** C2
Velenje Slovenia **62** C1
Veles Macedonia **63** D2
Vélez-Málaga Spain **60** C2
Velhas r. Brazil **155** D1
Velika Plana Serb. and Mont. **64** B2
Velikaya r. Rus. Fed. **42** C2
Velikiye Luki Rus. Fed. **43** D2
Velikiy Novgorod Rus. Fed. **43** D2
Velikiy Ustyug Rus. Fed. **40** D2
Veliko Tŭrnovo Bulg. **64** C2
Veli Lošinj Croatia **62** B2
Velizh Rus. Fed. **43** D2
Vellberg Ger. **55** D3
Vel'sk Rus. Fed. **40** D2
Velten Ger. **55** F1
Velykyy Burluk Ukr. **45** E1
Venafro Italy **62** B2
Venceslau Bráz Brazil **154** C2
Vendôme France **58** C2
Venev Rus. Fed. **43** E3
Venezia Italy see Venice
Venezuela country S. America **150** C2
Venezuela, Golfo de g. Venez. **150** B1
Venice Italy **62** B1
Venice U.S.A. **139** D3
Venice, Gulf of Europe **62** B1
Venlo Neth. **54** C2
Venray Neth. **54** B2
Venta r. Latvia/Lith. **42** B2
Venta Lith. **42** B2
Venterstad S. Africa **109** C3
Ventnor U.K. **53** C4
Ventspils Latvia **42** B2
Ventura U.S.A. **133** C4
Venustiano Carranza, Presa resr Mex.
    141 D3
Vera Spain **61** C2
Veracruz Mex. **143** C3
Veraval India **86** B2
Verbania Italy **62** A1
Vercelli Italy **62** A1
Vercors reg. France **59** D3
Verdalsøra Norway **46** C3

Verde r. Goiás Brazil **154** B1
Verde r. Mato Grosso do Sul Brazil **154** B2
Verde r. Mex. **142** B2
Verde r. U.S.A. **140** B2
Verde Grande r. Brazil **155** D1
Verden (Aller) Ger. **55** D2
Verdinho, Serra do mts Brazil **154** B1
Verdun France **59** D2
Vereeniging S. Africa **109** C2
Verín Spain **60** B1
Verkhnebakanskiy Rus. Fed. **45** E3
Verkhnetulomskiy Rus. Fed. **46** G2
Verkhniy Mamon Rus. Fed. **45** F1
Verkhov'ye Rus. Fed. **43** E3
Verkhoyna Ukr. **44** B2
Verkhoyanskiy Khrebet mts Rus. Fed.
95 K2
Vermand France **54** A3
Vermilion Can. **127** D2
Vermillion U.S.A. **135** D2
Vermillion Bay Can. **128** A2
Vermont state U.S.A. **137** F2
Vernal U.S.A. **132** E2
Vernon Can. **126** D2
Vernon U.S.A. **141** E2
Vero Beach U.S.A. **139** D3
Veroia Greece **65** B2
Verona Italy **62** B1
Versailles France **58** C2
Vert, Cape c. Senegal **96**
Vertou France **58** B2
Verulam S. Africa **109** D2
Verviers Belgium **54** B2
Vervins France **59** C2
Verzy France **54** B3
Vescovato France **59** D3
Veselaya, Gora mt. Rus. Fed. **41** E3
Vesele Ukr. **45** D2
Veselovskoye Vodokhranilishche resr
Rus. Fed. **45** F2
Veselyy Rus. Fed. **45** F2
Veshenskaya Rus. Fed. **45** F2
Vesoul France **59** D2
Vesterålen is Norway **46** C2
Vestfjorden sea chan. Norway **46** C2
Vestmanna Faroe Is **48** B1
Vestmannaeyjar is Iceland **36**
Vestnes Norway **46** B3
Vesuvius vol. Italy **62** B2
Ves'yegonsk Rus. Fed. **43** E2
Vetlanda Sweden **47** D4
Vetluga Rus. Fed. **40** D3
Veurne Belgium **54** A2
Vevey Switz. **59** D2
Veydelevka Rus. Fed. **45** E1
Vezirköprü Turkey **92** B1
Viana Brazil **151** E3
Viana do Castelo Port. **60** B1
Viangchan Laos see Vientiane
Viangphoukha Laos **74** B1
Vianópolis Brazil **154** C1
Viareggio Italy **62** B2
Viborg Denmark **47** B4
Vibo Valentia Italy **63** C3
Vic Spain **61** D1
Vicente Guerrero Mex. **142** A1
Vicenza Italy **62** B1
Vichuga Rus. Fed. **43** F2
Vichy France **59** C2
Vicksburg U.S.A. **138** B2
Viçosa Brazil **155** D2
Victor Harbor Austr. **116** B3
Victoria r. Austr. **114** C1
Victoria state Austr. **116** C3
Victoria Can. **126** B3
Victoria Chile **153** A4
Victoria Seychelles **99**
Victoria U.S.A. **141** E3
Victoria, Lake Africa **105** D3

Victoria, Lake Austr. **116** C2
Victoria, Mount Myanmar **74** A1
Victoria, Mount P.N.G. **71** D3
Victoria Falls Zambia/Zimbabwe
106 B1
Victoria Island Can. **124** E2
Victoria River Downs Austr. **114** C1
Victoria West S. Africa **108** B3
Victorville U.S.A. **133** C4
Videle Romania **44** C3
Viðidalsá Iceland **46** [inset]
Viechtach Ger. **55** F3
Viedma Arg. **153** B5
Viedma, Lago l. Arg. **153** A5
Vielsalm Belgium **54** B2
Vienenburg Ger. **55** E2
Vienna Austria **57** D3
Vienne France **59** C2
Vienne r. France **58** C2
Vientiane Laos **74** B2
Viersen Ger. **54** C2
Vierzon France **58** C2
Viesca Mex. **142** B2
Vieste Italy **63** C2
Vietnam country Asia **74** B2
Viêt Tri Vietnam **74** B1
Vigan Phil. **76** B2
Vigevano Italy **62** A1
Vigo Spain **60** B1
Vijayawada India **85** C3
Vik Iceland **46** [inset]
Viking Can. **127** D2
Vikøyri Norway **48** E1
Vila Franca de Xira Port. **60** B2
Vilagarcía de Arousa Spain **60** B1
Vilalba Spain **60** B1
Vila Nova de Gaia Port. **60** B1
Vilanova i la Geltrú Spain **61** D1
Vila Real Port. **60** B1
Vilar Formoso Port. **60** B1
Vila Velha Brazil **155** D2
Vilcabamba, Cordillera mts Peru
150 B4
Vil'cheka, Zemlya i. Rus. Fed. **94** G1
Vilhelmina Sweden **46** D3
Vilhena Brazil **150** C4
Viljandi Estonia **42** C1
Vilkaviškis Lith. **42** B3
Vil'kitskogo, Proliv str. Rus. Fed. **95** I1
Villa Ahumada Mex. **142** B1
Villablino Spain **60** B1
Villach Austria **56** C3
Villa de Cos Mex. **142** B2
Villa Dolores Arg. **152** B4
Villa Flores Mex. **143** C3
Villagrán Mex. **143** C2
Villahermosa Mex. **143** C3
Villa Insurgentes Mex. **142** A2
Villa María Arg. **152** B4
Villa Montes Bol. **152** B3
Villanueva Mex. **142** B2
Villanueva de la Serena Spain **60** B2
Villanueva de los Infantes Spain
60 C2
Villa Ocampo Arg. **152** C3
Villaputzu Italy **62** A3
Villarrica Para. **152** C3
Villarrobledo Spain **60** C2
Villa Unión Arg. **152** B3
Villa Unión Durango Mex. **142** B2
Villa Unión Sinaloa Mex. **142** B2
Villavicencio Col. **150** B2
Villazón Bol. **152** B3
Villefranche-sur-Saône France **56** A3
Villena Spain **61** C2
Villeneuve-sur-Lot France **58** C3
Ville Platte U.S.A. **138** B2
Villers-Cotterêts France **54** A3
Villeurbanne France **59** C2
Villingen Ger. **56** B3

Vilnius Lith. **42** C3
Vil'nohirs'k Ukr. **45** D2
Vil'nyans'k Ukr. **45** E2
Vilvoorde Belgium **54** B2
Vilyeyka Belarus **42** C3
Vilyuy r. Rus. Fed. **95** K2
Vimmerby Sweden **47** D4
Viña del Mar Chile **153** A4
Vinaròs Spain **61** D1
Vincennes U.S.A. **136** C3
Vineland U.S.A. **137** E3
Vinh Vietnam **74** B2
Vinh Long Vietnam **75** B2
Vinita U.S.A. **141** E1
Vinnytsya Ukr. **44** C2
Vinson Massif mt. Antarctica **119** K2
Vinstra Norway **47** B3
Vipiteno Italy **62** B1
Virac Phil. **76** B2
Virden Can. **127** E3
Vire France **58** B2
Virei Angola **106** A1
Virgem da Lapa Brazil **155** D1
Virgin r. U.S.A. **140** B1
Virginia S. Africa **109** C2
Virginia U.S.A. **135** E1
Virginia state U.S.A. **137** E3
Virginia Beach U.S.A. **137** E3
Virginia City U.S.A. **133** C3
Virgin Islands (U.K.) terr. West Indies
145 D3
Virgin Islands (U.S.A.) terr. West Indies
145 D3
Vîrôchey Cambodia **75** B2
Virovitica Croatia **63** C1
Virton Belgium **54** B3
Virtsu Estonia **42** B2
Vis i. Croatia **63** C2
Visaginas Lith. **42** C2
Visalia U.S.A. **133** C3
Visavadar India **86** B2
Visayan Sea Phil. **76** B2
Visby Sweden **47** D4
Viscount Melville Sound sea chan.
Can. **124** E2
Viseu Brazil **151** E3
Viseu Port. **60** B1
Vishakhapatnam India **85** C3
Viški Latvia **42** C2
Visoko Bos.-Herz. **63** C2
Vistula r. Pol. **57** D2
Viterbo Italy **62** B2
Viti Levu i. Fiji **158** E6
Vitim r. Rus. Fed. **95** J3
Vitória Brazil **155** D2
Vitória da Conquista Brazil **151** E4
Vitoria-Gasteiz Spain **60** C1
Vitré France **58** B2
Vitry-le-François France **59** C2
Vitsyebsk Belarus **43** D2
Vittel France **59** D2
Vittoria Italy **62** B3
Vittorio Veneto Italy **62** B1
Viveiro Spain **60** B1
Vizcaíno, Sierra mts Mex. **142** A2
Vize Turkey **64** C2
Vizianagaram India **85** C3
Vlaardingen Neth. **54** B2
Vladikavkaz Rus. Fed. **41** D4
Vladimir Rus. Fed. **43** F2
Vladivostok Rus. Fed. **78** B2
Vlasotince Serb. and Mont. **64** B2
Vlieland i. Neth. **54** A2
Vlissingen Neth. **54** A2
Vlorë Albania **65** A2
Vöcklabruck Austria **56** C3
Vogelsberg hills Ger. **55** D2
Vohimena, Tanjona c. Madag. **97**
Voi Kenya **105** D3
Voiron France **59** D2

Voisey Bay Can. **129** D1
Vojens Denmark **56** B1
Vojvodina *prov.* Serb. and Mont. **64** A1
Voknavolok Rus. Fed. **46** G3
Volcano Bay Japan *see* Uchiura-wan
Volda Norway **48** E1
Volga Rus. Fed. **43** E2
Volga *r.* Rus. Fed. **43** E2
Volgodonsk Rus. Fed. **41** D4
Volgograd Rus. Fed. **41** E4
Volkhov Rus. Fed. **43** D2
Volkhov *r.* Rus. Fed. **43** D1
Volkstedt Ger. **55** E2
Volnovakha Ukr. **45** E2
Volochys'k Ukr. **44** C2
Volodarsk Rus. Fed. **43** F2
Volodars'ke Ukr. **45** E2
Volodars'k-Volyns'kyy Ukr. **44** C1
Volodymyrets' Ukr. **44** C1
Volodymyr-Volyns'kyy Ukr. **44** B1
Vologda Rus. Fed. **43** E2
Volokolamsk Rus. Fed. **43** E2
Volokonovka Rus. Fed. **45** E1
Volos Greece **65** B3
Volosovo Rus. Fed. **42** C2
Volot Rus. Fed. **42** D2
Vol'sk Rus. Fed. **41** D3
Volta, Lake *resr* Ghana **100** C4
Volta Redonda Brazil **155** D2
Volzhskiy Rus. Fed. **41** D4
Vopnafjörður Iceland **46** [inset]
Voranava Belarus **42** C3
Voreioi Sporades *is* Greece **92** A2
Vorkuta Rus. Fed. **40** F2
Vorona *r.* Rus. Fed. **45** F1
Voronezh Rus. Fed. **43** E3
Voronezh *r.* Rus. Fed. **43** E3
Vorontsovka Rus. Fed. **45** F1
Vorskla *r.* Rus. Fed. **45** D2
Võrtsjärv *l.* Estonia **42** C2
Võru Estonia **42** C2
Vosburg S. Africa **108** B3
Vosges *mts* France **59** D2
Voss Norway **47** B4
Vostochno-Sibirskoye More *sea*
  Rus. Fed. *see* East Siberian Sea
Vostochnyy Sayan *mts* Rus. Fed. **95** I3
Vostok Rus. Fed. **78** C1
Votkinsk Rus. Fed. **40** E3
Votuporanga Brazil **154** C2
Vouziers France **54** B3
Voynitsa Rus. Fed. **46** G2
Voznesens'k Ukr. **45** D2
Voznesenskoye Rus. Fed. **43** F3
Vrådal Norway **47** B4
Vrangel' Rus. Fed. **78** B2
Vrangelya, Ostrov *i.* Rus. Fed. *see*
  Wrangel Island
Vranje Serb. and Mont. **64** B2
Vratnik *pass* Bulg. **64** C2
Vratsa Bulg. **64** B2
Vrbas *r.* Bos.-Herz. **63** C1
Vrbas Serb. and Mont. **64** A1
Vrede S. Africa **108** A3
Vredenburg S. Africa **108** A3
Vresse Belgium **54** B3
Vršac Serb. and Mont. **64** B1
Vryburg S. Africa **108** B2
Vryheid S. Africa **109** D2
Vsevolozhsk Rus. Fed. **43** D1
Vučitrn Serb. and Mont. **64** B2
Vukovar Croatia **63** C1
Vuktyl' Rus. Fed. **40** E2
Vukuzakhe S. Africa **109** C2
Vulcano, Isola *i.* Italy **62** B3
Vung Tau Vietnam **75** D2
Vyara India **86** B2

Vyatka Rus. Fed. *see* Kirov
Vyaz'ma Rus. Fed. **43** D2
Vyazniki Rus. Fed. **43** F2
Vyborg Rus. Fed. **42** C1
Vyerkhnyadzvinsk Belarus **42** C2
Vyksa Rus. Fed. **43** F2
Vylkove Ukr. **44** C2
Vynohradiv Ukr. **44** B2
Vypolzovo Rus. Fed. **43** D2
Vyritsa Rus. Fed. **43** D2
Vyselki Rus. Fed. **45** E2
Vyshhorod Ukr. **44** D1
Vyshniy-Volochek Rus. Fed. **43** D2
Vyškov Czech Rep. **57** D3
Vytegra Rus. Fed. **40** C2

W

Wa Ghana **100** B3
Waal *r.* Neth. **54** B2
Waalwijk Neth. **54** B2
Wabasca *r.* Can. **126** D2
Wabasca-Desmarais Can. **126** D2
Wabash *r.* U.S.A. **136** C3
Wabē Gestro *r.* Eth. **103** C4
Wabē Shebelē Wenz *r.* Eth. **103** C4
Wabowden Can. **127** F2
Waccasassa Bay U.S.A. **139** D3
Wächtersbach Ger. **55** D2
Waco U.S.A. **141** E2
Wad Pak. **86** A2
Waddān Libya **101** D2
Waddenzee *sea chan.* Neth. **54** B1
Waddington, Mount Can. **126** C2
Waddinxveen Neth. **54** B1
Wadena Can. **127** E2
Wadena U.S.A. **135** D1
Wadgassen Ger. **54** C3
Wadi Halfa Sudan **102** B2
Wad Medani Sudan **102** B3
Wafangdian China **82** C2
Wageningen Neth. **54** B2
Wagga Wagga Austr. **117** D3
Wahoo U.S.A. **135** D2
Wahpeton U.S.A. **135** D1
Waiau *r.* N.Z. **118** B3
Waigeo *i.* Indon. **71** C3
Waikabubak Indon. **73** C2
Waikerie Austr. **116** B2
Waimate N.Z. **118** B3
Wainganga *r.* India **87** B3
Waingapu Indon. **73** D2
Wainwright Can. **127** D2
Wainwright U.S.A. **124** B2
Waiouru N.Z. **118** C2
Waipara N.Z. **118** B3
Waipawa N.Z. **118** C2
Wairau *r.* N.Z. **118** B3
Wairoa N.Z. **118** C2
Waitaki *r.* N.Z. **118** B3
Waitara N.Z. **118** C2
Waiuku N.Z. **118** B2
Wajir Kenya **105** D2
Wakasa-wan *b.* Japan **79** C3
Wakatipu, Lake N.Z. **118** A4
Wakaw Can. **127** E2
Wakayama Japan **79** C4
WaKeeney U.S.A. **134** D3
Wakefield N.Z. **118** B3
Wakefield U.K. **52** C3
Wake Island *terr.*
  N. Pacific Ocean **112**
Wakkanai Japan **78** D1
Wakkerstroom S. Africa **109** D2
Wałbrzych Pol. **57** D2
Walcha Austr. **117** E2
Walchum Ger. **54** C1
Wałcz Pol. **57** D2

Wales *admin. div.* U.K. **53** B3
Walgett Austr. **117** D2
Walikale Dem. Rep. Congo **105** C3
Walker Lake U.S.A. **133** C3
Wallaroo Austr. **116** B2
Walla Walla U.S.A. **132** C1
Walldürn Ger. **55** D3
Wallendbeen Austr. **117** D2
Wallis, Îles *is* Wallis and Futuna Is **111**
Wallis and Futuna Islands *terr.*
  S. Pacific Ocean **113**
Walls U.K. **50** [inset]
Walney, Isle of *i.* U.K. **52** B2
Walsall U.K. **53** C3
Walsenburg U.S.A. **134** C3
Walsrode Ger. **55** D1
Walterboro U.S.A. **139** D2
Walvis Bay Namibia **106** A2
Wamba Dem. Rep. Congo **105** C2
Wanaaring Austr. **116** C1
Wanaka N.Z. **118** A3
Wanaka, Lake N.Z. **118** A3
Wanapitei Lake Can. **128** B2
Wanda Arg. **154** B3
Wanda Shan *mts* China **78** B1
Wanding China **74** A1
Wandlitz Ger. **55** F1
Wanganui N.Z. **118** C2
Wangaratta Austr. **117** D3
Wangqing China **77** B1
Wan Hsa-la Myanmar **74** A1
Wanning China **83** B4
Wanroij Neth. **54** B2
Wantage U.S.A. **53** C4
Wanxian China **82** A2
Wanyuan China **82** A2
Warangal India **85** B3
Warburg Ger. **55** D2
Warburton Austr. **114** B2
Warburton *watercourse* Austr. **116** B1
Wardha India **87** B2
Ward Hill U.K. **50** C1
Ware Can. **126** C2
Waren Ger. **55** F1
Warendorf Ger. **54** C2
Warialda Austr. **117** E1
Warmbad Namibia **108** A2
Warm Springs U.S.A. **133** C3
Warner Lakes U.S.A. **132** C2
Warner Robins U.S.A. **139** D2
Warnes Bol. **152** B2
Warracknabeal Austr. **116** C3
Warrego *r.* Austr. **117** D2
Warren Austr. **117** D2
Warren *AR* U.S.A. **138** B2
Warren *OH* U.S.A. **136** D2
Warren *PA* U.S.A. **137** E2
Warrenpoint U.K. **51** C1
Warrensburg U.S.A. **135** E3
Warrenton S. Africa **108** B2
Warri Nigeria **101** C4
Warrington U.K. **52** B3
Warrnambool Austr. **116** C3
Warsaw Pol. **57** E2
Warszawa Pol. *see* Warsaw
Warta *r.* Pol. **57** C2
Warwick Austr. **117** E1
Warwick U.K. **53** C3
Wasco U.S.A. **133** C3
Washburn U.S.A. **134** C1
Washington *DC* U.S.A. **137** E3
Washington *IA* U.S.A. **135** E2
Washington *IN* U.S.A. **136** C3
Washington *MO* U.S.A. **135** E3
Washington *NC* U.S.A. **139** E1
Washington *PA* U.S.A. **137** D2
Washington *state* U.S.A. **132** B1
Washington, Mount U.S.A. **137** F2
Washington Court House U.S.A.
  136 D3

Washuk Pak. 86 A2
Waskaganish Can. 128 C1
Waskaiowaka Lake Can. 127 F2
Wasser Namibia 108 A2
Waswanipi, Lac l. Can. 128 C2
Watampone Indon. 73 D2
Waterbury U.S.A. 137 F2
Waterbury Lake Can. 127 F2
Waterford Rep. of Ireland 51 C2
Waterford Harbour Rep. of Ireland
    51 C2
Waterloo U.S.A. 135 E2
Waterpoort S. Africa 109 C1
Watertown NY U.S.A. 137 E2
Watertown SD U.S.A. 135 D2
Watertown WI U.S.A. 136 C2
Waterville U.S.A. 137 G2
Watford U.K. 53 C4
Watford City U.S.A. 134 C1
Wathaman r. Can. 127 E2
Watonga U.S.A. 141 E1
Watrous Can. 127 E2
Watsa Dem. Rep. Congo 105 C2
Watseka U.S.A. 136 C2
Watsi Kengo Dem. Rep. Congo 104 C3
Watson Lake Can. 126 C1
Watsonville U.S.A. 133 B3
Watubela, Kepulauan is Indon. 71 C3
Wau P.N.G. 71 D3
Wau Sudan 103 A4
Wauchope Austr. 117 E2
Waukegan U.S.A. 136 C2
Waurika U.S.A. 141 E2
Wausau U.S.A. 136 C2
Waveney r. U.K. 53 D3
Waverly U.S.A. 135 E2
Waycross U.S.A. 139 D2
Wayne U.S.A. 136 D2
Waynesboro GA U.S.A. 139 D2
Waynesboro VA U.S.A. 137 E3
Waynesville U.S.A. 139 D1
Wazirabad Pak. 86 B1
Wear r. U.K. 52 C2
Weatherford U.S.A. 141 E2
Weaverville U.S.A. 132 B2
Webequie Can. 128 B1
Webster U.S.A. 135 D1
Webster City U.S.A. 135 E2
Weert Neth. 54 B2
Wee Waa Austr. 117 D2
Wegberg Ger. 54 C2
Węgorzewo Pol. 57 E2
Weiden in der Oberpfalz Ger. 55 F3
Weifang China 82 B2
Weihai China 82 C2
Weilmoringle Austr. 117 D1
Weimar Ger. 55 E2
Weinan China 82 A2
Weinsberg Ger. 55 D3
Weipa Austr. 115 D1
Weir r. Austr. 117 D1
Weirton U.S.A. 137 D2
Weishan China 74 B1
Weißenburg in Bayern Ger. 55 E3
Weißenfels Ger. 55 E2
Weißkugel mt. Austria/Italy 56 C3
Wejherowo Pol. 57 D2
Wekweti Can. 126 D1
Welch U.S.A. 136 D3
Weldiya Eth. 103 B3
Welkom S. Africa 109 C2
Welland r. U.K. 53 C3
Wellesley Islands Austr. 115 C1
Wellington Austr. 117 D2
Wellington N.Z. 118 B3
Wellington S. Africa 108 A3
Wellington U.S.A. 135 D3
Wellington, Isla i. Chile 153 A5
Wellington, Lake Austr. 117 D3

Wells Can. 126 C2
Wells U.K. 53 B4
Wells U.S.A. 132 D2
Wells, Lake salt flat Austr. 114 B2
Wellsford N.Z. 118 B2
Wells-next-the-Sea U.K. 52 D3
Wels Austria 56 C3
Welshpool U.K. 53 B3
Wembesi S. Africa 109 C2
Wemindji Can. 128 C1
Wenatchee U.S.A. 132 B1
Wenchang China 83 B4
Wenchi Ghana 100 B4
Wendelstein Ger. 55 E3
Wendeng China 82 C2
Wendisch Evern Ger. 55 E1
Wendo Eth. 103 B4
Wendover U.S.A. 132 D2
Wengyuan China 83 B3
Wenling China 83 C3
Wenshan China 83 A3
Wentworth Austr. 116 C2
Wenzhou China 83 C3
Wepener S. Africa 109 C2
Werda Botswana 108 B2
Werdau Ger. 55 F2
Werder Ger. 55 F1
Wernberg-Köblitz Ger. 55 F3
Wernigerode Ger. 55 E2
Werra r. Ger. 55 D2
Werris Creek Austr. 117 E2
Wertheim Ger. 55 D3
Wesel Ger. 54 C2
Wesendorf Ger. 55 E1
Weser r. Ger. 55 D1
Weser sea chan. Ger. 55 D1
Wessel, Cape Austr. 115 C1
Wessel Islands Austr. 115 C1
Wesselton S. Africa 109 C2
West Antarctica reg. Antarctica 119 I2
West Bank terr. Asia 92 B2
West Bend U.S.A. 136 C2
West Bromwich U.K. 53 C3
Westerburg Ger. 54 C2
Westerholt Ger. 54 C1
Western Australia state Austr. 114 B2
Western Cape prov. S. Africa 108 B3
Western Desert Egypt 102 A2
Western Ghats mts India 85 B3
Western Sahara terr. Africa 100 A2
Westerschelde est. Neth. 54 A2
Westerstede Ger. 54 C1
Westerwald hills Ger. 54 C2
West Falkland i. Falkland Is 153 B6
West Frankfort U.S.A. 136 C3
West Frisian Islands Neth. 54 B1
West Indies is Caribbean Sea 145 D2
West Loch Roag b. U.K. 50 A1
Westlock Can. 126 D2
Westmalle Belgium 54 B2
West Memphis U.S.A. 138 B1
Weston U.S.A. 137 D3
Weston-super-Mare U.K. 53 B4
West Palm Beach U.S.A. 139 D3
West Plains U.S.A. 135 E3
West Point U.S.A. 135 D2
Westport N.Z. 118 B3
Westport Rep. of Ireland 51 B2
Westray i. U.K. 50 C1
West Siberian Plain Rus. Fed. see
    Zapadno Sibirskaya Ravnina
West-Terschelling Neth. 54 B1
West Town Rep. of Ireland 51 B1
West Virginia state U.S.A. 137 D3
West Wyalong Austr. 117 D2
West Yellowstone U.S.A. 132 D2
Wetar i. Indon. 71 C3
Wetaskiwin Can. 126 D2
Wetzlar Ger. 55 D2

Wewak P.N.G. 71 D3
Wexford Rep. of Ireland 51 C2
Weyakwin Can. 127 E2
Weyburn Can. 124 F3
Weyhe Ger. 55 D1
Weymouth U.K. 53 B4
Whakatane N.Z. 118 C2
Whale Cove Can. 127 F1
Whalsay i. U.K. 50 [inset]
Whangarei N.Z. 118 B2
Wharfe r. U.K. 52 C3
Wharton U.S.A. 141 E3
Wha Ti Can. 126 D1
Wheatland U.S.A. 134 B2
Wheeler Peak NM U.S.A. 140 C1
Wheeler Peak NV U.S.A. 133 D3
Wheeling U.S.A. 137 D2
Whernside h. U.K. 52 B2
Whistler Can. 126 C2
Whitby U.K. 52 C2
White r. Can./U.S.A. 126 B1
White r. U.S.A. 138 B2
White, Lake salt flat Austr. 114 B2
White Bay Can. 129 E2
White Butte mt. U.S.A. 134 C1
White Cliffs Austr. 116 C2
Whitecourt Can. 126 D2
Whitefish U.S.A. 132 D1
Whitehaven U.K. 52 B2
Whitehead U.K. 51 D1
Whitehorse Can. 126 B1
White Lake U.S.A. 138 B3
White Mountain Peak U.S.A. 133 C3
White Nile r. Sudan/Uganda 103 B3
White Sea Rus. Fed. 40 C2
White Sulphur Springs U.S.A. 132 D1
Whiteville U.S.A. 139 E2
White Volta watercourse
    Burkina/Ghana 100 B3
Whitewater Baldy mt. U.S.A. 140 C2
Whitewater Lake Can. 128 B1
Whitewood Can. 127 E2
Whithorn U.K. 50 B3
Whitianga N.Z. 118 C2
Whitney, Mount U.S.A. 133 C3
Whitsunday Island Austr. 115 D2
Whyalla Austr. 116 B2
Wichelen Belgium 54 A2
Wichita U.S.A. 135 D3
Wichita Falls U.S.A. 141 E2
Wick U.K. 50 C1
Wickenburg U.S.A. 140 B2
Wicklow Rep. of Ireland 51 C2
Wicklow Head Rep. of Ireland 51 D2
Wicklow Mountains Rep. of Ireland
    51 C2
Widnes U.K. 52 B3
Wiehengebirge hills Ger. 55 D1
Wiehl Ger. 54 C2
Wieluń Pol. 57 D2
Wien Austria see Vienna
Wiener Neustadt Austria 57 D3
Wieringerwerf Neth. 54 B1
Wiesbaden Ger. 55 D2
Wiesloch Ger. 55 D3
Wiesmoor Ger. 54 C1
Wieżyca h. Pol. 57 D2
Wight, Isle of i. U.K. 53 C4
Wigtown U.K. 50 B3
Wijchen Neth. 54 B2
Wilcannia Austr. 116 C2
Wild Coast S. Africa 109 C3
Wilge r. S. Africa 109 C2
Wilhelm, Mount P.N.G. 110
Wilhelmshaven Ger. 54 D1
Wilkes-Barre U.S.A. 137 E2
Wilkes Land reg. Antarctica 119 G2
Wilkie Can. 127 E2
Willcox U.S.A. 140 C2
Willebroek Belgium 54 B2

Willemstad Neth. Antilles **145** D3
William, Mount Austr. **116** C3
William Creek Austr. **116** B1
Williams U.S.A. **140** B1
Williamsburg U.S.A. **137** E3
Williams Lake Can. **126** C2
Williamson U.S.A. **136** D3
Williamsport U.S.A. **137** E2
Williamston U.S.A. **139** E1
Williston S. Africa **108** B3
Williston U.S.A. **134** C1
Williston Lake Can. **126** C2
Willits U.S.A. **133** C3
Willmar U.S.A. **135** D1
Willowmore S. Africa **108** B3
Willowvale S. Africa **109** C3
Wills, Lake salt flat Austr. **114** B2
Willunga Austr. **116** B3
Wilmington Austr. **116** B2
Wilmington DE U.S.A. **137** E3
Wilmington NC U.S.A. **139** E2
Wilsdorf Ger. **54** D2
Wilson U.S.A. **139** E1
Wilson's Promontory pen. Austr. **117** D3
Wiltz Lux. **54** B3
Wiluna Austr. **114** B2
Winchester U.K. **53** C4
Winchester KY U.S.A. **136** D3
Winchester VA U.S.A. **137** E3
Wind r. Can. **126** B1
Windermere l. U.K. **52** B2
Windhoek Namibia **108** A1
Windom U.S.A. **135** D2
Windorah Austr. **115** D2
Wind River Range mts U.S.A. **134** B2
Windsor Austr. **117** E2
Windsor Can. **128** B2
Windward Islands Caribbean Sea **145** D3
Windward Passage Cuba/Haiti **145** C3
Winfield U.S.A. **135** D3
Wingene Belgium **54** A2
Wingham Austr. **117** E2
Winisk Can. **128** B1
Winisk r. Can. **128** B1
Winisk Lake Can. **128** B1
Winkana Myanmar **75** A2
Winkler Can. **127** F3
Winneba Ghana **100** B4
Winnebago, Lake U.S.A. **136** C2
Winnemucca U.S.A. **132** C2
Winner U.S.A. **134** C2
Winfield U.S.A. **141** E1
Winnibigoshish, Lake U.S.A. **135** E1
Winnipeg Can. **127** F3
Winnipeg r. Can. **127** F2
Winnipeg, Lake Can. **127** F2
Winnipegosis, Lake Can. **127** E2
Winnipesaukee, Lake U.S.A. **137** F2
Winnsboro U.S.A. **138** B2
Winona MN U.S.A. **135** E2
Winona MS U.S.A. **138** C2
Winschoten Neth. **54** C1
Winsen (Aller) Ger. **55** D1
Winsen (Luhe) Ger. **55** E1
Winslow U.S.A. **140** B1
Winston-Salem U.S.A. **139** D1
Winter Haven U.S.A. **139** D3
Winterberg Ger. **55** D2
Winterswijk Neth. **54** C2
Winterthur Switz. **59** D2
Winton Austr. **115** D2
Winton N.Z. **118** A4
Wirrabara Austr. **116** B2
Wisbech U.K. **53** D3
Wisconsin r. U.S.A. **136** B2
Wisconsin state U.S.A. **136** C2
Wisconsin Rapids U.S.A. **136** C2
Wista r. Pol. see Vistula

Wismar Ger. **56** C2
Witbank S. Africa **109** C2
Withernsea U.K. **52** D3
Witmarsum Neth. **54** B1
Witney U.K. **53** C4
Witrivier S. Africa **109** D2
Wittenberge Ger. **55** E1
Wittenburg Ger. **55** E1
Wittingen Ger. **55** E1
Wittlich Ger. **54** C3
Wittmund Ger. **54** C1
Wittstock Ger. **55** F1
Witvlei Namibia **108** A1
Witzenhausen Ger. **55** D2
Władysławowo Pol. **57** D2
Włocławek Pol. **57** D2
Wodonga Austr. **117** D3
Woippy France **54** C3
Wokam i. Indon. **71** C3
Woking U.K. **53** C4
Woldegk Ger. **55** F1
Wolfen Ger. **55** F2
Wolfenbüttel Ger. **55** E1
Wolfhagen Ger. **55** D2
Wolf Point U.S.A. **134** B1
Wolfsburg Ger. **55** E1
Wolfstein Ger. **54** C3
Wolfville Can. **129** D2
Wolgast Ger. **56** C2
Wolin Pol. **56** C2
Wollaston Lake Can. **127** E2
Wollaston Lake l. Can. **124** F3
Wollaston Peninsula Can. **124** C2
Wollongong Austr. **117** E2
Wolmirsleben Ger. **55** E2
Wolmirstedt Ger. **55** E1
Wolvega Neth. **54** C1
Wolverhampton U.K. **53** B3
Wönju S. Korea **77** B2
Wonowon Can. **126** C2
Wönsan N. Korea **77** B2
Wonthaggi Austr. **117** D3
Woocalla Austr. **116** B2
Woodah, Isle i. Austr. **115** C1
Woodbridge U.K. **53** D3
Woodland Park U.S.A. **134** B3
Woods, Lake salt flat Austr. **114** C1
Woods Point Austr. **117** D3
Woodstock Can. **137** G1
Woodville N.Z. **118** B3
Woodward U.S.A. **141** E1
Woolgoolga Austr. **117** E2
Woomera Austr. **116** B2
Wooster U.S.A. **136** D2
Worcester S. Africa **108** A3
Worcester U.K. **53** B3
Worcester U.S.A. **137** F2
Wörgl Austria **56** C3
Workington U.K. **52** B2
Worksop U.K. **52** C3
Worland U.S.A. **134** B2
Worms Ger. **55** D3
Wörth am Rhein Ger. **55** D3
Worthing U.K. **53** C4
Worthington U.S.A. **135** D2
Wotu Indon. **73** D2
Wowoni i. Indon. **73** D2
Wrangel Island Rus. Fed. **95** O2
Wrangell U.S.A. **126** B2
Wrangell Mountains U.S.A. **124** B3
Wrath, Cape U.K. **50** B1
Wray U.S.A. **134** C2
Wreck Point pt S. Africa **108** A2
Wrexham U.K. **52** B3
Wright U.S.A. **134** B3
Wrightmyo India **75** A2
Wrigley Can. **126** C1

Wrocław Pol. **57** D2
Września Pol. **57** D2
Wu'an China **82** B2
Wudu China **82** A2
Wuhai China **82** A2
Wuhan China **83** B2
Wuhu China **82** B2
Wukari Nigeria **101** C4
Wuli China **87** D1
Wuliang Shan mts China **74** B1
Wuliaru i. Indon. **71** C3
Wumeng Shan mts China **83** A3
Wunnummin Lake Can. **128** B1
Wunsiedel Ger. **55** F2
Wunstorf Ger. **55** D1
Wuntho Myanmar **74** A1
Wuppertal Ger. **54** C2
Wuppertal S. Africa **108** A3
Wurzbach Ger. **55** E2
Würzburg Ger. **55** D3
Wurzen Ger. **55** F2
Wuwei China **82** A2
Wuxi Chongqing China **82** A2
Wuxi Jiangsu China **82** C2
Wuxing China see Huzhou
Wuxuan China **83** B3
Wuyiling China **81** E1
Wuyishan China **83** B3
Wuyi Shan mts China **83** B3
Wuyuan China **82** A1
Wuzhishan China **83** A4
Wuzhong China **82** A2
Wuzhou China **83** B3
Wyangala Reservoir Austr. **117** D2
Wycheproof Austr. **116** C3
Wye r. U.K. **53** B4
Wyndham Austr. **114** B1
Wynne U.S.A. **138** B1
Wynyard Can. **127** E2
Wyoming state U.S.A. **134** B2
Wyszków Pol. **57** E2
Wytheville U.S.A. **136** D3

Xaafuun Somalia **103** D3
Xaignabouli Laos **74** B2
Xai-Xai Moz. **107** C2
Xamba China **82** A1
Xam Nua Laos **74** B1
Xanagas Botswana **108** B1
Xangongo Angola **106** A1
Xankändi Azer. **93** C2
Xanthi Greece **65** B2
Xanxerê Brazil **154** B3
Xapuri Brazil **150** C4
Xátiva Spain **61** C2
Xiamen China **83** B3
Xi'an China **82** A2
Xianfeng China **83** A3
Xiangfan China **82** B2
Xianggelila China **74** A1
Xianghuang Qi China see Xin Bulag
Xiangkhoang Laos **74** B2
Xiangtan China **83** B3
Xiantao China **83** B2
Xianyang China **82** A2
Xiaogan China **82** B2
Xiao Hinggan Ling mts China **81** E1
Xiaoshan China **83** C2
Xichang China **74** B1
Xicoténcatl Mex. **143** C2
Xifeng Gansu China **82** A2
Xifeng Guizhou China **83** A3
Xigazê China **87** C2
Xilinhot China **82** B1
Xin Bulag China **82** B1
Xincai China **82** B2

Xinghai China 80 C2
Xinghua China 82 B2
Xingning China 83 B3
Xingping China 82 A2
Xingtai China 82 B2
Xingu r. Brazil 151 D3
Xingyi China 83 A3
Xinhua China 83 B3
Xining China 80 C2
Xinjiang Uygur Zizhiqu aut. reg. China 87 C1
Xinmin China 77 A1
Xinning China 83 B3
Xintai China 82 B2
Xinxiang China 82 B2
Xinyang China 82 B2
Xinyu China 83 B3
Xinzhou Shanxi China 82 B2
Xinzhou Shanxi China 81 D2
Xinzo de Limia Spain 60 B1
Xiqing Shan mts China 80 C2
Xique Xique Brazil 151 E4
Xishanzui China 82 A1
Xi Ujimqin Qi China see Bayan Ul Hot
Xiushan China 83 A3
Xiuying China 83 B3
Xixia China 82 B2
Xizang Zizhiqu aut. reg. China 74 A1
Xo'jayli Uzbek. 88 C2
Xuancheng China 82 B2
Xuanwei China 83 A3
Xuchang China 82 B2
Xuddur Somalia 103 C4
Xun Jiang r. China 83 B3
Xunwu China 83 B3
Xuwen China 83 B3
Xuyong China 83 A3

Ya'an China 83 A2
Yabēlo Eth. 103 B4
Yablonovyy Khrebet mts Rus. Fed. 81 D1
Yadkin r. U.S.A. 139 D1
Yadong China 87 C2
Yagnitsa Rus. Fed. 43 E2
Yagoua Cameroon 104 B1
Yahk Can. 126 D3
Yahualica Mex. 142 B2
Yahyalı Turkey 92 B2
Yaizu Japan 79 C4
Yakima U.S.A. 134 B1
Yako Burkina 100 B3
Yakumo Japan 78 D2
Yakutat U.S.A. 126 B2
Yakutat Bay U.S.A. 126 A2
Yakutsk Rus. Fed. 95 K2
Yakymivka Ukr. 45 E2
Yala Thai. 75 B3
Yallourn Austr. 117 D3
Yalova Turkey 65 C2
Yalta Ukr. 45 D3
Yalu Jiang r. China/N. Korea 77 A1
Yamagata Japan 78 D3
Yamaguchi Japan 79 B4
Yamal, Poluostrov pen. Rus. Fed. see Yamal Peninsula
Yamal Peninsula Rus. Fed. 40 F1
Yamba Austr. 114 F2
Yambio Sudan 103 A4
Yamdi Bulg. 64 C2
Yamburg Rus. Fed. 40 G2
Yamethin Myanmar 74 A2
Yamoussoukro Côte d'Ivoire 100 B4
Yampil' Ukr. 44 C2
Yamuna r. India 87 C2
Yamzho Yumco l. China 87 D2

Yana r. Rus. Fed. 95 L2
Yan'an China 82 A2
Yanaoca Peru 150 B4
Yanbu' al Baḥr Saudi Arabia 90 A2
Yancheng China 82 C2
Yanchep Austr. 114 A3
Yangcheng China 82 B2
Yangchun China 83 B3
Yangdok N. Korea 77 B2
Yangjiang China 83 B3
Yangôn Myanmar see Rangoon
Yangquan China 82 B2
Yangshuo China 83 B3
Yangtze r. Qinghai China 80 C3
Yangtze r. China 83 C2
Yangtze r. China 74 B1
Yangtze, Mouth of the China 82 C2
Yangzhou China 82 B2
Yanji China 77 B1
Yankton U.S.A. 135 D2
Yano-Indigirskaya Nizmennost' lowland Rus. Fed. 95 L2
Yanskiy Zaliv g. Rus. Fed. 95 L2
Yantabulla Austr. 117 D1
Yantai China 82 C2
Yaoundé Cameroon 104 B2
Yap i. Micronesia 71 D2
Yapen i. Indon. 71 D3
Yapen, Selat sea chan. Indon. 71 D3
Yaqui r. Mex. 142 A2
Yaraka Austr. 115 D2
Yaransk Rus. Fed. 40 D3
Yaren Nauru 112
Yarim Yemen 90 B3
Yarkant He r. China 89 E3
Yarlung Zangbo r. China 80 C3
Yarmouth Can. 129 D2
Yarongo Rus. Fed. 40 F2
Yaroslavl' Rus. Fed. 43 E2
Yaroslavskiy Rus. Fed. 78 B2
Yarram Austr. 117 D3
Yartsevo Rus. Fed. 43 D2
Yasenogorsk Rus. Fed. 43 E3
Yasothon Thai. 75 B2
Yass Austr. 117 D2
Yatağan Turkey 65 C3
Yathkyed Lake Can. 127 F1
Yatsushiro Japan 79 B4
Yavari r. Brazil/Peru 150 C3
Yavatmal India 87 B2
Yavoriv Ukr. 44 B2
Yawatahama Japan 79 B4
Yazd Iran 93 D2
Yazoo City U.S.A. 138 B2
Ydra i. Greece 65 B3
Ye Myanmar 75 A2
Yecheng China 89 E3
Yécora Mex. 142 B2
Yefremov Rus. Fed. 43 E3
Yegorlyk r. Rus. Fed. 45 F2
Yegorlykskaya Rus. Fed. 45 F2
Yegor'yevsk Rus. Fed. 43 E2
Yei Sudan 103 B4
Yekaterinburg Rus. Fed. 40 F3
Yelets Rus. Fed. 43 E3
Yélimané Mali 100 A3
Yell i. U.K. 50 [inset]
Yellowknife Can. 126 D1
Yellow River r. China 82 B2
Yellow Sea N. Pacific Ocean 81 E2
Yellowstone r. U.S.A. 132 E1
Yellowstone Lake U.S.A. 134 A2
Yemen country Asia 90 B3
Yemva Rus. Fed. 40 E2
Yenakiyeve Ukr. 45 E2
Yenangyaung Myanmar 74 A1
Yên Bai Vietnam 74 B1
Yendi Ghana 100 B4

Yenice Turkey 65 C3
Yenifoça Turkey 65 C3
Yenisey r. Rus. Fed. 80 C1
Yeoval Austr. 117 D2
Yeovil U.K. 53 B4
Yeppoon Austr. 115 E2
Yerbogachen Rus. Fed. 95 J2
Yerevan Armenia 93 C1
Yereymentau Kazakh. 89 E1
Yermish' Rus. Fed. 43 F3
Yershov Rus. Fed. 41 D3
Yesan S. Korea 77 B2
Yesil' Kazakh. 89 D1
Yeşilova Turkey 65 C3
Yetman Austr. 117 E1
Ye-U Myanmar 74 A1
Yeu, Île d' i. France 58 B2
Yevlax Azer. 41 D4
Yevpatoriya Ukr. 45 D2
Yeysk Rus. Fed. 45 E2
Yezyaryshcha Belarus 42 C2
Yibin China 83 A3
Yichang China 82 B2
Yichun Heilong. China 81 E1
Yichun Jiangxi China 83 B3
Yilan China 78 C1
Yıldız Dağları mts Turkey 64 C2
Yıldızeli Turkey 92 B2
Yinchuan China 82 A2
Yingchengzi China 77 B1
Yingde China 83 B3
Yingkou China 82 C2
Yingtan Hubei China 82 B2
Yingshan Sichuan China 82 A2
Yingtan China 83 B3
Yining China 89 F2
Yirga Alem Eth. 103 B4
Yishui China 82 B2
Yitong China 77 B1
Yiwu China 80 C2
Yixing China 82 B2
Yiyang China 83 B3
Yizhou China 83 A3
Yli-Kitka i. Fin. 46 F2
Ylitornio Fin. 46 E2
Ylivieska Fin. 46 E3
Yogyakarta Indon. 73 C2
Yoko Cameroon 104 B2
Yokohama Japan 79 C3
Yola Nigeria 101 D4
Yonezawa Japan 79 D3
Yong'an China 83 B3
Yongchun China 83 B3
Yongdeng China 82 A2
Yŏngdŏk S. Korea 77 B2
Yongkang China 83 C3
Yongsheng China 74 B1
Yongzhou China 83 B3
Yopal Col. 150 B2
York Austr. 114 A3
York U.K. 52 C3
York NE U.S.A. 135 D2
York PA U.S.A. 137 E3
York, Cape Austr. 71 D3
Yorke Peninsula Austr. 116 B3
Yorketown Austr. 116 B3
Yorkshire Wolds hills U.K. 52 C3
Yorkton Can. 124 F3
Yoshkar-Ola Rus. Fed. 41 D3
Youghal Rep. of Ireland 51 C3
Young Austr. 117 D2
Younghusband Peninsula Austr. 116 B3
Youngstown U.S.A. 137 D2
Youvarou Mali 100 B3
Youyi Feng mt. China/Rus. Fed. 89 F2
Yozgat Turkey 92 B2
Ypé-Jhú Para. 154 A2
Yreka U.S.A. 132 B2
Yr Wyddfa mt. U.K. see Snowdon

ssingeaux France **59** C2
stad Sweden **47** C4
syk-Köl *salt l.* Kyrg. **89** E2
tri-Rangá *r.* Iceland **46** [inset]
uanjiang China **74** B1
uan Jiang *r.* China **74** B1
uanmou China **74** B1
uba City U.S.A. **133** B3
ubari Japan **78** D2
ucatán *pen.* Mex. **143** C3
ucatan Channel Cuba/Mex. **144** B2
uendumu Austr. **114** C2
ueyang China **83** B3
ugorsk Rus. Fed. **40** F2
ukagirskoye Ploskogor'ye *plat.*
 Rus. Fed. **95** M2
ukon *r.* Can./U.S.A. **126** B1
ukon Territory *admin. div.* Can.
 124 C2
ulin *Guangxi* China **83** B3
ulin *Shaanxi* China **83** B3
ulong Xueshan *mt.* China **74** B1
uma *AZ* U.S.A. **140** B2
uma *CO* U.S.A. **134** C2
umen China **80** C2
unak Turkey **92** B2
uncheng China **82** B2
unfu China **83** B3
ungas *reg.* Bol. **146**
unnan *prov.* China **83** A3
unta Austr. **116** B2
unyang China **82** B2
urimaguas Peru **150** B3
urungkax He *r.* China **87** C1
ur'yevets Rus. Fed. **43** F2
ü Shan *mt.* Taiwan **83** C3
ushkozero Rus. Fed. **46** G3
ushu China **80** C2
usufeli Turkey **93** C1
utian China **87** C1
uxi China **74** B1
uzha Rus. Fed. **43** F2
uzhno-Kuril'sk Rus. Fed. **78** E2
uzhno-Sakhalinsk Rus. Fed. **78** D1
uzhnoukrayins'k Ukr. **45** D2
uzhou China **82** B2
vetot France **58** C2

Z

aandam Neth. **54** B1
abaykal'sk Rus. Fed. **81** D1
abīd Yemen **90** B3
abol Iran **91** D1
abolī Iran **91** D2
acapa Guat. **143** D3
acatecas Mex. **142** B3
acatecas *state* Mex. **143** C3
acatepec Mex. **142** C3
acatlán Mex. **143** C3
acharo Greece **65** B3
acoalco Mex. **142** B2
acualtipán Mex. **143** C2
adar Croatia **62** C2
adetkyi Kyun *i.* Myanmar **75** A3
adonsk Rus. Fed. **43** E3
a'farānah Egypt **92** B3
afra Spain **60** B2
agreb Croatia **63** C1
agros, Kūhhā-ye *mts* Iran *see*
 Zagros Mountains
ahedān Iran **91** D2
ahlé Lebanon **92** B2
ahrān Saudi Arabia **90** B3
ahrez Chergui *salt pan* Alg. **61** D2
aječar Serb. and Mont. **64** B3
akharovo Rus. Fed. **43** E3

Zākhō Iraq **93** C2
Zakynthos Greece **65** B3
Zakynthos *i.* Greece **65** B3
Zalaegerszeg Hungary **57** D3
Zalău Romania **44** B2
Zalim Saudi Arabia **90** B2
Zalingei Sudan **103** A3
Zalma, Jabal az *mt.* Saudi Arabia
 90 A2
Zama City Can. **126** D2
Zambezi *r.* Angola *see* Zambezi
Zambezi *r.* Angola **107** B1
Zambezi Zambia **106** B1
Zambia *country* Africa **106** B1
Zamboanga Phil. **76** B3
Zamboanga Peninsula Phil. **76** B3
Zamora Spain **60** B1
Zamora de Hidalgo Mex. **142** B3
Zamość Pol. **57** E2
Zanda China **87** B1
Zandvliet Belgium **54** B2
Zanesville U.S.A. **136** D3
Zanjān Iran **93** C2
Zanskar Mountains India **87** B1
Zante *i.* Greece *see* Zakynthos
Zanzibar Tanz. **105** D3
Zanzibar Island Tanz. **105** D3
Zaokskiy Rus. Fed. **43** E3
Zaouatallaz Alg. **101** C2
Zaozhuang China **82** B2
Zapadnaya Dvina *r.* Europe **43** D2
Zapadnaya Dvina Rus. Fed. **43** D2
Zapadno Sibirskaya Ravnina *plain*
 Rus. Fed. **40** H2
Zapadnyy Sayan *reg.* Rus. Fed. **80** B1
Zapata U.S.A. **141** D3
Zapolyarnyy Rus. Fed. **46** G2
Zaporizhzhya Ukr. **45** D2
Zappendorf Ger. **55** E2
Zara Turkey **92** B2
Zaragoza Mex. **143** B2
Zaragoza Spain **61** C1
Zarand Iran **91** C1
Zaranj Afgh. **86** A1
Zarasai Lith. **42** C2
Zaraysk Rus. Fed. **43** E3
Zaraza Venez. **150** C2
Zaria Nigeria **101** C3
Zarichne Ukr. **44** C1
Zarqān Iran **93** D3
Zarubino Rus. Fed. **78** B2
Žary Pol. **56** D2
Zarzis Tunisia **101** D1
Zastron S. Africa **109** C3
Žatec Czech Rep. **55** F2
Zavitinsk Rus. Fed. **81** E1
Zavolzhsk Rus. Fed. **43** F2
Zawiercie Pol. **57** D2
Zaysan, Lake Kazakh. **89** F2
Zdolbuniv Ukr. **44** C1
Zealand *i.* Denmark **47** C4
Zeebrugge Belgium **54** A2
Zeerust S. Africa **109** C2
Zeil, Mount Austr. **114** C2
Zeitz Ger. **55** F2
Zelenogorsk Rus. Fed. **47** F3
Zelenogradsk Rus. Fed. **42** B3
Zemmora Alg. **61** D2
Zempoaltépetl, Nudo de *mt.* Mex.
 143 C3
Zengfeng Shan *mt.* China **77** B1
Zenzach Alg. **60** D2
Zereh, Gowd-e *depr.* Afgh. **86** A2
Zermatt Switz. **59** D2
Zernograd Rus. Fed. **45** F2
Zeulenroda Ger. **55** E2
Zeven Ger. **55** D1
Zevenaar Neth. **54** C1
Zeya Rus. Fed. **95** K3
Zeydābād Iran **93** D3

Zeyskoye Vodokhranilishche *resr*
 Rus. Fed. **95** K3
Zgierz Pol. **57** D2
Zhabinka Belarus **42** B3
Zhalpaktal Kazakh. **88** B2
Zhaltyr Kazakh. **89** D1
Zhanaozen Kazakh. **88** C2
Zhangjiajie China **83** B3
Zhangjiakou China **82** B1
Zhangping China **83** B3
Zhangshu China **83** B3
Zhangwu China **77** A1
Zhangye China **80** C2
Zhangzhou China **83** B3
Zhanibek Kazakh. **88** B2
Zhanjiang China **83** B3
Zhao'an China **83** B3
Zhaoqing China **83** B3
Zhaotong China **83** A3
Zhari Namco *salt l.* China **87** C1
Zharkent Kazakh. **89** F2
Zharkovskiy Rus. Fed. **43** D2
Zharma Kazakh. **89** F2
Zhashkiv Ukr. **44** D2
Zhejiang *prov.* China **83** C3
Zhelaniya, Mys *c.* Rus. Fed. **94** G1
Zheleznogorsk Rus. Fed. **43** E3
Zhenba China **82** A2
Zheng'an China **83** A3
Zhenghe China **83** B3
Zhengzhou China **82** B2
Zhenyuan China **83** A3
Zherdevka Rus. Fed. **43** F3
Zheshart Rus. Fed. **40** D2
Zhezkazgan *Karagandinskaya Oblast'*
 Kazakh. **89** D2
Zhezkazgan *Karagandinskaya Oblast'*
 Kazakh. **89** D2
Zhicheng China *see* Qingzhou
Zhigansk Rus. Fed. **95** K2
Zhitikara Kazakh. **88** D1
Zhlobin Belarus **43** D3
Zhmerynka Ukr. **44** C2
Zhob Pak. **86** A1
Zhokhova, Ostrov *i.* Rus. Fed. **95** M1
Zhongba China **87** C2
Zhongning China **82** A2
Zhongshan China **83** B3
Zhongwei China **82** A2
Zhoukou China **82** B2
Zhoushan China **83** C2
Zhovti Vody Ukr. **45** D2
Zhuanghe China **77** A2
Zhucheng China **82** B2
Zhukovka Rus. Fed. **43** D3
Zhukovskiy Rus. Fed. **43** E2
Zhumadian China **82** B2
Zhuzhou *Hunan* China **83** B3
Zhuzhou *Hunan* China **83** B3
Zhydachiv Ukr. **44** B2
Zhytkavichy Belarus **42** C3
Zhytomyr Ukr. **44** C1
Žiar nad Hronom Slovakia **57** D3
Zibo China **82** B2
Zielona Góra Pol. **57** D2
Zigaing Myanmar **74** A1
Zigong China **83** A3
Ziguinchor Senegal **100** A3
Zihuatanejo Mex. **142** B3
Žilina Slovakia **57** D3
Zillah Libya **101** D2
Zima Rus. Fed. **95** I3
Zimapán Mex. **143** C2
Zimbabwe *country* Africa **107** C2
Zimmi Sierra Leone **100** A4
Zimnicea Romania **44** C3
Zinder Niger **101** C3
Zinjibār Yemen **90** B3
Zirc Hungary **57** D3
Ziro India **74** A1

Zīr Rūd Iran **91** C2
Zistersdorf Austria **57** D3
Zitácuaro Mex. **143** B3
Zittau Ger. **56** C2
Zlatoust Rus. Fed. **41** E3
Zlín Czech Rep. **57** D3
Zlynka Rus. Fed. **43** D3
Zmiyevka Rus. Fed. **43** E3
Zmiyiv Ukr. **45** E2
Znamenka *Orlovskaya Oblast'* Rus. Fed. **43** E3
Znamenka *Tambovskaya Oblast'* Rus. Fed. **43** F3
Znam"yanka Ukr. **45** D2
Znojmo Czech Rep. **57** D3
Zolochiv *Kharkivs'ka Oblast'* Ukr. **45** E1
Zolochiv *L'vivs'ka Oblast'* Ukr. **44** B2
Zolotonosha Ukr. **45** D2

Zolotukhino Rus. Fed. **43** E3
Zomba Malawi **107** C1
Zonguldak Turkey **92** B1
Zonza France **59** D3
Zorzor Liberia **100** B4
Zossen Ger. **55** F1
Zouar Chad **101** D2
Zouérat Maur. **100** A2
Zrenjanin a **64** B1
Zubtsov Rus. Fed. **43** D2
Zug Switz. **59** D2
Zugdidi Georgia **93** C1
Zújar *r.* Spain **60** B2
Zülpich Ger. **54** C2
Zumpango Mex. **143** C3
Zumbo Moz. **107** C1
Zuni Mountains U.S.A. **140** C1
Zunyi China **83** A3

Županja Croatia **63** C1
Zürich Switz. **59** D2
Zutphen Neth. **54** C1
Zuwārah Libya **101** D1
Zvenyhorodka Ukr. **44** D2
Zvishavane Zimbabwe **107** C2
Zvolen Slovakia **57** D3
Zvornik Bos.-Herz. **63** C2
Zwedru Liberia **100** B4
Zweibrücken Ger. **54** C3
Zwelitsha S. Africa **109** C3
Zwettl Austria **56** D3
Zwickau Ger. **55** F2
Zwolle Neth. **54** C1
Zyryanka Rus. Fed. **95** M2